Behavior Modification

)

|

}

)03

FOURTH EDITION

Behavior Modification: What It Is and How to Do It

Garry Martin
Joseph Pear
University of Manitoba

Prentice-Hall International, Inc.

© 1992, 1988, 1983, 1978 by Prentice-Hall, Inc.
A Simon & Schuster Company
Englewood Cliffs, New Jersey 07632

Printed in the United States of America

10   9   8   7   6   5   4   3   2   1

ISBN   0-13-067232-7

Prentice-Hall International (UK) Limited, *London*
Prentice-Hall of Australia Pty. Limited, *Sydney*
Prentice-Hall Canada Inc., *Toronto*
Prentice-Hall Hispanoamericana, S.A., *Mexico*
Prentice-Hall of India Private Limited, *New Delhi*
Prentice-Hall of Japan, Inc., *Tokyo*
Simon & Schuster Asia Pte. Ltd., *Singapore*
Editora Prentice-Hall do Brasil, Ltda., *Rio de Janeiro*

To
Jack Michael, Lee Meyerson, Lynn Caldwell,
Dick Powers, and Reed Lawson, who taught us so
much and made learning so enjoyable

and

Toby, Todd, Kelly, Scott, Tana, and Jonathan,
who live in a world that is being made better
by such dedicated teachers

Contents

PART III   SOME PRELIMINARY CONSIDERATIONS TO EFFECTIVE
           PROGRAMMING STRATEGIES

PART V   PUTTING IT ALL TOGETHER

Preface

This fourth edition of *Behavior Modification*, like its predecessors, assumes no specific prior knowledge about psychology or behavior modification on the part of the reader. Those who want to know how to apply behavior modification effectively to their everyday concerns—from helping children learn life's necessary skills to solving some of their own personal behavior problems—will find the text useful. Mainly, however, this book is addressed to two audiences: (1) college and university students taking courses in behavior modification, behavior analysis, the psychology of learning, and related areas; and (2) students and practitioners of various helping professions (such as education, counseling, clinical psychology, medicine, psychiatry, nursing, psychiatric nursing, social work, speech therapy, physiotherapy, and occupational therapy) that are concerned directly with enhancing various forms of behavioral development.

From our separate experiences over the past 25 years in teaching members of both these groups, we are convinced that both groups learn the principles of behavior and how to apply them most effectively when the applications are explained with reference to the underlying behavior principles on which they are based. For this reason, as our title implies, this book deals equally with both the principles and the tactics (that is, the rules and guidelines for specific applications) of behavior modification.

Our goals, and the manner in which we have attempted to achieve them, can be summarized as follows:

1. To teach the elementary principles and procedures of behavior modification. Thus, we begin with the basic principles and procedures, illustrate them with numerous examples and applications, and increase the complexity of the material gradually. Study Questions at the end of each chapter promote the reader's mastery of the material and the reader's ability to generalize to situations not described in the text. These questions can also be used for examination purposes in formal courses.

    2. To teach practical how-to skills, such as observing and recording; recognizing instances of reinforcement, extinction, and punishment and their likely long-term effects; interpreting behavioral episodes in terms of behavioral principles and procedures; and designing, implementing, and evaluating behavioral programs. To accomplish this, we provide (a) Practice Exercises, which teach the reader about analyzing, interpreting, and developing programs for the behavior of others, and (b) Self-Modification Exercises, which encourage the reader to analyze, interpret, and develop programs for his or her own behavior.

    3. To provide advanced discussion and references to acquaint readers with some of the empirical and theoretical underpinnings of the field. This material is presented in the Extended Discussion and Notes sections at the end of the chapters. These sections, which contain numerous references to relevant articles and books, can be omitted without harm to the continuity of the text. Separate study questions on the notes are provided for those instructors who wish to use them and as aides for students wishing to broaden their understanding of behavior modification. The information given in the extended discussion sections can also be used by instructors as springboards for lecture material.

    4. To present the material in such a way that it will serve as an easy-to-use handbook for practitioners concerned with overcoming behavioral deficits and excesses in a wide variety of populations and settings.

    The book is divided into six parts:

    Part I introduces the behavioral orientation of the book and describes major areas of application of behavior modification techniques for improving a wide variety of behaviors of individuals in diverse settings.

    Part II covers the basic principles and procedures of behavior modification. Each of the chapters, except for Chapter 15, begins with a case history drawn from the fields of child development, mental retardation, childhood autism, early education, or coaching. Such examples readily lend themselves to simplified expositions of the principles. Moreover, undergraduate behavior modification projects are often concerned with populations in these areas. Numerous examples of how each principle operates in everyday life and how it can operate to the disadvantage of those who are ignorant of it are also given.

    Part III covers no new principles, but rather discusses more sophisticated ways in which to combine and apply the basic principles and procedures discussed in Part II.

    Part IV presents detailed procedures for assessing, recording, and graphing behavior. Chapter 20 explains how behavior modification research is typically carried out. Many instructors prefer to present much of this material quite early in their courses—sometimes at the very beginning. Therefore, we have written these chapters so that they can be read independently of the rest of the book; they do not depend on any of the other material. We recommend that students be required to read these chapters prior to carrying out any major projects for their courses.

Part V deals with how the basic principles, procedures, and assessment and recording techniques are incorporated into effective programming strategies. In keeping with the rigorously scientific nature of behavior modification, we have placed heavy emphasis on the importance of empirically validating program effectiveness. After describing general guidelines applicable to nearly all behavior modification programs, we describe the details of developing token economies in a wide variety of settings. Then, the chapters on self-control and self-desensitization expand on the self-modification exercises of the previous chapters and discuss recent applications to important clinical problems. The chapter on cognitive behavior modification attempts to show that the same behavioral approach that is so effective with public (overt) behavior is also applicable to private (covert) behavior. The final chapter in this section provides an overview of behavior therapy treatments for some of the most common clinical problems with outpatients.

Part VI expands the reader's perspective of behavior modification. It presents an overview of the history of behavior modification and contains a discussion of the ethical issues in the field. Although some instructors might feel that these chapters belong near the beginning of the book, we believe that the reader is more prepared to appreciate this material fully after obtaining a clear and thorough knowledge of behavior modification. We placed ethical issues at the end of the text not because we feel that this topic is less important than the others. On the contrary, we stress ethical issues throughout the book, and, thus, the last chapter provides a reiteration and elaboration of our views on this vital subject. We hope that, after reading the concluding chapter, the reader will be fully aware that the only justification for behavior modification is its usefulness in serving all humanity in general and its recipients in particular.

CHANGES IN THE FOURTH EDITION

This edition improves upon the third in several respects. We have updated the references and all the Extended Discussion and Notes sections in accordance with recent developments in the field. Examples have been added to several chapters to better illustrate the application of behavioral principles in everyday life (versus the way these principles have been harnessed by therapists to change behavior). Material has been added to many of the chapters to emphasize the importance of instructional and rule-governed control of behavior. Several chapters have been revised in response to feedback from students and instructors regarding sections that were somewhat difficult to understand, and two of the chapters on schedules of reinforcement have been rewritten as a single chapter to further enhance clarity. Finally, we have added material to the punishment chapter to reflect the current controversy regarding use of aversive vs. nonaversive methods in behavior management. All of our changes have been influenced by new developments in the discipline, and they have been incorporated into the text to enable the reader to talk about and apply behavior modification effectively.

ACKNOWLEDGMENTS

The writing of the four editions of this book was made possible by the help of many individuals. We gratefully acknowledge the cooperation and support of the staff at the Manitoba Developmental Centre, and Dr. Carl Stephens and the staff at the St. Amant Centre. Much of the material in this volume was generated while the authors were involved in these institutions; without the support of these staff members this book would not likely have been written.

Grateful acknowledgment is due to our many students and to Joan Lumsden, Lyle Wray, and Michael LeBow for their constructive feedback on earlier drafts; to Linda McDonald, who helped to gather some of the material for the guidelines sections; to Jim Rennie, for contributing a number of study questions; and especially to Jack Michael, Rob Hawkins, and Bill Leonhart for their many excellent suggestions for improvements. We also wish to thank Leila Krumm, Barb Roscoe, Beryl Lagassi, Vikki Wood, and Claudia Milton for their cheerful and efficient typing of various drafts of this text.

We are grateful to the following reviewers whose helpful criticism improved this fourth edition: Jay Alperson, *Poloniar College*, Nelson Smith, *University of Rhode Island* and Ross Vasta, *SUNY—Brockport*.

Completion of this book was facilitated by a research grant from the Medical Research Council (Grant No. MT-6353) of Canada to G. L. Martin.

TO THE STUDENT

This book is designed to help you learn to talk about and apply behavior modification effectively. You need no prior knowledge about behavior modification to read and understand this text from beginning to end. We are confident that students at all levels—from beginners to advanced—will find the text informative and useful.

Behavior modification is a very broad and complex field, with many ramifications. Realizing that some students will require or want a deeper knowledge of behavior modification than others will, we have separated the more elementary material from the material that demands more thought and study. The former material is presented in the main body of the text. The latter material is presented at the end of each chapter under the heading "Extended Discussion and Notes." Note numbers in the margin of the main text refer you to the correspondingly numbered passages in Extended Discussion and Notes sections. How you use these sections is up to you and your instructor. You can ignore them altogether and still obtain a good working knowledge of the principles and tactics of behavior modification, because the main text does not depend on the material in the Extended Discussion and Notes. However, we believe that many students will find these sections very informative and that many teachers will find the material useful in stimulating class discussion and imparting additional background information.

Another major way in which we have attempted to help you learn the material is by providing guidelines on the use of all the behavior modification methods discussed in the text. These guidelines should prove useful as summaries of the material as well as in helping you to actually apply the methods described in the text.

Numerous study questions and practice exercises (including "self-modification" exercises) are also presented in each chapter. The study questions are intended to help you check your knowledge of the material when preparing for quizzes and exams. The practice exercises and self-modification exercises are intended to help you develop the practical skills you will need to carry out behavior modification projects effectively.

To help make your study productive and enjoyable, we progress from the simpler and more intrinsically interesting material to the more difficult and complex material. This is also true of the writing style. But a word of caution: *Do not be misled by the seeming simplicity of the earlier chapters.* Students who conclude that they are skilled behavior modifiers after they have learned a few simple behavior modification principles unfortunately end up proving the old maxim that "a little knowledge is a dangerous thing." If we personally had to pick the most important chapter in this book, in terms of the knowledge and skills that define a competent behavior modifier, it would probably be Chapter 21. We therefore strongly suggest that you reserve judgment about your abilities as a behavior modifier until you have mastered Chapter 21 and all the preliminary material on which it is based.

With that word of caution, we wish you much success and enjoyment as you pursue your studies in this exciting and rapidly expanding field.

G.L.M.

J.J.P.

Prentice Hall and Drs. Loren E. Acker and Bram C. Goldwater [the Associates in Analysis of Behavior] are proud to announce a new addition to the practical learning experience of Martin and Pear's **BEHAVIOR MODIFICATION: WHAT IT IS AND HOW TO DO IT, Fourth Edition!**

BEHAVIOR MODIFICATION COMPUTER SIMULATIONS: THE WORLD OF SIDNEY SLUG AND HIS FRIENDS © is a microcomputer simulation game designed to teach the basic principles of learning and behavior change by allowing you to work on actual behaviors on a computer. **SIDNEY SLUG** has been used and enjoyed by thousands of students and professionals across North America because the program provides a compelling adjunct to courses in which behavior modification is considered.

The life-like SIDNEY SLUG program offers a "laboratory" experience not otherwise available. The techniques learned are those used in actual behavior modification. Learn by doing!

This interactive computer program provides on-line advice, evaluation of student input, and feedback to help the student shape behavior effectively. The on screen graphics and users manual provide animated and static simulations of behavior.

BEHAVIOR MODIFICATION COMPUTER SIMULATIONS: THE WORLD OF SIDNEY SLUG AND HIS FRIENDS © was developed by Drs. Acker and Goldwater of the Psychology Department, University of Victoria, British Columbia, Canada. Each has taught, researched, and applied behavioral principles for over 20 years. They bring to these lessons an acute understanding of behavioral techniques, and a sensitivity to the characteristics which make for effective educational materials.

This exciting classroom supplement is free upon adoption of the Martin and Pear **BEHAVIOR MODIFICATION** text. The program is available for IBM, MACINTOSH (IIe emulation mode), Apple II family, and compatibles.

The software provides a compelling adjunct to in-service personnel training and parenting workshops as well as to courses in Introductory Psychology, Applied Psychology, Learning and Motivation, Child Development, and Clinical Psychology, where behavior change is considered. It may also be purchased directly by contacting **ASSOCIATES IN ANALYSIS OF BEHAVIOR** at either of the following addresses:

Dr. Loren E. Acker	Dr. Bram C. Goldwater
#16 - 2330 Harbour Rd.	1422 Wende Rd.
Sidney, B.C.	Victoria, B.C.
Canada V9L 2P8	Canada V9P 3T5
(604) 721-7526	(604) 721-7531

CHAPTER 1

Introduction

What is the common element in situations involving the withdrawn behavior of a nursery school child, tardiness in a special education classroom, littering, ineffective studying, writing a novel, speeding, a phobia, migraine headaches, and staff management? Before attempting an answer, let's look at an example of each of these situations.

1. *Withdrawn Child.* A class of nursery school youngsters is in the playground. Some of the children are playing tag, others are swinging vigorously on the swings, a few are taking turns going down the slide, several are climbing on the monkey bars, and two or three are playing together in the sandbox. But one little boy sits quietly by himself, making no effort to join in the fun. A teacher tries conscientiously, as he has many times before, to coax this child into playing with the others. But his efforts this time, as before, are completely unsuccessful; the boy steadfastly maintains his social isolation from the other children.

2. *Tardiness.* Cathy is a seven-year-old girl who, because of her very poor visual-motor coordination, attends a school for developmentally handicapped children. Although she is able to take off her coat and boots and put them in their proper place each morning, she takes a great deal more time than is necessary to perform these simple functions. She has been known to spend as much as an hour in the cloakroom. To prevent her from missing a large part of the morning instruction, her teachers have taken to helping her remove and hang up her outside garments. Naturally, the teachers are not satisfied with this arrangement. Not only do they find that it takes too much time from their morning routine, but they also fear that it is interfering with Cathy's development of self-reliance. However, they are at a loss as to what

to do about the situation, since all their urgings do not make the child move any faster.

3. *Littering.* Tom and Sally have just arrived at the place where they intend to set up camp and are looking in disgust and amazement at the litter left by previous campers. "Don't they care about the environment?" asks Sally. "How can they enjoy nature and not want to let others enjoy it too?" "If people keep this up," Tom says, "there won't be any nature left for anyone to enjoy." Sadly they tell each other that something should be done about the problem, but neither can say what would solve it.

4. *Ineffective Studying.* With two term papers due next week and a midterm exam at the same time, Sam is wondering how he is ever going to make it through his first year of university. "Why didn't I start working on this stuff sooner, why didn't I?" he mutters over and over while sitting at his cluttered desk. Finally, unable to stand it any longer, he reaches over and flicks on the TV, thus escaping temporarily into its "mindless oblivion." The week before the exam he gets practically no sleep because of cramming every night, and just barely manages a C-minus on the test. But neither term paper is finished, and he is almost sure to lose marks for lateness even if his professors accept his overdue papers.

5. *Writing a Novel.* Karen works in a bank, but her real ambition is to write a novel. And not just a successful novel either, not just a publishable novel, but a *great* novel. Although most of her evenings and weekends are relatively free, she has not yet begun to write. Instead she spends all her spare time watching television, sewing, cooking, visiting friends, and going out on dates. She is waiting for the right "inspiration" to hit her—after all, a truly "great" writer only writes when "inspired," doesn't she? A box of sharpened pencils and a blank pad of paper lie on her desk in preparation for that important day when Karen will be inspired to write. Unfortunately, the pencils stay sharp and the paper stays blank, and it is becoming more and more apparent that Karen's ambition will never be realized.

6. *Speeding.* Accidents frequently occur on the highway approach into Pleasant City. Despite clearly posted reduce-speed signs, many motorists fail to slow down until they are well within the city limits. This is especially dangerous because a large number of children live in Pleasant City and there have been quite a few close calls in which cars speeding into the city have just narrowly missed a child. If this continues, eventually some child is going to be hurt seriously or killed.

7. *A Phobia.* Albert is a normal, healthy young man, but he has one quirk: he is terrified of airplanes. The mere thought of getting into a plane is enough to make him panic. If you were to ask him why he is afraid of airplanes, he would not be able to tell you. Rationally, he knows that it is unlikely that anything bad will happen to him when he is in one. Nevertheless, he cannot force himself to get in one. Not only is his airplane phobia inconvenient but it is also very embarrassing since his friends do not seem to understand why he will not ride in an airplane to go on vacation with them.

8. *Migraines.* While preparing dinner for her family, Betty Jackson was vaguely aware of an odd, yet familiar, feeling creeping up on her. At first she tried to ignore it, but this became increasingly difficult as the odd feeling intensified. Then, all at once, she felt nauseous. Fearfully she looked around, knowing from past experience what to expect, but still hoping it would not occur. The large blank regions in her field of vision, however, finally convinced her that she could no longer deny what was about to happen. "Tom, Jack," she called

to her sons watching TV in the living room, "you'll have to finish fixing dinner for yourselves and your father—I'm having another attack." As soon as she was satisfied that matters in the kitchen were being taken care of, she rushed up to the bedroom. Quickly she drew the blinds, for she knew that the light would soon be sheer torture to her, and lay down on the bed. A throbbing sensation in her right temple gradually intensified until it seemed that the whole right side of her head was about to explode. For hours she lay there completely alone in the dark, her pain almost unbearable. Yet no one came to comfort her, since her family knew that the slightest noise would make her pain even worse. Finally, after about six hours, her symptoms subsided and she was able to rejoin her family. But the threat of "another one of Mom's migraines" that could occur again unpredictably at any time still hung over the heads of the Jackson family.

9. *Staff Management.* Jack and Brenda were having coffee one morning at the Dairy Queen restaurant they owned. "We're going to have to do something about the evening staff," said Brenda. "When I came in this morning, the ice cream machine wasn't properly cleaned and the cups and lids weren't restocked."

"That's only the tip of the iceberg," said Jack. "You should see the grill! And the tables and both bathrooms could use a good scrubbing. Maybe we need more staff on the evening shift?"

"I don't think that's the problem. Sarah Johnson was in here the other night getting a sundae, and she said two of our staff were just standing around talking all the while she was here."

"Maybe we need a better training program. Or maybe we need some kind of a staff motivation program. We need something!"

Now, let us consider our initial question. What do the nine situations involving the withdrawn behavior of a nursery school child, tardiness in a special education classroom, littering, ineffective studying, writing a novel, speeding, a phobia, migraine headaches, and staff management have in common? It might seem at first that they are too diverse to have anything in common. Closer inspection, however, shows that each is concerned with some sort of human behavior. Together, they illustrate the range of problems with which specialists in behavior modification are trained to deal. In fact, if you read this book very carefully, you will find each of these types of behavioral problems discussed somewhere in the following pages, in terms of how it might be treated by means of behavior modification. Many other types of cases will also be discussed. Behavior modification, as you will see, has been found applicable to practically the entire range of human behavior.

WHAT IS BEHAVIOR?

Before we can talk about behavior modification, we must first ask, what do we mean by **behavior**? Some commonly used synonyms include "activity," "action," "performance," "responding," "response," and "reaction." Essentially, behavior is anything that a person says or does. Is the color of someone's eyes behavior? Is blinking behavior? Are the clothes someone is wearing behavior? Is dressing behavior? If you said no to the first and third questions and yes to the second and fourth, we are in agreement. One of the goals of this book is to encourage you to begin thinking and talking very specifically about behavior.

Now consider some examples that are a bit more difficult. Is intelligence behavior? Is an attitude behavior? Is motivation behavior? Is creativity behavior? If not, then what are they?

What do we mean when we say that a person is intelligent? To many people, intelligence is something that you are born with, a sort of "inherited brain power" or innate capacity for learning. But we never observe or directly measure any such thing. On an intelligence test, for example, we simply measure people's behavior—their answers to questions—as they take the test. The word "intelligent" is best used as an adverb describing how people behave under certain conditions, such as taking a test, not as a noun for some "thing." Perhaps a person described as intelligent readily solves problems that others find difficult, performs well on most course examinations, reads many books, talks knowledgeably about many topics, or scores well on an intelligence test. Depending on who uses the word, "intelligence" can mean any or all of these—but whatever it means, it refers to ways of behaving.

What about an attitude? Suppose that Johnny's teacher, Ms. Smith, reports that he has a bad attitude toward school. What does Ms. Smith mean by this? Perhaps she means that Johnny frequently skips school, refuses to do his classwork when he does attend, and swears at the teacher. Whatever she means when she talks about Johnny's "bad attitude," it is clearly his behavior with which she is really concerned.

Motivation and creativity also refer to the kinds of behavior in which a person is likely to engage under certain circumstances. The highly motivated student spends a great deal of time studying. The creative individual frequently emits behaviors that are novel or unusual and that, at the same time, have desirable effects.[1]

Note 1

What about mental retardation, autism, schizophrenia, learning disabilities, and emotional disturbances? These also are labels for certain ways of behaving. How do specialists decide that someone is severely retarded? They make the decision primarily because they might observe that the person, at a certain age,

cannot tie shoelaces;
is not toilet-trained;
eats only with the fingers or a spoon;
performs on psychological tests in such a way that the combined answers yield an IQ score of 35 or less.

How do specialists decide that someone has a learning disability? They make the decision on the basis of certain behaviors that they observe, such as attending to a task for only a few seconds or minutes (typically labeled a "short attention span");

staring at an item for many minutes (typically labeled "perseveration");

moving frequently from one position, location, or task to the next (labeled "hyperactivity");

confusing words while speaking, such as "thumb" for "tongue" (labeled "speech disability");

inverting words while reading, such as "saw" for "was" (labeled a "reading disability" or "dyslexia").

How do specialists decide that a child is autistic? They make this decision on the basis of certain behaviors that they observe. For example, they might observe that a child

frequently mimics particular questions rather than answering with an appropriate statement;

engages in various self-stimulatory behaviors, such as rocking back and forth, twirling objects with the fingers, or fluttering the hands in front of his or her eyes;

when called, does not respond, or moves away from the person doing the calling (more generally, shows antisocial behavior);

performs much below average on a variety of self-care tasks, such as dressing, grooming, and feeding.

Note 2   In all these cases, decisions are based on observable behavior, not on invisible "mental" abnormalities.[2] The behavior of people who are given the labels mentioned is compared with the behavior of others of approximately the same age and perhaps with a similar amount of training and educational background, and the comparison shows that individuals labeled "retarded," "austistic," or "learning disabled" have *behavior problems*—that is, *behavioral deficits* (too little behavior of a particular type), or *behavioral excesses* (too much behavior of a particular type), or both behavioral deficits and excesses. The same is true for individuals who are labeled "emotionally disturbed," "schizophrenic," "learning disabled," "neurotic," "psychotic," and so forth. The labels are applied when the person emits behaviors that are considered "abnormal." In all such cases, it is *behavior* that causes concern. Certain behaviors that parents see and hear often cause them to seek professional help for their children. Certain behaviors teachers see and hear often prompt them to have children removed from their classroom. Certain behaviors that can be seen or heard cause governments to set up institutions, clinics, community treatment centers, and special programs.

You may be wondering why we stress so strongly the importance of defining all types of problems, such as those mentioned above, in terms of behavior. The reason is that specific procedures are now available that can be used in school, in the workplace, in home settings—in fact, just about anywhere that there is a need to overcome behavior problems and to establish more desirable behaviors. These techniques are referred to collectively as *behavior modification.* Two terms that are closely related to behavior modification are "behavior therapy" and "applied behavior analysis." In our view, the term "behavior modification" has acquired a broader meaning than these other terms, and that is the term that we generally use throughout this book. (The historical use of these and similar terms is discussed at length in Chapter 27.)

The main purpose of this book is to describe behavior modification techniques in an enjoyable, readable, and practical manner. Since it has been written for people in various helping professions as well as for students, we intend to help readers learn not merely about behavior modification but also how to use it to overcome behavioral deficits and excesses in whatever field of specialization they may engage.

"Wait a minute," you may say. "From many of your examples it sounds as if this book is intended primarily for people concerned with helping severely handicapped individuals." In answer to such an observation, we wish to point out that the behavior modification procedures described in this volume can be used to solve behavior problems of any individual. Even people who are normal or average in most respects often have one or two annoying habits that they wish to correct. These habits can be considered either behavioral deficits or behavioral excesses. Here are examples of each type.

Examples of behavioral deficits

1. A child does not pronounce words clearly and does not interact with other children.
2. A teenager does not complete homework assignments, help around the house, work in the yard, or discuss problems and difficulties with her parents.
3. An adult does not pay attention to traffic regulations while driving, express sincere thanks to others, or meet his or her spouse at agreed-upon times.

Examples of behavioral excesses

1. A child frequently gets out of bed and throws tantrums at bedtime, throws food on the floor at mealtime, and plays with the controls for the television set.
2. A teenager frequently interrupts conversations between his parents and other adults, spends hours talking on the telephone in the evening, and uses abusive language.
3. An adult watches television continuously, frequently eats candies and other sweets between meals, smokes one cigarette after another, and bites his or her fingernails.

To identify a behavior as excessive or deficient, we must consider the context in which it occurs. For example, a child who uses a crayon to write on drawing paper shows appropriate behavior, but if a child uses a crayon to write on walls, that would be considered a behavioral excess. A normal teenager might interact appropriately with members of the same sex, but be extremely embarrassed and have difficulty talking to members of the opposite sex (a behavioral deficit). Some behavioral excesses, for example, self-injurious behavior, are inappropriate no matter what the context. In most cases, however, the point at which a particular behavior is considered deficient or excessive is determined primarily by the practices in our culture or by the ethical views of concerned individuals. The relationship between cultural practices, ethics, and behavior modification is discussed in detail in Chapter 28.

CHARACTERISTICS OF BEHAVIOR MODIFICATION

We would like to conclude our introduction by identifying defining characteristics of behavior modification for you. However, it is not easy to give a pat definition. There are many specialists in this field, and, as is true of members of any other large group, they do not always see eye to eye on every issue. In addition, other approaches have gradually begun to adopt some of the features that once clearly distinguished behavior modification. In our opinion, the most important characteristic of behavior modification is *its strong emphasis on defining problems in terms of behavior that can be measured in some way, and using changes in the behavioral measure of the problem as the best indicator of the extent to which the problem is being helped.*

Another important characteristic of behavior modification is that *its treatment procedures and techniques are ways of rearranging an individual's environment* to help that individual function more fully in society. The term **environment** refers to the specific physical variables in one's immediate surroundings. For example, the teacher, chalkboard, other students, and the furniture in a classroom are all part of a student's environment in a classroom setting. An individual's own behavior can also be a part of the environment influencing that individual's subsequent behavior. When hitting a forehand shot in tennis, for example, both the sight of the ball coming near *and* the behavior of completing your backswing provide environmental cues for you to complete the forehand shot and hit the ball over the net. Behavior modification procedures do *not* involve such things as psychosurgery, electroconvulsive therapy, or the use of drugs.[3]

Note 3

A third important characteristic of behavior modification is that *its methods and rationales can be described precisely.* This makes it possible for behavior modifiers to read descriptions of procedures used by their colleagues, replicate them, and get essentially the same results. It also makes it easier to teach behavior modification procedures than has been the case with many other forms of psychological treatment.

Curiously, the first and third features outlined above contribute to difficulties in deciding which methods to include in a discussion of behavior modification. Because behavior modifiers can specify their methods precisely, and measure the effectiveness of their methods in terms of actual improvements in the behaviors being worked on, the field is constantly changing as more effective methods are being developed and less effective methods are being discarded or deemphasized. While this process is going on, there is inevitably some disagreement in the field about what to include in a statement about the methods of behavior modification. However, all the behavior modifiers we know agree that the ultimate test of any behavior modification method is whether or not it can be proven to be effective in changing behavior in a desired manner. In addition, if two methods are both effective, then, other factors being equal (acceptance by the client, possible adverse side effects, etc.), the method that has been shown to be more effective in changing behavior must be used. In this book we stick mainly to methods that have been proven to be highly effective; moreover, in those instances in which we describe methods whose effectiveness has not yet been clearly established, we make this known to the reader.

There is a fourth important characteristic of behavior modification. To a large extent, *the techniques of behavior modification stem from basic laboratory research in the field known as experimental psychology.* For decades now, experimental psychologists working with humans as well as with animals have been measuring behavior precisely and attempting to develop principles and theories describing behavior. Therefore, it stands to reason that behavior modifiers in search of more effective techniques often, though certainly not always, draw upon procedures, findings, and theories of experimental psychology.

This brings us to a fifth characteristic of behavior modification. Within experimental psychology, *the psychology of learning in general and the principles of operant and Pavlovian conditioning in particular have thus far been most useful to the field of behavior modification.*[4] Therefore, in Part II we cover these principles in considerable detail and show how they are applicable to various types of behavior problems.

Note 4

Two final characteristics are that *behavior modification emphasizes scientific demonstration that a particular intervention was responsible for a particular behavior change,* and *it places high value on accountability for everyone involved in behavior modification programs*: client, staff, administrators, consultants, etc.*

THE APPROACH OF THIS BOOK

To summarize, the behavior modification approach focuses primarily on observable behavior and involves environmental (as opposed to medical, pharmacological, or genetic) manipulations to change behavior.[5] Individuals who are labeled mentally retarded, autistic, schizophrenic, neurotic, or whatever are individuals who show behavioral deficits or excesses. Behavior modification consists of a set of procedures that can be used to change behavior so that these individuals will be considered less retarded, less autistic, or less of whatever label has been given them. Some traditional psychologists have shown

Note 5

*We thank Rob Hawkins for bringing these last two points to our attention.

an excessive concern for labeling and classifying individuals. Regardless of the label given, the individual's behavior is still there and is still being influenced by the individual's immediate environment. The mother in Figure 1–1, for example, is still concerned about what to do with her child and how to handle the problem. That is where behavior modification comes in.

After the overview in the next chapter, Part II describes the principles and procedures of behavior modification. In essence, principles are procedures that are so simple that they cannot be broken down into simpler procedures and that have a consistent effect upon behavior. Principles are like laws in science. Most procedures used in behavior modification are combinations of the principles of behavior modification. These principles are almost never used in isolation from other principles in practical applications, especially with highly verbal individuals. Therefore, to better illustrate the principles under discussion, we have selected relatively simple lead cases for the chapters in Part II. After illustrating the principles involved in such cases, we

FIGURE 1–1 The experts "helping" mother with her child?

elaborate on how these principles are used with other types of problems. We also give numerous illustrations of these principles from normal behavior in everyday life. Later parts of the book show how highly complex programs are built from the principles and procedures introduced in Part II. In addition to these detailed programming strategies, ethical issues in their use are described. We hope that this book provides satisfactory answers to teachers, psychiatric nurses, students, teenagers, fathers, mothers, and others who say, "Thank you, Ms. or Mr. Expert, but what can I do about it?" (This is the question asked by the mother in Figure 1–1.) We hope also that the book will give introductory students of behavior modification an understanding of why the procedures are effective.

STUDY QUESTIONS

1. What is behavior? Give three synonyms for behavior.
2. Why would a behavior modifier say that we should talk about retarded behavior, not retarded children; or autistic behavior, not autistic children?
3. What is retarded behavior?
4. From a behavioral point of view, what is intelligence? creativity?
5. What is a behavioral deficit? Give two examples.
6. What is a behavioral excess? Give two examples.
7. What do behavior modifiers mean by the term *environment*? Give an example.
8. Describe seven defining characteristics of behavior modification.
9. Explain why two of the defining characteristics have contributed to difficulties in deciding which methods to include in a discussion of behavior modification.

PRACTICE EXERCISE

Consider someone who is personally close to you (e.g., a sister, a brother, or a lover). From your point of view, identify

a. two behavioral deficits to overcome in that person.
b. two behavioral excesses to decrease.

SELF-MODIFICATION EXERCISES

Assume that you would like to make yourself a better person. The first step would be to identify areas in which you would like to change.

1. List three specific behavioral deficits that you would like to overcome.
2. List three specific behavioral excesses that you would like to decrease or eliminate.

EXTENDED DISCUSSION AND NOTES

1. Creativity has sometimes been cited as an area of human endeavor that is beyond the scope of behavior modification. However, a number of published studies have examined creativity as behavior that can be developed with behavior modification techniques (Winston & Baker, 1985). Typically, these studies used either or both of two measures of creativity: (a) the variety of behaviors observed, such as when a child shows increased variety when drawing different geometric forms; and (b) occurrence of behaviors that are considered original or novel in the sense that they were not previously shown by that individual. For a critical analysis of behavioral studies of creativity, see Winston and Baker (1985).

2. The model in physical medicine in which germs, viruses, lesions, and other disturbances lead to the production of symptoms in the functioning of a normal human organism represented a major breakthrough in physical medicine during the nineteenth century. This model was adopted by Freud in his view of human beings and his attempt to describe the causes of abnormal behavior. Abnormal behavior was viewed as a symptom of an underlying disturbance in a personality mechanism. The implication of this view, which is called the *medical model*, was that one must treat the underlying personality disturbance rather than the observed symptom (the abnormal behavior). A behavioral approach, on the other hand, suggests that the abnormal behavior is a function of specifiable environment causes (at least primarily). Whether or not these causes can be identified, it is possible to rearrange the environment in such a way that the behavior can be changed.

3. While behavior modification procedures involve changing a person's environment, rather than giving a person drugs, there are some problems for which professional therapists might use a combination of behavior modification and drugs. In the treatment of severe depression, for example, antidepressants tend to produce faster results while cognitive behavior therapy (such as that of Beck's, discussed in Chapter 25) tends to produce less relapse (Roth, Bielski, Jones, Parker, & Osborn, 1982; Simons, Murphy, Levine, & Wetzel, 1986). Thus, the preferred treatment for severe depression appears to be a combination of cognitive behavior therapy and an antidepressant drug (Agras, 1987).

4. We do not mean to imply that the treatment procedures in all areas of behavior therapy or behavior modification are based solely on operant or Pavlovian conditioning. For example, such areas of experimental psychology as semantic conditioning, problem solving, information processing, and cognitive experimental psychology have been drawn upon to develop treatment techniques in the area referred to as cognitive behavior modification (see Chapter 25). Nevertheless, in our view, the laboratory findings and theoretical underpinnings of operant and Pavlovian conditioning provide the main part of the foundation on which behavior modification has been built.

5. Because behavior modifiers stress that changes in observable behavior constitute the criteria for judging the effectiveness of behavior modification techniques, it is often mistakenly assumed that behavior modifiers discount the importance of internal, covert, private, or subjective events (e.g., thoughts and feelings). Some behavior modifiers may tend in that direction, in that they adhere to a position that has been termed *methodological behaviorism* (Day, 1983). According to B. F.

Skinner, "Methodological behaviorism . . . ruled private events out of bounds because there could be no agreement about their validity" (1974, p. 18). Skinner advocated a different position, called *radical behaviorism*. According to Skinner, radical behaviorism does not reject events that we can observe introspectively in ourselves. It does not, however, regard these events to be nonphysical, as some psychologists and philosophers have maintained. In addition, it generally does not regard these introspectively observed events to be of special importance in explaining observable behavior. Rather, both covert and overt behaviors are assumed to be controlled by the external environment. (See Chapters 23 and 25 for further discussion of this issue.)

Behaviorists are also often accused of denying the importance of genetics in determining behavior. This mistaken impression may stem in part from the writings of John B. Watson. In 1913, Watson took psychology by storm when he published a paper entitled "Psychology as the Behaviorist Views It." Watson was dissatisfied with the introspective psychology of his day, and argued that the correct subject matter of psychology was observable behavior and only observable behavior. Watson also advocated an extreme form of environmentalism, summarized in the following famous (or infamous) claim:

> Give me a dozen healthy infants, well-formed, and my own specified world to bring them up in and I'll guarantee to take any one at random and train him to become any type of specialist I might select—doctor, lawyer, artist, merchant-chief, and, yes, even beggarman and thief, regardless of his talents, penchants, tendencies, abilities, vocations, and race of his ancestors. (Watson, 1930, p. 104)

However, Skinner (1974) pointed out that Watson himself admitted that this claim was exaggerated, and did not disregard the importance of genetics: "Watson himself had made important observations of instinctive behavior and was, indeed, one of the first ethologists in the modern spirit" (p. 5). Moreover, "Watson himself repeatedly referred to the 'heredity and habit equipment' of people" (p. 221). An appreciation by behavior modifiers of the importance of genetics was indicated by the publication of a mini-series on behavioral genetics in the journal *Behavior Therapy* (1986, vol. 17, no. 4). Included in the mini-series were articles on cardiovascular stress and genetics, childhood obesity and genetics, smoking and genetics, and alcoholism and genetics.

STUDY QUESTIONS ON NOTES

1. List two behavioral measures of creativity.
2. How does the behavioral approach to abnormal behavior differ from the medical model approach?
3. Is behavior modification the best treatment for all types of psychological problems? Discuss.
4. Do behavior modifiers ignore what goes on inside a person (i.e., thoughts and feelings)? Discuss.
5. Are all behavior modification procedures based on operant or Pavlovian conditioning? Justify your answer.
6. Are behavior modifiers concerned only with observable behavior? Discuss.
7. Do behavior modifiers deny the importance of genetics? Discuss.

CHAPTER 2

Areas of Application: An Overview

The value of behavior modification techniques for improving a wide variety of behaviors has been amply demonstrated in thousands of research reports. Successful applications have been documented with populations from the profoundly retarded to the exceptionally intelligent, with the very young and very old, both in highly controlled institutional programs and in uncontrolled community settings. The behaviors worked with have ranged from simple motor behaviors to complex intellectual problem solving. Applications are occurring with an ever-increasing frequency in such areas as education, social work, nursing, clinical psychology, psychiatry, community psychology, medicine, rehabilitation medicine, business, industry, and sports. This chapter briefly describes major areas of application in which behavior modification has a solid foundation and a promising future.

EDUCATION: FROM PRESCHOOL TO UNIVERSITY

Since the early 1960s, behavior modification applications in classrooms have progressed on several fronts. Many applications in grade school were designed to change student behaviors that were disruptive or incompatible with academic learning. Out-of-seat behavior, tantruming, aggressive behavior, excessive socializing—all have been successfully dealt with in classroom settings. Other applications have been concerned with modifying academic behavior directly, including oral reading, reading comprehension, spelling, handwriting, mathematics, English composition, creativity, and mastering science concepts. Considerable success has also been achieved in applications with individuals with special problems, such as learning disabled and hyperactive children.

Inroads have also been made in the use of behavior modification in physical education. The progress that has been made includes development of reliable observations for monitoring the behavior of physical education teachers and students so as to provide usable information on "what's happening in the gym?"; increased acceptance of "behavioral teaching skills" as important components for teacher preparation programs; and increased acceptance of behavioral strategies to help physical educators manage a variety of behavioral difficulties of students (Siedentop & Taggart, 1984).

An important innovation in behavioral approaches to teaching is that of *Personalized System of Instruction (PSI)*. PSI was developed by Fred S. Keller and his colleagues in the United States and Brazil in the 1960s as a behavior modification approach to university teaching (Keller, 1968). Since then it has spread to a wide variety of subject matters and levels of instruction (Keller & Sherman, 1982). The approach has a number of distinctive characteristics that make it possible for teachers to effectively use principles of behavior modification in improving classroom instruction. In particular, PSI: (1) identifies the target behaviors or learning requirements for a course in the form of study questions, such as the questions at the end of each chapter in this book; (2) requires students to study only a small amount of material before demonstrating mastery, such as the amount of material contained in a chapter or two and that might be studied in a week or two; (3) has frequent tests (such as once every week or two) in which students are required to demonstrate their knowledge of the answers to the study objectives; (4) has mastery criteria so that students must demonstrate mastery at a particular level before going on to the next level; (5) uses lectures primarily for motivation and demonstration, rather than as a major means of presenting new information; (6) uses a number of student assistants (called proctors) to assist in immediately scoring tests and providing feedback to students concerning test performance; and (7) incorporates a "go-at-your-own-pace" feature in which students are allowed to proceed through the course material at rates that suit their own particular abilities and time demands.

As originally conceived by Keller, PSI courses can require a good deal of labor to administer, especially with large classes, because of the extensive record keeping that PSI requires. With the rise of computer technology, some instructors have begun to automate much of the PSI procedure to make it more efficient. In addition, computers that are part of networks or that have time-sharing options (such as the mainframe computers on college and university campuses) have built-in telecommunications capabilities (e.g., electronic mail) that enable students to write and submit tests for marking, and that allow instructors and proctors to mark tests and provide rapid feedback, without the instructor, proctors, and students having to be at the same location or working on the course at the same time. This can be of great benefit to students who are unable to attend classes because of where they live, their job, or a disability. At the University of Manitoba, where it has been used for a number of years in several psychology courses, computer-aided PSI has been very popular with both on-campus and off-campus students (Kinsner & Pear, 1988; Pear & Kinsner, 1988).

Excellent "how-to-do-it" descriptions of behavior modification techniques for teachers have been published by Alberto and Troutman (1990) and Becker (1986). Reviews of research in several areas of behavior modification and education can be found in Witt, Elliot, and Gresham (1988), and Wielkiewicz (1986). Descriptions of PSI and its research foundation are contained in Keller and Sherman (1982), and Sherman, Ruskin, and Semb (1982).

SEVERE PROBLEMS: MENTAL RETARDATION, CHILDHOOD AUTISM, AND SCHIZOPHRENIA

Beginning in the 1960s, some of the most dramatic successes of behavior modification have occurred with applications to individuals with severe behavioral handicaps.

MENTAL RETARDATION

The diagnostic system of mental retardation used by the American Association on Mental Deficiency is based on an individual's performance on a standardized intelligence test, such as the Stanford-Binet Intelligence Scale or the Wechsler Intelligence Scale for Children (see Table 2–1). While a score on an intelligence test correlates with a general level of functioning, more useful assessment devices for training purposes are those that identify specific behavioral excesses and/or deficits, such as the Objective Behavioral Assessment Test (The OBA, Hardy, Martin, Yu, Leader, & Quinn, 1981). The OBA is described in more detail in Chapter 19.

Table 2-1 Incidence and Percentage of Mental Retardation by Categories

LEVEL	IQ OBTAINED STANFORD-BINET	WECHSLER	PERCENTAGE OF MENTALLY RETARDED	ESTIMATED NUMBER IN THE UNITED STATES
Mild	67–52	69–55	89.0	5,340,000
Moderate	51–36	54–40	6.0	360,000
Severe	35–20	39–25 (extrapolated)	3.5	200,000
Profound	19 and below	24 and below (extrapolated)	1.5	90,000

During the latter part of the nineteenth century, large institutions for mentally retarded persons began to be built. Until approximately the 1950s, treatment and training programs for all levels of retardation were minimal, and they were the most limited for the severe and profound levels. Fortunately, three forces materialized in the 1960s that, collectively, revolutionized the education of mentally handicapped persons. One force was represented by normalization advocates, such as Wolfensberger (1972), who argued that mentally handicapped persons should be helped to lead the most normative lives possible, and that traditional institutionalization is simply not normative. This led to a deinstitutionalization movement and the development of community living options for mentally handicapped persons. The second force was represented by civil rights advocates and parents of the mentally handicapped who, at least in the United States, successfully secured the legal right of the severely handicapped to receive an education. This meant that education programs for retarded persons had to be developed. The third force came primarily through the efforts of behavior modifiers who developed a technology that made it possible to demonstrate changes in the behavior of severely and profoundly retarded persons that experts in the field would have said were impossible just a few short years before. During the past three decades, many studies have successfully demonstrated the applicability of behavioral techniques for teaching mentally handicapped persons such behaviors as toileting, self-help skills (feeding, dressing, and personal hygiene), social skills, communication skills, vocational skills, leisure-time activities, and a variety of community survival behaviors. Reviews of the literature can be found in such sources as Cipani (1989), Matson (1990), and Whitman, Scibik, and Reid (1983), and in issues of *Research in Developmental Disabilities*.

CHILDHOOD AUTISM

Kanner (1943) first described infantile autism as a psychological disorder characterized by language and perceptual abnormalities, ritualistic behaviors, obsessive behaviors, and "an extreme autistic aloneness from birth." Children diagnosed as autistic show some behaviors similiar to children diagnosed as mentally handicapped in that they score much below average on a variety of self-care tasks, such as dressing, grooming, and feeding. However, they are also likely to show some combination of asocial behavior (e.g., not showing distress when their mother leaves the room), echolalia (repeating words or phrases without indicating that the words convey any meaning), under- or over-responsiveness to sensory contact, a flat or inappropriate emotional affect, abnormal play behaviors, and repetitive self-stimulatory behaviors (e.g., spinning objects in front of their eyes). Beginning in the 1960s, and continuing through to the present, Ivar Lovaas and others have developed behavioral treatments for autistic children. Using behavior change techniques, Lovaas focused on strategies to teach social behaviors, eliminate self-stimulatory behaviors, and develop language skills (Lovaas, 1977). When his intensive treatment programs have been applied to autistic children less than 30 months old, 50 percent of those children have been able to enter a regular classroom at the normal school age (Lovaas, 1982). No alternative treatment for autistic children has been shown to be as successful as behavior modification (Handleman, 1986; Lovaas & Smith, 1988, 1989).

SCHIZOPHRENIA

Beginning with a few case studies in the 1950s, major attention was directed toward schizophrenia by behavior therapists in the 1960s and early 1970s (Kazdin, 1978). During the late 1970s and early 1980s, however, interest in this area decreased and only a small number of behavioral articles were published (Bellack, 1986). There is, nevertheless, clear evidence of the success of behavior modification treatments with this population. Because inadequate social relationships are a prime contributor to the poor quality of life experienced by schizophrenics, they have been one of the behaviors targeted for change in behavior modification programs. Available research indicates considerable success in teaching patients social skills and in demonstrating their importance for effective communication and assertiveness (Bellack, Turner, Hersen, & Luber, 1984; Kelly & Lamparski, 1985; Morrison & Bellack, 1984). Other studies have demonstrated the effectiveness of behavioral treatments for teaching both social skills and job finding skills for schizophrenic patients (Bellack and co-workers, 1984; Bellack & Hersen, 1978; Jacobs, Kardashian, Kreinbring, Ponder, & Simpson, 1984). Such findings led Bellack to argue strongly that behavior therapy can make a significant contribution to the treatment, management, and rehabilitation of schizophrenic patients (Bellack, 1986, 1989).

CLINICAL BEHAVIOR THERAPY WITH OUTPATIENTS _____

Behavioral treatment of outpatients by clinical and counseling psychologists has come of age. In Chapter 26, we provide more detailed discussion of treatment of such clinical problems as anxiety disorders, obsessive-compulsive disorders, stress-related problems, depression, obesity, marital problems, sexual dysfunction, and personality disorders. More detailed discussion of these and other areas of clinical treatment can be found in Hersen and Bellack (1985), Kaplan (1986), Last and Hersen (1988), and Wolpe (1990). Presentation of the principles and procedures of child behavior therapy can be found in Hersen (1989) and Gross and Drabman (1990).

How common is behavior therapy among practicing psychologists? In his Presidential Address to the Association for Advancement of Behavior Therapy, Daniel O'Leary argued that behavior therapy has become one of the major theoretical orientations of psychologists treating children and adults and that behavioral psychologists should work with other professionals to inform the public of our progress (O'Leary, 1984). He pointed out that:

(a) a 1982 survey of clinical child psychologists revealed that the two major orientations of the respondents were behavioral and psychodynamic;

(b) a 1981 survey of pediatric psychologists indicated that 59% had a behavioral orientation, while 39% had a psychodynamic orientation;

(c) for psychologists treating adults, behavior therapy is one of the top two orientations, about on a par with the psychodynamic orientation;

(d) in 1983, in what some might consider to be the two main psychiatric and clinical psychological journals, *Archives of General Psychiatry* and *The Journal of Consulting and Clinical Psychology,* 81 percent of the articles directed at treatment-outcome research involving a minimum of five sessions were evaluations of behavior therapy procedures;

(e) over the past several years, approximately 70 percent of the psychosocial treatment research funded by the U.S. National Institute of Mental Health has been directed at behavior therapy.

How effective is behavior therapy with clinical populations? In their excellent review of earlier evaluations of behavior therapy, Kazdin and Wilson (1978) concluded that: (a) not a single study demonstrated that behavior therapy was significantly inferior to the alternative treatment to which it was compared, which was usually some form of verbal psychotherapy; (b) the majority of studies demonstrated that behavior therapy was marginally or considerably more effective than the alternative treatment; (c) there are clear problem areas (e.g., phobias, obsessive-compulsive disorders) where specific behavior therapy procedures are demonstrably superior to existing psychotherapeutic alternatives. These conclusions are as valid today as they were in 1978 (e.g., see Turner & Ascher, 1985; Giles, 1990).

SELF-MANAGEMENT OF PERSONAL PROBLEMS

Recall some of the problems described in the previous chapter. Sam had difficulty studying and finishing his term papers on time. Karen wasn't able to get started on that novel she wanted to write. And then there was Albert and his phobia of riding in airplanes. Many people would like to change something about themselves. How about you? Would you like to lose a few pounds? Get into an exercise program? Become more assertive? Are there skills you can learn to help you modify your behavior? A great deal of progress has been made in the area referred to as self-management, self-control, self-adjustment, self-modification, or self-direction. Successful self-modification requires a set of skills that can be learned. The skills involve ways of rearranging your environment to control your own subsequent behavior. Hundreds of successful self-modification projects directed at problems such as speaking up in class (Barrera & Glasgow, 1976), increasing exercise behavior (Kau &

Fischer, 1974), improving study habits (Richards, 1976), and eliminating tooth grinding (Pawlicki & Galotti, 1978) have been reported in the psychological literature. Self-modification for personal adjustment is described in more detail in Chapter 23. Extensive discussion of this topic can be found in Martin and Osborne (1989) and Watson and Tharp (1989).

MEDICINE AND HEALTH CARE

Traditionally, if a person suffered from chronic headaches, a respiratory disorder, or hypertension, that individual would see a physician. In the late 1960s, however, psychologists working with physicians began using behavior modification techniques to directly treat these and other medical problems— such as seizure disorders, chronic pain, addictive disorders, and sleep disorders (Doleys, Meredith, & Ciminero, 1982). This launched the discipline that came to be known as **behavioral medicine**, a broad interdisciplinary field concerned with the link among health, illness, and behavior. Behavioral psychologists practicing behavioral medicine work in close consultation with medical doctors, nurses, dieticians, sociologists, and others on problems that, until very recently, have been considered to be of a purely medical nature. Within the interdisciplinary field of behavioral medicine, **health psychology** considers how psychological factors can influence or cause illness, and how people can be encouraged to practice healthy behavior so as to prevent health problems such as heart disease (Feist & Brannon, 1988; Taylor, 1990). Health psychologists have applied behavioral principles in six major subareas.

Direct Treatment of Medical Problems. Do you suffer from headaches, backaches, or stomach problems during final exams? At one time it was thought that such problems were primarily psychological—existing mainly in the minds of those experiencing them. But the colds, headaches, and other symptoms and the accompanying pain are very real. Health psychologists are continuing the trend of the late 1960s of developing behavioral techniques to directly treat physical symptoms such as these (Feist & Brannon, 1988).

Establishing Treatment Compliance. Do you always keep your appointments with the dentist? Do you always take medication exactly as described by your doctor? As many as 50 percent of people don't (Sackett & Snow, 1979). But a drug that is 100 percent effective in curing a particular disease, for example, will be ineffective if the patient fails to take it as directed. Thus, an important part of health psychology is establishing treatment compliance with prescribed medical regimens. Because drug-taking is a behavior, promoting compliance with medical prescriptions is a natural for behavior modification.

Promotion of Healthy Living. Do you exercise at least three times per week? Do you eat properly and minimize your consumption of cholesterol and salt? Do you limit your consumption of alcohol, say, to no more than five drinks a week? Do you say no to tobacco and other drugs? If you can answer yes to these questions, and if you can continue to answer yes as the years go by, then you can considerably lengthen your life span (Figure 2–1). An important area of behavior modification involves the application of techniques to help people stay healthy, such as eating well-balanced meals and getting adequate exercise (Taylor, 1990).

Dealing with Aging and Chronic Illness.   Do you want to know what it's like to be old? Then "you should smear dirt on your glasses, stuff cotton in your ears, put on heavy shoes that are too big for you, and wear gloves, and then try to spend the day in a normal way" (Skinner & Vaughan, 1983, p. 38). As an increasing percentage of the population is made up of the elderly, more and more individuals must deal on a daily basis with loss of the skills and ability to function independently that occurs with old age or with chronic illness. Once again, behavior modification is involved. For example, habitual ways of performing daily routines at home or at work may no longer be possible. New routines must be developed and learned. Anxiety or fear about the possibility of failing to cope also might have to be dealt with. And new relationships might have to be developed with professional care staff. Behavioral techniques are being used increasingly to help the elderly and chronic-care patients to solve such problems.

Management of Caregivers.   Health psychologists are concerned not only with the behavior of the client or patient, but also with the behavior of those who have an impact on the medical condition of the client. Thus, health psychologists deal with the behavior of the client's family or friends as well as with various medical staff. Changing the behavior of nurses, psychiatric nurses, occupational therapists, and other medical personnel to improve service provided to patients is receiving increased attention (e.g., see Reid, Parsons, & Green, 1989).

Stress Management.   Like death and taxes, stress is one of the things that you can be sure of encountering in life. Stressors are conditions or events, such as excessive smog, a death in the family, pending examinations, large debts, and lack of sleep, that present coping difficulties for you. Stress reactions are the physiological and behavioral responses, such as fatigue, high blood pressure, and ulcers, that are brought on by stressors. An important area of health psychology concerns the study of stressors, their effect on behavior, and the development of behavioral strategies for coping with stressors (e.g., see Martin & Osborne, 1989). Some of these strategies are described in later chapters.

Although the broad interdisciplinary field of behavioral medicine and the subfield of health psychology are very young, they have the potential to make a profound contribution to the efficiency and effectiveness of modern medicine and health care (Taylor, 1990). For additional reading in this area, see issues of *The Journal of Behavioral Medicine*, as well as the books by Blechman and Brownell (1989); Cataldo and Coates (1986); and Reed (1990).

FIGURE 2-1   An important area of application of behavior modification stems from a desire to help people stay healthy, rather than waiting to treat them after they become ill. Behavioral strategies have been used effectively to help people to persist in physical fitness programs.

BEHAVIORAL COMMUNITY PSYCHOLOGY

In 1955 the Joint Commission on Mental Health and Illness was established by the U.S. Congress to study and make recommendations for the field of mental health. In 1961 the commission published its final report, which recommended that the size of the populations in state mental hospitals be reduced. This was to be accomplished, in part, by the construction and staffing of community mental health centers, whose mission would be to provide all necessary care for mental health problems while the clients remained in the community. In 1963 the U.S. Congress passed legislation that established three hundred community mental health centers, thereby paving the way for a number of psychologists to begin working at or in close connection with these centers and, therefore, to identify themselves as community psychologists. Because of its obvious importance and the widespread support for it, the area has generated a great deal of interest within psychology. In addition, the scope of community psychology has expanded beyond that of community mental health.

Martin and Osborne (1980) list three salient characteristics of community psychology. First, it emphasizes the early prevention of problems rather than the "fix-it" approach that is characteristic of much of clinical psychology and psychiatry. Second, it emphasizes the utilization of non-professionals in human service programs. Third, it tends, whenever possible, to seek out intervention strategies at the organizational level rather than at the individual level.

Although community psychologists are quite clear about their general approach to community problems, they have as a group been much less clear on the best techniques to use in dealing with those problems. In short, they have lacked a common and effective technology. With the development of behavior modification over the past three decades, however, increasing numbers of behavior modifiers have been entering this field. With them they have brought their technology. In addition, many formerly nonbehavioral community psychologists have begun to adopt some behavioral techniques. Thus, behavior modification may become the recognized technology within the field of community psychology.

For behavior modification to fulfill its promise as the technology of community psychology, however, certain adaptations must be made in the way in which behavior modification has often been done. With regard to the three characteristics of community psychology listed by Martin and Osborne, for example, community behavior modifiers should first de-emphasize the "fix-it" approach (e.g., by identifying individuals who may be unable to deal effectively with extremely stressful situations, and teaching them how to do so before they encounter such situations). With regard to the second characteristic, behavior modifiers frequently make use of nonprofessionals aspart of their general strategy for dealing with problems efficiently. Behavior modification techniques are extremely teachable, and it would seem desirable for community behavior modifiers to continue to emphasize this aspect of their technology. The third characteristic requires a shift from the usual focus of many behavior modifiers who are used to dealing with problems on an individual basis. Instead of dealing specifically with individual cases of aggression in a school setting, for example, a community behavior modifier would prefer to deal with the variables that tend to produce aggression in that particular school. This, of course, is a more efficient approach.

As mentioned, the scope of community psychology has expanded beyond that of community mental health. However, behavior modifiers have also dealt with a broad range of community problems. Important behavior modification projects have been done in such areas as littering, recycling, energy conservation, and job skills training.

Behavior modification has clearly expanded its focus from individual problems to community problems. If the present trend continues, behavior modification should become an important force in the community. For additional reading in the area, see the books by Geller, Winett, and Everett (1982); and Martin and Osborne (1980).

BUSINESS, INDUSTRY, AND GOVERNMENT

Behavior modification has also been applied to improve the performance of individuals in a wide variety of organizational settings. This general area has been referred to as **organizational behavior management** (OBM), which has been defined as the application of behavioral principles and methods to the study and control of individual or group behavior within organizational settings (Frederiksen & Lovett, 1980). Examples of the types of organizations involved range from small businesses to large corporations, and from small community centers (note the overlap with the previous section) to large state hospitals. Thus, OBM is concerned with organizations both small and large, and both private and public. According to Brandon L. Hall (1980, p. 145), former editor of the *Journal of Organizational Behavior Management*,

> The field of OBM consists of the development and evaluation of performance improvement procedures which are based on the principles of behavior discovered through the science of behavior analysis. These procedures are considered to be within the scope of OBM when they focus on improving individual or group performance within an organizational setting, whether that organization be a business, industrial setting, or human service setting, and whether that organization was established for profit or not.

One of the earliest studies in what was to become the field of OBM was carried out at the Emery Air Freight Company. According to an article entitled "Conversations with B. F. Skinner" in the 1973 issue of *Organizational Dynamics*, the desired behavior—employees' placement of packages in special containers—was increased from 45 percent to 95 percent through the use of positive reinforcement in the form of praise from supervisors.

Other studies since then have used behavioral techniques to, for example, improve productivity, decrease tardiness and absenteeism, increase sales volume, create new business, improve worker safety, reduce theft by employees, reduce shoplifting, and improve management-employee relations. For additional reading in this area, see issues of the *Journal of Organizational Behavior Management*, as well as books by Fredericksen (1982); Luthans and Kreitner (1985); and O'Brien, Dickenson, and Rosow (1982).

SPORT PSYCHOLOGY

Since the early 1970s, there has been a growing desire on the part of practicing coaches and athletes for more applied sport science experimentation, particularly in the area of sport psychology (Gowan, Botterill, & Blimke, 1979). *Applied sport psychology* has been defined as the use of psychological knowledge to enhance the development of performance and satisfaction of athletes and others associated with sports (Blimke, Gowan, Patterson, & Wood, 1984).

Behavior modification has made a number of contributions to this rapidly growing area.

Techniques for improving skills of athletes.   What is the most effective way to help an athlete learn new skills, eliminate bad habits and combine simple skills into complex patterns of execution? Considerable research has examined behavior modification techniques for effectively improving skills of athletes (Donahue, Gillis, & King, 1980; Martin & Hrycaiko, 1983) and practical strategies for applying these techniques have been described (Martin & Lumsden, 1987).

Strategies for motivating practice and endurance training.   How can a coach effectively improve attendance at practices, motivate athletes to get the most out of practice time, organize practices so that there is very little downtime in which athletes are inactive? Techniques for solving these types of problems include goal-setting strategies, effective use of reinforcement (or reward) strategies, self-recording and self-monitoring by individual athletes, and team-building sessions (Martin & Lumsden, 1987). All of these motivational techniques are based on principles described in later chapters of this book and can readily be learned by coaches.

Dealing with personal problems of athletes.   When most people hear the word "psychologist" they envision someone sitting in an office conducting therapy to help clients solve various personal problems of daily living. Obviously, athletes can also experience such problems and might seek help from a clinical psychologist to solve those problems. Because personal problems can detract from performance, some countries have psychologists travel with their teams to international competitions so that help is readily available to deal with any psychological problem that an athlete might experience. In this sense, a trained and licensed clinical psychologist is providing a service for athletes in the same way he or she would with any other individual.

Changing the behavior of coaches.   Coaches have a very difficult job. From a behavior modification perspective, a coach must effectively instruct, set goals, praise, reprimand, and perform other activities that, collectively, determine his or her effectiveness as a behavior modifier. Numerous research studies have been conducted in this area (Martin & Hrycaiko, 1983).

"Sports psyching" to prepare for competition.   We have all heard expressions like "The reason the team lost was because they were psyched-out," or "If you want to do your best, you have to get psyched-up." While we may have some general ideas as to what these kinds of phrases mean, knowing generally what they mean and learning how to teach psychological coping skills to athletes are two different things. A number of behavioral strategies have been described for helping athletes prepare for serious competition in sport (Harris & Harris, 1984; Orlick, 1986a, 1986b).

BEHAVIORAL ASSESSMENT

Behavioral assessment began to emerge during the 1960s as an alternative to traditional psychodiagnostic assessment. As indicated in Chapter 1 (note 2), psychoanalytic approaches to abnormal behavior originating from Freud and others viewed abnormal behavior as a symptom of an underlying mental disturbance in a personality mechanism. A major purpose of traditional psychodiagnostic assessment was to identify the type of mental disorder assumed to underly abnormal behavior. In contrast to this, behavioral assessment is concerned with obtaining a description of the problem behavior, identifying possible environmental causes of the behavior, selecting an appropriate behavioral treatment strategy to modify the behavior, and evaluating treatment outcome. As the interest in behavior therapy and behavior modification has expanded during the past three decades, so has the demand for guidelines for conducting behavioral assessments. For more information, refer to Chapters 18 and 19 of this text; the journals *Behavioral Assessment* and the *Journal of Behavioral Assessment*; or the books by Bellack and Hersen (1988); Hayes and Nelson (1986); and Hersen and Bellack (1981).

CONCLUSION

Note 1

The meteoric rise of behavior modification as a successful approach for dealing with a wide range of human problems has been remarkable.[1] Books and journal articles describe behavioral procedures and research ranging from child-raising (Norton, 1977) to coping with old age (Skinner & Vaughan, 1983), and from work (O'Brien et al., 1982) to play (Williams & Long, 1982). It has been used both with profoundly handicapped persons (Ciapani, 1985) and with gifted students (Belcastro, 1985), for self-improvement (Martin & Osborne; 1989), and to preserve the environment in which we live (Geller et al., 1982). Over 850 books have been published concerning basic, applied, and theoretical issues in behavior modification (Rutherford, 1984). A total of 23 journals are predominantly behavioral in their orientation (Wyatt, Hawkins, & Davis, 1986). Examples of applications in many of these areas are described and illustrated in the following chapters.

STUDY QUESTIONS

1. List at least five areas in which behavior modification is being applied.
2. List at least four behaviors that have been modified with behavior modification in education.
3. What is PSI, and who was its founder? State seven characteristics of PSI.
4. Briefly describe how PSI has made use of computer technology. State two benefits of this use of computer technology.

5. Briefly state the three forces that have revolutionized the education of mentally handicapped persons since the 1960s.

6. List at least four behaviors that have been modified by behavior modification with mentally retarded persons.

7. List at least four behaviors that have been modified by behavior modification with childhood autism.

8. List at least four behaviors that have been modified by behavior modification with schizophrenia.

9. State several types of evidence indicating the increasing prominence of behavior therapy in the clinical treatment of outpatients.

10. How effective is behavior therapy with clinical populations? Discuss.

11. List at least four behaviors that have been modified by behavior modification in the area of self-management of personal problems.

12. What is health psychology? Describe six areas of application within health psychology.

13. What are three salient characteristics of community psychology? How might behavior modification be adapted to fit these characteristics?

14. List at least four behaviors that have been modified by behavior modification in the area of behavioral community psychology.

15. Define organizational behavior management.

16. List at least four behaviors that have been modified by behavior modification in business, industry, or government.

17. List five general areas in which behavior modification has been applied in the area of sport psychology.

18. Distinguish between psychodiagnostic assessment and behavioral assessment.

EXTENDED DISCUSSION AND NOTE

1. To assess the impact that the behavioral approach has made on contemporary American culture, Lamal (1989) examined the orientation of psychologists in psychological associations, psychology job openings that required experience in behavior modification, the prevalence of behavioral approaches in business management, and book reviews and discussions of behavioral approaches in such sources as *The New York Review, Harper's, The Atlantic*, and *The New Yorker*. After considering the evidence, in spite of 30 years of impressive research studies, Lamal concluded that the behavioral approach had minimal impact on contemporary American culture, and that only a small minority of psychologists follow the approach. Lamal outlined a number of strategies that might be adopted to improve the dissemination and marketing of behavior modification—an outcome that is necessary if the potential of behavior modification for contributing to a better society is to be realized.

STUDY QUESTION ON NOTE

1. What has been the impact of the behavioral approach on contemporary American culture? Discuss.

CHAPTER 3

Getting a Behavior to Occur More Often with Positive Reinforcement

"Do you want this, Mommy?"

REINFORCING DARREN'S COOPERATIVE BEHAVIOR

Darren was a six-year-old boy who was extremely uncooperative with his parents.* They took him to the Gatzert Child Developmental Clinic at the University of Washington in the hope of learning how to deal more effectively with Darren's excessive commanding behavior. According to the parents, Darren virtually "ran the show," deciding when he would go to bed, what foods he would eat, when his parents could play with him, and so on. To obtain direct observations of Darren's behavior, both cooperative and uncooperative, Dr. Robert Wahler asked Darren's mother to spend some time with Darren in a playroom at the clinic. The playroom was equipped with adjoining observation rooms for data recording. During the first two 20-minute sessions (called baseline sessions), Darren's mother was instructed: "Just play with Darren as you might at home." Darren's "commanding" behavior was defined as any verbal or nonverbal instructions to his mother, such as pushing her into a chair, or saying such things as "You go over there and I'll stay here," or "No, that's wrong. Do it this way." Cooperative behavior was defined as any nonimperative statements, actions, or questions. To illustrate the consistency of Darren's behavior, we present a graph of the data collected in consecutive 10-minute intervals. As can be seen in Figure 3–1, Darren showed a very low rate of cooperative behavior during the baseline sessions. His commanding behavior (not shown in the figure), on the other hand, occurred at an extremely high rate. Following the baseline sessions, Darren's mother was asked to be very positive and supportive to any instances of cooperative behavior shown by Darren. At the same time, she was instructed to completely ignore his commanding

*This example is based on an article by Wahler, Winkel, Peterson, and Morrison (1965).

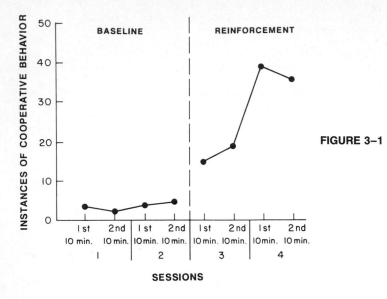

FIGURE 3–1 Darren's cooperative behavior. Each data point (dot) represents the total instances of Darren's cooperative behavior during a 10-minute interval within a session. Baseline refers to the observation phase prior to the reinforcement program. (Replotted from Wahler and others, 1965, Figure 1, p. 117.)

behavior. Over the next two sessions, Darren's cooperative behavior steadily increased. (During the same time, his commanding behavior decreased to near zero.) Further experimentation was done by Dr. Wahler and his colleagues to demonstrate that Darren's improvement was due to the positive consequences provided by his mother following instances of Darren's cooperative behavior (in conjunction with her ignoring of commanding behavior).

POSITIVE REINFORCEMENT

A **positive reinforcer** is an event that, when presented immediately following a behavior, causes the behavior to increase in frequency. The term *positive reinforcer* is roughly synonymous with the word **reward**. Once an event has been determined to function as a positive reinforcer for a particular individual in a particular situation, that event can be used to strengthen other behaviors of that individual in other situations. In conjunction with the concept of positive reinforcer, the principle called **positive reinforcement** states that *if, in a given situation, somebody does something that is followed immediately by a positive reinforcer, then that person is more likely to do the same thing again when he or she next encounters a similar situation.*

Although everyone has a commonsense notion of rewards, very few people are aware of just how frequently they are influenced by positive reinforcement during every hour of every day of their lives. Some examples of instances of positive reinforcement are shown in Table 3–1. (The terms "positive reinforcement" and "reinforcement" are often used interchangeably.)

The individuals in each of the examples in Table 3–1 were not con-

Table 3-1 Examples of Instances of Reinforcement of Desirable Behaviors

SITUATION	RESPONSE	IMMEDIATE CONSEQUENCES	LONG-TERM EFFECTS
1 Mother is busy ironing in the kitchen. Her three-year-old daughter is whining and attempting to get her attention.	The child gives up after five minutes and begins playing with baby sister.	Mother has just completed her ironing and sits down to play with daughter and baby sister for a brief period.	In the future, the daughter is more likely to play with baby sister rather than annoy mother because of the attention given when she began playing with her baby sister.
2 While you are waiting in a long line of cars for the light to change at a busy intersection, a car stops in the alley on your right.	You wave to the driver in the alley to pull into the line of traffic in front of you.	The driver nods and waves thanks to you and pulls into the line of traffic.	The pleasant feedback from the driver increases the likelihood that you will be courteous in similar situations in the future.
3 The students in a third-grade class have been given an assignment to complete.	Suzy, who is often quite disruptive, sits quietly in her desk and works on the assignment.	The teacher walks over to Suzy and pats her gently on the shoulder.	In the future, Suzy is more likely to work on the assignments given to her in class.
4 Father and child are shopping in a department store on a hot afternoon and both are very tired.	The child (uncharacteristically) follows father around the store quietly without complaining.	Father turns to the child and says, "Let's go and buy an ice cream cone and sit down for a while."	On future shopping excursions, the child is more likely to follow father quietly.
5 A woman has just tasted a batch of soup she made, and it tasted very bland.	She adds a little Worcestershire sauce.	"It tastes very tangy, just like minestrone soup," she says to herself.	There is an increased likelihood that, in similar situations in the future, she will add Worcestershire sauce to her soup.

Table 3-1   (*Continued*)

SITUATION	RESPONSE	IMMEDIATE CONSEQUENCES	LONG-TERM EFFECTS
6 A husband and wife are undressing and getting ready for bed.	The husband picks up her underthings and places them in the laundry hamper.	His wife pats him and murmurs her thanks.	In future evenings, the husband is more likely to put her underwear in the laundry hamper.
7 One of the authors of this book is attempting to dictate some material into the tape recorder, but the tape recorder is not working.	The author jiggles one of the wires attached to the microphone.	The tape recorder starts working.	The likelihood of wire jiggling increases in similar situations in the future.

sciously using the principle of reinforcement; they were just "doing what comes naturally." In each example, it might take several repetitions before there would be any really obvious increase in the reinforced response (that is, an increase that would be really noticeable to a casual observer). Nevertheless, the effect is still there. Every time we do something, no matter what it is, there are consequences that "turn us on" or "turn us off" or don't affect us one way or the other. Think about what you have done in the past hour, the past day, the past week, and think of the immediate consequences of some of those activities. Can you identify those consequences?

It is helpful to think about behavior in the same way that we think about other aspects of nature. What happens when you drop your shoe? It falls toward the earth. What happens to a lake when the temperature drops below zero degrees Celsius? The water freezes. These are things that we all know about and that physicists have studied extensively and formulated into laws, such as the law of gravity. The principle of positive reinforcement is

Note 1   also rapidly approaching the status of a law. Scientific psychology[1] has been studying this principle in great detail since the 1930s, and we know that it is the single most important part of the learning process. We also know of a number of factors that determine the degree of influence the principle of reinforcement will have on behavior. These factors have been formulated into guidelines to be followed when using positive reinforcement to strengthen desirable behavior.

FACTORS INFLUENCING THE EFFECTIVENESS OF POSITIVE REINFORCEMENT

1. SELECTING THE BEHAVIOR TO BE INCREASED

The behaviors to be reinforced must first be identified specifically. If you start with a general behavior category (e.g., being more friendly), you should then identify specific behaviors (e.g., smiling) which characterize that category. By being specific in this way, you (a) help to ensure the reliability of detecting instances of the behavior and changes in its frequency, which is the yardstick by which one judges reinforcer effectiveness; and (b) increase the likelihood that the reinforcement program will be applied consistently.

2. CHOOSING REINFORCERS ("DIFFERENT STROKES FOR DIFFERENT FOLKS")

Some stimuli are positive reinforcers for virtually everyone. Food is a positive reinforcer for almost every person who has not had anything to eat for several hours. Candy is a reinforcer for most children.

On the other hand, different individuals are frequently "turned on" by different things. Consider the case of Dianne, a six-year-old retarded girl who was in a project conducted by one of the authors. She was able to mimic a number of words, and we were trying to teach her to name pictures. Two reinforcers commonly used in the project were candy and bites of the child's supper, but neither of these proved effective with Dianne. She spat them out about as often as she ate them. After trying many other potential reinforcers, we finally discovered that allowing her to play with a toy purse for 15 seconds was very reinforcing. As a result, after many hours of training she is now speaking in phrases and complete sentences. For another child, listening to a music box for a few seconds turned out to be an effective reinforcer after other potential reinforcers failed. These stimuli might not have been reinforcing for everyone, but that is not important. The important thing is to use a reinforcer that is effective with the individual with whom you are working.

Most positive reinforcers can be classified under five somewhat overlapping headings: *consumable, activity, manipulative, possessional,* and *social.* Classified as consumable reinforcers are such things as candy, cookies, fruit, and soft drinks. Examples of activity reinforcers are the opportunities to watch television, look at a picture book, or even stare out of a window. Manipulative reinforcers include the opportunities to play with a favorite toy, color or paint, ride a tricycle, or tinker with a tape recorder. Possessional reinforcers refer to the opportunities to sit in one's favorite chair, wear a favorite shirt or dress, have a private room, or enjoy some other item that one can possess (at least temporarily). Social reinforcement includes affectionate pats and hugs, praise, nods, smiles, and even a simple glance or other indication of social attention.

Attention from others is a very strong reinforcer for almost everyone. As anyone who has visited an institution for the retarded knows, it is particularly powerful for retarded individuals. The high frequency at which these individuals demand attention from both staff and visitors tells us something about its high reinforcing effectiveness (Figure 3–2)

In choosing effective reinforcers for an individual, it is often helpful to examine a list of reinforcers used by others (see Table 3–2), or to complete a reinforcer survey. An example of such a survey is shown in Figure 3–3.

A considerable amount of trial and error may be involved in finding an appropriate reinforcer for a particular individual. Another method is simply to observe the individual in everyday activities and note those activities engaged in most often. This method makes use of a principle first formulated by David Premack (1959), which states that a behavior that occurs frequently can be used to reinforce a behavior that occurs less often.* For example, Johnson (1971) used this principle to help a depressed 17-year-old college

FIGURE 3–2 Praise is a powerful positive reinforcer for strengthening and maintaining valued behaviors in everyday life.

*The Premack principle is examined in Chapter 23.

Table 3-2   Reinforcers for Employees in a Variety of Work Settings

SPECIAL ATTENTION REINFORCERS	MONETARY REINFORCERS
Praise	Promotion
Praise in front of others	Paid days off
Special work assignments	Company stock
Reserved parking space	Company car
Choice of office	Pay for sick days not taken
Selection of own office furnishings	Pay for overtime accumulated
Invitation to higher-level meetings	Tickets to special events
Choice of work attire	Free raffle or lottery tickets
Social contacts with others	Extra furnishings for office
Solicitation of opinions and ideas	Gift certificates
Choice of work partner	Dinner for family at nice restaurant
Flexible job duties	Personalized license plate
COMPANY TIME REINFORCERS	Personalized gifts
	Desk calculator or computer terminal
Time off for work-related activities	Business cards
Time off for personal business	Expense account
Extra break time	*PARTICIPATION REINFORCERS*
Extra meal time	
Choice of working hours or days off	Voice in policy decisions
	Help set standards
	More responsibility
	Opportunity to learn new skill

student increase the frequency of positive self-statements. The student was required to imagine a positive thought (a low probability behavior) as prompted from a statement on an index card just before each instance of urinating (the high probability behavior). After a few days, the student spontaneously thought the positive self-statements just before urinating without the necessity of reviewing the index card. After two weeks of this procedure, the student reported that the positive thoughts were occurring at a high rate (and that the depressive thoughts had completely disappeared).

It is often quite effective to allow an individual to choose among a number of available reinforcers (Green et al., 1988). Variety is not only the spice of life; it is also a valuable asset to a training program. For example, a tray containing sliced fruits, peanuts, candy, and soft drinks can be presented to a severely retarded child after each desired response, with the instruction to take one item. The advantage of this is that at least one reinforcer among the selection is likely to be strong. If the individual can read, the reinforcers can be listed in the form of a "reinforcer menu," and the preferred reinforcers can be chosen in the same way that one would order a meal at a restaurant.

One last point to emphasize is that it is always the individual's per-

This questionnaire is designed to help you find some specific activities, objects, events, or individuals that can be used as reinforcers in an improvement program. Read each question carefully and then fill in the appropriate blanks.

A Consumable reinforcers: What does this person like to eat or drink?
   1   What things does this person like to eat most?
      a regular meal-type foods _____
      b health foods—dried fruits, nuts, cereals, etc. _____
            _____
      c junk foods—popcorn, potato chips, etc. _____
      d sweets—candies, ice cream, cookies, etc. _____
   2   What things does this person like to drink most?
      a milk _____   c juices _____
      b soft drinks _____   d other _____

B Activity reinforcers: What things does this person like to do?
   1   Activities in the home or residence
      a hobbies _____
      b crafts _____
      c redecorating _____
      d preparing food or drinks _____
      e housework _____
      f odd jobs _____
      g other _____
   2   Activities in the yard or courtyard
      a sports _____
      b gardening _____
      c barbecue _____
      d yardwork _____
      e other _____
   3   Free activities in the neighborhood (window shopping, walking, jogging, cycling, driving, swinging, teeter-tottering, etc.) _____
      _____
   4   Free activities farther away from home (hiking, snow shoeing, swimming, camping, going to the beach, etc.) _____
      _____
      _____
   5   Activities you pay to do (films, plays, sports events, night clubs, pubs, etc.) _____
   6   Passive activities (watching TV, listening to the radio, records, or tapes; sitting, talking, bathing, etc.) _____
      _____

C Manipulative reinforcers: What kinds of games or toys interest this person?
   1   Toy cars and trucks _____
   2   Dolls _____
   3   Wind-up toys _____
   4   Balloons _____

(Continued)

FIGURE 3–3 A Questionnaire to Help an Individual Identify Reinforcers

   5   Whistle _____
   6   Jump rope _____
   7   Coloring books and crayons _____
   8   Painting kit _____
   9   Puzzles _____
  10   Other _____
D Possessional reinforcers: What kinds of things does this person like to possess?
   1   Brush _____
   2   Nail clippers _____
   3   Hair clips _____
   4   Comb _____
   5   Perfume _____
   6   Belt _____
   7   Gloves _____
   8   Shoelaces _____
   9   Other _____
E Social reinforcers: What kinds of verbal or physical stimulation does this person like to receive from others? (specify who)
   1   Verbal stimulation
       a "Good girl (boy)" _____
       b "Good work" _____
       c "Good job" _____
       d "That's fine" _____
       e "Keep up the good work" _____
       f other _____
   2   Physical contact
       a hugging _____
       b kissing _____
       c tickling _____
       d patty-cake _____
       e wrestling _____
       f bouncing on knee _____
       g other _____

formance that tells you whether or not you have selected reinforcers wisely for that individual. When you are not sure if a particular item is reinforcing, you can always conduct an experimental test. Simply choose a behavior that the individual emits occasionally, record how often the behavior occurs without reinforcement over several trials, and then present the item following the behavior for a few additional trials and see what happens. If the individual begins to emit that behavior more often, then your item is indeed a reinforcer. If the performance does not increase, then you do not have an effective reinforcer. In our experience, not using an effective reinforcer is one of the most common errors of training programs. For example, a teacher may claim that a particular reinforcement program that he is trying to use is failing. Upon examination, the "reinforcer" used may turn out not to be a reinforcer for the student. No item should be assumed to be reinforcing without first being demonstrated to function as reinforcer for that person. In other words, an object or event *is defined as a reinforcer only by its effect on behavior.*

3. DEPRIVATION AND SATIATION

Most reinforcers will not be effective unless the individual has been deprived of them for some period of time prior to their use. In general, the longer the deprivation period, the more effective the reinforcer will be. Sweets will usually not be reinforcing to a child who has just eaten a large bag of candy. Playing with a purse would not have been an effective reinforcer for Dianne had she been allowed to play with one prior to the training session. We use the term *deprivation* to indicate the time, prior to a training session, during which an individual does not experience the reinforcer. The term *satiation* refers to that condition in which the individual has experienced the reinforcer to such an extent that it is no longer reinforcing. "Enough's enough," as the saying goes.

4. IMMEDIACY

For maximum effectiveness, a reinforcer should be given immediately after the desired response. Recall that Darren's mother followed this rule closely when working with him. A positive reinforcer strengthens any response that it immediately follows.

Sometimes it is possible to get an individual (who can follow instructions) to work for delayed reinforcement. Telling a child that if she (or he) cleans up her room in the morning her father will bring her a toy in the evening is sometimes effective. Of course, some people do work for very long delayed goals, such as college degrees. But it is a mistake to attribute such results to the direct effects of the principle of positive reinforcement. A reinforcer is not likely to have much direct effect on a behavior that precedes the reinforcer by anything much longer than 30 seconds (Chung, 1965; Hull, 1943; Perin, 1943; Michael, 1986). Knowledge of this fact can help prevent misinterpretations of causes of behavior change. For example, consider the case of Fernando. Fernando worked in an American-owned factory located in the outskirts of Mexico City.* Fernando was one of a group of 12 workers who had a chronic problem—they were frequently late for work. Annual bonuses given by the factory to the 40 workers who had the best attendance records had no effect on Fernando. Likewise, disciplinary interviews and one-

---

*This example is based on an article by Hermann, Montes, Dominguez, Montes, and Hopkins (1973).

day suspensions without pay failed to increase the frequency with which Fernando arrived on time. In fact, over a 12-week period while the latter condition was in effect, Fernando arrived on time less than 80 percent of the working days (see Figure 3–4, baseline phase). Jaime Hermann, with the support of managers at the factory, decided to implement a treatment program involving positive reinforcers. Jaime talked to Fernando (and the other workers who participated in the program) individually, and explained the procedure. Each day that Fernando punched in on time, he was immediately given a slip of paper indicating that he had earned approximately 2 pesos. At the end of each week, Fernando exchanged his slips for cash. As can be seen in Figure 3–4, the program had an immediate effect. Fernando arrived at work on time every day during the first eight weeks of the program. The program had a similar positive effect on the other 11 workers who had also frequently been late for work. Moreover, additional experimental phases demonstrated that the improvement was due to the treatment.

At first glance, Fernando's improvement may appear to represent a straightforward case of the direct effects of positive reinforcement. A closer analysis reveals the necessity for an alternative interpretation (Michael, 1986). What was the response that was directly reinforced? Punching the time clock? But punching the time clock more rapidly wouldn't have much effect on arrival time. How about walking more quickly from the parking lot to the factory entrance? But that response was not directly measured. Moreover, arriving at work on time is more likely a function of such behaviors as setting an alarm clock the night before to wake up earlier in the morning, perhaps taking less time to have breakfast, and leaving for work earlier than in the past. But these behaviors were not directly and immediately reinforced by the

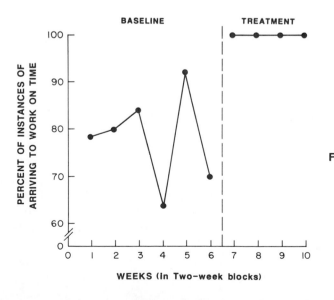

FIGURE 3–4 Fernando's instances of arriving at work on time. Each data point (dot) represents the percent of total instances that Fernando arrived at work on time during a 2-week period. (Replotted from Hermann and others, 1973, Figure 2, p. 568.)

receipt of the 2 pesos. Perhaps, because of Fernando's complex conditioning history concerning language, Jaime's description of the new program the day before it was put into effect increased the probability of certain self-instructional behavior on Fernando's part, both the night before he had to go to work and during the next morning at home, concerning the necessity of arriving on time. For example, before going to bed, Fernando might have said to himself, "I'm going to set the alarm half an hour early to make sure that I earn 2 extra pesos tomorrow," and he may have repeated something similar when he awoke the following morning. In other words, the positive effects of the program were due to the treatment. But the treatment was more complex than that of a positive reinforcer increasing the frequency of a re-

Note 2 sponse that immediately preceded it.[2]

5. INSTRUCTIONS: MAKE USE OF RULES

For reinforcement to increase an individual's behavior, it is *not* necessary that that individual be able to talk about or indicate an understanding of why he

Note 3 or she was reinforced.[3] After all, the principle has been shown to work quite effectively with animals that cannot talk (at least not in a human language). Nevertheless, instructions should generally be used.

Instructional influences on behavior will be easier for you to understand after reading the chapter on stimulus discrimination training (Chapter 8). But for now, let's view instructions as specific rules or guidelines that

Note 4 indicate that specific behaviors will pay off in particular situations.[4] For example, your professor might suggest the rule, "If you learn the answers to all of the study questions in this book, you will receive an A in the course."

Instructions can facilitate behavioral change in several ways. First, specific instructions will speed up the learning process for individuals who already understand them. For example, beginning tennis players practicing backhand shots showed little progress when simply told to "concentrate." But they showed rapid improvement when told to vocalize the word "ready" when the ball machine was about to present the next ball, the word "ball" when they saw the ball fired from the machine, the word "bounce" as they watched the ball contact the surface of the court, and the word "hit" when they observed the ball contacting their racquet while swinging their backhand (Ziegler, 1987). Second, as indicated above, instructions may influence an individual to work for delayed reinforcement. Getting an "A" in the course for which you are using this book, for example, is delayed several months from the beginning of the course. Daily rehearsing of the rule, "If I learn the answers to the questions at the end of each chapter, I'll likely get an A," may exert some influence over your study behavior. Third (as discussed further in Chapter 8), adding instructions to reinforcement programs may help to teach individuals (such as very young children or mentally retarded persons) to follow instructions.

6. WEANING THE STUDENT FROM THE PROGRAM AND CHANGING TO NATURAL REINFORCERS

The previous factors influence the effectiveness of positive reinforcement while it is being applied in a program. But what happens to the behavior when the reinforcement program terminates and the individual returns to his or her everyday environment? Most behaviors in everyday life are followed by reinforcers even though no one specifically or deliberately programmed the reinforcers to increase or maintain them. Reading signs is frequently reinforced by finding desired objects or directions. Eating is reinforced by the taste of food. Verbal and social behaviors are reinforced by the natural reactions of other people. Such events may be manipulated deliberately by psychologists, teachers, and others in behavior modification programs, and in such cases they would be referred to as arbitrary, contrived, or programmed reinforcers. Unprogrammed reinforcers that occur in the normal course of everyday living are called **natural reinforcers**, and the settings in which they occur are called the *natural environment*.

Note 5   After we have strengthened a behavior through proper use of positive reinforcement, it may then be possible for a reinforcer in the individual's natural environment to take over the maintenance of that behavior.[5] For example, sometimes it is necessary to use reinforcers such as edibles to strengthen picture naming in behaviorally retarded children. However, when the children leave the project and go back to their wards at the institution, they often say the words that they have learned and receive a great deal of attention from the aides. Eventually, the edibles may no longer be needed to reinforce the children for saying the names of pictures and objects. This, of course, is the ultimate goal of any training program. The teacher* should always try to ensure that the behavior being established in a training program will be reinforced and maintained in the natural environment. Because this problem is so important, it is discussed in much more detail in Chapter 12.

PITFALLS OF POSITIVE REINFORCEMENT

Note 6   Those who are aware of the principle of positive reinforcement can use it to bring about desirable changes in behavior. The principle operates equally well for those who are not aware of it. Unfortunately, those who are not aware of it are apt to use it unknowingly to strengthen undesirable behavior.[6] Table 3–3 presents some examples of how positive reinforcement may work against us in the long run.

*Throughout this book, the word *teacher* is sometimes used to refer to the individual (parent, teacher, nurse, aide, or whoever) who is helping someone to overcome a behavior problem. The word *student* is frequently used to refer to the individual who has the problem. Unless prompted otherwise, please do not think just of a typical classroom situation when you read about teachers and students in this book.

Table 3-3 Examples of Positive Reinforcement Following Undesirable Behavior

SITUATION	RESPONSE	IMMEDIATE CONSEQUENCES	LONG-TERM EFFECTS
1 A three-year-old child who has been playing with her coloring book gets up and looks around the living room.	The child goes over to the TV and begins fiddling with the dials.	Mother immediately comes over to her and says, "I guess you're tired of playing by yourself; let's go for a walk."	The chances of the child fiddling with the TV dials in the future increases because of the attention from mother.
2 While getting ready for work in the morning, a man cannot find his clean shirt.	He hollers loudly, "Where in the hell is my shirt?"	The wife immediately finds the husband's shirt.	In the future, the husband is more likely to holler and swear when he can't find his clothes.
3 A father is busy ironing, and his two young children are playing quietly.	One child hits his little brother over the head with a toy truck.	Father stops ironing and sits down to play with the child for a while.	The child is more likely to belt his little brother in the future to gain father's attention.
4 Mother and child are shopping in a department store.	Child begins to whine, "I want to go home; I want to go home."	Mother is embarrassed and leaves the store immediately with the child before making her purchases.	Child is more likely to whine in a similar situation in the future.
5 Severely retarded residents are eating their meal in the dining room at an institution.	One girl holds up her empty glass and grunts loudly, "Mmmmm, mmmmm, mmmmm."	One of the staff members immediately comes and fills the glass with milk.	The girl is likely to hold up her glass and make similar noises in future situations when she wants milk.
6 Father is watching a Stanley Cup playoff hockey game on TV.	Two of the children are playing in the same room and are being extremely noisy.	Father gives them each a dollar so that they will go to the store and not interfere with his TV watching.	The children are more likely to play very noisily when father is watching TV in similar situations in the future.

Table 3-3 *(Continued)*

SITUATION	RESPONSE	IMMEDIATE CONSEQUENCES	LONG-TERM EFFECTS
7 At a party, a husband becomes sullen when his wife is dancing flirtatiously with another man.	The husband shows signs of jealousy and angrily leaves the party.	The wife immediately follows him, and showers him with attention.	The husband is more likely to show jealousy and leave parties in similar situations in the future.

In our experience, the vast majority of undesirable activities of behaviorally deficient individuals is due to the social attention that such behavior evokes from aides, nurses, peers, teachers, parents, doctors, and others. This may be true even in cases where one would least expect it. Consider, for example, autistic and retarded children who exhibit extreme social withdrawal. One behavioral characteristic of such children is that they avoid looking at a person who is talking to them. Frequently, they move away from approaching adults. We might conclude that they don't want our attention. Actually, the withdrawn child's behavior probably gains him or her more social attention than would have been obtained by looking at the adult. In such cases it is only natural for adults to persist in attempting to get a child to look at them when they speak to the child. Unfortunately, this behavior is likely to reinforce the child's withdrawal behavior. The tendency to shower attention is sometimes maintained by the theory that social interaction is needed to "bring the child out of his or her withdrawn state." In reality, an appropriate treatment might involve withholding social attention for withdrawal behavior and presenting it only when the child engages in some sort of social-interaction behavior—such as looking in the direction of an adult who is attempting the interaction. The hard work of one aide or nurse using appropriate behavior techniques can be greatly hindered, or completely undone, by others who are reinforcing the wrong things. For example, an aide who attempts to reinforce eye contact in a withdrawn child is probably not going to have much effect if other people who interact with the child consistently reinforce looking-away behavior.

GUIDELINES FOR THE EFFECTIVE APPLICATION OF POSITIVE REINFORCEMENT

The following guidelines are offered for the use of parents, teachers, nurses, mental retardation workers, and others who wish to utilize positive reinforcement to increase occurrences of a particular behavior.

1. *Selecting the behavior to be increased.* As we indicated earlier in this chapter, the behavior selected should be a specific behavior (such as smiling) rather than a general category of behavior (such as socializing). Also, if possible, select a behavior that will come under the control of natural reinforcers after it has been increased in frequency. Finally, as shown with Darren's case, to judge the effectiveness of your reinforcer accurately, it is important to keep track of how often the behavior occurs prior to your program.

2. *Selecting a reinforcer.*
   a. If possible, complete the reinforcer survey presented in Figure 3–3 and select strong reinforcers that
      (1) are readily available.
      (2) can be presented immediately following the desired behavior.
      (3) can be used over and over again without causing rapid satiation.
      (4) do not require a great deal of time to consume (if it takes a half-hour to consume the reinforcer, this minimizes the training time).
   b. Use as many reinforcers as feasible, and, where appropriate, use a reinforcer tray or menu.

3. *Applying positive reinforcement.*
   a. Tell the individual about the plan before starting.
   b. Reinforce *immediately* following the desired behavior.
   c. Describe the desired behavior to the individual while the reinforcer is being given. (For example, say "You cleaned your room very nicely.")
   d. Use lots of praise and physical contact (if appropriate and if these are reinforcing to the individual) when dispensing the reinforcers. However, to avoid satiation, vary the phrases you use as social reinforcers. Don't always say "Good for you." (Some sample phrases: "Very nice"; "That's great"; "Right on"; "Tremendous.")

4. *Weaning the student from the program* (discussed more fully in Chapter 12).
   a. If, during the presentation of a dozen or so opportunities, a behavior has been occurring at a desirable rate, it might be possible to gradually eliminate tangible reinforcers (such as candy and toys) and maintain the behavior with social reinforcement.
   b. Look for other natural reinforcers in the environment that might also maintain the behavior once it has been increased in frequency.
   c. To ensure that the behavior is being reinforced occasionally and that the desired frequency is being maintained, plan periodic assessments of the behavior after the program has terminated.

STUDY QUESTIONS

1. What is a positive reinforcer?
2. What is the principle of positive reinforcement?
3. In what way is positive reinforcement like gravity?
4. Should you tell an individual with whom you are using reinforcement about the reinforcement program before putting it into effect? Why or why not?
5. What is the *best* way to determine if something is reinforcing for someone? (See section on "Choosing Reinforcers".)
6. List the two reasons for using a small amount of the reinforcer per reinforcement.

7. Is it correct to conclude that a withdrawn child does not like attention from other people? Explain.

8. "An object or event is defined as a reinforcer only by its effect on behavior" Explain what this means. (See section of "Choosing Reinforcers.")

9. How might you conduct a test to determine if the social attention of a particular adult is or is not reinforcing for a withdrawn child?

10. What do we mean by the *natural environment*? By *natural reinforcers*?

11. Briefly, what are six factors that influence the effectiveness of reinforcement?

12. Briefly describe the case of Fernando. Discuss whether this case is an example of the direct effects of the principle of positive reinforcement?

13. Why is it necessary to be specific when selecting a behavior for a reinforcement program?

14. Ideally, what four qualities should a reinforcer have (besides the necessary quality of functioning as a reinforcer)? (See p. 42.)

15. Describe two examples of positive reinforcement that you have encountered, one involving a desirable behavior and one involving an undesirable behavior. For each example, identify the situation, behavior, immediate consequence, and probable long-term effects (as shown in Tables 3–1 and 3–3). (The examples should not be from the text.)

16. What is plotted on the vertical axis in Figure 3–1?

17. What is plotted on the horizontal axis in Figure 3–1?

18. Describe three behavioral episodes in this chapter that involved natural reinforcers. Justify your choices.

PRACTICE EXERCISES

1. In a 15-minute period, use a pencil and paper to record your interactions with children. On the front of the paper, put a small mark each time you interact with (i.e., talk to, look at, or touch) a child immediately following a desirable behavior of the child. On the other side of the paper, put a small mark each time that you interact with a child immediately following an undesirable behavior of the child. At the end of the 15-minute period, count up the marks on each side of the paper. We hope that your instances of interaction following desirable behavior are five or six times as many as the interactions following undesirable behavior. If they are not, then we would encourage you to continue this daily exercise until this goal is reached.

2. How many times do you dispense social approval (nods, smiles, or kind words) to children during a day in which your total time with them is at least one hour. How many times do you dispense social disapproval (frown, harsh words, etc.) during a day? Again, use a small piece of paper and a pencil and record the instances in which you dispense social approval and those in which you dispense disapproval. Ideally, your social-approval total at the end of the day will be four or five times the social-disapproval total. We would encourage you to continue this daily exercise until you have achieved this ratio. Several studies have shown this ratio of reinforcers to reprimands to be beneficial (e.g., Madsen & Madsen, 1974; Stuart, 1971).

3. List 10 different phrases that you might use to express your enthusiastic approval to an individual. Practice varying these phrases until they come naturally to you.

SELF-MODIFICATION EXERCISES

1. Watch your own behavior for five one-minute periods while behaving naturally. At the end of each minute, describe a situation, a specific behavior, and the immediate consequences of that behavior. Choose behaviors whose consequences seemed pleasant (rather than neutral or unpleasant).
2. Complete the reinforcer questionnaire (Figure 3–3) for yourself.
3. Assume that someone (your husband, wife, friend, etc.) is going to reinforce one of your behaviors (such as making your bed daily, talking in conversation without swearing, or reading pages of this book). Select the two reinforcers from your completed questionnaire that best satisfy the above guidelines for selecting a reinforcer. Indicate how the guidelines have been satisfied.

EXTENDED DISCUSSION AND NOTES

1. What is scientific psychology? The best answer to this question might be found by examining the behavior of psychologists who consider themselves scientists. Although there is a good deal of agreement among individual scientific psychologists concerning the general characteristics of scientific psychology, there is also some disagreement. Some individuals have argued at length about what science and psychology are and are not. Others, many of whom have never conducted experiments or participated in other scientific activities, have made proposals concerning the manner in which scientific psychology should proceed. (These individuals are often called philosophers of science.) For more detailed discussion of the particular brand of scientific psychology subscribed to in this book, see Skinner (1953, pp. 1–22; 1956) and Sidman (1960). This approach, generally called the *experimental analysis of behavior*, emphasizes the value of studying the effects of manipulable aspects of the environment on observable behavior of individual organisms. Its immediate goals are to improve our prediction and control of the behavior of individual organisms. An additional goal is to improve our explanations of behavior. There are, however, different kinds of explanations. In one sense, a behavior is explained when one demonstrates its controlling variables or "causes." For example, Dr. Wahler explained Darren's commanding behavior by demonstrating that it was being reinforced by his mother's attention. In a second sense, a behavior is explained (or interpreted) when one postulates (but does not demonstrate) controlling variables or causes for that behavior. Much of Skinner's writings (e.g., 1953, 1957, 1969) consist of explanations of this type. That is, he offered plausible interpretations, but ones that he did not demonstrate as being correct. For example, Skinner postulated that one reason we make wishes is that our wishes are occasionally reinforced by coming true. For a discussion of different types of causes of behavior, see Moore (1990).

2. Malott (1984) and Michael (1986) have distinguished between the "direct acting" and the "indirect acting" effects of reinforcement. The direct acting effect of the principle of positive reinforcement is the increased frequency of a response because of its immediate reinforcing consequences. Indirect acting effects of positive reinforcement are those in which a treatment program involving a positive reinforcer influences some behavior (most often language) which in turn influences some other behavior (such as arriving on time). The "other" behavior may be desirable, but it does not occur as a direct-acting effect of positive reinforcement. Michael

(1986) has identified three clues to decide if a behavior change is due to indirect acting (vs. direct acting) effects: (a) the critical response precedes the reinforcer by more than 30 seconds (such as in the case of Fernando, where the critical response was leaving for work earlier than usual); (b) the behavior that is measured shows some increase in strength prior to the first occurrence of the consequence (such as Fernando arriving for work on time the very first morning of the program before he had even received the 2-peso consequence); and (c) a single occurrence of a consequence produces a large change in behavior (such as Fernando maintaining 100 percent arrival from the onset of the treatment). In later chapters we will discuss in more detail strategies that teachers can follow to increase the chances of obtaining indirect acting effects with procedures that involve a positive reinforcer.

3. Although at first it may seem strange to think of people learning without understanding, or being reinforced for emitting a certain behavior without their awareness of it, this is much easier to understand when we consider the following observations. First, from everyday experience as well as from basic experiments, it is obvious that animals can learn even though they are not able to verbalize an understanding or an awareness of their behavioral changes. Similarly, even the most profoundly retarded individuals who cannot speak have been shown to be affected by reinforcement (see Fuller, 1949). Finally, a number of experiments have demonstrated that normal adult humans can be influenced by reinforcement to show behavioral changes even if they are unable to verbalize them. For example, university students in an experiment were instructed to say words individually and not use sentences or phrases. When the experimenter nodded and said "Mmm-hmm" following particular types of words (such as plural nouns vs. adjectives), the students showed an increased frequency of saying that particular word. And yet, when questioned after the experiment, the students were unaware that their behavior was influenced (Greenspoon, 1951).

4. Skinner (1969, pp. 159 ff.) distinguished between what he called *contingency-shaped* and *rule-governed* behavior. Contingency-shaped behavior is behavior that has been strengthened simply because it has been followed by reinforcement. No verbalizations, either overt or covert, are involved in strengthening or evoking the behavior. Rule-governed behavior, on the other hand, is behavior that is controlled by descriptions of the contingencies (i.e., the relationships) between specific responses and specific reinforcers. These descriptions of contingencies can act as stimuli that evoke appropriate behavior, providing that the individual has received reinforcement for emitting appropriate behavior in the presence of (or immediately after) these descriptions or rules.

Rule-governed behavior is so common in most of us that it is almost impossible for us to imagine anyone responding simply on the basis of contingency-shaped behavior. The behavior of all of us, however, was necessarily entirely contingency shaped early in our lives. Rule-governed behavior is slowly developed out of contingency-shaped behavior. In the case of Fernando, the successful results may be partly due to rule-governed behavior.

This interpretation will be easier for you to understand after reading the chapter on stimulus discrimination training (Chapter 8). At present, it is important that you realize that some increases in behavior that may appear to be solely the result of reinforcement may be due at least partly to the existence of rule-governed behavior. For example, a child who has just cleaned her room and is told "Good girl for cleaning your room" may tend to engage in this behavior more frequently. The stimulus "Good girl for cleaning your room" seems to be acting as a reinforcer in this instance. But the child has also been given a rule—namely, "If I clean my room, I'll be a good girl" (and Mom and Dad will be nicer to me, etc.)—which tends to produce the room-cleaning behavior, quite apart from the reinforcing effect of praise. (This is why we would not use "Good girl for cleaning your room" as a reinforcer for the child doing her homework!) An excellent discussion of the importance of rule-governed behavior in everyday life can be found in Baldwin and Baldwin (1986). Detailed discussion of rule-governed behavior in general, and its usefulness in explaining how thoughts influence human behavior in particular, can be found in Hayes (1989a) and Zettle (1990).

5. Some researchers refer to the use of arbitrary or contrived reinforcers in a program as *extrinsic reinforcement*. Some critics of behavior modification (e.g., Deci & Ryan, 1985) have argued that the use of extrinsic reinforcers to increase a behavior may undermine *intrinsic motivation* to perform that behavior.

Unfortunately, the notion of intrinsic motivation is not well defined (Dickinson, 1989; Flora, 1990). Intrinsic motivation is usually proposed to explain a situation where an individual performs some behavior when there is no obvious extrinsic reinforcer maintaining that behavior. For example, a child might work at assembling a puzzle even though there is no obvious reinforcer other than the completed puzzle itself. Experiments that have been offered to support the criticism that extrinsic reinforcers undermine intrinsic motivation have often taken the following form. Subjects are given an activity that is assumed to be intrinsically motivating, such as assembling puzzles. One group is given some extrinsic reinforcer (such as an edible or some money) for assembling puzzles, while a second group assembles puzzles without the reward. Following the experimental session, both groups are again given an opportunity to assemble puzzles. In such studies, the subjects who were rewarded have sometimes spent less time in assembling puzzles when they are no longer rewarded in comparison to the control subjects, and the extrinsic rewards are said to have decreased intrinsic motivation.

The general notion that the use of extrinsic reinforcers undermines intrinsic motivation simply does not stand up either to experimental analysis or to careful analytical scrutiny. First, when performance on a task—such as assembling puzzles—is observed prior to extrinsic reinforcement, during extrinsic reinforcement for performing the task, and then after extrinsic reinforcement is withdrawn, the performance decreases following the withdrawal of extrinsic reinforcement to a level approximately equivalent to the prereinforcement level (Dickinson, 1989).

Second, for those studies in which extrinsic reinforcement did appear to undermine extrinsic reinforcement, alternative explanations of the finding are possible. Setting performance standards for extrinsic reinforcement to perform a task might make the task aversive and lead to a performance decrement when the reinforcement is withdrawn. If you tell a child, for example, "You can earn some candy, but only if you assemble puzzles continuously for the next 10 minutes," the child might assemble the puzzles in the short run, but avoid puzzle assembly after having earned the candy because of the aversiveness of being told what he or she "has to" do.

Third, as indicated in the section "Weaning the Student from the Program" (p. 39) behavior that has been reinforced extrinsically is generally more likely to come under the control of reinforcers in the natural environment and be maintained than behavior that has not been reinforced extrinsically.

Fourth, consider the preferences of the individuals to be reinforced (Mawhinney, 1990). Most people like to receive extrinsic reinforcers. As emphasized by Flora (1990), the notion that extrinsic reinforcers undermine intrinsic interest flies in the face of common sense. Consider, for example, those fortunate individuals who genuinely enjoy their work. If extrinsic reinforcers undermine intrinsic motivation, then these people should no longer accept their paycheck for their work—otherwise their intrinsic interest and enjoyment of their work will be lost.

Additional criticisms of the research purporting to demonstrate that extrinsic reinforcement undermines intrinsic motivation are discussed by Dickinson (1989) and Flora (1990).

6. Many studies have demonstrated that individuals who are unaware of the effects of reinforcement frequently and unknowingly strengthen undesirable behaviors by providing social attention as a reinforcer following those behaviors. A classic example was the early study by Zimmerman and Zimmerman (1958), in which teachers unknowingly maintained extreme tantrums in a child by paying attention to tantrumming behavior. Another classic study, conducted by Harris, Wolf, and Baer (1964), demonstrated clearly that nursery school teachers unknowingly maintained such behaviors as excessive crawling, crying and whining, isolate play, and excessive passivity by paying attention to those behaviors in their children. The authors of this study taught the teachers to ignore such behaviors and to attend to desirable alternative behaviors. The results in all cases were successful in increasing alternative desirable behaviors and decreasing the undesirable behaviors.

STUDY QUESTIONS ON NOTES

1. What two types of explanations are emphasized by the behavioral approach? Describe an example of each.
2. Distinguish between the direct acting and indirect acting effects of reinforcement.
3. What are three clues for deciding if a behavior change is due to indirect acting versus direct acting effects?
4. Discuss evidence that people's behavior can be modified without their being aware of it.
5. Distinguish between rule-governed and contingency-shaped behavior. Give an example of each. Give one reason why it is important for you to understand the distinction.
6. Briefly describe the type of experiment that appeared to demonstrate that extrinsic reinforcement undermines intrinsic motivation.
7. Describe several criticisms of the notion that extrinsic reinforcement undermines intrinsic motivation.
8. Describe a study that demonstrates that individuals who are unaware of the effects of reinforcement may unknowingly reinforce an undesirable behavior.

CHAPTER 4

Decreasing a Behavior with Extinction

"Peter, your tantrums are driving me crazy."

PETER'S CASE

Peter, a 10-year-old boy diagnosed as autistic, was a resident at the Manitoba Developmental Center.* One summer, he participated in a behavior modification program in which university students, under the supervision of one of the authors, attempted to teach him to talk and to engage in some basic kindergarten activities. One of the main problems encountered was that Peter frequently threw severe tantrums, during which he stamped, kicked, screamed, threw things, slapped his face, cried, and yelled "Cut," "Needle," or "Doctor" while pointing to his arm, leg, or some other part of his anatomy. These tantrums appeared to be provoked by mildly frustrating events—for instance, when he was prevented from leaving the room or when he failed to receive a reinforcer after emitting an incorrect verbal response.

Sessions were conducted initially in a small room. Peter sat in a tablet arm-chair desk that was placed against the wall so that he was prevented from wandering around. Whenever Peter began to tantrum, Veronica, the university student working with him, simply turned away and ignored him until the tantrum had ceased for a brief period. Following the tantrum and a period of at least 15 to 20 seconds during which Peter had been sitting quietly, Veronica would turn to him, say "Good boy!" and give him a poker chip which he could later exchange for food and candies. At the end of every 15- to 20-second period in which no tantrum occurred, Peter received another chip. As a result of this

*This report is based on a study by Martin, England, Kaprowy, Kilgour, and Pilek (1968). The Manitoba Developmental Center is a large residential and treatment center for retarded people in the province of Manitoba.

procedure of ignoring tantrums and reinforcing sitting quietly for brief periods, Peter's tantrum behavior gradually decreased in the teaching situation, making it possible to begin working on developing his verbal and other basic skills. The results of the procedure are shown in Figure 4–1.

EXTINCTION

The principle of **extinction** states that: (1) if, in a given situation, somebody emits a previously reinforced response and the response is not followed by a reinforcing consequence, then (2) that person is less likely to do the same thing again when he or she next encounters a similar situation. Stated differently, if a response has been increased in frequency through positive reinforcement, then completely ceasing to reinforce the response will cause it to decrease in frequency.[1]

Note 1

Observation of Peter's behavior on the ward indicated that he frequently received a lot of social attention from ward staff when he threw tantrums. It is likely that this attention was a positive reinforcer in maintaining the high frequency of this undesirable behavior. In the program described, Peter's tantrums no longer received attention and their frequency decreased to a very low level. As with positive reinforcement, very few of us are aware of just how frequently we are influenced by extinction during every hour of every day of our lives. Some examples of extinction appear in Table 4–1.

In each example in this table, the individuals are simply doing what comes naturally in their daily activities. In each example, it might take several repetitions of the behavior occurring and not being reinforced before there

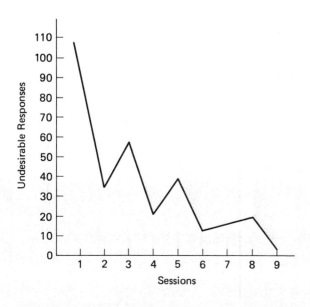

FIGURE 4–1 Extinction of undesirable verbal responses during tantrums. Each instance of Peter's "Cut," "Needle," or "Doctor" was counted as an undesirable response. A tantrum consisted of several such responses as well as crying, whining, and face slapping. The frequency of tantrums during the first nine sessions would therefore be somewhat less than the frequency of verbal responses.

Table 4-1 Examples of Extinction

	SITUATION	RESPONSE	IMMEDIATE CONSEQUENCES	LONG-TERM EFFECTS
1	A four-year-old child is lying in bed at night while the parents are sitting in the living room talking to guests.	The child begins to make loud animal noises while lying in bed.	The parents and guests ignore the child completely and continue to talk quietly.	The child is less likely to make animal noises in future situations of that sort.
2	The next evening, the same child and parents are having dinner at the dining room table. The child has just finished the main course.	The child holds up her empty plate and yells loudly, "Dessert, dessert, dessert."	The parents continue talking and ignore the child's loud demands. After the child sits quietly for a brief period, the mother serves dessert.	The behavior of demanding dessert is less likely to occur in similar situations in the future, and the behavior of waiting quietly until dessert is served is more likely to occur in similar situations in the future.
3	A husband is standing in the kitchen and begins to complain to his wife about the traffic on his way home from work.	The husband continues to stand in the kitchen and complain about the traffic.	The wife goes about the business of preparing supper and does not pay attention to any of his comments.	Continual (and probably unproductive) complaining by the husband is less likely to occur in the future.
4	A child in a third-grade classroom has just finished an assignment and raised his hand.	The child begins to snap his fingers.	The teacher ignores the child and responds to those children who raised their hand and are not snapping their fingers.	The child is less likely to snap his fingers in similar situations in the future.
5	A three-year-old child working on a plastic puzzle is attempting to put a piece in the wrong place.	The child rotates the piece to try to make it fit.	The piece still doesn't fit, no matter how many times it is rotated.	The likelihood of the child attempting to insert that piece in that position decreases.

would be any really obvious decrease in its frequency. Nevertheless, the effect is still there. Over a number of trials, behaviors that no longer "pay off" gradually decrease. Of course, this is highly desirable, for if we persisted in useless behavior, we would quickly "extinguish" as a race.

Extinction, like the principle of positive reinforcement, has been studied extensively by experimental psychologists over several decades, and we are able to describe a number of factors that influence its effectiveness. These are discussed now.

FACTORS INFLUENCING THE EFFECTIVENESS OF EXTINCTION

1. EXTINCTION COMBINED WITH POSITIVE REINFORCEMENT

Extinction is most effective when combined with positive reinforcement for some desirable alternative behavior. Thus, not only were Peter's tantrums ignored (extinction), but the behavior "sitting quietly" was positively reinforced. The combination of the two procedures probably decreased the frequency of the undesirable behavior much faster (and possibly to a lower level) than would have been the case had the extinction procedure been used alone.

It is often impractical to reinforce a child every few seconds for engaging in some desirable behavior (such as sitting or playing quietly) in place of disruptive behavior. It is possible, however, to begin with short intervals of desirable behavior and gradually increase them to longer, more manageable intervals. For example, a child who is engaging in inappropriate crying could be ignored until he had stopped crying for a period of 10 seconds. At the end of the 10-second interval, he could be reinforced with praise. On subsequent trials, the teacher could require successively longer periods of silence—15 seconds, then 25, then a minute, and so on—before presenting reinforcement. It is important that the increase in the requirement be very gradual; otherwise, the undesirable behavior will not decrease very rapidly. Also, care must be taken not to present the reinforcer immediately after the crying ceases, as this would tend to reinforce the crying, thereby increasing rather than reducing it.

2. CONTROLLING REINFORCERS FOR THE BEHAVIOR THAT IS TO BE DECREASED

Suppose that a four-year-old girl, Susie, has developed a great deal of whining behavior, especially in situations in which she wants something. Her mother has decided to ignore this behavior in the hope that it will go away. On three occasions during the afternoon, mother ignored the whining behavior until it ceased, and then, following a brief period of no whining, provided Susie with the item she desired. Things seemed to be progressing nicely until early evening, when father came home. While mother was in the kitchen, Susie approached mother and in a whiny tone asked for some popcorn to eat while watching TV. Although mother completely ignored Susie, father entered the room and said, "Mother, can't you hear your child? Come here, Susie, I'll get your popcorn." We are sure that you can now predict the effect this episode will have on Susie's whining behavior in the future (not to mention mother's anger toward father).[2]

Note 2

Reinforcers presented by other people or by the physical environment can undo your good efforts at applying extinction. Unfortunately, it is often very difficult to convince others of this if they are not familiar with the mechanics of positive reinforcement and extinction. For example, if several psychiatric nurses are ignoring a child's tantrumming behavior and another psychiatric nurse enters and says, "Oh, I can get this child to stop crying—here, Tommy, have a candy," then Tommy is likely to stop crying at that moment. But in the long run his crying may increase in frequency because of that reinforced trial. Since the nurse did get Tommy to stop crying, however, it would probably be difficult to convince her of the importance of extinction. In such cases, it is necessary either to control the behavior of these other individuals in some fashion, or to carry out the extinction procedure in their absence.[3]

Note 3

It is also important during the application of extinction to ensure that the reinforcers that you are withholding are the ones that were actually maintaining the undesirable behavior. Failure to do this can doom your extinction program, as shown in Figure 4–2.[4]

Note 4

Extinction is sometimes criticized on the grounds that it is cruel to deprive people of social attention during their time of need (this criticism usually assumes that an individual who is crying, whining, or showing various other behaviors that commonly evoke attention is in a time of need). In some cases, this might be a valid criticism. In many situations crying does indicate injury, emotional distress, and other forms of discomfort. We suggest that any behavior must be examined closely in terms of the desirability of decreasing it. If a decrease is desired, then extinction, along with positive reinforcement of an alternative behavior, frequently provides the right route to travel.

3. THE SETTING IN WHICH EXTINCTION IS CARRIED OUT

As indicated in the previous section, one reason for changing the setting in which extinction is carried out is to minimize the possibility that other people will reinforce the behavior you are trying to decrease. There is another reason for considering the setting. It would probably be unwise, for example, for a mother to initiate extinction of her child's temper tantrums in a downtown department store. The child is likely to display behavior in the department store such that the nasty looks from other shoppers and store clerks would

FIGURE 4–2 An extreme example of why attempts to apply extinction often fail. The actual reinforcer for the behavior must always be withheld.

decrease the chances of mother carrying through effectively. In other words, it is important to consider the setting in which extinction will be carried out, to (1) minimize the influence of alternative reinforcers on the undesirable behavior to be extinguished and (2) maximize the chances of the behavior modifier persisting with the program.

4. INSTRUCTIONS: MAKE USE OF RULES

Although it is not necessary that an individual be able to talk about or understand extinction, it will probably help to speed up the decrease in behavior if the person is initially told something like this: "Each time you do X, then Y (the reinforcing item) will no longer occur." Consider, for example, the third case described in Table 4–1. The husband complains excessively about the slow traffic each day upon arriving home from work. His wife would be adding instructional control to extinction if she said something like, "George, the traffic is the same each day, and it doesn't do any good complaining about it. I love to talk to you about other things. But each time that you come home and complain excessively about the traffic, I'm just going to ignore it." This should cause George's complaining to decrease rapidly. But remember that this procedure is more complex than simple extinction is. (Instructional control is discussed further in Chapters 8 and 16.)

5. EXTINCTION IS QUICKER AFTER CONTINUOUS REINFORCEMENT

Let us take another look at the case concerning Susie's whining behavior with mother. Before mother decided to introduce extinction, what happened when Susie was whining? Sometimes nothing would happen, because mother would be busy with other things, such as talking on the telephone. But at other times (often after five or six instances of whining), mother would attend to Susie and give her what she wanted. This is typical of many reinforcement situations in that it is clear that Susie was not reinforced following each instance of whining. Rather, she was reinforced occasionally, following several instances of whining. This type of situation is referred to as *intermittent reinforcement*, as opposed to continuous reinforcement, and is discussed in detail in Chapters 6 and 7. It is necessary to mention these two schedules of reinforcement here because the schedule can greatly influence the effectiveness of extinction.

The influence of the reinforcement schedule on extinction can easily be imagined if you consider a situation that you may have encountered. Suppose you are writing with a ball-point pen that suddenly stops. What do you do? You probably shake it up and down a couple of times and try to write with it a few more times. If it still doesn't write, you throw it away and get another pen. Now suppose that you are writing with another ball-point pen. In this second situation the pen occasionally skips. You shake it a few times and write some more, and then it misses some more. Each time you shake it, it writes a little more. Now comes the question. In which situation are you likely to persist longer in using the pen? Obviously, the second situation, because the pen occasionally quits but it usually writes again. When a behavior has always been reinforced and then is never reinforced (such as when a pen quits suddenly), behavior extinguishes fairly quickly. When intermittent reinforcement is involved in maintaining a behavior (such as a pen writing after shaking it), that behavior extinguishes more slowly.[5] Behavior that extin-

Note 5   guishes slowly is said to be *resistant to extinction*.

Now let us take a look at Susie's whining. It will take longer for extinction to completely eliminate her whining if it sometimes "paid off" and sometimes did not, than if it always paid off before being completely ignored. In other words, extinction is much quicker after continuous reinforcement (in which each response was reinforced) than after intermittent reinforcement (in which responses were reinforced only occasionally). If you try to extinguish a behavior that has been reinforced intermittently, you must be prepared for extinction to take longer.

PITFALLS OF EXTINCTION

As with the law of gravity, the principle of positive reinforcement, and other natural laws, the principle of extinction operates whether we are aware of it or not. Unfortunately, those who are not aware of extinction are apt to apply it unknowingly to the desirable behavior of friends, acquaintances, family, and others. Table 4–2 presents some examples of how extinction may, in the long run, work to decrease desirable behavior.

As these examples indicate, no one can escape the effects of extinction. Even in situations where some individuals are knowledgeably applying behavior modification in an effort to help behaviorally deficient individuals, their good works may be undone by others who are not knowledgeable about extinction. Suppose, for example, that a child in an institutional program for the retarded has been reinforced by a nurse's aide for dressing appropriately. Suppose, further, that this aide had been transferred or has gone on vacation and is replaced by an aide who is not familiar with the principles of positive reinforcement and extinction or with the particular program for the child. Confronted with a child who dresses himself and many children who do not, the new aide will quite likely spend a great deal of time helping the latter children but giving very little attention to the one child. It is a common human tendency to give plenty of attention to problems and to ignore situations in which things seem to be going well. It is easy to rationalize this selective attention. "After all," the aide may say, "why should I reinforce Johnny for doing something that he already knows how to do?" Despite this seemingly justifiable rationalization, we know that if the child's self-dressing behavior is to be maintained after it has been established, it must occasionally be reinforced.

A different kind of pitfall is the unexpected difficulties encountered by a behavior modifier trying to apply extinction. During extinction, behavior may increase before it begins to decrease. That is, things may get worse before they get better. Suppose that a child in the classroom is constantly raising her hand and snapping her fingers to gain the teacher's attention. If the teacher were to keep track of the frequency of finger snapping for a while, and then introduce extinction (that is, completely ignore the finger snapping), she would probably observe an increase in finger snapping during the first few minutes of extinction before the behavior gradually began to taper off. If something is no longer "paying off," a slight increase in the behavior may be sufficient to again bring the "payoff." This phenomenon has been studied extensively in laboratory situations, and it is something that everyone who attempts to apply an extinction procedure should be aware of. If the teacher decided to introduce extinction following finger snapping, and then observed an increase in this behavior during the next few minutes, she might erroneously conclude that extinction wasn't working and give up in the middle of the program. The effect of this action would be to reinforce the behavior when it gets worse. The rule to follow here is this: if you introduce extinction, don't give up the

Table 4-2 Examples of Undesirable Instances of Extinction

SITUATION	RESPONSE	IMMEDIATE CONSEQUENCES	LONG-TERM EFFECTS
1 The residents and nursing staff in an institution for the retarded are sitting in the TV room.	A particular resident has been sitting quietly for the past 20 minutes.	The nurses keep on talking, and no one responds to the child who has been sitting quietly.	The behavior of sitting quietly is less likely to occur in similar situations, in the future, owing to the lack of reinforcement for sitting quietly.
2 Two staff members are talking to each other in an institution for the retarded, and a resident approaches and stands nearby.	The resident stands and waits patiently beside the two staff members for several minutes. Finally, the resident interrupts.	The staff members continued talking while the resident waited patiently, and stopped talking and listened after the resident interrupted.	The response of standing beside the staff and waiting patiently is less likely to occur in the future, and the response of interrupting staff is more likely to occur in the future.
3 A man carrying several parcels is walking toward the exit door of a department store. A woman standing by the door waiting for the bus sees the man coming.	The woman opens the door for the man.	The man rushes out without saying a word.	The chances of the woman opening the door in similar situations in the future are decreased slightly.
4 A three-month-old baby is lying quietly in the crib just before feeding time.	The baby begins making cooing sounds (which, might be interpreted by eager parents as "mama" or "dada").	The mother, busily preparing a bottle, ignores the child. When the child is picked up later she is again quiet (or, more likely, crying).	The mother has just missed an opportunity to reinforce noise making that approximates speech. Instead, she reinforced lying quietly (or crying). Therefore, cooing is less likely to occur in the future.

ship in the middle of the storm. Usually things will get worse before they get better, but hang in there; doing so will pay off in the long run.

Another unexpected difficulty of extinction is that the procedure may produce mild aggression. Again, we have all experienced this. Probably all of us have experienced the act (or at least the desire) of pounding and kicking a vending machine that took our money and did not deliver the merchandise. If we reconsider the finger-snapping example, we might see some mild aggression. If a teacher ignores a child's finger snapping, the child might start snapping her fingers louder and louder and perhaps banging on the desk and hollering "Hey!" This characteristic of extinction has also been studied extensively in laboratory situations, and here again it is necessary that the teacher be prepared to "weather the storm." If an extinction procedure produces mild aggression, then giving up in the middle will not only reinforce the undesirable behavior on an intermittent schedule, it will also reinforce

Note 6   additional undesirable mild aggression.[6]

An additional difficulty is that a behavior that has completely decreased during an extinction session may reappear at the next opportunity for the behavior to occur. This reappearance of an extinguished behavior following a rest is called **spontaneous recovery**. Typically, the amount of behavior that recovers spontaneously is less than the amount that occurred during the previous extinction session. After several additional extinction sessions, spontaneous recovery is usually not a problem.

To oversimplify this and the preceding chapter, we suggest that, if you want behavior to happen more often, reinforce it; if you want behavior to happen less often, ignore it. But beware. There is much more to positive reinforcement and extinction than first meets the eye. For maximal effectiveness in the application of positive reinforcement and extinction, one should be aware of their pitfalls as well as the guidelines for the effective application of the two principles.

GUIDELINES FOR THE EFFECTIVE APPLICATION OF EXTINCTION

The following rules are offered as a checklist for individuals who wish to utilize extinction to decrease a particular undesirable behavior. As with the guidelines for positive reinforcement in Chapter 3, these rules assume that their user is a parent, teacher, or some other person who is working with individuals with behavior problems.

1. *Selecting the behavior to be decreased.*
   a. In choosing the behavior, be specific. Don't plan a major character improvement to take place at one time. For example, do not try to extinguish all of Johnny's trouble-making behavior in a classroom. Rather, choose a particular behavior, such as Johnny's finger snapping in the classroom.

   b. Remember that the behavior may get worse before it gets better and that aggressive behavior is sometimes produced during the extinction process. Therefore, make sure that the circumstances are such that you can follow through with your extinction procedure on the behavior chosen. For example, be very careful if the behavior is destructive to the individual or others. Will it be harmful for you to persist in your extinction program if the behavior gets worse? You should also consider the setting in which the behavior that you have selected is likely to occur. For example, it may be impractical to extinguish temper tantrums in a restaurant, because of obvious social pressures that you may be unable to resist. If you are concerned with decreasing a particular behavior but you cannot apply extinction because of the above considerations, do not despair. We will describe other procedures for decreasing behavior in Chapters 7, 13, and 17.

   c. Select a behavior for which you can control the reinforcers that are currently maintaining it.

2. *Preliminary considerations.*

   a. If possible, keep track of how often the undesirable behavior occurs prior to your extinction program. During this recording phase, do not attempt to withhold the reinforcer for the undesirable behavior.

   b. Try to identify what is currently reinforcing the undesirable behavior so that you can withhold the reinforcer during treatment. (If this is not possible, then, technically, the program does not have an extinction component.) The reinforcement history of the undesirable behavior might provide some idea of just how long extinction will take.

   c. Identify some desirable alternative behavior in which the individual can engage.

   d. Identify effective reinforcers that can be used for desirable alternative behavior by the individual.

   e. Try to select a setting in which extinction can be carried out successfully.

   f. Be sure that all the relevant individuals know, before the program starts, just which behavior is being extinguished and which behavior is being reinforced. Be sure that all who will be coming in contact with the individual have been prompted to ignore the undesirable behavior and to reinforce the desirable alternative behavior.

3. *Implementing the plan.*

   a. Tell the individual about the plan before starting.

   b. Regarding the positive reinforcement for the desirable alternative behavior, be sure that the rules in Chapter 3 for putting the plan into effect are followed.

   c. After initiating the program, be completely consistent in withholding reinforcement after all instances of the undesirable behavior and reinforcing the desirable alternative behavior.

4. *Weaning the student from the program* (discussed in more detail in Chapter 12).

   a. After the undesirable behavior has decreased to zero, there may be occasional relapses, so be prepared.

   b. Three possible reasons for the failure of your extinction procedure are:

     (1) the attention you are withholding following the undesirable behavior is not a reinforcer for the child.

     (2) the undesirable behavior is receiving intermittent reinforcement from another source.

     (3) the desired alternative behavior has not been strengthened appropriately.

If it is taking a long time for you to complete the extinction procedure successfully, then examine these reasons carefully.

        c. Regarding the reinforcement of the desirable alternative behavior, try to follow the rules in Chapter 3 for weaning the child from the program.

STUDY QUESTIONS

1. What are the two parts to the principle of extinction?
2. If you tell someone to stop eating candies and the person stops, is that an example of extinction? Explain why or why not on the basis of the definition of extinction.
3. When Peter ceased having tantrums, Veronica waited for 15 to 20 seconds before reinforcing Peter for sitting quietly. Why didn't Veronica reinforce Peter immediately after the tantrum had ceased?
4. Why did the mother's attempt to extinguish the child's cookie eating (as shown in Figure 4–2) fail?
5. Describe a particular behavior you would like to decrease in a child with whom you have contact. Would your extinction program require a special setting? Why or why not?
6. Why is it necessary to consider the setting as a factor influencing your extinction program?
7. If a behavior is not reinforced at least once in a while, what will happen to it?
8. Briefly describe four pitfalls of extinction.
9. Briefly explain five general factors influencing the effectiveness of extinction.
10. If you were recording some observations of an undesirable behavior prior to introducing an extinction program, what five things would you be looking for?
11. What are three possible reasons for the failure of an extinction program?
12. Extinction should not be applied to certain behaviors or situations. What types of behaviors and situations would these be? Give an example.
13. Describe two examples of extinction that you have encountered, one involving a desirable behavior and one involving an undesirable behavior. For each example, identify the situation, behavior, immediate consequence, and probable long-term effects, as is done in Tables 4–1 and 4–2. (Your examples should not be from the text.)
14. Examine Table 4–1. Which of those examples involve positive reinforcement for an alternative response? For those that do not, indicate how positive reinforcement for an alternative response might be introduced.

PRACTICE EXERCISE

Choose a situation in which you will be able to sit and watch an adult interact with one or more children for approximately half an hour. During this half-hour period, mark down the number of times that the adult pays attention to desirable behavior of the children and the number of times the adult ignores specific desirable behaviors of the children. This will give you some idea of how often we extinguish desirable behaviors of those around us.

SELF-MODIFICATION EXERCISES

1. Think of something you did today that did not pay off. Give a specific, complete description of the situation and behavior, following the examples in Table 4–1.

2. Select one of your behavioral excesses perhaps one that you listed at the end of Chapter 1.) Outline a complete extinction program that you (with a little help from your friends) might apply so as to decrease that behavior. Make sure that your plan follows the above guidelines for the effective application of extinction. However, do *not* try your plan at this time.

EXTENDED DISCUSSION AND NOTES

1. Extinction is but one way in which a behavior can be weakened. The reader should be careful not to confuse it with punishment or with forgetting. In punishment, a behavior is weakened by the presentation of an aversive event following the behavior. In forgetting, a behavior is weakened as a function of time following the last occurrence of the behavior. Extinction differs from both of these in that in extinction, behavior is weakened as a result of being emitted without being reinforced (see Skinner, 1953, p. 71).

2. One of the greatest hazards faced by an extinction program is reinforcement from a well-intentioned person who does not understand the program or its rationale. This obstacle was encountered in one of the earliest reports on the application of extinction to a child's temper tantrums. Williams (1959) reported the case of a 21-month-old infant who screamed and cried if his parents left the bedroom after putting him to bed at night. A program was initiated in which the parent left the room after bedtime pleasantries and did not reenter it, no matter how much the infant screamed and raged. The first time the child was put to bed under this extinction procedure, he screamed for 45 minutes. By the tenth night, however, he no longer cried, but rather smiled, as the parent left the room. But about a week later, when the parents were enjoying a much needed evening out, he screamed and fussed after his aunt, the baby-sitter, had put him to bed. The aunt reinforced the behavior by returning to the bedroom and remaining there until he went to sleep. It was then necessary to extinguish the behavior a second time, which took almost as long as the first time.

Ayllon and Michael (1959) observed the bad effect of unwanted reinforcement in extinction, which they called "bootleg reinforcement." A patient in a mental hospital engaged in such annoying psychotic talk (of the type referred to as delusional) that other patients had on several occasions beaten her in an effort to keep her quiet. To decrease her psychotic talk, the doctors instructed the nurses to ignore it and to pay attention only to sensible talk. As a result, the proportion of her speech that was psychotic decreased from 0.91 to 0.25. But later it increased to a high level, probably because of bootleg reinforcement from a social worker. This reinforcement came to light when the patient remarked to one of the nurses, "Well, you're not listening to me. I'll have to go and see Miss———[the social worker] again, 'cause she told me that if she listens to my past she could help me."

3. An example of a program in which significant others were trained to help carry out extinction was reported by Aubuchon, Haber, and Adams (1985). They successfully treated a 26-year-old female (referred to as L.) who had debilitating migraine headaches that occurred almost every day and that sometimes lasted from 8 to 12 hours. L. was an only child who began experiencing headaches at age 13. Over the next few years she received inordinate amounts of parental, social, and professional attention for her headaches, as well as being allowed to stay home from school—all powerful consequences that may have contributed to positive reinforcement of the problem. Various treatments had been tried unsuccessfully, including medication, acupuncture, chiropractic, psychotherapy, and electroconvulsive shock. Demerol appeared to provide temporary relief. During the three months prior to the treatment program described below, L. visited her physician for Demerol injections approximately three times per week. Following extensive behavioral assessment, L. agreed that her migraines may have been learned, and she agreed to try a behavioral treatment program. The treatment plan had several components. Concerning the extinction component, L.'s parents, husband, physician, and nurses were trained to ignore completely all pain behavior exhibited by L. Moreover, these same individuals provided praise and other reinforcers for "well" behaviors (such as domestic duties, work, etc.). L. signed a statement (called a behavioral contract, discussed more in Chapter 23) outlining the extinction and reinforcement components of the treatment. She also understood that her physician would no longer provide Demerol under any circumstances. The results of this program are shown in Figure 4–3. The results indicated that the multiple-component treatment program that included an extinction component was successful.

4. Extinction appears to be an important ingredient of an intervention technique called *gentle teaching* (McGee, Menolascino, Hobbs, & Menousek, 1987). Gentle teaching attempts to develop a social bonding between a disabled person and his or her caregiver. It also seeks to avoid any sort of punishing consequences by the caregiver, as this would interfere with bonding. Thus, in a procedure called "ignore-redirect-reward" the teacher may redirect his or her teaching efforts but would not alter them as a result of inappropriate behavior. For example, if a child left his or

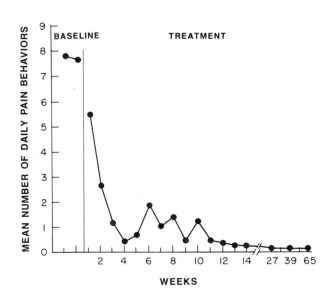

FIGURE 4–3 Mean number of daily pain behaviors as reported by spouse. Reprinted with permission from *Journal of Behavior Therapy and Experimental Psychiatry*, 16. P. Aubuchon, et al., "Can migraine headaches be modified by operant pain techniques?" © 1985, Pergamon Press, Ltd.

her desk in a special education classroom and sprawled out on the floor, the teacher might go to where the child was lying and continue with the lesson as though nothing had happened. Although gentle teaching seems not to have been influenced significantly by behavior modification, it appears to have much in common with it. For instance, reinforcement is also an important ingredient, although for the most part only natural reinforcers are used (see Walker, 1989, for a comparison of gentle teaching with behavior modification).

Advocates of gentle teaching have not stressed research as a way of testing their methods. Nevertheless, one study found that gentle teaching can be somewhat effective in reducing stereotypic behavior (e.g., hand flapping, finger flicking, staring into space, repetitive vocalizations) in mentally retarded persons (Jordan, Singh, & Repp, 1989). However, it was not as effective as a punishment procedure called *visual screening* in which the teacher places his or her hands over the individual's eyes when the individual engages in the stereotypic behavior (punishment is discussed in detail in Chapter 13). The reason for the relative ineffectiveness of gentle teaching in this study appears to be that, for some mentally retarded individuals, stereotypic behavior is reinforcing (Lovaas, Newsom, & Hickman, 1987). Thus, attempting to extinguish it is like the parent in the cartoon (Figure 4–2) who tried to extinguish cookie eating.

5. Kazdin and Polster (1973) demonstrated the extreme persistence of intermittently reinforced behavior in an applied setting. During daily breaks in a sheltered workshop, two retarded men who engaged in few social interactions received tokens for talking to peers. At first, every interaction was reinforced, and the daily average number of interactions generally increased. Then extinction was applied, and the behavior rapidly decreased. Next, reinforcement was reinstated. One man again received tokens for every interaction, but the other man was placed on an intermittent schedule, which was thinned gradually until, after three weeks, he received reinforcement at only one of the three daily breaks. Then, extinction was again carried out for both men. The man who had been on continuous reinforcement again showed a rapid decrease in social interactions. But the man who had been on an intermittent-reinforcement schedule maintained a high rate of interaction over a five-week period.

6. Studies with animals have shown that aggression toward animate and even inanimate objects can be produced by extinguishing a food-reinforced lever press. Similar results have also been demonstrated with humans. In one study, for example, four- and five-year-old children in an experimental room were taught to take marbles, dispensed individually from a toy clown's "mouth," and place them in a container on the opposite side of the room. If a child transferred a sufficient number of marbles during a session lasting approximately 20 minutes, the marbles could be exchanged for a toy. The room also contained a punching bag, suitably located in-between the clown marble dispenser and the marble storage container (so that a child had to pass the punching bag when transferring a marble from the clown to the container). Throughout a session, 1½ minutes of reinforcement (during which eight marbles were dispensed individually) alternated with 1½ minutes of extinction. During reinforcement periods, the children tended to work diligently collecting marbles. But during the extinction periods, the children often hit or shook the punching bag. In fact, five of the six children in the study hit the punching bag 2 to 10 times more often than they did during the marble-delivery periods (Todd, Morris, & Fenza, 1989). Thus, during extinction, a previously reinforced response will decrease. But some sort of aggressive behavior is a possible side effect.

STUDY QUESTIONS ON NOTES

1. How are extinction and forgetting similar, and how are they different?
2. What is bootleg reinforcement? Give an example.
3. What is gentle teaching? How does it use extinction? Why is gentle teaching not likely to be very effective in reducing stereotypic behavior in some mentally retarded individuals?
4. Describe how extinction was involved in a program to decrease migraine headaches.
5. How did Kazdin and Polster demonstrate that behavior is more persistent after intermittent reinforcement than after continuous reinforcement?
6. During extinction, aggression may occur. Describe an experiment that demonstrated this.

CHAPTER 5

Getting a New Behavior to Occur:
An Application of Shaping

"Valerie, walk by yourself to supper."

TEACHING VALERIE TO WALK

Valerie, a 16-year-old profoundly retarded girl with cerebral palsy, was partly paralyzed on her right side.* She had no speech, and although she had been taught to walk with support four years earlier, she would not move unless aided by staff. When a staff member let go, she simply dropped to the floor.

A procedure was devised to teach Valerie to walk by herself to the dining room. The following three steps summarize that procedure.

1. *Specifying the final desired behavior.* Walking unaided from the TV room to the dining room when told to do so was selected as the final desired behavior. Since this behavior never occurred, however, it was not possible to reinforce it. To get it to occur so that it could be reinforced, it was necessary to reinforce some other behavior first.

2. *Identifying a response that could be used as a starting point in working toward the final desired behavior.* Valerie would sometimes stand up and move from one chair to another if the two chairs were very close together, about a foot or two apart. The staff decided that this was a good response to begin with, since it was related to the desired behavior of walking to the dining room, in the sense that Valerie moved herself from one location to another.

3. *Reinforcing the starting response; then requiring closer and closer approximations until eventually the desired response occurs.* First, the

*This case was reported in Martin and Treffry (1970).

response of moving two feet, from one chair to another, was reinforced with food. This distance was gradually increased until, finally, Valerie would walk the entire distance from the TV room to the dining room.

At mealtimes, Valerie's food was placed on a table beside her chair so that she could walk from her chair to the chair next to the table. As can be seen in Figure 5–1, over a period of several days the table was moved farther and farther away.

Valerie continued to walk slightly farther each time, until the table was placed under the archway leading out of the TV room. At this point, Valerie missed six meals in a row.* It appeared that the staff might have to revert to an earlier approximation of the final desired behavior.

On the tenth day of the procedure, however, the staff gave Valerie a few spoonfuls of food before placing it on the table. (When a response has decreased to a zero level of occurrence, it is sometimes helpful to present a small amount of the reinforcer at the beginning of a session. This is termed

Note 1
reinforcer sampling.)[1] The same thing was done the next seven days, during which time Valerie usually obtained her meals. On the nineteenth day, reinforcer sampling was discontinued and Valerie obtained all three of her meals. On the twentieth day, the table was placed beside the stairs outside the archway leading to the dining room.

One day, after about two weeks in which Valerie had not missed a meal, she walked past the table with the meal on it, up the stairs, and into the dining room with the other children. This response was highly reinforced with praise and approval by the staff, and Valerie was given her meal in the dining room. Thereafter, Valerie was required to walk by herself to meals, which she continued to do and for which she received a great deal of approval from the staff. We are happy to report that more than five years later Valerie continued to improve and had had no relapses. She has received visits from her parents and has been much more of a joy for the staff and the other residents.

SHAPING

Shaping is a procedure used to establish a behavior that is not presently performed by an individual. Since the behavior has a zero level of occurrence, it is not possible to increase its frequency simply by waiting until it occurs and then reinforcing it. Therefore, the teacher begins by reinforcing a response that occurs with a greater than zero frequency and at least remotely resembles the final desired response. (Valerie, for example, was first reinforced for walking two feet because this behavior occurred occasionally and because it remotely approximated the behavior of walking the full distance from the TV room to the dining room.) When this initial response is occurring at a high frequency, the teacher stops reinforcing it and begins reinforcing a slightly closer approximation of the final desired response. Thus, the final desired response is eventually established by reinforcing successive approxi-

*However, a psychiatric nurse fed Valerie twice a day so that her good health would be ensured.

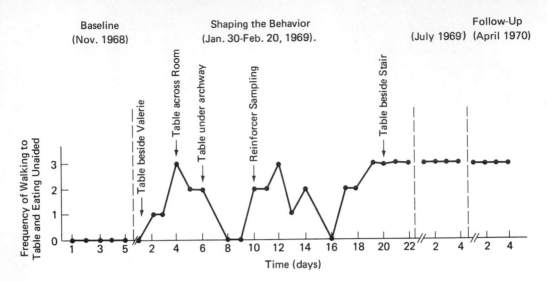

FIGURE 5–1 Control of Valerie's walking behavior. Each dot on the graph represents the number of times Valerie walked unaided to a table to eat her meal on any given day.

mations to it. For this reason, shaping is sometimes referred to as "the method of successive approximations." **Shaping** can be defined as the development of a new behavior by the successive reinforcement of closer approximations and the extinguishing of preceding approximations of the behavior.

The new behaviors that an individual acquires during a lifetime develop from a variety of sources and influences. Sometimes a new behavior develops when an individual emits some initial behavior and the environment (either the physical environment or other people) then reinforces slight variations in that behavior across a number of trials. Eventually that initial behavior may be shaped so that the final form no longer resembles it. For example, most parents use the shaping procedure in teaching their children to talk. When an infant first begins to babble, some of the sounds made remotely approximate words in the parents' native language. When this happens the parents usually reinforce the behavior excitedly with hugs, caresses, kisses, and smiles. The sounds "mmm" and "daa" typically receive exceptionally large doses of reinforcement from English-speaking parents. Eventually "ma-ma" and "da-da" occur and are strongly reinforced, and the more primitive "mmm" and "daa" are subjected to extinction. At a later stage, reinforcement is given after the child says "mommy" and "daddy," and "ma-ma" and "da-da" are extinguished.

The same process occurs with other words. First, the child passes through a stage in which very remote approximations of words in the parents' native language are reinforced. Then the child enters a stage in which "baby talk" (i.e., closer approximations of actual words) is reinforced. Finally, the child is required by the parents and others to pronounce words in accordance with the practices of the verbal community before reinforcement is given. For example, if a child says "wa-wa" at an early stage, she is given a glass of water, and if she is thirsty, that reinforces the response. At a later stage, "watah" rather than "wa-wa" is reinforced with water. Finally the child is required to say "water" before water reinforcement will be given.

Of course, this description greatly oversimplifies the way in which a child learns to talk. But it serves to illustrate the importance of shaping in the process by which normal children gradually progress from babbling to baby talk and finally to speaking in accordance with prevailing social conventions.

There are three aspects of behavior that can be shaped: topography, amount, and intensity. *Topography* refers to the spatial configuration or form of a particular response (i.e., the specific movements involved). Printing a word and writing the same word are examples of the same response made with two different topographies, and shaping a writing response from a printing response is an example of topography shaping. Shaping a child to say "mommy" instead of "ma-ma," as discussed above, is also an example of topography shaping.

The example of Valerie at the beginning of this chapter is an instance of shaping the *amount* of behavior: through shaping, the number of steps that Valerie took to the table was increased. Shaping the force of a response is an example of *intensity* shaping. Consider a young farm boy whose job it is to pump water out of a well with an old hand pump. When the pump was first installed, it was freshly oiled, the boy applied a certain amount of force to the handle, it moved up and down very easily, and water was produced. Let us suppose, however, that with rain, moisture, and lack of regular oiling the pump has gradually acquired a little rust. Each day, the boy probably applies the approximate amount of force he applied the previous day. When that force is no longer reinforced by the production of water, because of the addition of the small amount of rust that has made the pump handle more difficult to move, the boy would likely apply a little more force and find that it pays off. Over several months, the boy's behavior is gradually shaped so that he presses very hard on the first trial, a terminal behavior quite different from the initial behavior of moving the pump handle very easily.

Shaping is so common in everyday life that most people aren't even aware of it. Becoming a better dancer, learning to hit a tennis ball more accurately, changing gears smoothly when driving a car with a stickshift—all involve shaping. Sometimes the shaping procedure is applied systematically (as in the case of Valerie), sometimes nonsystematically (such as when parents shape correct pronunciation of words spoken by their children), and sometimes self-shaping occurs (you gradually perfect your method for making your own delicious spaghetti sauce).

FACTORS INFLUENCING THE EFFECTIVENESS OF SHAPING _____

1. SPECIFYING THE FINAL DESIRED BEHAVIOR

The first step in shaping is to identify clearly the final desired behavior, which is often referred to as the *terminal behavior*. In Valerie's case, the final desired behavior was walking unaided from the TV room to the dining room at mealtimes when told to do so. With a definition as specific as this, there was very little possibility that different staff members would develop different expectations regarding Valerie's performance. If different people working with the individual expect different things, or if one person is not consistent from one training session or situation to the next, then progress is likely to be retarded. A precise statement of the final desired behavior increases the chances for consistent reinforcement of successive approximations of that

Note 2   behavior.[2] The final desired behavior should be stated in such a way that all the characteristics of the behavior (its topography, amount, and intensity) are identified. In addition, the conditions under which the behavior is or is not to occur should be stated, and any other guidelines that appear to be necessary for consistency should be provided.

2. CHOOSING A STARTING BEHAVIOR

Because the final desired or terminal behavior does not occur initially, and because it is necessary to reinforce some behavior that approximates it, you must identify a starting point. This should be a behavior that occurs often enough to be reinforced within the session time allowed, and it should approximate the final desired behavior. For example, Valerie's behavior of standing up and moving from one chair to another (if the two chairs were very close together) is something that she would do. Since the terminal behavior was "extended walking" (at least from the TV room to the dining room), it was desirable to start with an approximation of walking—namely, standing up and taking a step or two.

In a shaping program it is crucial to know not only where you are going (the terminal behavior) but also the level at which the individual is performing at the present time. The purpose of the shaping program is to get the two together, by reinforcing successive approximations from the starting point to the final desired behavior, even though the starting point might

Note 3   be completely dissimilar to the terminal behavior.[3]

3. CHOOSING THE SHAPING STEPS

Before initiating the shaping program, it is helpful to outline the successive approximations through which the person will be moved in the attempt to approximate the final desired behavior. For example, suppose that the final desired behavior in a shaping program for a child is saying "daddy." It has been determined that the child says "daa," and this response is set as the starting behavior. Let us suppose that we decide to go from the initial behavior of "daa" through the following steps: "da-da," "dad," "dad-ee," and "daddy." To begin with, reinforcement is given on a number of occasions for emitting the initial behavior ("daa"). When this behavior is occurring repetitiously, the trainer moves on to step 2 ("da-da") and reinforces that approximation for several trials. This step-by-step procedure continues until the child finally says "daddy."

We are sure that some critical questions have already occurred to you. What is a reasonable step size? How many trials at each step should one reinforce before proceeding to the next step? Unfortunately there is no set of guidelines for identifying the ideal step size. In attempting to specify the behavioral steps from the initial behavior to the terminal behavior, the teacher might imagine what steps she herself would go through. Also, it is sometimes helpful to observe students who can already emit the terminal behavior and to ask them to emit the initial and subsequent approximations. Whatever guidelines or guesses are used, it is important to try to stick to them and yet be flexible if the trainee does not proceed quickly enough or is learning more quickly than had been expected. Some guidelines for moving through the behavioral program are offered in the following paragraphs.

4. MOVING ALONG AT THE CORRECT PACE

There are several rules of thumb to follow in reinforcing successive approximations of a final desired response:

   a. Do not move too soon (that is, after too few trials) from one approximation to the next. Trying to go to a new step before the previous approximation has been well established can result in losing the previous approximation through extinction without achieving the new approximation.
   b. Proceed in sufficiently small steps. Otherwise, the previous approximation will be lost through extinction before the present approximation has been achieved. However, do not make the steps unnecessarily small.
   c. If you lose a behavior because you are moving too fast or taking too large a step, return to an earlier approximation where you can pick up the behavior again.
   d. Items *a* and *b* caution against going too fast, and item *c* states how to correct for the bad effects of going too fast. It is also important not to progress too slowly. If one approximation is reinforced for so long that it becomes extremely strong, new approximations are less likely to appear.

These guidelines may not seem very helpful. On the one hand, it is advisable not to move too fast from one approximation to another; on the other hand, it is advisable not to move too slowly. If we could accompany these guidelines with a mathematical formula for calculating the exact size of

the steps that should be taken in any situation and exactly how many reinforcements should be given at each step, the guidelines would be much more
useful.[4] Unfortunately, the experiments necessary for providing this information have not yet been carried out. The teacher must observe the behavior
carefully and be prepared to make changes in the procedure—changing the
size of, slowing down, speeding up, or retracing steps—whenever the behavior
does not seem to be developing properly. Shaping requires a good deal of
practice and skill if it is to be performed with maximum effectiveness.[5]

Note 4

Note 5

PITFALLS OF SHAPING

As with other behavior principles and procedures, shaping can be misused
by people who are not aware of it. An example of this can be seen in Figure
5–2: a harmful behavior that might never have occurred without shaping is
gradually developed as a result of it. Another example of the misuse of shaping, one that is commonly observed in retarded children, leads to self-destructive behavior. Suppose, for example, that, because of an unusual and
unfortunate family situation, a small child receives very little social attention
when he emits appropriate behavior. Perhaps one day the child accidentally
falls and strikes his head lightly against a hard floor. Even if the child is not
injured seriously, an overly solicitous parent may come running quickly and
make a big fuss over the incident. Because of this reinforcement, and because
anything else the child does seldom evokes attention, he is likely to repeat the
response of striking his head lightly against the floor. The first few times this
occurs, the parent may continue to reinforce the response. Eventually, however, seeing that the child is not really hurting himself, the parent may stop
reinforcing it. Since the behavior has now been placed on extinction, the
intensity of the behavior may increase (see Chapter 4). That is, the child may
begin to hit his head more forcefully, and the slightly louder thud will cause
the parent to come running again. If this shaping process continues, the child
will eventually hit his head with sufficient force to cause physical injury. It is
extremely difficult, if not impossible, to use extinction to eliminate such violently self-destructive behavior. It would have been best never to have let
the behavior develop to the point where the child's parents were forced to
continue reinforcing it and increasing its strength.

Many undesirable behaviors commonly seen in special needs
children—for example, violent temper tantrums, hyperactivity, serious injury
inflicted by one child on another voluntary vomiting—are often products of
shaping. All these behaviors can be eliminated by a combination of extinction
of the undesirable behavior and positive reinforcement for desirable behavior.
Unfortunately, this is often difficult to do, because (1) the behavior is sometimes so harmful that it cannot be allowed to occur even once during the
period in which extinction is to take place, and (2) adults who are ignorant

FIGURE 5–2 A misapplication of shaping.

of behavior principles sometimes unknowingly foil the efforts of those who are conscientiously attempting to apply these principles.

As in medicine, the best cure is prevention. Ideally, all persons responsible for the care of other persons will be so thoroughly versed in behavior principles that they will refrain from shaping undesirable behavior.

Another kind of pitfall is the unknowing failure of a person to apply shaping when it should be applied. Some parents, for example, are simply not very responsive to their child's babbling behavior. Perhaps they expect too much from the child right from the beginning and are not inclined to reinforce extremely remote approximations of normal speech. (Some parents, for example, seem to expect their tiny new genius to say "Father!" right off the bat and are not at all impressed when the child says "da-da.") Or perhaps their personal problems interfere with their devoting the necessary attention to the child. The opposite type of problem also exists. Instead of not giving enough reinforcement for the right behavior, some parents give their children plenty of reinforcement for the wrong behavior. Perhaps they are so overly concerned about the child's well-being that they provide the child with all kinds of reinforcement without ever having to say or do anything for it. For example, they may continue to reinforce remote approximations of speech without ever demanding closer approximations. In other words, although shaping is a process that most parents apply in a more or less desirable fashion, without realizing it, there are some parents for whom this is not true. Thus, many variables can prevent a physically normal child from receiving the shaping that is necessary to establish normal speech behavior. If a child has not learned to talk by a certain age, he or she may be labeled as retarded or autistic. No one knows how many so-called mentally deficient individuals are in institutions not because of any genetic or physical defects, but simply because they were never exposed to effective shaping procedures.

Regardless of the causes of a child's failure to talk, much progress can usually be made by the use of a shaping procedure. We defer a detailed description of developing verbal behavior until other principles applicable to the development of normal verbal behavior have been discussed (see Chapters 8, 9, and 11).

GUIDELINES FOR THE EFFECTIVE APPLICATION OF SHAPING _____

1. *Select the terminal behavior.*
   a. Choose a specific behavior (such as working quietly at a desk for 10 minutes) rather than a general category of behavior (for example, "good" classroom behavior). Shaping is appropriate for changing amount and intensity of behavior, as well as for developing new behavior of a different topography (form).
   b. If possible, select a behavior that will come under the control of natural reinforcers after it has been shaped.
2. *Select an appropriate reinforcer.* See Figure 3-3 and the Guidelines for positive reinforcement, p. 41.
3. *The initial plan.*
   a. List successive approximations of the terminal behavior, beginning with the initial behavior. To choose the initial behavior, find a behavior already in the student's repertoire that resembles the terminal behavior most closely and that occurs at least once during an observation period. If your terminal behavior is a complex sequence of activities (such as making a bed) that you have broken down into sequential steps, and if your program amounts to linking the steps together in a particular order, then your program is not best described as shaping, nor is it best developed through a shaping program. Rather, it should be developed by chaining (see Chapter 11).
   b. Your initial steps or successive approximations are usually "educated

guesses." During your program, you can modify these according to the student's performance.

4. *Implementing the plan.*
   a. Tell the student about the plan before starting.
   b. Begin reinforcing immediately following each occurrence of the starting behavior.
   c. Never move to a new approximation until the student has mastered the previous approximation.
   d. If you are not sure when to move the student to a new approximation, utilize the following rule of thumb: move to the next step when the student performs the current step correctly in 6 out of 10 trials (usually with one or two trials less perfect than desired and one or two trials where the behavior is better than the current step).
   e. Do not reinforce too many times at any one step, and avoid underreinforcement at any one step.
   f. If the child stops working, you have moved up the steps too quickly, the steps are not the right size, or the reinforcer is ineffective.
      (1) First, check the effectiveness of your reinforcer.
      (2) If the student becomes inattentive or shows signs of boredom, the steps may be too small.
      (3) Inattention or boredom may also mean you have progressed too rapidly. If so, return to the previous step for a few more trials and then try the present step again.
      (4) If the student continues to have difficulty, despite "retraining" at previous steps, add more steps at the point of difficulty.

STUDY QUESTIONS

1. Identify the three basic steps in any shaping procedure, as presented at the start of this chapter, and describe them with an example (either the case of Valerie or an example of your own).
2. Explain how shaping involves successive applications of the principles of positive reinforcement and extinction.
3. What is another name for shaping?
4. Outline, according to the three steps in a shaping procedure, how parents might shape their child to say a particular word.
5. What one word characterizes all the variables plotted on the vertical axis of all the graphs in the book thus far?
6. List three aspects of behavior that can be shaped. Give an example of each.
7. What do behavior modifiers mean by "terminal behavior"?
8. Why bother with shaping? Why not just learn about the use of straightforward positive reinforcement to increase a behavior?
9. Define shaping.
10. How do you know you have enough successive approximations?
11. How do you know if you are allowing enough reinforced trials to occur at each of the approximations?
12. Give an example of how shaping might be accidentally used to develop an undesirable behavior.
13. Give an example of how the failure to apply shaping might have an undesirable result.

14. Give an example from your own experience of a terminal behavior that might best be developed through a procedure other than shaping. (See p. 72.)
15. Why is it necessary to avoid reinforcing too many times at any step?
16. Why is it necessary to avoid underreinforcement at any step?
17. Why do we refer to positive reinforcement and extinction as principles, and to shaping as a procedure? (Hint: see Chapter 1, p. 9.)

PRACTICE EXERCISE

Think of a normal child, one between the ages of two and seven, with whom you have had contact (for example, a sister, brother, or neighbor). Specify a realistic behavior that you might try to develop by utilizing a shaping procedure. Outline the starting point you would choose and the successive approximations you would go through.

SELF-MODIFICATION EXERCISES

1. Take a close look at many of your own behaviors—for example, sporting skills, personal-interaction skills, lovemaking skills, and study skills. Identify at least three specific behaviors of yours that were probably shaped by others, either knowingly or unknowingly. Identify at least three specific behaviors that were probably shaped by the natural environment. Put each of your examples in sentence form, approximately as follows: "I was probably shaped to hit a Ping-Pong ball with a good chop stroke. That is, after learning basic Ping-Pong skills, each time I tried a bit of a chop, the ball would fly off the table. Eventually, a slight chop was reinforced by the ball landing on the table and the other person hitting the ball into the net. As the other person learned to return my chops, I was reinforced for putting slightly increasing amounts of chop on the ball. In all cases, the reinforcement was returning the ball to the other side of the table and even greater reinforcement was returning it to the other side of the table so that the other person missed."
2. Select one of your behavioral deficits perhaps one that you listed at the end of Chapter 2. Outline a complete shaping program that you (with a little help from your friends) might use to overcome that deficit. Make sure that your plan follows the above guidelines for the effective application of shaping.

EXTENDED DISCUSSION AND NOTES

1. Recall from Chapter 3 the principle of positive reinforcement: if in a given situation somebody does something that is immediately followed by a positive reinforcer, then that person is more likely to do the same thing again when he or she next encounters a similar situation. This implies that the response should be maximally probable in a future situation that is most identical to the one in which reinforcement occurred, and that that situation typically includes sensory cues of the reinforcer. It was this reasoning that led Ayllon and Azrin (1968a) to suggest a procedure of briefly presenting a reinforcer before a response to increase the probability of the

response occurring, and then presenting the remainder of the reinforcer following the response. Ayllon and Azrin used the term *reinforcer sampling* to refer to this technique. In their experiment, mental hospital patients earned tokens that could be cashed in for a variety of reinforcers. Reinforcer sampling was used to increase the probability that the individuals would cash in the tokens for particular reinforcing activities.

2. Shaping appears to be useful in modifying not only external behavior but also internal behavior. For example, a study by Scott and colleagues (1973) indicated that shaping may be used to modify heart rate. Three individuals participated in the study—two normal male college students and a psychiatric patient suffering from chronic anxiety and manifesting a moderately elevated heart rate. During daily 20-minute experimental sessions (each of which was preceded by a 20-minute "adaptation" period), each man sat in a chair and watched television while his heart rate was recorded. After determining each man's baseline heart rate when he was watching television over a number of sessions, the experimenters wired the equipment in such a fashion that the sound portion of the TV program would be on continuously but the video portion would be on only when the individual's heart rate was five beats per minute *above* the baseline rate (for each of the college students) or five beats per minute *below* the baseline rate (for the psychiatric patient). (One of the college students was also reinforced with one cent for every 10 seconds that his heart rate was at the specified level, since he had complained about the standard television fare with which he was being presented.) This was shaping step 1. When the individual's heart rate remained at the designated high or low level for three consecutive sessions, the difference between the baseline level and the level required for reinforcement was increased by five beats per minute. This was shaping step 2. Shaping step 3 consisted of again increasing the requirement by five beats per minute, after the successful completion of shaping step 2. The outcome of the shaping procedure was that the heart rate of one of the college students was accelerated to an average of 17 beats per minute above baseline, that of the other college student was accelerated to an average of 16 beats per minute above baseline, and the heart rate of the psychiatric patient was decelerated to an average of 16 beats per minute below his baseline rate. In the next phase of the study, the experimenters permitted each man to view the video portion without having to behave in any specific manner. The heart rates of the two college students quickly returned to baseline levels. That of the psychiatric patient, however, remained at the low level to which it had been shaped. To demonstrate that the shaping procedure was responsible for this man's decrease in heart rate, the experimenters then used the procedure to shape his heart rate back to its original level. Interestingly, the experimenters noted that during the period that this patient's heart rate was decelerated, reports from his ward indicated that "he seemed less 'tense' and 'anxious' " and that "he made fewer requests for medication."

3. For example, in a classic study, Isaacs, Thomas, and Goldiamond (1960) used shaping to redevelop verbal behavior in a catatonic schizophrenic who had been mute for 19 years prior to training. Using chewing gum as a reinforcer, the experimenter shaped the patient through the behaviors of eye movement toward the gum, facial movement, mouth movements, lip movements, vocalizations, word utterance, and, finally, understandable speech.

4. How fast should you move from one step to the next? How large should step size be? One reason there are no specific answers to these questions is the difficulty of measuring specific step sizes and consistently reinforcing responses that satisfy a given step size. Human judgment is simply not fast enough or accurate enough to ensure that any given shaping procedure is being applied consistently in order to make comparisons between it and other consistently applied shaping procedures. This is particularly true when topography is the aspect of behavior that is being shaped. Computers, however, are both accurate and fast, and may therefore be useful in answering fundamental questions concerning which shaping procedures are most effective. One way of using computers to study topographical shaping was developed by Pear and Legris (1987). In their experiment, which demonstrated that a computer can shape where a pigeon moves its head in a test chamber, two video cameras were connected to a microcomputer that was programmed to detect the position of a bird's head within the test chamber. The reinforced response was moving the head into a "virtual sphere," that is, a spherical region in the test chamber that was defined by the computer. Gradual reductions in this sphere were used to shape the pigeons to put their heads into a small (3-cm diameter) target area in one back corner of the chamber. After every reinforcement, the radius of the sphere was reduced by a specific amount (1 cm), whereas after every 10-second period in which the bird did not contact the sphere the radius was increased by a specific amount (0.25 cm). The procedure was effective in producing contact with the target within four sessions for each of the three pigeons tested.

Another computerized method for studying the shaping of topography was developed by Midgley, Lea, and Kirby (1989). In their study, which demonstrated that a computer can be used to shape the depositing of ball bearings into a tube by rats, the computer did not actually detect the behavior of the animals as it did in the above study by Pear and Legris. Instead, the experimenter entered codes into the computer representing specific approximations to the target response (e.g., "touch ball bearing," "move ball bearing," "move toward hole"). However, following a shaping *algorithm* (i.e., a procedure that was programmed into it) the computer decided which responses to reinforce and which not to reinforce. In the two experiments Midgley and colleagues conducted with this procedure, it was found to be successful with 13 out of 15 rats that were tested, and one of the failures showed substantial progress toward making the terminal response

In addition to providing a methodology for studying shaping, the above studies suggest that computers may be able to shape at least some kinds of behavior as effectively as humans. Although the above studies were done with pigeons and rats, computers that can shape movements may prove useful in helping people with disabilities develop or redevelop certain functions. For example, a device that shapes movements may help a person regain the use of a limb that has been paralyzed due to a stroke or accident. Such a device would have the advantage over a human shaper in its precision, its ability to provide extremely rapid and systematic feedback, and its patience (i.e., computers are nonjudgmental and untiring).

5. Acker, Goldwater, and Agnew (1990) have developed a computer program that simulates many of the essential features of shaping. The student's task is to shape the movements of a simulated slug (named Sidney) so that the "animal" progresses from the left side of the computer screen to the right side. The student applies reinforcement by pressing a key after Sidney makes an approximation to the desired direction. If the student does not reinforce often enough, the slug throws a "tantrum" and shaping must begin all over again; if the student reinforces too frequently, the creature may become fixated on a particular direction and not move in the desired direction. The program appears to be an excellent method for helping even experienced behavior modifiers sharpen their shaping skills.

STUDY QUESTIONS ON NOTES

1. What is reinforcer sampling?
2. Give an example of reinforcer sampling described in this chapter.
3. Describe how Scott and colleagues used shaping to decrease the heart rate of a man suffering from chronic anxiety.
4. After using shaping to markedly alter the heart rate of three individuals, how did Scott and colleagues demonstrate that their procedure was responsible for this alteration?
5. What did Isaacs, Thomas, and Goldiamond do?
6. Describe how computer technology might be used to shape specific limb movements in a paralyzed person.
7. Describe how computer technology might be used to study shaping more accurately than can be done with the usual shaping procedures.
8. Briefly describe a computer program ("Sidney Slug") used to help teach shaping skills.

CHAPTER 6

Developing Behavioral Persistence Through the Use of Intermittent Reinforcement

"Fred, let's see how many wires you've stripped today."

IMPROVING FRED'S WORK RATE

Fred, a moderately retarded adult, worked in the wire-stripping operation of a sheltered workshop.* He was one of the clients in the workshop who worked at a lower rate, showing frequent pauses and periods of general inactivity. Because of his lower work output, he was selected to participate in a study on strategies to increase rates of worker performance.

Fred's task was to strip insulation from wire tips using wire-stripping pliers that had been modified to record a response each time they were used. In addition to learning to use the pliers to strip the wires, Fred had also learned about a green light and a counter located at his work station. Specifically, he had learned that at certain times the green light would flash to signal reinforcement, and the counter would advance by one. He had also learned that each tally on the counter could be exchanged for tokens at the end of work sessions, and that the tokens could be spent at the workshop store to buy a wide variety of items. Fred loved to be turned loose in the store with a bunch of tokens.

When it was clear that Fred knew all about the pliers, the points, and the token reinforcers, he was told that he could earn points (and subsequently tokens) for stripping the wires with the pliers, and that the counter would tell him how many tokens he had earned at any given time. Subsequently, Fred worked on the wire-stripping task for 10 one-hour periods per week. During the first week, the green light flashed and the counter advanced one each time that

*This case is based on a report by Schroeder (1972).

Fred completed stripping the fifth wire. In other words, a reinforcer was presented after every five work responses. During the second week, the schedule changed so that a reinforcer was presented following each 50th work response. During the third week, the schedule was advanced again so that Fred was reinforced following each 300th work response. Since changes in reinforcement rate also resulted in changes in total amount (money per hour) of reinforcement, this variable was controlled by adjusting the amount of reinforcement to the reinforcement rate. This made it possible to keep the total reinforcement amount per session nearly constant across all treatment sessions.

The payment schedule had a positive impact on Fred's work behavior. When Fred was paid following each fifth work response, he worked steadily. When the payment schedule required 50 responses for reinforcement, his work rate increased further. And when the schedule paid off following each 300th response, Fred showed the highest work rate of any of the three conditions.

SOME DEFINITIONS

The term **intermittent reinforcement** refers to the maintenance of a behavior by reinforcing it only occasionally (i.e., intermittently) rather than every time it occurs. Fred's work behavior, for example, was not reinforced after each work response. Instead, he was reinforced after a fixed number of responses had occurred. On this reinforcement schedule, Fred worked at a very steady rate.

To talk about intermittent reinforcement, we must first define **schedule of reinforcement**. A schedule of reinforcement is a rule specifying which occurrences of a given behavior, if any, will be reinforced. One of the two simplest schedules of reinforcement is **continuous reinforcement**. Had Fred received reinforcement each time he stripped a wire, we would say that he was on a continuous reinforcement schedule.

The second of the two simplest schedules of reinforcement is the opposite of continuous reinforcement. It is called **extinction**. As we have seen in Chapter 4, on an extinction schedule no instance of a given behavior is reinforced. The effect is that the behavior eventually decreases to a very low level or disappears altogether.

Between these two extremes—continuous reinforcement and extinction—lies intermittent reinforcement: one may reinforce certain instances of a given behavior while allowing other instances to go unreinforced. After all, it is often not practical to reinforce right away each occurrence of a desired response. Many real-life activities are not reinforced this way. You do not always get good grades after studying. You have to work for an hour before you earn an hourly wage, and you probably won't get your paycheck until the end of the week. Experiments on the effects of various strategies for reinforcing behaviors have been studied under the topic of *schedules of reinforcement*. Any rule specifying a procedure for occasionally reinforcing a

behavior is called an **intermittent-reinforcement schedule**. There are an unlimited number of such schedules (see Figure 6–1). Because each produces
its own characteristic behavior pattern, the different schedules are suitable

Note 1   for different types of applications.[1] In addition, certain schedules are more
practical to apply than others (e.g., some are more time-consuming or labor-
intensive than others).

Some intermittent-reinforcement schedules increase and maintain behavior, whereas others (to be discussed in the next chapter) decrease it. Intermittent schedules that increase and maintain behavior have several advantages
over continuous reinforcement: (1) the reinforcer remains effective longer
than with continuous reinforcement because satiation takes place more slowly;
(2) behavior that has been reinforced intermittently takes longer to extinguish
than behavior that has been continuously reinforced (see Note 5 of Chapter
4); (3) individuals work more consistently on certain intermittent schedules
than on continuous reinforcement; and (4) behavior that has been reinforced
intermittently persists more readily when transferred to reinforcers in the
natural environment. In this chapter we discuss four types of schedules for
increasing and maintaining behavior: ratio, simple interval, interval with limited hold, and duration. Each of these is subdivided into fixed and variable,
giving eight basic schedules.

RATIO SCHEDULES

The payment schedule for Fred (in the lead case at the beginning of this
chapter) was a *fixed-ratio (FR)* schedule. In an FR schedule, reinforcement
occurs each time a set number of responses of a particular type are emitted.
Recall that early in his program, Fred had to strip five wires for each reinforcement. This schedule is abbreviated: FR 5. Later he had to make 50 wire-
stripping responses for reinforcement. This is abbreviated: FR 50. Finally, he
had to make 300 responses, which is abbreviated FR 300. Note that the schedule was increased gradually. If Fred's wire stripping had been put on FR 300
immediately—i.e., without the intervening FR values—his behavior might
have deteriorated, and appeared very much as though he were on extinction.
This deterioration of responding from increasing an FR schedule too rapidly
is sometimes referred to as *ratio strain*.

FR schedules, when introduced gradually, produce (1) a high steady
rate until reinforcement, and (2) a postreinforcement pause—i.e., a pause in

Note 2   responding following reinforcement.[2] The length of the postreinforcement
pause depends on the value of the FR—the higher the value, the longer the
pause.

In a *variable-ratio (VR)* schedule, the number of responses required
to produce reinforcement changes unpredictably from one reinforcement to
the next. The number of responses required for each reinforcement in a VR
schedule varies around some mean value, and this value is specified in the

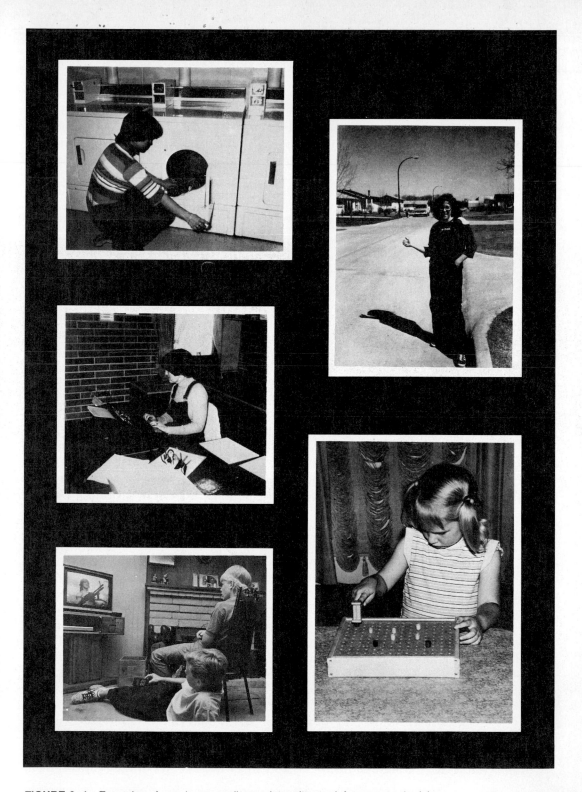

FIGURE 6–1 Examples of people responding on intermittent-reinforcement schedules.

designation of that particular VR schedule. For example, if a mean of 25 responses is required to produce reinforcement, the schedule is abbreviated: VR 25. VR, like FR, produces a high steady rate of responding. However, it also produces no (or at most a very small) postreinforcement pause. In addition, the value of a VR schedule can be increased somewhat more abruptly than that of an FR schedule without producing ratio strain, and the values of VR that can maintain responding are somewhat higher than those of FR.

The natural environment contains many common examples of ratio schedules. A common example of an FR schedule is paying an industrial worker for a specified number of completed parts (similar to the way Fred was given tokens for a certain number of stripped wires). The student who must do a specified number of problems or read a specified number of pages to complete a homework assignment is also performing on an FR schedule. Asking someone for a date is an example of behavior on a VR schedule, because (depending on one's popularity) one may have to ask an unpredictable number of different people to obtain an acceptance. Slot machines are programmed on VR schedules, in that the gambler has no way of predicting how many times he or she must put a coin in the slot and pull the lever to hit a payoff. Similarly, casting for fish is also reinforced on a VR schedule in that one must cast an unpredictable number of times in order to get a bite. A door-to-door salesperson who averages one sale every 10 houses is working on a VR 10 schedule, since he or she can never predict exactly when a sale will occur. Such individuals, as we all know, tend to be very persistent, which is a characteristic effect of the schedule.

Ratio schedules are used when one wants to generate a high rate of responding and one can monitor each response (since it is necessary to count the responses in order to know when to deliver reinforcement on a ratio schedule). The FR schedule is more commonly used in behavioral programs than VR because FR is simpler to administer. For example, ratio schedules have been used in a task designed to teach retarded children to name pictures of objects. The procedure involves presenting a carefully designed sequence of trials in which the teacher sometimes speaks the name of the picture for the child to imitate and sometimes requires that the child correctly name the picture. Correct responses are reinforced with praise (e.g., "Good!") and a treat; however, children make more correct responses and learn to name more pictures when correct responses are reinforced with a treat on a ratio schedule than when they are continuously reinforced with the treat. This is true, however, only if the ratio schedule does not require too many correct responses per reinforcement. As the response requirement increases, performance improves at first but then begins to show ratio strain (see Stephens, Pear, Wray, & Jackson, 1975). The optimal response requirement differs for different individuals and for different tasks. For example, Fred increased his response rate even when the FR was increased to 300. Many other individuals probably would have shown a decrease long before FR 300 was introduced. (Of course, it must be realized that the fact that the size of the reinforcement increased along with the size of the FR no doubt was a factor in Fred's high rate of responding on high FR schedules.) In general, the optimal FR value must be found by trial and error.

SIMPLE INTERVAL SCHEDULES

In a *fixed interval (FI)* schedule, the first response after a fixed period of time following the previous reinforcement is reinforced (see Figure 6–2), and a new interval begins. All that is required for reinforcement to occur is that the individual engage in the behavior after reinforcement has become available because of the passage of time. The value of the FI schedule is the amount of time that must elapse before reinforcement has become available (e.g., if one minute must elapse before the behavior can be reinforced, we call the schedule an FI 1-minute schedule). Note from Figure 6–2 that although the passage of a certain amount of time is necessary for reinforcement to occur in an FI schedule, the passage of time alone is not sufficient. For reinforcement to occur, a response must occur sometime after the specified time interval.[3] Note also that there is no limit on how long after the end of the interval a response can occur in order to be reinforced. Finally, note that a response

Note 3

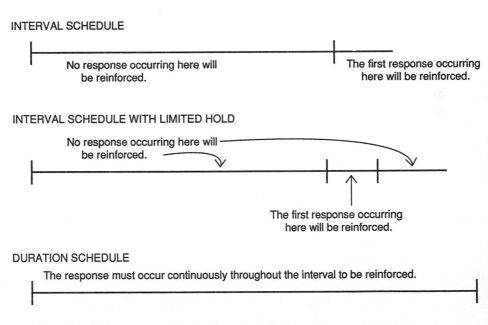

FIGURE 6–2   Diagrams illustrating the differences between the time-based schedules described in the text. In each diagram the horizontal line represents a period of time.

occurring before the specified interval is up has absolutely no effect on the occurrence of the reinforcer.

FI schedules produce (1) a rate of responding that increases gradually throughout the interval until reinforcement, and (2) a postreinforcement pause. The length of the postreinforcement pause depends on the value of the FI—the higher the value (i.e., the more time between reinforcers), the longer the pause.

In a *variable-interval (VI)* schedule, the length of the intervals changes unpredictably from one reinforcement to the next. The lengths of the intervals in a VI schedule vary around some mean value, and this value is specified in the designation of that particular VI schedule. For example, if a mean of 25 minutes is required before reinforcement becomes available, the schedule is abbreviated: VI 25 minutes. VI produces a moderate steady rate of responding and no (or at most a very small) postreinforcement pause.

Numerous examples of interval schedules can be found in the natural environment. A job that pays by the hour is sometimes cited as an example of an FI schedule, but this is not correct, because hourly pay assumes that the individual works during the hour. An FI schedule, however, requires only one response at the end of the interval. Going to pick up one's paycheck approximates an FI schedule in that the check is only ready after a certain period of time and going to the pay window does not make it ready any sooner. Checking one's mailbox is also an example of an FI schedule if mail is delivered at the same time each day. However, if one receives mail infrequently, checking one's mailbox approximates a VI schedule, since one cannot predict when there will be any letters in the mailbox. Checking one's answering machine is also an example of a VI schedule, since phone messages may be left at any time.

Simple interval schedules are not often used in behavior modification programs for several reasons: (1) FI produces postreinforcement pauses; (2) although VI does not produce postreinforcement pauses, it does generate lower response rates than ratio schedules do; and (3) interval schedules require continuous monitoring of behavior after the end of each interval until a response occurs.

INTERVAL SCHEDULES WITH LIMITED HOLD

An interval schedule with a limited hold is the same as a simple interval schedule with a slight modification, but one that has a powerful effect on behavior. As with simple FI and VI schedules, behavior is reinforced only if it occurs after a certain time interval following the previous reinforcement. However, as indicated in Figure 6–2, to be reinforced the behavior must also occur within an interval following the first interval. That is, once a reinforcement is "set up" its availability is "held" only for a limited period (hence the term "limited hold"). The addition of a limited hold to an interval schedule is indicated by writing the abbreviation for the schedule followed by "/LH" and the value of the limited hold. For example, if a limited hold of 2 seconds is added to an FI 1-minute schedule, the resulting schedule is abbreviated: FI 1 minute/LH 2 seconds.

Interval schedules with limited hold produce similar effects to those produced by ratio schedules (including strain if large increases in interval size are introduced abruptly). FI/LH produces effects similar to those produced by FR schedules, and VI/LH produces effects similar to those produced by VR schedules. Thus, interval schedules with limited hold are sometimes used when a teacher wants to produce ratiolike behavior but is unable to count each instance of the behavior (e.g., when the teacher can only monitor the behavior periodically or at irregular intervals).

In the natural environment, a good approximation of an FI/LH schedule is waiting for a bus. Buses usually run on a regular schedule—e.g., one every 20 minutes. An individual may arrive at the bus stop early, just before the bus is due, or just after it arrives—it makes no difference, for that person will still catch the bus. So far, this is just like a simple FI schedule. However, the bus will wait only a limited time—perhaps one minute. If the individual is not at the bus stop within this limited period of time, the bus goes on and the person must wait for the next one. A good approximation of behavior on a VI/LH schedule is telephoning a friend whose line is busy. Note that as long as the line is busy, we will not get through to our friend no matter how many times we dial, and that we have no way of predicting how long the line will be busy. However, after finishing the call, our friend may leave or may receive another call. In each case, if we do not call during one of the limited periods in which the line is free and the friend is at home, we miss the reinforcement of talking to our friend and must wait another unpredictable period before we again have an opportunity to gain this particular reinforcement.

Interval schedules with limited hold are common in behavior modification projects. For example, a teacher faced with a class full of rambunctious young students might use an FI 30-minutes/LH 2-seconds schedule to reinforce in-seat behavior. That is, if the children were quiet sometime during a 2-second period after a 30-minute interval, they would receive some desirable item such as points that could be accumulated toward early dismissal or extra free time. However, with this schedule, the students would likely learn to be out of their seats for much of the first part of the 30-minute interval. A better schedule to use would be a VI 30-minutes/LH 2-seconds, since this schedule **Note 4** would be less likely to produce such "pausing."[4]

DURATION SCHEDULES

In a duration schedule, reinforcement occurs after the behavior has been engaged in for a continuous period of time. In a *fixed-duration (FD)* schedule, the period that the behavior must be engaged in is fixed from reinforcement to reinforcement. The value of the FD schedule is the amount of time that the behavior must be engaged in continuously before reinforcement occurs (e.g., if it is one minute we call the schedule an FD 1-minute schedule). In a *variable-duration (VD)* schedule the interval of time that the behavior must be engaged in continuously changes unpredictably from reinforcement to reinforcement. The mean interval is specified in the designation of the VD schedule. For example, if the mean is one minute, the schedule is abbreviated: VD 1 minute. Both FD and VD schedules produce long periods of continuous behavior. The FD schedule, however, produces a postreinforcement pause **Note 5** whereas the VD schedule does not (or, at most, a very short one).[5]

The natural environment provides a number of examples of duration schedules. For instance, the behavior of a worker who is paid by the hour might be considered to be on an FD schedule. Melting solder might also be an example of behavior on an FD schedule. To melt the solder, one must hold the tip of the soldering iron on the solder for a continuous fixed period of time. If the tip is removed, the solder cools quickly and the person has to start over again and apply heat for the same continuous period. An example of a VD schedule might be rubbing two sticks together to produce fire, since the amount of time this takes varies as a function of factors such as the size, shape, and dryness of the sticks). Another example of a VD schedule is waiting for traffic to clear before crossing a busy street.

In behavior modification programs, duration schedules are useful only when the target behavior can be measured continuously and reinforced on the basis of its duration. One should not assume that this is the case for any target behavior. Presenting reinforcement contingent on a child studying or practicing the piano for an hour *may* work. However, it may also only reinforce sitting at the desk or in front of the piano. This is particularly true of something like studying, where it is difficult for the parent or teacher to observe whether the desired behavior is occurring (the child may be day-dreaming or reading a comic book hidden in the text). Practicing the piano is easier to monitor because the parent or teacher can hear whether the child is doing the lesson.

Eye contact is a behavior that is commonly reinforced on duration schedules in training programs with retarded and autistic children. Many such children do not make eye contact with others, and any attempt by an adult to initiate this behavior causes the children to quickly avert their eyes from the adult. Eye contact is important as a prerequisite to further social development.

OVERVIEW OF THE EIGHT BASIC SCHEDULES
FOR INCREASING AND MAINTAINING BEHAVIOR

The eight schedules we discuss in this chapter and their characteristic effects **Note 6** are illustrated in Table 6–1.[6] Note that the eight basic schedules have been classified as either ratio, simple interval, interval with limited hold, or duration schedules, and as either fixed or variable. **Ratio schedules** make reinforcement contingent on a certain number of responses being completed; **simple interval schedules** make reinforcement contingent on a response being made after a certain time period has elapsed; **interval schedules with limited hold** make reinforcement contingent on a response occurring within a limited period of time after a certain time period has elapsed; and **duration schedules** make reinforcement contingent on a response being made for a certain continuous period of time.

Note 6

Thus, the schedules in each of the categories listed along the side of Table 6–1 have certain requirements based on either number of responses (i.e., ratio schedules) or time (i.e., simple interval schedules, interval schedules with limited hold, and duration schedules) that must be met in order for reinforcement to occur.

Table 6-1 Characteristic Effects and Applications of Basic Reinforcement Schedules for Increasing and Maintaining Behavior

	FIXED	VARIABLE	APPLICATION

Ratio	high steady rate
	postreinforcement
	  pause
	ratio strain with large
	  increases in the re-
	  sponse require-
	  ment
	High R.T.E.*
		high steady rate
		no postreinforcement
		  pause
		less ratio strain with
		  large increases in
		  the response re-
		  quirement
		High R.T.E.
			to increase and main-
			  tain rate of specific
			  responses, such as
			  Fred's wire strip-
			  ping

Simple
Interval
	gradually increasing
	  rate
	postreinforcement
	  pause
	Moderate R.T.E.
		moderate steady rate
		no postreinforcement
		  pause
		High R.T.E.
			not commonly used in
			  behavioral pro-
			  grams

Interval
with
Limited
Hold
	high steady rate
	postreinforcement
	  pause
	strain with large in-
	  creases in the in-
	  terval
	Moderate R.T.E.
		high steady rate
		no postreinforcement
		  pause
		less strain with large
		  increases in the
		  mean interval
		High R.T.E.
			to increase duration of
			  behaviors, such as
			  on-task behavior of
			  children in a class-
			  room

Duration	continuous behavior
	postreinforcement
	  pause
	strain with large in-
	  creases in the du-
	  ration
	Moderate R.T.E.
		continuous behavior
		no postreinforcement
		  pause
		less strain with in-
		  creases in the
		  mean duration
		High R.T.E.
			to increase behaviors
			  that should persist
			  throughout a period
			  of time, such as
			  practicing piano
			  lessons

*R.T.E. = Resistance to Extinction.

PITFALLS OF INTERMITTENT REINFORCEMENT

The most common pitfall of intermittent reinforcement often traps not only the uninitiated but also those with some knowledge of behavior modification. It involves what may be described as inconsistent use of extinction. For example, a parent may at first attempt to ignore a child's tantrums. But the child persists, and in despair the parent finally "gives in" to the child's obnoxious demands for attention, candy, or whatever. Thus, the child obtains reinforcement on a VR or VD schedule, and this leads to further persistent tantrumming in the future. Many times, parents and staff say that they had to give in to the child's demands because "extinction was not working." However, the resulting intermittent reinforcement produces behavior that is even more persistent and hence takes much longer to extinguish than behavior that has been continuously reinforced.

In our work, we have encountered cases in which children have screamed until exhausted and then, as soon as they've rested, done the same thing again. (This is called spontaneous recovery; see p. 00.) Eventually, even such severe tantrums can be eliminated by extinction, but this requires a good deal of time and patience. We suspect that such persistent undesirable behavior would not occur in the first place were it not for the inadvertent application of intermittent reinforcement.

GUIDELINES FOR THE EFFECTIVE USE OF INTERMITTENT REINFORCEMENT

To use intermittent schedules effectively in generating and maintaining desired behaviors, it is important to observe the following rules:

1. Choose a schedule that is appropriate to the behavior you wish to strengthen and maintain.
2. Choose a schedule that is convenient to administer (but, of course, remain consistent with the first rule).
3. Use appropriate instruments and materials to determine accurately and conveniently when the behavior should be reinforced. For example, if you are using a ratio schedule, make sure that you have a counter of some sort—be it a fancy wrist counter (as used for keeping golf scores), a string of beads, or simply pencil and paper. Similarly, if you are using an interval or duration schedule, make sure that you have an accurate timer appropriate to your schedule. If you are using a variable schedule, make sure that you have arranged to follow a sequence of random numbers that vary around the mean you have chosen.
4. The frequency of reinforcement should initially be high enough to maintain the desired behavior and should then be decreased gradually until the final desired amount of behavior per reinforcement is being maintained. (Recall that for Fred, the fixed ratio was at first very small and was then increased.) Always remain at each stage long enough to ensure that the behavior is strong.

If you increase the requirement too rapidly, the behavior will deteriorate and you will have to return to an earlier stage (possibly continuous reinforcement) to recapture it. This is similar to the shaping procedure described in Chapter 5.

5. Inform the individual in language that he or she can understand of the schedule you are using. A number of studies (Pouthas, Droit, Jacquet, & Wearden, 1990; Shimoff, Matthews, & Catania, 1986; Wearden, 1988) indicate that people perform more efficiently on various schedules if they have specific rules to follow regarding the schedule in effect (see discussion of instruction and rule-governed behavior on p. 38, 45, and 53–54).

STUDY QUESTIONS

1. Describe the payment schedules used to increase Fred's work rate. What type of schedule of reinforcement does this payment schedule represent?
2. Define and give an example of each of the following:
   a. intermittent reinforcement
   b. schedule of reinforcement
   c. continuous reinforcement
   d. extinction
3. What are the two simplest schedules of reinforcement?
4. Name the schedules of reinforcement described in this chapter.
5. Explain what an FR schedule is. Give two examples of FR schedules in everyday life (at least one of which is not in the text).
6. What is the characteristic effect of an FR schedule?
7. What is ratio strain?
8. Explain why FR would not be used to teach students to sit at their desks.
9. Explain what a VR schedule is. Give two examples of VR schedules in everyday life (at least one of which is not in the text).
10. Describe how a VR schedule is similar to an FR schedule, procedurally. Describe how it is different, procedurally.
11. What is the characteristic effect of a VR schedule?
12. Describe two examples of how FR or VR might be applied in training programs.
13. What is an FI schedule? What is its characteristic effect?
14. What is a VI schedule? What is its characteristic effect?
15. Explain why simple FI schedules are not often applied in training programs.
16. Explain what an FI/LH schedule is, and give two examples from everyday life (at least one of which is not in the text). (*Hint:* Think of behaviors that occur at certain fixed times, such as arriving for meals, plane departures, and cooking.)
17. Describe how an FI/LH schedule is similar to a simple FI schedule, procedurally. Describe how it differs, procedurally.
18. Explain what a VI/LH schedule is. Give two examples of VI/LH schedules that occur in everyday life (at least one of which is not in the text).
19. What is the characteristic effect of a VI/LH schedule?
20. Describe two examples of how VI/LH might be applied in training programs.

21. Explain what an FD schedule is. Give two examples of FD schedules that occur in everyday life (at least one of which is not in the text).
22. Explain why FD might not be a very good schedule for reinforcing study behavior.
23. Describe two examples of how FD might be applied in training programs.
24. Explain what a VD schedule is. Give two examples of VD schedules that occur in everyday life (at least one of which is not in the text).
25. Describe how intermittent reinforcement works to the disadvantage of people who are ignorant of its effects. Give an example.
26. For each of the photos in Figure 6–1, identify the response, then the probable reinforcer, and finally the schedule of reinforcement that appears to be operating. In each case, justify your choice of schedule.

PRACTICE EXERCISES

Assume that the following behaviors have been established:

a. dishwashing behavior of roommate or spouse
b. dusting behavior of son or daughter
c. completion of a mathematics assignment by a student

You are now faced with the task of maintaining them. Following the guidelines for the effective use of intermittent reinforcement, describe in detail the best schedules to use and how you might apply them for each of the above behaviors.

SELF-MODIFICATION EXERCISE

Assume that you have been assigned a 400-page book to read during the next few days. Select an appropriate reinforcer for yourself, and identify the best schedule on which to dispense the reinforcer. Describe the reasons for your selections, and outline the mechanics of how you might implement the program and complete it successfully.

EXTENDED DISCUSSION AND NOTES

1. The effects of the various schedules of reinforcement have been worked out mainly with animals. The classic authoritative work on this topic, written by Ferster and Skinner (1957), deals mostly with pigeons pecking on a response key to obtain reinforcement in the form of a few seconds access to grain. A number of experiments have been conducted to determine whether humans show the same patterns of responding that other animals do when exposed to basic schedules of reinforcement. In one common procedure, for example, a human volunteer presses a lever to produce points that can be exchanged for money or some other reinforcing item. In many cases, however, humans responding under these conditions do not show the behavior described in this chapter. In particular, humans often do not show decreased response rates and pauses in responding where animals typically show them (see reviews by Baron & Galizio, 1983; Lowe, 1979). One possible reason for these differences between humans and animals has to do with the complex verbal behavior humans have typically been conditioned to emit and to respond to—that is, humans can verbalize rules that may prevent them from showing the same behavior patterns that animals show when exposed to various reinforcement schedules (Michael, 1987). Thus, humans may make statements to themselves about the schedule of reinforcement in effect and respond to those statements rather than to the actual schedule itself. For example, humans may tell themselves that the experimenter will be pleased if they respond at a high rate throughout the session—even though the schedule may be one that normally generates a low rate of responding—and this self-instruction may then produce a high rate (see discussion of rule-governed behavior in Chapter 3). Evidence for this view comes from data indicating that the patterns shown by preverbal infants are similar to those shown by animals (Lowe, Beasty, & Bentall, 1983), and gradually become less similar as children become increasingly verbal (Bentall, Lowe, & Beasty, 1985). Moreover, Laties and Weiss (1963) found that adult humans given a counting task to perform while responding on a schedule tended to show patterns typical of animals. Presumably, the counting task interfered with whatever rules the human subjects might have verbalized to themselves while responding on the schedule.

In addition, rate and patterns of responding on various schedules of reinforcement can be very much influenced by instructions (Catania, Matthews, & Shimoff, 1982; Hayes, Brownstein, Zettle, Rosenfarb, & Korn, 1986), although whether and to what extent they are may depend on the type of schedule and whether the instructions are given by the experimenter or by a computer (Torgrud & Holborn, 1990).

2. An analysis of records kept by the novelist Irving Wallace suggests that novel writing follows a fixed-ratio pattern (Wallace & Pear, 1977). Wallace typically stopped writing immediately after completing each chapter of a book he was working on. After a brief pause of a day or so he resumed writing at a high rate, which he maintained until the next chapter was completed. In addition, longer pauses typically occurred after a draft of a manuscript was completed. Thus, one might reasonably argue that completed chapters and completed drafts of manuscripts are reinforcements for novel writing and that these reinforcements occur according to FR schedules. It should, of course, be recognized that novel writing is a complex behavior and that other factors are also involved.

3. What happens if we present the reinforcer at the end of the interval regardless of what the individual is doing? Skinner (1948) performed just such an experiment with eight pigeons. The pigeons, who had been deprived of food, were placed in a chamber in which they received some mixed grain every 15 seconds regardless of their behavior. The result was that after being exposed to this procedure awhile, six of the birds developed very consistent responses: One bird made counterclockwise turns between reinforcements; another repeatedly thrust its head into one of the corners of the chamber; another made tossing movements with its head; two birds swung their heads back and forth; and the sixth bird made pecking or brushing movements toward the floor. Skinner concluded from these results that reinforcement acts in an automatic manner, strengthening any response that it follows closely in time *even if the response has nothing to do with producing the reinforcer.* Skinner reasoned that if the interval between reinforcements is short (as it was in his experiment), a response that had been *adventitiously* (i.e., accidentally) reinforced in this manner would probably still be occurring when the next reinforcer occurred. Therefore, it would likely be strengthened again. In most cases, this process would lead to an arbitrary response becoming very strongly established.

Skinner used the term *superstitious behavior* to describe responses developed in this manner by adventitious reinforcement. He believed that the process operates in humans as well as in experimental animals. For example, he would infer that an entertainer who engages in a superstitious ritual before each performance is probably doing this because the behavior is being adventitiously reinforced by the favorable reaction of audiences to the performance. Plausible as this interpretation may sound in accounting for a good deal of otherwise unexplainable human behavior, the concept of superstitious behavior has encountered some difficulty in the basic research laboratory. Most notably, a number of basic researchers have been unable to replicate Skinner's finding that pigeons develop arbitrary behaviors when given periodic free reinforcement. For example, Staddon and Simmelhag (1971) found that their pigeons engaged mainly in pecking during the latter part of the interval between reinforcements. Timberlake and Lucas (1985), on the other hand, reported that their pigeons engaged predominantly in a restricted set of behaviors directed toward the wall on which the feeder was located (e.g., bumping the wall with their breasts while stepping side to side). Studies such as these suggest that there may be a strong genetic contribution to superstitious behavior, at least as far as nonhuman animals are concerned.

4. Wolf, Hanley, King, Lachowicz, and Giles (1970) used this method, which they called the "timer-game," to increase the in-seat behavior of 16 low-achieving children in a remedial class. The timer-game was not uniformly effective for all the children. But one child whose out-of-seat behavior remained high when her in-seat behavior earned her points for herself showed good improvement when her in-seat behavior also earned points for the four students who sat closest to her. Speculating about this, the authors remarked, "The peer points condition resulted in more control over Sue's out-of-seat behavior than the individual points condition. Exactly what the peers contributed to the effect must await further analysis. Our impression was that they provided a number of consequences and other functions for Sue. For example, if she stood up, she was immediately reminded to sit down. If she broke her pencil, which she often did, one of the four peers would volunteer to sharpen it for her. If she went to the lavatory, she was reminded to hurry. However, the extent of their attending behavior was not determined."

5. There is evidence that, when FR and FD both appear to be applicable, the former schedule is preferable. Semb and Semb (1975) compared two methods of scheduling workbook assignments for elementary school children. In one method, which they called "fixed-page assignment," each child was instructed to work until he finished 15 pages. In the other method, "fixed-time assignment," each child was instructed to work until the teacher told him to stop. The amount of time he was required to work was equal to the average amount of time he spent working during the fixed-page condition. In both methods, each child received free time if he or she answered correctly at least 18 of 20 randomly selected workbook frames; otherwise, the child had to redo the entire assignment. On the whole, the children completed more work and made more correct responses under the fixed-page condition than under the fixed-time condition.

6. Schedules of reinforcement can help us understand behavior that has frequently been attributed to inner motivational states. This can be illustrated by several rather familiar examples.

a. A college student named Jill works very hard at her studies and achieves top marks. An equally bright student named Jack hardly cracks a book, receives low marks, and eventually drops out of school. It might be said that Jill has more internal motivation than Jack does. However, the actual reason for the different scholastic performances of the two students might lie in their histories of reinforcement schedules. Perhaps in grade school Jill had teachers who reinforced her frequently for studying behavior, and then gradually less frequently as she progressed through grade school and high school. When she entered college her reinforcement frequency was decreased still further, but the transition occurred gradually enough that her studying was still maintained at a high rate. Perhaps Jack was not so fortunate. Perhaps, for example, his reinforcement frequency was decreased too sharply when he entered high school. This would have caused his studying to suffer a decline, thus providing him with even fewer reinforcements and causing an even further weakening of the behavior. When he entered college his studying behavior was just too weak to be maintained by the very sparse reinforcement schedules that unfortunately are characteristic of many higher educational institutions. The result was that Jack's studying behavior, already weakened in high school, suffered severe ratio strain and he dropped out.

b. Similar considerations can help us understand the behavior of the dedicated scientist, artist, business person, etc. For example, the scientist's behavior is on a high VR schedule. He or she works sometimes for months, even years, on each experiment. And many experiments are unsuccessful. When we consider that most scientific behavior has been adjusted to such schedules more or less by accident, it is little wonder that there are so few dedicated scientists. Knowledge of schedules of reinforcement will help us learn how to develop more dedicated scientists without having to wait for accidental environmental events to develop them for us.

c. Schedules of reinforcement can also help us understand the causes of much behavior we might label "undesirable." Consider the pathological gambler, for instance. Because this individual is obviously acting against his or her own best interests, it is sometimes said that he or she has an inner motive of masochism—a need for self-punishment. However, it seems that (at least in many cases) the pathological gambler is a victim of an accidental adjustment to a high VR schedule. Perhaps when first introduced to gambling, this individual won several large sums in a row. Over time, however, the gambler won bets less frequently until now his or her gambling is being maintained at a high rate by very infrequent reinforcements.

STUDY QUESTIONS ON NOTES

1. Who wrote the classic authoritative work on schedules of reinforcement, and what is the title of their book?
2. What may account for the failures to obtain the schedule effects in basic research with humans that are typically found in basic research with animals?
3. Describe how FR schedules may be involved in novel writing.
4. What is adventitious reinforcement? What is superstitious behavior? Explain both with reference to an example.
5. What difficulty has been encountered in attempts to replicate Skinner's study on superstitious behavior?
6. Might it be better to reinforce a child for dusting the living room furniture for a fixed period of time or for a fixed number of items dusted? Explain your answer.

7. Describe the "timer-game" of Wolf and colleagues.

8. Is it accurate to say that Sue (in the Wolf et al. study) received "bootleg reinforcement"? Why or why not? (*Hint:* Read note 2 in Chapter 4.)

9. Briefly describe how schedules of reinforcement can help us understand behavior that has frequently been attributed to inner motivational states.

CHAPTER 7

Types of Intermittent Reinforcement to Decrease Behavior

"Tommy, a little less talking out, please!"

DECREASING TOMMY'S TALKING OUT

Tommy, an 11-year-old boy classified as trainable mentally retarded, was judged by his teacher to be the most disruptive student in his special education classroom.* He frequently engaged in inappropriate talking and other vocalizations during class. The behavior was troublesome not so much because of its nature, but because of the high rate at which it occurred. A program was therefore undertaken, not to eliminate it, but rather to reduce it to a less bothersome level.

The undesirable behavior, "talking out," was given the following precise behavioral definition: "talking to the teacher or classmates without the teacher's permission; talking, singing, or humming to oneself; and making statements not related to the ongoing class discussion." A practice teacher located in the back of the room recorded Tommy's talk-outs during one 50-minute session per day. (A second trained observer also recorded Tommy's talk-outs, to ensure the accuracy of the observations.)

In phase 1 of the program, the behavior was recorded for 10 sessions. It was found that Tommy averaged about one talk-out every nine minutes (or about 0.11 per minute). In phase 2, Tommy was told the definition of a talk-out and instructed that he would be allowed five minutes of free play time at or near the end of the day if at the end of the 50-minute session he had made three or fewer talk-outs (i.e., less than about one every 17 minutes). At the end of each

---

*This case is based on Deitz and Repp (1973).

session, Tommy was told by the teacher whether he had met the requirement, but during the session he was never told the number of talk-outs recorded.

This procedure was quite effective. During phase 2, which lasted 15 sessions, Tommy averaged about one talk-out every 54 minutes (0.02 per minute). Moreover, he never exceeded the upper limit of three per session.

In the third and final phase, the reinforcement schedule was removed and Tommy was told that he would no longer receive free time for low rates of talk-outs. Over the eight sessions of this phase for which data were taken, his rate of talking out increased to an average of one every 33 minutes (0.03 per minute). Although this rate was higher than the rate during the treatment procedure (phase 2), it was still a great deal lower than the rate before the procedure was introduced (phase 1). Thus, the treatment had a beneficial effect even after reinforcement was removed.

DIFFERENTIAL REINFORCEMENT OF LOW RATES

If reinforcement occurs only when responding is occurring at a low rate, responding will subsequently tend to occur at a low rate. This phenomenon is called **differential reinforcement of low rates**. Tommy's case illustrates one way in which low-rate behavior can be reinforced differentially. In that case, an interval was specified/50 minutes) and reinforcement occurred at the end of the interval if it contained fewer than a specified number of responses **Note 1** (three talk-outs).[1]

This method, like those discussed in Chapter 6, involves a schedule of intermittent reinforcement. However, the schedules in Chapter 6 are used to increase and maintain appropriate behavior. The schedules in this chapter are used to decrease responding that is inappropriate (see O'Brien & Repp, 1990). One class of schedules for decreasing responding is called *differential-reinforcement-of-low-rates (DRL)* schedules. There are two main ways in which DRL can be programmed: *limited-responding* DRL and *spaced-responding* DRL. Limited-responding DRL is the type of schedule used with Tommy. The total number of talk-outs each session was recorded, and reinforcement was given if that total was limited to not more than some specific number, which, in this case, was three.

In limited-responding DRL, the maximum allowable number of responses for reinforcement to occur can be specified for an entire session, or for separate intervals throughout a session. For example, it would have been possible to divide Tommy's 50-minute session into three intervals, approximately 17 minutes long, and to give Tommy reinforcement at the end of each interval in which a limit of one talk-out occurred.

Limited-responding DRL is useful when two conditions hold: (1) some of the behavior is tolerable but (2) less of it is better. In Tommy's case, the teacher felt that three talk-outs per session would not be too disruptive; no doubt she would have preferred none at all, but she did not wish to impose too stringent a requirement on Tommy. Therefore, Tommy would hear that he had earned his five minutes of free time by making three, two, one, or zero talk-outs during any given session.

Spaced-responding DRL is useful when the behavior you want to reduce is actually desirable, provided that it does not occur at too high a rate. In other words, following an interval in which the behavior does not occur, an instance of the behavior is required for reinforcement. For example, a student who always volunteers the correct answer deprives classmates of the chance to respond to the teacher's questions. Naturally we would not wish to eliminate this child's behavior; we would hope, rather, to reduce it to a more appropriate level. We might do this by placing the behavior on the following type of DRL schedule: any target response that occurs after five minutes of the previous target response is immediately reinforced; any target response that occurs within five minutes of the previous target response is *not* reinforced. This is called a spaced-responding DRL 1-response/5-minute schedule. This type of schedule requires that responses be emitted in order for reinforcement to occur. On the type of schedule used with Tommy, the individual need not respond at all to obtain reinforcement.

Another example of the use of spaced-responding DRL is the reinforcement of slow speech in a student who speaks too rapidly. The student would be asked questions such as "How are you?" or "Where do you live?" for which standard responses are reinforced—but only if they encompass a certain minimum time period whose length is determined by what the teacher regards as a normally acceptable rate of speech. Thus, the sequence of respond–wait–respond is reinforced (provided that the wait is long enough).

DIFFERENTIAL REINFORCEMENT OF ZERO RESPONDING

The type of DRL schedule used with Tommy might have specified a limit of zero rather than three talk-outs per 50-minute period. This schedule is used frequently enough to merit a special name—DRO (pronounced "dee-are-oh"), which stands for **Differential Reinforcement of Zero Responding**. Had this schedule been used with Tommy, it would have been called a DRO 50-minute schedule.

If an undesirable behavior occurs often and for long intervals, it would be desirable to begin with a DRO of short duration. For example, DRO 15 seconds might be used to eliminate tantrum behavior. This procedure could be carried out by resetting a stopwatch to zero each time a tantrum occurred and allowing it to "tick off" seconds when the tantrum stopped. Reinforcement would occur when a continuous 15 seconds had elapsed with no tantrumming. When the nonoccurrence of the behavior is under good control of this contingency, the schedule should be increased—for example, to DRO 30 seconds. The size of DRO should continue to be increased in this fashion until (1) the behavior is occurring very rarely or not at all and (2) a minimum amount of

Note 2　reinforcement is being given for its nonoccurrence.[2]

DIFFERENTIAL REINFORCEMENT OF INCOMPATIBLE RESPONDING

Sometimes the "O" in DRO is said to stand for *other* responding rather than *zero* responding. This is because, in reinforcing the "nonoccurrence" of a target response, what we are actually doing is reinforcing the occurrence of some *other* response(s) whose emission is incompatible with the target response. When we say that two responses are incompatible, we mean that they are opposites, that they compete with each other, that they cannot both be emitted at the same time. For example, sitting and standing are incompatible behaviors. If we were to put sitting on a DRO, standing might be the behavior that we would actually be reinforcing, even though standing was not actually specified as the behavior to be reinforced.

Suppose, however, that we specify explicitly the incompatible response that is to be reinforced in eliminating a particular target response. Then, rather than DRO, the procedure would be called "DRI"—which stands for **Differential Reinforcement of Incompatible Responding**. Suppose, for example, that you are a grade school teacher who wants to eliminate the running-around-the-room behavior of a so-called hyperactive child in your classroom. One possibility would be to put the unwanted behavior on a DRO schedule; however, it might be replaced by an incompatible behavior that is also undesirable—such as, for example, lying on the floor. To avoid this, you might use DRI, instead of DRO, by specifying the incompatible behavior that is to be reinforced. You might, for example, reinforce sitting quietly at one's desk. An even better choice would be completing large amounts of school

Note 3   work, since this behavior is more useful to the child.[3]

The use of DRI to eliminate an undesirable behavior is essentially what we recommended in Chapter 4 when we stated: "Extinction is most effective when combined with positive reinforcement for some desirable alternative behavior" (p. 5). Technically, providing that you can withhold the reinforcer maintaining a behavior, DRI is the extinction of that behavior while at the same time reinforcing an alternative or incompatible behavior. The choice of schedule for reinforcing the incompatible behavior should be based on considerations discussed in Chapter 6.

PITFALLS OF SCHEDULES FOR DECREASING BEHAVIOR

Pitfalls of DRO and DRI are similar to the pitfalls already discussed for reinforcement (Chapter 3), extinction (Chapter 4), and schedules of intermittent reinforcement to increase behavior (Chapter 6). One interesting pitfall that is unique to DRL should be described here. Understanding it may help us to appreciate how "underachievers" are frequently generated in our society.

Consider what happens when a child starts performing well in school—by giving correct answers to questions, for example. At first, the teacher is quite impressed and enthusiastically reinforces the behavior. But as the rate of the behavior increases, the teacher gradually becomes less impressed. This is "obviously a bright child," and so one expects a high rate of good behavior from her. Thus, the reinforcement gradually decreases, perhaps to zero, as the rate of the behavior increases. Eventually, the child learns that she obtains more reinforcement if she performs at a low rate, because the teacher is more impressed with good behavior when it occurs infrequently than when it occurs frequently. Many kids breeze through school showing only occasional "flashes of brilliance" instead of developing to their full potential. To avoid this type of inadvertent DRL schedule, teachers should define precisely the behavior they want to maintain at a high rate. They should then make sure that they reinforce this behavior on an appropriate schedule, whether or not they happen to be "impressed" with it on any particular occasion.

GUIDELINES FOR THE EFFECTIVE USE OF INTERMITTENT SCHEDULES TO DECREASE BEHAVIOR

1. Decide which type of schedule should be used to reduce the target behavior. Use limited-responding DRL if some of the target behavior is tolerable, but the less the better. Use spaced-responding DRL if the behavior is desirable as long as it does not occur too rapidly or too frequently. Use DRO if the behavior should be eliminated and there is no danger that the DRO procedure might result in the reinforcement of an undesirable alternative behavior. Use DRI if the behavior should be eliminated and there is a danger that DRO would strengthen undesirable alternative behavior.

2. Having chosen which schedule to use, proceed as follows:
   a. If a limited-responding DRL schedule is to be used,
      (1) record as baseline data the number of target responses per session for several sessions or more to obtain an initial value for the DRL schedule that will ensure frequent reinforcement.
      (2) gradually decrease the responses allowed on the DRL in such a way that reinforcement occurs frequently enough throughout the procedure to ensure adequate progress by the student.
      (3) gradually increase the size of the interval to decrease response rate below that obtained with (2).
   c. If a spaced-responding DRL schedule is to be used,
      (1) record baseline data over several sessions or more, determine the average time between responses, and use this average as the starting value of the DRL schedule.
      (2) gradually increase the value of the DRL schedule in such a way that reinforcement occurs frequently enough throughout the procedure to ensure adequate progress by the student.
   d. If DRO is to be used,
      (1) record baseline data over several sessions or more to obtain an initial interval for the DRO.
      (2) use DRO starting values that are approximately equal to the mean value between instances of the target behaviors during baseline.
      (3) gradually increase the size of the interval in such a way that reinforcement occurs frequently enough to ensure adequate progress by the student.

    e. If DRI is to be used,

        (1) choose an appropriate behavior to be strengthened that is incompatible with the behavior to be eliminated.

        (2) take baseline data of the appropriate behaviors over several sessions or more to determine how frequently the appropriate behavior should be reinforced to raise it to a level at which it will replace the inappropriate behavior.

        (3) select a suitable schedule of reinforcement for increasing the appropriate behavior (see Chapter 6).

        (4) gradually increase the schedule requirement for the appropriate behavior in such a manner that it continues to replace the inappropriate behavior as the reinforcement frequency decreases.

3. If possible, inform the individual, in a manner that he or she is able to understand, of the procedure that you are using.

STUDY QUESTIONS

1. Describe briefly, point by point, how Tommy's talking out in class was reduced.
2. Explain, in general, what a DRL schedule is. Give an example of a DRL schedule that occurs in everyday life.
3. Distinguish between limited-responding DRL and spaced-responding DRL.
4. How is a spaced-responding DRL different from an FI schedule, procedurally?
5. Give two examples (at least one of which is not in the text) of how DRL would be useful in treating a behavior problem.
6. Explain what a DRO schedule is. Give an example of a DRO schedule that occurs in everyday life.
7. Give two examples (at least one of which is not in the text) of how DRO might be useful in treating a behavior problem.
8. What does the "O" in DRO stand for? Explain your answer.
9. Explain what a DRI schedule is. Give an example.
10. What happens if the frequency of reinforcement on DRL or DRO or DRI is too low or is decreased too rapidly?
11. Describe how DRL works to the disadvantage of people who are ignorant of its effects. Give an example.
12. Explain how DRL, DRO, and DRI differ from the intermittent-reinforcement schedules discussed in Chapter 6.

PRACTICE EXERCISES

1. For each of the two types of DRL schedules cited in Study Question 3, describe a possible application in training programs with retarded children. Describe in detail how you would program and administer DRL in these situations.
2. Describe two possible applications of DRO in programs of early-childhood education. Describe in detail how you would program and administer DRO in these situations.
3. Explain what sort of instruments and materials you might use, and how you might use them, to implement DRL and DRO.

EXTENDED DISCUSSION AND NOTES

1. One might think that the five minutes of free play that occurred near the end of the day functioned as a reinforcer for decreasing Tommy's talk-outs much earlier in the day. Recall from Chapter 3, however, that the direct effects of reinforcement operate only over very short intervals. Therefore, the procedure described in this chapter with Tommy was probably effective because of Tommy's complex history of reinforcement and language training. This is, when Tommy had fewer than three talk-outs within a 50-minute session, the immediate consequence was probably praise and attention from the teacher, who might have said, "Gee, that's great, Tommy; you've just earned another five minutes of free play near the end of the school day. Just think of how much fun you're going to have." The praise may be a reinforcer for Tommy. Moreover, hearing someone talk about how much fun it is to play has probably been paired with playing many times in the past. In this way, the teacher's reminder about having fun might also have become a reinforcer. This process is known as establishing a neutral stimulus as a conditioned reinforcer and is described in more detail in Chapter 10. In addition, Tommy might spend much of the time in between the session in which talk-outs were measured to the end of the day telling himself how much fun he's going to have. This rehearsal of a rule (see note 4 in Chapter 3) may help to bridge the time gap between the occurrence of desirable behavior during the 50-minute session and a reinforcer such as extra playtime that is dispensed on a much delayed basis.

2. In a basic experiment with pigeons, Zeiler (1971) compared spaced-nonresponding DRO with extinction as response-elimination procedures. Two responses were reinforced until they occurred at a high rate. One response was then placed on extinction, and the other was reinforced on a DRO 30-second schedule. The behavior on DRO decreased more quickly than the extinguished behavior.

Weiher and Harmon (1975) applied a DRO schedule to reduce the head banging of a 14-year-old retarded child. The boy's head was a mass of scar tissue as a result of his self-destructive behavior and, consequently, he was kept in restraints. Prior to the DRO program, the boy was fitted with a padded cap that allowed freedom of movement but prevented injury. During observation sessions in which the boy wore the protective cap, he banged his head at a rate of approximately 15 "thumps" per minute. Training sessions were then initiated, again with the boy wearing the protective cap to prevent injury. During the first seven sessions, reinforcement (a half-teaspoon of applesauce dispensed through a baby's bottle) was presented on a DRO 3-seconds for head banging. Sessions were conducted twice per day and varied in duration from several minutes to 25 minutes. During the next few sessions the DRO was increased gradually and then made variable. By the fiftieth session, the DRO varied from 15 to 90 seconds. The results were highly successful in eliminating this dangerous behavior. As a result of this treatment, the boy was able to enter training programs designed to establish a variety of useful skills.

Not all uses of DRO have proved so successful. Repp, Deitz, and Deitz (1976) noted two important differences between "successful" and "unsuccessful" studies of DRO reported in the applied literature: (1) the unsuccessful studies used larger starting values for the DRO schedule than did the successful studies, and (2) the successful studies used DRO starting values that were approximately equal to the mean intervals between instances of the target behaviors prior to the introduction of the DRO schedule. Following these rules, Repp and colleagues successfully used interval DRO to reduce behaviors such as hair twirling, hand biting, thumb sucking, and disruptive behavior in retarded individuals.

3. A great deal of behavior modification is concerned with finding techniques that can be used by ordinary people in the community (i.e., the nonspecialist). Friman and Altman (1990) demonstrated that the parents of a four-year-old severely handicapped boy, with no functional expressive speech, could use DRI to treat the high-rate disruptive behavior of their son. The youngster, Bill, was described as "a child perpetually in motion who would not sit still for play or instruction." The parents worked with Bill in treatment sessions under the experimenters' guidance. Toys were present beside Bill's chair, and the parents provided reinforcement (apple juice, raisins, etc.) for specified intervals that Bill spent seated in the chair. For the first 28 sessions, average length of the intervals was 10 seconds (VD 10 seconds), after which it was increased to 20 seconds (VD 20 seconds).

If Bill left his seat, the parents quickly reseated him and did not give him reinforcement. The DRI procedure resulted not only in a dramatic decrease in out-of-seat behavior but also produced a large decrease in two other undesirable behaviors (mouthing and throwing objects) and an increase in toy play. The experimenters speculated that Bill's undesirable behavior "was a high-rate search for reinforcers, especially edibles and adult attention. The parents, delivering edibles and attention in the DRI, taught Bill an effective and acceptable method for obtaining these reinforcers: remaining in his seat. As the program progressed, Bill's sitting appeared to come under the control of more naturally occurring reinforcers, specifically toy play" (Friman & Altman, 1990, pp. 253–254).

STUDY QUESTIONS ON NOTES

1. What might account for the effectiveness of the delayed reinforcement contingency applied to Tommy's talk-outs? (There are at least two points.)
2. If you wanted to decrease a behavior, would you apply an extinction program or a DRO schedule? Justify your choice. (*Hint:* There are two points to be made.)
3. What are two differences between the successful and unsuccessful attempts to apply DRO?
4. Briefly describe how parents of an excessively active child used DRI to decrease out-of-seat behavior.

CHAPTER 8

Doing the Right Thing at the Right Time and Place Is a Matter for Stimulus Discrimination Training

"Now, children, please work at your desks."

LEARNING TO FOLLOW TEACHER'S INSTRUCTIONS

The teacher in a regular third-grade class in an Auckland suburban elementary school had a problem.* When she was giving instructions to the class, she wanted the children to listen attentively from their seats. At other times, she wanted them to work quietly on their own. But 9 of the 34 children posed special problems of inattention and poor in-seat behavior. These youngsters frequently argued, shouted, hit and kicked other youngsters, banged furniture, and left the classroom without permission. They did listen attentively and work quietly occasionally, but not often and usually not when the teacher wanted them to. This was clearly a situation, then, in which the desired behavior (listening attentively or working quietly) was in the children's repertoire (i.e., they could do it), but did not occur at the desired times.

A procedure for getting the desired behavior to occur at the desired time was introduced during an oral and written language lesson from 9:30 to 10:20 every morning. During several mornings, observers recorded the *on-task* behavior of the nine problem children *during teacher instruction*, when they were to remain silently in their seats and attend to the teacher, and *during work periods*, when they were to write a story, draw a picture, or perform other activities prescribed by the teacher. The problem children were typically on-task less than 50 percent of the time. The teacher then introduced an interesting system to the children. She made a large chart, on one side of which was printed with red letters:

*This study was taken from Glynn and Thomas (1974).

LOOK AT THE TEACHER
STAY IN YOUR SEAT
BE QUIET

On the other side, in green letters, was:

WORK AT YOUR PLACE
WRITE IN YOUR BOOKS
READ INSTRUCTIONS ON THE BLACKBOARD

The children were each given a 10-by-12-inch card with several rows of squares on it, one row for each day of the week, and the definitions of on-task behaviors during teacher instruction and during work periods were explained to them. The children were told that a "beep" would be heard several times throughout the lesson. When they heard a "beep" they were to mark themselves on-task by placing a checkmark in one of the squares if they were "doing what the chart says" when a beep occurred. The beeps occurred on average of once every two minutes. The children were also told that, at the end of the lesson, they would be able to cash in each checkmark for one minute of free play time in a nearby room that contained a variety of games and toys. The program was introduced for all of the children in the class, although data were taken only on the nine problem children. In very short order, the sign telling them what to do exerted strong control over their behavior, influencing them to perform the desired behavior at the desired times. The program increased the on-task behavior of the nine problem children to approximately 91 percent.

STIMULUS DISCRIMINATION TRAINING AND STIMULUS CONTROL

As we have seen in previous chapters, behavior is strongly affected by its consequences. Behavior that is reinforced increases. Behavior that is not reinforced undergoes extinction and decreases. However, any behavior is valuable only if it occurs at the right times and in appropriate situations. For instance, at an intersection it is desirable if you stop the car when the light is red, not when the light is green. Executing a perfect double back flip will earn you valuable points in a gymnastics routine, but it probably won't have the same effect in your first corporate-level job interview. As we acquire new behaviors, we also learn to produce those behaviors at the right time and place. How do we learn to do this successfully?

To understand the process, we must first recognize that there are always other people, places, or things that are around when behavior is reinforced or extinguished. For example, when little Johnny is playing in the street with his friends, swearing is likely to be reinforced by laughter and attention. When little Johnny is sitting at the dinner table at Grandpa and Grandma's on Sunday, his swearing is not likely to be reinforced, and may even be punished. After several such experiences, the people and things that were around during reinforcement and extinction come to cue the behavior—swearing by Johnny becomes highly probable in the presence of the kids on the street, and very improbable in Grandma and Grandpa's house.

Any situation in which behavior occurs can be analyzed in terms of three sets of events: (1) the conditions that exist just prior to the occurrence of the behavior (such as the street scene or the dinner table at Grandma and Grandpa's house just before Johnny swore), (2) the behavior itself (Johnny's swearing), and (3) the consequences of the behavior (either approval from Johnny's friends, or nonapproval from Grandma and Grandpa). Objects and events that can affect an individual's behavior are called **stimuli** (plural of **stimulus**). Books, lights, pens, people, trees, and shoes are all stimuli, as are all types of sounds, smells, tastes, and physical contacts with the body. That is, anything that can be detected by a sense organ is potentially a stimulus. When a behavior is reinforced in the presence of a stimulus and not others, that stimulus begins to exert control over the occurrence of the behavior. For example, in the program at the Auckland elementary school, when the children saw the sign in big red letters saying LOOK AT THE TEACHER (etc.), they listened carefully to what the teacher had to say, because doing so was reinforced in the presence of that stimulus. We say that that stimulus exerted control over the behavior. When a particular behavior is more likely to occur in the presence of a particular stimulus and not others, we say that the behavior is under the control of that stimulus.

We use the term *stimulus control* to refer to the control of a stimulus over a behavior as a result of that behavior having been reinforced in the presence of that stimulus. For example, suppose that you have just put money into a vending machine and you are looking for your favorite candy bar. You see the name of that bar beside a particular button, and you press that button. The sign exerted stimulus control over your button-pressing behavior. Similarly, in the lead example for this chapter, the sign LOOK AT THE TEACHER (etc.) exerted stimulus control over the children's behavior of paying attention.

While some stimuli are consistent predictors that a particular behavior will be reinforced, other stimuli are consistent predictors that a particular behavior will not be reinforced. An OUT OF ORDER sign on a vending machine is a cue that the behavior of inserting money into the machine will not be reinforced. The appearance of an empty cup is consistently associated with the absence of reinforcement for raising the cup to your lips to obtain a drink. Thus, stimulus control also exists when a particular stimulus controls the absence of a particular behavior.

In general terms, a behavior is likely to occur in the presence of stimuli that were present when previous instances of that behavior were reinforced; a behavior is likely not to occur in the presence of stimuli that were present when previous instances of that behavior were not reinforced. The procedure by which we learn to emit appropriate behavior in the presence of some stimuli, and not in the presence of other stimuli, is called *stimulus discrimination training*. There are names for the two types of stimuli associated with reinforcement and nonreinforcement of a particular response. If an event is a stimulus in the presence of which the occurence of a specified response will be reinforced, then that event is called an S^D (pronounced "ess-dee") for that response. Loosely speaking, an **S^D** is a signal that a particular response will pay off. If an event is a stimulus in the presence of which a specified response will *not* be reinforced, then that event is called an S^Δ (pronounced "ess-delta") for that response. Thus an **S^Δ** is a signal that a particular response will not pay off.[1] The symbol S^D is an abbreviation for the term *discriminative stimulus*. The symbol Δ is the Greek letter D. Thus, there are two types of discriminative stimuli: S^Ds, which are associated with reinforcement, and S^Δs, which are associated with extinction or nonreinforcement. Through discrimination training, individuals learn to emit responses in the presence of S^Ds and learn not to emit them in the presence of S^Δs.

Note 1

In our example of Johnny's swearing, the stimulus of the kids in the street is an S^D for the response of swearing because that response will be reinforced by their laughter and attention. The stimulus of Grandpa and Grandma is an S^Δ for the response of swearing because swearing will not be reinforced in their presence. This can be diagrammed as follows:

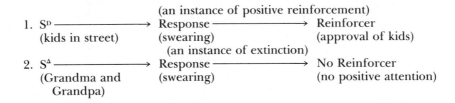

1. S^D ⟶ Response ⟶ Reinforcer
   (kids in street) (swearing) (approval of kids)
   (an instance of positive reinforcement)

2. S^Δ ⟶ Response ⟶ No Reinforcer
   (Grandma and Grandpa) (swearing) (no positive attention)
   (an instance of extinction)

A stimulus can simultaneously be an S^D for one response and an S^Δ for another; that is, in the presence of a particular stimulus, one response will be reinforced while another will not be reinforced. For example, when the teacher in the Auckland classroom presented the sign LOOK AT THE TEACHER (etc.), that stimulus was an S^D for the children's on-task behavior (staying in their seats and attending to the teacher), and it was an S^Δ for their off-task behavior (writing in their books, running around the room, etc.). This may be diagrammed as follows:

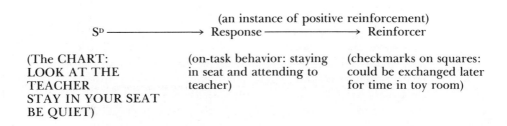

(an instance of positive reinforcement)

S^D ⟶ Response ⟶ Reinforcer

(The CHART: LOOK AT THE TEACHER STAY IN YOUR SEAT BE QUIET)

(on-task behavior: staying in seat and attending to teacher)

(checkmarks on squares: could be exchanged later for time in toy room)

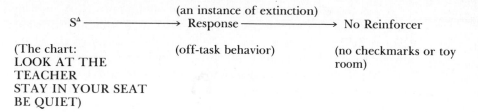

$S^\Delta \xrightarrow[\hspace{3cm}]{\text{(an instance of extinction)}} \text{Response} \xrightarrow{\hspace{3cm}} \text{No Reinforcer}$

(The chart: (off-task behavior)   (no checkmarks or toy
LOOK AT THE   room)
TEACHER
STAY IN YOUR SEAT
BE QUIET)

A phrase that is frequently used in connection with the type of diagram shown above is *contingency of reinforcement*. According to Skinner (1969, p. 7), an "adequate formulation of the interaction between an [individual] and [his or her] environment must always specify three things: (1) the occasion upon which a response occurs, (2) the response itself, and (3) the reinforcing consequences. The interrelationships among them are the 'contingencies of reinforcement.' " Thus, all the reinforcement schedules (including extinction) discussed earlier in combination with the contexts in which they occur are contingencies of reinforcement, as is any arrangement among stimulus, response, and consequences.

Note 2   It is an interesting exercise to take any situation in which we find ourselves and examine the stimulus control of some of our behaviors.[2] Consider the typical awakening-in-the-morning scene for most of us. Stimuli indicating morning—such as daylight in the window, specific configurations on clocks, and the sound of an alarm clock—are S^Ds for the behavior of rising and getting dressed. The call to breakfast is an S^D for entering the dining area and eating. The cues associated with having just eaten breakfast are S^Ds for washing, brushing one's teeth, and combing one's hair. Pressure on the bladder and distention of the bowels are S^Ds for going to the toilet.

Our culture and physical environment set up stimuli as S^Ds and S^Δs for our behavior, but we are not always "appropriately" controlled by those S^Ds and S^Δs. Suppose that a child finishes the main course at mealtime and demands of his mother, "Gimme dessert!" instead of asking, "Please may I have my dessert?" Let us suppose, further, that the parents decide that when the child has finished his main course, only a polite request for dessert ("Please may I have my dessert?") will be reinforced. In other words, the empty plate in that situation is an S^D by definition in that it is a stimulus signaling that a particular response (such as asking "Please may I have my dessert?") will be reinforced. Although the parents have set up that stimulus as an S^D it may take several trials (and perhaps some instruction by the parents) before the child finally emits the appropriate behavior. Thus, stimuli may be set up as S^Ds by one's parents (or peer group), but they do not necessarily control one's behavior. In many situations, a person standing beside a door with an armful of groceries is an S^D for someone to open the door, and that behavior is likely to be reinforced with social approval. The sight of a famous singer is an S^D for a fan to ask for an autograph, which may be reinforced by the singer giving one.

Examples of this sort could be cited at length. Although many of the stimuli in these examples are S^Ds by definition, in that appropriate responses emitted in their presence would be followed by reinforcement, these stimuli frequently do not actually control the behavior of the individuals of concern. It is, therefore, helpful to distinguish between stimuli that are S^Ds or S^Δs only by definition and those that function as controlling stimuli for some behavior. Controlling stimuli are sometimes referred to as *effective* S^Ds and S^Δs, whereas S^Ds and S^Δs that are such by definition but do not control the behavior are often called *ineffective*. Some examples of ineffective S^Ds and S^Δs are shown in Figure 8–1.

The failure of one individual to respond to the discriminative stimuli provided by another can be a major source of difficulty in a variety of inter-personal situations. For example, husbands and wives often provide each other with ineffective S^Ds and S^Δs. Even though a spouse may not be "in the mood" for lovemaking, the partner may not respond to the subtle cues provided. Individuals often are preoccupied with other matters, tired, depressed, excited, and so forth. Sometimes these private behaviors are signaled very obviously, and sometimes the signals are not so obvious. When other individuals do not respond to the S^Ds and S^Δs provided, unpleasant interactions frequently follow. A comment, a glance, a touch, or a smile may mean far more or less than was intended. Misinterpretations occur between lovers, parents and children, friends, and employers and employees. It is often extremely helpful to analyze these situations in terms of the problems of stimulus control, for at least one of the individuals in such situations has not learned to provide appropriate discriminative stimuli, or to respond appropriately to the discriminative stimuli provided. Some of the reasons for inappropriate responses to S^Ds and S^Δs are discussed later in this chapter.

Stimulus-control problems such as the above might be described as instances of *failure to discriminate*. Other difficulties arise from *failure to generalize*. These difficulties will be discussed in Chapter 12.

FACTORS DETERMINING THE EFFECTIVENESS OF STIMULUS DISCRIMINATION TRAINING

1. CHOOSING DISTINCT SIGNALS

If it is important to develop stimulus control of a particular behavior, it is desirable to identify controlling S^Ds that are very distinctive. For example, in the case of the parents who wanted to teach their child to ask, "Please may I have my dessert?" only when the child has eaten all of his or her dinner, it might be advisable for the parents to make the child's empty dinner plate distinctive. For instance, one of the parents might run to the child, wipe the empty plate clean, and say "Boy, do you ever have a clean plate!" Would you like your dessert now?" If, on the other hand, the parents sometimes provide

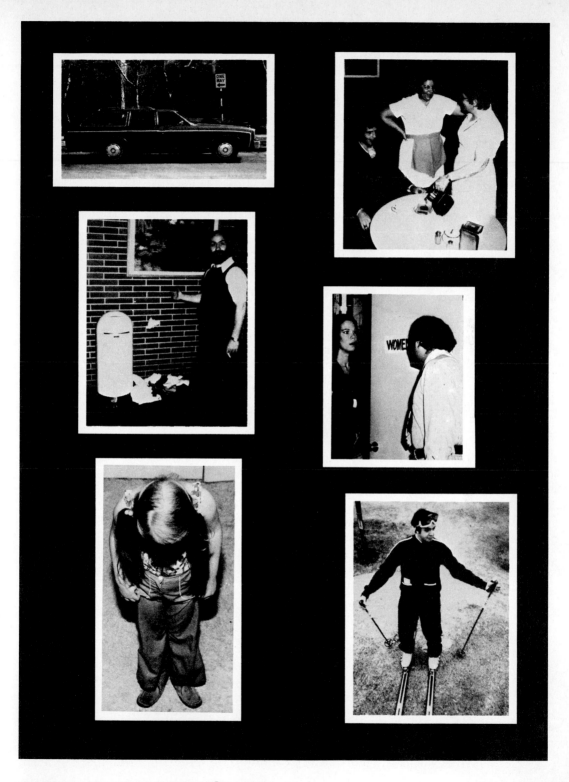

FIGURE 8–1 Examples of ineffective S^Ds and S^Δs.

the dessert when a few pieces of food are left on the plate, then the stimulus that they wish to function as an S^D for the response of asking for dessert is much more difficult to discriminate from other stimuli (namely, having slightly more food on the plate), and the discrimination training is likely to go more slowly. Similarly, some of the misunderstandings among lovers, friends, and others might be averted if the stimuli that were meant as S^Ds were made much more distinctive and described to the other person. (Techniques that help people to present clearer discriminative stimuli to indicate their needs and feelings to others are collectively called *assertiveness training*.)

When considering a stimulus to be set up as an S^D for the behavior of another person, you might ask yourself the following questions:

Note 3

1. Is the stimulus different from other stimuli along more than one dimension? That is, is it different in location, size, color, and sensory modality (vision, hearing, touch, and so on)?[3]
2. Is the stimulus one that can be presented only (or at least mainly) on occasions when the desired response should occur, so that confusion with the occurrence of the stimulus on other occasions is avoided?
3. Is the stimulus such that there is a high probability of the person attending to it when it is presented?
4. Are there any undesirable responses that might be controlled by the chosen stimulus? If some undesirable response follows the stimulus, it will interfere with the development of new stimulus control with the desired response.

Note 4

Careful attention to these questions will increase the chances that your stimulus control will be effective.[4]

2. MINIMIZING THE OPPORTUNITIES FOR ERROR

Consider the example of a child learning to answer a phone when it rings, but not if it doesn't ring. The response of picking up the phone if the phone has not been ringing is a response to an S^Δ. This type of response is typically referred to as an "error." Stimulus control can be developed much more effectively when the teacher attempts to minimize the possibility of errors on the part of the student. For example, if a parent is trying to teach a child to appropriately answer the phone, the parent might move the phone out of reach if the phone is not ringing and add verbal prompts of this sort: "Now remember, we don't answer telephones when they are not ringing. We only answer them just after they've begun to ring." Then, as soon as the phone rings (perhaps a phone call from a friend, made specifically for training purposes), the parent can immediately place the phone in front of the child and say, "The phone is ringing. Now you should answer it."

At this point you might be thinking, "But often we want to teach people to respond to subtle cues. Why should we then maximize distinctive signals?" Let us simply reply that choosing distinctive cues and minimizing errors will lead to more effective stimulus control than might otherwise occur.

In Chapter 9, we discuss techniques for gradually introducing discriminations involving very subtle cues. For the moment, it is important to keep in mind that efforts to choose distinctive signals and to minimize errors will lead to the development of effective stimulus control more quickly and with much less frustration for the student (and the teacher too) than attempts to develop discriminations that involve very subtle cues.

3. MAXIMIZING THE NUMBER OF TRIALS

As we mentioned in Chapters 3 and 4, a number of instances of positive reinforcement or extinction are usually necessary before any really obvious behavior change is noticeable to a casual observer. Likewise, effective stimulus control is developed after a person is reinforced for emitting the desired behavior in the presence of S^Ds on a number of trials and alternatively experiences extinction of that behavior in the presence of S^Δs on a number of trials. In general, it is well accepted that a number of reinforced trials are necessary for the development of consistent behaviors in retarded and other behaviorally deficient individuals. What many people forget is that this is true for all of us when we are acquiring new discriminations. In the example of a husband and wife, one of whom is "not in the mood," it is important for that partner to realize that the other partner may not learn to respond to subtle cues, or even obvious cues, with just one or two trials. (In fact, some learning theorists have hypothesized that one-trial discrimination learning never occurs.) After a number of instances of reinforcement for correct responding to the S^Ds, those S^Ds will likely control the response on subsequent trials, if reinforcement continues at least on an intermittent basis.

4. MAKE USE OF RULES: DESCRIBE THE CONTINGENCIES

The development of stimulus control often involves trial and error—several trials of positive reinforcement for a behavior in the presence of an S^D, and several trials of that behavior going unreinforced in the presence of an S^Δ. In the case of Johnny's swearing, for example, his swearing behavior came under the control of the kids in the street as S^Ds (and came not to occur in the presence of Grandma and Grandpa as S^Δs) through trial and error. But the children in the classroom example at the start of this chapter did not take a few trials to show evidence of stimulus control. During the very first session after the teacher explained the new set of classroom rules, the children showed an immediate increase in on-task behavior in the presence of the appropriate signs (e.g., LOOK AT THE TEACHER, etc.), and they immediately earned reinforcement for doing so. Johnny's swearing illustrates what Skinner called *contingency-shaped behavior*, while the children in the classroom illustrate what Skinner called *rule-governed behavior* (see note 4 in Chapter 3). A rule describes a contingency of reinforcement—stimuli, behavior, and consequences. When you wish to develop stimulus control over a particular behavior, you should always provide the individual with a rule or set of rules stating what behaviors in what situations will lead to what consequences. Because of our complex conditioning histories for following instructions, the addition of a set of rules to a stimulus discrimination program may lead to instantaneous stimulus control. Use of rules is discussed further in Chapter 16.

PITFALLS OF STIMULUS DISCRIMINATION TRAINING

Any effective method can be misapplied, and stimulus discrimination training is no exception. An example of this is the case, observed by one of the authors, of a seven-year-old retarded boy who banged his head against hard surfaces unless an adult was with him and holding his hand. As soon as the adult dropped the child's hand and moved away, the child would immediately dive to the floor and begin banging his head hard enough to cause considerable bleeding. This behavior occurred only when the child was standing on a hard floor or on concrete. It did not occur when he was standing on a rug or on grass. The reason for this is easy to see. No one would come running to give him attention if he banged his head on a soft carpet or on grass, since he did not injure himself when he did that. Of course, the staff had no choice but to give him attention when he banged his head on hard surfaces. Otherwise, he would have injured himself seriously. The staff had thus inadvertently taught the boy the following discrimination:

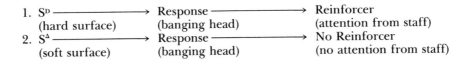

1. S^D ⟶ Response ⟶ Reinforcer
   (hard surface)   (banging head)   (attention from staff)
2. S$^\Delta$ ⟶ Response ⟶ No Reinforcer
   (soft surface)   (banging head)   (no attention from staff)

There are numerous examples of situations in which people inadvertently teach others to respond inappropriately to particular cues. If they were aware of what they were doing, they would not teach those discriminations. Behavioral episodes of the following sort are common in many households with young children: Terry, a three-year-old boy, is playing with the adjustment dials on the TV set. Mother says quietly, "Terry, please leave those dials alone." Terry continues to fiddle with the dials. A few minutes later, Mother hollers a little louder and a little less politely, "Terry, get away from that TV set." Terry continues to fiddle with the dials, screwing up the color, the contrast, and the horizontal focusing. A minute or two later, Mother says, this time loudly and with a threatening look, "Terry, for the last time get away from the TV set before I come and spank your bum!" Terry finally moves away from the TV set and Mother says, "Now, that's better, Terry. Mommy loves you much better when you do what I tell you; why didn't you do that in the first place?" It is probably obvious to you that Mother has just reinforced

Terry for responding to her third-level threats. The discrimination Terry is learning is that of waiting until Mother is really angry and threatening before attending to her requests.

Consider another behavioral episode that some of you may recognize. At a neighborhood party for a half-dozen or so couples, Jack gets a little drunk and begins to "hustle" one of the other wives. Jack's wife, Brenda, gives him a couple of stern glances. Jack continues to hustle. A little later, Brenda looks at Jack with her hands on her hips and says, "Jaaack!" Jack continues to hustle. Finally, Brenda takes Jack aside, gives him a stern lecture, and threatens to go home, following which Jack stops hustling and attends more to Brenda. After some discussion, Brenda expresses her confidence in Jack and shows him some affectionate attention. Question: What discrimination is being developed in Jack?

If you feel that you have to tell an individual something many times before he or she responds, or that nobody listens to you, or that others are not doing the right thing at the right time and place, you should closely examine your interactions with these individuals for instances of misapplication of stimulus discrimination training.

GUIDELINES FOR EFFECTIVE STIMULUS DISCRIMINATION TRAINING

1. *Choose distinct signals.* Specify the S^Ds and at least one S^Δ. (In other words, specify conditions under which the behavior should and should not occur.)
2. *Select an appropriate reinforcer.* See Figure 3-3.
3. *Develop the discrimination.*
   a. Arrange for the student to receive several reinforced trials in the presence of the S^D.
      (1) Specify clearly in a rule the S^D-desirable-response-reinforcer sequence.
      (2) To teach the student to act at a specific time, present additional cues for correct performance just before the action is to occur rather than after he or she has performed incorrectly.
      (3) Help identify the cues that differentiate the circumstances for the behavior and use instructions where appropriate to teach him or her to act in a particular way under one set of circumstances but not under another.[5]

Note 5

      (4) Recognize that stimulus control over the student's behavior will not develop if the student is not attending to the cues; therefore, use dramatic gestures to emphasize the cues.
      (5) Keep verbal cues constant initially.
      (6) Post the rules in a conspicuous place, and review them regularly.
   b. When the S^Δ is presented, make the change from the S^D very obvious and follow the rules for extinction for the behavior of concern. Stimuli that can acquire control over behavior include such things as geographical location of training place; physical characteristics and location of furniture, equipment, and people in the training room; time of day of training; and sequence of events that precede and accompany training. A change in any of these may disrupt stimulus control.

4. *Weaning the person from the program* (discussed in more detail in Chapter 12).
   a. If the behavior occurs in the right place at the right time at a desirable rate during a dozen or so of the opportunities for the behavior, and if it is not occurring in S^{Δ} situations, it might be possible to gradually eliminate contrived reinforcers and maintain the behavior with social approval.
   b. Look for other natural reinforcers in the environment that might maintain the behavior once it is occurring in the presence of S^Ds and not in the presence of S^{Δ}s.
   c. Plan periodic assessments of the behavior after the program is terminated in order to ensure that it is occasionally being reinforced, and that the desired frequency of the behavior in the presence of S^Ds is being maintained.

STUDY QUESTIONS

1. What is the difference between a stimulus and a discriminative stimulus?
2. What is the difference between stimulus control and stimulus discrimination training?
3. Shaping and stimulus discrimination training are similar in that they both involve successive applications of reinforcement and extinction. In what two ways are they dissimilar?
4. What is a synonym for an effective S^D?
5. For any two stimuli that have been set up as an S^D and an S^{Δ} but whose relationship to the behavior is described best as ineffective stimulus control, what would be the behavior in the presence of these stimuli?
6. Define and give an example of an S^D. Identify the response in the example.
7. Define and give an example of an S^{Δ}. Identify the response in the example.
8. What are "contingencies of reinforcement"? Explain.
9. Identify examples of S^Ds and S^{Δ}s as follows: two S^Ds from Table 3–1, two S^Ds from Table 3–3, two S^{Δ}s from Table 4–1, and two S^{Δ}s from Table 4–2.
10. What questions might you ask yourself when you are considering the selection of a stimulus to be set up as an S^D for the behavior of another person? (See p. 110).
11. For each of the questions that you asked yourself in the preceding question, provide an example from your own experience.
12. What do we mean by an error in discrimination training?
13. Consider the task of teaching a child to discriminate the proper placement of a knife, fork, and spoon at a table setting. There are a number of things that one might do, before and during training, to minimize the possibility of errors. Describe the details of three such things.
14. With examples, distinguish between rule-governed and contingency-shaped behavior (see also note 4 in Chapter 3).
15. Was the children's high on-task behavior to the posted rule in the Auckland classroom likely rule-governed or contingency-shaped? Justify your choice.
16. Describe an example of how ignorance of stimulus discrimination training may work to one's disadvantage.
17. Say how the examples in Figure 8–1 represent examples of ineffective S^Ds and S^{Δ}s.

PRACTICE EXERCISES

1. Identify five S^Ds that controlled your behavior during the past day or two. Clearly identify the general situation, the controlling S^D, the behavior controlled, and the reinforcement contingency.
2. Identify five situations in which you presented an S^D that controlled the behavior of some other person. Write the situations clearly as in the previous exercise.
3. Describe five situations in which you presented an S^Δ to some other person. Label the situations clearly, as in Practice Exercises 1 and 2, and indicate whether or not the S^Δ controlled the behavior appropriately.
4. Briefly describe a situation in which someone close to you has not been doing the things that you would like him or her to do, and you suspect the problem is that you are not presenting clear-cut S^Ds and S^Δs. Describe how you might develop better stimulus control over the desired behavior in that person.

SELF-MODIFICATION EXERCISES

1. Choose an excessive behavior of yours that you might like to decrease. For that behavior, carefully monitor those situations in which the behavior occurs and does not occur over a two- or three-day period. Clearly identify the controlling S^Ds, and, if possible, some controlling S^Δs for the behavior. Such information will prove to be extremely helpful if you decide later to set up a self-control program after completing this book.
2. On the basis of the material you have read thus far in this book, describe in detail how you might set up specific control of your study behavior so as to improve your learning of the discriminations that are necessary in mastering the remainder of the material in this book. (*Hint:* Consider stimulus control, reinforcement, extinction, incompatible behaviors, and schedules of reinforcement.)

EXTENDED DISCUSSION AND NOTES

1. It is important to note that we are "speaking loosely" here to help make the terminology more understandable. In general, one should be very careful to use well-defined behavioral terminology when speaking of an S^D. As Michael (1982) has pointed out, saying that a stimulus is "an S^D for reinforcement," "a cue for reinforcement," or "a stimulus for reinforcement" is sloppy use of the terminology because it omits reference to the response controlled by the S^D. Instead, one should say that a stimulus is an S^D for a *response* because the response has been reinforced in its presence and not in its absence.

Likewise, Michael points out that it is inappropriate to say that an S^D is a stimulus that signals reinforcement or predicts reinforcement. These expressions are borrowed from cognitive psychology, which is to be distinguished from behavioral psychology by the former's focus on hypothetical intervening processes. In saying that a stimulus signals reinforcement, for example, one is implying that the individual is taking in some sort of information and processing it. According to Michael, "What action occurs as a result of this information and how this action is controlled by the information is generally left for future study, or, in flirtation with a nondeterministic position, 'left to the organism' " (p. 48). One might argue about whether such an approach is useful; in any case, it seems advisable to avoid mixing behavioral and cognitive terminologies. (In Chapter 25 we discuss attempts to integrate cognitive psychology and behavior modification.) It should be noted, however, that our use of the word *signal* on page 106 does specify the response and is therefore not as objectionable as the examples Michael cites. Besides, as we indicated, we were speaking loosely to help make the behavioral terminology clear to the reader.

2. Often, behaviors that appear perplexing to the uninformed are easy to understand to an individual knowledgeable about stimulus control. For example, some children may be little angels with one parent and little monsters with the other. Relatives, outside viewers of the situation, and often parents themselves find it difficult to comprehend the Dr. Jekyll and Mr. Hyde behaviors of the children. Such contrasts are easily understood in terms of stimulus control. To illustrate, let us consider an experiment by Redd and Birnbrauer (1969).

   In this study, two adults worked with the same retarded children, but at different times. One adult provided candy, ice cream, or sips of soft drinks along with much praise when the children played cooperatively with other children. The second adult provided the same reinforcers, but did so on a time basis, which was independent of the children's behavior. That is, the second adult provided the reinforcers on a noncontingent basis with respect to the children's responses. This meant that behaviors other than cooperative play would be reinforced at least as often, if not more often, than cooperative play behavior. The result was that the adults gradually acquired stimulus control over the play behavior of the children: whenever the first adult appeared, the children showed a great deal of cooperative play behavior (which was the behavior reinforced in that adult's presence); when the second adult was present, the cooperative play behavior of the children occured at a much lower level. Thus, it is clear that different individuals can become S^Ds and S^Δs for completely different behaviors of others. In the presence of particular adults, children generally emit the behavior that those adults are likely to reinforce. If a child is a "monster" in your presence, check the reinforcement contingencies that you are applying.

3. Some forms of stimulus control are more complex than a single stimulus (such as a green light or a sign in a window) controlling a single response (such as crossing a street or going into a shop to buy something). One complex type of stimulus control, called *contextual control*, is that in which the general setting or context may alter the manner in which an individual responds to particular stimuli (Baer, Wolf, & Risley, 1987; Michael, 1982). For example, when you drive in Great Britain, the highway dividing line is an S^Δ to steer to the left of it, whereas when you drive in other countries, it is an S^Δ to steer to the right of it. In this example, the country in which you are driving is the context that determines how a particular stimulus controls your behavior. Knowledge of contextual control can be important in designing effective behavioral treatments. For example, Haring and Kennedy (1990) found that a procedure that was effective in reducing an autistic girl's self-stimulatory behavior when she was performing classroom tasks was not effective in reducing it when she was doing leisure activities; and, conversely, a procedure that was effective in reducing her self-stimulatory behavior when she was doing leisure activities was not effective in reducing it when she was performing classroom tasks. (For further discussion of contextual control, see chapter 16).

4. A stimulus comes to control a response if that response is reinforced in its presence—but we know that many of our responses very rapidly come under the control of stimuli without having to be reinforced in the presence of those stimuli (or even any similar stimuli), at least not initially. How does this occur? One way in which we can perhaps understand this is by considering the following type of experiment. Suppose that an individual is given a task in which a light may be either red or green. In the presence of the red or green light, the individual has to choose between two geometric shapes: a circle and a square. When the light is red, the circle is correct; when it is green the square is correct. After this person has learned this task, he or she is given a task in which either a circle or a square is presented and the person has to choose between two printed nonsense words: "bix" and "zak." When the circle is presented, "bix" is correct; when the square is present, "zak" is correct. After the individual has learned this task, the following test is conducted: the person is presented with the red or green light and asked to choose between "bix" and "zak." The result is that when the red light is presented the individual chooses "bix" and when the green light is presented the person chooses "zak." This demonstrates what, in logic, is known as *transitivity*—as a result of having learned to match A to B (i.e., red and green to the circle and square, respectively), and B to C (i.e., the circle to "bix" and the square to "zak," respectively), the individual now matched A to C without specific training to do so. Similar testing reveals that the individual behaves in accordance with two other principles of logic without specific training to do so: *symmetry* (matching B to A, and C to B) and *reflexivity* (matching A to A, B to B, and C to C). A person who can respond in accordance with all three of these logical relations in this type of testing situation is said to possess or show *stimulus equivalence*, and the stimuli that are matched together (red, circle, and "bix," and green, square, and "zak," in the above example) are said to form *stimulus equivalence classes* (Sidman, 1971; Sidman & Tailby, 1982). Stimulus equivalence can be readily demonstrated in verbally competent individuals, but it has not been demonstrated conclusively with language-disabled individuals or with animals (Devany, Hayes, & Nelson, 1986; Hayes, 1989b).

5. An interesting application of this step was reported by Borkovec, Wilkinson, Folensbee, and Lerman (1983) in their report of stimulus control applications to the treatment of worry. A group of chronic worriers were instructed to establish a one-half-hour worry period to take place at the same time and in the same location each day. When the subjects experienced worrisome thoughts (both self-statements and images), they deliberately engaged in self-instruction to postpone the worry behavior to their preset "worry" time. In place of the worry behavior at all other times, they learned to focus on present-moment experiences. During the "worry period," they engaged in half an hour of problem solving to eliminate the causes of worry behavior. These attempts to get worry behavior under stimulus control were successful. Daily worry reports declined significantly among treated subjects relative to controls.

STUDY QUESTIONS ON NOTES

1. Give examples of a precise use of the term S^D and imprecise uses of the term. What is wrong with the imprecise uses?
2. How might you explain the behavior of a child who is usually a "perfect angel" with one parent and a "holy terror" with the other? Outline an experiment supporting your explanation.

3. What is meant by the term "contextual control"? Illustrate with an example.
4. Describe how stimulus control can be used in the treatment of excessive worrying.
5. Describe an example of an experiment demonstrating transitivity. How would you demonstrate symmetry and reflexivity in an experiment?
6. Briefly, what is a *stimulus equivalence class*?

CHAPTER 9

Developing Appropriate Behavior with Fading

"Peter, what's your name?"

TEACHING PETER HIS NAME

Peter possessed an extensive mimicking repertoire (he could repeat many of the words other people said) but had little other verbal behavior.* He would mimic many words, even when it was not appropriate. For example, when asked "What's your name?" he would reply "Name." Sometimes he would repeat the entire question, "What's your name?" This was a problem of stimulus control in which questions (stimuli) evoked mimicking responses rather than appropriate answers.

Using the following procedure, a university student, Veronica, taught Peter to respond appropriately to the question "What's your name?" First, Veronica identified an effective reinforcer. Since Peter had been taught to work for plastic tokens that could be exchanged for treats such as candy and popcorn, Veronica decided to use the tokens as reinforcers.

Peter sat at a small table in a quiet room, and Veronica sat across from him. In a very soft whisper, Veronica asked, "What's your name?" then, very loudly and quickly and before Peter could respond, she shouted, "PETER!" Of course, Peter mimicked the word "Peter," and Veronica reinforced this with "Good boy!" and a token. You may wonder how this could represent any progress, since the boy was still only mimicking the student. However, over

---

*This case is taken from Martin, England, Kaprowy, Kilgour, and Pilek (1968) and utilizes procedures first described by Risley and Wolf in a paper to the American Psychological Association in 1964 and reprinted in Ulrich, Stachnik, and Mabry (1966, pp. 193–198).

several trials Veronica began asking the question "What's your name?" more loudly and began supplying the answer "Peter" more quietly. In each case, she continued to reinforce the correct response—"Peter." Eventually, Veronica asked loudly, "What's your name?" and simply mouthed the word "Peter." Nevertheless, the boy responded with the correct answer, "Peter." Over several trials, Veronica ceased even mouthing the correct answer, but Peter still responded correctly to the question "What's your name?"

FADING

Fading is the gradual change, on successive trials, of a stimulus that controls a response, so that the response eventually occurs to a partially changed or completely new stimulus (Deitz & Malone, 1985; Rilling, 1977). In the case described above, Peter would at first say his name only when it was said to him. Through a fading process, the stimulus control over the response "Peter" was gradually transferred from the stimulus "Peter" to the stimulus "What's your name?"

In any situation in which a stimulus exerts strong control over a response, fading can be a very useful procedure for changing the stimulus control. The discovery and development of fading techniques have led to some dramatic changes in educators' views regarding the learning process. At one time, it was felt that people had to make mistakes while learning to know what not to do. However, errorless transfer of a discrimination can occur, and it has at least three advantages over procedures involving trial and error. First, errors consume valuable time. Second, if an error occurs once, it tends to occur many times, even though it is being extinguished. (Remember from Chapter 4 that, during extinction, "things may get worse before they get better.") Third, the nonreinforcement that occurs when errors are being extinguished often produces emotional side effects such as tantrums, aggressive behavior, and attempts to escape from the situation.

We have used fading procedures in many learning situations in our programs with retarded and autistic individuals and very young children. In teaching students to name an item of clothing—a shirt, for example—teachers might proceed according to the following instructions:

1. Point to your shirt and say "shirt." Keep doing this until the student consistently mimics "shirt" a number of times, and immediately reinforce each correct response. (This assumes that you have a student who is able to mimic this particular word. It also assumes that the student has been trained to look at any item you point to.)

2. When the student consistently mimics "shirt," present the stimulus that you want to control the response, and at the same time gradually fade out the stimulus "shirt." That is, you might say, "What's this? Shirt" while pointing to the shirt. In response, the student usually mimics "shirt." Over several trials, gradually decrease the intensity of the stimulus "shirt" to zero, so that

the student eventually responds with the answer "shirt" to the stimulus of someone pointing at his shirt and asking "What's this?" Again, each appropriate response is to be reinforced.

Fading can also be used to teach tracing, copying, and drawing circles, lines, squares, triangles, numerals, and letters of the alphabet. To teach a student to trace a circle, the teacher might begin with a large number of sheets on each of which is a heavily dotted circle. The teacher places a pencil in the student's hand, says "Trace the circle," and then guides his hand so that the pencil traces the circle by connecting the dots. Immediately after this, of course, the student receives a reinforcer. After several such trials, the teacher fades out the pressure of her hand as a cue controlling the student's tracing, by

1. lightly holding the student's hand for several trials;
2. touching her fingertips to the back of the student's hand for several trials;
3. pointing to the item to be traced;
4. finally, simply giving the instruction, "Trace the circle." (Steps 1, 2, and 3 are always accompanied by this instruction.)

Once the teacher has taught the student to trace, she can teach the student to draw or copy by fading out the dotted cues that guide the tracing. For example, the teacher might use a sheet on which there are several dotted circles. The circles progress from a heavily dotted circle on the left to a circle with very few dots on the right. The teacher points to the most heavily dotted circle and instructs the student, "Trace the circle here." The desired response is reinforced, and the procedure is repeated for each of the more lightly dotted circles. On subsequent steps, the dots can be faded out completely so that the student will draw a circle in the absence of dots. It is then a simple matter to fade in the instruction "Draw a circle" to this newly acquired response. The instruction "Copy a circle," said while the teacher points to a circle, can also be faded in and come to control the response. Teaching the student to copy many different figures in this fashion will eventually enable him to copy adequately figures that he has had little experience copying.

Thus far, we have talked of fading in a rather restricted sense—that is, in the sense that fading can be used to change stimulus control when a specific response occurs to a rather specific stimulus (such as in the example in which the specific response "Peter" was brought under the control of the specific stimulus "What's your name?"). Fading can also be used to maintain appropriate behaviors when the general situation changes. For example, in one of the authors' programs with autistic children, we wanted to have a group of autistic boys respond appropriately in a classroom setting (Martin et al., 1968). But these boys were very disruptive, especially in a group situation. This being the case, we could not at first place them in a classroom setting. Thus, we decided first to obtain the desired behavior from each child in an individual situation and then fade in the classroom setting.

Our initial training sessions were conducted in a small room in which there were several chairs and tablet-arm desks. Two or three teachers (university students) worked individually with two or three students on a one-to-one ratio. The procedures involved eliminating tantrums through extinction and reinforcing sitting attentively, appropriate verbal behavior, drawing, copying, and other desirable behaviors. Each child's desk was placed against the wall in such a fashion as to make it difficult for him to leave the situation.

Within one week, the children learned to sit quietly, attend to the teacher, and mimic words in verbal training. Stimulus control was established between the general training situation and the children's attentiveness. But our goal at that time was to teach the children to function appropriately in a regular classroom situation with one teacher at the front of the class. If we had switched immediately to this situation after the first week, however, much inattentiveness and disruptive behavior would no doubt have occurred. Therefore, over a period of four weeks, we gradually changed from one small room with three students and three teachers to a standard-sized classroom with seven students and one teacher. This fading occurred along two stimulus dimensions.

One dimension was the physical structure of the room. We moved the children from the small room to the regular large classroom. However, we did so by first placing the three tablet-arm desks against the wall of the regular classroom, just as we had done in the small room. The three chairs that the teachers sat in were also moved to the regular classroom. The rest of the classroom was empty. Over several days, the tablet-arm desks were gradually moved away from the wall and toward the center of the room until, finally, the three desks were side by side. Additional desks and furnishings were added one at a time until the children were finally sitting in desks in a normally furnished classroom.

The second dimension was the number of children per teacher. Fading along this dimension was carried out at the same time that fading along the first dimension took place. At first, one teacher worked with one student for several sessions. The teacher then worked with two students, alternating questions between them for several sessions. In this fashion, the student-teacher ratio was increased gradually until only one teacher worked with as **Note 1** many as seven children in a classroom situation.[1]

Care should be taken to avoid confusing fading with shaping. Both are procedures of gradual change. However, as described in Chapter 5, shaping involves reinforcement of slight changes in a behavior so that it gradually comes to resemble the target behavior. The stimulus situation generally stays about the same, and the behavior changes from an initial behavior (not necessarily resembling the target) to the final target behavior. Fading, on the other hand, involves reinforcement of a specific response in the presence of slight changes in a stimulus so that the stimulus gradually comes to resemble the stimulus that you wish to control that particular response. Thus, *shaping involves the gradual change of a response while the stimulus stays about the same; fading involves the gradual change of a stimulus while the response stays about the same.*

USING FADING PROCEDURES TO TEACH VERBAL SKILLS

The lead case to this chapter showed how fading was used to teach an autistic child to respond appropriately to the question "What's your name?" Fading can be used in a similar manner to teach a wide variety of appropriate responses to questions. If a child can imitate a given object's name, for example, fading can be used to teach the child to vocally identify that object when asked what it is. Sometimes, of course, an individual cannot even imitate a particular verbal response—in that case, shaping is generally used to establish the imitative behavior prior to establishing the naming behavior.

Fading can also be used to teach fairly complex verbal skills. Consider the following use of fading to teach an eight-year-old autistic boy to count objects.* Danny had participated in a token-reinforcement program in which he earned poker chips that could be exchanged for food, candy, and other goodies. His attention span had been increased and he had learned to identify and recite the numerals 1 through 10. To teach Danny to count up to 10 objects, the teachers developed a detailed training procedure that utilized fading. Danny was required to complete 10 consecutive correct trials at each of six steps before progressing to the next step. Whenever Danny made an error on any step after step 1, he was moved back to the previous step and again required to complete that step correctly on 10 consecutive trials in order to advance. After Danny had progressed successfully through all six steps for a given numeral, he was returned to step 1 for the next numeral. The steps were as follows:

Step 1

Danny received a sheet of white paper with a numeral printed on the upper right-hand corner and a corresponding number of circles drawn on the paper (see Figure 9–1A). A trial began with the teacher pointing to the numeral, such as 5, in the upper right-hand corner of the page and asking, "Danny, what number is this?" Danny consistently identified the numeral 5 correctly, to which the teacher responded, "Good boy Danny. Put five circles on the paper." Danny then filled the outlined circles with circles cut from orange felt and received approval and a token. If Danny responded incorrectly, the teacher said "no" and demonstrated the correct response. After 10 consecutive correct trials, Danny was moved to step 2 of the training procedure for that particular numeral.

*This case is taken from Murrell, Hardy, and Martin (1974) and is paraphrased by permission of the publisher.

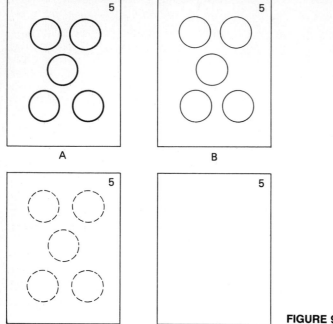

FIGURE 9–1 The stimulus sheets used in Danny's fading program.

Step 2

The procedure remained the same as in step 1, except that the outlines of the circles were finer (see Figure 9–1B).

Step 3

The procedure was the same as in step 1, except that the outlines of the circles were now broken lines (see Figure 9–1C).

Step 4

The procedure was the same as in step 1, except that the paper on Danny's desk was now blank, with only the numeral printed in the top right-hand corner (see Figure 9–1D).

Step 5

The procedure was the same as in step 1, except that the sheet of paper was not placed on Danny's desk. Instead, at the start of the trial Danny was shown the appropriate numeral cut from the felt material and asked, "Danny, what number is this?" When Danny correctly identified the numeral, such as 5, the teacher said, "Good boy, Danny. Now place five circles on your desk." After doing this correctly, he received reinforcement. As in all previous steps, Danny had to complete 10 consecutive trials correctly before moving on to the next step.

Step 6

The procedure was the same as in step 5, except that Danny was required to place the appropriate number of orange circles in the teacher's hand rather than on the desk. Following Danny's correct identification of the numeral, such as 5, the teacher held out her hand and said, "Good boy, Danny. Now give me five circles." On the first trial of step 6, the teacher held her hand on the desk. During the second through the fifth trials, the teacher gradually raised her hand off the desk and held it in midair directly in front of Danny. During the last few trials, Danny was taking the correct number of circles from a pile and placing them in the teacher's hand.

After Danny completed 10 consecutive trials on step 6, the numeral was considered learned. He was then taught to count the next numeral, proceeding through the same six steps. In this way, Danny learned to count objects for all of the numerals 1 through 10. Danny made only six errors in the entire training program. You can see how fading was utilized in several different ways in this program.

FACTORS INFLUENCING THE EFFECTIVENESS OF FADING

1. CHOOSING THE FINAL DESIRED STIMULUS

The *final desired stimulus* (i.e., the stimulus we want to evoke or produce the behavior at the end of the fading procedure) should be chosen carefully. It is important to select the final desired stimulus so that the occurrence of the response to that particular stimulus is likely to be maintained in the natural environment. Some fading programs make the error of stopping with a stimulus that does *not* include some aspect of the situation that the student will frequently encounter in the natural environment. Consider Danny's case. It would have been easy for the teachers to stop training after step 5, for Danny was clearly counting out the correct number of circles and placing them on his desk when asked to do so. However, classroom observation indicates that a more natural occurrence is for a teacher to approach a student, hold out her hand, and ask the student to give her a specific number of objects. The training program was therefore carried on through step 6. Moreover, the teachers conducted further training with Danny: following step 6, he was asked to count out other items (such as bingo chips, wooden blocks, and puzzle pieces of varying sizes, shapes, and colors) under the training procedure utilized in step 6.

2. CHOOSING THE STARTING STIMULUS

It is important to select a *starting stimulus* that reliably evokes the desired behavior. In Danny's training program, the teacher knew that Danny would place a felt circle on the heavy outline of a circle if there was such an outline on the piece of paper in front of him. Therefore, the heavy outline of a circle was the starting stimulus selected to teach Danny to count. In the task of teaching Peter his name, Veronica knew that Peter would mimic the last word of a question if that word was spoken loudly. Therefore, the starting stimulus with Peter was the question "What's your name?" said very softly and followed quickly by the shouted answer, "Peter!"

Supplemental stimuli that control the desired behavior but that are not a part of the final desired stimulus are sometimes referred to as **prompts** (Touchette & Howard, 1984). It is helpful to distinguish among *verbal prompts*, which are verbal hints or cues; *gestural prompts*, certain motions the teacher makes without touching the student; *environmental prompts*, in which the environment is altered in a manner that will evoke the desired behavior; and *physical prompts* (also called *physical guidance*), in which she touches the student to guide him. The teacher may provide any or all of these types of prompts to ensure the correct response. For example, suppose that the teacher wishes to develop appropriate stimulus control of the instruction "Touch your head" over the response of the student touching his head. The teacher might initiate training by saying, "Touch your head. Raise your hand and put it on your head like this," while touching his own head. In this example, "Raise your hand and put it on your head like this" is a verbal prompt, the teacher's action of putting his hand on his head is a gestural prompt. Selecting several kinds of prompts that, together, reliably produce the desired response will minimize **Note 2**   errors and maximize the success of the fading program.[2]

3. CHOOSING THE FADING STEPS

When the desired response is occurring reliably to the prompts given at the onset of the training program, the prompts can then be gradually removed over trials. The steps through which the prompts are to be eliminated should **Note 3**   be carefully chosen.[3] Unfortunately, effective use of fading is, like effective use of shaping, still somewhat of an art. It is very important to monitor the student's performance closely to determine the speed at which fading should be carried out. If the student begins to make errors, the prompts have been faded too quickly or through too few fading steps. It is then necessary to backtrack until the behavior is again well established before continuing with fading. On the other hand, if too many steps are introduced or too many prompts are provided over a number of trials, the student might become overly dependent on the prompts. Consider the example of teaching a child to touch his head when asked to do so. If the teacher spends a great many trials providing the prompt of touching her own head, the child may become dependent on it and attend much less to the instruction "Touch your head."

PITFALLS OF FADING

Just as other behavior principles and procedures can be applied unknowingly by those who are not familiar with them, so can fading be misused. However, it appears to be more difficult to misuse fading inadvertently because the necessary gradual change in cues rarely occurs by chance.

The case of the child who banged his head on hard surfaces (described in Chapter 8) might be an example of the effects of the misuse of fading. In Chapter 5 we pointed out that shaping might produce such behavior. It is also possible that fading is responsible for it. Suppose that the child began attracting attention initially by hitting his head on soft surfaces, such as grass. At first, this behavior may have caused adults to come running to see if the child had injured himself. When they eventually learned that no injury resulted from this behavior, they ceased providing it with attention. The child may then have progressed to hitting his head with the same force but on slightly harder surfaces, such as carpeted floors. For awhile, this perhaps increased the amount of attention elicited from adults, but this amount of attention may eventually have decreased when the adults learned that the child did not injure himself in this way. Only when the child graduated to hitting his head on surfaces such as hard floors and even concrete, which caused real and serious self-injury, did the adults give him continued attention. Note that throughout this example there was a gradual change in the stimulus (the type of floor surface) evoking the undesired behavior; eventually, the behavior was evoked by the most undesirable stimulus possible. Thus, this example clearly fits the technical definition of fading.

GUIDELINES FOR THE EFFECTIVE APPLICATION OF FADING

1. *Choosing the final desired stimulus.* Specify very clearly the stimuli in the presence of which the target behavior should eventually occur.
2. *Selecting an appropriate reinforcer* (See Chapter 3).
3. *Choosing the starting stimulus and fading steps.*
   a. Specify clearly the conditions under which the desired behavior now occurs—that is, what people, words, physical guidance, and so forth, are necessary, at present, to evoke the desired behavior.
   b. Specify clearly the dimensions (such as color, people, and room size) that you will fade to reach the desired stimulus control.
   c. Outline the specific fading steps to be followed and the rules for moving from one step to the next.
4. *Putting the plan into effect.*
   a. The fading of cues should be so gradual that there are as few errors as possible. However, if an error occurs, move back to the previous step for several trials and provide additional prompts.
   b. When the desired stimulus control is obtained, review the guidelines in previous chapters for weaning the student from the program (a topic that is discussed in more detail in Chapter 12).

STUDY QUESTIONS

1. Define fading and give an example of it.
2. Why is it advantageous to establish stimulus control without errors?
3. Identify three stimulus dimensions along which fading occurred in the examples cited in the first two sections of this chapter.
4. Describe an example from this chapter in which the training situation remained constant but a specific stimulus dimension was faded.
5. Describe an example from this chapter in which the general training situation was faded but the specific training stimuli remained relatively constant.
6. Describe how you might use fading to teach your pet to perform a trick. Describe how you might use shaping to teach your pet to perform another trick. Drawing from your examples, distinguish clearly between fading and shaping.
7. Assume that you have an 18-month-old child who will imitate the word "chip." Describe in detail how you might use fading to teach your child to correctly identify a chip (i.e., a potato chip) when you point to it and ask "What's that?"
8. Describe two ways in which fading was used in the program through which Danny learned to count.
9. What do we mean by *final desired stimulus*? Give an example.
10. What do we mean by *starting stimulus*? Give an example.
11. Define the four major categories of prompts. Give examples from this chapter.
12. How many reinforced trials should occur at any given fading step before the stimuli of that particular step are changed? (*Hint*: What suggestions were made in the examples in this chapter?)

PRACTICE EXERCISES

1. Suppose that a two-year-old child has reached the stage at which he is beginning to "explore" the surrounding neighborhood. The child has already learned some speech, and you wish to teach him to answer the question "Where do you live?" Outline a fading program with which you could teach the answer to this question; indicate what you would use as a reinforcer, the number of trials you would have at each fading step, and so forth.
2. Assume that you must teach a severely retarded child, or a very young normal child, to eat with a spoon. Outline a program in which you would use all four of the major categories of prompts. Describe how each of the prompts would be faded.
3. Suppose that the official temperature scale has been switched recently from degrees Fahrenheit to degrees Celsius. The government has assigned you the job of designing an effective program for teaching citizens to respond knowledgably to the Celsius scale. You have been given complete freedom to work with the radio and television weather announcers. Describe a plan that would accomplish this task. Include a precise statement of your target stimulus control, your starting stimulus control, and the fading steps you would use.

EXTENDED DISCUSSION AND NOTES

1. In addition to being used for teaching, fading has also been used for diagnostic purposes. For example, Meyerson and Michael (1964) used it to diagnose the level of hearing of children who were presumed to be moderately retarded. These authors wanted to determine if the behavioral problems of the children were due to poor hearing or to other conditions. The authors first designed an experimental testing room in which two small levers were placed directly below two light bulbs, each arranged on a console so that it was difficult to press both levers simultaneously. The children were taught to press the lever underneath the light bulb that was lit. When they did so, they were reinforced with candy, toys, and other items. The children soon learned to press the lever under the light that was lit and to switch to the other lever when that light bulb went off and the opposite light bulb went on. The schedule of reinforcement was then changed to VR 8. The next step in the program consisted of presenting a loud sound (one that was approximately in the middle of the frequency range of normal hearing) each time the light bulb on the left was illuminated. When that light went off and the opposite light was illuminated, the sound terminated. Fading was then introduced: over a number of alternations of the two lights, during which the loud tone was presented whenever the left light was illuminated and was not presented whenever the right light was illuminated, the intensity of the lights was gradually diminished until they were not presented at all. The result of this fading procedure was that the children learned to press the left lever when the tone was presented and to press the right lever when there was no sound. The children were finally ready to be tested for their hearing. Over a number of trials, the intensity of the sound was gradually changed. In other trials, the frequency of the sound was changed as well. At the point where the children's lever pressing no longer correlated with the presence or absence of the tone, Meyerson and Michael knew that they had encountered a hearing deficiency. Thus, by using a fading technique Meyerson and Michael were able to determine that some of the children had been diagnosed as moderately retarded due to brain damage when in fact their behavioral handicaps were due at least in part to poor hearing.

2. Etzel and LeBlanc (1979) distinguished between fading and what they termed "stimulus shaping." According to them, in fading the overall structure or configuration of a stimulus is not changed, whereas it is changed in stimulus shaping. An example of stimulus shaping would be a procedure for teaching an individual to discriminate between a circle and an oval. At first, a discrimination might be established between a circle and a rectangle (because this is an easier discrimination to make). Gradually, over trials, the corners of the rectangle would become increasingly rounded and its sides would become increasingly curved until eventually its shape had been changed to that of an oval. Although the term *stimulus shaping* is now common in the literature, not all behavior analysts agree that it should be considered as distinct from fading. For example, in an article discussing these and other stimulus-control terms, Deitz and Malone (1985) concluded that the distinction between fading and stimulus shaping is potentially confusing and neither necessary nor useful.

3. There are at least four different methods of removing prompts gradually. (1) decreasing assistance; (2) increasing assistance; (3) graduated guidance; and (4) time delay. *Decreasing assistance*—in which a starting stimulus that evokes the response is gradually removed or changed until the response is evoked by the

final desired stimulus—is the method that is illustrated by all the examples of this chapter. *Increasing assistance* takes the opposite approach: the teacher begins with the final desired stimulus, and introduces prompts only if the student fails to respond appropriately to the final desired stimulus. The level of the prompts is gradually increased during a trial in which the student failed to respond at the preceding level until eventually the student responds to the prompt. *Graduated guidance* is similar to the method of decreasing assistance, except that the teacher's physical guidance is gradually adjusted from moment to moment within a trial as needed, and then faded across trials. For example, the teacher may grasp the student's hand firmly at the beginning of the trial, and gradually reduce the force on the student's arm as the trial progresses. With *time delay*, the final desired stimulus and the starting stimulus are presented together at first; then, rather than changing the starting stimulus, the time interval between the final desired stimulus and the starting stimulus is gradually increased until eventually the individual is responding only to the final desired stimulus. Many studies have indicated little or no difference in the effectiveness of these different prompt-removal methods (for a review, see Demchak, 1990).

STUDY QUESTIONS ON NOTES

1. Describe how the Meyerson-Michael procedure might be adapted so as to test for red-green color blindness in severely retarded children who have very little speech.
2. Describe an example of what some behavior analysts call "stimulus shaping." Would all behavior analysts agree that this is different from fading?
3. Which of the prompt-removal procedures fit the definition of fading given at the beginning of this chapter, and which do not? Explain.

CHAPTER 10

Developing and Maintaining Behavior with Conditioned Reinforcement

"OK, team! Here's how you can earn an Eagle Effort Award."

COACH DAWSON'S POINT PROGRAM*

"Let's see a little concentration out there. You should hardly ever miss lay-ups in drills!" shouted Jim Dawson at basketball practice. Jim was coach of a Clinton Junior High basketball team in Columbus, Ohio. He was concerned about the players' performance during a series of drills that he used to open each practice. There was also an attitude problem. "Some of them just aren't team players," he thought to himself. "Some of them really have a bad attitude."

With the help of Dr. Daryl Siedentop of Ohio State University, he worked out a motivational system in which players could earn points for performance in lay-up drills, jump-shooting drills, and free-throw drills at daily practice. In addition, they could earn points by being a "team player" and encouraging their teammates by making "supportive comments." Points were deducted if Coach Dawson saw a lack of "hustle" or a "bad attitude." The points were recorded by student volunteers who served as managers for the team. All of this was explained to the players in detail. At the end of a practice, the coach praised players who earned a lot of points, as well as players who earned more points than in the previous practice. In addition to reviewing their records of points earned at each practice, players who earned a sufficient number of points had their names posted in a conspicuous place on the "Eagle Effort" board in the hall leading to the gymnasium and were rewarded with an "Eagle Effort" award

*This example is based on a report by Siedentop (1978), and is paraphrased from Martin & Lumsden (1987).

at a post-season banquet. Overall, the system was highly effective. Performance in lay-up drills improved from an average of 68 percent before the system to an average of 80 percent. Jump-shooting performance improved from 37 to 51 percent. Free-throw shooting at practices improved from 59 to 67 percent. However, the most dramatic improvement was in the "team player" category: The number of supporting comments increased rapidly to such an extent that the managers could not monitor them all. In addition, while at first most of the comments were "pretty phony," over sessions they became increasingly sincere. By the end of the season the players were exhibiting good-attitude behaviors to a remarkable extent and, in Coach Dawson's words, "We were more together than I ever could have imagined."

CONDITIONED REINFORCEMENT

The points that Coach Dawson used at basketball practices were probably not by themselves reinforcing to the players. We doubt that the players would have worked very hard, if at all, to get points for their own sake. The players worked hard because the points were associated with other reinforcers, called *backup reinforcers*, that made the points into reinforcers. The backup reinforcers for the points included praise from Coach Dawson, the "Eagle Effort" award at the postseason banquet, and the posting of the players' names on

Note 1 the "Eagle Effort" board in the hall leading to the gymnasium.[1]

When working with children, reinforcers such as popcorn and candy are usually reinforcing in themselves. Most children just "naturally" like them. Stimuli such as these, whose reinforcing power is biologically determined, are called *primary reinforcers*.* Backup reinforcers can be, but need not be, primary reinforcers. Stimuli that are not originally reinforcing but acquire reinforcing power through association with backup reinforcers are called *conditioned reinforcers*.

Conditioned reinforcers that can be accumulated and exchanged for backup reinforcers are called *tokens*. A behavior modification program that uses tokens is called a *token system* (in Chapter 22, we discuss *token economies*, which are token systems designed for groups of individuals). Just about anything that can be accumulated can be used as the medium of exchange in a token system (see Figure 10–1). In some token systems individuals earn plastic discs (such as poker chips), which they can retain until they are ready to cash them in for backup reinforcers (see Martin et al., 1968). In other token systems they are paid with "paper money," on which is written the amount earned, the individual's name, the name of the employee who paid him, the date, and the task the individual performed to earn the token (see Logan, 1970). In still others, as in Coach Dawson's program, individuals receive points, which are recorded on a chart beside their names or in notebooks they keep with them (see Philips, 1968).

*Another name for primary reinforcer is *unconditioned reinforcer* (that is, a stimulus that is reinforcing without being conditioned).

FIGURE 10–1 Examples of tokens.

Tokens constitute one type of conditioned reinforcer, but stimuli that cannot be accumulated can also be conditioned reinforcers. A common example, already mentioned, is praise. A mother who expresses pleasure at her child's good behavior is simultaneously disposed to smile at the child, hug him, play with him, and give him a treat or a toy. Praise is normally established as a conditioned reinforcer during childhood, but it continues to be maintained as one for adults. This is because, when people praise us, they are generally more likely to favor us in various ways than when they do not praise us.[2]

Note 2

Although it is normal for praise to become a conditioned reinforcer, this does not hold true in the case of some behaviorally handicapped people. Perhaps for them, no one ever associated praise with effective backup reinforcers. Indeed, this may be one reason for their behavioral handicaps. Praise is used so commonly as a reinforcer in our society that any individual for whom it is not reinforcing cannot be expected to acquire very many socially desirable behaviors. It would seem that such an individual would almost necessarily become behaviorally handicapped—no matter what the "innate potential" for her intellectual and other social development might be. Of course, if her "innate potential" is not very great to begin with, she may emit socially desirable behavior so rarely that people in her natural environment seldom or never praise her. Thus, her lack of contact with praise precludes it from becoming a conditioned reinforcer, which makes it even more difficult for her to develop socially desirable behaviors. It follows that those working with others should ensure that praise becomes and remains a conditioned reinforcer for them. In training programs, this is typically done by praising desirable behavior just prior to presenting other types of reinforcement.

Before closing this section we might mention briefly the principle of *conditioned punishment*, which is very similar to that of conditioned reinforcement. Just as a stimulus that is paired with reinforcement becomes reinforcing itself, so a stimulus that is paired with punishment becomes punishing itself. "No!" and "Stop that!" are examples of stimuli that become conditioned punishers, because they are often followed by punishment if the individual continues to engage in the behavior that provoked them. Moreover, punishing tokens as well as reinforcing ones are possible. The demerit system used in the military is an example of a punishing-token system. There are, however, problems associated with the use of punishment (see Chapter 13).

FACTORS INFLUENCING THE EFFECTIVENESS OF CONDITIONED REINFORCEMENT

1. THE STRENGTH OF THE BACKUP REINFORCERS

The reinforcing power of a conditioned reinforcer depends in part upon the reinforcing power of the backup reinforcer(s) on which it is based. For example, suppose that Coach Dawson had used only praise as a backup reinforcer for those players who earned points. In that case, the points would have been effective reinforcers only for the players for whom the coach's praise was an effective reinforcer.

2. THE VARIETY OF BACKUP REINFORCERS

The reinforcing power of a conditioned reinforcer depends in part on the number of different backup reinforcers available for it. This factor is related to the preceding one in that, if there are many different backup reinforcers available, then at any given time at least one of them will probably be strong enough to maintain tokens at a high reinforcing strength for any individual in the program. A conditioned reinforcer that is based on a number of different backup reinforcers is called a ***generalized reinforcer***. Thus, the points in Coach Dawson's program were generalized reinforcers. Money is another example of a generalized reinforcer because it can be exchanged for an almost unlimited variety of reinforcers. This is why it can keep people occupied day after day in its pursuit.

3. THE SCHEDULE OF PAIRING WITH THE BACKUP REINFORCER

In Chapter 6, we saw that behavior is more persistent if reinforcement docs not follow every occurrence of the target behavior. Likewise, conditioned reinforcement is more effective if backup reinforcement does not follow each occurrence of the conditioned reinforcer. For example, the players in Coach Dawson's program had to earn a certain number of points before they were given backup reinforcement.

4. EXTINCTION OF THE CONDITIONED REINFORCER

For a conditioned reinforcer to remain effective, it must continue to be associated with a suitable backup reinforcer. Had Coach Dawson discontinued the backup reinforcers of his praise and the "Eagle Effort" program, the players may eventually have stopped working for the points. Ceasing to provide backup reinforcement for a conditioned reinforcer is called *extinction of a conditioned reinforcer* and is similar to the procedure described in Chapter 4 for extinguishing a response.

PITFALLS OF CONDITIONED REINFORCEMENT

People who are unfamiliar with the principle of conditioned reinforcement may unknowingly misapply it in various ways. One very common misapplication occurs when an adult scolds a child for behaving inappropriately, but

(1) does not provide any type of "backup punishment" (see Chapter 13) along with the scolding and (2) does not reinforce desirable alternative behavior. The scolding, no doubt, is given in the expectation that it will be punishing, but often this is not the case. Indeed, the attention that accompanies such negative verbal stimuli may even be highly reinforcing, especially for behaviorally handicapped individuals, who often do not receive much attention from adults. In this way, scoldings and other negative verbal stimuli (such as "No!") can become conditioned reinforcers, and the individual will behave inappropriately to obtain them.

Indeed, even stimuli that are normally punishing can become conditioned reinforcers through association with powerful primary reinforcers. The classic example is the parent who spanks a child for misbehavior and then, "feeling guilty" from the ensuing piteous crying, immediately hugs the child and gives her ice cream or some other treat. The possible outcome of this unthinking procedure is that the child will develop a "liking for lickings"; that is, the spanking could become a conditioned reinforcer that would maintain, not eliminate, the misbehavior it follows.

Extinction of a conditioned reinforcer can be unknowingly applied with unfortunate results by those who are unfamiliar with this aspect of conditioned reinforcement. An example of this is a teacher who awards stars for good behavior but fails to use effective backup reinforcers. The result is that the stars eventually lose whatever reinforcing power they may have had when they were first introduced. Failure to use effective backup reinforcers can account for the lack of motivation students sometimes show on certain token systems.[3]

Note 3

GUIDELINES FOR THE EFFECTIVE USE OF CONDITIONED REINFORCEMENT

The following guidelines should be observed in applying conditioned reinforcement.

1. A conditioned reinforcer should be a stimulus that can be managed and administered easily in the situation in which you plan to use it. For example, points were ideally suited for the players in Coach Dawson's program.
2. As much as possible, use the same conditioned reinforcers that the individual will encounter in the natural environment. For example, it is desirable in training programs to transfer control from artificial-token systems to the monetary-token system used in the natural environment.
3. In the early stages of establishing a conditioned reinforcer, backup reinforcement should be presented as quickly as possible after the presentation of the conditioned reinforcer. Later, the delay between conditioned reinforcement and the backup reinforcement can be increased gradually, if desired.
4. Use generalized conditioned reinforcers wherever possible; that is, use many different types of backup reinforcers, not just one. This way, at least one of

the backup reinforcers will probably be strong enough at any given time to maintain the power of the conditioned reinforcer.

5. When the program involves more than one individual (as was the case in Coach Dawson's program), avoid destructive competition for conditioned and backup reinforcers. If one person receives reinforcement to the detriment of another, that may evoke aggressive behavior in the second individual and/ or his desirable behavior may extinguish. This rule implies in particular that one should avoid making an issue out of the fact that one individual is earning more conditioned and backup reinforcement than another. Of course, people differ in their abilities, but the bad effects of these differences can be minimized by designing programs so that each individual earns a good deal of reinforcement for performing at his or her own level.

6. In addition to the above rules, one should follow the same rules for conditioned reinforcers that apply to any positive reinforcer (see Chapter 3). Additional details for establishing token economies are described in Chapter 22.

STUDY QUESTIONS

1. Explain what a conditioned reinforcer is. Give and explain two examples.
2. Explain what a backup reinforcer is. Give two examples.
3. What were the conditioned reinforcers and backup reinforcers in Coach Dawson's program?
4. If Coach Dawson had not paired praise and the "Eagle Effort" program with the points, the players may have continued to work because of a variety of natural reinforcers that may have been paired with the points. What might these natural reinforcers have been?
5. Explain what a primary reinforcer is. Give two examples.
6. Which of the reinforcers in Figure 3-3 are primary reinforcers and which are conditioned reinforcers? Defend your answer.
7. Explain why money is a conditioned reinforcer.
8. What are tokens? Explain in two or three sentences what a token system is.
9. Give two examples of stimuli that are conditioned reinforcers but not tokens. Explain why they are conditioned reinforcers.
10. Why is it important for those working with the behaviorally handicapped to ensure that praise becomes a conditioned reinforcer for them?
11. Explain what a conditioned punisher is. Give and explain two examples.
12. Explain what a generalized reinforcer is. Explain why a conditioned reinforcer that is a generalized reinforcer is more effective than one that is not.
13. Explain what extinction of a conditioned reinforcer is.
14. How does the schedule of pairing a conditioned and backup reinforcer affect the strength of the conditioned reinforcer?

SELF-MODIFICATION EXERCISE

Self-modification Exercise 2 in Chapter 3 required you to complete the reinforcer questionnaire for yourself. Self-modification Exercise 2 in Chapter 5 required you to outline a detailed shaping program for overcoming one of your deficiencies. Now select several reinforcers from your reinforcer questionnaire and describe how they might be used in a plausible token system to carry out your shaping program from Chapter 5.

EXTENDED DISCUSSION AND NOTES

1. There is little doubt that the points functioned as conditioned reinforcers for the basketball players. It is likely, however, that more than the direct-acting effect of the points as positive reinforcers was involved in the improvement of the basketball players at practice (see Michael, 1986). You will recall from Chapter 3 that positive reinforcers have a direct-acting effect on behaviors that immediately precede them. However, the points in Coach Dawson's program were not awarded until the end of practice. Why then did the players show improvement in performance?

   Perhaps they noticed managers recording points just after a correct behavior was performed, which may have served as a conditioned reinforcer. As positive peer comments increased, these likely served as conditioned reinforcers for improved performance. A part of the answer may also lie in the indirect-acting effect of the points as reinforcers (see Chapter 3). Perhaps the players verbally rehearsed rules such as, "If I make more jump shots I'll earn more points," and such statements may have exerted rule-governed control over the improved performance (see Chapter 3). Thus, while the overall improvement might be attributed to the point program, and while the points were conditioned positive reinforcers, the improved performance of the players in practice may not have been due to a direct-acting effect of those points as conditioned reinforcers for the behaviors of lay-ups, jump-shooting, free-throws, and peer support.

2. Even the mild murmur "mmm-hmm," if used as an expression of interest or approval, can have measurable reinforcing effects. As described in detail in Chapter 3, Greenspoon (1951) demonstrated this in a classic experiment in which he instructed college students to "free-associate" and then said "mmm-hmm" contingent upon the emission of plural nouns. The frequency of plural nouns increased even for those students who appeared (on the basis of testing) not to have been aware of the reinforcement contingency. Moreover, the frequency of plural nouns decreased when Greenspoon extinguished this behavior by withholding "mmm-hmm."

3. We discussed earlier how knowledge of schedules of reinforcement can help us to understand behavior that has often been attributed to inner motivational states (see Chapter 6, note 6). Knowledge of conditioned reinforcement can also help us to understand such behavior. For an industrious college student, for example, good grades and the praise of relatives and teachers were associated with powerful reinforcers. In this person's childhood, a good report was probably followed by words of endearment, hugs, and special treats. Now that he or she is a young adult, the backup reinforcers that maintain grades and praise as conditioned reinforcers may be more difficult to identify, but they are still just as powerful (especially when combined with the schedule effects discussed in Chapter 6).

Study Questions on Notes

1. Can we attribute the improved performance of Coach Dawson's basketball players entirely to the direct-acting effects of points as condition reinforcers? Why or why not?

2. Describe how Greenspoon demonstrated that "mmm-hmm" can be a reinforcer.

3. Describe how knowledge of conditioned reinforcement can help us to understand behavior that is often attributed to inner motivational states.

CHAPTER 11

Getting a New Behavior to Occur with **Behavioral Chaining**

"Agnes, please make a coffee pack for me."

TEACHING AGNES TO ASSEMBLE A COFFEE PACK

Agnes was a severely retarded woman with an IQ of 22 who lived in a group home with several other severely retarded women.* The group home staff was told that if Agnes could learn to perform vocational tasks, she might be able to attend a sheltered workshop that had a contract with an airline company to assemble coffee packs. This task involved appropriately stuffing a plastic bag with a folded paper napkin, coffee whitener, a sugar pack, and a plastic stir stick. These coffee packs were used by the airline company to serve with coffee on their domestic flights. Angela Pallotta-Cornick, a graduate student, decided to try to teach Agnes to perform this task, partly because Agnes would follow simple instructions.

Before beginning training, Angela conducted a test to see what Agnes could do without any training at all. She placed some samples of each of the components of the task in front of Agnes. She then showed Agnes a completed coffee pack and asked her to make one just like it. Agnes promptly stuffed the plastic bag with plastic stir sticks. It seemed clear that Agnes could not assemble the coffee pack appropriately, at least under the test conditions.

Assembling a coffee pack consists of a sequence of responses that must be followed, one response at a time, in the proper order. It was apparent that, before any progress could be made, this sequence would have to be specified. Therefore, the entire process of assembling a coffee pack was divided into the following 15 sequential units or steps.

*This example is taken from Pallotta-Cornick (1978).

1. Pick up one napkin.
2. Fold napkin in half (making it narrower).
3. Sharpen crease with forefinger.
4. Fold napkin in half (making it shorter).
5. Pick up one plastic bag.
6. Open plastic bag.
7. Pick up folded napkin.
8. Put napkin into plastic bag with folded end first.
9. Pick up one coffee whitener.
10. Put coffee whitener into plastic bag.
11. Pick up one sugar pack.
12. Put sugar pack into bag over napkin, with logo on sugar pack clearly visible.
13. Pick up one stir stick.
14. Put stir stick into the bag.
15. Lift plastic bag so that contents all go to the bottom.

The training procedure carried out by Angela involved a series of trials, on each of which Agnes was required to perform all fifteen steps in the appropriate sequence. At each step, Angela verbally prompted Agnes to perform the step. If Agnes performed the step appropriately, she was praised and then prompted to perform the next step. If Agnes performed the step inappropriately, Angela used verbal instructions and physical guidance to help Agnes perform the correct response, and then Agnes was required to go on to the next step. Incorrect performance of a step was not followed by praise. Following successful completion of step 15, Agnes received more praise and also an edible of her choice. In this way, Agnes practiced assembling coffee packs over a number of trials, performing each of the steps in the appropriate order on each trial. As Agnes became increasingly proficient at performing the steps, Angela provided less and less verbal help. Eventually, all Angela had to say was "Do all you can" and Agnes would perform all 15 steps correctly. Even though Agnes was severely retarded, she learned to assemble the coffee packs appropriately after approximately six 20-minute sessions.

STIMULUS-RESPONSE CHAINING

Note 1

A stimulus-response chain is a sequence of discriminative stimuli (S^Ds) and responses (Rs) in which each response except the last produces the S^D for the next response. The last response is followed typically by a reinforcer.[1] What Agnes had acquired in learning to assemble a coffee pack was such a sequence of stimuli and responses. The first stimulus (S^D_1) for the entire sequence was the instruction, "Please assemble the coffee pack"; this was the instruction that was given in the presence of a completely unassembled coffee pack. The response (R_1) to that stimulus was "picking up one napkin." The napkin in hand was the stimulus for the response "folding the napkin in half." The napkin in half was the stimulus for the response "sharpening the crease with the forefinger." And so on until the entire coffee pack was assembled, at which point Agnes received edible reinforcers and extra praise. The reason for calling this procedure a stimulus-response chain can be seen by writing it out as follows:

$$S_1^D \longrightarrow R_1 \longrightarrow S_2^D \longrightarrow R_2 \longrightarrow S_3^D \longrightarrow R_3 \ldots S_{13}^D \longrightarrow R_{15} \longrightarrow S^+$$

The stimulus-response connections are the "links" that hold the chain together. As the saying goes, "a chain is only as strong as its weakest link." Similarly, if any response is so weak that it fails to be evoked by the S^D preceding it, the next S^D will not be produced and the rest of the chain will not occur. The chain will be broken at the point of its weakest link. The only way in which to repair the chain is to strengthen the weak stimulus-response connection by means of an effective training procedure.

The symbol S^+ at the far right of the diagram symbolizes the positive reinforcer that follows the last response in the chain. It designates the "oil" that one must apply regularly to keep the chain rust free and strong.

There are three major methods of teaching a stimulus-response chain. One method is called ***total task presentation***. With this method, the client attempts all the steps from the beginning to the end of the chain on each trial and continues with total task trials until all steps are mastered. This was the strategy used to teach Agnes to assemble coffee packs.

A second major method of teaching a stimulus-response chain is called ***backward chaining***. This method gradually constructs the chain in a reverse order from that in which the chain is performed; that is, the last step is established first, then the next-to-last step is taught and linked to the last step, then the third-from-last step is taught and linked to the last two steps, and so on, progressing backward toward the beginning of the chain. Backward chaining has been used in numerous programs, including teaching various dressing, grooming, and verbal behaviors to retarded individuals. To teach a boy to put on a pair of slacks, for example, we break down the task into the following nine steps:

1. Taking the slacks from the dresser drawer.
2. Holding the slacks upright with the front facing away from the individual.
3. Putting one leg in the slacks.
4. Putting the other leg in the slacks.
5. Pulling the slacks to the knees.
6. Pulling the slacks to the thighs.
7. Pulling the slacks all the way up.
8. Doing up the button or snap.
9. Doing up the zipper.

When we use backward chaining to teach an individual this chain, we start with the last step. The trainer helps the individual to put on the slacks so that all the steps are completed except for step 9. The individual is then taught to finish by doing up the zipper. When this has been taught, the trainer then starts the individual from step 8 and teaches him to finish from there. That is, the individual is taught to do up the button (step 8), which is the S^D for doing up the zipper, and to finish. When he consistently makes both responses in sequence, the slacks are pulled down to his thighs. He is then taught to pull them all the way up (step 7), which is the S^D for the response of step 8. On each trial, the individual completes *all* the steps learned previously. The training proceeds in this backward fashion, with one step being added at a time, until the individual can perform all nine steps.

Students often find backward chaining strange, apparently because they think that it teaches an individual to perform the chain backward, as the name suggests. Naturally, this is not true. There is a very good theoretical rationale for using backward chaining. Consider the example of teaching a retarded boy to put on a pair of slacks. By starting with step 9, the response of "doing up the zipper" was reinforced in the presence of the snap done up. Therefore, the sight of "the snap done up" became an S^D for step 9, "doing up the zipper." On the basis of the principle of conditioned reinforcement, the sight of "the snap done up" also became a conditioned reinforcer for whatever preceded it. After several trials at step 9, the trainer went on to step 8. The behavior of "doing up the snap" produced the stimulus, sight of "the snap done up." The sight of "the snap done up" had become a conditioned reinforcer, and it immediately followed performing step 8. Thus, when one uses backward chaining, the reinforcement of the last step in the presence of the appropriate stimulus, over trials, establishes that stimulus as a discriminative stimulus for the last step and as a conditioned reinforcer for the next-to-the-last step. When the step before the last step is added, the S^D in that step also becomes a conditioned reinforcer, and so on. Thus, the power of the positive reinforcer that is presented at the end of the chain is transferred "down the line" to each S^D as it is added to the chain. In this way, backward chaining has a theoretical advantage of always having a readily available conditioned reinforcer to strengthen each new response that is added to the sequence.

The third major method of teaching a stimulus-response chain is called *forward chaining*. With this method, the initial step of the sequence is taught first, then the first and second steps are taught and linked together, then the first three steps, and so on until the entire chain is acquired. At least partly because backward chaining resembles a reversal of the natural order of things, forward chaining and total task presentation are used more often in everyday situations outside the behavior modification setting. Among the many examples that can be cited to illustrate forward chaining, consider the way in which a child might be taught to pronounce a word, such as "milk."

Note 2   He might be first taught to say "mm," then "mi," then "mil," and finally "milk."[2]

The three major chaining formats are diagrammed in Figure 11–1. Which is most effective? Bellamy, Horner, and Inman (1979) concluded that total task presentation has several practical advantages over the other chaining

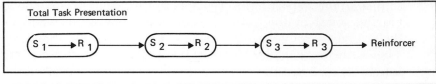

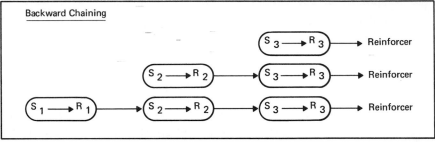

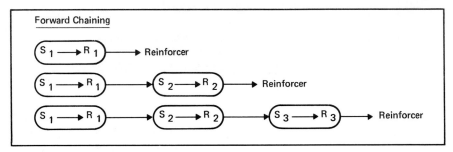

FIGURE 11–1 A diagram of the three major chaining formats.

formats for teaching retarded persons. Total task presentation requires the trainer to spend less time in partial assembly or disassembly to prepare the task for training; it appears to focus on teaching response topography and response sequence simultaneously and, therefore, should produce results more quickly; and it appears to maximize the learner's independence early in training, especially if some steps are already familiar to the learner. Moreover, several studies have demonstrated that total task presentation is at least as good as, or better than, backward chaining or forward chaining for teaching various tasks to retarded persons (Martin, Koop, Turner, & Hanel, 1981; Spooner, 1984; Yu, Martin, Suthons, Koop, & Pallotta-Cornick, 1980). In general, total task presentation is probably the method of choice for nonretarded individuals as well. But there are some clear exceptions. For example, when giving driving instructions it is highly advisable to teach the use of the **Note 3** brake prior to the use of the accelerator (for obvious reasons!).[3]

CHAINING COMPARED WITH FADING AND SHAPING

Chaining, fading, and shaping are sometimes called the *gradual change procedures* because they each involve progressing gradually through a series of steps to produce a behavior that did not occur previously. It is important to keep clear the distinctions among the three gradual change procedures.

In shaping, the steps consist of reinforcing closer and closer approximations to the final desired response (see Chapter 5). In fading, the steps consist of reinforcing the final desired response in the presence of closer and closer approximations to the final desired stimulus for that response (see Chapter 9). In chaining, the steps usually consist of reinforcing more and more of the specific stimulus-response links that comprise the chain. An exception to this is the method of total task presentation; in this case all the links are taught right from the beginning of training, and shaping or fading may be used to develop the responses or to bring them under the control of their appropriate stimuli. Since shaping or fading is used, the procedure is still a gradual change procedure. Table 11–1 summarizes some of the similarities and differences of the three procedures as they are typically applied.

FACTORS INFLUENCING THE EFFECTIVENESS OF CHAINING

1. DO A TASK ANALYSIS: IDENTIFY THE COMPONENTS OF THE FINAL SEQUENCE

The behavioral sequence you wish to develop must be broken down into individual components, and the proper order of the sequence must be kept. The process of breaking a task down into smaller steps or component responses to facilitate training is referred to as *task analysis* (see Bellamy and others, 1979; Popovich, 1981). As with the selection of shaping steps (discussed in Chapter 5), the selection of chaining steps or components is somewhat subjective. The components should be simple enough to be learned without great difficulty. If you wanted to teach a severely retarded child to brush her teeth, for example, it would be a mistake to consider the task in terms of the three gross steps of putting toothpaste on the brush, brushing, and rinsing. For the child to master the chain, each of these steps would have to be subdivided into even smaller steps. The components should also be selected so that there is a clear-cut stimulus or set of stimuli signaling the completion of each component. This will facilitate the development of those stimuli as conditioned reinforcers for preceding responses and as S^Ds for subsequent responses throughout the chain. For example, in utilizing chaining to teach a child appropriate hand-washing behavior, you might select putting water in the sink as one of the components. It would be important to specify a particular level of water, and perhaps even make a mark (at least temporarily) approximately halfway up the sink, to provide a very clear stimulus that terminates the end of this particular component (which you might define as "holding the water taps on until the water level reaches the halfway mark").

After completing your task analysis, review each of the controlling stimuli for each of the responses in the sequence. Ideally, each controlling stimulus should be clearly distinctive from the other controlling stimuli. If

Table 11-1 Similarities and Differences Among Shaping, Fading, and Chaining

	SHAPING	FADING	CHAINING
Terminal behavior	1 New behavior along some physical dimension, such as topography, amount, or intensity. 2 The final behavior consists of only the last shaping step.	1 New stimulus control of a particular behavior. 2 The fading steps do not necessarily form part of the terminal stimulus control.	1 New sequence of responses, with a "clear-cut" stimulus signaling the end of each response and the start of the next. 2 The final behavior consists of all the chaining steps.
General training procedure	1 Often involves an unstructured environment in which the student has the opportunity to emit a variety of behaviors. 2 Proceeds in a forward fashion in terms of the "natural order" of behavior.	1 Typically involves a structured environment since the stimuli present must be controlled precisely. 2 Proceeds in a forward fashion in terms of the "natural order" of behavior.	1 Typically involves a semistructured or structured teaching environment. 2 May proceed in a forward or backward fashion in terms of "the natural order" of behavior.
Other procedural considerations	1 Often involves instructional control; may involve some physical prompting at successive steps, but usually minimally. May also involve some fading at successive steps, but this is unusual. 2 Involves successive application of reinforcement and extinction.	1 May involve some shaping, although this would be very unusual. 2 Involves successive application of reinforcement; if extinction has to be used, fading has not proceeded optimally.	1 Frequently involves verbal and physical prompts, physical guidance, fading, and perhaps shaping at successive steps. 2 Typically involves fewer extinction trials than in shaping, because of the strong simulus control established by prompting and fading at successive steps.

similar stimuli control different responses, there is a greater chance for error and confusion by the client. If, in your task analysis, two of the controlling stimuli are quite similar and there appears to be nothing you can do about it, then consider artificially coding one of the stimuli in some way to make acquisition of the chain easier.

2. CONDUCT A PRELIMINARY MODELING TRIAL

Before requiring your client to perform a sequence of responses, model the entire sequence while verbally describing the performance of each step. (Guidelines for modeling are described in Chapter 16.) If only one sample of the training task is available, the task must be disassembled after the modeling trial and components rearranged for the client to perform the task. Otherwise, the client can be trained using alternative samples of the task.

3. BEGIN TRAINING THE BEHAVIORAL CHAIN

Give the client an initial request to begin work and to complete the steps of the task.* For example, "Okay, Agnes, please assemble the coffee pack." If at any step the client stops responding or appears distracted, you should first provide a pacing prompt such as "What's next?" or "Carry on." If the client performs a response incorrectly or fails to begin responding at any step within a reasonable period of time, you should proceed with error correction. Provide the necessary instructional and/or physical guidance to help the client perform

Note 4 that step correctly. After an error is corrected, go on to the next step.[4]

4. USE AMPLE SOCIAL AND OTHER REINFORCERS

During each trial, the correct completion of each step should be praised immediately. In addition, the client should receive an additional reinforcer (such as an edible) contingent upon successful completion of the last step in the chain. As the client becomes more skillful in performing the steps, the praise can be eliminated gradually so that performance of the chain is eventually maintained by the single reinforcer at the end of the chain.

5. DECREASE EXTRA ASSISTANCE AT INDIVIDUAL STEPS AS QUICKLY AS POSSIBLE

Depending on the details of the task analysis, it will likely be necessary to provide some additional instruction or physical assistance in correcting errors with clients. Across successive trials, this extra assistance should be faded as quickly as possible. It is important not to provide assistance to the point where you create a dependency in your client. That is, be careful not to reinforce the client for making errors or for waiting for your help at particular steps.

---

*The step or steps to begin with will depend on whether you use total task presentation, backward chaining, or forward chaining.

PITFALLS OF CHAINING

Just as relatively simple undesirable responses are often established inadvertently through the thoughtless administration of positive reinforcement, so also are undesirable chains. Probably the most common kind of undesirable chaining occurs when an inappropriate response precedes an appropriate response that is reinforced; both responses are thereby strengthened together. An example of this type of chaining is the distracting habit exhibited by some speakers of prefacing each remark with "uh." A similar though somewhat more serious example is the making of bizarre facial expressions prior to each utterance.

Sometimes the application of other behavior modification procedures results in accidental undesirable chaining. For example, a procedure commonly used to teach names of pictures involves two types of trials, called *probe* trials and *prompt* trials. On a probe trial, an individual is shown a picture to name and is asked, "What's this?" A prompt trial is the same as a probe trial except that the correct response is modeled immediately after the question (e.g., "What's this? Cat."). Prompt trials are given after errors are made on probe trials. Olenick and Pear (1980) observed that some children made a large number of errors even when it appeared that they could name the pictures appropriately. The researchers suggested that, for these youngsters, a chain had developed in which errors on probe trials were reinforced by prompt trials because an easier response (imitation) was reinforced on prompt trials. Olenick and Pear solved this problem by lowering the reinforcement rate for correct responses on prompt trials, while maintaining a high reinforcement rate for correct responses on probe trials.

Self-control problems that plague many people provide several other examples of undesirable behavioral chains. Consider the problem of overeating. Although there are undoubtedly a variety of possible reasons for overeating, one of the more frequent causes may be the inadvertent development of undesirable behavioral chains. For example, it has been observed that some overweight people eat very rapidly. An examination of the behavioral sequence involved suggests the following chains: loading food onto the utensil, placing food in the mouth, reloading utensil while chewing the food, simultaneously swallowing the food while raising the next load of food to the mouth, placing food in the mouth, and so forth. This behavioral chain has been broken successfully by extending the chain and introducing delays. A more desirable chain might be the following: loading food onto the utensil, placing food in the mouth, putting down the utensil, chewing the food, swallowing, waiting three seconds, reloading the utensil, and so on. In other words, in the undesirable chain the person gets ready to consume the next mouthful before even finishing the present one. A more desirable chain separates these components and introduces brief delays.

Another undesirable behavioral chain that is manifested by some overweight people consists of watching TV until a commercial comes on, going to the kitchen during the commercial, getting a snack, and returning to the TV (a very powerful reinforcer in itself). Another example, one that is commonly observed in homemakers who eat excessively, consists of preparing a snack, taking the snack to the telephone, calling a neighbor or relative, and eating the snack while talking on the telephone (again, thereby supplementing the reinforcement value of the food itself). There are a variety of procedures for solving such self-control problems, and these are discussed more fully in Chapter 23. The point to remember here is that undesirable behaviors are frequently components of unintentionally developed behavioral chains.

GUIDELINES FOR THE EFFECTIVE USE OF CHAINING

One should observe the following rules when developing stimulus-response chains.

1. Identify the units of the chain that are simple enough to be learned without great difficulty by the individual to whom you are teaching the chain.
2. The units must be taught in the proper sequence. Otherwise, poor stimulus control will develop in that when one step is completed it will not necessarily be a discriminative stimulus for the next step, but rather may control some other step (as when a young child learns to count incorrectly, for example, 1, 2, 4, 3).
3. To expedite learning, use a fading procedure to decrease extra help that may be needed by a client to perform some of the steps.
4. If you are using backward or forward chaining, make sure that on each trial the student performs the entire set of components learned up to that point.
5. Early in training, use ample reinforcement for correct performance of individual steps. Gradually decrease this reinforcement as the client becomes more skillful.
6. Make sure that the reinforcement provided at the end of the chain conforms to the guidelines for the effective application of positive reinforcement given in Chapter 3. The more effective this terminal reinforcement, the more stable the chain of responses. This does not mean, however, that once a chain is developed it must be reinforced each time it occurs in order to be maintained. After Agnes had been taught to assemble a coffee pack, for example, coffee pack assembly could be viewed as a single response, which could, if desired, be put on any intermittent reinforcement schedule.

STUDY QUESTIONS

1. Why was the coffee pack assembly program for Agnes divided into 15 steps (as opposed to, say, 4 or 40 steps)?
2. Briefly describe the chaining procedure used to teach Agnes to assemble coffee packs.
3. Describe or define a stimulus-response chain, and give an example other than the examples in this chapter.

4. Why do you suppose a behavioral chain is called a chain?

5. In a chain, a given stimulus is both an S^D and a conditioned reinforcer. How can this be? Explain with an example.

6. In the behavioral chain of driving a car, accelerating it, and changing gears (assume that you have a four-speed transmission), how is the chain of the driver who has a tachometer (and uses it) different from the chain of the driver who does not have a tachometer?

7. Name and describe briefly three major chaining methods.

8. Describe how each of the three major chaining methods might be used to teach bed-making.

9. Which of the major chaining methods do the authors recommend, and why?

10. Distinguish among the types of terminal behavior typically established by shaping, fading, and chaining.

11. List and briefly describe five factors influencing the effectiveness of chaining.

12. What is meant by the term "task analysis"? Describe a plausible task analysis appropriate for teaching a three-year-old child the behavior of tying a knot in a shoelace.

13. Give an example of a pitfall of chaining. Explain how this pitfall can be avoided.

PRACTICE EXERCISES

1. Describe how you might use chaining to teach a child to lace his or her shoes.

2. Describe how you might use chaining to teach a child to tie a knot.

3. Describe how you might use chaining to teach a child to tie a bow.

4. Try out your chaining programs in Practice Exercises 1–3 and see how they work.

SELF-MODIFICATION EXERCISE

Identify a behavioral deficit of yours that might be amenable to a chaining procedure. Describe in detail how you might use the guidelines for the effective use of chaining to overcome this deficit.

EXTENDED DISCUSSION AND NOTES

1. Some sequences of stimuli and responses that appear to be chains are not really chains. In his continuing efforts to increase the effectiveness of behavioral language, Michael (1982) proposed two behavioral terms relating to S^Ds, primary reinforcement, and conditioned reinforcement: (a) establishing operation and (b) establishing stimulus.

An *establishing operation* is an operation that (a) increases the effectiveness of some object or event as a primary reinforcer and (b) evokes behavior that in the past has been followed by that object or event. An example would be feeding a child very salty food, which would establish water as a reinforcer and also evoke behavior (e.g., asking for a drink, turning on the water tap) that has previously been followed by water. An establishing operation is not to be confused with an S^D. The latter evokes behavior that in the past has been followed by a particular reinforcement, but it does not increase the effectiveness of that object or event as reinforcement. Thus eating potato chips followed by drinking a soda is not a chain.

   An *establishing stimulus* is an object or event that (a) increases the effectiveness of another object or event as a conditioned reinforcer and (b) evokes behavior that in the past has been followed by that object or event. An example is a teacher asking a student to write a test. This stimulus establishes pen and paper as reinforcers and also evokes behavior (e.g., rummaging through one's purse, asking one's neighbor for a piece of paper) that has in the past produced these objects. Note that the example of a teacher asking the student to write a test does not fit the definition of an S^D for rummaging through one's purse or asking for a piece of paper (see the definition of S^D on p. 106). The teacher asking a student to write a test is not a stimulus that is correlated with an increased frequency of obtaining pen and paper by rummaging through one's purse or asking for these objects. Thus the sequence of "teacher asking student to write test, followed by student getting pen and paper, followed by student writing test" is not an example of a chain.

2. In a variation on forward chaining referred to as the *pure part* method, different parts of a chain are taught separately and then all are combined to form a whole. Suppose, for example, that you wished to teach someone to swim using a front crawl stroke. Using appropriate guidance and flotation devices, the student might first be taught the proper arm stroke, then the proper kick, and then proper head turning and breathing. Finally, all three parts would be put together into one entire or whole sequence. Weld and Evans (1990) compared pure part learning to total task presentation (also called "whole method of instruction") to teach severely and moderately retarded adolescents to prepare a bag lunch, and to make a greeting card. Half of the students were taught the two tasks using the pure part method, and the other half were taught using the whole learning method. Overall, the group taught using the whole method performed slightly better (although differences were not significant). Interestingly, students taught the pure part method tended to show fewer problem behaviors during training sessions. This finding suggests that future studies that compare different training strategies should also carefully monitor whether those strategies produce side effects, such as increased frequency of problem behaviors.

3. As we mentioned, backward chaining has the theoretical advantage over forward chaining and total task presentation of always having a readily available conditioned reinforcer to strengthen each new response that is added to the sequence in a backward order. For this reason, basic operant conditioning texts in the past frequently cited backward chaining as the procedure of choice for teaching behavioral chains (e.g., see Ferster & Perrott, 1968; Millenson, 1967; Powers & Osborne, 1976; Skinner, 1938; Whaley & Malott, 1971). The first edition of this text also made that recommendation. Since then, however, we have reconsidered. Praise is a generalized conditioned reinforcer that is readily available for most humans. It therefore seems unreasonable to teach behavioral chains to humans in practical settings using only a single reinforcer presented following the last step of a behavioral chain such as was typically recommended with lower organisms in basic operant texts. As recommended by Bellamy et al. (1979), and demonstrated by Koop, Martin, Yu, and Suthons (1980), teaching behavioral chains should, at least initially, be accompanied by frequent reinforcement for correctly

performed steps throughout the chain as well as following successful completion of the chain.

4. The question arises as to how many trials you should conduct within a training session. It has been common in special-education programs to employ multiple trials within a session for individuals with severe handicaps (Gaylord-Ross & Holvoet, 1985). Others have suggested that it might be better to teach a skill only in the context in which it naturally occurs (e.g., Sailor & Guess, 1983). If the skill being taught occurs only once a day in a student's normal activities, then a single training trial per day would be conducted. Kayser, Billingsley, and Neel (1986) conducted research to compare these two approaches. Severely handicapped children were taught to perform the steps for making a snack in their regular classrooms. Some of the steps of the task were taught with backward chaining in a multiple trial training format (10 consecutive trials per session). Other steps of the task were taught in a total-task, single-trial training format. Under this latter condition, a single trial was conducted once a day during the school week for each student. The total-task, single-trial strategy produced markedly superior results for three of eight students, moderately superior results for two additional students, and no differences for the remaining three students. These results suggest that one trial per day using total-task presentation in the natural environment may be better than several trials per day using backward chaining.

STUDY QUESTIONS ON NOTES

1. What is the theoretical advantage of backward chaining over the other two major chaining methods? (Also, see p. 143.)
2. Why might backward chaining be more effective with lower organisms while total task presentation might be more effective with humans?
3. What does Michael mean by the term *establishing operation*? Explain with reference to an example.
4. What does Michael mean by the term *establishing stimulus*? Explain with reference to an example.
5. Why is the sequence of drinking soda after eating potato chips not likely a chain?
6. Why is the sequence of "a teacher announcing an exam, followed by a student asking a friend for a pen, followed by the student getting paper," and so on not a chain?
7. Describe the pure-part method of chaining. How does it differ from standard forward chaining?
8. Which procedure works better in a natural context: single-trial, total-task presentation, or a multiple-trial, backward chaining procedure?

CHAPTER 12

Transferring Behavior to New Settings and Making It Last: **Generality** of Behavior Change

---

"Hi, there. I have a nice surprise for you in my car."

TEACHING STAN TO PROTECT HIMSELF

During recess time, four-year-old Stan was playing with a toy near the edge of his preschool playground, unaware that a stranger was observing him intently from a distance. No teacher was in sight. Gradually, the stranger approached until he was standing beside Stan.

"Hi, there," said the stranger, "What's your name?"

"Stan," the boy replied.

"Nice day, isn't it, Stan?"

The stranger engaged Stan in small talk for a few minutes. Then, casting his eyes around the school yard, the stranger casually asked, "Stan, how would you like to go for a walk with me?"

The stranger seemed friendly and Stan was used to taking directions from adults. He stood up and approached the stranger. Just then, a teacher appeared and the stranger quickly moved away.

An attempted child abduction? Not exactly. The stranger was actually an assistant in an experiment designed to study a method of teaching self-protection to young children, and Stan was being tested to determine his suitability for the experiment.* He and two other children (Patti and John), who also appeared susceptible to lures often used by child molestors, were included in the experiment. The children were tested several times to verify that they would go with a stranger who approached them using any of several kinds of lures (e.g., "Your teacher said it was all right for you to come with me" and "I

---

*This case is based on an experiment by Poche, Brouwer, and Swearingen (1981).

have a nice surprise in my car. Would you like to come and see it?"). Then training was begun. Two adult trainers acted out a scene in which one trainer approached the other and used one of the lures. The other trainer responded with, "No, I have to go ask my teacher," and ran toward the school building. The child was then instructed to respond in the same way as the second trainer to the lure of the first trainer, and was provided with social reinforcement (e.g., praise) that was occasionally followed with material and activity reinforcement (e.g., stickers, playing on the swings) when he or she did so.

Responses were trained to one lure per day. When a child consistently responded correctly to the first lure, responding was trained to a second lure, and then to a third lure. In addition to the lures being varied in this manner, the exact location of each session on the school grounds was also varied by approximately 75 feet. After training was completed, each child was tested in a community setting to determine whether the response established during training would be performed in a novel setting. All three children responded correctly to the lures in that setting. After 12 weeks, Stan and Patti were tested again in the community setting. Stan continued to respond perfectly, whereas Patti made the correct verbal response but stayed in the vicinity of the stranger.

GENERALITY: STIMULUS GENERALIZATION, RESPONSE GENERALIZATION, AND BEHAVIOR MAINTENANCE

We say that training produces *generality* when it leads to the development of behavior that has *not* been specifically trained or when the trained behavior is maintained. There are several types of generality.

When establishing a behavior in the presence of a particular stimulus or situation causes the behavior to occur more readily in the presence of another stimulus or situation, we say that the behavior has *generalized* from the first to the second stimulus or situation. **Stimulus generalization** occurs when behavior becomes more probable in the presence of one stimulus or situation as a result of having been reinforced in the presence of another stimulus or situation. For example, Stan responded correctly to a stranger's lures in the community setting even though he had been trained to do so to a different stranger in a different setting. A follow-up study (Poche & colleagues, 1988) has shown that the training stimulus need not be a real person; many children will appropriately reject a stranger's lures when the training is by videotape.

Stimulus generalization is the opposite of stimulus discrimination. As explained in Chapter 8, when a behavior occurs in the presence of one stimulus or situation more readily than in the presence of another, we say that the individual has *discriminated* between the two stimuli or situations.

There are many examples of stimulus generalization in everyday life. Consider a case that is familiar to many parents: an infant learns to say "doggie" to a hairy, four-legged creature with floppy ears and a friendly bark. Later, the infant sees a different kind of dog and says "doggie." This is an instance of stimulus generalization because a previously reinforced response ("doggie") was emitted in the presence of a new stimulus (a new kind of dog). Still later, the infant sees a horse and again says "doggie." This is another instance of stimulus generalization, even though the response in this case is incorrect, which proves that not all instances of stimulus generalization are favorable and illustrates why it is necessary to teach discriminations, as de-

Note 1   scribed in Chapter 8.[1]

Not to be confused with stimulus generalization is a phenomenon called ***response generalization***. This occurs when a behavior becomes more probable in the presence of a stimulus or situation as a result of a similar behavior having been strengthened in the presence of that stimulus or situation. It would take place if, for example, improvement of articulation of specific words in a clinical setting led to improvement in the articulation of untreated words in that setting. If a stranger tried to lure Stan when he was playing in his yard, and Stan said, "No, I have to ask my mother [instead of "my teacher"]," he would be showing response generalization.

To be effective, a therapeutic behavioral change must show stimulus generalization from the training situation to the natural environment, and it must also sometimes show response generalization to new behaviors. Therapeutic behavioral change must also be MAINTAINED in the natural environment. ***Programming for generality*** of behavior change is concerned with these three areas: *stimulus generalization, response generalization*, and *behavior*

Note 2   *maintenance*.[2] Specifically, "a behavioral change may be said to have generality if it proves durable over time, if it appears in a wide variety of possible environments, or if it spreads to a wide variety of related behaviors" (Baer, Wolf, & Risley, 1968, p. 96). Looking back through the previous chapters, one can see that programming for generality of behavior change is an important consideration in every training program. For example, it was desirable for Peter (Chapter 4) to decrease his tantrumming in situations other than the classroom. Unfortunately, Peter failed to show stimulus generalization and continued to tantrum when back on the ward. These, and similar examples, illustrate that failure to obtain generality of behavior change is a major problem facing behavior modifiers. How do we solve the problem?

FACTORS INFLUENCING THE EFFECTIVENESS OF PROGRAMMING GENERALITY OF BEHAVIOR CHANGE

1. PROGRAMMING STIMULUS GENERALIZATION

In discussing generality, we distinguish two situations: (1) the *training* situation and (2) the *target* situation—a situation in which we want generality to occur. The target situation is usually, but not necessarily, the natural environment. The initial occurrence of stimulus generalization depends critically on the physical similarity between the training and target situations. The more similar they are, the more initial stimulus generalization (and hence the less discrim-

Note 3   ination) there will be between them.[3]

a. Train in the target situation.   Thus, the first effort of the behavior modifier attempting to program stimulus generalization should be to make the final stages of the training situation similar to the target situation in as many ways as possible. Other things being equal, the best way in which to do this is to train in the target situation.

b. Vary the training conditions.   This might be done by conducting training sessions with relatively little control over the stimuli presented in the presence of which correct responses are reinforced. If behaviors are brought under the control of a greater variety of stimuli during training, then there is an increased probability of some of those stimuli being present in the target situation. Thus, in the lead case for this chapter, no attempt was made to control background stimuli, such as playground and traffic noise, as might be done in more basic research.

c. Program common stimuli.   A third tactic is to program common stimuli deliberately by developing the behavior to specific stimuli that are present in both the training and target settings. For example, Walker and Buckley (1972) described a program in which social and academic classroom behavior were taught to children in a remedial classroom. Stimulus generalization to the regular academic classroom was assured by establishing common stimuli between the remedial classroom and the regular classroom by using the same academic materials in both classrooms.

d. Train sufficient stimulus exemplars.   A fourth tactic, and one that Stokes and Baer (1977) considered to be perhaps one of the most valuable areas for programming generality, is called "train sufficient stimulus exemplars." With this technique, "generalization to untrained stimulus conditions . . . is programmed by the training of sufficient exemplars (rather than all) of these stimulus conditions." Thus, in the lead case for this chapter, training occurred in several different places in the schoolyard and with several dif-

Note 4   ferent lures.[4]

2. PROGRAMMING RESPONSE GENERALIZATION

It appears that there has been less concern in the literature for tactics for programming response generalization than there has been for programming stimulus generalization. This may be because there is a great emphasis in our educational system on teaching students the "correct" answers to questions. Variations on correct answers (that may show response generalization) are either not accepted or are followed by reinforcers of an inferior quality (such as a "B" instead of an "A" as a grade on a mathematics exam). Nevertheless, there are some strategies for programming response generalization, two of which are described now.

   a. Train sufficient response exemplars.   A strategy for programming response generalization is similar to that of training sufficient stimulus exemplars. This is referred to as training sufficient response exemplars (Stokes & Baer, 1977). For example, Guess, Sailor, Rutherford, and Baer (1968) taught a retarded girl to use plural nouns correctly in speech with this technique. With appropriate prompting and reinforcement, they first taught the girl to name objects correctly in the singular and the plural when presented with one object (e.g., cup) and two objects (e.g., cups). They continued in this way until, after a number of exemplars of the correct singular and plural labels had been taught, the girl appropriately named new objects in the plural even though only the singular labels for these objects had been taught. Thus,

Note 5   the girl showed response generalization.[5]

   b. Vary the acceptable responses during training.   Another strategy is to vary deliberately the responses that are acceptable during training. For example, in developing creativity, Goetz and Baer (1973) deliberately reinforced children during block building in a nursery school setting for any response that was different from prior block building responses. This tactic led to an increase in the creative block building demonstrated by the children. (For more on creativity, see Chapter 1, note 1.)

3. PROGRAMMING BEHAVIOR MAINTENANCE

It's one thing to program stimulus generalization to a new setting, or response generalization to new behaviors. It's another thing for a therapeutic behavior change to last (in those new settings or with those new behaviors). Maintenance depends critically on whether the behavior will continue to be reinforced. Each time you program generality to a new setting, that's stimulus generalization. But making it last in that new setting is a problem of maintenance. There are four general approaches to the problem of achieving lasting generality or maintenance in target situations.

   a. Allow natural contingencies of reinforcement to take effect.   One approach is to make use of the reinforcement the natural environment already provides for the target behavior. In many cases, such contingencies are probably operating at least to a minimal extent. Talking is an obvious example of behavior that is heavily reinforced in most environments. Yet a child may not learn to talk because of what are, at least for him, deficient contingencies. Nevertheless, after speech has been established in a training situation, it continues unabated in the natural environment because of the natural contingencies of reinforcement for it there. Indeed, it often seems necessary only to establish vocal imitation and a few object-naming responses for the natural contingencies of reinforcement to take over and develop very functional speech behavior.

　　Many fears can be overcome permanently if the natural contingencies are allowed to take over after the individual has been gradually induced to engage in the previously feared activity. Such activities often provide their own sources of reinforcement once they are no longer feared. For example, playing with other children is a behavior that might gradually be shaped in a very shy child. Once this behavior is strongly established, however, the behavior modifier probably will not have to worry about reinforcing it further. The other children will take care of that themselves in the course of their play, for, indeed, that is what social play is all about. This approach to the problem of maintenance has been called *trapping*, because it involves developing behavior that in a sense falls into the "behavioral trap" represented by the contingencies in the natural environment (Baer & Wolf, 1970). The approach requires the behavior modifier to tailor the target behavior to fit these contingencies after he or she has appraised them realistically. (An example

Note 6   of behavioral trapping is shown in Figure 12–1.)[6]

　　b. Change the behavior of people in the natural environment.   A second approach to the problem of achieving lasting generality is usually more difficult than the first. It involves actually changing the contingencies in the target situation so that they will maintain the behavior that has generalized from the training situation. In following this approach, it is necessary to work with people in the target situation—ward staff, parents, teachers, neighbors, and others who have contact with the target behavior. The behavior modifier must teach these individuals how to reinforce the behavior (if it is desirable) or how to extinguish it (if it is undesirable) appropriately. The behavior modifier must also occasionally reinforce the appropriate behavior of these individuals—at least until it comes into contact with the improved target behavior, which will then, ideally, reinforce their continued application of the

Note 7   appropriate procedures.[7]

　　As an example of this second approach, consider the case of a child living at home who has little behavior in her repertoire except tantrumming. Possibly this is her sole means of gaining attention and other reinforcers from her parents. There is little doubt that more desirable behaviors could be established in a training situation, but such behaviors would not be maintained in the home situation unless the contingencies operating there were changed. A behavior modifier called in on this case might therefore adopt the following plan.

　　In a training situation designed to teach the child to play with toys rather than to tantrum, the behavior modifier would first adjust the desired behavior to an appropriate schedule—for instance, VI/LH with infrequent reinforcement (since it will not be practical for the parents to give frequent reinforcement in the home environment). Having accomplished this, the behavior modifier would begin generalization training in the home environment.

FIGURE 12–1 An example of behavioral trapping.

The behavior modifier would show the mother how to keep accurate records of the child's desirable and undesirable behavior. At first, the mother, with the help and prompting of the behavior modifier, would frequently reinforce the child for playing nicely with her toys in the living room. Gradually, she would decrease the frequency of reinforcement to have more time for activities that did not involve the child. She would use a kitchen timer, or similar device, to remind herself to reinforce the child. Throughout this procedure, the behavior modifier would frequently reinforce the mother for appropriately managing and recording the child's behavior. Then the behavior modifier would fade out of the situation by visiting less and less frequently to check the mother's records. But if the program deteriorated, he or she would temporarily stop the fading process and spend enough time in the training situation to correct matters. Ideally, the mother's behavior of appropriately reinforcing the target behavior would eventually be maintained by the child's good play behavior and her decreased whining, crying, and tantrumming.[8]

Note 8

c. Use schedules of reinforcement in the target situation.   After a behavior has generalized to a target situation it may be desirable to reinforce the behavior deliberately in the target situation on an intermittent schedule for at least a few reinforced trials. The intermittent schedule should make that behavior more persistent in the target situation and thereby increase the probability of the behavior lasting until it can come under the control of natural reinforcers.

d. Give the control to the individual.   A subarea within behavior modification has been concerned with helping individuals to apply behavior modification to themselves. This area, which has been referred to as *self-management*, *self-modification*, and behavioral *self-control*, has produced many books containing easy-to-follow "how-to-do-it" procedures that help individuals to manage their own behavior. This area is discussed more fully in Chapter 23. Concerning the problem of maintaining behavior in target situations, giving the control to the individual might occur in one of two major ways. First, it might be possible to teach an individual to assess and record instances of his or her own generalized behavior and apply a specific procedure to that behavior as suggested in Chapter 23. Second, as suggested by Stokes and Baer (1977), it might be possible to teach an individual a means of *recruiting a natural community of reinforcement* to maintain generalized responding. For example, in a study by Hildebrand, Martin, Furer, and Hazen (1990) some of the mentally retarded workers in a sheltered workshop usually showed very low productivity. On the few occasions when they worked at a high rate, they received very little feedback from staff. Hildebrand and colleagues taught the workers to meet a productivity goal, and then to call staff members' attention to their good work. This led to increased feedback for the workers from the staff, and helped to maintain a higher level of productivity by the workers.

PITFALLS OF GENERALITY

All the components of generality have potential pitfalls as well as positive aspects. Consider stimulus generalization. Without stimulus generalization, learning would be of very limited value. No matter how perfectly a person learned something, he or she would have to learn it all over again every time the situation changed even slightly. (Just imagine how annoying it would be to have spent much time learning a skill only to discover that you no longer possessed it after moving to a new city to begin a job that depended on that skill.) But stimulus generalization has its disadvantages too, in that a behavior learned in a situation in which it is appropriate may then emerge inconveniently in a situation in which it is inappropriate.

A conspicuous example of the stimulus generalization of a desirable behavior to an inappropriate situation that can often be seen among retarded individuals lies in the area of greetings and displays of affection. Of course, it is highly desirable for these behaviors to occur under appropriate circumstances, but when an individual walks up to and hugs a total stranger, the results can be less than favorable for a number of obvious reasons. The solution to this problem is to teach the individual to discriminate between situations in which different forms of greetings and expressions of affection are appropriate and situations in which they are inappropriate.

The opposite type of problem is the stimulus generalization of undesirable behavior to a situation where a desirable alternative is appropriate. For example, the suppression through punishment of displays of affection may cause an individual to be cold and withdrawn in situations that warrant affectionate behavior. Perhaps this sort of generalization is at the root of certain so-called emotional disturbances. Again, the solution is to teach the individual when and how to express emotional behavior such as affection, as well as when not to.

Another example of inappropriate stimulus generalization may be the destructive competitiveness demonstrated frequently by some individuals and occasionally by all of us. Such behavior may stem in part from the strong reinforcement given in our culture for winning in sports and in achieving high grades in our educational system. As a wise person once remarked, "It may be true that wars have been won on the playing fields of Eton, but they have also been started there."

Another pitfall stems from a lack of desirable stimulus generalization. This can be seen in the typical study habits of students. Frequently, students cram for exams the night before the examination. They memorize certain verbal chains in response to certain prompts and questions. What they frequently fail to consider is the importance of bringing their knowledge of the material under broader stimulus control than just one or two questions, that is, they do not program for generalization. A great many people have had the same experience with learning a second language. One of the authors was among the many who took a second language during four years of high school. At the end of that time, he was clearly incapable of speaking the language. He had a certain repertoire for answering questions on French exams, translating English articles into French, and translating French articles into English, but this repertoire had not been brought under the stimulus control of a typical conversational setting.

Another example of lack of desirable stimulus generalization occurs in the interaction between parents and their children. In various social situations, such as restaurants, parents frequently do not present the same stimuli to their children, or provide the same contingencies of reinforcement, that they present at mealtimes in the home situation. Consequently, the children frequently do not generalize their table manners and good behaviors that occur at home to the restaurant or other social settings. It is not uncommon to hear a parent lament, "I thought I taught you how to be a good child, and now look at you." We hope that, after reading this book and performing the study questions and study exercises, the same parents will do a much better job of programming stimulus generalization. (If not, you will probably hear us lament, "I thought I taught you how to be a good behavior modifier, and now look at you.")

The pitfalls listed above indicate how stimulus generalization can work to the disadvantage of those who are ignorant of it. There are also many pitfalls for programming maintenance of behavior change. These were described at the end of Chapters 6 and 7 concerning schedules of reinforcement.

GUIDELINES FOR PROGRAMMING GENERALITY OF BEHAVIOR CHANGE

To ensure stimulus and reponse generalization from the training situation to the natural environment, and to ensure behavior maintenance, the behavior modifier should observe the following rules as closely as possible:

1. Choose target behaviors that are clearly useful to the individual, as these are the behaviors that are most likely to be reinforced in the natural environment.
2. Teach the target behavior in a situation that is as similar as possible to the environment in which you want the behavior to occur.
3. Vary the training conditions so as to maximally sample relevant stimulus dimensions for transfer to other situations and to reinforce various forms of the desirable behavior.
4. Establish the target behavior successively in as many situations as is feasible, starting with the easiest and progressing to the most difficult.
5. Gradually reduce the frequency of reinforcement in the training situation until it is less than that occurring in the natural environment.
6. When changing to a new situation, increase the frequency of reinforcement to offset the tendency of the individual to discriminate the new situation from the previous training situation.
7. Make sure that sufficient reinforcement for maintaining the target behavior occurs in the natural environment. This rule requires especially close attention in the early stages of transferring the target behavior from the training situation to the natural environment. Add reinforcement as necessary, including reinforcement to those people (such as parents and teachers) who are responsible for maintaining the target behavior in the natural environment,

and then decrease this reinforcement slowly enough to prevent the target behavior from deteriorating.

STUDY QUESTIONS

1. What is behavioral generality? Briefly describe how behavioral generality was demonstrated in the experiment on teaching self-protection skills to children.
2. List, define, and give an example of each of three components or areas of behavioral generality.
3. Explain the difference between stimulus generalization and stimulus discrimination. Describe examples illustrating the difference.
4. Explain the difference between stimulus generalization and response generalization. Describe examples illustrating the difference.
5. Briefly describe four tactics for programming stimulus generalization. Give an example of each.
6. Briefly describe two tactics for programming response generalization. Give an example of each.
7. Briefly describe four tactics for programming behavior maintenance in a target situation. Give an example of each.
8. What do we mean by behavioral trapping? Give an example.
9. Give two examples of a pitfall of stimulus generalization, one of which involves generalization of a desirable behavior to an inappropriate situation and the other of which involves generalization of an undesirable behavior.
10. Give an example of a pitfall of response generalization.
11. Give an example of a pitfall of behavior maintenance.

PRACTICE EXERCISES

1. Describe a recent situation in which you generalized in desirable ways. Clearly identify the behavior, the training situation, and the test situation.
2. Describe a recent situation in which you generalized in an undesirable way (in other words, the outcome was undesirable). Again, identify the behavior, training situation, and test situation.
3. Choose one of the cases described in the previous chapters in which there was no effort to program stimulus generalization. Outline a specific plausible program for producing stimulus generalization in that case, taking into account the factors influencing the effectiveness of generalization training.

SELF-MODIFICATION EXERCISE

Consider the behavior deficit for which you outlined a shaping program at the end of Chapter 5. Assuming that your shaping program will be successful, discuss what you might do to program generality. (See the factors influencing the effectiveness of generality that were discussed earlier in this chapter.)

EXTENDED DISCUSSION AND NOTES

1. Teaching concepts such as "dog" and "red" can be described in terms of teaching individuals to respond appropriately to stimulus classes representing the concepts to be taught. A *stimulus class* is a set of stimuli, all of which have some characteristic in common. For example, look around the room in which you are and list the objects you see that are red. These objects constitute the stimulus class that we might label "red objects." Although these objects are different in many respects, they all have in common the color red (defined physically in terms of a particular wavelength of light). When an individual can appropriately identify all red objects, we say that that individual has the *concept* "red." Stated differently, if an individual emits an appropriate response to all the members of a particular stimulus class, and does not emit that response to stimuli that do not belong to the class (for instance, in the example above the individual does not respond "red" to green objects, blue objects, etc.), then the individual generalizes to all of the members within a stimulus class (or concept) and discriminates between stimulus classes (for instance, between all red objects and all blue objects), and we say that the individual is showing conceptual behavior (Keller & Schoenfeld, 1950, p. 155). For a more detailed discussion of conceptual behavior, see Whaley and Malott (1971, pp. 171–192) or Malott and Whaley (1983, chapters 13–15).

2. Our definitions of stimulus and response generalization closely follow the traditional operant conceptualizations (Keller & Schoenfeld, 1950; Skinner, 1953). In an influential article titled "An Implicit Technology of Generalization," Stokes and Baer (1977, p. 350) defined generalization somewhat differently:

> Generalization will be considered to be the occurrence of relevant behavior under different, non-training conditions (i.e., across subjects, settings, people, behaviors, and/or time) without the scheduling of the same events in those conditions as had been scheduled in the training conditions. Thus, generalization may be claimed when no extra training manipulations are needed for extra training changes; or may be claimed when some extra manipulations are necessary, but their cost or extent is clearly less than that of the direct intervention. Generalization will not be claimed when similar events are necessary for similar effects across conditions.

In other words, generalization to Stokes and Baer refers to what we have included under stimulus generalization, response generalization, and behavior maintenance. Stokes and Baer then went on to summarize from the applied literature a number of general strategies for producing desired responding in "non-training" settings (i.e., for "programming generalization"). In a subsequent article, Johnston (1979) criticized Stokes and Baer for defining generalization in conflict with its traditional operant conceptualization. Johnston argued that such terminological slippage between a basic science of behavior and behavior modification may make it difficult for these areas to maintain desirable symbiotic relations, that Stokes and Baer's definition discourages an understanding of behavioral processes that are at work in training and nontraining settings, and that it encourages a "technological literature more in a bag of tricks style than in the behavior analytic style." We tend to agree with Johnston and with the position expressed by Baer, Wolf, and Risley (1968) that there are advantages to being conceptually systematic in behavior modification (i.e., to relating applied procedures to basic behavioral concepts in a consistent manner). Consequently, our organization of factors influencing the effectiveness of programming generality of behavior change that appear in this chapter is somewhat different from that presented by Stokes and Baer (1977). We would encourage serious students of behavior modification to study the Stokes and Baer paper, as well as the insightful commentary by Johnston (1979), with care.

3. An example of this occurred in a study by Welch and Pear (1980) in which objects, pictures of objects, and photographs of the objects were compared as training stimuli for naming responses in four severely retarded children in a special training room. It was found that three of the four children displayed considerably more generalization to the objects in their natural environment when they were trained with the objects rather than the pictures or photographs of the objects. The fourth child, who was also the most proficient, linguistically, displayed substantial generalization regardless of the type of training stimulus used. A follow-up study by Salmon, Pear, and Kuhn (1986) indicates that training with objects also produces more generalization to untrained objects in the same stimulus class than does training with pictures. The results therefore suggest that parents and teachers of severely retarded children should use objects as training stimuli as much as possible whenever generalization to these stimuli is desired.

4. Lowther and Martin (1980) conducted a study on exemplars that addressess the following question: "Will training across more than one setting, with only one trainer involved, lead to generalization of the response to new settings *and* trainers? Alternatively, will the use of more than one trainer within a single setting lead to generalization across both trainers *and* settings?" Six severely retarded participants took part in two experiments; three participants in each. All the participants were taught to emit the simple verbal greeting "Hi!" when a staff member approached, and the probability of this occurring became the dependent variable by means of which stimulus generalization was assessed. The first experiment investigated the effects on subsequent generalization, across settings and individuals, of training by additional trainers in a single setting. The second experiment investigated the effect on subsequent generalization, across settings and individuals, of training by one trainer across additional settings. Both variables investigated produced widespread stimulus generalization across settings and trainers. In summary, the study demonstrated that generalization of a single greeting response with retarded persons was accomplished either by programming the response to two or more trainers in one setting or to one trainer in two or more settings.

5. This instance of response generalization is somewhat more complex than our straightforward definition given at the beginning of this chapter. It does appear, in this example, that the reinforcement of a specific response has increased the probability of similar responses. However, the new form of the response (the plural for a new object) is also occurring to a new stimulus (the new object itself).

6. Kohler and Greenwood (1986) have called for more extensive study of behavioral traps. They point out that researchers have often postulated a behavioral trap as the reason that the behavior of someone has been maintained over time, or has generalized to other behaviors or settings. Some researchers have even identified the social contingencies in the natural environment that may be responsible for trapping the behavior of concern. Few studies, however, have experimentally demonstrated that the generality was really due to behavioral trapping. Kohler and Greenwood argue that in order to conclude convincingly that generality is due to behavioral trapping, either of two new types of experimental evidence are needed:

(a) the social stimuli in the natural environment thought to be responsible for trapping the behavior could be experimentally withdrawn to see if the originally trained behavior reverses in the predicted direction; (b) the social stimuli thought to be responsible for trapping of a behavior in the natural environment could be experimentally demonstrated to be responsible for trapping additional behaviors of additional individuals.

7. Martin (1972) discussed the importance of reinforcing the behavior of the behavior modifier. Psychiatric nurses and nursing attendants who used behavior modification procedures to improve the behavior of retarded individuals did so much more consistently when their own behavior was reinforced in a structured staff-incentive program. For additional discussion and research of factors important in maintaining staff behaviors in residential treatment programs, see McInnis (1976) and Prue, Krapfl, Noah, Cannon, and Maley (1980).

8. Many studies have been conducted to examine programs to teach parents to use behavior modification to manage the behavior of their children in the home (see Daniel & Polster, 1984). In addition, children, when appropriately trained, can also be an extremely useful resource in helping to maintain generality of behavior change in their peers (see Fowler, 1988).

STUDY QUESTIONS ON NOTES

1. What do we mean by stimulus class? By conceptual behavior?
2. Describe how you might teach each of the following concepts to a child, using the behavioral definition of conceptual behavior: (a) green; (b) wet; (c) honest.
3. Distinguish between the approach of Stokes and Baer and that of this text toward defining generalization. What are the relative advantages of the two approaches?
4. What rule for programming stimulus generalization is exemplified by the study in which object and picture names were taught to retarded children? Explain.
5. Which is more effective, programming stimulus generalization across settings or trainers?
6. What two types of evidence would demonstrate the effectiveness of behavioral trapping?
7. Describe a plausible example of how you might teach children in a preschool to maintain a desired behavior change in one of their peers.

CHAPTER 13

Eliminating Inappropriate Behavior Through **Punishment**

"Ben, don't be so aggressive."

ELIMINATING BEN'S AGGRESSIVENESS

Ben was a seven-year-old boy enrolled in a public school program for severely disturbed children.* He had been diagnosed as developmentally delayed, and the staff in the school had noticed an increase in the frequency with which Ben aggressively hit other children and/or the staff. In fact, during baseline observations over approximately three weeks, the frequency of Ben's hits averaged about 30 per day. Something had to be done.

Although painful and noxious consequences have been demonstrated to reduce undesirable behaviors when presented as punishers, such consequences have been found to be unacceptable in a number of situations including many public school classrooms. Therefore, the staff decided to examine whether contingent exercise might decrease Ben's hitting behavior.

A number of precautions were taken to ensure that the contingent exercise would in no way be detrimental to Ben's health. The procedures were explained thoroughly to the parents, and parental consent was obtained for Ben's participation in the program. The procedures were also reviewed and approved by the ethical review board of the school district in which the program was carried out. The program was conducted at Ben's school throughout the school day. On the day that the contingent exercise was introduced, the first hit by Ben led the nearest adult to say, "Ben, no hitting. Stand up and sit down 10 times." The adult then held Ben's hand and lifted it over his head to prompt standing up, and then pulled his upper body forward to prompt sitting down,

*This example is based on an article by Luce, Delquadri, and Hall (1980).

167

while at the same time saying "Stand up, sit down" for the 10 exercises. Although Ben showed some verbal resistance to the exercise on a few occasions, the staff reported that physical prompting was necessary only on the first few training trials. On subsequent days, only verbal reminders were necessary to prompt the exercise task. From an average of approximately 30 hits per day during baseline, Ben's hits dropped to a frequency of 11 on the first day of the exercise program, 10 on the second day, 1 on the third day, and either 0 or 1 thereafter.

After two weeks of the procedure, the staff stopped applying the contingent exercise program to see what would happen to Ben's hits. The frequency of hits remained low for four days, but then they began to increase over the next four days. The staff reinstituted the contingent exercise program and observed an immediate drop in the frequency of hitting to near zero. The program continued formally for another two months, and the staff recorded one hit on each of three days during that entire time. Ben could run about and interact with other children and no longer showed the distressful aggressiveness characteristic of his past behavior.

THE PRINCIPLE OF PUNISHMENT

A *punisher* is an event that, when presented immediately following a behavior, causes the behavior to decrease in frequency. Once an event has been determined to function as a punisher for a particular behavior of an individual in a particular situation, that event can be used to decrease other behaviors of that individual in other situations. Associated with the concept of a punisher is the *principle of punishment*, which states: *if, in a given situation, somebody does something that is immediately followed by a punisher, then that person is less likely to do the same thing again when he or she next encounters a similar situation.* In Ben's case, contingent exercise was a punisher for his aggressive hitting behavior.

Like positive reinforcement, punishment affects our learning throughout life. The immediate consequences of touching a hot stove, for example, teaches us not to do this again. As infants, the bruises from a few falls helped to teach us better balance while learning to walk. A light swat on your behind from concerned parents may have taught you not to run into the street during heavy traffic. And we've all had our behavior affected by revoked privileges or reprimands from teachers. But it is important to recognize that there is a great deal of controversy within the field of behavior modification regarding the *deliberate* use of punishment. Some people have gone so far as to suggest, or at least strongly imply, that punishment should never be used deliberately. We shall return to this issue later in this chapter, after discussing the different types of punishment and the factors that influence the effects of punishment in suppressing behavior.

TYPES OF PUNISHERS

Many kinds of events, when delivered as consequences for behavior, fit the definition of punisher given above. Most of these events can be classified into the following categories (see Van Houten, 1983): (1) physical punishment, (2) reprimands, (3) timeout, and (4) response cost. Although there is some overlap among these categories, they provide a convenient way in which to organize punishment procedures. We now consider each category in turn.

PHYSICAL (AVERSIVE) PUNISHMENT

This category includes all punishers that activate pain receptors or other sense receptors that typically evoke feelings of discomfort. Physical punishers are also referred to as aversive stimuli, aversive punishers, or simply—aversives. Some examples of aversive punishers are spankings, pinches, electric shock, ammonia vapor, cool baths, loud or harsh sounds, prolonged tickling, and hair tugging.

Aversive punishment is not pleasant for the client or the therapist; nevertheless, there are cases in which clients have benefitted greatly from the procedure. A dramatic example is what may have been the lifesaving treatment of a six-month-old baby (Sajwaj, Libet, & Agras, 1974). Sandra was admitted to a hospital because of a failure to gain weight that was associated with the constant bringing up of food (ruminating). She was underweight and undernourished, and death was a distinct possibility. Preliminary observations indicated that a few minutes after being given milk, Sandra would begin ruminating and would continue for about 20 to 40 minutes until she had apparently lost all the milk she had consumed. Sajwaj and colleagues decided to administer lemon juice as a punisher. During treatment, Sandra's mouth was filled with lemon juice immediately after staff members detected the vigorous tongue movements that reliably preceded her rumination. After 16 feedings with lemon juice, the rumination had decreased to a very low level. To ensure that the improvement was due to the treatment program, Sajwaj and co-workers suspended the use of lemon juice for two feedings. The result was a dramatic increase in rumination. Following additional treatment, Sandra was discharged to foster parents, who maintained the treatment until it was no longer necessary. Five months later, Sandra was returned to her natural parents, a much improved little girl.

REPRIMANDS

Reprimands are strong negative verbal stimuli (e.g., "No! That was bad!") contingent on inappropriate behavior. They also usually include a fixed stare and, sometimes, a firm grasp. In Chapter 10 it was mentioned that a stimulus

Note 1 paired with punishment becomes itself a punisher.[1] Such a stimulus is called a *conditioned punisher*. It is likely that the verbal component and the fixed stare of a reprimand are conditioned punishers, in part because of their being paired with the other component (the firm grasp), which may be a form of physical punishment. In some cases, the effectiveness of reprimands has been increased by pairing them with other forms of punishment. For example, Dorsey, Iwata, Ong, and McSween (1980) paired reprimands with a water mist spray to suppress self-injurious behavior in retarded individuals. This caused the reprimands to become effective not only in the original setting but also in a setting where the mist had not been used.

TIMEOUT

Timeout involves transferring an individual from a more reinforcing to a less reinforcing situation following a particular behavior (Van Houten, 1983, p. 28). There are two types of timeouts: exclusionary and nonexclusionary. *Exclusionary timeout* consists of removing the individual from the situation in which reinforcement is occurring for a short time (e.g., five minutes). Often a special room, called a *timeout room*, is used for this purpose. The timeout room is bare of anything that might serve as a reinforcer, and may be padded to prevent self-injury. The period of detention in the timeout room should

Note 2 not be very long; about five minutes is usually quite effective.[2] *Nonexclusionary* timeout consists of introducing into the situation a stimulus associated with less reinforcement. An example of this is the *timeout ribbon* introduced by Foxx and Shapiro (1978). Children in a classroom wore a ribbon that was removed for a short time when a child was disruptive. When not wearing the ribbon, the child was not allowed to participate in classroom activities and was ignored

Note 3 by the teacher.[3]

RESPONSE COST

Response cost involves the removal of a specified amount of reinforcer following a particular behavior. Examples of response cost in everyday life are library fines, traffic tickets, and charges for overdrawn checking accounts. Response cost is sometimes used in behavior modification programs in which clients earn tokens as reinforcers (Weiner, 1962, 1963). Note that response cost differs from timeout in that there is no change in the prevailing reinforcement contingencies when it is administered.

FACTORS INFLUENCING THE EFFECTIVENESS OF PUNISHMENT

1. MAXIMIZING THE CONDITIONS FOR A DESIRABLE ALTERNATIVE RESPONSE

To decrease an undesirable response, it is maximally effective to concurrently increase some desirable alternative response. This means that you should identify some desirable response that will compete with the undesirable behavior to be eliminated. You should also attempt to identify powerful S^Ds that control the desirable behavior and present these to increase the likelihood that the behavior will occur. To maintain the desirable behavior, you should also have effective positive reinforcers that can be presented on an effective schedule. Because the staff members in Ben's case were concerned with examining contingent exercise as a punisher by itself, they did not incorporate a specific positive reinforcement contingency for a desirable alternative to Ben's hitting. However, they might easily have done so.

When consulted by individuals who are thinking about using a punishment procedure to decrease an undesirable behavior, we have always recommended that they first design effective positive reinforcement and stimulus control programs for desirable alternative behaviors (see Figure 13–1). Thus, if you are considering developing and using a punishment program to decrease someone's undesirable behavior, we strongly urge you first to review and apply the information in the earlier chapters concerning positive reinforcement and stimulus control. You should also familiarize yourself with the arguments against the use of punishment, which are summarized later in this chapter.

FIGURE 13–1 An example of the reinforcement of a desirable alternative behavior.

2. MINIMIZING THE CAUSE OF THE RESPONSE TO BE PUNISHED

To maximize the opportunity for the desirable alternative behavior to occur, anyone attempting a punishment program should first minimize the causes of the punished behavior. This implies two things. First, one should try to identify the current stimulus control of the punished behavior. Second, one should next try to identify existing reinforcers for the undesirable behavior. If the behavior is occurring, it is likely that occasional reinforcers are maintaining it.[4] In Ben's case, the teachers were unable to identify S^Ds that consistently evoked hitting, nor could they identify maintaining reinforcement contingencies.

Note 4

It is important to note that, in many situations in which someone is emitting undesirable behavior, punishment may not be necessary. Maximizing the conditions for a desirable alternative response and minimizing the causes of the response to be punished may yield some desirable alternative behavior that competes so strongly with the behavior to be decreased that punishment will never have to be used.

3. SELECTING A PUNISHER

It is very important to be sure that the punisher is effective. Some stimuli may seem to be punishing when in fact they are not. For example, a parent may say "No! Naughty boy! Stop that!" to a child who is engaging in an undesirable behavior. The child may immediately cease the undesirable behavior and emit some other, desired behavior that will continue to receive the attention of the adult. The adult might then conclude that the reprimand was an effective punisher. However, if the adult were to keep track of the frequency of that undesirable behavior in the future, he or she might find that the verbal reprimand was not a punisher, but in fact a reinforcer. The child may have stopped temporarily because, having obtained the attention of the adult, he can emit other behavior that will maintain the adult's attention, at least for a short time. In other words, the verbal reprimand may function as an S^D for subsequent desirable behaviors of the child, regardless of the effects of the verbal reprimand as a punisher or a reinforcer on the preceding undesirable behavior. Several studies indicate that verbal reprimands often function as positive reinforcers and that the long-term frequency of the undesirable behavior that evoked the reprimand is therefore likely to increase.[5] This is not to say that verbal reprimands or threats are never punishing. However, the situations in which they are effective seem to be those in which they are consistently backed up by a strong punisher.

Note 5

To be effective, the punishing stimulus should be fairly intense. Frequently, individuals start with a weak punisher in the belief that they can increase its strength if it is not effective. The following is familiar to many parents. A child emits some undesirable behavior, which is followed by a mild reprimand by the parent. The behavior reoccurs, and the parent provides a stronger reprimand, perhaps coupled with a frown. The behavior is repeated, and the parent severely scolds the child. The behavior is repeated, and the child receives a scolding and a mild slap. The behavior is repeated until finally the parent delivers a severe spanking. There are two problems here. One is that the undesirable behavior may be very harmful or dangerous; if that behavior consists, for example, of running out in the street and playing in the traffic, then the long-term consequences of allowing it to occur many times are potentially disastrous. The second problem is that the severe punisher, the spanking, may have lost a good deal of its effectiveness by the time it is applied. Gradually increasing the intensity of a punisher is not nearly as effective as introducing the punisher in its final form on the first occasion (Azrin & Holz, 1966).

The punisher selected should be one that can be presented immediately following the undesirable behavior. The punisher should also be one that can be presented in a manner such that it is in no way paired with positive reinforcement. This requirement often presents difficulties in situations in which the punisher is delivered by an adult and the individual being punished receives very little adult attention. If a child has received a lot of loving attention from an adult during a period of time prior to the occurrence of the undesired behavior, and the adult immediately presents a strong verbal reprimand following the undesirable behavior, then the verbal reprimand might be punishing. On the other hand, if that reprimand is the only adult attention that has been received by the child for an extended period of time, then that reprimand is a form of adult attention and may in fact be reinforcing.

Contingent exercise turned out to be a very suitable punisher for Ben. It was highly effective, could be presented immediately following the undesirable behavior, and could be presented in a manner such that it was in no way paired with positive reinforcement. The care and attention that the staff gave to choosing the actual exercise task obviously paid off. The staff chose the task because it could be prompted by a voice command from a staff member, Ben frequently performed the behavior in various play situations, it could be carried out in a variety of settings, and it appeared to tire Ben quickly without causing any unnecessary strain.

4. DELIVERING THE PUNISHER

Punishment is most effective when the punisher is presented immediately following the undesirable behavior. If the punisher is delayed, some more desirable behavior may occur prior to the punisher and this desirable behavior may be affected by the punisher to a much greater extent than the prior undesirable behavior. The classic example of this is the mother who asks her husband, as he returns home from work, to spank their son, who has been bad earlier in the day. This request is doubly disastrous: not only does the child receive punishment, even though he may now be engaging in good behavior, but the father is punished for coming home from work. We do not mean to imply that delayed punishment is completely ineffective. As we pointed out in our previous discussions of rule-governed behavior, most humans are adept at bridging rather large time gaps between their behavior and its consequences. Even so, immediate punishment is much more effective than delayed punishment.

The punisher should be delivered after *every* instance of the undesirable behavior (see, for example, Kircher, Pear, & Martin, 1971). Occasional punishment is not nearly as effective as punishment that follows every instance of the undesirable behavior. This implies that, if the teacher is unable to detect most instances of the behavior to be punished, he or she should have serious doubts about the value of implementing a punishment procedure.

The delivery of the punishment should in no way be paired with positive reinforcement. As already mentioned, such a pairing weakens the punisher. In addition, the person administering the punishment should remain calm when doing so. Anger and frustration on the part of the punisher may reinforce the undesirable behavior or inappropriately alter the consistency of intensity of the punishment. A calm, matter-of-fact approach ensures that a punishment program will be followed as it has been designed, and that the person administering the punishment will be less likely to apply a punisher at inappropriate times (i.e., when angry or annoyed) rather than immediately following an occasion of undesirable behavior.

SHOULD PUNISHMENT BE USED?

The use of punishment has always been highly controversial, even before the advent of behavior modification, but the controversy appears to have intensified in recent years (Repp & Singh, 1990). A number of organizations concerned with helping people have formulated, or appear to be in the process of formulating, official statements against at least some uses of punishment. For example, the Practice Directorate of the American Psychological Association and the National Association of School Psychologists have provided testimony to the United States Congress in support of an amendment banning the use of corporal (that is, physical) punishment for emotionally disturbed children ("PD Supports Ban on Corporal Punishment," 1990). In 1990, the American Association on Mental Retardation adopted a policy statement condemning "aversive procedures which cause physical damage, pain, or illness" and "[p]rocedures which are dehumanizing—social degradation, verbal abuse and excessive reactions" ("AAMR Revises Policy," 1990).

There are some who argue that nonaversive methods for eliminating unacceptable behavior are always at least as effective as aversive methods and that, therefore, there is never any justification for using aversive forms of punishment (see Guess, Helmstetter, Turnbull, & Knowlton, 1986; Guess, Turnbull, & Helmstetter, 1990). No humane person would think it is ethical to use aversive methods if nonaversive methods that are equally effective are available. However, it appears that there are some extremely harmful behaviors which, in some cases, can be suppressed only with aversive punishment. For example, there are some retarded and autistic individuals who repeatedly engage in severe self-injurious behavior—damaging their vision by gouging their eyes; damaging their hearing by clapping their hands against their ears; causing tissue damage and bleeding by banging their heads on hard objects or tearing at their flesh; becoming malnourished by inducing vomiting after eating—that places them in great danger of either disabling or killing themselves. A number of studies in the literature demonstrate that these behaviors can be suppressed by aversive punishment (see Favell and others, 1982). Once the self-injurious behavior is suppressed, positive reinforcement is then used to maintain desirable alternative behavior, but this cannot be done until the self-injurious behavior has been suppressed.[6] The only alternative to using aversive punishment, in many cases, appears to be restraint—for example, tying heavily padded mittens to the individual's hands, or even tying the individual to a wheelchair or bed—but this effectively prevents the person from ever learning desirable behavior to replace the undesirable behavior.

Note 6

Several books describe methods that the authors of the books claim can effectively replace all forms of aversive control (see McGee, Menolascino, Hobbs, & Menousek, 1987; Meyer & Evans, 1989). For the most part, the methods described are based on the behavior principles discussed in Chapters 3 to 12 of this text. Although these authors provide many good examples of alternatives that should be tried before resorting to aversive methods, it is not clear that the methods they propose can effectively replace aversive methods in all cases. What is clear is that the decision to use or not use aversive methods in a particular case requires considerable professional training and expertise and should not be made by unqualified individuals. Treatment of severe behavior problems, which are the only type for which aversive punishment should be considered, is therefore best left to professionals who have advanced degrees in psychology or other helping professions from accredited universities and who are members of accredited professional organizations (Griffith & Spreat, 1989).

While much intense controversy centers on aversive punishment, other forms of punishment are also under attack. Few people would argue that all forms of punishment can be eliminated. However, it is extremely difficult to specify the exact degree of punishment that is appropriate in a given situation. For example, regarding timeout, Meyer and Evans (1989, p. 102) state: "the time-out area need not be incredibly comfortable and desirable, but also should not be extremely unpleasant." Clearly, this recommendation leaves a great deal of room for subjectivity in selecting a timeout area. Meyer and Evans also oppose the use of exercise as a punisher—such as in the example of Ben given at the beginning of the chapter—although they regard exercise as beneficial if used to "calm" an individual following inappropriate behavior (p. 137). Unfortunately, it is very difficult—perhaps even impossible—to distinguish between these two functions of exercise, since requiring someone to exercise for the purpose of "calming" him or her may also *punish* (according to the technical definition of punishment given at the beginning of this chapter) behavior that it follows. It appears that what Meyer and Evans are actually concerned with is that if punishment has to be used, it must never be used in a humiliating or degrading (that is, punitive) manner. We certainly concur in this. Regardless of the nature of a person's disability, or the inappropriateness of his or her behavior, everyone should always be treated in a manner that shows respect for the person as a human being.

While the use of punishment is highly controversial, it is clear that punishment can have a number of potentially harmful effects. These may be summarized as follows:

1. Strong punishment tends to elicit aggressive behavior. Experiments with animals show that painful stimuli cause them to attack other animals—even though these other animals had nothing to do with inflicting the painful stimuli (Azrin, 1967). If this finding also applies to humans, then we should not be surprised to observe individuals who have just been punished attacking other individuals. Clearly, such behavior is a very undesirable side effect of punishment.

2. Strong punishment can produce other undesirable emotional side effects, such as crying and general fearfulness. Not only are these side effects unpleasant for all concerned, they frequently interfere with desirable behavior—especially if it is of a complex nature.

3. Punishment may cause the situation and people associated with the aversive stimulus to become conditioned punishers. For example, if you are trying to teach a child to read, and if you punish the child whenever he or she makes a mistake, anything associated with this situation—such as printed words, books, the person who delivers the punishment, the type of room in which the punishment occurs—will tend to become punishing. The child may attempt to escape or avoid these stimuli (see Chapter 14). Thus, instead of helping the individual to learn, punishment may drive him or her away from people, objects, and events associated with the learning situation.

4. Punishment does not establish any new behavior; it only suppresses old behavior. In other words, punishment does not teach an individual what to do; at best, it only teaches what not to do. For example, the main defining characteristic of the retarded is that they lack behavior that nonretarded people have. The primary emphasis for these individuals, then, should be on establishing new behavior rather than on merely eliminating old behavior. Reinforcement is required to accomplish this task.

5. Children often model or imitate adults. If adults apply punishment to children, the children are apt to do the same to others. Thus, in punishing children we may inadvertently be providing a model for them to follow in showing aggression toward others (Bandura, 1965, 1969). For example, chil-

dren who were taught a game in which they were fined for incorrect behavior fined other children to whom they taught the game (Gelfand, Hartmann, Lamb, Smith, Mahan, & Paul, 1974).

6. Because punishment results in quick suppression of undesirable behavior, it can tempt the user to rely heavily on it and neglect the use of positive reinforcement for desirable behavior. However, the undesirable behavior may return after only a temporary suppression, or some other undesirable behavior could occur. The person administering punishment may then resort to progressively heavier doses, thereby creating a vicious circle with disastrous side effects.

Some behavior modifiers maintain that all the problems listed above can be eliminated or greatly reduced with the proper use of punishment (e.g., Johnston, 1985; Van Houten, 1983), and considerable data support this contention (Axelrod & Apsche, 1983). However, because punishment is so easy to abuse, we recommend that it be used only as a last resort, and then only by appropriately trained and accredited professionals.

PITFALLS OF PUNISHMENT

We have discussed extensively the many potentially harmful side effects lying in wait for those who try to use punishment without being familiar with its properties. At least as serious are the many instances in which punishment is applied by people who are not aware that they are applying it. A common example of this is criticizing or ridiculing a person for inadequate behavior. Since criticism and ridicule are generally punishing, they will likely suppress future instances of that behavior and tend to drive the individual away from the person administering them. Yet the inadequate behavior that is criticized and ridiculed may be an approximation of more adequate behavior. Suppressing it could destroy the individual's opportunity to obtain the adequate behavior through the use of shaping. In everyday language, the individual becomes "discouraged" and "gives up" in his or her "attempt" to develop adequate behavior. In addition, because he or she will attempt to escape from and avoid the person administering the criticism and ridicule (see Chapter 14), that person will have lost a great deal of potential reinforcing effectiveness.

Another example of someone's applying punishment without being aware of it is the person who says "That was good, but. . . ." Suppose that a teenager helps a parent with the dishes and the parent replies, "Thanks for helping, but next time don't be so slow." We are sure that, based on the foregoing discussion, you can describe a much more effective and pleasant way for the parent to react.

In our view, punishment should be applied only in conjunction with positive reinforcement for a desirable behavior, and only for the purpose of eliminating undesirable behaviors that cannot be reduced in other ways.

GUIDELINES FOR THE EFFECTIVE APPLICATION OF PUNISHMENT PROCEDURES

The rules for the effective use of punishment are probably violated more than those for other principles. Therefore, if you propose a punishment procedure (even one involving a mild punisher), you owe it to yourself and the person whose behavior is to be punished to do an effective job.

1. *Selecting a response.* Punishment is most effective with a specific behavior (such as jumping on the arm of the chair) rather than a general category of behavior (such as wrecking furniture).
2. *Maximize the conditions for a desirable (nonpunished) alternative response.*
   a. Select a desirable alternative behavior that competes with the behavior to be punished such that the alternative behavior can be reinforced. If possible, select a behavior that will be maintained by the natural environment after the termination of your reinforcement program.
   b. Provide strong prompts to increase the likelihood that the desirable alternative behavior will occur.
   c. Reinforce the desirable behavior with a powerful reinforcer on an appropriate schedule.
3. *Minimize the causes of the response to be punished.*
   a. Try to identify and eliminate many or all of the stimuli controlling the undesirable behavior, at least early in the training program.
   b. Try to eliminate any possible reinforcement for the undesirable behavior.
4. *Select an effective punisher.*
   a. Choose an effective punisher that can be presented immediately following the undesirable behavior.
   b. The punisher should be one that will in no way be paired with positive reinforcement following the undesirable behavior.
   c. Select a punisher that can be presented following every instance of the undesirable behavior.
5. *Delivering the punisher.*
   a. The punisher should be presented *immediately* following *every* instance of the response to be decreased.
   b. The individual administering the punisher should do so in a calm and matter-of-fact manner.
   c. The person doing the punishing should also be associated with a lot of positive reinforcement for alternative behaviors, so that he or she does not become a conditioned punisher.
   d. The administering individual should take care not to pair punishment with reinforcement.
6. In all programs involving punishment, careful data should be taken on the effects of the program. The conditions under which the program should be applied must be stated clearly, written down, and adhered to.

STUDY QUESTIONS

1. Describe how Ben's aggressive behavior was eliminated.
2. How was stimulus control an important part of the punishment contingency for Ben?

3. What is a punisher? State the principle of punishment.
4. Describe four different types of punishers and illustrate each with an example.
5. Under which of the four categories of punishment would you put the type of punishment used with Ben? Justify your choice.
6. Define conditioned punisher and illustrate with an example.
7. Distinguish between exclusionary and nonexclusionary timeout.
8. If you do a good job of attending to the first two factors influencing the effectiveness of punishment, you may not have to apply punishment. Discuss.
9. What are the problems with gradually increasing the intensity of the punishing stimulus over successive applications of that stimulus?
10. How would you determine if a verbal reprimand was a punisher for a particular child?
11. In the subsection "Selecting a Punisher," we described a sequence (involving a potential reprimand) of events and behaviors that might be characterized as a behavioral chain. What was the sequence?
12. What is a common example of the response-contingent withdrawal of positive reinforcement that is applied as punishment by parents to their children?
13. In the subsection "Delivering the Punisher," we suggested that, if the teacher is unable to detect most instances of a behavior to be punished, then the teacher should have serious doubts about the value of implementing a punishment procedure.
   a. From the information in this chapter, what reasons can you cite to support this suggestion?
   b. What alternative means of managing the situation are available to the teacher?
14. What are four concerns of the teacher in regard to delivering a punisher?
15. In view of the controversy regarding the use of punishment, do you agree with the way punishment was used with Ben? Defend your answer.
16. Cite six potentially harmful side effects of the application of punishment.
17. Describe an example illustrating how punishment is applied by people who are not aware that they are applying it.

PRACTICE EXERCISES

1. Consider the behavior of speeding (driving a car in excess of the speed limit) in our culture.
   a. Briefly outline the current contingencies with respect to speeding.
   b. Compare the current contingencies for speeding with the guidelines for the effective application of punishment procedures. Identify those guidelines that were either ignored or flagrantly violated by the lawmakers and law enforcers.
2. Consider the behavior of littering the highways in your area. Answer the questions that you answered for speeding in Exercise 1.

SELF-MODIFICATION EXERCISE

Choose a behavior of yours that you would like to decrease. With the help of a friend, describe in detail a punishment program that would likely decrease that behavior. (Make the program as realistic as possible, but do not apply it.) Your punishment program should be consistent with all the guidelines for the effective application of punishment.

EXTENDED DISCUSSION AND NOTES

1. This was demonstrated very clearly in an experiment by Lovaas, Schaeffer, and Simmons (1965) with autistic children. In the first part of the experiment, the children were reinforced with candy for pressing a lever, and they demonstrated very high lever-pressing rates. On several occasions, immediately following a lever press the experimenter said "No!" which had practically no effect on the rate of lever pressing. The severely disturbed children were then given a training session in which their extreme self-stimulation and tantrumming behaviors were followed by a "No!" and a brief electric shock punisher. After several pairings of the word "No!" with the shock in these sessions, the children were again given an opportunity to press a lever for candy reinforcement. When their lever pressing was occurring at a high rate, the experimenter said "No!" and the presentation of this verbal stimulus now had a very strong suppressing effect on the lever pressing.

2. Bostow and Bailey (1969) successfully applied timeouts of two minutes duration (plus an additional 15 seconds of quiet behavior at the end of that time) for disruptive and aggressive behaviors of two retarded patients in a state hospital ward setting. In another study, White, Nielsen, and Johnson (1972) compared the effectiveness of timeout durations of 1 minute, 15 minutes, and 30 minutes in controlling deviant behaviors in a group of 20 institutionalized retarded individuals. They found that 1-minute timeouts were not as effective in general as were 15- and 30-minute timeouts, but there was little difference between the two longer timeout intervals. Thus, excessively long timeouts do not necessarily increase the effectiveness of the timeout as a punisher. After reviewing studies that examined various durations of timeouts in punishment programs, Brantner and Doherty (1983) concluded that, from a wide spectrum of populations and behavior problems, relatively short durations of timeout have generally been effective. Also, as indicated by White and others (1972), ethical considerations (such as avoiding durations of timeout in excess of what is necessary) and practical considerations (such as avoiding lengthy timeouts that take the individual away from a learning environment) must also be considered in selecting a particular timeout duration.

3. It has sometimes been argued that timeout should not be ended if the individual is engaging in undesirable behavior (such as tantrumming) when the specified timeout period has elapsed. Otherwise, it is argued, the undesirable behavior might be reinforced. However, Mace, Page, Ivancic, & O'Brien (1986) indicated that timeout without a contingent delay is just as effective as timeout with a contingent delay.

4. It is also possible that a client might show undesirable behavior because the behavior allows him or her to escape from or avoid some unpleasant or aversive consequences. These contingencies are referred to as escape and avoidance contingencies and they are discussed in Chapter 14.

5. The potential reinforcing value of reprimands was demonstrated nicely in a study by Madsen, Becker, Thomas, Koser, and Plager (1970). A teacher was instructed

to increase her use of the reprimand "Sit down!" when the children were out of their seats. As a consequence of the teacher saying "Sit down!" more often, the children's out-of-seat behavior increased.

6. A highly controversial device termed the *Self-Injurious Behavior Inhibiting System (SIBIS)* has appeared on the market. The device, which is strapped to the head, is designed to detect self-injurious blows to the head and deliver an aversive electric shock to the arm or leg, contingent on such blows. Despite the controversy concerning the SIBIS, a group of researchers (Linscheid, Iwata, Ricketts, Williams, & Griffin, 1990) tested it with five individuals whose severely self-injurious head-beating had not been responsive to nonaversive treatments. The data indicated that the device was effective in completely eliminating the self-injurious behavior and produced no detrimental side effects.

STUDY QUESTIONS ON NOTES

1. Describe contingencies other than positive reinforcement that might maintain undesirable behaviors.
2. How did Madsen and colleagues demonstrate that reprimands can actually be reinforcing?
3. Discuss whether long timeouts are more effective than short timeouts.
4. Briefly describe how Lovaas and co-workers demonstrated that a stimulus paired with punishment will itself become punishing. What is such a stimulus called?
5. What is the Self-Injurious Behavior Inhibiting System? In view of the controversy regarding the use of punishment, do you believe that testing and using this device is appropriate? Defend your answer.

CHAPTER 14

Establishing a Desirable Behavior by Using **Escape** and **Avoidance** Conditioning

"Scotty, would you like to play with your new toy?"

A NEW TOY FOR SCOTTY

Scotty was a seven-year-old institutionalized severely retarded boy, diagnosed as having Down's syndrome, who habitually beat his head with his hands.* This self-destructiveness was so severe that Scotty spent 24 hours a day in a crib with his hands tied to his waist and a modified football helmet on his head. Because of the severity of the problem, the staff psychologist designed a behavioral procedure involving electric-shock punishment. This quickly eliminated Scotty's head beating in the training situation. But what about other situations?

The psychologist realized that it would not be safe to let the boy run freely on the ward until some desirable alternative behavior to head beating was developed. To accomplish this, staff members placed Scotty in a highchair and put a large metal truck on the tray in front of him. An electric timer wired to the truck measured how long the boy touched the truck. Since Scotty engaged in this activity hardly at all, it was clear that special procedures would be required to get him to do so. Before describing these procedures, we should emphasize that prior to being implemented they were reviewed and approved by the Ethical Review Committee of the institution. This committee also monitored the program throughout the time that it was in effect. (As we point out in Chapter 28, all behavior modification programs should be subject to appropriate ethical controls. This is especially critical when aversive events such as shock are to be used.)

*This case is described in Whaley and Malott (1971).

At the beginning of the program, Scotty was given trials in which a mild electric shock was presented through electrodes attached to his leg; simultaneously, a buzzer sounded. When Scotty touched the truck, the buzzer and the shock turned off automatically. At first, it was necessary to prompt Scotty by guiding his hand to the truck when the buzzer and shock came on. After about a dozen trials, however, he did this himself immediately upon the presentation of the two stimuli. After each trial, Scotty's hand was taken from the truck, if necessary, before a new trial was begun.

This procedure is called escape conditioning because Scotty escaped the shock (that is, he removed or terminated it) by placing his hand on the truck. When he escaped consistently, the escape procedure was changed to what is called avoidance conditioning. To keep the buzzer off and prevent shock from occurring, Scotty had to keep his hand on the truck. The instant he removed it the buzzer sounded, and three seconds later shock occurred. By keeping his hand on the truck continuously, Scotty could avoid shock altogether.

Although at the beginning of the program Scotty practically never touched the truck, during the subsequent avoidance procedure he kept his hand on it almost continuously for up to several hours—depending on how long the session lasted. During that time, he did not beat his head. The next step was to teach Scotty to touch another toy. The truck was replaced with a toy tiger stuffed with metal shavings so that it could be used, as was the truck, to electrically record the amount of time Scotty held his hand on it. As with the truck, Scotty kept his hand on the toy constantly and did not beat his head.

Gradually, Scotty began to grasp and manipulate the toy tiger. At times, he was observed to even hug and kiss it. The shocker was then disconnected, although the buzzer remained operative. Since Scotty never released the toy long enough to learn that the shock would no longer occur, it appeared that the shock contingency was no longer necessary. Next, the buzzer was disconnected. Nevertheless, the boy continued to hold the tiger about as much as before.

Other stuffed animals were then faded in. Occasionally, it was necessary to present a short booster session with shock, but this quickly reestablished the desired behavior and thus was required infrequently. The psychologist, therefore, decided that the time had come to let Scotty roam the ward freely with a stuffed toy. The boy clutched the toy wherever he went and did not beat himself.

Some readers might think it cruel to make a child dependent on a toy through electric shock. Actually, the child was much better off with this dependency than without it. No longer did he have to be restrained in bed 24 hours a day. He could run, play, and learn social interaction and other vital skills. At first, he was extremely dependent on his toy; in fact, once when accidentally deprived of it he beat his head frantically. But over the span of about a year, he gradually became less and less dependent on his toy, and eventually, did not beat his head even when without it.

ESCAPE AND AVOIDANCE

Two principles were used in Scotty's case: escape conditioning and avoidance conditioning. The principle of *escape conditioning* states that there are certain stimuli whose removal immediately after the occurrence of a response will increase the likelihood of the response. In the escape procedure used with Scotty, the removal of shock following the response of touching the truck increased the probability that Scotty would touch the truck each time shock was presented.

Note that escape conditioning is similar to aversive punishment in that both procedures involve the use of some sort of aversive event. However, escape conditioning is just the opposite of punishment. In the punishment procedure, the likelihood of future behavior is *decreased* as a result of *presenting* a punisher following past instances of behavior. In the escape-conditioning procedure, the likelihood of a behavior is *increased* as a result of terminating **Note 1** or *removing* a punisher following past instances of the behavior.[1]

Escape conditioning has the disadvantage that the aversive stimulus must be present for the desired response to occur. For example, when Scotty was on the escape procedure, shock had to be presented before he would touch the toy. Therefore, escape conditioning is generally used not as a terminal contingency but rather as preparatory training for the introduction of avoidance conditioning. Thus, Scotty was given avoidance conditioning after he had acquired escape behavior.

In *avoidance conditioning*, a response prevents the occurrence of a punisher. This increases the probability of occurrence of the response if it is low and maintains that probability at a high level. Thus, the principle of **avoidance conditioning** states that a behavior will increase in frequency if it prevents a punisher from occurring. During the avoidance procedure with Scotty, touching a toy prevented shock from occurring. When Scotty took his hand off the truck, the buzzer sounded and shock occurred three seconds later.

The sound of the buzzer when Scotty removed his hand from the toy was a *warning stimulus*: it signaled the occurrence of shock three seconds later. Other names for warning stimulus are *conditioned aversive stimulus* and *conditioned punisher*. Eventually, Scotty would keep his hands on the toy just to avoid the sound of the buzzer, and it was thus possible to dispense with the shock altogether. This type of avoidance conditioning, which includes a warning signal that enables the individual to discriminate a forthcoming punisher, is **Note 2** called *discriminated avoidance conditioning*.[2] Finally, the buzzer itself was disconnected and the behavior was maintained without either buzzer or shock —except, as we mentioned, for an occasional booster session as new toys were faded in.

How was it possible to eventually maintain the behavior of toy touching without shock or the buzzer? There are two probable answers. First, it is in the nature of an avoidance procedure that, when the behavior occurs regularly, the punisher does not occur. Therefore, when the procedure no longer applies, it takes quite some time to discover that performing the behavior is not what keeps the punisher from occurring. Second, after Scotty began holding the toy, he probably came in contact with *positive* reinforcers that tended to maintain the behavior apart from the termination of the shock.

After all, normal youngsters enjoy hugging stuffed animals, and it seems reasonable to suspect that this activity became reinforcing for Scotty too. Also, other people may have frequently praised Scotty for the nice way he was playing with his toys, or commented on his cute toy. Thus, two things—the tendency for an avoidance response to be very resistant to extinction and the availability of positive reinforcement for desirable behavior—probably account for the fact that Scotty continued to hold stuffed animals long after this behavior no longer prevented shock from occurring.

You may also wonder why Scotty eventually ceased beating his head, even when he did not have his toy with him. The answer would seem to be related to why he beat his head in the first place. This behavior was probably reinforced by the attention Scotty received for it. Moreover, because he had to be severely restrained, he had no opportunity to learn to obtain attention in other ways. However, when he could move about freely without beating his head, more desirable behaviors could occur and be reinforced with attention. Eventually, these more desirable behaviors took precedence over the gruesome one of head beating.

Although escape conditioning seems to be less frequent than avoidance conditioning in our society, there are examples of escape conditioning with which we are familiar (see Table 14–1).

Avoidance conditioning influences us every day. Unfortunately, it is common in the classroom, where children may be required to give the right answer to avoid the teacher's ridicule or anger and to avoid a poor mark. Our legal system is based entirely on avoidance conditioning. We pay our taxes to avoid going to jail. We put money in parking meters to avoid getting a ticket. We pay our parking fines in order to avoid a court summons.

Escape and avoidance conditioning involve the use of *punishers*, as defined in Chapter 13. Therefore, the controversy regarding the use of punishment (see Chapter 13) applies, as well, to escape and avoidance conditioning. In addition, escape and avoidance conditioning suffer from much the same disadvantages as punishment (see Chapter 13). Aversive stimuli can produce undesirable emotional behaviors, such as aggression and general fearfulness, which, among other things, interfere with the learning process. Moreover, any stimulus associated with punishment tends to become punishment itself. Thus, an individual will tend to avoid or escape any situation or person associated with the use of punishers. Clearly, this does not further an individual's social, emotional, and intellectual development.

It is encouraging to note that Scotty did not show any of these side effects of aversive stimulation. He evidenced no hesitation in going to experimental sessions. In fact, he showed a great deal of affection toward the person who worked with him, such as by approaching him with outstretched arms when spotting him among a group of people. Nevertheless, escape and avoidance, like punishment, should generally be thought of as last-resort procedures: they should not be used if positive reinforcement will do the job.

Table 14-1 Examples of Escape Conditioning

	AVERSIVE SITUATION	ESCAPE RESPONSES BY INDIVIDUAL	REMOVAL OF AVERSIVE SITUATION	LONG-TERM EFFECTS
1	A child sees an adult with a bag of candies. The child begins to scream, "candy, candy, candy."	To terminate the screaming, the adult gives the screaming child a candy.	The child stops screaming.	In the future, the adult is more likely "to give in to" the screaming child (and the child is more likely to scream when she sees a candy bag, because of the positive reinforcement she gains for doing so).
2	Child A slaps (and continues to slap) child B.	Child B cries loudly.	An adult removes child A from the vicinity of child B.	Child B is likely to cry more quickly in future situations in which she is slapped.
3	A retarded child has had shoes put on her that are too tight and are pinching her toes.	The child makes loud noises in the presence of an adult and points to her toes.	The adult removes the shoes (and perhaps puts on larger shoes).	The child is more likely to make loud noises and point to her sore feet (or to other areas of pain) more quickly in similar situations in the future.
4	An adult frowns at a child and says, "Pick up that paper you threw on the floor."	The child picks up the paper.	The adult stops frowning.	The response of picking up the paper (or obeying the adult) is likely to occur more quickly in future situations in which the adult frowns while giving instructions.
5	A staff member in an institution comes upon a pile of smelly feces on the floor.	The staff member walks away without cleaning it up.	The staff member does not have to clean up the feces, and escapes the aversive smell.	In the future, the staff member will likely walk away from feces on the floor.

PITFALLS OF ESCAPE AND AVOIDANCE

Often, people inadvertently use escape and avoidance conditioning to establish behaviors that they probably would rather not see established.

Children often learn to escape and avoid punishment in ways that are not particularly desirable. An everyday example is the child who desperately promises "I'll be good; I won't do it again" to escape or avoid punishment for some infraction of parental authority. When such pleas are successful, the pleading behavior is strengthened and thus increased in frequency under similar circumstances, but the undesirable behavior the parent meant to decrease has probably been affected very little or not at all. Verbal behavior having little relation to reality may be increased while the undesirable target response may persist in strength.

Prisoners may learn to make the "right" verbal statements to obtain early parole, but sometimes it is merely their verbal behavior that has been modified, not their antisocial behaviors (e.g., assaults, property destruction). Apologies, confessions, and the "guilty look" characteristic of transgressors in all walks of life can be traced to similar contingencies. Lying or misrepresenting the facts is another way of avoiding punishment, if one can get away with it.

Another pitfall of escape and avoidance is the inadvertent establishment of conditioned aversive stimuli, to which an individual then responds in such a way as to escape or avoid them. By their excessive use of punishment, some teachers transform themselves, their classroom, and the learning materials they use into conditioned aversive stimuli. All too frequently, this situation produces individuals who avoid teachers, school, and books, and who therefore fail to advance academically. Clearly, this is a most unfortunate consequence of escape and avoidance conditioning.

A final pitfall of escape conditioning is that in many situations it maintains undesirable behaviors of the teacher. This can easily be seen in the first example in Table 14–1.

GUIDELINES FOR THE EFFECTIVE APPLICATION OF ESCAPE AND AVOIDANCE

The following rules should be observed by any person who applies escape and avoidance:

1. Given a choice between maintaining behavior on an escape or an avoidance procedure, the latter is to be preferred. There are two reasons for this. First, in escape conditioning the punisher must be present prior to the target response, whereas in avoidance conditioning the punisher occurs only when the target response fails to occur. Second, in escape conditioning the target response does not occur when the punisher is not present, whereas in avoidance conditioning responding decreases very slowly when the punisher may no longer be forthcoming.

2. The target behavior should be established by escape conditioning before it is put on an avoidance procedure. Avoidance behavior is usually easier to establish if escape behavior is established first, as was done in the case of Scotty.

3. During avoidance conditioning, a conditioned punishing stimulus should signal the impending punisher. This enhances conditioning by providing a "warning" that failure to respond will result in aversive stimulation. An example from the natural environment is the printed word VIOLATION on a parking meter, which indicates that the motorist may receive a parking ticket if he or she does not put a coin in the meter. The buzzer served a similar function for Scotty, indicating that shock would occur three seconds after he removed his hand from the toy. (Presumably, although the authors of the study don't say whether this was so, if Scotty placed his hand back on the toy within three seconds, the buzzer would shut off and shock would be prevented. Similarly, putting a coin in a parking meter removes the VIOLATION sign and prevents a ticket.)

4. Escape and avoidance conditioning, like punishment, should be used cautiously. Because these procedures involve aversive stimuli, they can result in harmful side effects, such as aggression, fearfulness, and a tendency to avoid or escape any person or thing associated with the procedure.

5. Positive reinforcement for the target response should be used in conjunction with escape and avoidance conditioning. Not only will it help to strengthen the desired behavior, but it will also tend to counteract the undesirable side effects mentioned.

6. As with all the procedures described in this text, the individual concerned should be told—to the best of his or her understanding—about the contingencies in effect. However, again, as with all these procedures, instructions are not necessary for escape and avoidance conditioning to work.

STUDY QUESTIONS

1. How is escape conditioning similar to the punishment procedure? How do their effects differ?

2. Procedurally, in what two ways is escape conditioning different from positive reinforcement? How are their effects similar?

3. Procedurally, what are two differences between escape conditioning and avoidance conditioning?

4. How are conditioned positive reinforcers and conditioned punishers similar, and how are they different?

5. Give two other names for "conditioned punisher."

6. What two factors probably account for the observation that Scotty eventually continued to touch the toy even without the application of a shock or the buzzer?

7. Explain in behavioral terms, with an example of your own, why individuals frequently reinforce the undesirable behavior of other individuals. (Hint: See the first example in Table 14–1.)

8. Explain how escape conditioning might maintain an adult's behavior of responding inappropriately to a child's extreme social withdrawal.

9. Why should escape- and avoidance-conditioning procedures be considered only as a last resort?

10. In view of the controversy regarding the use of aversive punishers (see Chapter 13), do you agree with the escape and avoidance procedure used with Scotty? Defend your answer.

11. Briefly describe at least three pitfalls of escape and avoidance. (If possible, use examples other than those in the text.)

12. Why is an avoidance procedure generally preferred to an escape procedure?

PRACTICE EXERCISES

1. Construct a chart similar to Table 14–1 in which you present five examples of avoidance conditioning that have influenced your behavior. Present each example in terms of the categories of situation, warning signal, response, consequences, and long-term effects.

2. Successful avoidance behavior means that an individual has been conditioned to respond (probably to a warning signal) in such a way as to avoid the occurrence of a punisher. This means that the avoidance behavior might persist even if (for whatever reasons) the environment has changed such that the punisher will no longer be presented, regardless of the individual's behavior. Why is this so? Give two examples from your own experience.

SELF-MODIFICATION EXERCISE

Identify a fear or anxiety reaction that you experienced recently. Describe your reaction and its stimulus control in some detail. Is your reaction analyzed best as positively reinforced, avoidance, or escape behavior? Justify your analysis with reference to behavioral principles and procedures.

EXTENDED DISCUSSION AND NOTES

1. Unfortunately for the student striving for a clear understanding of behavioral psychology, a variety of technical terms are used in reference to punishing events. To make matters worse, there are often rather subtle differences in the manner in which different authorities define these different terms. For example, Skinner uses the term "negative reinforcer," which he defined and distinguished from "positive reinforcer" as follows (1953, p. 73):

> Events which are found to be reinforcing are of two sorts. Some reinforcements consist of *presenting* stimuli, of adding something—for example, food, water, sexual contact—to the situation. These we call *positive* reinforcers. Others consist of removing something—for example, a loud noise, a very bright light, extreme cold or heat, or electric shock—from the situation. These we call *negative* reinforcers. In both cases the effect of reinforcement is the same thing—the probability of response is increased.

Thus, negative reinforcement is equivalent to what this text refers to as escape conditioning (that is, increasing the probability of a response by making the removal of a particular type of stimulus—which is called a punisher, an aversive stimulus, or a negative reinforcer—contingent on that response). However, there is disagreement among behaviorists on the logical validity of distinguishing between positive and negative reinforcement. Most notably, Michael (1975) has argued against the distinction on the basis that it is logically meaningless to distinguish between cases in which a stimulus is removed and cases in which a stimulus is presented. The removal of one stimulus (for example, extreme cold or heat) always logically implies the presentation of another stimulus (in this case, a more moderate temperature), and vice versa. Thus, instead of distinguishing between presenting and removing stimuli, Michael would speak only of events involving changes in the stimuli present in a situation. Such stimulus-change events are reinforcing when they increase the probability of responses they follow, and they are punishing when they decrease the probability of responses they follow. Thus, Michael would get rid of the distinction between positive and negative reinforcement, but would retain the distinction between reinforcement and punishment.

The manner in which we defined punishment in Chapter 13 is consistent with Michael's definition of that term (as well as with that of other writers, such as Azrin and Holz, 1966, and Van Houten, 1983). However, Skinner's definition of punishment is different. He does not define it in terms of its effect in reducing behavior. Rather, he defines punishment as the presentation of a negative reinforcer or the removal of a positive reinforcer following a response. According to this definition, to say that presenting or removing a particular stimulus constitutes punishment, it is necessary first to show that that stimulus is a negative or positive reinforcer, respectively.

2. A less common type of avoidance conditioning does not involve a warning signal. This type of avoidance is known as Sidman avoidance (after Murray Sidman, who studied this type of avoidance extensively with lower organisms; e.g., Sidman, 1953). An interesting experiment was conducted with Sidman avoidance by Hefferline, Keenan, and Harford (1959). In this experiment, individual normal adults sat in chairs and listened to music. Attached to their thumbs were tiny wire electrodes that measured extremely small thumb twitches. The individuals were instructed to listen to the music through earphones, and were told the music might occasionally be interrupted by noise. (Other participants were given somewhat different instructions, but for our purposes their results will not be described.) During the first few minutes, the music continued uninterrupted and Hefferline and colleagues recorded the number of thumb twitches. Then, during an experimental period, thumb twitches affected music and noise according to an escape/Sidman-avoidance procedure. When the noise was superimposed on the music, a thumb twitch would enable the individual to escape from the noise for 15 seconds. Subsequent thumb twitches during that time (without any warning signal) would continue to postpone the noise for 15-second intervals. Under these conditions, the rate of the thumb twitching increased greatly—to the extent that the individuals were able to listen to the music without interruption. (An interesting sidelight to this experiment was that the individuals were completely unaware—that is, they were unable to verbalize the fact—that they had been conditioned to thumb twitch in the fashion described.)

3. In an investigation of self-injurious behavior with seven developmentally disabled individuals, Iwata, Pace, Kalsher, Cowdery and Cataldo (1990) found that the self-injurious behavior occurred more often when certain demands (for example, academic tasks) were made on the individuals than when attention was made contingent on the self-injurious behavior or during play. The experimenters inferred that the self-injurious behavior was reinforced by escape from a demand condition rather than positively reinforced. This was confirmed by showing that the behavior was decreased by an extinction procedure in which the demand continued when the person engaged in the self-injurious behavior.

STUDY QUESTIONS ON NOTES

1. What is the difference between the definition of a punisher in this text and Skinner's definition of a negative reinforcer?
2. Why did Michael recommend that we dispose of the term "negative reinforcer"? Discuss.
3. What is Sidman avoidance conditioning?
4. Describe two situations in which you were influenced by Sidman avoidance conditioning.
5. How is the experiment by Hefferline and others related to the Greenspoon experiment described in Chapter 3, note 3?
6. Briefly describe how self-injurious behavior maintained by an escape contingency was extinguished. What sort of precautions do you think would be necessary in carrying out such a procedure?

CHAPTER 15

Procedures Based on
Principles of
Respondent Conditioning

The principles and procedures described in the previous pages of this book are mainly those of *operant conditioning*. The term operant conditioning was initially used by Skinner (1938) in a very special sense, namely to refer to the observation that behavior could be modified by its consequences. As we have seen, consequences that cause a behavior to increase are called reinforcers, and those that cause it to decrease are called punishers. Behaviors that operate on the environment to generate consequences, and are in turn controlled by those consequences, are called *operant behaviors*.

While operant principles have widespread applicability, some behavior does not seem to fit the model of operant conditioning. Some of our behaviors seem to be reflexive (that is, elicited by prior stimuli quite apart from the consequences of the behaviors). These are called *respondent behaviors*, and a different set of principles seems to apply to them. Principles governing respondent behavior grew out of the work of the Russian physiologist Ivan Pavlov (1927). In this chapter we briefly describe these principles and how they differ from those of operant conditioning. In addition, we highlight some of the applications of these principles.

PRINCIPLES OF RESPONDENT CONDITIONING

Respondent-conditioning principles are based on the fact that certain stimuli automatically elicit certain responses apart from any prior learning or conditioning experience. These "automatic" stimulus-response relationships are called ***unconditioned reflexes***. Examples of such reflexes are shown in Figure 15–1.

The reflexes in Figure 15–1 are unconditioned in the sense that the stimuli elicit the responses without prior conditioning (in other words, they are inborn). A stimulus that elicits a response without prior learning or con-

UNCONDITIONED REFLEX

Unconditioned Stimulus ·········> Unconditioned Response

Digestive system

Food ···································> salivation
Bad Food ·····························> sickness, nausea
Object in esophagus ···············> vomiting

Reproductive system

Genital stimulation ··················> vaginal lubrication, penile erection, orgasm

Nipple stimulation···················> milk release (in lactating women)

Circulatory system

High temperature ····················> sweating, flushing
Sudden loud noise ···················> blanching, pounding heart

Respiratory system

Irritation in nose·····················> sneeze
Throat clogged ······················> cough
Allergens ····························> asthma attack

Muscular system

Low temperature ····················> shivering
Blows or burns ······················> withdrawal
Tap on patellar tendon···············> knee jerk
Light to eye··························> pupil constriction
Novel stimulation ····················> reflexive orienting

Infant reflexes

Stroking the cheek ··················> head turning
Object touches lips···················> sucking
Food in mouth ······················> swallowing
Object in the hand ··················> grasping
Held vertically, feet touching ground ·····> stepping

FIGURE 15–1   A partial list of unconditioned reflexes. John D. Baldwin and Janice I. Baldwin, *Behavior Principles in Everyday Life*, 2nd ed. © 1986, p. 44. Reprinted by permission of Prentice-Hall, Inc., Englewood Cliffs, N.J.

ditioning is called an ***unconditioned stimulus*** (US). A response elicited by such a stimulus is called an ***unconditioned response*** (UR).

Respondent Conditioning. For each of the responses in Figure 15–1, there are stimuli that do not elicit them. In that sense, such stimuli are considered ***neutral***. For example, assume that a particular stimulus (such as the sound of classical music) is neutral in the sense that it does not elicit a particular response (salivation) in a particular individual. The principle of ***respondent conditioning*** states that if that stimulus (the sound of clasical music) is followed closely in time by a US (food in the mouth), which does elicit the response of salivation, then the previously neutral stimulus (sound of classical music) will also tend to elicit the response of salivation in the future.* Of course, it may take more than just one pairing of classical music with food before the sound of classical music would elicit any noticeable amount of salivation. A diagram illustrating respondent conditioning is shown in Figure 15–2.

If a salivation response was in fact conditioned to the sound of classical music, the stimulus-response relationship would be referred to as a ***conditioned reflex***. The stimulus in a conditioned reflex is called a ***conditioned stimulus*** (CS, e.g., the sound of the classical music), and the response in a conditioned reflex is referred to as a ***conditioned response*** (CR, e.g., salivation to the classical music).

CSs and S^Ds. Note that CSs are like S^Ds in that both produce responses that have been conditioned to them. The conditioning procedures that established them differ, however. In addition, the ways in which CSs and S^Ds produce their responses seem to differ. Responses produced by CSs frequently seem to be more automatic or consistent. To capture this difference, standard behavioral terminology refers to CSs as *eliciting* the responses conditioned to them, whereas S^Ds are said to *evoke* the responses conditioned to them. In addition, operant behavior is sometimes said to be *emitted* by an individual, whereas respondent behavior is *elicited* by a stimulus. Throughout this text, we have been consistent in the use of the terms "elicit," "evoke," and "emit."

Factors Influencing Respondent Conditioning. There are several variables that influence the development of a conditioned reflex. First, *the greater the number of pairings of a CS with a US, the greater is the ability of the CS to elicit the CR*, until a maximum strength of the conditioned reflex has been reached.[1] If a child is scared several times by the loud barking of a dog, for example, sight of the dog will elicit a stronger fear than if the child had only been scared by the dog just once.

Second, *stronger conditioning occurs if the CS just precedes the US by up to*

Note 1

---

*Respondent conditioning is also commonly referred to as *classical conditioning* or *Pavlovian conditioning*.

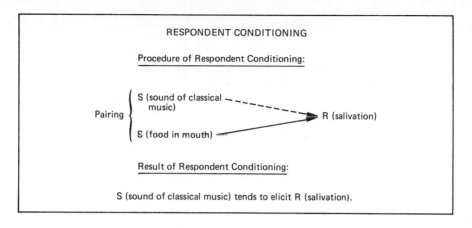

FIGURE 15–2　Respondent conditioning model.

a few seconds, rather than by a longer time or rather than following the US. Conditioning in the latter case is difficult to attain. If a child sees a dog, and then is frightened by the dog's loud barking, sight of the dog is likely to become a CS with fear as a CR. On the other hand, if the child hears loud barking of a dog hidden from view, and a few seconds later sees a dog trot around the corner of a building, the fear caused by the loud barking is not likely to be transferred to the sight of the dog.

　　Third, *a CS acquires greater ability to elicit a CR if the CS is always paired with a given US than if it is only occasionally paired with the US.* If a couple, for example, consistently light a candle in the bedroom just before having sex, and not at other times, then the candlelight is likely to become a CS eliciting sexual arousal. On the other hand, if they light a candle in the bedroom every night but have sex there only one or two nights each week, then the candlelight will be a weaker CS for sexual arousal.

Note 2　　　Fourth, *when several neutral stimuli precede a US, the stimulus that is most consistently associated with the US is the one most likely to become a strong CS.*[2] A child, for example, may experience thunderstorms in which dark clouds and lightning are usually followed by loud claps of thunder, which cause fear. On other occasions, the child sees dark clouds, but there is no lightning or thunder. The child will acquire a stronger fear of lightning than of the dark clouds because lightning is more consistently paired with thunder.

　　Respondent Conditioning and Emotions.　Many unconditioned reflexes involve that part of our nervous system referred to as the *autonomic nervous system.* Our autonomic nervous system is involved in the activities of our internal functioning, such as heart beat, breathing, digestion, and glandular activity. These physiological activities are also involved when we experience what we label "emotional behavior." What happens inside you, for example, in a moment of great fear? Your body is physically aroused—mobilized for action. Your adrenal glands secrete adrenalin into your bloodstream for extra energy. Your heart rate increases dramatically. At the same time, you breathe much more rapidly, providing an increased supply of oxygen to the blood. This oxygen surges through your body with the increased heart rate, supplying more oxygen to your muscles.

At the same time that these changes are occurring, you get that "queasy" feeling in your stomach. Blood vessels to the stomach and intestines constrict and the process of digestion is interrupted, diverting blood from your internal organs to your muscles. Your mouth becomes dry as the action of the salivary glands is impeded. You might even temporarily lose bowel and/or bladder control. These internal reactions of the body mobilize your resources to prepare you to fight or to flee.

While the exact number of inherited emotional reflexes must await further research, there is no doubt about the importance of respondent conditioning for attaching physiological components of emotions to new stimuli. Since the time of Pavlov, Russian researchers have demonstrated that nearly every organ and gland controlled by the autonomic nervous system (see Figure 15–1) is susceptible to respondent conditioning (Airapetyantz & Bykov, 1966). When experimenters have demonstrated respondent conditioning of emotions with humans, they have often relied on the visible signs of the physiological changes to demonstrate that learning has occurred. Consider, for example, a classic experiment by Watson and Rayner (1920). They were interested in demonstrating that fears could be learned through Pavlovian procedures. They conducted their experiment with "Little Albert," an 11-month-old infant. During preliminary observations, it was demonstrated that Albert was not afraid of a variety of items that were placed in his vicinity when he was happily playing on a rug on the floor. Watson then introduced a white rat (of which Albert had previously shown no fear) and, while Albert was watching the rat closely, Watson banged a steel bar with a hammer just behind Albert's head. The loud noise caused startle, crying, and other fearful behavior in Albert. After a total of seven pairings of the loud noises within the sight of the rat over two separate sessions approximately one week apart, Albert showed a very strong fear reaction to the rat. Whenever the rat appeared, Albert cried, trembled, and showed the facial expression for fear. When other items were introduced, for which Albert had previously shown no fear, Albert's fear had spread to these items as well. In particular, this fear was transferred to a rabbit, a dog, a seal skin coat, and a piece of cotton. Unfortunately, Albert's parents moved away before Watson and Rayner had a chance to decondition the fear.[3]

Note 3

Following the Watson and Rayner experiment, Mary Cover Jones (1924) followed up some of Watson's suggestions and demonstrated a procedure to eliminate fear reactions in infants. The procedure is referred to as *respondent extinction.*

RESPONDENT EXTINCTION

The procedure of *respondent extinction* involves presenting a CS while withholding the US. After a number of such presentations, the CS gradually loses its capability of eliciting the CR. Let's suppose, for example, that a child reaches out to touch a large dog just as the dog barks very loudly, scaring the child. As a function of the pairing of the loud bark with the sight of the big dog, the sight of the big dog alone now elicits crying and trembling, a Pavlovian conditioned response that we label fear. Now let's suppose that the parent takes the child to a dog show. Although there are lots of large dogs around, they have been trained to walk and sit quietly while on display. Repeated contact with these dogs will help the child overcome fear of the sight of dogs. Sight of dogs loses its capability of functioning as a CS to elicit the fear reaction as a CR. Many of the fears that we acquire during childhood—fears of the dentist, the dark, thunder and lightning, etc.—undergo reflexive extinction as we grow older, as a function of repeated exposure to these things in the absence of dire consequences.

COUNTERCONDITIONING

Recall from Chapter 4 that operant extinction proceeds more quickly and effectively if an alternative response is reinforced. A similar rule holds for respondent extinction: A conditioned response may be eliminated more effectively if a new response is conditioned to the conditioned stimulus at the same time that the former conditioned response is being extinguished. This process is called *counterconditioning*. Stated technically, a CS will lose its capability to elicit a CR if that CS is paired with a stimulus that elicits a response that is incompatible with the CR. To illustrate this process, suppose that instead of simply exposing the child in the above example to dogs, we encouraged the child to play with another child who has a dog. As the child plays with his or her friend and the friend's dog, some of the positive emotions elicited by the friend will become conditioned to the friend's dog. These positive conditioned emotional responses will help counteract the negative conditioned emotional responses previously elicited by the dog, and thus more quickly and more effectively eliminate those responses.

RESPONDENT AND OPERANT CONDITIONING COMPARED

Respondent and operant conditioning procedures appear to influence two different kinds of behaviors. Nevertheless, there are a number of parallels between the procedures. Some of the differences and parallels between respondent and operant conditioning are presented in Figure 15–3.

	OPERANT	RESPONDENT
Type of Behavior	Behavior that is emitted by the individual; sometimes referred to as voluntary.	Respondent or reflexive; said to be elicited by prior stimuli; referred to as involuntary.
Reinforcement	*Procedure*: Presentation of a positive reinforce following a response (or the removal of an aversive stimulus following a response). *Result*: Behavior increases in frequency.	*Procedure*: Pairing of previously neutral stimulus with an unconditioned stimulus. *Result*: Neutral stimulus acquires capability of eliciting a conditioned response, and the stimulus is then called a conditioned stimulus.
Extinction	*Procedure*: Reinforcer is withheld following a previously reinforced response. *Result*: Response decreases in frequency.	*Procedure*: Conditioned stimulus is presented without further pairings with the unconditioned stimulus. *Result*: Conditioned stimulus loses capability of eliciting conditioned response.
Spontaneous recovery	*Procedure*: A "rest" period is introduced following an extinction session in which a behavior had completely decreased. *Result*: Following the rest, the previously extinguished response will again occur, although to a lesser extent than during the extinction session.	*Procedure*: A rest period is introduced following an extinction session in which trials occurred until a conditioned stimulus no longer elicited a conditioned response. *Result*: Following the rest, the conditioned stimulus again elicits a conditioned response, although to a lesser extend than during the extinction session.

FIGURE 15–3 Operant and respondent conditioning compared.

Any behavioral sequence is likely to include both respondent and operant conditioning. In some situations, we might select certain stimuli and responses from a sequence to study respondent conditioning. Or we might examine that same sequence somewhat differently and study operant conditioning. Consider the behavior sequence shown in Figure 15–4. As you can see, the sound of the bell in Figure 15–4 appears to be involved in both respondent and operant conditioning.

Another example of a behavioral sequence that involves both respondent and operant conditioning might be as follows. Suppose that a small child runs to pet a large dog. Never having had any reason to fear dogs, the child shows no fear now. Suppose, however, that the dog playfully jumps at the child and knocks him down. Quite naturally, the child will begin crying because of the pain and surprise of this rough treatment. Now what will happen the next time the child sees the dog or one that resembles it? Of course, the child will probably start crying and showing other types of fear behavior. Thus, a stimulus (sight of dog) that previously did not elicit a particular response (crying and other types of fear behavior) has come to do so because it was paired with a stimulus (suddenly being knocked down) that did elicit that response.

It is important to note that, in this example, the child's experience with the dog will have two important effects on the youngster's behavior. First, as we mentioned, the child will have a fear reaction (consisting of trembling, crying, the secretion of adrenalin into the blood, and an increased rate of heartbeat, among other things) whenever he sees a dog that resembles the one that knocked him down. This fear reaction to dogs is, as we mentioned, a response that has been respondently conditioned. Second, any behavior

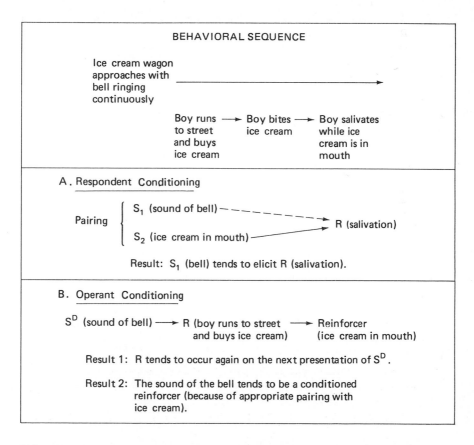

FIGURE 15–4 A behavioral sequence that includes both operant and respondent conditioning.

(such as looking over a backyard fence) that leads to the sight of a dog resembling the one that knocked him down will likely decrease in frequency. Moreover, the child will tend to avoid or get away from such dogs. In other words, those dogs will have become conditioned punishers for the child. In Chapter 13, we stated that a stimulus that is not punishing can become punishing if it is paired with a stimulus that is punishing. Some psychologists would theorize that the sight of the dog has become a conditioned punisher because it elicits fear as a result of respondent conditioning and that the fear

Note 4 so elicited is aversive.[4]

It is evident that the same procedure that will cause a stimulus to elicit fear will also cause that stimulus to be a conditioned punisher. This is illustrated in Figure 15–5.

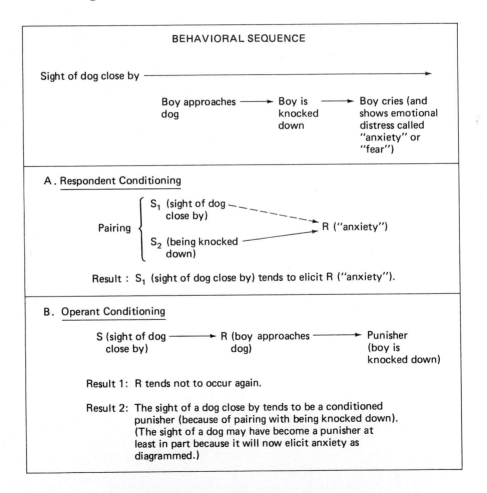

FIGURE 15–5 The development of a stimulus as a conditioned punisher. Some psychologists would theorize that, in this example, the sight of the dog has become a conditioned punisher because it elicits anxiety as a result of respondent conditioning.

It is not always possible to discuss a behavioral sequence just in terms of operant conditioning. For example, it might be said that the child in the preceding example had been punished for approaching dogs by having been knocked down by a dog. Although this might explain why the child no longer approaches dogs, it does not explain why he experiences fear (which can be measured in terms of internal bodily reactions, such as increased level of adrenaline in the blood and an increased rate of heartbeat) when he sees a dog. It therefore appears that it is necessary to add the principle of respondent conditioning to our list of basic behavioral principles (cf. Pear & Eldridge, 1984).

The behavior modification procedures described in subsequent pages of this chapter seem to be based in large measure on respondent conditioning. This is not to say that they do not also involve operant conditioning or that respondent conditioning was not operating in some of the procedures described previously in this book. Both types of conditioning are present and probably interact in virtually all behavior modification procedures. Although this complicates the description of behavior modification procedures, it probably does not hinder the practice of behavior modification. Indeed, as we have seen repeatedly throughout this book, increasing the number of principles that are applied to a behavior problem generally increases the likelihood that the treatment will be successful.

APPLICATIONS OF RESPONDENT CONDITIONING PRINCIPLES

AVERSION THERAPY

Certain kinds of positive reinforcers can be very troublesome. People who find pastries and other sweets overly reinforcing tend to eat too many fattening foods and become overweight. Similarly, people who find cigarettes, alcohol, and other harmful commodities overly reinforcing tend to overindulge in these reinforcers to the detriment of their health and well-being. People who obtain sexual reinforcement in socially unacceptable ways—for instance, by seducing children—tend to endanger others, by exposing them to potentially harmful experiences, and themselves, by risking imprisonment and other social sanctions.

Aversion therapy was developed largely as an attempt to counteract the power of undesirable reinforcers (those that tend to be overindulged in or that harm others). Before describing some of the methods of aversion therapy, we should caution the reader that their safe and effective use requires special expertise. These procedures, as the label aversion therapy implies, involve the use of aversive stimulation. As we have seen in Chapter 13, there are serious dangers in the use of aversive stimulation. It should therefore be used only by qualified experts who know when and how it is most likely to be effective, and how to guard against potentially harmful side effects.

Basically, aversion therapy involves the repeated pairing (that is, over a number of trials) of an undesirable reinforcer with an aversive event. The rationale of aversion therapy is counterconditioning; that is, it is assumed that the undesirable reinforcer should then become less reinforcing, because it will come to elicit a response similar to that elicited by the aversive stimulus.

For example, in the treatment of alcoholism, a person may be given a drug that will make him nauseous. Just before the drug takes effect, he is given a sip of an alcoholic beverage. Thus, the sight, smell, and taste of the drink is followed immediately by nausea. This pairing of alcohol with nausea is repeated over a number of sessions. Eventually, alcohol itself should tend to elicit nausea, which would tend to cause the individual to avoid alcohol. How well the therapy works in any given case probably depends, at least in part, on other treatment factors—such as whether the client continues taking the drug after leaving the hospital; and on operant processes operating in the natural environment—such as whether the client receives social reinforcement for his subsequent choosing of nonalcoholic over alcoholic beverages at parties, restaurants, and bars.

For instance, in a study in which alcoholics experienced the pairing of alcohol drinking with disulfiram (Antabuse) medication, less than 1 percent of the clients continued to take the drug after release from a hospital (Lubetkin, Rivers, & Rosenberg, 1971). In another study, only 7 percent of the patients continued to take disulfiram after one year (Ludwig, Levine, & Stark, 1970). However, an aversion-conditioning component involving disulfiram proved to be a valuable addition to a program for treating alcoholics that included a multiple-component behavior therapy program with procedures directed toward job finding, marital counseling, social and recreational programming, and a buddy system (Azrin, 1976; Azrin, Sisson, Meyers, & Godley, 1982). Similar results have also been obtained for cigarette smoking. The aversion-conditioning procedure in this case involved requiring subjects to rapidly smoke one cigarette after another until nausea occurred. In this way, the smell and flavor of cigarettes was paired with an aversive stimulus (nausea). This procedure, called rapid smoking aversion therapy, caused short-term cessation of smoking but did not show successful long-term effects (Danaher, 1977). However, when the rapid smoking aversion procedure was added to a multiple-component behavioral counseling program for quitting smoking, both short-term and long-term results were better than with the behavior counseling program alone (Tiffany, Martin, & Baker, 1986).

Symbolic representations (such as pictures, slides, and filmstrips) of the undesirable reinforcers, rather than the actual reinforcers themselves, are commonly used in aversion therapy. This is largely a matter of convenience. Hundreds of slides or filmstrips dealing with a wide variety of troublesome reinforcers can easily be stored in the therapist's office. Moreover, it is relatively easy to make new slides or filmstrips appropriate to individual cases. These stimuli can then be presented at specified intervals and for specified durations and can be associated with the onset or termination of the aversive stimulus in a precisely controlled manner. Moreover, their use precludes various problems that would arise if the actual undesirable reinforcers were used during therapy. To give an extreme example, one obviously would not use real children in treating a child molester. It is generally acceptable, however, to use pictures of children in various poses.

In many cases, aversion therapy is conducted not only in the absence of the actual undesirable reinforcers, but even in the absence of *external* representations of those reinforcers. Instead, *internal* representations are used. Most people can visualize internal pictures called images. Moreover, these internal images need not be merely visual; they can also be auditory (that is, one can imagine various sounds), tactile (one can imagine touching or being touched), kinesthetic (one can imagine making various movements), and so forth.

A procedure called *covert sensitization* (Cautela, 1966) involves having the client imagine both the undesirable reinforcer and the aversive stimulus. This procedure is so named because the pairing of the stimuli occurs only in the client's imagination (in other words, it is "covert") and the anticipated result of this covert pairing process is that the undesirable reinforcer becomes aversive (that is, the client becomes "sensitized" to it). One use of the procedure is with clients who wish to give up smoking (as described by Irey, 1972). For example, during a particular trial the client might be instructed to vividly imagine lighting a cigarette after dinner in a restaurant, inhaling, and then suddenly becoming so violently ill that he vomits all over his hands, his clothes, the tablecloth, and the other people at the table. He continues to vomit, and then, when his stomach is empty, to gag while the other people in the restaurant stare at him in amazement and disgust. In short, the scene is made extremely realistic and aversive. When the maximum degree of aversiveness is felt, the client is instructed to imagine turning away from his cigarette and immediately beginning to feel better. The scene concludes with the client washing up in the bathroom, without his cigarettes, and feeling tremendous
Note 5   relief.[5]

SYSTEMATIC DESENSITIZATION

As explained, aversion therapy works primarily by causing an undesirable reinforcer to become aversive, or at least less reinforcing. Often, however, the opposite type of problem is encountered: a stimulus that the client wishes to be reinforcing, or at least neutral, elicits a strong aversive reaction. A little boy who was bitten by a dog may continue long afterward to have a strong fear of dogs. It would, of course, be unfortunate if this fear prevented him from enjoying dogs who posed no real threat to him. Many people have fears that are so intense that they are virtually incapacitated by them. For example, a person might have such an intense fear of heights that he cannot walk up a single flight of stairs or look out of a second-story window without experiencing acute anxiety. Or, to take another example, a person might be so terrified of crowds that she cannot bear to go into public places. Surprising as it may seem, trying to convince these people that their fears are irrational often has no beneficial effect. They usually know that their fears have no rational basis and would like to control them but cannot because the fears are automatically elicited by specific stimuli. Such intense, irrational, incapacitating fears, are called *phobias*.

One method that has proved quite effective for treating phobias was developed by Wolpe (1958). (For a brief history of this method, see Chapter 27.) Wolpe based his treatment on the process of counterconditioning. He hypothesized that a reasonable treatment for phobias was to identify responses that were opposite to fear and to teach the client to engage in those responses in situations that normally produced fear. The three classes of responses that he used to inhibit fear were relaxation, assertion responses, and sexual responses. The fear-antagonistic behavior that Wolpe found most suitable to his purpose was relaxation, and the term used to describe his therapy that incorporates relaxation is *systematic desensitization*.

A procedure for training people to relax their muscles completely had been developed previously by Jacobson (1938), and Wolpe (1958, 1990) adapted this procedure for use with his clients who experienced debilitating fears. In general, the relaxation procedures require a client to tense and then relax a set of muscles so that they are more deeply relaxed following the tensing than before. The client is taught to apply this tension-relaxation exercise to muscles of all major areas of the body (such as arms, neck, face, and shoulders). By following the appropriate procedures during several training sessions, many individuals can eventually learn to relax deeply in a matter of minutes. (A more detailed description of this procedure is given in Chapter 24.)

Systematic desensitization first involves teaching the client to readily induce deep muscle relaxation. In addition, by interviewing the client thoroughly, the therapist obtains a detailed description of all the stimuli and situations that are related to the debilitating fear or anxiety that the client experiences. Thus, the therapist identifies not only those stimuli that elicit the most intense anxiety, but also related stimuli that elicit lesser degrees of anxiety. The client then rates these stimuli on a 100-point scale in which a rating of 0 indicates that the stimulus elicits no amount of anxiety and a rating of 100 indicates that it elicits the greatest amount of anxiety. The anxiety-eliciting stimuli or situations are then arranged in a hierarchy, with those that elicit the least anxiety at the bottom and those that elicit the most anxiety at the top. The following hierarchy might be constructed for a client who is terrified of riding in crowded elevators:

9. Being pressed against the wall in an elevator that is filled to capacity.
8. Being in an elevator that is three-fourths full.
7. Being the only passenger in an elevator.

6. Being in an elevator that has four people in it.

5. Being in an elevator that has two people in it.

4. Standing outside an elevator door waiting for the elevator to arrive.

3. Walking toward an elevator 20 feet away.

2. Walking toward an elevator from the front door of the building in which it is located.

1. Walking to an appointment on the top floor of a tall building that has an elevator.

Note that, although the client in this hypothetical example is most afraid of being in an elevator that is filled to capacity, he is also more frightened of being the only passenger in an elevator than of being in an elevator with several other people. This illustrates that it is important to construct a hierarchy that is valid for the particular client. A hierarchy that is valid for one client may not be valid for another, even though both may have the same general type of phobia. (For an example of a more complex hierarchy from an actual case, see Chapter 24, Table 24-1.)

After the therapist has taught the client how to induce self-relaxation and has constructed a hierarchy of anxiety-eliciting stimuli (or several hierarchies, if the client has more than one type of debilitating fear), therapy begins. While relaxing on a couch, the client is instructed to imagine clearly the first scene in the hierarchy. If the client experiences any anxiety whatsoever while visualizing the scene, he signals this to the therapist by raising one finger (this minimal signaling response is used so that the client does not disrupt his relaxed state). If no anxiety has been signaled, then the therapist, after about 7 to 10 seconds, signals the client to relax and to stop imagining the scene. Following approximately 15 to 30 seconds of relaxation, the client is again requested to imagine the scene. After two successes of imagining a scene (with a 15- to 30-second period of relaxation after each presentation), the therapist then instructs the client to clearly imagine the next scene in the hierarchy. At the first indication of anxiety, the therapist immediately instructs the client to cease imagining the scene. Then, after the client is again completely relaxed, the therapist instructs him to imagine the previous scene. If no anxiety is experienced with that scene, the next scene in the hierarchy is attempted again. In this manner of alternately imagining scenes and then relaxing without imagining them, the client proceeds gradually through the least anxiety-eliciting to the most anxiety-eliciting scenes. At each step, relaxation counteracts the anxiety elicited by that scene. When the client finishes the last scene in the hierarchy, he can generally encounter the actual feared **Note 6** situations without undue distress.[6] No doubt the positive reinforcement he then receives helps to maintain his continued interactions with the stimuli that previously elicited intense, debilitating fear.

A variation on the systematic desensitization procedure is referred to as "in vivo desensitization." This is a procedure in which the individual desensitizes a fear in "real life" (in vivo) rather than desensitizing the fear in his or her imagination, as described in this chapter. The steps for in vivo desensitization are very similar to those described above, except that rather than progressing through a hierarchy of imagined fear situations, the individual actually approaches the fear-producing stimuli. In vivo desensitization has been used to overcome fears of darkness, birds, animals, and a variety of other situations for which it is relatively easy to arrange for real-life hierarchies.

Guidelines for using systematic desensitization are presented in Chapter 24.

OTHER RESPONDENT-CONDITIONING APPLICATIONS

Most applied respondent-conditioning procedures presently in use involve the establishment or elimination of aversive reactions to specific stimuli. It would be a mistake, however, to think that this exhausts the possibilities. Therefore, this chapter concludes with two examples of other uses of respondent conditioning.[7]

Note 7

One example is a treatment for chronic constipation that was developed by Quarti and Renaud (1964). Defecation, the desired response in cases of constipation, can be elicited by administering a laxative. However, reliance on such drugs to achieve regularity is not the healthiest solution because of the undesirable side effects that often result. Quarti and Renaud therefore had their clients present themselves with a distinctive electrical stimulus—a mild, nonpainful electric current—immediately prior to defecating. Defecation was initially elicited by a laxative, and then the amount of the drug was gradually decreased until defecation was elicited by the electrical stimulus alone. Then, by applying the electrical stimulus at the same time each day, several of the clients were also able to get rid of the electrical stimulus, because the natural environment stimuli characteristically present at that time each day acquired control over the behavior of defecating. Thus, these clients achieved regularity without the continued use of artificial stimulation. (Also see Rovetto, 1979).

The second example of a respondent-conditioning treatment that does not involve conditioning or counterconditioning of aversive states is a treatment for enuresis (bed-wetting). One possible explanation for enuresis, a problem that is rather common in young children, is that pressure on the child's bladder when he is asleep and has to urinate does not provide sufficient stimulation to awaken him. A device that seems to be effective for many enuretic children consists of a buzzer connected to a special pad under the bottom sheet on the child's bed (see, for instance, Mowrer, 1938; Wickes, 1958). The apparatus is wired so that the buzzer sounds and awakens the child as soon as the first drop of urine makes contact with the pad. Eventually, in many cases the child will awaken before he urinates—apparently because the response of waking up has been conditioned to the stimulus of pressure

FIGURE 15–6 An example of a failure to identify all anxiety-eliciting stimuli prior to desensitization.

on the bladder. Naturally, the procedure should be supplemented with reinforcement to the child when he goes to the toilet at night so that this behavior will occur instead of bed-wetting.

Some general guidelines for using respondent conditioning are as follows:

1. Identify a stimulus (S_2) that reliably elicits the response that you desire to condition.
2. Identify a stimulus (S_1) that does not presently elicit the response but that would be convenient or desirable to have elicit the response.
3. Repeatedly pair the two stimuli by presenting S_1 first and quickly (within 0.5 to 1.0 seconds) follow it with S_2 (see also the subsection "Factors Influencing Respondent Conditioning").
4. Gradually decrease the number of trials during which S_2 is presented, but continue to present S_1 so that it alone will eventually elicit the response.

A CAUTIONARY NOTE

Chapters 3 through 13 of this book described basic principles and procedures of operant conditioning, along with guidelines for their application. Chapter 14 presented information on escape and avoidance conditioning, and Chapter 15 presented information on aversion therapy (including covert sensitization) and systematic desensitization. Chapters 16 through 25 describe additional information for designing and executing behavioral programs. We believe that mastery of the material in Chapters 3 through 13 and 16 through 25 will enable the reader to design, implement, and maintain a variety of behavior modification programs effectively. We do not make such a claim for the material in Chapters 14 and 15. Additional information and guidance are necessary before the reader attempts to carry out programs involving escape or avoidance conditioning, aversion therapy (including covert sensitization) and systematic desensitization. Chapter 24 provides information for carrying out a self-desensitization program.

STUDY QUESTIONS

1. What is the basic tenet of operant conditioning?
2. Give five examples of unconditioned reflexes (two of which are not in the text). Describe both the stimulus and the response.
3. State the principle of respondent conditioning. Clearly describe and diagram three examples of respondent conditioning (one of which is not in the text).
4. In a sentence each, briefly describe four variables that influence the development of a conditioned reflex.
5. State the principle of respondent extinction. Describe an example of respondent extinction.
6. Define and give an example of the following: unconditioned stimulus, unconditioned response, conditioned stimulus, conditioned response.
7. Compare respondent and operant conditioning in terms of behavior, reinforcement, extinction, and spontaneous recovery.
8. Explain how respondent conditioning and operant conditioning can interact to cause an individual to escape or avoid a particular stimulus. Use diagrams and examples to clarify your explanation.

9. For what general type of problem is aversion therapy used? Give three examples (one of which is not in the text).
10. Why should aversion therapy be used only by competent professional practitioners?
11. Describe the basic procedure and rationale of aversion therapy. Give an example of aversion therapy.
12. Describe the basic procedure and rationale of covert sensitization. Give an example of covert sensitization.
13. For what general type of problem is systematic desensitization used? Give an example.
14. Explain why relaxation is used in systematic desensitization.
15. Explain how a hierarchy of aversive situations is constructed in systematic desensitization.
16. In one page or less, summarize the basic procedure of systematic desensitization.
17. Who developed systematic desensitization?
18. What is in vivo desensitization?
19. Briefly describe a respondent-conditioning procedure for treating constipation.
20. Describe a respondent-conditioning procedure for treating enuresis.

EXTENDED DISCUSSION AND NOTES

1. Experiments by Pavlov and his followers seemed to indicate that just about any stimulus could be readily established as a CS in just about any species, provided that the stimulus preceded a US by a few seconds on several trials. Modern research, however, has indicated that organisms are biologically predisposed to be more readily conditioned to some stimuli than to others. Rats, for example, are foragers. Because they will eat almost anything, the probability is high that they will eat something that might poison them. From an evolutionary point of view, rats that evolve with a great sensitivity to any taste associated with food that makes them sick are rats that will be more likely to survive. And, sure enough, giving a rat a taste of something just before making it sick will establish that taste as a CS, causing the rats to develop an aversion to the taste (Garcia, Hankins, & Rusiniak, 1974). This occurs with just a single pairing between the taste and the sickness. And tastes can easily become CSs for nausea in rats even though those tastes occur up to an hour or more before the rats become sick (Garcia, Ervin, & Koelling, 1966). On the other hand, because rats tend to live much of their lives in dark passages, the sight of their food plays a less important role than does its taste. It's not surprising, then, that rats are more easily conditioned to show aversion to tastes than to visual cues (Garcia & Koelling, 1966).

Birds, conversely, rely greatly on their vision in obtaining food. It's not surprising that, with them, it is easier to condition food aversion to the color of food than to its taste (Wilcoxin, Dragoin, & Kral, 1971). What about humans? Are we biologically predisposed to be more readily conditioned to some neutral stimuli than to others? In some cases, at least, it appears that we are. Some experiments on learning fears, for example, have shown that humans are very quick to learn fears to stimuli that may have posed a threat to our survival during our evolution, such as snakes, insects, and heights, while we are much slower to learn fears to stimuli that were likely nonthreatening in our history, such as pictures of flowers (Hugdahl & Ohman, 1977; Ohman, Dimberg, & Ost, 1984).

2. Pavlov thought that the simple pairing of a neutral stimulus with a US automatically led to conditioning. However, this appears not to be the case. Consider an experiment on a phenomenon called *blocking*. In the first part of an experiment a group of rats is given a number of tone-shock pairings. As Pavlov would predict, the tone quickly becomes a CS eliciting fear as a CR. In the second part of the experiment, each time that the tone is paired with the shock, a light is simultaneously presented with a tone. Will the light (because it is also paired with shock) become a CS eliciting fear? Pavlov would say yes. Surprisingly, however, even after many trials, the light elicits very little fear in the animals in comparison to the tone (Halas & Eberhardt, 1987). It is as though the association between tone and shock "blocks" any association between light and shock. Stated differently, the tone was already a good predictor that shock would follow. Merely adding a light to the tone did not improve the predictability of the occurrence of the shock. These and other such findings have led Robert Rescorla to argue that conditioning occurs between the CS and US "not simply because they occur contiguously in time, but rather because the CS provides information about the US" (1987, p. 121). While Rescorla's interpretation has its critics (Furedy & Riley, 1987; Wasserman, 1989; also see note 1 of Chapter 8 for commentary regarding problems with mixing such cognitive terms as "information" with well-defined behavioral terms), there is no doubt that our understanding of Pavlovian conditioning has changed over the years. We now have many research findings that enable us to specify the conditions under which Pavlovian conditioning will and will not occur (Turkkan, 1989).

3. Most instances of what we would refer to as emotional behavior involve both respondent and operant components. Some event (either a CS or a US) elicits an internal reaction (a reflexive response that consists of some activity of the autonomic nervous system), and the internal reaction often has visible counterparts that we interpret as an immediate expression of emotion (a red face, clenched jaw, narrowed eyes, etc.). Operant components of emotion are involved in secondary displays of emotion. These are the different ways that individuals have learned to deal with emotional situations. To a situation that causes the reaction that we might call anger, for example, one person might shout, swear, and throw things. Another person in that same situation might simply count to ten silently to himself or herself. The form of these operant components depends on the individual's reinforcement history. For a more detailed behavioral analysis of emotional behavior, see Martin and Osborne (1989).

4. This theoretical description of how an interaction between respondent and operant processes can result in escape behavior, avoidance behavior, and punishment was first formulated systematically by Mowrer (1960). The theory is called *two-factor theory* because it is based on two principles of conditioning. It should be noted that this theory is not accepted by some learning theorists. For a discussion of data and theory concerning operant-respondent interactions, see Pear and Eldridge (1984).

5. Covert sensitization has also been conceptualized as a covert punishment procedure (Walker, Hedberg, Clement, & Wright, 1981). Within this conceptualization, the individual is prompted to imagine (a) a particular stimulus situation (such as being at home alone at night); (b) then emitting an approach behavior in that situation (such as walking to the liquor cabinet, taking out some wine, pouring it into a glass); (c) then experiencing an aversive stimulus as a punishing consequence for the approach behavior (such as seeing worms crawl out of the wine

glass and slither up the individual's hand and arm); (d) then escaping from that scene and emitting some other alternative behavior that is associated with relief.

6. Turner, Ditomasso, and Deluty (1985) reviewed research on the efficacy of systematic desensitization for specific disorders. As in previous reviews, they indicated that the desensitization literature consisted largely of uncontrolled case studies. Where experimental studies were conducted, they suffered from methodological problems inherent in much of psychotherapy research, as well as procedural problems concerning the alternative treatments to which desensitization was compared. Nevertheless, they concluded that systematic desensitization was an effective procedure for a number of disorders. Specifically, there is strong evidence that desensitization is an effective treatment for a variety of adult phobic disorders. An exception is agoraphobia, for which desensitization is not generally successful. Both speech anxiety and test anxiety also respond well to systematic desensitization. Desensitization appears to be an effective adjunct to treatment of sexual disorders in which anxiety is a major component. Numerous uncontrolled case studies suggest that desensitization produces a positive treatment effect with obsessive-compulsive disorder and depression, but controlled experimental trials are lacking with these disorders. Case studies have also been conducted concerning desensitization with muscle contraction disorders, Gilles de la Tourette's syndrome, and seizure disorders, but no controlled experimental trials were reported. In conclusion, desensitization still appears to be an effective treatment for a number of disorders. Additional controlled research, however, is needed in a number of areas.

7. Ader and Cohen (1982) demonstrated that Pavlovian conditioning procedures may affect the functioning of our immune system. In an experiment with rats, they paired saccharine-sweetened drinking water with injections of a drug known to suppress immune functioning (the drug also caused nausea, which they were studying at the time). After a number of trials, the rats developed a taste aversion for the saccharine (presumably because of its association with nausea). To eliminate the taste aversion to the saccharine, the experimenters force-fed the rats saccharine for several days. Unexpectedly, some of the animals died approximately 40 days after the study. Subsequent experiments indicated that the pairing of saccharine with the immune-suppressive drug established saccharine as a conditioned stimulus eliciting immune suppression. Force-feeding the rats on this conditioned stimulus weakened the rats sufficiently that the experimental animals could no longer resist the invasion of pathogens. Other studies have also successfully demonstrated classical conditioning of various aspects of immune responses in other species (Ader & Cohen, 1985; Turkkan, 1989). This exciting new area of research on the effects of conditioning processes on the functioning of the body's immune system is called *psychoimmunology*, or *psychoneuroimmunology*. Ader and Cohen (1985) have raised some fascinating questions concerning this new area. If it is possible to demonstrate that a neutral stimulus like saccharine can be conditioned to suppress immune system functioning, is it also possible to respondently condition our immune system to be even more effective in battling invaders? If so, might such a procedure help our bodies fight cancerous growths and other diseases? Could this provide a mechanism for treating acquired immune deficiency syndrome (AIDS). Future research will address such questions.

STUDY QUESTIONS ON NOTES

1. Briefly describe some evidence indicating that organisms are biologically predisposed to be more readily conditioned to some neutral stimuli than to others.

2. Briefly describe the respondent conditioning experiment on "blocking." How does Robert Rescorla interpret the results of this and other experiments on respondent conditioning?

3. Illustrate with an example how emotional behavior might include both respondent and operant components.

4. Describe how covert sensitization might be conceptualized as a punishment procedure.

5. In a sentence, what is the field known as psychoimmunology?

CHAPTER 16

Short-Cut Tactics with Stimulus Control:
Instruction, Modeling, Guidance, and Situational Inducement

Consider the following general categories of behavior problems:

1. A desired behavior occurs too infrequently.
2. An undesired behavior occurs too frequently.
3. A desired behavior never occurs.
4. A desired behavior occurs, but in the presence of inappropriate stimuli and not in the presence of appropriate stimuli.

Thus far, what basic procedures for dealing with such problems has this book given you? For category 1, you will probably answer "reinforcement." For 2, you will probably say "extinction, reinforcement of alternative behavior, DRL, DRO, DRI, punishment, and counterconditioning." For 3, you will probably reply "chaining and shaping." And for category 4, you will probably respond "stimulus discrimination training and fading."

A perfect score—very good! (Of course, we gave you some modeling just in case you needed it—but more about that later.) Before rushing ahead with a program based on these techniques, let us reflect on whether there might not be some faster or easier way in which to achieve your objective. Specifically, what we have in mind is looking for stimuli that already control the desired behavior and, if possible, devising a strategy that incorporates them. Such use of existing forms of stimulus control can be conveniently discussed under the headings of instruction, modeling, physical guidance, and situational inducement.

INSTRUCTION

In Chapter 3 we defined instructions as rules or guidelines (i.e., verbal stimuli) that indicate that specific behaviors will pay off in particular situations. When we were infants, instructions were meaningless to us. But as we grew older, we learned that following instructions often led to rewards ("If you eat all your potatoes, you can have an extra dessert"), or enabled us to avoid punishers ("If you don't be quiet, I'll send you to your room"). In other words, instructions or rules were S^Ds, and they gradually acquired stimulus control over our behavior.

Sometimes rules clearly identify reinforcers or punishers associated with following the rules, as illustrated in the above examples. In other cases, consequences are implied. When a parent says to a child in an excited voice, "Wow! Would you look at that!," looking in the implied direction will likely enable the child to see something interesting. On the other hand, if a parent sternly says to a child, "Don't touch that!," the instruction carries the implication that the child touching the implied item is likely to lead to a punisher. By the time we are adults, we all follow instructions to a high degree, and we all use instructions to influence the behavior of others. Many people, however, do not fully appreciate what a powerful behavior modification procedure instruction is. Powerful instructional control was demonstrated quite humorously numerous times on the television program "Candid Camera." For example, in one stunt the signs MEN and WOMEN were placed on two adjacent telephone booths. The result was that some people stayed out of the booth designated for the opposite sex even when it was unoccupied and they had to wait in line to use the phone in the other booth.

Contextual stimuli, described in Note 3 of Chapter 8, can influence the extent to which we follow instructions. You are more likely to follow advice regarding your career if it is given to you by a close friend, for example, rather than by a stranger in the street. On the other hand, if you and your friend are visiting a foreign city, you are more likely to follow directions to find a particular restaurant if you are instructed by a stranger in the street, rather than by your friend. Contextual influences on the effects of instruction can also be seen with children who are obedient with adults at school but not with their parents at home.

You may have heard parents complain: "I don't know how many times I've told that kid _____ (insert "to pick up his clothes"; "to mow the grass"; "to do his homework"; "to come home at a decent hour"; "not to track mud into the house"; "not to play his stereo so loud"; "not to stay on the phone so long"; "not to slam the door"; etc.) but he never listens." To the behavior modifier, it is no mystery that such instruction is not effective: in the past, the parent probably has not consistently reinforced appropriate responses **Note 1**   and extinguished inappropriate responses to instructions.[1]

As we indicated in earlier chapters, behavior modification programs should always include instruction in the form of rules that can be followed easily. Correct use of rules can produce behavior change much more rapidly than shaping or trial-and-error experiences with reinforcement and extinction. This was illustrated by an experience of one of the authors when he was a graduate student in the 1960s. While doing research for his master's thesis at an institution for retarded people, he decided to demonstrate the effectiveness of positive reinforcement to some of the other students. A retarded girl named Shirley who was working in the kitchen generally piled all the plates, dishes, cups, and utensils in one particular area after drying them. The author decided to use social approval to reinforce putting the plates and dishes in one area and the cups and utensils in another area. After each meal, the author faithfully stood around the kitchen ignoring Shirley when she put everything in one pile, but smiling and nodding his approval when she put the articles in appropriate separate piles. Very little progress occurred over several meals, and the author could see that the training process was probably going to be anything but rapid. At about this time, one of the nurses came into the kitchen and asked the author what he was trying to do. After he told her, she immediately said, "Oh, if that's all you want, that's simple. Shirley, from now on, put the plates and dishes here and the cups and utensils over there." From then on, Shirley did just that. The moral is obvious: if you want someone to do something, first try giving instructions. It may not always work, but when it does, it takes much less time and effort than painstakingly waiting for the behavior to occur before you reinforce it. Of course, reinforcement should be applied just the same to ensure the maintenance of the behavior at a high level.

Here are some general guidelines for the effective use of instruction:

1. Instruction should be within the understanding of the individual to whom it is applied.
2. Instruction should specify the behavior in which the individual is to engage.
3. Instruction should specify contingencies involved in complying (or not complying) with it, and these contingencies should be applied consistently.
4. Complex instruction should be broken down into easy-to-follow steps.
5. Instruction should be sequenced so that it proceeds gradually from very easy to more difficult behavior for the individual being treated.
6. Instruction should be delivered in a pleasant, courteous manner.
7. Fading should be used as necessary to phase out instruction if you want other stimuli that are present to take control of the behavior.

MODELING

Modeling is a procedure whereby a sample of a given behavior is presented to an individual to induce that individual to engage in a similar behavior. As **Note 2** is true for instruction, it can be quite powerful.[2] You may convince yourself of this by performing the following simple experiments:

1. For an entire day speak only in a whisper, and note how often people around you also whisper (this is a good experiment to try when you have laryngitis).
2. Yawn conspicuously in the presence of other people, and note their frequency of yawning.
3. Stand looking in a window of an empty department store for an hour, and note how many people stop and also look in the window.

In each case, compare the data obtained with data obtained under comparable circumstances when the behavior is not being modeled.

Note 3   As with instruction, modeling is in such common use by the general public that few people (other than behavior modifiers) think of it as a behavior modification procedure.[3] Parents, for example, use it rather unsystematically, but quite effectively in many cases, to teach language and other behavior to their children. Behavior modifiers use it in much the same way, although more systematically, to teach a variety of behaviors, as described in Chapter 9.

Modeling often involves having an individual observe a peer who is performing appropriately. For example, consider the case of an extremely withdrawn nursery school child who almost never interacts with other children. This behavior problem could be treated with shaping. A method that can perhaps produce faster results, however, is to have the child observe several instances of another child joining in the activities of a group of children. The group should be responding to the model in a reinforcing manner (for example, by offering her play material, talking to her, and smiling). To ensure that the modeling occurs under opportune circumstances and in a suitable fashion, it may be necessary to instruct certain children to perform as models and to instruct the children in the group to behave in a conspicuously reinforcing manner to the models. It is sometimes convenient and effective to film or videotape a number of such episodes for viewing by socially withdrawn children (see O'Connor, 1969). The presentation of modeling scenes through film, videotape, and other media is called *symbolic modeling*. Studies

Note 4   show that this type of modeling can sometimes be as effective as the real thing[4] (see, for instance, Masters & Driscoll, 1971).

Modeling is frequently used with adults who possess highly developed behavioral repertoires. The following excerpt from a therapy session illustrates this (Masters, Burrish, Hollon, & Rimm, 1987, pp. 100–101. The client being treated was a male college student who had difficulty asking for dates over the telephone. In the excerpt, the client is rehearsing asking for a date. Note how the therapist combines instruction and shaping with modeling.

Client: By the way (pause) I don't suppose you want to go out Saturday night?

Therapist: Up to actually asking for the date you were very good. However, if I were the woman, I think I might have been a bit offended when you said "By the way." It's like your asking her out is pretty casual. Also, the way you phrased the question, you are kind of suggesting to her that she doesn't want to go out with you. Pretend for the moment I'm you. Now, how does this sound: "There's a movie at the Varsity Theater this Saturday that I want to see. If you don't have other plans, I'd very much like to take you."

Client: That sounded good. Like you were sure of yourself and liked the woman too.

Therapist: Why don't you try it.

Client: You know that movie at the Varsity? Well, I'd like to go, and I'd like to take you Saturday, if you don't have anything better to do.

Therapist: Well, that certainly was better. Your tone of voice was especially good. But the last line, "if you don't have anything better to do," sounded like you don't think you have much to offer. Why not run through it one more time?

Client: I'd like to see the show at the Varsity, Saturday, and, if you haven't made other plans, I'd like to take you.

Therapist: Much better. Excellent, in fact. You were confident, forceful, and sincere.

Here are some general guidelines for the effective use of modeling:

1. The complexity of the modeled behavior should be suitable for the behavioral level of the client.
2. Combine instructions with modeling.
3. Reinforcement should be given for correct imitation of the modeled behavior.
4. The modeling episode should be sequenced from very easy to more difficult behavior for the individual being treated.
5. To enhance stimulus generalization the modeling scenes should be as realistic as possible.
6. Use fading as necessary so that stimuli other than the model can take control over the desired behavior.

PHYSICAL GUIDANCE

Physical guidance is the application of physical contact to induce an individual to go through the motions of the desired behavior. Some familiar examples of guidance are a dance instructor leading a pupil through a new dance step, a golf instructor grasping the novice's arms and moving them through the proper swing and follow-through, and a parent holding a child's hand while teaching her to cross the street safely. Guidance is always only one component of a teaching procedure. Both the dance instructor and the golf instructor will also use instruction (they will tell the student what to do and give her "pointers"), modeling (they will demonstrate the appropriate physical postures and motions), and reinforcement for correct responses or approximations to them (such as "Excellent!" or "Much better!"). Likewise, the parent teaching her child to cross the street safely will use instruction (for example, by saying, "Look both ways") and modeling (for example, by looking both ways in an exaggerated manner).

Some uses of guidance in behavior modification programs were given in Chapter 9—for example, using guidance and fading to teach a child to touch his head upon request. Guidance is generally used in procedures for teaching instruction following and model imitation, so that instruction and modeling can then be used to establish other behaviors. For example, in one procedure for teaching instruction following, a child is placed in a chair opposite the teacher. At the beginning of a trial the teacher says, "Johnny, stand up" and then lifts the child onto his feet. Reinforcement is then presented immediately, as though the child himself had performed the response. Next, the teacher says, "Johnny, sit down," and grasping the child's shoulders the teacher gently but firmly presses him down on the chair. Again, immediate reinforcement is presented. The process is repeated over numerous trials while guidance is faded out (see Kazdin & Erickson, 1975). After this set of instructions is learned, the behavior modifier teaches another set (such as "Come here" and "Go there"), using a similar procedure. Less and less fading may be required to teach successive instructions, until eventually even fairly complex instruction-following behavior can be taught with little guidance.

As in teaching instruction following, the teacher who uses guidance to teach model imitation starts with a few simple imitations (such as touching one's head, clapping one's hands, tapping the table, standing up, and sitting down) and adds new imitations as the previous ones are learned. This can involve teaching instruction following and model imitation at the same time, depending on the verbal stimuli presented. For example, the individual will learn to follow an instruction to imitate behavioral displays if the teacher says "Do this" while modeling the behavior. This might facilitate the development of **generalized imitation**, whereby an individual, after learning to imitate a number of behaviors (perhaps with some shaping, fading, guidance, and reinforcement), learns to imitate a new response on the first trial without reinforcement (Baer, Peterson & Sherman, 1967).

Another common application of guidance is in helping individuals to overcome fears. For example, helping a person who is terrified of water might involve gradually leading her by the hand into the shallow end of a swimming pool and supporting her while she floats. The least fear-provoking aspects of a situation should be introduced first, and the more fear-provoking aspects later in a very gradual manner. One should never try to force an individual **Note 5** to do more than she feels comfortable doing.[5] The more fearful the person is, the more gradual the process should be. In the case of a very fearful individual one may have to spend many sessions simply sitting with her on the edge of the pool.

Some general guidelines for the effective use of guidance are as follows:

1. Reinforcement should be given immediately after the successful completion of the guided response.
2. Guidance should be sequenced gradually from very easy to more difficult behavior for the individual being treated.
3. The stimuli you want to eventually control the behavior should be conspicuously present during guidance.
4. Use fading as necessary so that other stimuli can take control over the behavior.

SITUATIONAL INDUCEMENT

Largely because of our similar histories of reinforcement and punishment, there are numerous situations and occasions in our society that control similar behavior in many of us. The interiors of certain public buildings, such as churches, museums, and libraries, tend to suppress loud talking. Parties tend to evoke socializing and jovial, carefree behavior. Catchy melodies prompt humming and singing, and strident march music tends to incite participation in a foot-stamping parade. The assorted stimuli associated with Christmas induce cheerfulness, friendliness, and gift buying.

The term *situational inducement* refers to influencing a behavior by using situations and occasions that already exert control over the behavior. Such techniques, like others we have discussed, no doubt predate recorded history. Ceremonious gatherings involving singing and dancing probably served to strengthen "togetherness" in ancient tribes, just as they do today in almost all cultures. Monasteries and convents have been used for centuries to promote asexual religious behavior by providing an environment conducive to reading religious texts and meditating and by restricting opportunities for the sexes to interact.

Supermarkets and department stores use many situational features to induce buying. Among these are the attention-evoking manner in which the products are displayed and pictures showing the products in an attractive way. Fine restaurants provide a relaxing atmosphere to induce leisurely enjoyment of a full-course meal. If the restaurant becomes crowded and people are waiting for tables, fast music may be played to induce rapid eating.

Examples of situational inducement can also be found in the home. Many people have unusual objects in their living room that function as "conversation pieces." If the conversation lags when guests are present, a rare decorative vase may stimulate someone to initiate a new line of conversation with a remark such as, "Oh, where did you get that beautiful Ming vase?" or "I saw one just like it on my recent trip to China." Such fragile conversation pieces tend also to induce undesirable handling behavior, especially in children. When this happens, the host may use situational inducement by quickly handling the potential offender something less expensive, such as a toy or a drink.

Situational inducement has been used in a number of imaginative and effective ways in behavior modification programs to help increase or decrease target behaviors, or to bring them under appropriate stimulus control. Examples can be discussed conveniently under four somewhat overlapping categories: (1) rearranging the existing surroundings, (2) moving the activity to a new location, (3) relocating people, and (4) changing the time of the activity.

REARRANGING THE EXISTING SURROUNDINGS

An interesting example in the first category occurred in a case reported by the well-known behaviorist Israel Goldiamond (1965). Goldiamond was consulted by a married couple who were having a problem in their relationship.* When the couple were together in the house, the husband could not refrain from screaming at his wife over her once having gone to bed with his best friend. One of the goals that was decided upon, therefore, was to replace screaming with civilized conversational behavior. Goldiamond reasoned that the husband's screaming had probably come under the control of the S^Ds in the home environment and that one way in which to weaken the behavior in that situation would be to change those S^Ds. He therefore instructed the couple to rearrange the rooms and furniture in the house to make it appear considerably different. The wife went one step further and bought herself a new outfit. Goldiamond then provided for the reinforcement of civilized conversation in the presence of these new S^Ds that were not associated so strongly with screaming (how he did this is explained more fully in the next section). It was important to do this as quickly as possible, because if screaming occurred too often in the presence of the new S^Ds, it would become conditioned to them just as it had been conditioned to the old S^Ds.

Another example of rearranging the existing surroundings is altering the furniture and other items in one's room to promote better and more persistent studying behavior. One might, for example, improve the lighting, clear one's desk of irrelevant material, move the bed as far as possible from the desk, and have the desk facing away from the bed. Better yet, if possible, one should not even have the bed in the same room as the desk because the bed is an S^D for sleeping. To prevent nonstudy behaviors from being conditioned to the new stimuli, one should engage only in studying behavior when in the rearranged environment (see Goldiamond, 1965).

---

*It should not be thought that this simplified example from the early days of behavior modification is representative of contemporary applications of behavior modification to marital counseling. More detailed discussion of this topic is given in Chapter 26, and in Bornstein and Bornstein (1986).

Letter writing is a behavior that is difficult to maintain because it involves a long delay of reinforcement (it takes at least several days to get a return letter). One way in which to strengthen your tendency to write, however, is to place before you a picture of the person to whom you are writing. This is another example of rearranging stimuli to control behavior. (Other examples are illustrated in Figure 16–1).[6]

Note 6

MOVING THE ACTIVITY TO A NEW LOCATION

The second category of situational inducement is illustrated by another part of the procedure Goldiamond used in the case of the husband who screamed at his wife. The spouses were instructed that, immediately after rearranging the furniture at their home, they were to go to a place that would induce civilized conversation. It was hoped that this behavior would continue until they returned home, and would then come under the control of the new S^Ds in the home.

To quote from Goldiamond's report (1965, p. 856),

> Since it was impossible for [the husband] to converse in a civilized manner with his wife, we discussed a program of going to one evening spot on Monday, another on Tuesday, and another on Wednesday.
>
> "Oh," he said, "you want us to be together. We'll go bowling on Thursday."
>
> "On the contrary," I said, "I am interested in your subjecting yourself to an environment where civilized chit-chat is maintained. Such is not the case at a bowling alley."
>
> I also asked if there was any topic of conversation which once started would maintain itself. He commented on his mother-in-law's crazy ideas about farming. He was then given an index card and instructed to write "farm" on it and to attach a $20 bill to that card. The $20 was to be used to pay the waitress on Thursday, at which point he was to start the "farm" discussion which hopefully would continue into the taxi and home.

Changing the location of the activity is one approach to problems relating to studying. The student using this approach should select a special place that is conducive to studying and that has distinctive stimuli that are not associated with any behavior other than studying. A reserved carrel in a university library is ideal for this purpose, although any other well-lit, quiet area with adequate working space would be suitable. Depending on the extent of appropriate study behavior in the student's repertoire, it may be necessary to combine relocating the activity with some of the basic procedures discussed in Part II of this text. For severe deficiencies, behavior incorporating good study skills should first be shaped and then placed on either a low-duration or a low-ratio schedule in the special studying area. The value of the schedule should then be increased gradually so that the behavior will eventually be maintained at the desired level. Appropriate reinforcement (such as coffee with a friend) should be arranged to occur immediately after the schedule

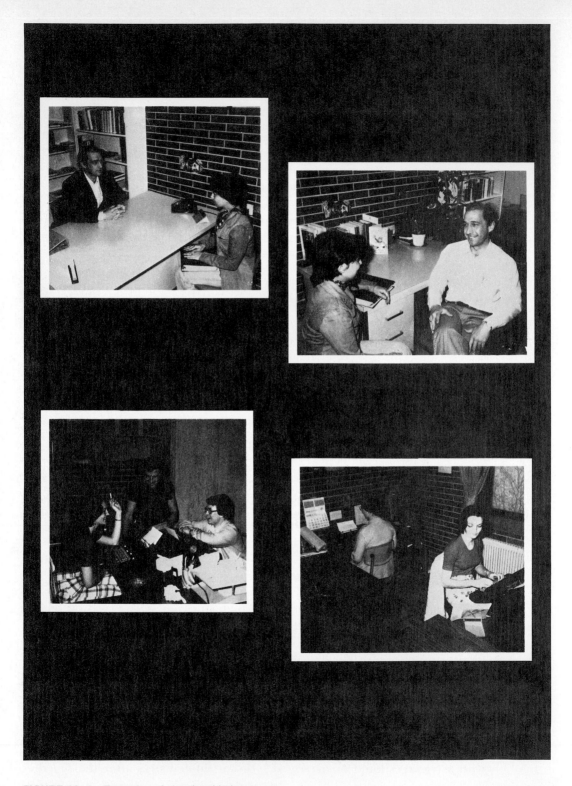

FIGURE 16–1 Examples of situational inducement.

requirement has been met. Should one experience a tendency to daydream or to engage in other nonstudy behavior while in the studying area, one should do a little more productive studying and then leave immediately so that daydreaming does not become conditioned to the stimuli in the studying area (see Fox, 1962). Similarly, the husband in the case reported by Goldiamond was instructed to go to the garage and sit on a specially designated "sulking" stool whenever he was in the house and felt a tendency to sulk—this being a behavior that was threatening the recently strengthened conversational behavior after screaming had been eliminated.

RELOCATING PEOPLE

The third category of situational inducement was not illustrated in Goldiamond's case study. The procedures used in that case were effective; therefore, a separation of the spouses was not necessary. Although relocating the participants is generally a measure of last resort when dealing with individuals who wish to maintain their respective relationships, it is sometimes the most practical tactic in other circumstances. If you just cannot get along with Sam Jones, and there is no particular reason for you to associate with him anyway, then why try to change his behavior and/or yours to make the two of you more compatible? Both of you will probably be happier respecting each other from a distance. Relocating people can also be used to bring about the opposite effect, that is, to bring people together. For example, getting dates is a problem for many college students. To deal with this problem, therapists often recommend to clients to increase their contact with the opposite sex.[7]

Note 7

Classroom teachers of small children often change seating arrangements to relocate pupils whose close proximity leads to various types of disruptions. This is usually much easier than designing and carrying out reinforcement and/or punishment programs to eliminate undesirable interactions, and the end result may be just as effective, or more so.

CHANGING THE TIME OF THE ACTIVITY

The final category of situational inducement involves taking advantage of the fact that certain stimuli and behavioral tendencies change predictably with the passage of time. For example, two sexual partners may find that sexual activity is better for them in the morning than at night when one of them is "too tired." Changing the time of an activity has been used effectively in weight-control programs. People who cook for their families sometimes put on excess weight by "nibbling" while preparing meals and then sitting down for a full-course dinner. Rather than foregoing dinner with one's family, a partial solution to this problem is to do the preparation, except for the actual cooking, shortly after having eaten the previous meal, while the tendency to eat is still relatively weak (see LeBow, 1981, 1989).

Situational inducement covers a very broad set of procedures. Its use, therefore, is considerably less straightforward than is that of the other methods discussed in this chapter. In short, a good deal of imagination is typically required if it is to be used effectively. We suggest the following guidelines:

1. Insofar as this is practical, arrange for the individual of concern to be exposed to locations and environmental arrangements that already control the target behavior in the desired way and to avoid locations and arrangements that do not have this control.

2. Determine whether it is necessary or desirable to extend the behavior to situations that do not presently exert desirable control over the behavior, and, if it is, take appropriate steps to bring this about.

3. Make sure that undesirable behavior never occurs in the presence of situations introduced to strengthen the desirable behavior.

STUDY QUESTIONS

1. What basic procedures discussed in Chapters 3–14 of this text might be used to
   a. increase an infrequent behavior?
   b. decrease an excessive behavior?
   c. develop a behavior that never occurs?
   d. get a desired behavior to occur in the presence of appropriate stimuli?

2. A teacher of a second-grade class complains to you, "When I tell the children to stay in their desks and work, they never listen to me." Describe the contingencies that are likely operating with respect to that instruction from the teacher to the kids in the class.

3. Explain (in terms of your past experiences with S^Ds, S^Δs, reinforcement, and extinction) why the tone of voice of someone giving you instructions might determine whether you will follow the instructions appropriately.

4. Describe two recent situations in which you were influenced by modeling to emit a behavior.

5. Describe the specific steps you might go through in using modeling to overcome the extreme withdrawal behavior of a nursery school child who never interacts with other children. Identify the basic principles and procedures being applied in your program.

6. In the dialogue between the client and the therapist concerning the client's difficulty in asking for dates, briefly describe
   a. how modeling was involved.
   b. how instructions were involved.
   c. how shaping was involved.

7. What is meant by symbolic modeling? Describe how this might explain how a city-dwelling child might learn to fear snakes.

8. What is meant by physical guidance? How does it differ from gestural prompting (see p. 126).

9. What is generalized imitation? Describe an example.

10. Identify a behavior that you were recently influenced to perform as a result of instructions, modeling, and physical guidance. Describe how each tactic was involved.

11. What do we mean by the term situational inducement? Which term given previously in this book has essentially the same meaning? (See p. 126)

12. Describe each of the four proposed categories of situational inducement.

13. Give an example from your own experience of each of the four categories of situational inducement.

14. For each of the following examples, identify the category of situational inducement in which it might best be placed and indicate why.
   a. On Saturday afternoon, an exercise buff can't seem to "get up the energy" to lift his weights. To increase his likelihood of weight-lifting, he places the weights in the center of the den (where he usually exercises), turns on the TV to the Saturday afternoon wrestling matches, and opens his *Muscle Beach* magazine to the Mr. America centerfold.
   b. It is said that Victor Hugo, the famous writer, controlled his work habits in his study by having his servant take his clothes away and not bring them back until the end of the day (Wallace, 1971, pp. 68–69).
   c. To stop drinking, an alcoholic surrounds himself with members of Alcoholics Anonymous and stops seeing his old drinking buddies.
   d. Another exercise buff has decided to jog a mile every night before going to bed. Alas, "the road to hell [or perhaps to heart attack] is paved with good intentions." Late nights, good TV, wine with dinner, and other delights take their toll. Three months later, our "exercise buff" is still fat and out of shape because of many missed jogging nights. He therefore changes the routine and begins jogging each day immediately upon arriving home and before eating dinner.
   e. After many interruptions while working on this book at the university, the authors began working at one of their homes.

15. According to the proposed guidelines for the use of instruction, modeling, and physical guidance,
   a. What behavioral principle is used with all three procedures?
   b. What two other behavioral procedures are likely to be used with all three procedures?

PRACTICE EXERCISES

1. Outline a program that a parent might follow to teach a two-year-old child to respond consistently to the instruction "Please bring me your shoes." Indicate how your program might use instructions, modeling, and guidance, and how it follows the guidelines for the effective application of each.

2. Select two behaviors from the following list:
   a. doing the dishes immediately after a meal
   b. getting up when the alarm rings
   c. feeling happy
   d. cleaning up your bedroom twice per week
   e. doing some exercises daily
   f. decreasing your cigarette smoking
   For each behavior, describe how you might influence the behavior by combining at least three of the following tactics: modeling, guidance, rearranging the existing surroundings, moving the activity to a new location, relocating people, and changing the time of the activity. Make your suggestions highly plausible in regard to the situation.

SELF-MODIFICATION EXERCISE

Identify one of your behaviors that you would like to modify (a deficit or an excess). Describe a plausible program that you might use successfully to modify that behavior. Include in your program at least five of the following procedures, and indicate how each is involved: instructions, modeling, guidance, rearranging the existing surroundings, moving the activity to a new location, relocating people, and changing the time of the behavior.

EXTENDED DISCUSSION AND NOTES

1. That instruction alone is not always effective has been demonstrated empirically numerous times. O'Leary, Becker, Evans, and Saudargas (1969) found that rules did not alter disruptive classroom behavior, whereas token reinforcement for desirable behavior decreased the undesirable behavior. Phillips (1968) reported on a token system used in Achievement Place, a residential unit for "predelinquents" (boys who were judged guilty of minor offenses and deemed likely to advance to more serious crimes). One of his findings was that instructions (for example, "Stop that kind of talk") did not effectively reduce aggressive statements (such as "I'll kill you") by the boys. However, aggressive statements were markedly reduced when fines (the loss of tokens) were charged for them. In another study conducted with boys at the same residential unit, Bailey, Wolf, and Phillips (1970) found that giving them a number of classroom rules to follow (such as "Do not talk without permission" and "Do not look out the window") did not effectively decrease the specified undesirable behaviors. However, the undesirable behaviors were reduced markedly when the boys could earn tokens for engaging in them less than 10 percent of the time.

2. An interesting application of modeling concerned the modification of the rate at which a "regular" at the local tavern consumed draft beer (DeRicco & Niemann, 1980). The subject, a 35-year-old real estate saleswoman and part-time student, drank beer regularly with six other women at a small local tavern on Friday afternoons. Since she was also taking a course on behavior modification with the other women that involved a study on alcohol drinking, she knew that something was being studied, but she was totally unaware that it was her own drinking behavior. During several sessions of baseline, she invariably approximated 72 oz. of beer in an hour. During the first experimental phase, a confederate modeled a drinking rate of exactly half that of the subject. The subject's drinking was not affected. Similarly, the subject was unaffected when two confederates modeled drinking rates exactly half that of the subject. However, when four confederates modeled drinking rates of exactly half of the subject's, the subject's drinking rate itself was cut in half, to an average of approximately 36 oz. of beer in an hour. The study indicates that modeling may prove to be a useful tool in the prevention of excessive alcohol consumption. Strong modeling influences on alcoholics' rates of alcoholic consumption were also demonstrated by Caudill and Lipscome (1980).

3. Historically, learning by imitation has been given an important place in a number of different psychological theories, not just behavioristic ones. In Freudian (psychoanalytic) theory, for example, a male child typically develops certain "male" behavior patterns through identification with his father, whereas a female child develops female behavior patterns through identification with her mother. Thus, for example, the absence of a strong male figure with whom to identify could (in theory) lead to feminine traits—even homosexuality—in a boy who identifies excessively with the mother. Gestalt psychologists considered imitative learning to be innate in higher species and attempted to show, for example, that chimpanzees could learn to solve problems by watching other chimpanzees solve them. More behavioristically oriented psychologists, however, have tended toward the view that imitation is itself a learned behavior.

There are several processes by which imitative behavior might be learned. First, an individual is frequently reinforced when he or she performs the same actions that another individual performs; hence, other people's actions tend to become S^Ds for engaging in similar actions. (For example, a child who watches someone open a door to go outside receives the reinforcement of going outside when he or she performs the same action.) Second, to the extent that other people are reinforcing to us, their actions acquire conditioned reinforcing properties; hence, we receive conditioned reinforcement when we perform the same actions. A third possibility is that, once we have learned to imitate simple responses, we can then imitate more complex behaviors, provided that these are composed of the simpler responses. (For example, once an individual has learned to imitate "al," "li," "ga," and "tor" as single syllables, or as units of various words, she can then imitate the word "alligator" the first time she hears it) (Skinner, 1957). A fourth possibility is that imitative behavior is not just a set of separate stimulus-response relationships but is itself an operant class of responses. In other words, it is possible that, once a person is reinforced for imitating some behaviors, he or she will then tend to imitate other behaviors, even if they contain no elements in common with the imitative behaviors that were reinforced.

Regardless of theoretical orientation, there is no doubt that model imitation is an important factor in human behavioral development (Kymissis & Poulson, 1990). Exactly how, and under what conditions, it influences behavior is an important practical question that is receiving intensive experimental study. Experimental psychologist Albert Bandura and his co-workers have contributed greatly to our understanding of this important aspect of human behavior. (For an early review of Bandura's and others' studies in this area, see Bandura, 1969.) Modeling has also been used effectively as a therapy technique (for a review, see Perry & Furukawa, 1986).

4. If symbolic modeling is effective, what about the effects of one of the biggest sources of it . . . what the average American household watches for seven hours a day (Oskamp, 1984) . . . what the average American child spends more time watching than attending school (Liebert & Poulos, 1975)—the television set? Research supports the position that watching large doses of violence and aggression on television increases the chances that a viewer will behave aggressively (Friedrich-Cofer, 1986). In one study, for example, a group of seven- and eight-year-old boys who watched a violent TV program were much more aggressive later during a game of floor hockey than were boys who had watched a TV program that did not contain violence (Josephson, 1987). There is certainly an enormous amount of violence on television. The average American child will watch over 20,000 TV shootings before becoming an adult (Liebert, 1986). Others (Freedman, 1984, for example), have argued that rather than observation of violence on television causing aggression, it may simply be that people who are already aggressive tend to watch television programs that show lots of violence. While we must recognize concerns like those of Freedman's, the fact remains that many studies suggest that violence can be influenced from watching television and films.

5. Not all behavior therapists agree with this view. For example, if a client has a strong fear of something (such as looking out from high places), some therapists encourage the client to form very vivid images of specific situations that cause the fear (looking down from the top of a very tall building, feeling dizzy, feeling more and more anxious, and so forth). It is assumed that this approach will extinguish the anxiety reactions of the client to the scenes imagined in the therapist's office, and that the results will generalize to the real world. This approach of having a client imagine himself in a very fearful and anxiety-producing situation is called *implosive therapy* (Stampfl & Levis, 1967). Implosive therapy differs from a procedure termed *flooding*, in which the therapist requires the patient to encounter the actual feared situation either in vivo or in imagination and maintains that situation for long periods of time. With implosive therapy, instead of requiring the client to imagine realistic scenes, the therapist requires the client to imagine high-anxiety scenes from an exaggerated unrealistic verbal description that the therapist provides. The literature does not indicate implosive therapy to be as successful as systematic desensitization (Morganstern, 1973, 1974). Moreover, studies have indicated that the inclusion of implosion-type material in a flooding procedure to treat phobias either had no effect, or impaired treatment outcome (Wilson, 1982). In view of these findings, we do not recommend the use of implosive therapy.

6. Melin and Gotestam (1981) demonstrated the positive therapeutic effects of rearranging the environment on the behavior of 21 psychogeriatric patients at a large state mental hospital. The patients, the majority of whom were diagnosed as senile dementia, showed very little communication with each other and/or with the staff. The ward was decorated sparsely, with what little furniture there was generally placed along the walls. Meals were standardized and served from a tray that was often placed over the patient's chair or wheelchair. Following a baseline during which the frequency of communication and the degree of skill in eating behavior were monitored, the physical environment was rearranged in several ways. Patients in the experimental group were placed around small tables rather than along the walls of the wards. In addition, coffee was no longer served on the individual eating trays. Cups, saucers, sugar, cream, coffee, and buns were placed on a table in a special room so that the patients could serve themselves and have coffee together around their small tables. The results showed that both the frequency of communication and the individual eating behavior of patients improved significantly, both in comparison to original baselines and in comparison to the control group.

7. In some cases, however, increasing contact with the opposite sex may not be sufficient to increase the frequency of dates. It also may be necessary to learn ways to communicate that you are available and would accept an invitation. Muehlenhard, Koralewski, Andrews, and Burdick (1986) have identified a number of verbal and nonverbal behaviors that women may use to convey interest in dating. The effectiveness of these behaviors was rated by college men who viewed videotapes of women engaging in them. Examples of verbal behaviors that received high ratings were: (a) the woman compliments the man; (b) she keeps talking rather than ending the conversation quickly; and (c) she asks him questions about himself. Examples of nonverbal behaviors that received high ratings were: (a) the woman looks at the man almost constantly; (b) she smiles almost constantly; and (c) she stands about 18 inches (as opposed to 4 feet or 7 feet) from him.

STUDY QUESTIONS ON NOTES

1. In a sentence, what is often required to ensure the effectiveness of instruction? Give an example from note 1.

2. Describe the results of the study of modeling of alcohol drinking by DeRicco and Niemann.

3. Describe four processes by which imitative behavior might be learned, and give an example of each.

4. What experimental psychologist has contributed greatly to our understanding of modeling?

5. Can symbolic modeling influence people to be more violent? Discuss.

6. What is implosive therapy? How does it differ from systematic desensitization (pp. 204–205)? How does it differ from flooding?

7. What category of situational inducement was demonstrated by Melin and Gotestam with the psychogeriatric patients? Defend your choice.

8. Indicate how one might use existing forms of stimulus control to increase the frequency of being asked out on dates.

CHAPTER 17

Alternative Strategies
for Decreasing Behavior

Many problems referred to behavior modifiers are phrased in terms of behavioral excesses. This is probably due largely to the habitual way in which the average person thinks about behavior problems. That is, people tend to focus more on what is "wrong" about what a person is doing rather than on what they would like that person to be doing instead. A teacher might complain, for example, that "Susie keeps running around the room during class" and "Johnny just sits staring into space."

Greenspoon (1976, p. 176) commented, "The specification of desired behaviors . . . is not an easy task. The difficulty is well illustrated by the parent who spent 30 minutes telling the psychologist all the behaviors that her son emitted that she did not like. When asked what she wanted the boy to do, she replied, 'Well, I just want him to be a good boy.' When asked what behaviors constituted a 'good boy,' she conceded that she didn't know and would have to think about it."

When referrals are presented in this way, the skillful behavior modifier does not automatically think, "Aha! Here's a behavioral excess to be decreased." Rather, she asks the teacher or parent, "What is the appropriate behavior to increase in this situation?" Through such examination, it may be found that the teacher, for example, is really concerned about Susie's and Johnny's "undesirable" behaviors only to the extent that they keep these children from engaging in more desirable behaviors (such as completing their classwork assignments). So the behavior modifier would reformulate the problem in terms of increasing a behavior that doesn't occur frequently enough rather than decreasing a behavior that occurs too frequently (see Goldiamond, 1975).

Although one should always think in terms of increasing desirable behavior, it is sometimes necessary to focus also on decreasing undesirable behavior. This does not mean, however, that the first thought that should come to mind is to use extinction or punishment. As explained in Chapters 4 and 13 these procedures have a number of drawbacks. They frequently produce undesirable side effects, and they frequently require many trials before the undesirable behavior decreases to zero (or at least to a tolerable level). Moreover, it is not always easy to apply them effectively. Consider, for example, the use of timeout punishment. Timeout may be impractical if a suitable timeout room is not available. Additionally, an individual receives attention while being placed in a timeout room, and this attention, being immediately contingent upon the undesirable behavior, may therefore serve to maintain it. The application of timeout may also be quite variable, depending upon the behavior modification skills of the individual using it. A teacher in a good mood might say, "Now, now, you're being naughty. You know you shouldn't do that. I'm going to have to put you in the timeout room. Come on, let's go." Then the teacher takes the student gently by the hand and leads him to the timeout room. On the other hand, imagine how the same teacher might take a child to a timout room on a day when the teacher is in a bad mood.

Due to the difficulties associated with extinction and punishment, it is important to explore alternative ways of managing undesirable behavior. Some of these alternatives might include a component of extinction, together with other principles. Others might involve partial rather than complete suppression of behavior. All the alternatives to be discussed later in this chapter focus on increasing desirable behavior as a part of the strategy of decreasing undesirable behavior. As expressed by Dunlap (1990), behavior problems can best be understood as behavioral *deficits* instead of behavioral excesses, in the sense that the person showing the behavior problem lacks effective behavior for achieving desirable outcomes.

After pointing out some reasons for considering the causes of behavior, we discuss some of these alternatives. At the end of the chapter, we list guidelines indicating the order in which we believe the methods described in this and the preceding chapters should generally be considered in selecting a method to decrease a particular undesirable behavior.

IT HELPS TO CONSIDER THE CAUSES OF BEHAVIOR

In Part II of this book, we gave many examples of how ignorance of the basic principles and procedures of behavior modification can lead to behavior problems. The knowledge thus generated about the causes of those problems can clearly be useful: it can help to prevent those problems. Ultimately, prevention may be the most important reason for considering the causes of behavior.

Even after a problem behavior has been detected, however, knowledge of the causes of that behavior can often help in deciding how to deal with it.

For example, if the sources of reinforcement for the behavior can be identified, it may be possible to alter or eliminate them so that extinction may
proceed. Sometimes, however, consideration of the causes will indicate that
extinction is not the best strategy because the sources of reinforcement cannot
be effectively changed—at least not in the situation in which the behavior is
occurring. For example, the individual may be receiving reinforcement from
his peers, and it may not be feasible to get them to stop reinforcing him.

Due consideration to the causes of behavior may also lead one to the
appropriate conclusion that specialists more competent than oneself should
deal with the problem. For example, if a person is troubled by thoughts of
suicide, the novice behavior modifier should not attempt to extinguish that
behavior on the reasoning that "he's just trying to get my sympathy; well, I'll
withhold it and he'll stop talking that way." Obviously, such an approach could
prove disastrous. It would be much more ethical to refer the person to an
experienced behavior therapist, who is qualified to identify the sources controlling the behavior and to undertake appropriate measures to counteract
those sources.

Likewise, the novice behavior modifier should not attempt to eliminate
behaviors that may have medical causes. Sneezing, vomiting, and seizures are
obvious examples of behaviors for which the application of extinction or
punishment might be as ridiculous as this tongue-in-cheek advice from Lewis
Carroll:

> Speak roughly to your little boy,
>   And beat him when he sneezes:
> He only does it to annoy,
>   Because he knows it teases.

It is true that cases of almost continuous sneezing for which there are no
known medical causes have been reported. Vomiting controlled entirely by
nondeliberate reinforcement is not uncommon in institutions for the retarded.
We have also observed retarded children whose "seizures" are not true seizures
at all, but rather very realistic fake seizures reinforced by the attention they
attract from attendants, nurses, and doctors. However, it would be unethical
for any behavior modifier to attempt to treat such cases without first consulting
Note 1 the appropriate medical authorities.[1]

ALTERNATIVE STRATEGIES FOR DECREASING BEHAVIOR

SITUATIONAL INDUCEMENT

In Chapter 16, we described four somewhat overlapping categories of situational inducement: rearranging the existing surroundings, moving the activity to a new location, relocating people, and changing the time of the activity.

As was illustrated by many of the examples in that chapter, it is frequently possible to decrease behavior by identifying stimuli that already control desirable alternative behaviors, and using these stimuli according to one or more of the situational-inducement procedures (for example, recall the efforts of Goldiamond to decrease a man's screaming at his wife).

If an undesirable behavior occurs in response to particular stimuli in very specific situations, it is sometimes possible to eliminate the behavior simply by changing the stimulus and eliminating the opportunity to emit the behavior. Consider the case of Edward, an eight-year-old mildly retarded boy who was in a special education class.* His teacher, Ms. Millan, reported to one of the authors that Edward consistently (three or four times a day) emitted undesirable, classroom-disturbing behaviors. After some discussion with Ms. Millan, it became clear that the disturbing behaviors that she was concerned about involved a loud approximation of "Tarzan" noises. It was also clear that Edward made the Tarzan noises whenever he was asked questions for which he did not know the answer. Rather than giving wrong answers, Edward would burst out with "Eeee-ah, eeee-ah." Needless to say, the Tarzan noises disrupted the class. (Ms. Millan reported that one of the other boys climbed on a desk and jumped up and down while scratching himself underneath the armpits and making noises like Cheetah the chimp.) The program Ms. Millan implemented was simply to eliminate the occasion for the undesirable behavior to occur. She stopped asking questions for which Edward did not know the answers and took him aside for some individual sessions regarding the work to be done the next day. During these sessions, she quizzed Edward on his knowledge of the subject matter. Although he would occasionally make mistakes, he did not make Tarzan noises. Since only he and Ms. Millan were present during these sessions, the behavior apparently was under the stimulus control of the presence of the other class members.

During class, over a two-week period, Ms. Millan asked Edward questions to which he knew the answers and gave him a great deal of approval for correct answers. Then, over the next two weeks, Ms. Millan began fading in slightly more difficult questions, each of which she prefaced with a strong prompt, such as "Now, Edward, here is a question that's a little difficult. But I'm sure you can answer it, and if you can't we will figure out the answer together, won't we class." Thus, if Edward eventually did give a wrong answer, he was immediately engaged with the teacher and the rest of the class in an attempt to figure out the answer. This gave Edward the opportunity to receive the attention of the class for desirable behavior, rather than for the undesirable Tarzan noises. That, coupled with his recent history of receiving reinforcement for giving correct answers, solved the problem. The project required approximately a month of careful attention from Ms. Millan. Thereafter,

---

*The details of this case were provided by a student in a behavior modification course for resource teachers taught by G. Martin at the Winnipeg School Division No. 1, Winnipeg, Manitoba, January–March 1973.

Edward required no special attention. To maintain his good behavior, however, Ms. Millan made sure that she periodically asked Edward questions to which he knew the answers.

INSTRUCTION, MODELING, AND ROLE PLAYING

Toby, the son of one of the authors, was attending nursery school three mornings each week. His parents (Garry and Nickie) were somewhat dismayed when Toby frequently reported that he had been fighting in school with a boy named Karl. Because of their concern, Garry and Nickie approached the nursery school teacher, Mona, and asked if they could come and watch Toby's activities. Sure enough, they observed that Toby frequently engaged in rough-housing with a boy named Karl. They also observed that Toby was not the instigator. During certain activities Karl would grab Toby and Toby would retaliate. The two children would then begin wrestling and playfully rolling along the floor in a boisterous fashion.

The problem was handled at home by means of a few sessions of instruction, modeling, and role playing involving Toby, Garry, and Nickie. One evening, Garry instructed Toby as follows: "Toby, let's pretend that Nickie is Mona and that we're at nursery school. Okay? Let's pretend that you and I are the kids at nursery school. You pretend to be Karl and I'll pretend to be you. Now, let's pretend that we are making animal noises like Mona sometimes tells us to." At this point, Nickie, playing the role of Mona, gave the appropriate instructions for the children to get down on the floor and pretend that they were tigers and to make tiger noises. Garry then said, "Now, Toby, remember you're Karl. What does Karl do when you're making animal noises?" "He usually comes and tries to pretend he's eating me up like a tiger," said Toby. Garry replied, "OK, Toby, you do that to me." Toby responded vigorously, as though he were Karl. At that point Garry said, "Now, Toby, here's what I want you to do when Karl does that to you." Garry (playing the role of Toby) immediately stood up and said, "No, Karl. My dad doesn't like me to fight in school. Right, Mona?" To this, Nickie (playing the role of Mona) immediately responded with, "Good for you, Toby. Yes, that's right."

After several repetitions of the role playing, the roles were reversed and Toby was instructed to pretend and act as though he were "Toby at school." Garry assumed the role of Karl, and Nickie continued to play Mona. Over several trails and several different "typical nursery school" activities, Garry played the role of an aggressive Karl and grabbed Toby in an attempt to start to wrestle. Toby was prompted to immediately stand up and say, "No, Karl. My dad doesn't want me to fight in school. Right, Mona?" After a number of trials, Toby's reaction became quite automatic. During a period of approximately a week, Toby's fighting with Karl in the classroom decreased to nearly zero. Toby began emitting more desirable classroom behaviors and, in turn, received more reinforcement from Mona. Six weeks after this program, Toby's fighting in school was still under good control.

ELININATE AN EARLY COMPONENT OF A CHAIN

Note 2

Sometimes, an undesirable behavior is part of a consistent behavioral chain. It is therefore sometimes possible to eliminate an undesirable behavior by eliminating an earlier component of the chain that leads up to it.[2]

Such a case was described to one of the authors by a mother of a retarded child who was living at home. Frequently during the day, and always just when the mother was busy in the kitchen, the child would go to the mother's bedroom, take a piece of jewelry out of the jewelry box, carry it to the bathroom, and flush it down the toilet. She would then come and tell her mother what she had done. Since the sequence of behaviors appeared to be quite consistent, the strategy employed was that of dealing with an earlier component of the chain, so as to indirectly rather than directly eliminate the actual behavior of flushing the jewelry down the toilet. Specifically, the girl was given several prompted trails during which, when mother and daughter were both in the kitchen, the mother took the daughter by the hand, went into the bedroom, prompted the daughter to take a piece of jewelry out of the box, and guided the daughter to bring the jewelry into the kitchen and place it in a jar on the kitchen table. This behavior was highly reinforced.

After several guided trials, mother was able to initiate the sequence of behaviors by instructing the child while they were both in the kitchen. The guidance and instruction trials occurred over a two-day period during which the child was not given an opportunity to go into the bedroom on her own. On the start of the third day, the child was instructed that anytime she wanted to, when mom was in the kitchen, she could get some jewelry, place it in the jar in the kitchen, and receive a "treat" from mom. In addition, the mother took a photograph of the daughter putting the jewelry into the jar on the kitchen table and placed the picture beside the jewelry box in the bedroom. During the next three weeks, the daughter continued periodically to bring jewelry to the kitchen and to receive "treats" for doing so. Not once did she flush jewelry down the toilet. Eventually, the girl stopped playing with mother's jewelry altogether.

STIMULUS CONTROL AND PARTIAL ELIMINATION

Lori was an attractive, severely retarded little girl with a very angelic face.* She was small for her age, slightly chubby, and had short blond hair and irresistible appeal. Perhaps in part because of these characteristics, she had gradually been shaped to be extremely persistent in her approach to the staff, so much so that she became a chronic pest. The following sequence was typical. While Bonnie, the nurse in charge of the ward, sat working in her office, Lori peeked in and said, "Hi." "Hi, Lori, I'm busy now but I'll talk to you later," said Bonnie. "You busy now?" said Lori. There was no response from Bonnie,

*This example is based on an unpublished case report at Cedar Cottage, The Manitoba Developmental Center, Portage la Prairie, Manitoba, 1971.

who was trying to work and to ignore Lori's pestering. "You work hard?" asked Lori. (No response from Bonnie.) "Hi," said Lori. (No response from Bonnie.) "You don't love me?" said Lori with a sad look. "Of course I love you, Lori," said Bonnie, unable to resist any longer.

This type of interaction between Lori and the staff was very common. Although the staff attempted to ignore Lori's excessive pestering it was almost impossible to do so consistently unless one were exceptionally cold-hearted toward cute little girls. Many undesirable behaviors are developed simply because repetitions of the behavior will finally produce a consequence. Lori was so cute in her approach and so persistent in her pestering that she inevitably received intermittent reinforcement from the staff for her pestering behavior.

Since total extinction would, therefore, have been extremely difficult, the staff designed a procedure for eliminating the behavior only partially— that is, eliminating it only when it was most disruptive. Each staff member received a two-by-four-inch card to be pinned to his or her shirt or dress. The card was red on one side and green on the other. In general, during certain intervals throughout the day, all the staff members would turn their cards to the green side and Lori's pestering would be reinforced. At other times of the day, the staff would turn their cards to the red side and no pestering would be reinforced. On the first morning of the procedure, a staff member walked toward Lori very quickly, before she had a chance to begin pestering, and said very quickly, and firmly, "Hi, Lori. See my card (while pointing to the card)? I can't talk to you because the card is red. I'll see you later." The staff member then quickly turned and walked away, leaving Lori standing there in a state of stunned silence. Within just a few seconds, the staff member returned with the green side of the card showing. Smiling pleasantly, she said, "Hi, Lori. See my card? It's on the green side, so now I can talk to you." The staff member then proceeded to engage Lori in a brief conversation. When there was a pause in the conversation, the staff member suddenly assumed an appearance of sternness and a businesslike attitude. Turning the card to the red side, she said, "I can't talk to you now, Lori. My card will be red for a while. I'll see you later." The staff member then quickly walked away before Lori had a chance to respond. All the staff members repeated this type of interaction with Lori throughout the day. Moreover, when all the staff had their cards turned to the red side, if Lori attempted to approach one of them, that person immediately pointed to his or her card and instructed Lori that no conversation was possible. The staff member then left the vicinity immediately. Any conversation on Lori's part was consistently extinguished in those situations.

During the first few days of the procedure, the green side was usually showing. Over several days, the staff introduced the red side for longer and longer periods of time. After two weeks, the staff had started managing their red and green cards individually. Lori quickly learned to discriminate whether a nearby staff member was available for conversation, and she responded appropriately. Not only did the procedure effectively manage Lori's pestering, but it also introduced a new reinforcer for her desirable behavior. During times when cards were red, if Lori emitted some desirable behavior on the ward (such as helping with the cleaning or playing appropriately with another child), a staff member would often approach Lori, turn the card green, and begin interacting with her. The presentation of the green side of the card had become a conditioned reinforcer. Moreover, over time, Lori appeared to learn more subtle discriminations—such as distinguishing between staff behaviors when they were busy vs. when they were relaxed or socializing. Lori appeared to learn what the staff were doing, even though the red or green card might not have been visible, and if the staff were busy, she would refrain from pestering. If the staff appeared not to be busy, Lori would approach further, check for the green card, and begin to socialize.

There are many other examples of high-frequency behaviors that are disruptive for teachers, parents, and others. A useful strategy in many of these situations is to develop stimulus control and partial elimination of behavior. Implementing such a program is not only much easier than attempting to totally extinguish the behavior, it is usually much more pleasant for all concerned and it may lead to the development of a desirable conditioned reinforcer, as it did in Lori's case.

OVERCORRECTION: POSITIVE PRACTICE AND RESTITUTION

At an institution for retarded people, the floor of Ward 2B was littered with reclining, sitting, or sprawling individuals despite the ample availability of unoccupied chairs and sofas.* Not only was this unsightly, but it was also dangerous in that residents lying or sitting on the floor have been injured accidentally by other residents trying to step around them. Therefore, the psychologists at the institution set up a program to reduce or eliminate this undesirable behavior. First, they took baseline data for 12 days of floor sprawling by the 11 residents who showed the highest frequency of this behavior. During this baseline phase, only simple correction was used; that is, a resident sprawling on the floor was simply lifted into a standing position and given a statement of disapproval. Residents observed sitting in chairs were frequently praised by one of two therapists. However, the undesirable behavior showed little or no tendency to decrease as a result of this procedure. Therefore, in the next phase a procedure called positive practice was introduced. Two trainers continuously monitored the residents' behavior. Whenever a resident sat down on the floor, one of the trainers would go up to the resident, tell him or her not to do that, and require the resident to sit in a nearby chair

---

*This case is based on a report by Azrin and Wesolowski (1975).

for one minute. When the one-minute period was over, the resident had to walk to another chair and sit on it for one minute, then another chair for one minute, and so on, until the resident had sat in 10 chairs. The resident was left sitting in the last chair.

Over 12 days the prompting given to the residents to sit in the chairs was faded out, and after the first four days only verbal prompts were needed. During the first four days, physical guidance was necessary for some individuals. At the end of the 12-day period, the regular ward staff took over the program.

The data recorded indicated that the positive practice procedure was very effective. Sprawling on the floor was eliminated after eight days and the residents used the chairs instead.

Positive practice is one component of a general method called *overcorrection*, which was pioneered by Azrin and Foxx (1971) and their collegues (for a review, see Foxx & Bechtel, 1982). Another type of overcorrection is called *restitution* overcorrection. Where possible both are combined into one procedure, although sometimes only positive practice can be applied as in the above example.

Restitution consists of correcting or "setting right" whatever in the environment has been disturbed or disrupted by the undesirable behavior, and doing this in such a manner that more is corrected than was actually disturbed or disrupted. This is why the method is called *overcorrection*. For example, if an individual deliberately kicks over a chair, he or she would be required not only to put the chair back in its place but also to straighten out other pieces of furniture in the room. The individual would not be reinforced in any way for this restituting behavior since to do so might constitute reinforcement for the undesirable behavior that made it necessary in the first place.

In positive practice, the individual is required to repeat over and over again a desirable alternative behavior; thus in the example cited, the individual might be required to practice sitting down in the chair a number of times. Again, the individual would not be reinforced in any way for this positive practice of the desirable alternative behavior, since to do so might constitute reinforcement for the undesirable behavior.

At this point you might be wondering how one gets the individual to engage in restitution or positive practice if he or she is not to be reinforced for doing so. The answer that Azrin and Foxx give is to use the minimum force necessary to get the individual to overcorrect. Thus, if instruction suffices, use that; if, however, that doesn't work, then try gestural or environmental prompting; if neither of these works, then use physical prompting. If none of these works—for example, if you are a 95-lb nurse trying to overcorrect a 250-lb psychopathic killer who refuses to be overcorrected—then overcorrection is probably *not* the procedure you would want to use in this

Note 3 particular instance.[3]

HABIT REVERSAL

Azrin and Nunn (1973) developed a method to reduce or eliminate various sorts of nervous habits or tics in otherwise normal individuals. This method, which is called *habit reversal*, involves practicing a reaction that competes with (i.e., is incompatible with) the nervous habit or tic. For example, to correct "shoulder jerking," the client would be instructed to "contract shoulders by depressing the shoulders down as far as they will go while keeping the arms close to the body"; to correct "wrist tic," the client would be instructed to "push hands on arms of chairs, desk, leg, and so on, and contract the muscles so that hands are pushing opposite the tic movement (i.e., contract hands down if the wrist jerks upward)" (Azrin, Nunn, & Frantz, 1980, p. 174). The competing reactions are practiced daily in front of a mirror at home and also performed immediately after the occurrence of the tic movement or just before it is likely to occur. In addition to the practice of a competing response, habit reversal also involves some more general procedures such as reviewing the inconvenience caused by the tic, identifying situations and events associated with presence or absence of the tic, deliberately performing and describing the tic in front of a mirror (negative practice), relaxation training, relaxation exercises, having a family member present for social support during treatment, and self-recording and graphing the daily number of tic episodes.[4] In a study involving 11 clients, Azrin and Nunn (1973) found that the habit reversal method resulted in a mean decrease of 90 percent of the nervous habits or tics on the first day, 95 percent after one month, and 99 percent after three months. Moreover, Azrin, Nunn, and Frantz (1980) found the habit-reversal method to be much more effective than simple negative practice, in which the clients purposely performed the tic in front of a mirror while saying to themselves, "This is what I'm not supposed to do." Azrin and Nunn (1977) outlined step-by-step procedures for the layperson to follow to use habit reversal to decrease stuttering, nail biting, hair pulling, muscular tics, and other nervous habits.

Note 4

GUIDELINES FOR DECREASING BEHAVIOR

Throughout this text, a number of different procedures for decreasing undesirable behaviors have been described. Prior to deciding upon a particular procedure for a particular undesirable behavior, one should consider two questions:

1. How can the problem be formulated in terms of increasing a desirable alternative behavior?
2. What are the likely causes of the undesirable behavior?

Depending on the answers to these questions, one might next (if appropriate) consider the following procedures listed. In general, for optimum results they should be considered in the order listed. Procedures appear higher on the list for one or more of the following reasons: demonstrated effectiveness, emphasis on increasing desirable alternative behavior, minimum restrictiveness for the client.

1. *Shortcut tactics*
   a. Instruction
   b. Situational inducement
      (1) Relocate people
      (2) Change time of activity
      (3) Move activity to new location
      (4) Rearrange surroundings
   c. Habit reversal
   d. Instruction, modeling, and role playing
   e. Instuction and physical guidance
2. *Indirect tactics*
   a. Eliminate early component of a chain
   b. Establish new stimulus control and use partial elimination.
3. *Reinforcement schedules combined with extinction*
   a. DRO (Chapter 7)
   b. DRL (Chapter 7)
   c. Extinguish undesirable behavior while reinforcing desirable alternative behavior (Chapter 3, Chapter 7 for DRI).
4. *Punishment*
   a. Overcorrection
   b. Timeout (Chapter 13)
   c. Aversive stimulation (Chapter 13)

STUDY QUESTIONS

1. What should be a behavior modifier's first question after being given a thorough description of an undesirable behavior to be decreased? Explain with an example.
2. Discuss why extinction and punishment should not be among the first procedures to be considered for reducing an undesirable behavior.
3. State three broad reasons why it is important to consider the causes of undesirable behavior.
4. Give two examples (at least one of which is not from the text) of the use of situational inducement to reduce an undesirable behavior.
5. Give an example of the use of instruction, modeling, and role playing to reduce an undesirable behavior.
6. Give an example of reducing an undesirable behavior by eliminating an early component of a chain. Draw a diagram resembling those in Chapter 11 to illustrate your example.
7. Give an example of the use of stimulus control to partially eliminate an undesirable behavior. Draw a diagram resembling those in Chapter 8 to illustrate your example.

8. Using examples, distinguish between positive practice overcorrection and restitution overcorrection.
9. Describe all of the components included by Azrin and Nunn in the multiple-component procedure they call "habit reversal." Describe two examples.
10. Before deciding on a particular procedure for decreasing an undesirable behavior, what two things should you consider?
11. Why do authors of this text recommend that situational inducement be considered before overcorrection as a strategy for reducing a problem behavior of a client? (Hint: There are three possible reasons.)

PRACTICE EXERCISES

1. Identify two undesirable behaviors of someone you know well (but do not identify that person). Try to construct plausible explanations for (i.e., causes of) those behaviors. State which of the behaviors you think would be especially difficult or inappropriate to eliminate by extinction or punishment, and say why.
2. Design a program or programs for eliminating one or both of the undesirable behaviors in Exercise 1. Incorporate one or more of the following procedures:
   a. situational inducement
   b. instruction, modeling, and role playing
   c. eliminating an early component of a chain
   d. stimulus control and partial elimination

SELF-MODIFICATION EXERCISES

1. Do Practice Exercise 1 for two of your own undesirable behaviors.
2. Do Exercise 2 for the undesirable behaviors you listed for yourself.

EXTENDED DISCUSSION AND NOTES

1. However, the existence of a medical cause need not mean that a behavioral treatment will be ineffective. Nor, for that matter, does the existence of a purely environmental cause necessarily mean that a medical treatment will be ineffective (see Stolz, Wienckowski, & Brown, 1975, p. 1034). For a discussion of behavioral approaches to medical problems, see Chapter 2.

2. For example, there is evidence that seizures can be modified in this way. Seizures are sometimes preceded by very clearly defined behaviors. Zlutnick, Mayville, and Moffat (1975) found that they could often prevent the onset of a child's seizure by shouting "No!" and shaking the child vigorously immediately upon the occurrence of a preseizure behavior (which in one case consisted of a fixed gaze at a flat surface, such as a table top or a wall). In some cases, the preseizure behavior also decreased, suggesting that the procedure may have been punishing.

3. Marholin, Luiselli, and Townsend (1980) concluded that overcorrection "is an effective procedure for reducing and eliminating a wide range of maladaptive behaviors" (p. 72). However, it seems to be composed of several more basic procedures. First, although Azrin and Besalel (1980) have argued that overcorrection is different from simple punishment, it appears definitely to involve punishment (Foxx & Bechtel, 1982). Second, it involves prompting to influence a client to engage in a desired behavior that is incompatible with the behavior being corrected. However, the rules for prompting the desired behavior are not specified clearly (see Murphy, 1978). In addition, overcorrection often involves fading in that the guidance and stimuli that control positive practice are gradually withdrawn.

Thus, overcorrection appears to be a punishment procedure, in combination with other procedures, with no particular advantage over other punishment procedures, except for claims that it may be more socially acceptable than other forms of punishment (e.g., Webster & Azrin, 1973). MacKenzie-Keating and McDonald (1990) argued that the term "overcorrection" should be eliminated completely from the behavior modification vocabulary. They recommend that the term be replaced by three separate procedures labeled "restitution training," "positive practice of functional behavior," and "guided movement training." Restitution training would be recognized as a punishment procedure in which, contingent upon an undesirable behavior, the individual would be required to restore the environment so that it is the same or better than it was prior to the undesirable behavior. Positive practice of a functional behavior is a punishment procedure in which an individual, contingent upon an undesirable behavior, would be required repeatedly to practice a positive, functional, alternative behavior. Guided movement training is a punishment procedure in which an individual, contingent upon an undesirable behavior, would be required repeatedly to practice an incompatible gross motor movement. Positive practice of a functional behavior is different from guided movement training in that the behavior required to be repeated in the latter would not necessarily serve a useful purpose in the individual's environment (an example might be repeated movement of arms or fingers). This revised terminology would improve communication among practitioners who use the techniques, and it would more clearly indicate that the procedures involve punishment and therefore should be used with the same ethical considerations that apply to other punishment procedures (see Chapters 13 and 28).

4. Miltenberger, Fuqua, and McKinley (1985) compared a habit-reversal package to a simplified package consisting of just two components, awareness and competing-response training, in the treatment of muscle tics. The results of their study indicated that the simplified package was just as effective as the multiple-component treatment package proposed by Azrin and Nunn. Miltenberger and co-workers identified three practical reasons why it is important for researchers to try to identify the behaviorally active components of a complex multiple-component procedure, such as habit reversal. First, a simpler behavior change package is easier to teach to clients and therapists than a more complex package, which may result in more accurate application of procedures. Second, they cited evidence indicating that patients will comply better with simpler treatment packages than with more complex ones, thus making it very worthwhile to identify the unnecessary components in a complex package, and to omit them from further applications. Third, the identification of the active-treatment components in a package may help to clarify the behavioral principles responsible for the treatment's effectiveness, thus contributing to our theoretical understanding of the procedure.

STUDY QUESTIONS ON NOTES

1. Is it true that problem behaviors with medical causes must receive medical treatment? Explain.
2. Briefly describe some evidence that seizures function like a behavioral chain.
3. Describe how several basic behavioral principles and/or procedures appear to be involved in the overcorrection procedures.
4. Describe MacKenzie-Keating and McDonald's recommendation for talking about overcorrection procedures. What are the advantages of their recommendations?
5. Why is it important for researchers to try to identify the behaviorally active components of a multiple-component treatment package such as habit reversal?

CHAPTER 18

Behavioral Assessment:
Initial Considerations

Throughout this book, numerous examples illustrate the effectiveness of behavior modification procedures. Many of these examples are accompanied by graphs showing the changes (increases or decreases) that occurred in behavior when particular procedures were applied. Some of the graphs also include follow-up observations indicating that the improvements were maintained after the programs had terminated. The graphs were not presented just to make it easier for you to understand the material. Precise records of behavior are an inseparable part of behavior modification procedures. Indeed, some people have gone so far as to say that the major contribution of behavior modification has been the insistence on accurately recording specific behaviors and making decisions on the basis of recorded data rather than merely on the basis of subjective impressions. As with Linus and his blanket in the popular Peanuts cartoons, the behavior modifier and the data sheet are inseparable.

MINIMAL COMPONENTS OF A PROGRAM: ASSESSMENT, INTERVENTION, AND FOLLOW-UP

A successful behavior modification program typically involves at least three components during which behavior is recorded: (1) a baseline, or preprogram behavioral-assessment phase, (2) a treatment phase, and (3) a follow-up phase. During the *baseline* phase, the behavior modifier assesses the behavior to determine its level prior to the introduction of the program or treatment. Ideally, after making a precise baseline assessment a behavior modifier will design an effective *treatment* program to bring about the desired behavior change. In educational settings, such a program is referred to typically as a training or teaching program. In community and clinical settings, the program is referred to more often as an intervention strategy or a therapy program. Finally, the *follow-up* phase is carried out to determine whether the improvements achieved during treatment are maintained after the termination of the program.

These three phases follow from the importance that behavior modifiers place on directly measuring the behavior of concern, and from using changes in the measures as the best indicator that the problem is being helped (see Chapter 1, p. 7). For example, concerning phase 1, if a child is having difficulty in school, the behavior modifier would be considerably more interested in the specific behavioral excesses or deficits that constitute the problem (e.g., low reading proficiency) than in the child's score on an intelligence test (although the behavior modifier would probably not be disinterested in the latter information).

Concerning phase 2, behavior modification programs typically provide for frequent observation and monitoring of the behavior of interest during training or treatment. In some cases, the difference between behavior modification and other approaches on this point is primarily a matter of degree. Traditional educational practices typically involve periodic assessment during the teaching program for the purpose of monitoring the performance of the students. Certain clinical treatment programs involve periodic assessment of the clients at various intervals. Moreover, some programs that have been labeled behavior modification have consisted primarily of before-and-after measures and have lacked precise, ongoing recording during treatment. Nevertheless, many behavior modifiers have emphasized and practiced, to a degree seldom found in other approaches, frequent monitoring of the behavior during the application of the specific treatment or intervention strategies.

Phase 3 reflects the strong emphasis that behavior modifiers give to assessment *after* the termination of the treatment or intervention phase whenever possible, since a problem has not really been solved if the improvement is not permanent. Thus, behavior modification experts agree that programs should include a follow-up phase in which the persistence of the desirable behavior changes following termination of the program are evaluated.

In many cases, such as behavioral programs involving one or two behaviors and a small number of individuals, it is both possible and desirable to gather reliable follow-up information. In some cases, this might consist of precise observation or assessment under natural circumstances in which the behavior is expected to occur. In other projects, however, precise follow-up observations simply are not possible. Consider a behavior modification program set up for an entire classroom and conducted for many months. At the end of the program, the children may go on to another class, graduate to another program, leave the school, or in some other way become unavailable for follow-up observation. Under these circumstances, it would simply be impossible to do anything other than conduct a test that would sample a few of the behaviors developed by the behavior modification program.

DATA! DATA! DATA! WHY BOTHER?

There are a number of reasons for recording accurate data during the baseline and throughout a program. First, *an accurate behavioral assessment provides a description of the problem that will help the behavior modifier to decide whether or not he or she is the appropriate one to design a treatment program.* Relevant considerations are described in more detail in Chapter 21.

Sometimes an accurate baseline will indicate that what someone thought to be a problem is actually not a problem. For example, a teacher may say, "I don't know what to do with Johnny; he's always hitting the other kids." But after taking a baseline, the teacher may discover that the behavior actually occurs so rarely that it does not merit a special program. Both of the authors have experienced this phenomenon more than once. Others have too, as illustrated by the following example from Greenspoon (1976, p. 177).

> The reliance on casual observation led a woman to complain to a psychologist that her husband rarely talked to her during mealtime. She said that his failure to talk to her was becoming an increasing source of annoyance to her and she wanted to do something about it. The psychologist suggested that she prepare a chart and record on the chart the number of times that he initiated a conversation or responded to the verbal behavior that she emitted. She agreed to the suggestions. At the end of a week, she called back to inform the psychologist that she was surprised and pleased to report that she had been in error. It turned out that her husband both initiated conversation and responded to her verbal emissions at a very high rate.

A second reason for assessing and recording behavior carefully is that *the initial assessment process often helps the behavior modifier to identify the best treatment strategy.* Discovering potential reinforcers for a behavior during the baseline phase is clearly useful for designing an effective intervention program. Precise baseline observation can also help greatly in deciding upon a particular procedure, as described in other chapters.

A third reason for recording accurate data during the baseline and throughout a program is that *accurate baseline data provide a means for clearly determining whether the program has produced, or is producing, the desired change in behavior.* Sometimes people claim that they do not need to record data to know whether a desirable change in behavior has occurred. No doubt this is often true. A mother obviously needs no data sheet or graphs to tell her that her child is completely toilet-trained: there is ample evidence (or, it is hoped, lack of it) in the child's pants.

But not all cases are so clear-cut—at least not immediately. Suppose that a child is acquiring toileting behavior very slowly. The parent may think that the program is not working and abandon it prematurely. With accurate data, this type of mistake can be avoided. This point is illustrated nicely by the following case.*

Dr. Lynn Caldwell was consulted by a woman whose six-year-old son was, in her words, "driving me up a wall with his constant slamming of the kitchen door everytime he goes out of the kitchen." Dr. Caldwell asked the mother to obtain a baseline of the target behavior by tallying each instance of it on a sheet of paper attached to the refrigerator. Over a three-day period, the total number of door slams was 123. Dr. Caldwell then instructed the mother to provide approval each time the boy went through the door without slamming it. But she was to administer a brief timeout whenever he slammed the door (he was to go back and remain for three minutes in whichever room he had just left, and the mother was to ignore him during that time), and then require him to proceed through the door without slamming it. After applying this procedure for three days, the mother brought the tally sheet to Dr. Caldwell. "This behavior modification stuff doesn't work," she complained, pointing to the large number of tally marks on the data sheet. "He's just as bad as he ever was." But when the tally marks were counted, there were only 87 of them over the three days of treatment, compared with the 123 that were entered over the three days of baseline. Encouraged by this observation, the mother continued the program, and the behavior quickly dropped to an acceptable level of about 5 per day (after which the satisfied mother did not make further contact with Dr. Caldwell).

Without accurate data, one might also make the opposite type of error. One might conclude that a procedure is working and continue it when in fact it is ineffective and should be abandoned or modified. For example, Harris, Wolf, and Baer (1964) described the case of a boy in a laboratory preschool who had the annoying habit of pinching adults. His teachers decided to use a behavior modification procedure to encourage him to pat rather than pinch. After the procedure had been in effect for some time, the teachers agreed that they had succeeded in reducing pinching by substituting patting. When they looked at the data recorded by an outside observer, however, they saw clearly that, although patting was considerably above the level it had been during the baseline recordings, pinching had not decreased from its baseline level. Perhaps concentrating on the procedure and/or the patting so diverted the teachers that they had failed to notice the pinching as much as they had before introducing the procedure. In any case, had it not been for the recorded data, the teachers probably would have wasted a great deal more time and effort than they did on an ineffective procedure.[1]

Note 1

The above three reasons for recording accurate data during the baseline and throughout the program correspond to what Ciminero (1977) has

---

*This case was described by Dr. Lynn Caldwell, Department of Rehabilitation Medicine, University of Washington, in a taped presentation to the first Manitoba Behavior Change Conference, Portage la Prairie, Manitoba, 1971.

identified as the three main functions of behavioral assessment: *description* of the problem, *selection* of a treatment strategy, and *evaluation* of treatment outcome.

A fourth reason for accurately recording and graphing behavior is that *publicly posted results can be both prompts and reinforcers for the behavior modifier for carrying out a program* (see Figure 18–1). Staff in institutions for the retarded, for example, often become more conscientious in applying procedures when up-to-date charts or graphs clearly showing the effects of the procedures are posted conspicuously on the wards. Parents and teachers alike may find that their efforts to modify children's behavior are reinforced by graphic representation of the improved behavior.

Note 2   A fifth reason for recording and graphing behavior is that *the displayed data may lead to improvements apart from any further treatment program.*[2] Students who graph their own study behavior (for instance, by recording the daily number of paragraphs or pages studied, or the amount of time spent studying) may find increases in the graph to be reinforcing. Data that are presented appropriately can be reinforcing even to young children. For example, an occupational therapist at a school for handicapped children once consulted one of the authors concerning a seven-year-old girl who each morning took an excessive amount of time taking off her outside garments and hanging them up. It appeared that the teachers could not be persuaded to stop attending to the child when she was in the cloakroom. The author suggested that the therapist somehow attempt to influence the child with a graph of the amount of time she spent in the cloakroom each morning. The procedure that the therapist devised proved to be as effective as it was ingenious.*

A large chart was hung on the wall. The chart was colored green so as to represent grass, and a carrot patch was depicted near the bottom of it. Days were indicated along the bottom of the chart and the amount of time in the cloakroom was indicated along the side. Each day, a circle was marked on the chart to indicate the amount of time spent in the cloakroom in the morning, and a small paper rabbit was attached to the most recent circle. Using simple language, the therapist explained the procedure to the child and concluded by saying, "Now let's see if you can get the bunny down to eat the carrots." When the rabbit was down to the level of the carrots, the child was encouraged to keep him there: "Remember, the longer the bunny stays in the carrot patch, the more he can eat." A follow-up showed that the improved behavior persisted over a period of one year.

Behavior modifiers were not the first to discover the usefulness of recording one's behavior to help modify that behavior. As with many other supposedly "new" psychological discoveries, the real credit should perhaps go to the writers of great literature. For example, in his autobiography, first published in 1883, Anthony Trollope (1946, p. 116) stated:

---

*We are grateful to Nancy Staisey for providing us with the details of this procedure.

FIGURE 18–1 Examples of individuals being reinforced by publicly posted data.

When I have commenced a new book, I have always prepared a diary, divided into weeks, and carried on for the period which I have allowed myself for the completion of the work. In this I have entered, day by day, the number of pages I have written, so that if at any time I have slipped into idleness for a day or two, the record of that idleness has been there, staring me in the face, and demanding of me increased labour, so that the deficiency might be supplied. According to the circumstances of the time,—whether my other business might then be heavy or light, or whether the book I was writing was or was not wanted with speed,—I have allotted myself so many pages a week. The average number has been about 40. It has been placed as low as 20, and has risen to 112. And as a page is an ambiguous term, my page has been made to contain 250 words; and as words, if not watched, will have a tendency to straggle, I have had every word counted as I went. . . . There has ever been the record before me, and a week passed with an insufficient number of pages has been a blister to my eye and a month so disgraced would have been a sorrow to my heart.

Ernest Hemingway is another novelist who used self-recording to help maintain his literary output. One of his interviewers reported (Plimpton, 1965, p. 219):

He keeps track of his daily progress—"so as not to kid myself"—on a large chart made out of the side of a cardboard packing case and set up against the wall under the nose of a mounted gazelle head. The numbers on the chart showing the daily output of words differ from 450, 575, 462, 1250, back to 512, the higher figures on days Hemingway puts in extra work so he won't feel guilty spending the following day fishing on the gulf stream.

The well-known author Irving Wallace used self-recording even before he was aware that others had done the same. In a book touching on his writing methods (Wallace, 1971, pp. 65–66), he commented:

I kept a work chart when I wrote my first book—which remains unpublished—at the age of nineteen. I maintained work charts while writing my first four published books. These charts showed the date I started each chapter, the date I finished it, and number of pages written in that period. With my fifth book, I started keeping a more detailed chart which also showed how many pages I had written by the end of every working day. I am not sure why I started keeping such records. I suspect that it was because, as a free-lance writer, entirely on my own, without employer or deadline, I wanted to create disciplines for myself, ones that were guilt-making when ignored. A chart on the wall served as such a discipline, its figures scolding me or encouraging me.

SOURCES OF INFORMATION FOR BASELINE ASSESSMENT

Up to now we have talked about the three minimal components of a behavior modification program; namely, baseline, treatment or intervention, and follow-up. In many cases, however, a prebaseline phase is also necessary to determine whether to conduct a baseline on a particular behavior of an individual. This prebaseline phase is called *screening and general disposition* assessment (see Hawkins, 1979). If done by an agency, the screening and general disposition phase serves to determine whether this particular agency is the appropriate one to deal with this individual's behavior. It also provides information as to which behavior(s) should be baselined, if indeed this is the appropriate agency to deal with the problem, or what agency the client should be referred to if this isn't the appropriate one. For example, a behaviorally oriented center for children with learning difficulties might screen a child referred to it to determine whether his or her academic skills are unusual enough to require some sort of program that is not ordinarily provided by the school. To achieve this initial assessment, the agency might use a number of different preliminary indicators, ranging from teachers' reports to the child's IQ score (although these indicators would, of course, be interpreted simply as rather crude measures of behavior rather than as measures of underlying traits). To take an example at the other extreme, a center for gifted children might perform a similar screening and disposition assessment to determine whether a special program quite different from the one just described is required for a particular child. In this latter case one might question our use of the term "problem"; however, note that we are using the term to indicate that a special program may be needed, not that the behavior that calls for it is undesirable.

As indicated, behavior modifiers may make use of traditional tests, such as intelligence tests, in their screening and general disposition assessments—although they typically do not interpret them in the traditional manner. Behavior modifiers also use other assessment devices to aid in pinpointing specific behaviors of interest. These may be either direct or indirect assessment procedures.

DIRECT ASSESSMENT PROCEDURES

Throughout this book we have emphasized direct observation and recording of behavior. Each of the case histories at the beginning of Chapters 3 through 14 concern specific behaviors that were precisely defined and directly observed by individuals charged with the responsibility for designing and implementing **Note 3** behavior modification programs.[3] In observing behavior directly, we can measure its frequency, duration, latency, quality, and stimulus control. Chapter 19 is devoted entirely to discussion of strategies for directly assessing behavior.

INDIRECT ASSESSMENT PROCEDURES

Unless you are a therapist who sees clients in your office, direct observation is usually feasible in all the situations in which one would apply behavior modification principles (for example, as a nurse, a teacher, a parent, or anyone else who works directly with people and situations in which the behavior of interest occurs). Professional therapists, however, frequently do not find it practical to observe their clients regularly in the situation in which the target

Note 4 behaviors occur.[4] Typically, the clients of a behavior therapist visit the therapist in his or her office at regularly scheduled appointment times (for example, one hour per week as is the case for other types of professional therapists). Therefore, behavior therapists have made considerable use of indirect assessment procedures. The more common among these are interviews with the client and significant others, questionnaires, role playing, obtaining information from consulting professionals, and client self-monitoring. We now discuss each of these procedures briefly.

Interviews with the Client and Significant Others.   Observation of an initial interview across a random sample of behavior therapists and therapists of other orientations is likely to show numerous commonalities. Because many clients are anxious when first meeting a therapist, the therapist typically does much of the initial talking. The therapist might begin by describing briefly the types of problems with which he or she typically works. The therapist might then ask a number of simple questions concerning the background of the client, or the therapist might ask the client to complete a simple demographic referral form. The therapist might next invite the client to describe, in general terms, what the problem is. During initial interviews, behavior therapists and traditional therapists are likely to use similar techniques to help the client feel at ease and to gain information about the problem, such as being a good listener, asking open-ended questions, requesting clarification, expressing concern for and acknowledging the validity of the client's feelings and problems.

In interviewing the client and significant others (the client's spouse, parents, or anyone else directly concerned with the client's welfare), behavior therapists attempt to establish and maintain *rapport* (that is, a relationship of mutual trust) with the client and any significant others included, just as do traditionally oriented therapists. This relationship can be facilitated by the therapist's being especially attentive to the client's description of the problem while refraining from expressing personal values that may unduly influence the client, showing empathy by communicating some understanding of the client's feelings to the client, and emphasizing the confidentiality of the client-therapist relationship (Bernstein, Bernstein, & Dana, 1974).

Some behavior therapists deliberately keep the discussion during the initial interview at a general level. Others lead the discussion more directly to the presenting problem. Although there are individual differences among behavior therapists in this respect, it is probably accurate to say that behavior therapists are likely to focus discussion on the specific behaviors that characterize the problem or problems of a client sooner in the therapeutic relationship than do more traditional therapists. This can be done by asking a number of questions about a problem and its controlling variables. At some point in the interviewing process, the behavior therapist will help the client to identify major problem areas; select one or two problem areas for initial treatment focus; translate the problem areas into specific behavioral deficits or excesses; attempt to identify controlling variables of the problem behavior; and identify some specific behavioral objectives for treatment.[5] Specific behavioral questionnaires and role playing are often used to facilitate this process.

Note 5

Questionnaires.   A well-designed questionnaire can provide information that may be useful in assessing a client's problem and developing the behavioral program for the client. Several types of questionnaires are popular with behavior therapists:

Life history questionnaires provide demographic data such as marital status, vocational status, and religious affiliation, and background data such as sexual, health, and educational histories. Two notable examples of such questionnaires are Cautela's Behavioral Analysis History Questionnaire (1977) and Wolpe's Life History Questionnaire (see Wolpe, 1982).

Problem checklists have the client indicate which problem applies to him or her from among detailed lists of problems. Such questionnaires are particularly useful in helping the therapist completely specify the problem or problems for which the client is seeking therapy. An example of such a questionnaire is the Behavior Self-Rating Checklist (Upper, Cautela, & Brook, 1975).

Survey schedules provide the therapist with information needed to conduct a particular therapeutic technique with the client. The questionnaire shown in Figure 3-3, for example, provides information useful in applying positive reinforcement procedures. Other types of survey schedules are designed to provide information preparatory to using such procedures as systematic desensitization and convert sensitization (e.g., the Fear Survey Schedule, Wolpe & Lang, 1964). Different types of survey schedules can be found in Cautela (1977, 1981).

Third-party rating scales have been designed to permit significant others and professionals involved with the client to assess subjectively the frequency and/or quality of certain behaviors. A popular example of such a checklist for use with retarded persons is the Adaptive Behavior Scale (Nihira, Foster, Shellhaas, & Leland, 1969). In fact, most assessment instruments for measuring adaptive behavior of retarded persons rely on behavior ratings from third-party informants who are familiar with the behavior of the client being evaluated. Halpern, Irvin, and Landman (1979) argued that we should have more research to examine the extent to which ratings of behavioral competencies of students agree with direct measures of those competencies. One such behavioral assessment instrument of adaptive behavior for retarded persons that has been field-tested adequately both as a rating form and as a direct observation instrument is the OBA (*Objective Behavioral Assessment of the Severely and Moderately Mentally Handicapped*) (Hardy, Martin, Yu, Leader, & Quinn, 1981).

Role Playing. If it is not feasible for the therapist to observe the client in the actual situation in which the problem occurs, an alternative is to recreate that situation (or at least certain crucial aspects of it) in the therapist's office. That, essentially, is the rationale behind role playing in which the client and therapist enact interpersonal interactions related to the client's problem. For example, the client may enact himself or herself being interviewed for a job with the therapist playing the role of the interviewer. Not only is role playing frequently used in conjunction with behavioral interviews in assessing a problem, but it is also used in treating it (for example, see pp. 216–217).

Information from Consulting Professionals. If other professionals (e.g., physicians, physiotherapists, teachers, nurses, social workers) have been dealing with the client in any way related to the problem, relevant information should be obtained from them. For example, a client's problem might be related to some medical factor about which his or her physician could provide extremely important information for dealing with the problem. Before such steps are taken, however, appropriate permission should always be obtained from the client.

Client Self-monitoring. Self-monitoring may be the next best thing to direct observation by the therapist. In fact, it is direct observation by the client of his or her own behavior. We mention it under indirect assessment procedures, however, because the therapist does not observe the behavior directly. Thus, as with the other indirect assessment procedures, the therapist cannot have as much confidence in the observations as would be the case if she or some other trained observer had made them.

The characteristics of behavior that might be self-monitored are the same as those characteristics that would be observed directly by a trained observer—namely, frequency, duration, latency, quality, and stimulus control. Strategies and examples for monitoring these characteristics directly are described in Chapter 19. Additional examples of self-monitoring are provided in Chapter 23.

STUDY QUESTIONS

1. Describe the minimal components of a behavior modification program.
2. What is the difference among a training program, a therapy program, and an intervention strategy?
3. Give five reasons for collecting accurate data during a baseline and throughout a program.
4. What type of error is exemplified by the case of Dr. Caldwell and the door-slammer's mother? Explain how accurately recorded data counteracted this error.
5. What type of error is exemplified by the case of the boy who went around pinching adults? Explain how accurately recorded data counteracted this error.

6. Briefly describe the details of the clever graphing system devised for the child who got the rabbit to the carrot patch.
7. Describe how self-recording was used by Anthony Trollope, Ernest Hemingway, and Irving Wallace to help them maintain their writing behavior.
8. What is a prebaseline phase often called, and what functions does it serve?
9. Briefly distinguish between direct and indirect assessment procedures. What determines which is used?
10. List and describe briefly the five main types of indirect assessment procedures.
11. List and describe briefly four types of questionnaires used in behavioral assessments.

EXTENDED DISCUSSION AND NOTES

1. The two types of errors illustrated here are so common that they have been given special names: type I errors and type II errors. A type I error is that of concluding that a given procedure is effective when in fact it is not. A type II error is that of concluding that a given procedure is not effective when in fact it is. From our experience, we would advise the novice to be especially wary of making type II errors. It seems that beginning behavior modifiers tend to give up on a procedure if dramatic results are not obtained quickly. Even programs that are ultimately very effective may take some time to begin showing tangible results.

2. Van Houten and Nau (1981) reported a situation in which displayed data leads to improvement. They found that the percentage of drivers speeding was greatly reduced by erecting along the highway a sign that listed the percentage of drivers not speeding during the preceding week and the best record to date. This study was done in Canada. Later, Sherer, Friedman, Rolider, and Van Houten (1984) replicated the finding in Israel. However, Roque and Roberts (1989) did not obtain the effect when they repeated the study under similar conditions in the United States. The reason for this failure to replicate is not presently known.

3. In describing the dimensions of applied behavior analysis, Baer, Wolf, and Risley, (1968, p. 93) suggested that a person's "verbal description of his own nonverbal behavior usually would not be accepted as a measure of his actual behavior unless it were independently substantiated. Hence, there is little applied value in demonstrating that an impotent man can be made to say that he is no longer impotent. The relevant question is not what he can say, but what he can do. Application has not been achieved until this question has been answered satisfactorily."

4. As indicated earlier in this book (Chapter 1, note 2; and Chapter 2), a major purpose of traditional psychodiagnostic assessment was to identify the type of mental disorder assumed to underlie abnormal behavior. To help practicing clinicians diagnose clients with different types of presumed mental illness, the American Psychiatric Association developed the *Diagnostic and Statistical Manual of Mental Disorders* (DSM I, 1952). The manual was later revised as the DSM II (1968). Behavior therapists rejected the psychiatric scheme for diagnosis for several reasons. First, they did not accept the medical model of abnormal behavior that suggests that problem behavior is a symptom of an underlying disturbance in a personality mechanism. Rather, they assumed that abnormal behavior is primarily a function of specifiable environmental causes. Second, they were impressed by the strong evidence that the psychiatric scheme for diagnosis was lacking in reliability, validity, and treatment implications (Hersen, 1976). In 1980, the American Psychiatric Association published the DSM III, which is different from the two previous versions in several respects. First, it attempts to be generally atheoretical rather than being grounded in psychodiagnostic theorizing. Emphasis is placed on describing and categorizing the specific problems rather than making assumptions about their causes. Second, a comprehensive description of individual disorders is provided, including such information as essential and correlated features, age of onset, course, impairment, complications, predisposing factors, prevalence, sex ratio, familial patterns, and requirements for differential diagnosis. Third, the system is multidimensional. The first two dimensions include all of the various disorders included in the DSM II. The third dimension requires identification of physical disorders and conditions as well. The fourth dimension requires identification of "psychosocial stressors" that may contribute to the problem. The fifth dimension requires the therapist to rate the individual's level of adaptive functioning when that individual is functioning at his or her best. These last two dimensions provide additional information for planning treatment, managing the case, and predicting outcome. In consideration of the improvements of the DSM III over its predecessors, several prominent behavior therapists have argued that it behooves behavioral clinicians to classify their patients according to the DSM III in addition to conducting detailed behavioral assessments (Hersen & Last, 1985; Hersen & Turner, 1984; Kazdin, 1983). However, this advice may be premature. There has now arrived on the scene the DSM III-R ("R" is for "revised") (American Psychiatric Association, 1987). As we noted above, the DSM III was considered to be an advance over earlier editions because it attempted to be atheoretical. There appears to have been some retreat from this position in the DSM III-R (Nathan, 1987). Moreover, DSM III was an attempt to utilize an empirical basis for diagnostic categories. There appears to be a retreat also from this position. This is evidenced by the inclusion of several new categories of problem behavior that are likely to be controversial and are not well supported at this time by data (Nathan, 1987). One of these attempts is to categorize premenstrual syndrome (PMS) as a disorder. Nathan (1987, p. 205) observes that these changes "foreshadow a marked return to unsubstantiated theory in the development of DSM IV [the next revision]."

5. Numerous studies have examined the effects of the behaviors of the interviewer on the performance of the interviewee. These studies in conjunction with behavioral analyses of the goals of interviewing procedures in behavior therapy have been used to provide detailed guides for individuals interested in behavioral approaches to interviewing. Specific guidelines for behavioral interviewing can be found in Cormier and Cormier (1979).

STUDY QUESTIONS ON NOTES

1. What was an example of a type I error given in this chapter?
2. What was an example of a type II error given in this chapter?
3. Describe how feedback has been used to reduce speeding.
4. Why did behavior therapists reject traditional psychodiagnostic assessments as exemplified by the DSM I and DSM II?
5. How does DSM III differ from DSM I and DSM II?
6. According to Nathan, how does DSM III-R differ from DSM III?

CHAPTER 19

Direct Behavioral Assessment: What to Record and How

Let us suppose that you have chosen a particular behavior on which to work. How do you directly measure, assess, or evaluate that behavior?

As we mentioned in Chapter 18, behavior modifiers generally prefer direct to indirect measurement of a behavior whenever direct measurement is feasible. In measuring behavior directly, there are four general characteristics to consider: frequency, quality, duration, and stimulus control.

CHARACTERISTICS OF BEHAVIOR TO BE RECORDED

FREQUENCY

A measure that is often useful is the number of instances of the behavior that occur in a given period of time. If you are interested in teaching self-feeding to a child, for example, you might examine the frequency of slopping and the frequency of eating with the hands during mealtime. (Another word, often used interchangeably with frequency, is *rate*.) The first step would be to attempt to define slopping and eating with hands in such a way that you or anyone else could observe the child and decide when either of these responses occur. Let us suppose that you define the responses in the following way:

1. *Slopping food.* An instance of slopping is to be recorded whenever food drops and lands anywhere except in the mouth or back on the plate, as a result of

a. the child moving a utensil from her plate to her mouth, or vice versa;
b. the child loading her utensil with food or attempting to cut through it;
c. the child moving her plate around;
d. the child dropping food from her mouth.

Each of these occurrences is to be counted as one instance of slopping, regardless of the actual amount of food that may be dropped on any one occasion.

2. *Eating with the hands.* An instance of eating with the hands will be recorded each time the student touches food with his hand(s) while putting the food in his mouth. If the student slops while using his hands, then we record an instance of slopping as well as an instance of eating with the hands.

Now you know what behaviors to look for. Your next step is to take a baseline of how many slops and how many instances of eating with hands occur during several meals. If you have a helper to observe your student during the meal, he or she might use a data sheet such as that shown in Figure 19–1.

In many situations, an individual simply doesn't have a helper or the time to take data with paper and pencil. Fortunately, there are other ways of measuring quantity that require minimal time. One such method is to use a counter, such as the relatively inexpensive wristwatch type used by golfers to record their score. With these counters you can count up to 99 simply by pressing a button for each instance of the behavior. Another easy recording technique is to transfer an item, such as a bead, from one pocket to another. At the end of the session, or at the end of the day, depending on the particular behavior being recorded, the number of beads in the second pocket is counted and recorded. You could also use an electronic calculator. Press "+1" each time an instance of the behavior occurs and the calculator keeps track of the

Date: *January 1*   Observer: *John H.*

Student: *Corrine*

			Observation	
	Instances	Total	Time	Additional Comments
Slops:	~~LHT~~ ~~LHT~~ //	12	20 min	*Evening meal, three other students at the table. Meal: soup, mashed potatoes, hamburger, veg., jello, milk.*
Eating With Hands	///	3	20 min	*Evening meal, three other students at the table. Meal: same as above.*

FIGURE 19–1 A sample data sheet for recording slopping and eating with the hands of mealtimes.

total. Hand-held computers have been used to record more than one behavior or the behavior of more than one individual, along with the times at which each instance of behavior occurs (Paggeot, Kvale, Mace, & Sharkey, 1988; Repp, Karsh, Felce, & Ludewig, 1989). There is usually no excuse for not taking data. Adequate ways of measuring behavior that require little of the observer's time can almost always be found.

    After the daily data have been tallied, they are transformed to a graph. Let us suppose that, over 10 meals, our observer recorded the following number of slops: 21, 27, 19, 18, 20, 24, 26, 16, 17, 23. Let us assume, further, that during the next 10 meals the student was presented with a brief timeout (in which she and her chair were pulled back from the table and held there for 10 seconds) following each slopping response. (In this example, we assume that the child could eat properly, so that no shaping was necessary.) During this program of timeout, the slops per meal were as follows: 10, 8, 5, 3, 1, 3, 2, 5, 6, 4. As shown in Figure 19–2, these data might be graphed in either of two ways. Figure 19–2A is called a *cumulative record* since each of the responses cumulate, or are added to the previous response. For example, consider meal 1. During meal 1, 21 slops occurred; therefore, a dot is made up the side at 21 and across the bottom at meal 1 (see point A). At meal 2, 27 slops occurred. These 27 slops cumulate (i.e., are added) to the 21 slops at meal 1, making a total of 48 slops. Therefore, our second dot is placed so that it corresponds to 48 at the side and to meal 2 across the bottom (see point B). During meal 3, 19 slops occurred, and these 19 are added to the cumulative total, 48, from the previous two meals. Thus, our third dot is placed at a spot corresponding to 67 on the vertical line and meal 3 on the horizontal line. In this way, the performance during any one meal is added to the total performance during previous meals to be graphed on the cumulative record.

    The first 10 points of the graph describe the child's performance during the evening meal, when no attempt was made to influence slopping. An inspection of the performance on the first ten meals of the cumulative record shows a medium slope (not too steep and not too low) of the graph line. The slope of the line gives us an idea of how many responses occurred over a given period of time. In other words, it provides an indication of the rate of response. The rate of response is directly related to the slope of the graph line: a steep slope indicates a very high rate of response and a low slope indicates a low rate of response. In Figure 19–2A, the medium slope during our initial observations indicated a medium rate of responding. One feature of the cumulative record should be noted: the line can never decrease. If the child is not performing at all, in which case there is no response cumulating with what is already there, then the line would be flat.

    The next 10 points of the graph describe the child's performance during the treatment program. During meals 11–20, each time the child slopped, her chair was pulled back from the table and held there for 10 seconds. If the child was quiet at the end of 10 seconds, she was allowed to move up to the table again and resume her meal. This brief timeout clearly

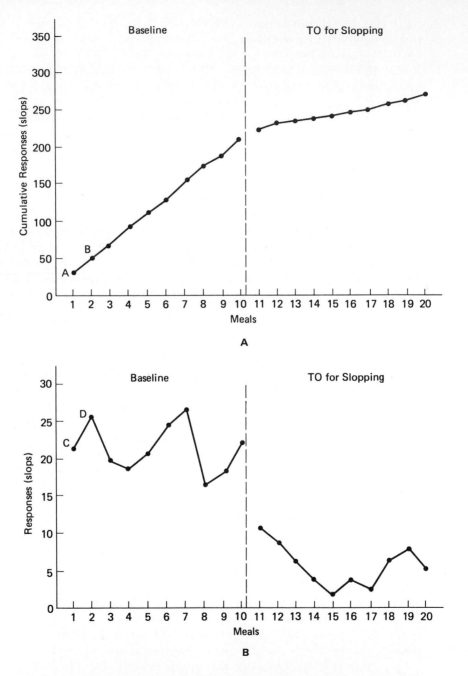

FIGURE 19–2 A cumulative graph (A) and a frequency graph (B) of the same data.

served as a punishment for slopping and decreased the slopping behavior (e.g., see Martin, McDonald, & Omichinski, 1971). This is represented on the cumulative record by a very low slope.

A second type of graph is shown in Figure 19–2B. We call it a *frequency graph*. The features of this graph will become obvious if we consider how each of the points is plotted. Since 21 slops occurred during meal 1, a point is made corresponding to 21 on the vertical line and meal 1 on the horizontal line (see point C). Since 27 slops occurred during the second meal, a point is made corresponding to 27 on the vertical axis and meal 2 on the horizontal axis. Thus, the line can decrease, increase, or stay flat, depending on the number of instances of the response during successive meals. The differences and similarities between a cumulative record and frequency graph can be seen by

Note 1   comparing Figure 19–2A with Figure 19–2B.[1]

It is sometimes possible to design a recording sheet that both records the raw data and serves as a final graph. Let us consider the fictitious case of a child, Jackie, who engaged in frequent biting attacks on other children. Let us suppose that a bite was defined as any instance of Jackie touching his teeth to the skin or clothes of another child and that staff members were requested to watch Jackie as closely as possible during the day. Each time they observed an instance of biting, they were to go to the chart in the main office and place an *X* in the appropriate place. The chart is shown in Figure 19–3.

As you can see from Figure 19–3, the instances of biting were recorded up the side of the graph and the days of the program were recorded across the bottom of the graph. Each time an instance of biting occurred, the staff member would simply add an *X* for the appropriate day to the number of *X*s that were already on the chart for that particular day. The graph shows clearly that the hypothetical treatment program of placing Jackie in a timeout room (a small, empty room) for three minutes following each instance of biting worked quite well to decrease the biting attacks to zero. This type of graph is especially useful for those who do not have the time to rechart their behavior tallies from their data sheet to a graph.

Each instance of a behavior that is recorded in terms of frequency, such as slopping or biting as defined, is a separate, individually distinct behavior that is easy to tally in a given period of time. Behavior modifiers have recorded the frequency of such behaviors as saying a particular word, swearing, throwing objects, completing arithmetic problems, mouthfuls of food, puffs on a cigarette, and nervous twitches. Each of these behaviors has characteristics such that successive occurrences of the given behavior are relatively discrete and the amount of time that it takes to perform the behavior is relatively similar from one occasion to the next.

QUALITY

Many general evaluations of whether or not a person is good at something or poor at something relate to how many times they tend to emit some behavior

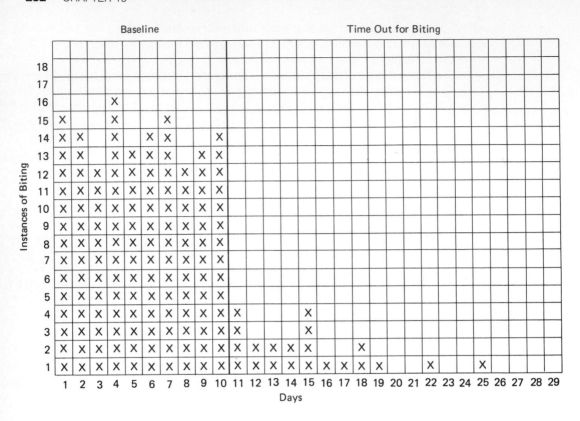

FIGURE 19–3 Jackie's biting behavior. Each X represents one bite.

in a given period of time. For example, the person who is a good student is most likely someone who shows a high frequency of studying and answering test questions correctly. An individual who is said to be a "cooperative child" is one who shows a high frequency of doing what he is told. In assessing the quality of eating performance, we might arbitrarily decide that any child who slops more than two times per meal shows a poor quality of eating behavior. This involves a measurement and graphing of the actual number of slops—in other words, a frequency graph as described in the previous section. A more refined variation of quality assessment would be to specify a particular behavior and then to identify different levels of the quality of that behavior.[2] For example, consider the behavior of arm raising in terms of the steps shown in Table 19–1.

     In Table 19–1, arm raising is analyzed in terms of the steps that a severely handicapped child might go through in gradually acquiring an arm-raising response. A level 1 response is the poorest quality of arm raising, and a level 6 response is the finest quality of arm raising. One could keep track of the individual's performance over a number of trials simply by recording which of the various levels of response the child achieves. This would provide

Note 2

Table 19-1 Levels of Arm Raising from Poor Quality to Good Quality

1	While sitting at a table and resting both arms on the table,	the student raises an arm so that the hand and forearm are two inches off the table.
2	While sitting at a table and resting both arms on the table,	the student raises an arm so that it is approximately at the student's chin level.
3	While sitting at a table and resting both arms on the table,	the student raises an arm so that it is approximately at the student's eye level.
4	While sitting at a table and resting both arms on the table,	the student raises an arm so that his hand is slightly above his head.
5	While sitting at a table and resting both arms on the table,	the student raises an arm so that it is pointing upward with his hand six inches above his head, but the elbow is still bent.
6	While sitting at a table and resting both arms on the table,	the student raises an arm so that it is pointing straight above his head.

us with an indication of the quality of arm raising at any point in time on any given training trial.

In some cases, one might assess quality by utilizing instrumentation to make the appropriate judgments. For example, when voice loudness is the behavior of concern, decibel level can be measured by a device called a *voice meter*.

Recently, one of the authors developed detailed checklists for evaluating swimming strokes in normal children taking swimming lessons. A noteworthy feature of these checklists is that they use pictures to aid the observers in assessing the quality of the behavior. Figure 19–4 shows the checklist for the backstroke.

DURATION

In dealing with a behavior such as temper tantrumming, for example, you may not be particularly concerned (at least initially) with its frequency (how often it occurs) or with its quality (e.g., severity), but you might be quite concerned with how long it lasts. Other examples of situations in which duration of responding is important are attention span, sitting in one's seat in a classroom, watching television, talking on the telephone, and taking coffee breaks.

If you are concerned with recording the duration of a behavior in sessions, then the type of data sheet shown in Figure 19–5 might be appropriate. However, if you are concerned simply with keeping track of the total duration of some activity over successive sessions, or days, then you might easily tabulate and present these data for effective visual display on a combined

Hands: Fingers together
Arms: Roll shoulder into your ear
(Recovery) Arm comes over straight
Arm comes over close to ear
Little finger enters water first

Arms: Lower arm bends to almost 90 degrees under shoulder
(Pull) As arm straightens underwater, snap wrist at thigh and down

Legs: Leg action begins at the hips
Knees move up and down very little
Knees don't break the surface
Toes point down at bottom of kick
Toes just break surface at top of kick

Body: Hips kept high in the water
Hips kept as flat as possible
Head: Tilted up slightly, ears in water
Head kept stationary, don't rock

FIGURE 19–4 Checklist for the backstroke.

data sheet/graph. For example, an individual concerned with monitoring his TV watching might prepare a chart showing cumulative minutes of TV watching up the side and days across the bottom.

Another aspect of duration is the amount of time an individual takes to respond appropriately to a particular stimulus after it is presented. (This is sometimes referred to as the *latency* of the response.) For example, a child in a classroom might work effectively once she gets started; the problem is that she shows a very long latency; that is, after the teacher asks her to do something, she fools around "forever" before starting. Ordinary stopwatches or clocks are usually used to record time.

STIMULUS CONTROL

Frequently, we wish to assess a behavior in terms of the conditions under which it might be observed to occur. As we pointed out in Chapter 8, the term *stimulus control* is used to indicate that certain behaviors occur in some situations and not in others. Hardy and others (1981) designed a detailed system called the *Objective Behavioral Assessment of the Severely and Moderately Mentally Handicapped* (OBA). The OBA assesses the stimulus control of basic self-care skills, social and advanced self-care skills, sheltered domestic skills, prevocational motor dexterity skills, and sheltered work performance of severely and moderately mentally handicapped persons. In this test, the student

Teacher: *Mary*   Student: *Agnes*   Date: *Jan 5/82*

Attention Span	Session (minutes)																				
	0			1			2			3			4			5					
1–2 sec	///		/																		
3–4 sec		//	X	/	//																
5–6 sec					/	/	/		/												
7–8 sec							X	/	/	/				/		/					
9–10 sec										/	/	X		X		/	/				

Procedure: While sitting in front of the student (S) (who has his hands on the table), hold a reinforcer (e.g., a candy) at eye level until S looks at it for the specified duration (beginning with 1–2 seconds), then give S a reinforcer other than the one attended to. After three consecutive reinforced trials at a given attention span, move down to the next level. If a 15-second interval passes without a reinforced trial, return to the previous attention span for one reinforced trial. Record the data in the appropriate column throughout a 5—minute session.

FIGURE 19–5   A data sheet and procedure used to increase the attention span of a severely retarded student.

is instructed to perform a particular behavior—for example, "Please put on your socks." The student's behavior is then scored as shown in Table 19–2.

Hardy and co-workers (1981) identified specific behaviors that appear to be taught in many training programs with severely and moderately mentally handicapped persons. Those target behaviors were then specified in the behavior test, instructions were prepared for the tester, and definitions of the different types of prompts were standardized so that the behaviors could all be assessed on the basis of the rating system just described. This testing system for identifying the conditions under which the behavior will occur is very useful for placement and evaluation of students in individualized training programs. Moreover, as indicated in Chapter 18, the OBA has been field tested both as a rating form for indirect assessment and as a direct observation instrument. The OBA also presents a self-instructional, self-testing program that teaches the reader to use the assessment system accurately and easily.

In many cases, behavior modification programs concerned with the development of preverbal and verbal skills are typically preceded by behavior assessments of the stimulus control of the student's verbal behavior. Tests are available that determine the conditions under which the students will emit appropriate imitative behavior, echoic behavior, or object identification (for example, see Kaprowy, 1975). For that matter, any test in which a student is given instructions, some paper, and a pencil and is asked to answer the questions is a test of the stimulus control of behavior—are the correct answers under the control of the questions? In many training programs, the critical measure of behavior is whether or not the student identifies some pictorial or printed stimulus correctly. In such cases, the student's identification response is said to be controlled by the stimulus that the student is identifying.

CONTINUOUS RECORDING, INTERVAL RECORDING, AND TIME-SAMPLING RECORDING

For any given behavior, one could attempt to record that behavior continuously, day and night. In most cases, this method is far too ambitious for our

Table 19-2 Scoring Student Behavior from the OBA

TEST ITEM	SCORE
The test item was performed approximately in all respects without further prompting or guidance of any kind after a specific instruction was presented.	3
The test item was performed appropriately only after the instruction and a verbal prompt were provided by the tester.	2
The test item was performed appropriately only after the instruction and a prescriptive verbal prompt (similar to the verbal prompt except that it provides much more detail) were given concurrently with modeling of the desired behavior.	1
The test item was not performed appropriately to the preceding level of prompting.	0

time and resources. One alternative is to designate a specific segment of time, such as a one-hour training session, an afternoon, a mealtime, or a recess time, and attempt to record every instance of the specified behavior throughout that interval. Recording every instance of a behavior during a specified time segment is called *continuous recording*.

An alternative strategy is *interval recording*. Here, a specific block of time is selected (such as a 30-minute observation period). This time is then divided into equal intervals of relatively short duration (frequently, intervals of 10 seconds). A specified behavior is then recorded a maximum of once per interval throughout the observation period, regardless of how many times the behavior might occur during each interval and regardless of the duration of the behavior. An observer might use a tape recorder that plays a prerecorded beep (or some such signal) every 10 seconds. Let us suppose that the behavior of concern is an appropriately defined social-interaction response. If the response occurs once during a 10-second interval, a tally is made on the data sheet (for a sample data sheet, see Figure 19–7). If several responses or continuous social interaction occurs during the 10-second interval, the observer still makes only one tally. As soon as the beep is heard, indicating the start of the next 10-second interval, the behavior is again recorded either 1 or 0 depending on its occurrence. Behavior recorded in this way is typically graphed in terms of the percentage of observation intervals in which it is observed.

Another behavior-observation technique frequently used is *time sampling* (e.g., see Powell, Martindale, & Kulp, 1975; Schaefer & Martin, 1969). In time-sampling recording, a behavior is scored as occurring or not occurring during very brief observation intervals, each of which is separated from the others by some longer period of time. For example, a parent of a preschool child might be concerned about the frequency of the child's sitting and rocking back and forth (a self-stimulation behavior). It might be useful to have records of this behavior whenever it occurs and for as long as it occurs throughout the child's waking hours, but in general this is not realistic. An alternative is for the parent to seek out the child once every hour and make a note of whether or not the child shows any sitting and rocking behavior during a 15-second observation interval: each observation interval is separated from the next by approximately one hour. This type of observational technique enables one observer to observe one or more behaviors of one or more students, even though the observer has many other commitments during the day. An example of a data sheet for time sampling appears in Figure 19–6.

Frequently, a recording procedure somewhat intermediate to interval recording and time-sampling recording is used. One reason for this is the possibility of missing observations while recording data according to a strict interval-recording system. For example, assume that an observer is attempting to record the occurrence or nonoccurrence of a behavior during 10-second intervals. The behavior might occur at the start of the next 10-second interval, while the observer is recording the results of the previous interval, and the

DATE _____

Time	Behavior			Location			Comments
	Sitting	Standing	Rocking	Kitchen	Living Room	Bedroom	
8:00 AM							
9:00							
10:00							
11:00							
12:00 PM							
1:00							
2:00							
3:00							
4:00							
5:00							
6:00							
7:00							
8:00							
9:00 PM							

FIGURE 19–6 A time-sampling data sheet for recording behavior of a child who frequently sits and rocks.

observer might therefore miss the occurrence of the behavior. Thus, it is common for an observer to watch the student for a specified interval (say, 10 seconds) and then to record the behavior during the next interval (the next 10 seconds) over a given period of time (for instance, half an hour). Another reason for combining the two systems is that one observer may wish to record the behavior of several students. In such a case, the observer might watch one student for 10 seconds and then record a behavior as occurring or not occurring, watch another student for 10 seconds and record a behavior as occurring or not occurring, and so forth, until all the students have been observed once. All of the students would then be observed a second time, a third time, and so forth, throughout the observation period. Strictly speaking, such an observation system could also be described as time sampling with a very brief time between observation intervals.

ASSESSING THE ACCURACY OF OBSERVATIONS

Hawkins and Dotson (1975) identified three sources of error that can affect the accuracy of observations. First, the *response definition* might be vague, subjective, or incomplete, so that the observer has problems in taking accurate observations. Second, the *observational situation* might be such that it is difficult for an observer to detect the behavior because of distractions or other obstructions to the observing process, or because the behavior is too subtle or complex to be observed accurately in that situation. Third, the *observer* might be poorly trained, unmotivated, biased, or generally incompetent. We might also add two other possible sources of error: poorly designed *data sheets* and cumbersome *recording procedures*. Because any one of these sources of error, or a combination of them, might be present in any behavior modification project, behavior modifiers frequently conduct what are referred to as **inter-observer-reliability (IOR)** estimates. Two independent observers might record observations of the same behavior of the same student during a given session. They are careful not to influence or signal each other while they are recording or to peek at each other's observations. The question is, given their best efforts while using the available behavior definitions and recording procedures, and considering their own training, how closely will their scores compare? There are several ways of comparing their scores, but two are more common than the others.

Let us return to our example of the observer who is recording the number of slops, as defined earlier in this chapter. On day 1 our observer recorded 21 slops. Let us suppose that on day 2 we bring in a second observer, who stands on the other side of the table and watches our student. The second observer is familiar with the definition of slopping and uses exactly the same data-recording sheet as our first observer. At the end of the meal, our first observer recorded 27 slops. Let us suppose that our second observer scored 29 slops. This can be converted to an estimate of our IOR by dividing the smaller number by the larger number and multiplying by 100 percent: IOR equals 27 divided by 29 times 100 percent equals 93 percent. Now it is important to ask what this IOR score means. It means that the two observers agreed quite closely (almost 100 percent) on the total *number* of slops. It does not mean that they agreed on 27 specific responses, with the second observer counting 2 extra to make 29. It is quite possible, for example, that one observer recorded a slop and that the second observer missed it. The second observer could then have counted a slop that the first observer missed. This could have gone on throughout the meal, in which case the two observers would have disagreed completely. Nevertheless, their agreement on the total gives us more confidence in the actual total number of slops that were tallied, in spite of the possible disagreement on individual cases. This approach of counting two totals and then dividing the smaller by the larger and multiplying by 100 percent is quite common when the two observers are counting the frequency of a particular response over a period of time.

The second IOR procedure is used with interval recording. Recall that in interval-recording procedures, one and only one response can be recorded during each brief period of time (usually 5 or 10 seconds) over an extended observation period. If we have two independent observers recording the same behavior, and each is using an interval-recording procedure, then the question is: How do their successive intervals compare in terms of those that contain a response versus those that do not? Let us suppose that two observers are recording two types of social interaction for one child. The behaviors are defined as touching another child and vocalizing in the direction of the other child. Their interval scores are shown in Figure 19–7.

As you can see, the first observer counted 18 instances of touching, as did the second observer. However, the two observers agreed on only 16 of these 18 instances. Each counted 2 instances that the other missed, yielding a total of four disagreements. Our IOR is obtained by dividing the number of intervals on which they agree that the behavior occurred, by the total number of intervals on which either recorded a behavior (agreements divided by agreements plus disagreements on the occurrence of a behavior), and multiplying by 100 percent:

$$\text{IOR} = \frac{16}{16+4} \times 100\% = \frac{16}{20} \times 100\% = 80\%$$

What is considered an acceptable IOR in behavior modification studies? It has been suggested that by convention IOR should be between 80 and 100 percent (Kazdin, 1989, p. 71). However, potential variation in computational procedures renders the final IOR value potentially misleading when **Note 3** considered by itself.[3] We would suggest that readers of behavior modification literature consider the response definitions, observer-training procedures, recording system, method of calculating IOR, and the final IOR value as a total package when judging the reliability of reported data. Defects in any of these might make the results suspect.

Observer 1

Observation Intervals (ten seconds each) Total Behavior

	5	10	15	20	25	30	35	40	45	Total Behavior
Touching										18
Vocalizing										

Observer 2

Observation Intervals (ten seconds each) Total Behavior

	5	10	15	20	25	30	35	40	45	Total Behavior
Touching										18
Vocalizing										

FIGURE 19–7 Sample data sheet for interval recording.

STUDY QUESTIONS

1. Describe three ways of keeping track of the number of times a certain response occurs during a day.
2. Prepare a cumulative graph of the following instances of a behavior that were observed during successive sessions: 3, 7, 19, 0, 0, 0, 27, 12, 12, 6.
3. Describe at least four ways in which a cumulative graph of a set of data differs from a frequency graph of the same data.
4. On a cumulative graph, what can you infer from the following?
   a. a steep slope
   b. a low slope
   c. a flat line
5. Draw and describe briefly a data sheet that would also serve as a graph.
6. In what two major ways is timing important? Give examples of each.
7. What do we mean by the latency of a response? Give an example.
8. What behavioral characteristic does the OBA assess? Explain your answer.
9. Describe with an example the continuous-recording system.
10. Describe with an example the interval-recording system.
11. Describe with an example the time-sampling-recording system.
12. Describe with an example how a procedure intermediate to interval recording and time-sampling might be used.
13. When would one likely select an interval-recording system over a continuous-recording system?
14. Describe five sources of error in recording observations.
15. In a sentence or two, what do we mean by interobserver reliability? (Describe it in words, and don't give the procedures for calculating IORs.)
16. Using the procedure described in the text for computing IORs with interval data, compute an IOR for the data of vocalizing, as recorded by observers 1 and 2 (Figure 19–7). Show all your computations.
17. According to convention, what is an acceptable IOR in a research program? What does "by convention" mean?

PRACTICE EXERCISE

Select a behavioral deficit or excess that was modified successfully (for example, Peter's tantrums), as described in one of the other chapters. For that behavior:

a. Design in a plausible data sheet.
b. Prepare a summary of some representative data (real or hypothesized).
c. Graph your data in a frequency graph.
d. Graph your data in a cumulative graph.

SELF-MODIFICATION EXERCISE

Select one of your own behavioral excesses or deficits. For that behavior, answer questions a–d above.

EXTENDED DISCUSSION AND NOTES

1. Simple frequency graphs are much more common than cumulative graphs in behavior modification studies. In some situations, however, a cumulative graph is more advantageous. For example, when continuous recording is being used, a cumulative graph can give one a direct impression of rate of response more easily than a frequency graph because in a cumulative graph changes in rate can be inferred from changes in the slope of the line. A cumulative graph may also be preferred when an experimenter is comparing two or more behaviors or conditions concurrently. For example, one of the authors conducted an experiment in which severely retarded and autistic children were taught to identify pictures of antonyms (wet versus dry, big versus small, etc.; Martin, 1975). The children received two training sessions per day, one training session utilizing one set of antonyms, and the other training session being used to teach a second set. The procedure in both cases was the same, except for one factor. With one set of antonyms, wrong responses were followed by a brief timeout (5 to 10 seconds) in which the teacher simply turned her head from the child and ignored him. With the second set of antonyms, wrong responses by the child resulted in a longer timeout (15 to 20 seconds). The question being asked was which of the two timeout durations would have a greater suppression effect on error responding. The results for one child, Roger, are plotted cumulatively in Figure 19–8.

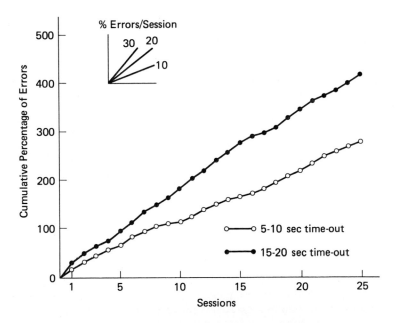

FIGURE 19–8   Cumulative percentage of errors by Roger during a picture-naming task under two experimental condtions.

It can be seen from Figure 19–8 that Roger consistently made fewer errors when errors were followed by the shorter timeout. Although the differences were small within any one session, the gradual spread of the cumulative graphs clearly showed the consistent effect. If these results were plotted as frequency graphs, the effect would be more difficult to detect visually, because the two lines would be very close to each other across the graph and would frequently overlap. For further discussion of the role of cumulative graphs in a science of behavior, see Killeen (1985).

2. Thierman and Martin (1989) devised a different system for measuring quality of household cleaning by four severely mentally handicapped adults living in a community residence. To assess quality of cleaning, inconspicuous "markers" were placed on the surfaces to be cleaned. The markers were small amounts of substances which resembled commonly found dirt in each task. Soap smears were used in the bathtub, as this is a substance often found in "dirty" tubs. Carpet freshener was used in dusting, as it resembles dust. Toothpaste smears were used in the mirror-cleaning task, as these are often found on dirty mirrors in the bathroom. And in the kitchen-cleaning task, several different food markers were scattered around, including sugar, ketchup, rice, crumbs, vegetables, coffee grounds, and water. After a client had performed a cleaning task, a percentage score was derived by counting the number of markers cleaned in comparison to the total number of markers that had been inconspicuously dispersed prior to cleaning. In their research, Thierman and Martin were able to demonstrate that an intervention self-management package made up of picture prompts, self-monitoring, and public posting of results was an effective strategy for teaching severely mentally handicapped adults to improve the quality of their household cleaning.

3. The procedure that we have suggested for computing IOR during interval recording is that of dividing the number of intervals on which observers agree that a behavior occurred by the total number of intervals on which either recorded a behavior (agreements plus disagreements on a behavior) and multiplying by 100 percent. Some researchers, however, include in their measure of agreements, agreements between two observers that no behavior occurred—in other words, agreements on blank intervals. However, when very few behaviors have been recorded, this can greatly inflate a reliability score. For example, consider the 45 observation intervals given in Figure 19–7. Let us suppose that observer 1 recorded an instance of touching during interval 5 and that observer 2 recorded an instance of touching during interval 6. No other instances of touching were recorded. In such a case, the two observers would disagree completely on the occurrence of the behavior; the IOR would be zero if IOR is computed as suggested in the text. However, if agreements on blank intervals are included, their IOR equals 43 agreements divided by 43 agreements plus 2 disagreement times 100 percent, equals 95.6 percent. Because of this distortion, many researchers follow the proposal that we have suggested in the text for computing IOR and do *not* count agreements on blank intervals. In other words, intervals in which neither observer scores a behavior are ignored. An acceptable exception to this would be when one is concerned with decreasing a behavior and having agreement that the behavior did not occur. These points and other comments on the complexity of computing IOR are discussed in more detail in Barlow, Hayes, and Nelson (1984), Barlow and Hersen (1984), and Poling and Fuqua (1986).

STUDY QUESTIONS ON NOTES

1. What are two types of situations in which a cumulative graph might be more informative than a frequency graph in terms of the direct impression obtained from viewing the graph?

2. Describe how Thierman and Martin used "markers" to assess quality of household cleaning by severely mentally handicapped persons.

3. When is it especially misleading to include agreement on blank intervals in computing the IOR? Give an example.

4. For the data given in Figure 19–7, compute the IOR but include agreements on blank intervals in your number of agreements. Now, compute IOR but include only agreements on intervals during which behavior occurred. How do your two measures compare?

5. When might it be acceptable to include agreement on blank intervals in your computation of IOR? Why would this be acceptable?

CHAPTER 20

Doing **Research** in Behavior Modification

In Chapter 18, as in many places in this text, we emphasize that a minimal behavior modification program should have at least three phases: a *baseline phase*, for determining the initial level of the behavior prior to the program; a *treatment phase*, in which the intervention strategy is initiated; and a *follow-up phase*, for evaluating the persistence of the desirable behavior changes following termination of the program. If a behavior modifier has done a good job of programming for generalization (described in Chapter 12), then the follow-up phase should show that the improved behavior is persisting. However, many publications concerning behavior modification go beyond these three minimal phases and describe data that demonstrate convincingly that it was indeed the treatment that caused a particular change in behavior. This emphasis on scientific demonstration that a particular treatment was responsible for a specific behavioral change has produced a continual refinement of behavior modification procedures to their present highly effective level. The value of such demonstrations might be illustrated best with a hypothetical example.

Our example involves a second-grade student's frequency of successfully completing addition and subtraction problems in daily half-hour math classes. The student, Billie, was performing at a much lower level than were any of the other students and was showing a great deal of disruptive behavior during the class. The teacher, Ms. Johnson, reasoned that an increase in Billie's performance at solving the assigned math problems might make it more pleasurable for Billie to work at the problems and might thereby decrease his disruptive interactions with those around him. During a one-week baseline,

Ms. Johnson assigned a certain number of problems to the class and recorded the number that Billie completed successfully during each half-hour period. Billie averaged successful completion of seven math problems per half-hour. Ms. Johnson next introduced a reinforcement program. She told Billie that for each math problem he completed successfully he could add one extra minute of time to his physical education class on Friday afternoon, an activity that appeared to be highly pleasurable for him. Billie's performance improved during the first week of the program. During the second week, he averaged 19 correct math problems per half-hour class.

Can the teacher attribute the improvement in Billie's performance to the treatment? Our initial tendency might be to say "yes," in that performance is much better now than it was during the original baseline. Consider, however, that the improvement may have been due to other factors. For example, Billie may have had a bad cold during baseline and may have started to get over his illness during the first week of the program; his recovery could have resulted in the subsequent mathematical improvements. Or a new student who set a good example for Billie to model may have been seated near him during the treatment phase but not during the baseline. Or perhaps the problems assigned during the treatment phase were easier than those assigned during baseline. Or perhaps something that the teacher could not possibly have been aware of was responsible for his improved performance.

In any program in which a treatment phase is introduced for the purpose of modifying the behavior of some individual, it is quite possible for some uncontrolled or interfering variable or condition to occur concurrently with the treatment, such that the change in the behavior is due to the uncontrolled variable rather than the treatment itself. A behavior modification research project attempts to demonstrate convincingly that it was the treatment, rather than some uncontrolled variable, that was responsible for the

Note 1 change in the behavior in question.[1]

THE REVERSAL-REPLICATION (ABAB) RESEARCH DESIGN _____

Let us suppose that Ms. Johnson, being scientifically inclined, is aware of the possibilities noted above, and would like to demonstrate convincingly that it was indeed her program that was responsible for Billie's improvement. (Besides satisfying her curiosity, there are several practical reasons why she might have wanted to demonstrate the success of her program. For example, such a demonstration would indicate whether she should try a similar procedure with another problem Billie might have, whether she should recommend similar procedures to Billie's other teachers, and whether she should try similar procedures with other students in her class.) Therefore, at the end of the second week of the reinforcement program, she eliminated the reinforcement and returned to the baseline condition. Let us suppose that the hypothetical results of this manipulation by the teacher are those shown in Figure 20–1.

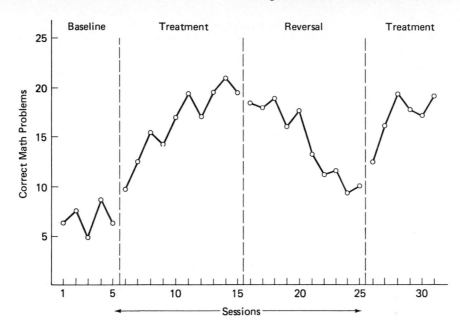

FIGURE 20–1   Hypothetical data showing a reversal-replication (ABAB) design for Billie.

By the end of the second week of return to the baseline conditions (which is called a *reversal*), Billie was performing at a level approximately that of his original baseline. Ms. Johnson then reintroduced the treatment phase, just as it had been before, and, as can be seen in Figure 20–1, Billie again improved his performance. Ms. Johnson had replicated both the original baseline and the original treatment effects. If some uncontrolled variable was operating, one must hypothesize that it was occurring mysteriously at exactly the same time the treatment program was operative and was not occurring when the treatment program was removed. This becomes much less plausible with each successful replication of the effect. We now have much more confidence that it was indeed the teacher's procedure that produced the desired behavior change. Ms. Johnson demonstrated a cause-effect relationship be-tween a particular behavior, sometimes referred to as a *dependent variable*, and
Note 2   her treatment program, sometimes referred to as the *independent variable*.[2]

The type of experimental strategy that Ms. Johnson employed is called a **reversal-replication** design. It is so named because it includes a reversal to baseline conditions followed by a replication of the treatment phase (and, it is hoped, of the effect). The baseline condition is often abbreviated "A," and
Note 3   the treatment condition "B." Hence, this design is also called an **ABAB** design.[3]

Although the reversal-replication design appears simple at first glance, beginning students doing behavior modification research quickly encounter several questions that are not very easy to answer. Assuming that problems of response definition, observer accuracy, and data recording (discussed in

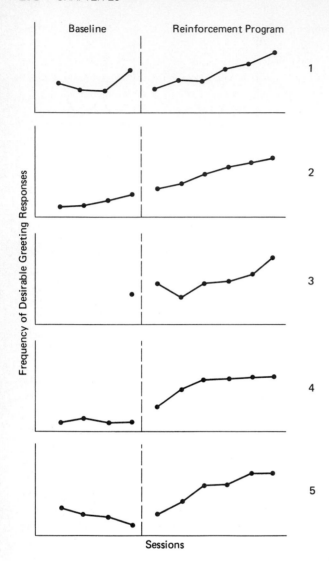

FIGURE 20–2 Hypothetical data for five children.

Chapter 19) have been solved, the first question is this: How long should the baseline phase last? The difficulties of answering this question might be appreciated best by viewing Figure 20–2. Which of the baselines in Figure 20–2 do you consider to be the most adequate? If you selected baselines 4 and 5, we agree. Baseline 4 is acceptable because the pattern of behavior appears stable and predictable. Baseline 5 is acceptable because the trend observed is in a direction opposite to the effect caused by the independent variable. Ideally then, a baseline phase should continue until the pattern of performance is stable or until it shows a trend in the direction opposite to that predicted when the independent variable is introduced.

However, other considerations may lead one to shorten or lengthen a baseline in any applied research project. First, there are scientific considerations related to the newness of the behavior and the independent variables being studied. One might be more comfortable conducting a shorter baseline in a new study of behavior that has already been well researched than in a study of a less explored area. Second, practical considerations might limit the length of baseline observations. The available time of the experimenter, the availability of observers, restrictions on students for completing projects on time, and any of a number of other factors might lead one to limit or extend the baseline for nonscientific reasons. Finally, ethical considerations often affect baseline length. For example, if one is attempting to manage the self-abusive behavior of a retarded child, then an extended baseline phase is ethically unacceptable.

Another question that a beginning student in behavior modification research will encounter is this: How many reversals and replications are necessary? Again, there is no easy answer to this question. If one observes a very large effect when the independent variable is introduced, and if the area is one that has been explored before, then one replication may be sufficient. Other combinations of factors might lead the student to conduct several replications in order to convincingly demonstrate a cause-effect relationship.

Although a reversal-replication design is the most common behavior modification research strategy, it does have limitations that make it inappropriate in certain situations. First, it may be undesirable to reverse to baseline conditions following a treatment phase. For example, when treating a retarded child's self-abusiveness, it would be ethically unacceptable to reverse to baseline immediately following a successful treatment.

Second, it may be impossible to obtain a reversal. For example, "behavioral trapping" may prevent a reversal. In Chapter 12, we described how a shy child might be taught to interact with his peers; once the teacher's reinforcement produces the desirable interaction, the child's behavior might be "trapped" by his peers who maintain it after the withdrawal of the teacher's attention. Other behaviors may not reverse to baseline conditions because the behavior has become "self-reinforcing." Once a golf pro has taught a novice golfer to hit a golf ball over 200 yards, it is unlikely that the golfer will deliberately return to his original, unorthodox swing, which produced a 150-yard drive. Occasionally, it may be impossible to do a reversal because of changes in body structure. For example, it is impossible to use the reversal-replication design to investigate the effects of an appendectomy on emotional behavior.

MULTIPLE-BASELINE DESIGNS

As we noted, a major purpose of behavior modification research is to demonstrate the control imposed on behavior by a particular treatment. Multiple-baseline designs are used to accomplish this without reversing to baseline conditions.

A MULTIPLE BASELINE ACROSS BEHAVIORS

Let us suppose that Ms. Johnson was concerned with demonstrating the effects of her reinforcement procedure on Billie's academic performance, but did not want to do a reversal and risk losing the improvement shown by Billie. She might have accomplished her demonstration of treatment control over improved performance by constructing a **multiple baseline across behaviors**. Her first step would have been to baseline two or more behaviors concurrently. Specifically, she might have recorded Billie's performance in solving math problems during math class, his performance in spelling correctly during English class, and his sentence writing during creative writing class. These baselines might have been those shown in Figure 20–3. The multiple-baseline design across behaviors calls for the introduction of the treatment sequentially across two or more behaviors. The extra minute of physical education class per correct problem might have been introduced in the math class while the baseline condition was continued during spelling and writing classes. If the results were those shown in Figure 20-3, the teacher might next have introduced the treatment for the second behavior—correct spelling.

Finally, the teacher might have introduced the treatment for the third behavior—sentence writing. If performance was as indicated in Figure 20–3, then it clearly indicated that the behavior changed only when the treatment was introduced. This provides a very clear demonstration of the control of the treatment over several behaviors.

The application of this design assumes that the behaviors are relatively independent. If Ms. Johnson had applied the treatment program to one behavior while the other two behaviors were kept at baseline conditions, and if an improvement had been observed in all three behaviors, then she could not have confidently attributed the improvement to the treatment itself. An example of such generalization across behaviors was reported by Nordquist (1971).

A MULTIPLE BASELINE ACROSS SITUATIONS

Another variety of multiple-baseline design studies the effects of a treatment on a single behavior that occurs in several situations. For example, Corte, Wolf, and Locke (1971) were concerned with eliminating the self-abusive, face-hitting responses of a profoundly retarded adolescent in an institution. A number of procedures had been unsuccessful in eliminating this behavior. As a last resort, the authors designed a very carefully controlled program utilizing brief electric shock punishment to decrease the self-abusive behavior. Because of the obvious practical value of scientifically researching a treatment

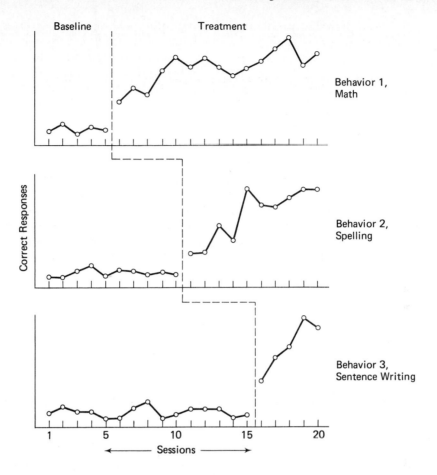

FIGURE 20–3 Hypothetical data illustrating a multiple-baseline-across-behaviors design for Billie.

for eliminating self-abuse; because the authors did not want other therapists to use electric shock punishment unless there was strong evidence for its success (where other procedures had failed); and because a reversal design was unacceptable, the authors decided to use a **multiple baseline across situations** to evaluate the effects of the treatment. They recorded self-abusive behavior in two settings: a small session room and a general ward. Self-abusiveness occurred at a high rate in both settings. The shock procedure was then introduced in the session room; the other setting continued to be baselined. Following the successful reduction of the self-abusive behavior as a consequence of the treatment program in the session room, the shock was introduced in the general ward setting. The treatment program led to a decrease in the second setting as well as the first, demonstrating that the successful treatment of the self-abusiveness was due to the shock contingency.

A potential problem with a multiple baseline across settings is that, when the treatment is applied to the behavior in the first setting, it may cause subsequent improvement in all settings. When this happens, the experimenter is not able to conclude that the improvement was necessarily due to the treatment.

A MULTIPLE BASELINE ACROSS PEOPLE

Yet another multiple-baseline design demonstrates the effectiveness of a treatment by applying it sequentially to individuals. For example, Fawcett and Miller (1975) used a **multiple baseline across people design** to demonstrate the effectiveness of a combination of procedures (called a treatment package) designed to improve public speaking behaviors. Public speaking skills of three individuals were recorded during initial public speaking sessions. The first individual was then given the package while the others continued on baseline. Exposure to the treatment improved the public speaking behaviors of the first individual. The package was introduced sequentially to the second person, and then to the third person, and each time it led to an improvement in public speaking behaviors. This demonstration of improvement in individuals who receive treatment sequentially across time is also a convincing demonstration of the effectiveness of a treatment program. A potential problem with this design is that the individuals involved might deliberately communicate with or otherwise influence other individuals who are being baselined and thereby cause these other individuals to show a change in behavior prior to the introduction of the treatment program (for example, see Kazdin, 1973a).

The obvious advantage of these three multiple-baseline designs over a reversal-replication design is that they eliminate the need for reversing to baseline conditions. On the other hand, it is not always possible to find two or more behaviors, two or more settings, or two or more individuals that can be multiple-baselined such that there is complete independence between the multiple measures. Moreover, it often takes additional time and/or observers to gather the necessary data for multiple baselines.

MULTI-ELEMENT DESIGNS

The preceding research designs are ideally suited for demonstrating that a particular treatment was indeed responsible for a specific behavioral change. But what if one wanted to compare the effects of different treatments within an individual? The previous designs are not well suited for this purpose. An alternative design for such a concern is the **multi-element design**. This design has also been referred to as a multiple schedule design (Hersen & Barlow, 1976), **alternating treatment design** (Barlow & Hayes, 1979; Barlow & Hersen, 1984), and a **simultaneous treatment design** (Kazdin & Hartmann, 1978). As these various names suggest, this design involves alternating two or more treatment conditions considerably more rapidly than would be done in a reversal-replication design. For example, Wrighton (1978) was concerned with comparing several treatments for decreasing self-stimulatory behavior of a retarded teenager during classroom periods for posture training. Two of the treatments that were compared consisted of demerit points (exchanged for a three-minute timeout on a variable-ratio schedule) delivered by a teacher contingent upon self-stimulatory behavior and extinction (no particular consequences were given for the self-stimulation). These two conditions were programmed in randomly alternating sessions. To minimize the possibility of generalization of the results of treatment in one session to the alternative treatment in another session, Wrighton provided very distinctive stimuli associated with the different sessions: she wore a poncho and a black wig under the extinction condition and a yellow ski suit (with her normal red hair) during the demerit point condition. In this way, it was possible for her to compare the relative effects of the two treatments by having each in effect as one element of a multi-element design in randomly alternating sessions. The results can be seen in the top panel of Figure 20–4.

A potential problem with this design is that differential effects of the two treatments observed might be due, in part, to control exerted by the different stimuli associated with the treatment effects. Another problem is that the two conditions may interact, that is, that one of the treatments may produce an effect either because of the contrast to the other treatment in alternating sessions or because of generalization across conditions. And in many studies using multi-element designs, interactions have occurred (Hains & Baer, 1989). In other words, if just one of the treatments had been applied, the effects observed may have been very different. Anticipating these potential problems, Wrighton conducted two additional phases, one of which preceded the data shown in the top panel of Figure 20–4. A baseline and a reversal phase were conducted in which she wore the appropriate clothes but did not apply the demerit point contingency. During the baseline and reversal phase, extinction of the self-stimulatory behavior occurred in all sessions. The results can be seen in the bottom panel of Figure 20–4. These results demonstrate that the separation of the curves in the treatment phase was not due to differential effects of the associated stimulus conditions and that the extinction

Note 4 sessions were not affected by the contrast with the demerit sessions.[4]

As suggested by Sidman (1960, p. 326), it is possible to use the multi-element design to study topographically different forms of behavior. An example of such an application was described briefly in note 1 of Chapter 19. Other examples were described by Koop, Martin, Yu, and Suthons (1980); Martin, Koop, Turner, and Hanel (1981); Stephens, Pear, Wray, and Jackson

Note 5 (1975); and Yu, Martin, Suthons, Koop, and Pallotta-Cornick (1980).[5]

DATA ANALYSIS AND INTERPRETATION

Researchers who employ the behavior modification research designs described typically analyze their data without the use of statistical techniques that are

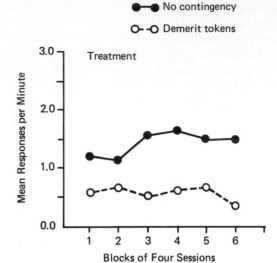

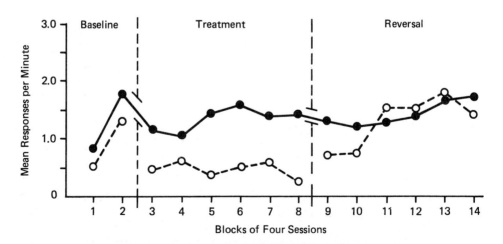

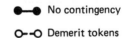

FIGURE 20–4 Self-stimulatory behavior of a retarded teenager during posture-training sessions. The top panel shows data from a multi-element design comparing two treatments. These data were the middle phase of an experiment combining an ABA reversal design with a multi-element design, as shown in the bottom panel. (Adapted from Wrighton, 1978.)

Note 6   more common in other areas of psychology.[6] The evaluation of the effect of a particular treatment is typically made on the basis of two major sets of criteria: scientific and practical. Scientific criteria are used to evaluate whether or not there has been a convincing demonstration that the treatment was responsible for producing a reliable effect on the dependent variable. This judgment is commonly made by visually inspecting the graph of the results. Problems in deciding whether a treatment produced a reliable effect on a dependent variable might best be appreciated by examining Figure 20–5. Most observers of the five graphs contained therein would probably agree that there is a clear, large effect in graph 1, a reliable though small effect in graph 2, and questionable effects in the remaining graphs.

Although there appear to be no consistently applied guidelines for inspecting one's data to judge whether or not a significant effect has occurred, a number of scientific considerations should be kept in mind. One has greater confidence that an effect has been observed, the greater number of times that it is replicated; the fewer the overlapping points between baseline and treatment phases; the sooner the effect is observed following the introduction of the treatment; the larger the effect in comparison to baseline; the more pre-

Note 7   cisely the treatment procedures and response measures are specified[7]; and the more consistent the findings with existing data and accepted behavioral theory.

Judging whether or not a significant effect has occurred from a scientific point of view is one thing; evaluating the importance of behavior change to the client or other significant individuals in the client's life is something else again. In evaluating the clinical effectiveness of the treatment, we must consider more than just the experimental reliability of the treatment's effect on behavior. That is, if graph 2 in Figure 20–5 were a graph of self-abusive behavior, the reliable cause-effect relationship demonstrated therein might be of little clinical significance. If the individual is still extremely self-abusive, as indicated by the performance during treatment phases, then the people responsible for caring for that child would not be satisfied. Judgments about the clinical or applied importance of behavior change have come to be referred to as judgments of *social validity*.

Wolf (1978) has suggested that behavior modifiers need to socially validate their work on at least three levels: (1) they must examine the extent to which target behaviors identified for treatment programs are really the most important for the client and/or society; (2) they must be concerned with the acceptability to the client of the particular procedures used, especially when alternative procedures can accomplish approximately the same results; and (3) they must ensure that the consumers (the clients and/or their caregivers) are satisfied with the results. One social validation procedure involves subjective evaluation in which clients or other significant individuals are asked about their satisfaction with the goals, procedures, and results. A related procedure is to conduct preference tests with clients and to determine which of the two or more alternatives they prefer. In a third procedure, the goals

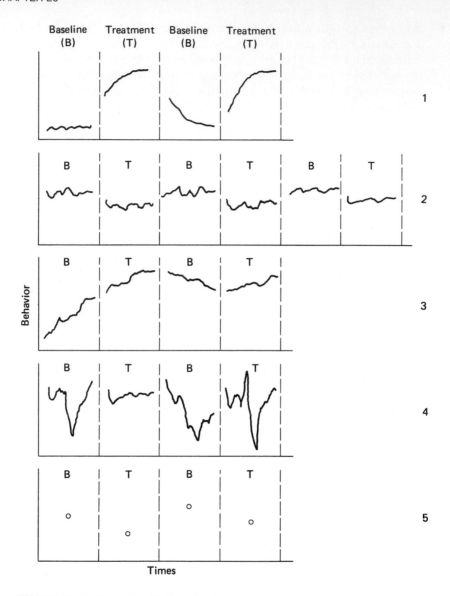

FIGURE 20–5 Some hypothetical data.

as well as the results of treatment are validated socially by comparing results with clients to the average performance of some comparison group, such as nondeviant peers. These strategies are discussed in more detail by Kazdin (1977b) and Wolf (1978).

STUDY QUESTIONS

1. Briefly, describe the minimal components of a behavior modification program?
2. In two or three sentences, distinguish between a minimal behavior modification program and behavior modification research.
3. In two or three sentences, explain why we cannot necessarily claim that a change in behavior during a minimal behavior modification program was due to the treatment.
4. Describe briefly, with reference to an example, the four components of the reversal-replication design.
5. Ideally, how long should the baseline phase of the reversal-replication design continue?
6. In a sentence or two each, describe why baselines 1, 2, and 3 from Figure 20–2 are inadequate.
7. What scientific, practical, and ethical considerations might lead one to lengthen or shorten a baseline?
8. How many reversals and replications are necessary in a reversal-replication design?
9. Identify two limitations of the reversal-replication design, and give a brief example of each.
10. Describe briefly, with reference to an example, a multiple-baseline-across-behaviors design.
11. When is a multiple-baseline-across-behaviors design inappropriate?
12. Describe briefly, with reference to an example, a multiple-baseline-across-situation design.
13. When is a multiple-baseline-across-situation design inappropriate?
14. Describe briefly, with reference to an example, a multiple-baseline-across-people design.
15. When is a multiple-baseline-across-people design inappropriate?
16. Describe briefly, with reference to an example, a multi-element design. Give two other names for multi-element design.
17. Briefly describe two potential problems with the multi-element design.
18. In a sentence or two each, what are the scientific and practical criteria for evaluating the effects of a particular treatment?
19. For each of graphs 3, 4, and 5 in Figure 20–5, describe why it is difficult to draw conclusions about the effects of the treatments.
20. Let us suppose that you have conducted an ABAB design to analyze the effects of a treatment. You are now inspecting your data to judge whether or not a significant effect has occurred. Meeting what six criteria would give you maximum confidence that the treatment had produced a significant effect on the dependent variable?
21. What are the three levels of social validation and why are they important?

PRACTICE EXERCISE

Suppose that you are teaching some students about doing research that ultilizes reversal and multiple-baseline designs. Your students must do a research project in which they select a dependent variable and then evaluate the effects of some treatment upon that dependent variable. Your task as teacher is to analyze the material in this chapter to prepare a guide that will help the students to select the appropriate research design. Your guide should take the form of a series of questions that they might ask, the answers to which would lead to a particular design. For example, if (a) and (b), then choose a reversal design; but if (c), (d), and (e), then choose a multiple-baseline design; and so forth.

SELF-MODIFICATION EXERCISE

As described in Chapter 18, self-recording without any additional behavioral procedures sometimes leads to behavioral change. Let us suppose you have decided to describe a self-recording procedure and then to investigate that as a treatment in a self-modification program. Describe a plausible multiple-baseline design that would enable you to assess self-recording as an effective self-control treatment.

EXTENDED DISCUSSION AND NOTES

1. Actually, there are a number of reasons for conducting behavior modification research. Most often, the research is probably conducted to demonstrate that a particular treatment was responsible for a specific behavioral change. In addition, however, research might be conducted to determine which components of the treatment may have been responsible for the behavioral change observed; to assess the relative effects derived from a particular treatment in relationship to the costs (this type of research is called cost-effectiveness research); to help students complete master's theses and Ph.D. dissertations to obtain advanced degrees; to enable researchers to obtain research grants; to enable one to publish, so as not to perish in one's professorial profession; and for a host of other reasons.

2. Two considerations in evaluating a possible cause-effect relationship are *internal validity* and *external validity*. A finding is internally valid if the independent variable did in fact cause observed changes in the dependent variable. Campbell and Stanley (1963) listed several classes of variables that threaten internal validity. Paraphrased slightly, these are:

a. *History*: the specific events (such as a new student moving beside Billie, as described on p. 276) occurring between the baseline and treatment measures in addition to the treatment variable.
b. *Maturation*: processes within the student (such as Billie overcoming his cold, as described on p. 276) operating as a function of the passage of time, such as growing older, growing hungrier, or growing more tired.
c. *Testing*: the effects of being assessed upon one's performance in subsequent assessments (for example, Billie saying to himself, "Gee, Ms. Johnson is starting to keep my scores every math class. I guess I better shape up").
d. *Instrumentation*: changes in the calibration of a measuring instrument or in the observer's criteria (for example, Ms. Johnson may have asked easier questions during treatment).

e. *Statistical regression*: a statistical law stating that a person who has been selected on the basis of his extreme scores will tend to score less deviantly upon further measurement.

A finding is externally valid to the extent that it can be generalized to other behaviors, individuals, settings, or treatments.

3. In a reversal-replication research design, the reversal phase frequently involves a return to baseline conditions, as we have described in the text. However, there are two other alternatives, either of which might be appropriate for particular research problems. To illustrate the first alternative, consider Ms. Johnson's program for improving Billie's mathematics performance. Following the treatment phase, Ms. Johnson eliminated the reinforcement program. However, she might simply have delivered the one-minute additions to the physical education program (the reinforcers) on a noncontingent basis. This delivery of reinforcers independent of behavior during the reversal is one alternative to completely eliminating the reinforcers, as described in the text, and is referred to as an ABCB design.

   A second alternative is for the researcher to continue delivering the reinforcer during the reversal phase, but to deliver it for any behavior other than the behavior that was reinforced during treatment (such as *not* doing math problems, in Billie's case). This type of reinforcement schedule, called DRO, is discussed in Chapter 7. A complete reversal of the reinforcement rule during the reversal phase is likely to demonstrate very quickly whether or not the treatment was responsible for a behavior change, in that the reinforcer is now presented contingent on any behavior "other" than the behavior influenced during treatment. Examples of this variation during the reversal phase can be found in Bostow and Bailey (1969) and Kazdin (1973b). Leitenberg (1973) called this alternative a "true reversal design," and called the reversal-replication design described in the text a "withdrawal design."

4. What if it is not practical to do a baseline, but you still want to compare two independent variables in a relatively brief period of time? Wacker and his colleagues (1990) recommend a *sequential alternating treatments design* as a possible solution. With this design, two treatments are randomly alternated across sessions, such as illustrated for the middle phase in the study by Wrighton (see Figure 20–4). Then, in a multiple-baseline design across subjects, only one of the treatments is applied for several sessions. Finally, in the multiple-baseline design across subjects, the other treatment is applied for several sessions. This design has proven useful for comparing the effects of two treatments within a relatively short period of time (Wacker and others, 1990).

5. Another type of design is the *changing-criterion design* (see Axelrod, Hall, Weis, & Rohrer, 1974; Barlow & Hersen, 1984). This design attempts to demonstrate stepwise changes in the dependent variable corresponding to stepwise changes in the treatment. Axelrod and colleagues demonstrated control over cigarette smoking with this design by reducing the daily cigarettes allowed in a stepwise fashion. If more than the allowed number of cigarettes was smoked per day, the client was required to tear up a dollar bill for each cigarette smoked over the daily allowed amount. A research design that is common in other areas of psychology is the *control-group design*. This design typically involves at least two groups, one that receives the treatment and one that does not. The average performance of the two groups is then compared according to appropriate statistical procedures. Each of the other research designs described in this chapter focuses on the behavior of individuals. Control-group designs focus on the *average* performance of groups. For this and other reasons, control-group designs have not been popular in be-

havior modification research. For additional discussion of a variety of control-group designs suitable for applied research, see Campbell and Stanley (1963) or Kazdin (1980b).

Reversal-replication and multiple-baseline designs, as well as the two designs described above, are directed toward evaluating the effects of independent variables on behavior change while the treatments are being applied. However, there has been relatively little discussion of experimental designs for assessing response maintenance. Rusch and Kazdin (1981) suggested several designs for evaluating response maintenance after experimental control has been adequately addressed. In maintenance studies, the concern is to demonstrate that behavior is maintained after an intervention has been withdrawn. One design is referred to as the *sequential-withdrawal* design. In this design, one component of a treatment having a number of components is withdrawn initially, then a second, and so on until all components have been withdrawn. By withdrawing each component sequentially in consecutive experimental phases, an experimenter can determine the extent to which individual components are critical to response maintenance. A second maintenance design has been labeled the *partial-withdrawal* design. This design is recommended for a multiple-baseline design and consists of withdrawing part of the intervention or the entire intervention from one of the baselines following a demonstrable behavior change. This enables an investigator to determine what might happen were the treatment withdrawn from all the baselines, but it reduces the risks of losing the behavior since the treatment (or a component of it) is only withdrawn from one of the baselines. A third maintenance design has been labeled the *partial-sequential-withdrawal* design, and this is essentially a combination of the partial and sequential-withdrawal designs described previously. The advantages and limitations of these designs are discussed by Rusch and Kazdin (1981).

6. This is not meant to imply that statistical research designs are not utilized in behavior modification research. The "odd" statistical research design can be found in the *Journal of Applied Behavior Analysis* since its inception in 1968. Moreover, there have been suggestions of appropriate statistical techniques for research in applied behavior analysis (for example, see Johnson & Pennypacker, 1981; Kazdin, 1984). However, Michael (1974) noted that the experimental and applied analyses of behavior have developed increasingly sophisticated and reliable methods of behavioral control, and have done so largely without the use of statistical research designs that characterize other areas of psychology. He argued, further, that because of this, and because the value of statistical-inference procedures for behavior modification has not been empirically demonstrated, applied behavior analysis should continue utilizing research designs such as those described in this chapter, rather than adopting statistical-inference procedures that are currently being recommended by some researchers. Moreover, in his presidential address to the Association for Advancement of Behavior Therapy, David Barlow (1980) emphasized this point from the point of view of the practicing clinician. He argued that the gap between clinical reality and the production and use of scientific data will not be bridged as long as our science emphasizes factorial design, multivariant statistics, and the 0.05 level of probability, for these will never be used in the private office or clinic. (also, see Barlow & Hersen, 1984.) Finally, we might note that, in addition to arguments that applied behavior analysts should *resist* using statistical inference techniques in their research, Hawkins (1989) issued an invitation to clinical researchers to begin using *more* single-subject designs than group statistical designs. While listing the many benefits of single-subject designs, Hawkins argued convincingly that their use is likely to lead to a more powerful behavior change technology.

7. Baer, Wolf, and Risley (1968) have labeled this criterion of an applied study as *technological*. A study is technological when the procedures have been specified precisely enough so that a "typically trained reader could replicate the procedure well enough to produce the same results, given only a reading of the description."

STUDY QUESTIONS ON NOTES

1. What do we mean by *internal validity? external validity*?
2. List and describe briefly the five classes of variables cited by Campbell and Stanley that threaten internal validity.
3. What are some of the reasons people do behavior modification research?
4. Describe the details of the ABAB research design that Ms. Johnson might have applied in which the second A phase would have been noncontingent reinforcement. Can you say why, from a research point of view, this might have been an improvement over the design she used?
5. Briefly describe the steps that might be followed in a sequential alternating treatments design.
6. Describe briefly, with reference to an example, the changing-criterion design.
7. Distinguish briefly between the partial-withdrawal design and the sequential-withdrawal design.
8. Why did Michael and Barlow argue against the use of statistical research designs in behavior modification research?
9. What is a technological study?

CHAPTER 21

Designing a Program
to Overcome a
Behavioral Handicap

In previous chapters we described a variety of principles and procedures for overcoming behavioral handicaps (that is, behavioral deficits or excesses). It is probably obvious by now that most behavioral applications involve combinations of principles and basic procedures. We suspect that it is also obvious that one must make a number of decisions in designing and implementing a program that are not really a part of the scientific principles and procedures themselves. Some behavior modifiers are better than others at the "art" of program design and implementation. In the next four chapters we present a number of guidelines that will help you to become proficient at designing *specific* types of behavior programs. This chapter provides *general* guidelines that should be followed when designing *any type* of behavioral program. The client might be a retarded child, a mental hospital patient, a normal child at home, a normal child in a classroom setting, or perhaps a normal adult. The situation is one in which you, the behavior modifier, or a mediator (parent, teacher, or some other person) would be largely responsible for carrying out the program.

A PROBLEM HAS BEEN REFERRED: SHOULD YOU DESIGN A PROGRAM?

Behavioral handicaps have a variety of causes, exist in a variety of different forms, and differ widely in degree of complexity and severity. The fact that a problem has been referred is not always sufficient reason for proceeding with program design and implementation. To decide where to begin or, indeed, if one should begin at all, it is helpful to try to answer the following questions. It is usually possible to obtain answers to these questions during the screening and general disposition phase of behavioral assessment described in Chapter 18.

1. Was the problem referred primarily for the benefit of the client?
2. Can the problem and the goal be specified such that you are dealing with a specific behavior or set of behaviors that can be counted, timed, or measured in some other way?
3. Is the problem important to the client or to others?
4. Have you eliminated the possibility that there are medical or psychological complications involved in this problem that would necessitate referring the problem to another specialist? (In other words, are you the appropriate person to deal with this problem?)
5. Is the problem one that would appear to be easily manageable?
6. If the goal is reached, might it be easily generalized and maintained?
7. Can you identify significant individuals (such as relatives, friends, and teachers) in the client's natural environment who might help to record observations and manage controlling stimuli and reinforcers?
8. If there are individuals who might hinder the program, can you identify ways of minimizing their potential interference?
9. On the basis of your tentative answers to these eight questions, do your training qualifications, daily schedule, and available time seem adequate for you to participate in the program?

If you answered yes to all these questions, then you might proceed. But let us consider the questions in more detail. Regarding question 1, if the problem was referred by others, then you must determine if the accomplishment of the goal will be for the benefit of the client. If the accomplishment of the goal is for the benefit of others, it should *at least* be neutral for the client. One must be very careful about one's ethics, and some referrals might simply stop here.

Concerning question 2, many referrals are very vague, subjective, and general, such as, "Johnny is hyperactive"; "My child is driving me up a wall"; "I'm really an unorganized person"; "I don't want Teddy to be so darn stubborn." If the problem is initially vague (for example, if it is merely labeled "aggression"), you must specify a component behavior(s) (for example, kicking furniture) that can be measured or assessed behaviorally. However, in such cases it is extremely important then to ask whether dealing with the component(s) will solve the general problem in the eyes of the referring agent or agencies. If it is impossible to agree with the agent on the component behaviors that define the problem, then you should probably stop here. If you do achieve agreement, it should be specified in writing, because people are sometimes forgetful and may later feel that you did not deal with the problem that they referred to you.

Concerning question 3, there are several questions that one might ask, to evaluate the importance of the problem. If the problem is an undesirable behavior, does it usually lead to much immediate aversiveness for the client or others? Will solving the problem lead to much more positive reinforcement for the client or others? Will solving the problem be likely to stimulate other desirable behaviors, directly or indirectly? If the answers to these questions are yes, then it is likely that the problem is important. If the answer is no to some of these questions, then you might reconsider your involvement with that particular problem.

Concerning question 4, it should be obvious that if there is any chance that the problem has serious medical complications (for instance, excessive weight gain or loss) or serious psychological complications (for instance, the danger of suicide), the appropriate type of specialist should be consulted. You should then proceed to treat the problem, if at all, only in a manner that is consistent with the recommendation of that specialist.

Concerning question 5, you might consider the following: If the major problem is to decrease an undesirable behavior, has the behavior been occurring for a short time, under narrow stimulus control, and with few instances of intermittent reinforcement? A problem having these characteristics is likely to be much easier to solve than is an undesirable behavior that has been occurring for a long time, under the control of many stimulus situations, and with a history of intermittent reinforcement. Moreover, you should be able to identify desirable behaviors that can replace the undesirable behavior. If the problem is to teach a new behavior, you should assess whether or not the client has the prerequisite skills.

Concerning question 6, you should consider the following: Can the problem and the improved behavior be managed in the natural environment? If not, can a special training setting be developed that can easily be faded into the natural environment? You should also consider whether there are natural contingencies that will likely maintain the behavioral objective after it has been achieved, whether you can change the people in the natural environment so that they help maintain the desired behavior, and whether it is possible for the client to learn a self-control program (discussed in Chapter 23) so that the improved behavior will persist.

Concerning question 7, you must consider who is available to help manage a program. When designing programs for children, for example, **Note 1** parents can often successfully implement and maintain the program.[1] On the other hand, it makes little sense to accept a referral concerned with the development of a language-training program that will require approximately an hour of concentrated effort per day, if you have only about 10 minutes each day to spend on the project, if the mother and father are separated, and if the mother works full time during the day and has four other children who **Note 2** occupy her attention in the evening.[2]

Concerning question 8, it makes little sense for you to design a program if people are going to be sabotaging it all the time. When a behavior modifier first enters a ward for the retarded, the home of a family with a problem child, or the classroom of a second-grade teacher, the behavioral problems and the number and complexity of potentially disruptive influences are often mind-boggling. For obvious reasons, it is better to start simply so as to succeed in a small way rather than to attempt too much and risk failing gloriously. A careful evaluation of the initial referral in terms of these questions and considerations can often contribute greatly to the initial success of the behavior program.

Concerning question 9, you should only accept those referrals for which you have appropriate training and adequate time to carry out an effective program.

SELECTING AND IMPLEMENTING AN ASSESSMENT PROCEDURE

Let us suppose that you have decided to proceed with designing and implementing a behavioral program for a behavioral handicap referred to you. You might then proceed through the following steps:

1. Define the behavioral handicap in precise behavioral terms, for reliable baselining.
2. Select an appropriate baseline procedure (see Chapters 18 and 19).
3. Select appropriate baseline procedures for monitoring potential side effects of the program.
4. Design recording procedures that will enable you to log the amount of time devoted to the project by the professionals working on it (such as teachers and behavior modifiers). This will help you when you do a cost-effective analysis.
5. Ensure that the observers have received appropriate training in identifying critical aspects of the behavior, applying the recording procedures, and graphing data.
6. Select a procedure for increasing and maintaining the strength of the record-keeping behavior of the data recorders.
7. Select a procedure for ensuring the reliability of the baseline observations (see Chapter 19).
8. Ensure, if appropriate, that your baseline procedure will allow you to identify the current stimulus control and the consequences of the problem behavior.
9. After beginning to collect baseline data, analyze those data carefully to select an appropriate intervention strategy and decide when to terminate the baseline phase and begin the intervention phase.

We reviewed the guidelines for defining, recording, and graphing behaviors in Chapters 18 and 19, and we will not repeat them here. However, there are some additional considerations that a behavior modifier should review before, and during, assessment procedures.

What daily times can the mediator(s) schedule for this project? If, for example, a teacher has about 10 minutes each day just before lunchtime to devote to the project, it is senseless to design time-sampling data sheets that require her to assess behavior throughout the day. It is also senseless to gather data on a wide variety of behaviors that the teacher will never have time to examine. Some behavior modification projects are killed before they start when the behavior modifier designs complex data collection systems that the teacher doesn't have a hope of using.

Will others in the situation help or hinder your data collection? There is no sense in designing a baseline procedure to record the duration of a child's tantrumming in a home situation if a grandmother, an aunt, a brother, or other relatives are going to give the child a candy to stop tantrums because "they can't stand seeing the poor little boy upset." On the other hand, friends and relatives can often be extremely helpful, either by recording data directly or by reminding others to do so. If the help of others is to be utilized, posting data sheets and a summary of the recording procedures where everyone involved in the project can see them (such as in a conspicuous place in the kitchen) is usually a very desirable practice.

Will the physical environment help or hinder your assessment? Let us suppose that you wish to take a baseline on the frequency and timing of a child's urinating and defecating throughout the day. If the house has many rooms and the child wanders through them, it may be difficult to immediately detect instances of the "dirty deed." Or suppose that someone wishes to take a baseline of smoking behavior, but during the baseline spends some time in the house of a friend who doesn't smoke and doesn't have ashtrays around. Obviously this is not ideal for assessment procedures. If you wish to assess the basic self-dressing skills of a severely retarded individual by presenting clothing items with appropriate instructions, and the child's favorite TV program is blaring in the background, then your assessment is not likely to be accurate.

What is the nature of the existing behavior? It is a behavior that occurs frequently throughout the day in many situations, such as thumb-sucking, fingernail biting, whining, or pestering? Or is it one that occurs once every two or three weeks, such as occasional but severe tantrums, stealing, or running away from home? Is the behavior one that requires a quality assessment, such as dusting furniture or washing and drying dishes? In some cases, your answers to these questions might influence you to scrap the project. For example, a problem behavior that occurs very rarely can be extremely difficult to treat if you have very limited time available for the project. Certainly the nature of the behavior will dictate the type of recording procedure to be selected, as described in Chapter 19.

How rapidly should the behavior change? Does the behavior require immediate attention because of its inherent danger (as, for example, in the case of self-abuse)? Or is the behavior one whose immediate change would be extremely convenient for those concerned (for instance, parents who want to toilet-train their child just before going on vacation)? If the behavior is one that has been occurring for many years, and if another few days or weeks more or less won't make much difference, then you might be more diligent in the design of a detailed data-recording system to reliably assess baseline levels of performance. Examples of this latter type of behavior might include smoking, excessive TV watching, and poor housecleaning.

PRELIMINARY CONSIDERATIONS OF PROGRAM DESIGN

Let us suppose that you have completed your assessment of the current level of performance concerning the problem. Before writing out the details of your program, you should review a number of preliminary design considerations:

1. Review the target behavior and the desired stimulus control.
2. Identify individuals (relatives, teachers, and others) who might help to manage controlling stimuli and reinforcers. Also, identify individuals who might hinder the program.
3. Review alternative combinations of principles and procedures.
   a. If you are overcoming a behavioral deficit,
      i. Think of short-cut tactics first:
         (a) instruction (oral and/or written)
         (b) situational inducement (rearrange the surroundings, move the activity to a new location, relocate people, and/or change the time of the activity)
         (c) modeling
         (d) guidance
      ii. Consider whether you want to increase the frequency of an existing behavior or establish a new behavior.
      iii. Decide whether shaping or chaining is more appropriate.
   b. If you are decreasing a behavioral excess,
      i. Think of short-cut tactics first:
         (a) instruction
         (b) situational inducement (relocate people, change time of activity, move activity to a new location, and/or rearrange existing surroundings)
         (c) instruction and modeling
         (d) instruction and guidance
         (e) habit reversal
      ii. Can you try an indirect or partial solution?
         (a) Eliminate early component of a chain.
         (b) For high-frequency behaviors, introduce new stimulus control and partial elimination.
      iii. Consider alternative desirable behavior to be increased.
      iv. Decide whether DRL, DRO, or DRI can be used.
      v. Should punishment be used? Remember that punishment is only acceptable (if at all) as a last resort and under appropriate professional supervision with appropriate ethical approval.

c. If you are changing the stimulus control of an existing behavior,
   i. Select the controlling S^Ds such that they
      (a) are different from other stimuli along more than one dimension.
      (b) are encountered mainly in situations in which the desired stimulus control should occur.
      (c) evoke attending behavior.
      (d) do not evoke undesirable behavior.
   ii. Determine the current stimulus control of the desired behavior.
   iii. Decide how the current stimulus control can be faded so as to achieve the target stimulus control. (Remember that fading can occur along any dimension: color, sound, room size, number of people, appearance of people, gestures, furniture arrangements, familiarity, and so on.)
4. Review the guidelines for the effective application of the selected principles at the end of Chapters 3 to 13.
5. Review ethical considerations of program design.

Let us suppose that your problem is to overcome a behavioral deficit. The behavior that you wish to occur is not now occurring. You should then ask a number of questions designed to determine if one or more of the short-cut tactics cited might be appropriate. Do any of the significant individuals in the client's life know of any instructions that might produce the desired behavior? Is there any significant individual whose modeling of the desired behavior the client might readily imitate? Is there any easily administered physical guidance procedure that, combined with fading, would produce the desired end product? Would the desired behavior occur if the existing surroundings were rearranged? If the activity were moved to a new location or a new time? If significant people were made more obvious or less obvious? If anything from these short-cut tactics might be identified that will produce the desired behavior, then the problem might be phrased primarily in terms of item 3c—changing the stimulus control of the existing behavior. That is, if some short-cut tactics will produce the behavior, then it should be possible to identify some dimensions along which those controlling stimuli can be faded to achieve the desired stimulus control and behavioral objective. If so, then you should examine very carefully the surrounding individuals and the surrounding environment in relationship to the client to select controlling S^Ds according to the guidelines cited.

If your major concern is decreasing some undesirable behavior, there are also a number of preliminary considerations that should be reviewed. These inevitably amount to various strategies for increasing some desirable alternative behavior, as opposed to concentrating on the use of extinction or punishment to decrease the undesirable behavior. A thorough review of the problem behavior in terms of these considerations (see item 3b and Chapter 17) will frequently lead to effective and rapid decelerating procedures such that extinction and/or punishment are not the primary focus of attention.

After an appropriate combination of principles and procedures has been selected, the guidelines for their effective application should be reviewed prior to the explicit design and implementation of a program. Finally, you should review your choice of treatment methods in terms of relevant ethical considerations, such as the ethical issues for human services listed in Table 28-1.

STRATEGIES OF PROGRAM DESIGN AND IMPLEMENTATION

Some behavior modifiers appear to be extremely skillfull at designing effective programs "off the top of their heads"—that is, identifying the program details critical to their success and designing programs that show quick, desirable results. There is probably no set of guidelines for you to follow that will immediately turn you into that kind of behavior modifier. Nor are there any rigid sets of guidelines to which you should adhere for every program you design. Many behaviors can be managed successfully with a very minor rearrangement of existing contingencies; others require much creativity. The following guidelines will help you to design an effective program.

1. Define the goal and identify the target behaviors and identify its (their) desired level of occurrence (i.e., frequency) and stimulus control. Then answer these questions:
   a. Is the description precise?
   b. On what grounds was the goal chosen, and how is that in the client's best interests?
   c. Has the client been given all possible information about the goal?
   d. What are potential side effects of accomplishing the goal, for both the client and others?
   e. Do the answers to these questions suggest that you should proceed?
      If so, then continue, keeping in mind the answers to considerations 2, 3, and 4 in the preceding section.
2. Specify the short-cut tactics and/or positive alternatives (if any) that will be tried (see Chapters 16 and 17 and considerations 3a and 3b in the preceding section).
3. Specify the details of the behavioral-programming steps by answering these questions:
   a. What reinforcers will be used?
   b. How will shaping, fading, chaining, token training, and schedules of reinforcement be used?
   c. What are the necessary precurrent behaviors, and how will they be developed?
   d. What problems might arise, and how can they be managed?
4. Specify the details of the data-recording and data-graphing procedures.
5. Specify the training setting. What environmental rearrangement will be necessary to maximize the desired behavior, minimize errors and competing behavior, and maximize proper recording and stimulus management by the mediators (those directly carrying out the program)?
6. Specify the reinforcer system by answering the following questions:
   a. How will reinforcers be selected? (See Chapter 3.)
   b. How will reinforcer effectiveness be continually monitored and by whom? (See Chapter 3.)

  c. How will reinforcers be stored and dispensed, and by whom?

  d. If a token system is used, what are the details of its implementation?

7. Describe how you will program generality of behavior change (Chapter 12) by:

  a. Programming stimulus generalization

   i. training in the test situation

   ii. varying the training conditions

   iii.programming common stimuli

   iv.training sufficient stimulus exemplars

  b. Programming response generalization

   i. training sufficient response exemplars

   ii. varying the acceptable responses during training

  c. Programming maintenance (generality over time)

   i. using natural contingencies of reinforcement

   ii. training the people in the natural environment

   iii.using schedules of reinforcement in the natural environment

   iv.giving the control to the individual

8. Collect the necessary materials (such as reinforcers, a reinforcer-storage system, data sheets and graphs, and curriculum materials).

9. Make checklists of rules and responsibilities for all participants in the program (staff, teachers, parents, peers, students, the client, and others).

10. Specify the dates for data and program reviews, and identify those who will attend.

11. Identify some contingencies that will reinforce the behavior modifiers and mediators (in addition to feedback related to the data and program reviews).

12. Review the potential cost of the program as designed (cost of materials, teacher time, professional consulting time, and so forth), and judge its merit against its cost. Reprogram as necessary or desired on the basis of this review.

13. Sign a behavioral contract.

14. Implement the program.

  If you have followed all these guidelines, the program is ready to go. However, step 13, signing a behavioral contract, requires some additional discussion. Behavioral contracting was described initially as a strategy for scheduling the exchange of reinforcers between two or more individuals, such as between a teacher and students (Homme, Csanyi, Gonzales, & Rechs, 1969) or between parents and children (Dardig & Heward, 1976; DeRisi & Butz, 1975). Such contracts typically provide a very clear statement of what behaviors of what individuals will produce what reinforcers and who will deliver those reinforcers. However, written agreements between therapists and clients are also increasingly recommended as a strategy for ensuring that the therapist is responsible or accountable to the client (Sulzer-Azaroff and Reese, 1982; O'Banion and Whaley, 1981). Richard Stuart (1975) has developed a client-therapist treatment contract with provision for clearly outlining the objectives and methods of treatment, the framework of the service to be provided, and contingencies for remuneration that may be forthcoming to the therapist. When the agreement is signed, both the client and the therapist have secured basic protections of their rights. We recommend that behavior modifiers prepare such a written agreement with the appropriate individual(s) prior to implementing a program.

   The implementation of your program also requires a great deal of consideration. This might be done in two parts. First, you must be certain that those responsible for carrying out the program, the mediators, are emitting appropriate behavior. This might involve a detailed discussion and review session with the mediators. It may also involve some modeling and demonstration on your part, perhaps some role playing on the part of the mediators (depending on the complexity of the programs), and finally some monitoring and on-the-spot feedback when the program is actually implemented, so that parents and/or teachers and/or others are encouraged to follow the program and are reinforced for doing so (see Martin, 1972). The second aspect of program implementation is introducing it to the client. It is obviously very important that the initial contact of the client with the program be highly

Note 3 reinforcing, so that the probability of further contacts is increased.[3] Presumably, a well-designed program will include a great deal of specific information for introducing the programming steps (as suggested in guideline 3) to the client.

PROGRAM MAINTENANCE AND EVALUATION _____

Is your program having a satisfactory effect? This is not always an easy question to answer. It is also not always easy to decide, by some criterion or other, what to do if the program is not having a satisfactory effect. We suggest reviewing the following guidelines to assess a program that has been implemented:

1. Monitor your data to determine whether the recorded behaviors are changing in the desired direction.
2. Consult the people who must deal with the behavioral handicap, and determine if they are satisfied with the progress.
3. Consult the behavioral journals, professional behavior modifiers, or others with experience in using similar procedures on similar problems to determine if your results are reasonable in terms of the amount of behavior change during the period the program has been in effect.
4. If on the basis of guidelines 1, 2, and 3 the results are satisfactory, proceed directly to guideline 8.
5. If on the basis of guidelines 1, 2, or 3 your results are unsatisfactory, answer the following questions and make the appropriate adjustment for any yes answer:
   a. Have the reinforcers that are being used lost their appeal?
   b. Are the procedures being applied incorrectly?
   c. Is there outside interference from others that is disrupting the program?
   d. Are there any subjective variables—staff attitudes, teacher enthusiasm, and so forth—that might be affecting the program?
6. If none of the answers to these four questions is yes, check to see whether

additional programming steps need to be added or removed. The data may show excessive error rates, which would suggest the need for additional programming steps. Or they may show very high rates of correct responses, which might indicate that the program is too easy and that a certain amount of boredom is occurring. Add, remove, or modify steps as necessary.

7. If the results are now satisfactory, proceed to guideline 8; otherwise consult with a colleague and/or consider redesigning the entire program.

8. Identify the schedule that will enable you to provide appropriate program maintenance until the behavioral objective is reached.

9. Following attainment of the behavioral goal, outline an appropriate arrangement for assessing performance during follow-up observations.

10. After successful follow-up observations have been obtained, do a cost-effective analysis on the basis of all the information available. Also, socially validate the procedures and results as described on pp. 285–286.

11. Where possible and appropriate, analyze your data and communicate your specific procedures and results to other behavior modifiers and interested individuals.

STUDY QUESTIONS

1. What is the purpose of this chapter, and how does this chapter relate to the other chapters in the book?

Evaluating the Referral

2. Assume that you are a professional behavior modifier. List at least four possible conditions under which you would *not* treat a behavior problem that has been referred to you.

3. What does a behavior modifier do when given a vague problem (such as "aggression") to work on?

4. How does a behavior modifier evaluate the importance of a problem?

5. How does a behavior modifier evaluate the ease with which a problem might be solved?

6. How does a behavior modifier evaluate the ease with which the desired behavior change might be generalized to, and maintained in, the natural environment?

Preliminary Considerations of Program Design

7. If you are thinking of overcoming a behavioral deficit, state four short-cut tactics that you might consider.

8. If you are thinking of decreasing a behavioral excess, describe two indirect or partial solutions you might consider.

9. If you are thinking of changing the stimulus control of an existing behavior, what three steps should you consider—and in what order? (Do not list the substeps.)

Strategies of Program Design and Implementation

10. You are about to design a treatment program. After defining the target behavior and identifying its desired level of occurrence and stimulus control, what four questions should you answer before proceeding to the design?

11. In designing a behavioral program, for what three reasons might you decide to rearrange the training environment (guideline 5)? Give an example of each.

12. What factors should you consider in programming for generalization?

13. What strategy is recommended to ensure accountability of the therapist?

14. How can you increase the likelihood that the client's initial contact with the program will be favorable?

Program Maintenance and Evaluation

15. After a program has been implemented, what three things should be done to determine whether it is producing satisfactory results? (see guidelines 1, 2, and 3.)

16. If a program is producing satisfactory results, what two things should be done prior to successfully terminating the program? (see guidelines 8 and 9.)

17. Describe in detail the steps that should be followed if a program is not producing satisfactory results (guidelines 5, 6, and 7).

PRACTICE EXERCISE

Suppose that you are a behavior modifier. The mother of a "normal" four-year-old child asks for your help in designing a program to overcome the child's extreme disobedience. Construct realistic but hypothetical details of the behavior problem and take it through *all* steps in each of the following stages of programming:

a. Deciding whether you should design a program to treat the problem.
b. Selecting and implementing an assessment procedure.
c. Determining preliminary considerations of program design.
d. Developing strategies of program design and implementation.
e. Establishing program maintenance and evaluation.

(*Note*: The problem will have to be fairly complex for you to take it through *all* the steps in each of these stages.)

EXTENDED DISCUSSION AND NOTES

1. For example, Love, Matson, and West (1990) demonstrated that mothers could learn to be effective therapists for autistic children's phobias. In one case, Ronnie, a six-year-old autistic boy, was extremely afraid at the sight and sound of a running bathroom shower. If the shower was turned on when Ronnie was in or near the bathroom, he would scream and run from the area. Ronnie's mother was given instruction in the use of modeling, reinforcement procedures, and role playing. Over the course of 13 sessions, Ronnie's mother modeled successive approximations to the shower and reinforced Ronnie for imitating her (this approach to fear reduction is described in more detail in Chapter 24). By the end of the program, Ronnie was able to get into the tub and take a shower all by himself.

2. Even if significant others are not required to implement a program, their availability can be extremely valuable for programming generality. Consider, for example, the problem of developing effective behavioral weight-loss programs for children (for a review of this area, see LeBow, 1984). Israel, Stolmaker, and Adrian (1985) introduced two groups of overweight children (from 8 to 12 years of age) to an eight-week intensive multicomponent, behavioral weight-reduction program. The parents of the second group were also presented with a short course on behavioral child management skills. At the end of the eight-week treatment program, both groups of children had lost approximately the same amount of weight. After a one-year follow-up, however, maintenance of improved weight status was superior for the children whose parents had been introduced to the behavioral child management procedures.

3. The problem of a client's motivation for behavior change is of special concern if you are a behavior therapist helping a client as an outpatient. In such cases, it is important that the client cooperate fully in practicing the behavior modification procedures outside of your office. As indicated by Kanfer and Grimm (1980), treatment may fail, not because a client's problem is intractable, but because the therapist has neglected to establish appropriate prerequisites for change. Behavior therapists and traditional therapists are equally aware of this problem. In describing a behavioral problem-solving approach to managing clinical change, Kanfer and Grimm have outlined seven overlapping phases:

(1) role structuring and creating a therapeutic alliance,
(2) developing a commitment for change,
(3) conducting a behavioral analysis,
(4) negotiating treatment objectives,
(5) executing treatment and maintaining motivation,
(6) monitoring progress, and
(7) programming for generalization and treatment termination.

These phases offer a potentially useful conceptual guide for therapists to ensure that appropriate attention is given to the client's motivation to change in various aspects of therapy. Another useful device is the Motivation for Behavior Change Scale described by Cautela and Upper (1975). This scale prompts the therapist to monitor a number of behaviors of the client to assess the degree of cooperation during the course of treatment.

STUDY QUESTIONS ON NOTES

1. Briefly describe how Ronnie's mother helped him to overcome his fear of a running bathroom shower.
2. How did Israel and colleagues demonstrate that utilizing significant others in a program can enhance generality?
3. Which of Kanfer and Grimm's problem-solving phases deal with the problem of motivation? (There are at least two.) Describe briefly how these might be carried out.

CHAPTER 22

Token Economies

Conditioned reinforcement was first defined and discussed in Chapter 10. In that chapter, a conditioned reinforcer was defined as a stimulus that is not originally reinforcing but that acquires reinforcing power from being paired appropriately with other reinforcers. Some conditioned reinforcers, such as praise, are quite brief. The stimulus is gone almost as soon as it is presented. Other conditioned reinforcers, such as money, endure until they are exchanged for backup reinforcers, such as food. Conditioned reinforcers of the latter type are called tokens. A program employing tokens with a group of individuals is called a *token economy*.

There are two major advantages to using token reinforcers. First, they can be given immediately after a desirable behavior occurs and cashed in at a later time for a backup reinforcer. Thus they can be used to "bridge" very long delays between the target response and the backup reinforcer, which is especially important when it is impractical or impossible to deliver the backup reinforcer immediately after the behavior. Second, tokens make it easier to administer consistent and effective reinforcers when dealing with a group of individuals.

Kazdin (1977a, 1985) discussed the impressively wide variety of setting in which token economies have been used. They have been used on psychiatric **Note 1** wards,[1] in institutions and classrooms for the mentally retarded, in normal classroom settings ranging from preschool all the way to college and university classes, in homes for predelinquents (that is, juveniles who have engaged in antisocial behaviors), in prisons, in the military, on wards for the treatment of drug addicts and alcoholics, in nursing homes, in convalescent centers, in normal family homes to control children's behavior and to treat marital discord, and in various work settings to decrease absenteeism and to enhance on-the-job performance. Although developed primarily in institutional settings, the techniques used in token economies have been extended to various community settings to decrease littering, to increase recycling of wastes, to increase energy conservation, to increase use of mass transportation, to decrease noise pollution, to increase racial integration, to increase behaviors involved in gaining employment, and to increase self-help behaviors in people who are disadvantaged by the present economic system. Token economies have even been extended to community living situations. One such extension is Twin Oaks (Kinkade, 1973), a farm-based community modeled after the fictitious experimental community described in the novel *Walden Two* by Skinner (1948). Another example is the University of Kansas Experimental Living Project, a behaviorally managed experimental community of 30 college students (Johnson, Welch, Miller, and Altur, 1991; Thomas & Miller, 1980).

In this chapter we cannot do justice to the extremely wide range of behaviors and situations to which the techniques of token economies apply. What we intend to do, however, is to give a general introduction to the use of token economies in various settings. For more specific details on establishing a token economy in a particular setting, the reader is referred to any of the excellent handbooks that are now available for that purpose in several areas

Note 2 of application.[2]

INITIAL STEPS IN SETTING UP A TOKEN ECONOMY

DECIDING ON THE TARGET BEHAVIORS

The target behaviors will be determined largely by the type of individuals with whom you are working; by the short-range and long-range objectives you wish to accomplish with those individuals; and by specific behavior problems you are encountering that interfere with the realization of those objectives. For example, if you are the classroom teacher of a group of rambunctious first-graders, your objectives will likely include teaching reading, printing, counting, addition, subtraction, and constructive social interaction. Your target behaviors would include behaviors that are involved in these skills or are prerequisite to them. Thus, at least one of your target behaviors might be "sitting quietly when the teacher gives out instructions." A more advanced target behavior might be "correctly completing problems in a workbook."

The more homogeneous the group with which you are dealing, the easier it is to standardize the rules concerning which specific responses will be reinforced with what specific number of tokens. From this perspective, at least, it is fortunate that many groups for whom token economies are appropriate are composed of individuals who are at roughly the same behavioral level (for example, severely retarded individuals, or college students enrolled in a PSI course—see p. 14). However, even with very homogeneous groups, it will probably be necessary to have some specific reinforcement rules for certain individuals, according to their respective behavioral needs. This necessity for individualizing programs adds to the complexity of administering a token economy, but the resulting difficulties are not serious if a staff member is not required to handle too many radically different individual programs at once. Assigning special cases to special-treatment groups may be one efficient way in which to solve the problem of individualization in certain types of settings.

TAKING BASELINES

Just as one does before initiating other procedures, one should obtain baseline data on the specific target behaviors before initiating a token economy. It may be that your clients are already performing at a satisfactory level and that the potential benefits to be gained from setting up a token economy do not justify the time, effort, and cost involved in doing so. After the program has been started, comparing the data with the baseline data will enable you to determine the effectiveness of the program.

SELECTING BACKUP REINFORCERS

The methods for selecting backup reinforcers are essentially the same as the methods for selecting reinforcers (described in Chapter 3). Keep in mind, however, that a token system will generally increase the variety of practical reinforcers that you can use, since they need not be limited to those that can be delivered immediately following a desired response.

In considering reinforcers that are normally available, one should take extreme caution to avoid the serious ethical problems that can arise. For example, several states have passed legislation affirming the rights of mental patients to have access to meals, comfortable beds, TV, and so on. Furthermore, a number of court decisions have upheld these civil rights of patients. One should, therefore, never plan a program that might involve depriving an individual of something that already legally and morally belongs to him or her.

After having established what your backup reinforcers are going to be and how you are going to obtain them, you should next consider the general method of dispensing them. A store or commissary is an essential feature of most token economies. In a small token economy, such as a classroom, the store can be quite simple, say, a box located on the teacher's desk or another table in the room. In a larger token economy, such as a mental institution, the store would typically be much larger, perhaps occupying one or more rooms. Regardless of the size of the store, a definite method of keeping records of purchases must be devised so that an adequate inventory (especially of items in high demand) can be maintained at all times, within the limit of your budget.

SELECTING THE TYPE OF TOKENS TO USE

Tokens can take on any of the forms that money has assumed (including clam shells, if nothing better is available). Poker chips are often used, but personal "checks," entries in a "bankbook," marks on a chart on the wall or in notebooks carried by clients, stars or stamps to be pasted in booklets—all these and numerous other possibilities may suit the needs of your particular token economy, depending mainly on the type of client involved.

In general, tokens should be attractive, lightweight, portable, durable, easy to handle, and, of course, not easily counterfeited (see Figure 22–1). If automatic dispensers of backup reinforcement are used, you should ensure that your tokens will operate those devices. You should also ensure that you have an adequate number of tokens for your clients. Stainback, Payne, Stainbeck, and Payne (1973) suggest that one should have on hand about 100 tokens per child when starting a token economy in a classroom.

One should also acquire the necessary accessories for handling and storing tokens. For example, school children may need boxes, bags, or purses in which to store the tokens they have earned.

IDENTIFYING AVAILABLE HELP

Help from other individuals may not be essential in a small token economy, such as a classroom, but is certainly to be desired especially in the initial stages of the program. In a large token economy, such as a large ward in a mental institution, such help is essential.

There are a number of sources from which help may be obtained: (1) people already assigned to work with the clients (e.g., teachers' aides, nurses' aides, teaching assistants); (2) volunteers (e.g., homemakers, retired couples, senior citizens, members of civic organizations and community action groups); (3) behaviorally advanced individuals within the institution (e.g., conscientious fifth-graders assigned to help manage a token economy for first-graders); and (4) members of the token economy itself. In some cases, clients have been taught to deliver tokens to themselves contingent on appropriate **Note 3**   behavior.[3]

After the token economy begins to function smoothly, more and more of its members will gradually become able to assume more and more responsibility in helping to achieve its goals. For example, at Achievement Place, a group home for predelinquent boys, some of the youths supervised others in carrying out routine household tasks. The supervisor, or "manager," as he was called, had the authority to both administer and remove tokens for his peers' performances. Of the several methods that were studied for selecting

FIGURE 22–1 Tokens should not be easily counterfeited.

managers, democratic elections proved to be best in terms of the performances of the youths and their effectiveness in accomplishing their tasks (Phillips, Phillips, Wolf, & Fixsen, 1973). In another experiment at Achievement Place, some youths served with remarkable effectiveness, despite their having very little adult supervision and no specific training, as therapists for others who had speech problems (Bailey, Timbers, Phillips, & Wolf, 1971). In some courses that use PSI (see p. 14), students who are among the first to master an assignment have served to evaluate the performance of other students on that assignment and to give them immediate feedback concerning their performance. Another method used in college and university classes is to give the students a test near the beginning of the term on the first several sections of the course material. Those students who demonstrate on this test that they can readily master the course material are each put in charge of a small group of students, whom they help to tutor and supervise throughout the remainder of the course (Johnson & Ruskin, 1977).

In deciding how you are going to obtain workers who will help to manage your token economy, you will need to consider how their helping behavior is to be reinforced. Your approval is, of course, a potential reinforcer that should be used generously. Permission to continue working in the token economy and to work at desired jobs are additional reinforcers at your disposal.

CHOOSING THE LOCATIONS

No special locations are essential for a token economy, which is nice since the designer of a token economy often has little or no choice in its location. Some locations are better than others, however, depending on the type of token economy under consideration. For example, college instructors using token economies often arrange to have their courses scheduled in lecture halls or very large classrooms designed originally for at least twice as many students as the number anticipated to attend class at any given time. Movable desks are generally preferred over stationary ones because they enable students to work easily in small groups. Classrooms with token economies are often very noisy places and give the initial impression of mass confusion to a casual observer. Surprising as it may seem, however, almost all students soon adjust quite well to the noise, so that it does not prevent them from working with great efficiency.

SPECIFIC IMPLEMENTATION PROCEDURES ───────────────

Before and during the implementation of a token economy there are, as with any other new program, a number of specific procedures to be decided upon and implemented. These can be categorized as follows.

Keeping Data. Here we are concerned with what sort of data sheets should be used, who is to record the data, and when the data are to be recorded.

The Reinforcing Agent. It is important to decide who is going to administer reinforcement, and for what behaviors. For example, Ayllon and Azrin recommend that, in situations where several managers dispense tokens to several clients (such as on a hospital ward), only one person should be assigned to reinforce a particular response at a particular time. Otherwise, "no one individual can be held responsible for failure to administer the reinforcement procedures properly, since any deviation, omission, or modification is easily attributed to the behavior of some other employee" (Ayllon & Azrin, 1968b, p. 136).

In addition, care should be taken to ensure that tokens are always delivered in a positive and conspicuous manner immediately following a desired response. Friendly, smiling approval should be administered at the same time the token is given, and the client should be told (at least in the initial stages) why she or he is receiving the token.

Amount or Frequency of Tokens to Pay.   There are several important considerations concerning the amount of tokens to give for a particular behavior. One consideration is the stage of the economy; that is, how accustomed the clients are to receiving tokens. Stainback and others (1973) recommended that 25 to 75 tokens per child is not excessive on the first day of a token economy in a classroom. They recommended further that the number be decreased gradually to 15 to 30 each day. Other considerations are the therapeutic value of the behavior being reinforced and the likelihood that the client will engage in it without tokens.

Managing the Backup Reinforcers.   Here we have to consider how frequently backup reinforcers will be available to be purchased (that is, how frequently "store time" should be scheduled). In the beginning, the frequency should probably be quite high, then decreased gradually. For example, for school children, Stainback and others (1973) recommended that store time be held once or twice per day for the first three or four days and then decreased gradually in frequency until it is held only once each week (Friday afternoon) by the third week of the token economy.

It is also necessary to decide how many tokens each backup reinforcer will cost. In addition to the monetary cost, which is of course the most obvious consideration in assigning token values to backup reinforcers, two other factors should be considered. One is supply and demand. That is, charge more for items whose demand exceeds the supply and less for items whose supply exceeds the demand. This will help to maintain an adequate supply of effective reinforcers and promote optimal utilization of the reinforcing power of each backup reinforcer. The other factor to consider is the therapeutic value of the backup reinforcer. A client should be charged very little for a backup reinforcer that is beneficial to him or her. This will help to induce the client to partake of the reinforcer. For example, a client may be charged only a few tokens for admission to a party because of the important social skills that participating in this event may help to develop.

Possible Punishment Contingencies.   The use of tokens provides the possibility of using fines as punishment for inappropriate behavior. This type of punishment may be preferable, from an ethical point of view, to physical punishment and timeout. As with all forms of punishment, it should be used sparingly and only for clearly defined behaviors (see Chapter 13).

If fines are used in a token economy, it may be necessary to add training contingencies that teach clients how to accept fines in a relatively nonemotional, nonaggressive manner. Such contingencies were described by

Phillips, Phillips, Fixsen, and Wolf (1973) for their token economy with pre-delinquent youths. In that economy, the contingencies related to fines probably helped to teach youths an important social skill: how to accept reprimands from law enforcers in society.

Supervision of Staff.   The managers of a token economy, no less than the clients, are subject to the laws of behavior. They must receive frequent reinforcement for appropriate behavior, and their inappropriate behavior must be corrected if the token economy is to function effectively. Their duties must therefore be specified clearly, and they must be supervised in the performance of those duties.

Continuous supervision is generally impractical. Therefore, time sampling should be used. The director of the economy should start with frequent supervision and then gradually reduce its frequency. A desirable schedule of staff supervision and reinforcement might be a VI/LH to maintain a high, steady rate of appropriate staff performance (see Ayllon & Azrin, 1968b, p. 151).

Handling Potential Problems.   In the design of a token economy, as with any complex procedure, it is wise to plan for potential problems. Some of the problems that are likely to arise in a token economy are (1) confusion, especially during the first few days after the initiation of the economy; (2) staff shortages; (3) attempts by clients to get tokens they have not earned or backup reinforcers for which they do not have enough tokens; (4) clients playing with tokens and manipulating them in other distracting ways; and (5) failure to purchase backup reinforcers. All these and other problems that may arise can almost always be managed by careful planning beforehand.

PREPARING A MANUAL

The final stage to complete before implementing the token economy is to prepare a manual or written set of rules describing exactly how the economy is to run. This manual should explain in detail what behaviors are to be reinforced, how they are to be reinforced with tokens and backup reinforcers, the times at which reinforcement is to be available, what data are to be recorded, how and when they are to be recorded, and the responsibilities and duties of every staff member. Each rule should be reasonable and acceptable to clients and staff. Every staff member should be given a copy of the manual or a clear and accurate version of those portions of it pertaining to his or her specific duties and responsibilities. If feasible, each client should be given a clear and accurate version of those portions of the manual pertaining to him or her. If the client is not able to read fluently but can understand the spoken language, a clear explanation of those portions of the manual that are relevant should be provided.

The manual should include definite procedures for evaluating whether the rules are being followed adequately and procedures for ensuring that they are. Methods for arbitrating disputes concerning the rules should be included in the manual, and the participation of clients in the arbitration procedures should be provided for to the greatest extent that is practical and consistent with the goals of the token economy. Effecting such client participation is a step toward developing the behaviors involved in individual initiative, self-government, and other skills that are so highly prized in the natural environment. Toward this end, it is desirable at some stage in the token economy to have the clients themselves participate in constructively revising old rules and designing new rules for running the economy. The rules should also be capable of modification when there is evidence that a change is desirable. However, sudden and drastic changes can generate undesirable emotional behavior in clients. Moreover, clients may become disinclined to follow the rules when they are changed frequently or arbitrarily. So that rule modifications may occur in the smoothest manner possible, it seems advisable to have the manual itself specify the basis on which it will be revised. Advance notification of impending rule changes should be given to all concerned, and revisions and additions to the manual should be explained, discussed, justified, put in writing, and disseminated prior to being put into effect.

PROGRAMMING GENERALITY TO THE NATURAL ENVIRONMENT

Token economies are sometimes regarded as ways in which to manage problem behavior in institutional settings. They do serve this function, but this observation should not let us neglect their more important function of helping clients to adjust to the natural environment beyond the institution. Because social reinforcement, not tokens, prevails in the natural environment, a token economy should be designed so that social reinforcement gradually replaces token reinforcement.[4]

Note 4

There appear to be two general ways of weaning the client from tokens. One is to eliminate them gradually. The second is to decrease their value gradually. The first alternative can be accomplished by gradually making the schedule of token delivery more and more intermittent, by gradually decreasing the number of behaviors that earn tokens, or by gradually increasing the delay between the target behavior and token delivery. The second alternative can be accomplished by gradually decreasing the amount of backup reinforcement that a given number of tokens can purchase or by gradually increasing the delay between token acquisition and the purchase of backup reinforcers. At present, we cannot say which method or combination of methods produces the best results. In addition, all the considerations involved in programming generality (discussed in Chapter 12) should be reviewed.

Gradually transferring control to the clients themselves so that they plan and administer their own reinforcements is another step in preparing clients for the natural environment. An individual who can evaluate his or her own behavior, decide rationally what changes need to be made in it, and program effectively for these changes is clearly in a good position to cope with almost any environment. Methods for establishing these skills are discussed in Chapter 23.

ETHICAL CONSIDERATIONS

Token economies involve the systematic application of behavior modification techniques on a relatively large scale. The possibilities of abusing the techniques, even unintentionally, are thereby magnified. Precautions should be taken to avoid such abuse. One such precaution is to make the system completely open to public scrutiny, provided that such openness is subject to the approval of clients or their advocates. Visits by outsiders, including newspaper reporters and other representatives of the media, should be encouraged, within the accepted boundaries of confidentiality between client and therapist. Visitors should be allowed free access to the manual of rules governing the token economy. Their questions and criticisms should be answered satisfactorily by the administrators of the economy. Visitors should also be permitted to talk to the clients of the economy and obtain their impressions of it. Ayllon and Azrin even adopted the commendable policy of giving visitors tours conducted by the clients themselves. An open-door policy of this sort will help not only to ensure high ethical standards but also to allay the fears and suspicions about behavior modification that too often exist in the minds of the public in general and the relatives of the clients in particular. Sometimes clients find even well-designed token economies aversive, which may give rise to anger, complaints, and resistance to the program. This problem has been dealt with in some programs by providing clients with the option of leaving the program without penalty (see Ayllon, Milan, Roberts, & McKee, 1979), and permitting clients to suggest or negotiate changes in the contingencies of the token economy (e.g., Karraker, 1977; Kazdin, 1977a).

Another precaution is to inform the clients clearly of their legal and moral rights. Furthermore, clients and managers should be instructed to report any infringements of those rights. Such reports, as well as other complaints and criticisms, should be listened to and acted upon quickly in a morally responsible fashion.

The ends of a token economy and the suitability to those ends of the means for obtaining them constitute the "acid test" of the ethics of the token economy. Thus, the ethics of a token economy will ultimately be judged on the basis of how effectively and humanely the transfer to the natural environment is carried out. For additional discussion of ethical issues concerned with behavior modification, see Chapter 28.

A SUMMARY OF CONSIDERATIONS IN DESIGNING A TOKEN ECONOMY

1. Review some appropriate literature.
2. Identify your target behaviors.
   a. List some short-range and long-range objectives.
   b. Arrange your objectives in order of priority.
   c. Select those objectives that are most important for the clients and that are prerequisites for later objectives.
   d. Identify several of the priority objectives on which to start, emphasizing those that can be accomplished quickly.
   e. Pinpoint a number of target behaviors for each of the starting objectives.
3. Take a baseline of your target behaviors.
4. Select your backup reinforcers.
   a. Use reinforcers that are usually effective with the population of interest.
   b. Use the Premack principle (see Chapter 3).
   c. Collect verbal information from the clients concerning their reinforcers.
   d. Give the clients catalogues that will help them to identify reinforcers.
   e. Identify a variety of "free-time" reinforcers.
   f. Identify natural reinforcers that might be programmed.
   g. Consider the ethics and legalities regarding the reinforcers on your list.
   h. Design an appropriate store to keep, display, and dispense your backup reinforcers.
5. Select the most appropriate type of token for your client. (They should be attractive, lightweight, portable, durable, easy to handle, and not easy to counterfeit.)
6. Identify those who are available to help manage the program.
   a. Existing staff
   b. Volunteers
   c. University students
   d. Residents of the institution
   e. Members of the token economy themselves
7. Obtain an appropriate location and necessary equipment.
   a. Accept the location with the greater space.
   b. Equipment and furnishings should be easily movable.
   c. Rearrange the setting so that behaviors of the clients can be detected most easily and reinforced immediately.
8. Decide on specific implementation procedures.
   a. Design appropriate data sheets and determine who will take data and how and when it will be recorded.
   b. Decide who is going to administer reinforcement, how it will be administered, and for what behaviors.
   c. Decide upon the number of tokens that can be earned per behavior per client per day.
   d. Establish "store" procedures and determine the token value of backup reinforcers.
   e. Be wary of punishment contingencies. Use them sparingly, only for clearly defined behaviors, and only when it is ethically justifiable to do so.

f. Ensure that staff duties are clearly defined and that a desirable schedule of staff supervision and reinforcement is implemented.
g. Plan for potential problems.
9. Prepare a token economy manual for the clients and the staff.
10. Institute your token economy.
11. Plan strategies for obtaining generality to the natural environment.
12. Monitor and practice relevant ethical guidelines at each step.

STUDY QUESTIONS

1. What is a token economy?
2. What are two major advantages to using token reinforcers?
3. List a number of settings in which token economies have been used (at least five).
4. List a number of behaviors that token economies have been designed to develop (at least five).
5. List and briefly describe six initial steps in setting up a token economy.
6. What is the store of a token economy? Give examples.
7. What six characteristics should a token have?
8. Identify three sources of potential volunteer help in managing a token economy.
9. What do you think are some advantages in having the members of the token economy themselves function as the main source of help?
10. Before and during implementation of a token economy, what eight specific procedures must be decided upon and implemented?
11. What are some of the advantages and disadvantages of assigning only one person to reinforce a particular response at a particular time in a token economy on an institutional ward?
12. How should tokens be delivered?
13. How many tokens should you have for each student in the group?
14. According to Stainback and others, how often should store time be held during the first few days of a token economy?
15. For a token economy on a ward in an institution (for the retarded, mental patients, or juvenile delinquents), describe a plausible VI/LH schedule of staff supervision.
16. Why would a VI/LH schedule be preferred to an FI/LH schedule for staff supervision?
17. Describe two general methods of weaning clients from tokens when transferring behavior to the natural environment.
18. If one decides to effect a gradual decrease in the number of behaviors that earn tokens, what general guidelines might be followed in deciding which behaviors no longer require token reinforcement? That is, where do you start and on which behaviors do you start?
19. What precautions should you take to help ensure high ethical standards for your token economy?

PRACTICE EXERCISES

1. For a group of individuals of your choosing (for instance, in an elementary school classroom, a university class, or a ward in an institution for the retarded), identify five plausible goals for a token economy.
2. Define precisely the target behaviors related to each of the five goals listed in Exercise 1.
3. Describe a number of things you might do to identify backup reinforcers for the group of individuals you choose in Exercise 1.

EXTENDED DISCUSSION AND NOTES

1. Paul and Lentz (1977) described more than 10 years of intensive research on the treatment of chronic psychotic inpatients at a state mental hospital. Their use of a token economy was successful in terms of both effectiveness and cost for treating patients and moving many of them from the ward into a more productive lifestyle. Although their program was more effective than the active milieu treatment and the usual medications/custodial-care routine typically given those types of patients, token-economy programs have not become common at mental hospitals. In a study of Veterans Administration medical centers, Boudewyns, Fry, and Nightingale (1986) estimated that only approximately 1 percent of all psychiatric patients treated are offered some form of behavior modification/token-economy therapy. They concluded that a major factor accounting for the low number of such programs may be that of staff resistance to implementing and managing the programs.

Glynn (1990) suggested that other reasons for the decline in the number of token economies in psychiatric settings include reduced length of inpatient admissions, greater emphasis on community-based treatments, economic constraints, and legal and ethical challenges.

2. Much of the material in this chapter is covered in greater detail in the following major works on token economies: Ayllon and Azrin (1968b), which deals with token economies in mental hospitals; Stainback, Payne, Stainback, and Payne (1973), which deals with token economies in elementary school classrooms; Welch and Gist (1974), which deals primarily with token economies in sheltered workshops; Ayllon and others (1979), which describes token programs in prisons; and Kazdin (1977a), which presents a comprehensive review of token-economy research. For more information on the use of token-economy procedures in college and high school courses, in which systems incorporating these procedures are sometimes called Personalized System of Instruction or (PSI), see Keller and Sherman (1982), Sherman, Ruskin and Semb (1982), and p. 14 of this book.

3. For example, Rae, Martin, and Smyk (1990) designed a program to pay tokens to mentally retarded clients in a sheltered workshop for showing improved on-task performance. The tokens could be redeemed for items in the workshop cafeteria. But the workshop had insufficient staff to reliably keep track of those clients who were on-task and those who were not. A solution was to teach the workers to self-monitor their own on-task performance. A pencil and a sheet with squares on it were placed in front of each worker. The workers were taught that, when a buzzer sounded, they should mark an *X* on one of the squares if they were on-task. The buzzer was set to go off at six random times during a half-day. When a worker earned six *X*'s, they could be exchanged for a token. The total program proved to be very effective for increasing the on-task behavior of the workers on a variety of workshop tasks.

4. Levine and Fasnacht (1974) argued that the use of tokens to reinforce a behavior may impede the generalization of that behavior to the natural environment. However, Kazdin (1985) has summarized a large amount of data indicating that token economies are effective with diverse populations, and that the gains achieved with token economies are often maintained for at least several years following the termination of the program. There is no evidence that token economies are better with one type of client or problem than another either with regard to amount of improvement achieved or the amount maintained after termination of the program. However, Kazdin points out that more data on the long-term effects of token economies are needed, especially for programs implemented for only short periods.

STUDY QUESTIONS ON NOTES

1. Considering their effectiveness, state the major factors in accounting for the low number of token economies in psychiatric settings.
2. What source texts might you recommend for someone interested in developing a token economy in a mental hospital? In an elementary school classroom? In a sheltered workshop? in a prison?
3. Describe a token program in which clients in a sheltered workshop administered tokens to themselves.
4. Discuss whether using tokens to reinforce behavior can impede the generalization of that behavior to the natural environment.

CHAPTER 23

Helping an Individual to Develop **Self-Control**

Al and Mary were sitting in the campus cafeteria. "I think I'll have another doughnut," said Al. "Maybe it'll take my mind off that test."

"What's the matter, you think you failed?" asked Mary.

"Not really. Guess I just feel like having another doughnut."

"You often feel like having another doughnut. How much do you weigh now—about 20 or 30 pounds more than last year?" asked Mary.

"At least! But I just don't have the will power to resist. Sally's been after me to go see her boss about it. You know, he's the guy I told you about that teaches psychology."

"Think he can help?" asked Mary.

"I dunno. Can't hurt and maybe it'll help. I think I'll go talk to him."

Many problems of self-control are similar to the problem faced by Al. That is, they involve self-restraint—learning to decrease excessive behaviors that have immediate gratification—such as excessive smoking, eating, drinking, and TV watching.

Other problems of self-control require behavior change in the opposite direction—responses that need to be increased—such as studying, exercising, being assertive, and performing household chores. Many people speak as though there's some magical force within us—called *will power*—responsible for overcoming such problems. People probably believe this, in

Material in this chapter was described by Martin and Osborne (1989) and is paraphrased with permission.

part, because others are always telling us things like, "If you had more will power you could get rid of that bad habit." Or "If you had more will power you could improve yourself and get some better habits." Most of us have heard such advice many times. Unfortunately, it's usually not very helpful advice because the person offering it almost always neglects to tell us how we can get more of this so-called will power. It is more useful to look at how problems of self-control stem from differences between immediate consequences of a behavior and its delayed consequences (Brigham, 1982). From such a starting point, we proceed to a model for self-control.[1] Finally, we describe how most successful self-control programs proceed through six basic steps.

Note 1

CAUSES OF SELF-CONTROL PROBLEMS ⎯⎯⎯⎯⎯⎯⎯⎯⎯⎯⎯⎯⎯⎯⎯⎯⎯

"I just *can't* resist having an extra dessert."

"I *really* should get into an exercise program. I wish I wasn't so lazy."

"My term paper is due, I have a big midterm, and I *have* to finish writing up that lab assignment. What am I doing here at this bar? Why aren't I home studying?"

Do any of these sound familiar? If you're like most people, you've probably heard yourself say such things many times. These are the sorts of situations where we're tempted to talk about not having enough "will power." Most such situations exemplify a conflict between immediate and delayed consequences of the behaviors of concern.

IMMEDIATE SMALL REINFORCERS VS. DELAYED STRONG PUNISHERS

Why is obesity one of the major health problems facing Americans today? In part it's because eating is a behavior for which the immediate consequences are positive (all that tasty food). Even though potential delayed consequences of overeating are clearly negative (obesity and other health risks), immediate consequences affect a response much more strongly than do delayed consequences. Thus, when the immediate consequences are reinforcing and the delayed consequences are punishing, the immediate reinforcers frequently win out—even when the immediate consequences represent *small* reinforcers while the delayed consequences are *major* punishers. Many problems of self-control stem from this fact (Brigham, 1982). The immediate consequences of smoking, for example, are positive for most smokers. Major punishers such as shortness of breath, sore throat, and coughing, not to mention possible lung cancer, are long delayed. The immediate enjoyable consequences of drinking alcoholic beverages override the delayed punishing consequences of a hangover. The immediate reinforcing consequences from sexual behavior with a best friend's mate may override the delayed hurt and emotional anguish when your friend finds out and is no longer your friend.

IMMEDIATE SMALL REINFORCERS VS. DELAYED STRONGER REINFORCERS

For some types of self-control problems, you can do one thing and receive immediate small reinforcers, or you can do something else and receive delayed but much higher valued reinforcers. For example, you can spend your money in the present and frequently enjoy a night on the town, dinner and dancing, and many other immediate short-term reinforcers. Alternatively, you can save your money and receive a delayed but much stronger reinforcer (such as a new car or a down payment on a house). As another example, you can enjoy drinking and socializing almost every night. Alternatively, you can stay home and study and receive much higher grades along with other delayed reinforcers like scholarships to graduate school, better jobs, etc. For these types of self-control problems, the two alternative behaviors are usually incompatible.

IMMEDIATE PUNISHERS VS. DELAYED REINFORCERS

Why are some people so hesitant to try a new dance step? To take up a new sport? To make new friends? To try something different? This type of problem occurs because learning new skills frequently involves minor punishing consequences (perhaps from initially looking foolish, from not knowing what to do, from "put-downs" from onlookers, etc.), while potentially reinforcing consequences are delayed (e.g., it takes a while to get good enough at a new skill before you can really enjoy it).

IMMEDIATE WEAK PUNISHERS VS. DELAYED STRONGER PUNISHERS

Why do many people tend to postpone such activities as going to the dentist or scheduling minor surgery? In this type of self-control problem, there are immediate weak punishers contingent upon performing. It hurts when you go to the dentist. The delayed consequences, of course, can be much more aversive (your teeth can fall out). However, once again, the immediate consequences win out.

A MODEL FOR SELF-CONTROL _____

An effective model of self-control must deal satisfactorily with the causes of self-control problems described in the preceding section. The model that we describe has two parts. The first part of the model requires clear specification of the problem as behavior to be controlled. The second part of this model of self-control requires that you apply behavioral techniques to manage the problem behavior. In that sense, this model of self-control consists of doing something (applying techniques of behavior change) to increase the chances that you will do something else (change the problem behavior). An individual must behave in some way that arranges the environment to manage his or her own subsequent behavior. It means emitting a *controlling behavior* to effect a change in a *behavior to be controlled* (Skinner, 1953).

This presents the problem of *controlling the controlling behavior*. That is, since self-control implies that some components of a person's behavior control other components of his or her behavior, the question arises as to what is to control this controlling behavior. If it is answered that the individual is to control his or her own controlling behavior, then what is being said is that the controlling behavior is itself to be controlled by controlling behavior. But then the question is what is to control *that* controlling behavior. Thus, in matters of self-control, the problem of controlling the controlling behavior is **Note 2** always present and must be taken into account.[2]

Controlling behaviors include all the ways of managing antecedents and consequences discussed previously in this text. When individuals attempt to manage consequences for their own behaviors, however, they encounter a difficulty not encountered to the same degree when people manage consequences for others. This difficulty is that of *short-circuiting of contingencies*. The process can be easily seen in the following two simple examples:

1. Suppose that you want to study more efficiently because this behavior will eventually bring you a great deal of reinforcement—such as getting the kind of job you want, being able to talk intelligently with other people, and understanding events in the world around you. But this reinforcement is far in the future. It is therefore very difficult for it to compete with the weaker but more immediate reinforcement of even a moderately entertaining TV program. It might seem logical to use your TV watching to reinforce your studying behavior. On the other hand, studying does not turn on the TV; flicking the power switch on the TV set or remote control does. There is a good chance, therefore, that the reinforcement contingency will be short-circuited, in the sense that the reinforcer will be consumed without the desired behavior having occurred, as illustrated in Figure 23–1.

2. Suppose that you want to decrease your food intake because you know that overeating can cause health problems and make you less attractive physically to other people. But these punishers are long delayed. Therefore, they have a hard time competing with the reinforcement residing in that piece of pie sitting in front of you. You might decide to bring some more immediate punishment to bear on the problem by pinching yourself each time you take a bite of pie. But the pain that you feel punishes the skin squeezing (pinching) as much as it punishes pie eating. There is a good chance, therefore, that the punishment contingency will be short-circuited in the sense that the undesirable behavior will occur and the punisher will not follow it. The pinching disappears while you, feeling perhaps a little guilty, continue to enjoy the pie.

FIGURE 23–1 An example of short-circuiting.

Despite this difficulty, however, self-control can be achieved and is well worth the effort involved. The ideal person to carry out a behavior modification program with a client is someone who is intimately concerned with the welfare of the client and who can observe him or her 24 hours a day. Everyone has such a person; it is, of course, oneself.

STEPS IN A SELF-CONTROL PROGRAM

Unlike most of the cases considered previously in this book, the candidate for a self-control program realizes that he or she has a problem and has probably attempted to solve it himself. Failing in that effort, the individual has, let us assume, come to a behavior modifier or behavior therapist for help. The role of the therapist is to help develop and strengthen the controlling behavior.

The therapist does not attempt to solve the problem directly but, rather, acts more as a consultant, providing the client with the procedures he or she must undertake to solve the problem. At each step in the treatment, the therapist should not just give advice; she should also explain to the client the reasons for that advice and should proceed only with the client's informed consent. This is desirable (1) because of the consultant-client nature of their relationship, (2) because the client might carry out the procedures more accurately if he understands and accepts their rational, and (3) because this approach should help the client to learn how to solve other behavior problems that he may encounter.

Note 3

Although a therapist could help a client implement the procedures in this chapter, we will assume that you are implementing them by yourself without the aid of a therapist. (Perhaps you are consulting not only this text but also one of the many self-help books that are available for managing personal problems.)[3] We will describe how to do so through the following steps. (1) specifying the problem, (2) making a commitment to change, (3) taking data on the problem, (4) designing and implementing a treatment plan, (5) ensuring support for the program, and (6) programming for long-term success.

1. SPECIFY THE PROBLEM

What is it that you would like to change? How will you know if you have succeeded? To answer these questions, you need to try to specify the problem in quantitative terms. For Al (in the example beginning this chapter), this was relatively easy—he wanted to lose 30 pounds. Stated more precisely, he wanted to use about 1,000 calories more each day than he consumed to give a weight loss of about two pounds each week. Many problems of self-control can be easily specified in quantitative terms. It's relatively easy, for example, to set specific goals in the areas of weight control and exercise. In contrast, other self-improvement goals are more difficult to measure. These would include things like "having a more positive attitude towards school," "becoming less nervous," or "improving a relationship." Mager (1972) refers to such vague abstractions as "fuzzies." A fuzzy is an acceptable starting point for identifying a self-control problem. However, you must then "unfuzzify" the abstraction by identifying the performances that would cause you to agree that your goal has been achieved. Mager outlined a number of useful steps for the process of "unfuzzification." These include:

a. Write out the goal.
b. Make a list of the things that you should say or do that clearly indicate that you've met the goal. That is, what would you take as evidence that your goal has been achieved?
c. Given a number of people with the same goal, how would you decide who had met the goal and who hadn't?
d. If your goal is an outcome (rather than something that you do) such as achieving a certain weight, accumulating a certain amount of money, or hav-

ing a clean room, then make a list of specific behaviors that will help you to achieve that outcome.

2. MAKE A COMMITMENT TO CHANGE

Note 4

By *commitment to change* we refer to a rule one states to oneself (and perhaps to others) that one will change one's behavior.[4] Perri and Richards (1977) demonstrated that *both* a commitment to change *and* a knowledge of change techniques were important for successful accomplishment of self-modification projects by undergraduate psychology students. In problem areas such as eating, smoking, studying, or dating, successful self-managers had both a stronger commitment to change and used more behavior change techniques than did unsuccessful self-managers (Perri & Richards, 1977).

A high probability of success in changing your behavior requires that you do things to keep your commitment strong. First, make your commitment to change public (Shelton & Levy, 1981). Increasing the number of people who can remind you to stick to your program increases your chances of success (Passman, 1977). Second, rearrange your environment to provide frequent reminders of your commitment and your goal (Graziano, 1975). Also, make sure those reminders are associated with the positive benefits of reaching your goal. Third, invest considerable time and energy into planning your project initially (Cooper & Axsom, 1982; Kelley, 1983). Prepare a list of statements related to your investment in your project so that you can use those statements to help strengthen and maintain your commitment (e.g., "I've put so much into it, it would be a shame to quit now"). Fourth, because you will undoubtedly encounter temptations to quit your project, plan ahead for various ways to deal with the temptation to disregard your commitment (Kelly, 1983; Patterson & Mischel, 1975; Shiffman, 1984).

3. TAKE DATA AND ANALYZE CAUSES

The next step is to take data on the occurrence of the problem—when, where, and how often it occurs. This is especially important when the goal is to decrease excessive behaviors. As indicated in Chapter 18, there are a number of reasons for keeping track of the problem behavior, not the least of which is to provide a reference point for evaluating progress. For many self-control projects, a 3-by-5-inch card and a pencil may serve nicely for tallying instances of the problem as they occur throughout the day.

There are a number of techniques for increasing the strength of record keeping. For example, if the problem behavior is smoking, you should record each cigarette before it is smoked, so that the behavior will reinforce recording it. You might set up external reinforcers that are controlled by other people. For example, you might give control of your spending money to someone who can monitor your behavior continuously for extended periods of time and who could return your money contingent upon consistent data taking. You might also get other people to reinforce your recording behavior by (1) telling friends about your self-modification project, (2) keeping your recording chart or graph in an obvious place to increase the likelihood of feedback from friends, and (3) keeping your friends informed on how the project and results are progressing. Contingencies mediated by other people are an important safeguard against the short-circuiting processes described at the beginning of this chapter.

In some cases (as pointed out in Chapter 18), recording and graphing the behavior may be all that's needed to bring about improvement. A convincing demonstration of this effect was made by Maletsky (1974). Three of the five cases he studied were completed successfully, even though Maletsky was careful not to introduce any treatment other than the counting and graphing of unwanted behaviors. The first case concerned repetitive scratching that resulted in unsightly lesions on the arms and legs of a 52-year-old woman. The woman had been suffering with this problem for 30 years. The second case concerned a nine-year-old boy's repetitive hand-raising in class. (Often he didn't know the answers to the teacher's questions.) The third case involved the out-of-seat behavior in school of a hyperactive 11-year-old girl. In all three cases, the behavior decreased over a six-week period as a result of the daily counting and graphing. In some cases, it might even be possible to count each thought, desire, or urge to emit a behavior before the behavior occurs. For example, McFall (1970) reported a study in which recording each urge to have a cigarette was sufficient to decrease not only the likelihood of subsequently taking a cigarette, but also the number of urges.

When recording the frequency of the problem during these initial observations, you should take a close look at the immediate consequences that might be maintaining the problem. From this exercise often comes suggestions for successful programming strategies.

Let's take a look at Al's situation. Since in our example Al was eating a doughnut right after a test, there is a possibility that, for him, eating was somehow involved in the reduction of anxiety. But there is another explanation of Al's excessive eating. When Al began examining the circumstances in which he typically snacked, he made a surprising finding: The great majority of instances of eating were followed immediately by some other reinforcing event.

> A bit of a doughnut—then a sip of coffee;
> Another potato chip while watching TV—his favorite basketball player just scores another basket;
> Another candy to munch on while in his car—the stop light turns green and Al drives away;
> And so on.

Al ate while drinking coffee, while drinking beer, while talking to friends, while talking on the phone, while riding in a car . . . in other words, while coming into contact with a wide variety of reinforcing events in the natural environment. As we indicated in earlier chapters, the effects of reinforcers are automatic and do not depend on an individual's awareness. No wonder Al had trouble dieting.

Thus, during preliminary observations, it's important to analyze immediate consequences that might maintain the undesired behavior to be eliminated as well as the immediate consequences (or lack of them) of the behavior that you wish to develop. This information can be very useful in the next step of your program.

4. DESIGN A PROGRAM

Throughout your life, in certain *situations* certain *behaviors* have had certain *consequences*. Each of these three variables provides a fertile area for selecting self-control techniques.

Manage the Situation.   When we defined stimulus control in Chapter 8, we said that certain responses occur in the presence of some stimuli and not others. Because this is so, it is possible for you to capitalize on the stimuli that control your responses when planning self-control programs. As indicated in Chapter 16, it is helpful to think of major classes of stimuli that control our behavior, such as instructions, modeling, our immediate surroundings, other people, and the time of day.

Instructions. We have already indicated how you can capitalize on instructions to change a variety of behaviors (see Chapter 16). Meichenbaum (1977) argues that almost every self-modification program should include some self-instructions. Self-instructions have been used in formal self-management projects to increase exercise and study behavior (Cohen, DeJames, Nocera, & Ramberger, 1980), reduce fears (Arrick, Voss, & Rimm, 1981), reduce nail-biting (Harris & McReynolds, 1977), and improve a variety of other behaviors (Dush, Hirt, & Schroeder, 1983).

Modeling. Modeled behavior is another class of stimulus events that is useful in self-control programs. For example, do you want to improve your skills at introducing yourself to an attractive person at social gatherings? Find someone who's good at it, observe that person's behavior, and try to imitate it. A procedure called *participant modeling* (Leitenberg, 1976) is an especially effective method for reducing fears. With this procedure, the fearful person observes a model interact with the fear-inducing stimulus and then imitates the model.

Our Immediate Surroundings. Do you have trouble studying at home? Try going to the library, where studying is a high-probability behavior (Brigham, 1982). Many people have a particular behavior they would like to decrease. That behavior occurs in particular situations. An alternative desirable behavior occurs in other situations. A useful strategy is to rearrange the environment to present cues for the desirable alternative behaviors.

Other People. As we said above, modeling is one way of providing strong prompts for you to engage in some behavior. Another strategy is to simply change the people around you. You've learned to behave in one way with some people and in another way with others. For example, you're likely to talk without swearing when in conversation with Grandma and Grandpa, but are more likely to swear when shooting the breeze with the gang. In some cases, your self-adjustment program will consist of minimizing contact with certain people. Marlatt and Parks (1982), for example, have indicated that people with addictive behaviors are more likely to show a relapse if they hang out with others engaging in those behaviors.

The Time of Day. We've all learned to do certain things at certain times. Sometimes our problems are related to that fact. Sometimes it's possible to achieve successful self-control by changing the time of the activity. For example, many students are most alert in the morning. Yet they spend their free time during the mornings having coffee with friends and socializing, and leave their studying to the evening when they are less alert. Successful self-control of studying for such students might be accomplished by moving studying to mornings and socializing to evenings.

Manage the Behavior. If the behavior of concern is relatively simple—such as swearing—you're likely to focus more on antecedents and consequences. If the behavior is complex, you need to spend some time focusing on the behavior itself. If your goal is to acquire some complex skills, it's helpful to consider task analysis, mastery criteria, and chaining. *Mastery criteria* are performance requirements for practicing a skill such that if the criteria are met, the behavior has been learned. Consider, for example, the task of learning to play golf. Simek and O'Brien (1981) task-analyzed "playing golf" into 22 components. They arranged these in a behavioral progression for instructional purposes and identified mastery criteria for each component (see Table 23–1).

Then they taught a group of novices by starting with 10-inch putts rather than by teaching them to swing a club, as is often done by golf pros. Why? For two reasons. First, it seemed like the simplest response—and the general rule is to start with the simple and proceed to the complex. Second, it incorporated a powerful natural reinforcer for performing the response correctly—namely, hitting the ball into the hole (note that this is similar to the argument for using backward chaining—see Chapter 11). Gradually, as mastery criteria for simple responses were met, the length of the shot was increased to longer putts, then to short chip shots, to longer chip shots, to short pitch shots, to longer pitch shots, to middle iron shots, and eventually to hitting fairway woods, and finally a driver. "But how well did they score when put on a golf course?" one might ask. In a study with 12 novice golfers, six of the golfers completed the behavioral progression and mastery criteria in eight lessons. The other six golfers received eight lessons of traditional instruction from a golfer who had taught golf for several years. All 12 then

Table 23-1   A Behavioral Progression and Mastery Criteria for Learning Golf*

	COMPLETE GOLF CHAIN AND MASTERY CRITERION	
Step	Shot	Mastery Criterion
1	10-inch putt (between clubs optional)	4 putts consecutively holed
2	16-inch putt (between clubs optional)	4 putts consecutively holed
3	2-foot putt clubs removed	4 putts consecutively holed
4	3-foot putt	4 putts consecutively holed
5	4-foot putt some break	2 holed, 2 out of 4 within 6 inches
6	6-foot putt	4 consecutively within 6 inches
7	10-foot putt	4 consecutively within 12 inches
8	15-foot putt	4 consecutively within 15 inches
9	20-foot putt	4 consecutively within 18 inches
10	30-foot putt	4 consecutively within 24 inches
11	35-foot chip 5 feet off green 7-iron	4 out of 6 within 6 feet
12	35-foot chip 15 feet off green wedge	4 out of 6 within 6 feet
13	65-foot chip	4 out of 6 within 6 feet
14	25-yard pitch	4 out of 6 within 10 feet
15	35-yard pitch	4 out of 6 within 15 feet
16	50-yard pitch	4 out of 6 within 15 feet
17	75-yard shot	4 out of 6 within 30 feet
18	100-yard shot	4 out of 6 within 40 feet
19	125-yard shot	4 out of 6 within 45 feet
20	150-yard shot	4 out of 6 within 54 feet
21	175-yard shot	4 out of 6 within 66 feet
22	200-yard shot (if within your range)	4 out of 5 within 90 feet

*Reprinted with permission from Simek and O'Brien (1981).

played a complete, 18-hole round of golf. The behavioral progression group "whipped" the traditional group handily, beating them by an average of 17 strokes.

Shaping is an important strategy for self-improvement projects in which your ultimate goal involves a large behavioral change from your starting point. Important rules of thumb to keep in mind include: start small, meet mastery criterion before moving up a step, and keep progressive steps small. Studies of dieters, for example, have reported that those who set small, gradual shaping steps for reducing calories are more likely to develop self-control of binge eating than subjects who set large steps (Gormally, Black, Daston, & Rardin, 1982; Hawkins & Clement, 1980).

Manage the Consequences.   One strategy for manipulating consequent events is to eliminate certain reinforcers that may inadvertently strengthen a particularly undesirable behavior in a particular situation. Do you remember Al's discovery when he analyzed his eating problem? He noticed that in addition to the taste of food itself, other reinforcers (TV, pleasant conversation, etc.) were usually associated with eating. A major feature of Al's dieting control program, therefore, should be to disassociate eating from these extra activities.

Recommendations by LeBow (1981) to accomplish this include: (1) develop an eating place in the home that is to be used only for that purpose, and eat only there when at home; (2) use the same eating utensils and placemats at each meal; (3) eat only at designated times; and (4) keep food out of every room but the kitchen.

A second way of manipulating consequences is by self-recording and self-graphing the target behavior (e.g., see McLaughlin, Burgess, & Sackville-West, 1981; Maletsky, 1974; McFall, 1970; Paquin, 1982; Rosen, 1981; Zohn & Bornstein, 1980). Seeing a line that shows gradual improvement can serve as a prompt to think a variety of positive, self-confidence thoughts. It can also serve as a prompt for extra social attention from others for sticking to a self-control program.

A third way of manipulating consequences involves arranging for specific reinforcers to be earned by you for showing improvement, or even for just sticking to the program (see Heffernan & Richards, 1981; Sohn & Lamal, 1982). Consider, for example, a self-control program initiated by one of the authors. During the winter, he began an exercise program that involved running two miles (14 laps) three times a week at the university's underground track. The author found that after 9 or 10 laps, fatigue thoughts would come to mind and he would frequently talk himself out of doing the last few laps, saying such things as, "Oh well, I've done pretty well by running 11 laps." He decided to try a self-reinforcement program to increase the frequency of "antifatigue" thoughts during the last few laps. Specifically, during the tenth through fourteenth laps, he would think some antifatigue thought and then follow it with a pleasurable thought. The particular antifatigue thought that he chose was about a TV physical fitness commercial claiming that "the average 60-year-old Swede is in the same physical condition as the average 30-year-old Canadian" (we have since learned that the claim is false, but this is not important to our illustration). Each time the author got to a particular spot on the track, he thought about the very healthy Swede jogging merrily along. At the next turn, he thought about something enjoyable, such as making love to a beautiful woman. He enjoyed the pleasurable thought across the end of the track and then would simply not think the Swede thought or the reinforcing thought down the other side of the track. In this way he was able to engage in a private behavior that counteracted the fatigue thoughts and was able to strengthen that behavior. After practicing this determinedly for about two weeks, he was able to put the fatigue thoughts completely out of mind.

Was the effectiveness of this program really due to self-reinforcement? Not necessarily. There are at least three other possibilities: (1) the program might have worked equally well if the author had not thought the "reinforcing" thoughts—perhaps thinking the antifatigue thoughts themselves would have been sufficient; (2) the "reinforcing" thoughts may have been effective because they increased the distinctiveness of the antifatigue thoughts that were reinforcing for other reasons (this is essentially the process discussed under the second way of manipulating consequent events); (3) the

Note 5

"reinforcing" thoughts may have increased the conditioned reinforcing properties of the antifatigue thoughts through association with them (this would
be similar to having a pleasant meal on an airplane to help enhance the
conditioned reinforcing aspects of flying so as to overcome a fear of flying).[5]

A common strategy for incorporating reinforcers into self-control
programs is to request others to dispense the rewards (see S. M. Hall, 1980;
Mermelstein, Lichtenstein, & McIntyre, 1983; Weisz & Bucher, 1980; and
Wood, Hardin, & Wong, 1984). For example, Mary decided to initiate a
jogging program. She also decided that she would receive money immediately
after jogging. Also, if she jogged every day, she could select and engage in
one of several possible social activities with her husband. If she met her goals,
Mary's husband dispensed the reinforcers. The program was quite successful
(Kau & Fischer, 1974).

Some rules of thumb for incorporating reinforcers into your program
include: (1) make it possible for you to earn specific reinforcers on a daily
basis; (2) set up bonuses that can be earned for progress on a weekly basis;
(3) vary the reinforcers from one day to the next and one week to the next
so as to prevent boredom with the entire system; (4) if possible and desirable,
have other individuals dispense the reinforcers to you for meeting your goals;
and (5) tell others about your progress.

Recall the Premack principle from Chapter 3. The Premack principle
states that any activity that you are more likely to perform can be used to
strengthen a behavior that you are less likely to perform. This strategy can
also be used in self-control programs. High-frequency behaviors used in documented cases of self-improvement have involved, for example, smoking and
making telephone calls (Todd, 1972), urinating (Johnson, 1971), opening daily
mail at the office (Spinelli & Packard, 1975), and sitting on a particular chair
(Horan & Johnson, 1971).

5. ENSURE SUPPORT FOR THE PROGRAM

Let's suppose you have started your self-control program and are making
some progress. The question is, will you stick to it? Unfortunately, relapses
are common in self-control programs (Marlatt & Parks, 1982). By *relapse*, we
mean going back to the unwanted behavior at approximately the same rate
that you were at before you started your program. We're not talking here
about an occasional slip.

One way of preventing a relapse is to practice all of the things that
we recommended in the subsection on making a commitment. A particularly
effective strategy is to sign a behavioral contract. A **behavioral contract** is a
clear written statement of what behaviors of what individuals will produce
what rewards, and who will deliver those rewards. It usually involves two or
more people, although "self-contracts" have also been used. A contract usually
involves a clear statement of the following:

a. the target behaviors;
b. the method of data collection;
c. the reinforcers to be used, their schedule of delivery, and who will deliver them (i.e. the *mediator*);
d. potential problems and their resolutions;
e. bonus and/or penalty clauses;
f. a schedule of review for progress; and
g. the signatures of all persons involved, and the date of the agreement.

The contract serves at least four important S^D functions:

1. It ensures that all parties involved agree to the goals and procedures and that they do not lose sight of them during the course of the treatment.
2. Because the goals are specified behaviorally, the contract also ensures that throughout the program all parties will agree on how close they are to reaching the goals.
3. The contract provides the client with a realistic estimate of the cost of the program to him or her in time, effort, and money.
4. The signatures on the contract help to ensure that all parties will faithfully follow the specified procedures, because in our society signing a document is a strong S^D indicating a commitment.

As we have stressed in previous chapters, behavior modification procedures should be revised in appropriate ways when the data indicate that they are not producing satisfactory results. Thus, the contract should be open to renegotiation at any time. If, for example, a signatory finds that she simply cannot meet some commitment specified in the contract, she should so inform the other signatories at the next meeting with the therapist. The difficulty would then be discussed, and, if it seemed desirable, a new contract replacing the previous one would be negotiated, drafted, and signed.

The contract shown in Table 23–2 was prepared by a student in a course on behavior modification and self-control taught by one of the authors. This student worked in a mental-retardation institution, where she had experienced considerable difficulty because of her tendency to become upset with other staff members. After preparing a baseline of the problem behaviors, the student prepared and followed the program described in this contract.

Sometimes a therapist and a client may design a program and prepare a contract that produces completely successful and satisfactory results. Often, however, the initial contract may have to be revised before success is likely to be achieved. If problems arise in following the contract and implementing the program, a number of relevant factors might be discussed at the review meetings. DeRisi and Butz (1975) have suggested that the client and therapist might examine the following "trouble-shooting guide" when satisfactory progress is not being made.

Table 23-2   Sample Contract

A   PROBLEM AND GOAL

Achieving a frequency of zero instances per day of anger in response to hearing someone lying or being dishonest or in response to remembering an instance of someone lying or being dishonest.

Definitions:

Anger: muscle tension, particularly in the hands and face, in response to hearing someone lie.

One instance: an uninterrupted episode of anger—that is, an episode not interrupted by thinking about something else that did not cause anger.

Lying: any statement, verbal omission, or shake or nod of the head that I consider to be a lie. Note: Whether or not the other person is lying is based on my own feeling that it is a lie.

B   DATA COLLECTION

Each instance of anger is recorded as one count on a wrist counter (golf scorer) that I am allowed to wear. These instances will be graphed each evening before I go to bed.

C   REINFORCERS AND THEIR DELIVERY

1   *Daily.* If the target for that day, as described in the shaping steps below, is reached, I permit myself to have my pillow when I go to sleep. If it is not reached, I must place my pillow in the kitchen cupboard and sleep without it.

2   *Weekly.* I have given $400, which I saved up to buy a stereo, to Sally. As I meet the weekly criterion for each step, I will receive portions of the money back, as specified below:

Reaching criterion for Step   1: $ 10
Reaching criterion for Step   2:   10
Reaching criterion for Step   3:   10
Reaching criterion for Step   4:   10
Reaching criterion for Step   5:   20
Reaching criterion for Step   6:   20
Reaching criterion for Step   7:   40
Reaching criterion for Step   8:   60
Reaching criterion for Step   9:   80
Reaching criterion for Step 10:   140

Steps:

Step   1:   6 instances or less per day for one week.
Step   2:   5 instances or less per day for one week.
Step   3:   4 instances or less per day for one week.
Step   4:   3 instances or less per day for one week.
Step   5:   2 instances or less per day for one week.
Step   6:   1 instance or less per day for one week.
Step   7:   0 instances per day for one week.
Step   8:   0 instances per day for the second consecutive week.
Step   9:   0 instances per day for the third consecutive week.
Step 10:   0 instances per day for the fourth consecutive week.

Continued

D POTENTIAL PROBLEMS AND THEIR RESOLUTIONS

    1 I have guarded against the feeling of being strongly punished by the fact that if I do not meet my criterion for that week, I do not lose the money; I am simply delayed in buying the stereo.

    2 I will minimize the two problems of short-circuiting as follows. (a) I will control taking my pillow when I have not earned it by putting the pillow in the kitchen cupboard at the far end of my apartment so that I have to walk a far distance to get it. (b) I will control buying the stereo before the program is complete by reminding myself that if I bought the stereo prematurely I would not be able to get as good a quality stereo, because I would not have all the money returned to me. Also, I will inform several of my friends about my project and my progress to avoid doing this.

    3 I have encountered a problem in deciding on which day I should begin my week. My baseline shows Wednesday to be a "high day." That is, counts are typically higher on Wednesday than any other day. My week, therefore, will begin on Thursday and run until Wednesday afternoon. This will be an incentive not to "blow a week's work in the last day of the week."

E BONUS OR PENALTY CLAUSES

    None, other than specified above.

F SCHEDULE FOR REVIEW OF PROGRESS

    Every Wednesday evening with Sally.

G SIGNATURES OF ALL INVOLVED AND THE DATES OF THE AGREEMENT

Client Suzy   Date January 30th

Others Involved Sally   Date January 30th

                                         Date

Therapist   Date

TROUBLESHOOTING GUIDE*

The following questions may help you to spot the problems in your contracting system:

    The contract

1. Was the target behavior specified clearly?
2. Did the contract provide for immediate reinforcement?
3. Did it ask for small approximations to the desired behavior?
4. Was reinforcement frequent and in small amounts?
5. Did the contract call for and reward accomplishment rather than obedience?
6. Was the performance rewarded after its occurrence?
7. Was the contract fair?
8. Were the terms of the contract clear?
9. Was the contract honest?
10. Was the contract positive?

    *Adapted from DeRisi and Butz, *Writing Behavioral Contracts: A Case Simulation Practice Manual* (1975, pp. 58–60).

11. Was contracting as a method being used systematically?
12. Was the contract negotiated mutually?
13. Was the penalty clause too punitive?

The client

1. Did the client understand the contract?
2. Is the client getting the reinforcer from some other source?
3. Do the reinforcers have to be reevaluated?
4. Has a new problem behavior developed that is drawing the mediator's attention away from the target behavior?

The mediator

1. Did the mediator understand the contract?
2. Did the mediator dispense the kind and amount of reinforcement specified in the contract?
3. Did the mediator dispense it according to instructions, at the rate specified, and with consistency?
4. Did punishment accidentally accompany the performance being reinforced?
5. Did the mediator stop mediating?
6. Is a new mediator required?

Measurement

1. Have the data been verified as accurate?
2. Did your data collector understand what he or she was supposed to count?
3. Did you rehearse the counting task with the data collector?
4. Did you reinforce the data collector for his or her behavior?
5. Is the data collection task too complex or too difficult?
6. Should you try to get another data collector?

6. MAKE IT LAST

Let's suppose you have met your goal: you've lost those 20 pounds you wanted to; or you haven't had a cigarette in three months; or your studying has paid off and you got an "A" on your last two exams. Now the question is, will it last? Will you be able to maintain your gains over the long run? One thing is certain. Your gains from your self-control program are more likely to be maintained if you take some deliberate steps to make them last.

One strategy to "make it last" is to set specific dates for postchecks and to list specific strategies to follow if the post checks are unfavorable. For example, if your self-control program was one of weight reduction, you might continue to weigh yourself once a week. If your weight increases to a specified level, then immediately return to your program for a week. Another strategy is to set up a "buddy" system. Find a friend or relative with a similar problem and set mutual maintenance goals. Once a month, get together and check each other's progress. If your progress has been maintained, celebrate in a previously agreed-upon way. In a study of smokers, Karol and Richards (1978) found that smokers who quit with a buddy and who telephoned encouragement to each other showed greater reduction of smoking in an eight-month follow-up than did smokers who tried to quit on their own. A third strategy is to practice the self-control steps outlined in this chapter to improve additional behaviors. You are more likely to continue using self-control techniques if you practice them on more than one self-control project (Barone, 1982). Moreover, you are more likely to be able to deal with a relapse if you are skillful in the self-control techniques that brought about the improvement in the first place. Additional strategies for programming maintenance are described in Chapter 12.

CIRCUMVENTING THE THERAPIST

So far we have considered only very simple examples of self-management. Some problems, however, require a step-by-step self-modification project that may last several months or more. Such cases may involve a therapist providing instructions, some modeling, and an opportunity for behavioral rehearsal and role playing by the client. Recall the example in Chapter 16 in which the therapist utilized instructions, modeling, shaping, and role playing to help a college student learn how to ask for a date over the telephone. In other cases, a therapist might interact extensively with a client to help him or her develop self-control over self-verbalizations. Cognitive psychologists generally describe this approach (which we discuss in more detail in Chapter 25) as helping individuals to change their behavior by changing their beliefs or thoughts. In some cases, therapists helping clients in complex self-control programs might go through all the steps in the guidelines in Chapter 21, especially those cited in the section entitled "Strategies of Program Design and Implementation."

However, it should be clear from the preceding sections in this chapter that many people who have mastered some behavior modification principles can use them to control their own behavior without having to see a therapist. For example, the student who has mastered this and previous chapters should have little difficulty in handling a simple behavior problem that has been bothering her (although we would still recommend seeing a therapist about serious problems). Perhaps the student would like to decrease her smoking, nail biting, swearing, or abusive remarks to others. Or perhaps she would like to enhance her studying, exercising, personal tidiness, consideration of others, or public speaking. She probably does not really need a therapist to help her accomplish these goals.

A person who has read this book already knows how to take data; he does not need a therapist to help him do that. He knows also how to plan a program and evaluate its effectiveness. He knows a large number of behavior modification principles and techniques and how to apply them; hence, it is likely that he can apply an appropriate combination of them to his own case. Moreover, the present chapter has made him aware of short-circuiting, a major difficulty in self-control programs, and has illustrated how contracting can minimize this difficulty. A behavioral contract can be negotiated with any person who is close to you and wants to help you change your behavior. In short, many people can be their own behavior therapist.

STUDY QUESTIONS

1. What do people seem to be talking about when they talk about "will power"? Is will power a useful concept? Why or why not?
2. Describe four causes of self-control problems and illustrate each with reference to an example.
3. What are the two types of short-circuiting? Give an example of each.
4. In two or three sentences, describe the model of self-management presented in this chapter.
5. List six steps that characterize many programs in self-adjustment.
6. List the steps that Mager recommends to "unfuzzify" a vaguely stated problem or self-control goal.
7. How does this book define "commitment"?
8. Describe four steps that you could take to strengthen and maintain your commitment to a program of self-control.
9. Illustrate how Al was inadvertently reinforced for eating numerous times throughout the day.
10. List five major classes of stimuli that you might consider when planning how to manage the situation in a self-control program.
11. Define and give an example of mastery criterion.
12. In a sentence or two each, describe three different ways of manipulating consequences in self-control programs.
13. Describe three strategies that you might follow to increase the chances that your success with a self-control program will last.
14. Briefly describe a self-control program for reinforcing "antifatigue" thoughts.
15. What is a behavioral contract? Describe its essential features.
16. What important stimulus-control functions does a behavioral contract serve?
17. How did the behavioral contract for controlling the student's anger attempt to alleviate potential problems of short-circuiting?
18. Describe several ways in which another person can be used to help prevent short-circuiting in a self-control program.
19. Is it plausible to suggest that many individuals can become their own behavior therapists? Justify your answer.

SELF-MODIFICATION EXERCISES

1. Using the information in this and the preceding chapters, describe how you might go about following all six steps of a self-control program for bringing

about successful self-adjustment for a behavior of yours that you would like to change.

2. Implement your program and take data for a minimum of three weeks. Then write a summary report of the results (approximately 5 to 10 pages, plus graphs).

EXTENDED DISCUSSION AND NOTES

1. The first important behavioral analysis of the area of self-control was provided by Skinner in his book *Science and Human Behavior* (Skinner, 1953). The first major report on some clinical applications of Skinner's theoretical treatment of self-control was written by Goldiamond (1965). In the early 1970s, several books on self-control were published (e.g., Watson & Tharp, 1972; Mahoney & Thoreson, 1974; Thoreson & Mahoney, 1974) and the topic received a great deal of attention in the behavior modification journals. New labels were also introduced to refer to this general area. Some writers have used the terms self-control, self-management, self-modification, and self-regulation interchangeably. Others have argued that such terms should be used to denote separate processes (Baer, 1984; Brigham, 1982; Kanfer & Gaelick, 1986).

2. Suggestions for controlling the controlling behavior occur throughout this chapter. Theoretically, we assume that most of the contingencies that teach us and maintain our controlling behaviors are provided by the society in which we live. As stated by Skinner (1953, p. 240),

> We make this controlling behavior more probable by arranging special contingencies of reinforcement. By punishing drinking—perhaps merely with "disapproval"—we arrange for the automatic reinforcement of behavior which controls drinking because such behavior then reduces conditioned aversive stimulation. Some of these additional consequences are supplied by nature, but in general they are arranged by the community. This is indeed the whole point of ethical training. It appears, therefore, that society is responsible for the larger part of the behavior of self-control. If this is correct, little ultimate control remains with the individual. A man may spend a great deal of time designing his own life—he may choose the circumstances in which he is to live with great care, and he may manipulate his daily environment on an extensive scale. Such activity appears to exemplify a high order of self-determination. But it is also behavior, and we account for it in terms of other variables in the environment and history of the individual. It is these variables which provide the ultimate control.

3. Although there has been a proliferation of self-help manuals on the market, there has been little quality field testing of the effectiveness of such manuals or research comparing them to each other so as to provide guidelines for consumer choice (Glasgow & Rosen, 1978, 1979). As reported by Glasgow, Swaney, and Schafer (1981), their study contains both "good" and "bad" news for developers and users of self-help behavior therapy manuals. They compared the effectiveness of two commercially published manuals for the control of fingernail-biting (Azrin & Nunn, 1977; Perkins & Perkins, 1976) with each other as well as with a self-observation

control condition. One group was exposed to each condition. Moreover, each group was subdivided into self-administered subjects versus therapist-administered subjects. The self-administered subjects followed the procedures on their own over a three-week period. The therapist-administered subjects attended three weekly small-group meetings at which subjects were praised for completing homework assignments and were guided in following the procedures and discussing difficulties. The report contained "good" news and "bad" news for authors of self-help behavior modification manuals. The "good" news is that all groups showed significant progress and results were maintained at a six-week follow-up. The self-administered treatments appeared to be as effective as therapist-administered treatments. The "bad" news was that self-observation procedures in which clients simply recorded and graphed their nail-biting were as effective as the programs contained in the commercially published self-help manuals. We do not mean to imply that all that is needed to achieve self-control is self-monitoring. Other research has indicated that self-monitoring is not always sufficient to bring about desired behavior change. For certain, more research is needed in this area.

4. A commitment is verbal behavior that corresponds to other behavior that one later engages in if the commitment is kept. A number of studies have been conducted on training a correspondence between stated intentions (commitments) and later behavior. For example, Ward and Stare (1990) prompted a group of kindergarten children to state that they were going to play in a certain designated area. Specifically, the children were prompted to say, "I'm going to play at the workbench today." The children received a token if they made this statement. After four minutes of play, children who played at the workbench received another token for playing at the workbench after saying that this is what they would do. Compared to a group of children who simply received tokens for playing in the designated area, the group that received correspondence training showed more instances of following through on stated intentions to engage in another activity (playing with toys), even though they received no tokens for following through on this commitment. The results thus showed that correspondence training on one response can generalize to a new response. This tendency to generalize correspondence training may be what makes it possible for us to keep commitments for behavior change that we have made to ourselves.

5. Catania (1975, 1976) and Goldiamond (1976), have argued that it is inappropriate to use the label "self-reinforcement" to refer to a procedure in which an individual emits some behavior and then presents a reinforcing consequence immediately after, such as in the case of the author thinking of the Swede and then thinking about a pleasurable event. Certainly it is possible for an individual to consume a reinforcer following some behavior. A professor grading papers might decide to grade five papers and then to eat a handful of peanuts. However, if paper grading increases in frequency, it is inappropriate to attribute the increase to "self-reinforcement." The problem is that this implies that the increase is due to positive reinforcement as conceptualized theoretically and in basic and applied research. However, we must remember that short-circuiting can occur at any time (also, see Skinner, 1953, p. 238). In a review of the experimental literature on this point, Brigham (1980) noted that "To date, unequivocal empirical evidence to support the notion of self-reinforcement as an effective applied procedure is almost nonexistent and certainly does not justify the major role it is given in most treatments of self-control" (p. 29).

STUDY QUESTIONS ON NOTES

1. Who wrote the first important behavioral analysis of the area of self-control? Who wrote the first major report on some applications of Skinner's theoretical treatment of self-control?

2. In this chapter, self-control refers to an individual behaving in some way that arranges the environment to control his or her own subsequent behavior. According to Skinner, what provides the ultimate control over this controlling behavior? Discuss.

3. In what sense does the study by Glasgow and others on the evaluation of self-help manuals contain both good news and bad news for the authors of those manuals?

4. What is correspondence training? Briefly describe how generalized correspondence was demonstrated in kindergarten children.

5. Given the problem of short-circuiting, is self-reinforcement possible? Defend your answer.

CHAPTER 24

Systematic Self-Desensitization

In Chapter 15, we explained that systematic desensitization is a procedure in which a client gradually progresses through a hierarchy of *imagined* anxiety-producing situations, arranged from those that elicit the least anxiety to those that elicit the most anxiety, while maintaining a completely relaxed state in order to counteract the anxiety. Systematic *self*-desensitization is essentially the same procedure, except that the client progresses through the various desensitization stages by him or herself. In other words, it is a self-modification procedure that is much like the self-modification procedures discussed in Chapter 23, except that it focuses strictly on problematic fears. We therefore explain the procedure by assuming that you have an undesirable fear that you would like to eliminate (for example, a fear of flying).

Note 1   It is now recognized that there are methods for overcoming phobias that are generally more effective than systematic desensitization.[1] (We discuss some of these methods in Chapter 26.) However, only systematic desensitization has been adapted to be applicable in a self-management program. The steps outlined below are suitable for problematic fears that are not too intense or debilitating (for severe phobias, we recommend that professional help be obtained). Your systematic self-desensitization program will take you through the following phases: (1) constructing a fear hierarchy, (2) learning deep muscle relaxation, and (3) carrying out the actual therapy steps of the self-desensitization process.

CONSTRUCTING THE FEAR HIERARCHY _____

To construct a fear hierarchy, first list from 10 to 30 fear-producing situations related to your undesirable fear. Then arrange these situations in order, starting with the situation that causes the least fear and ending with the situation that causes the most fear. To accomplish this task, get a stack of 3-by-5-inch index cards and proceed as follows.

1. Take one of the index cards, and on the front write a brief phrase about the fear-eliciting situation that makes you only slightly nervous. For example, if your fear is that of flying, the phrase might be "sitting at home and phoning the airline to make a reservation." Now turn the index card over, and on the back list several stimuli that will help prompt you to realistically imagine yourself actually experiencing the phone call. The prompts might include such things as the color of your phone and the sound of a voice saying, "Airline reservations desk—may I help you?" A sample index card is shown in Figure 24–1.

2. Take another index card, and list a situation that elicits a slightly larger amount of fear. Again, on the back of that card provide yourself with some verbal prompts that will help you clearly imagine experiencing that situation. Continue in this manner until all the fear-producing situations are listed on note cards arranged so that each situation produces a little more anxiety than the preceding one. You now have a fear hierarchy. An example of a fear hierarchy for an individual who was afraid of flying is shown in Table 24–1.

Note that each item in Table 24–1 refers to a specific, concrete situation that can be imagined in vivid detail, rather than a vague general idea. For example, item 10 is to be preferred to "waiting for the plane," for it is more likely to prompt specific images of sitting in the lobby, listening to the announcements of flight numbers, and so forth.

3. Your next step is to validate your fear hierarchy by making sure that your cards have been arranged in the proper order (they should start with the situation that produces the least anxiety and end with the situation that generates the most anxiety), and that the steps between them are sufficiently small (no "jump" in anxiety level from one item to the next should be too large). This should be done as follows:

a. Rate each item in your hierarchy on a scale from 0 to 100, where 100 means that the situation elicits the maximum conceivable amount of anxiety (extreme panic and absolute terror) when encountered in the natural environment, and 0 means that the situation produces absolutely no emotion when encountered in real life. This value is referred to as the number of *subjective units of discomfort* (suds) elicited by the situation.[2]

Note 2

b. Check whether your original order of items in the hierarchy and your suds ratings are consistent (each item in the hierarchy should have a higher suds ranking than the item below it and a lower ranking than the item above it). If they are not consistent, redo both the hierarchy and the suds ratings until they are completely consistent.

Talking to the travel agent, making reservations

Front side

1. Phoning the travel agent — dial number, call answered.

2. Giving particulars of destination, dates of trip.

3. Writing down flight numbers and times.

4. Marking calendar with dates, flight times, and flight numbers.

Back side

FIGURE 24–1   A sample index card for a fear-producing situation.

Note 3

c. Use your suds ratings to ensure that the distances between items in the hierarchy are sufficiently small and approximately equal (rule of thumb: distances between items should be no greater than 5 to 10 suds).[3] Construct new items and insert them between any items that are greater than 10 suds apart.

d. Number each of the cards in order, starting with the card causing the least anxiety as number 1.

e. If you cannot make suds ratings without apparent inconsistencies between the ratings and your hierarchy, or within the ratings themselves, cease your attempt at self-desensitization and seek professional clinical desensitization (since it would appear that several major anxieties are present and interacting—a condition that may be too complex to be dealt with by the nonprofessional).

Table 24-1 Example of a Fear-of-Flying Hierarchy*

1   The plane has landed and stopped at the terminal. I get off the plane and enter the terminal, where I am met by friends.
2   A trip has been planned, and I have examined the possible methods of travel and decided "out loud" to travel by plane.
3   I have called the travel agent and told him of my plans. He gives me the times and flight numbers.
4   It is the day before the trip, and I pack my suitcase, close it, and lock it.
5   It is 10 days before the trip, and I receive the tickets in the mail. I note the return address, open the envelope, and check the tickets for the correct dates, times, and flight numbers.
6   It is the day of the flight, I am leaving home. I lock the house, put the bags in the car, and make sure that I have the tickets and money.
7   I am driving to the airport for my flight. I am aware of every plane I see. As I get close to the airport, I see several planes—some taking off, some landing, and some just sitting on the ground by the terminal.
8   I am entering the terminal. I am carrying my bags and tickets.
9   I proceed to the airline desk, wait in line, and have the agent check my tickets and then weigh and check my bags.
10 I am in the lounge with many other people, some with bags also waiting for flights. I hear the announcements over the intercom and listen for my flight number to be called.
11 I hear my flight number announced, and I proceed to the security checkpoint with my hand luggage.
12 I approach the airline desk beyond the security checkpoint, and the agent asks me to choose a seat from the "map" of the plane.
13 I walk down the ramp leading to the plane and enter the door of the plane.
14 I am now inside the plane. I look at the interior of the plane and walk down the aisle, looking for my seat number. I then move in from the aisle and sit down in my assigned seat.
15 The plane is in flight, and I decide to leave my seat and walk to the washroom at the back of the plane.
16 I notice the seat-belt signs light up, so I fasten my seat belt and I notice the sound of the motors starting.
17 Everyone is seated with their seat belts fastened, and the plane slowly moves away from the terminal.
18 I notice the seat-belt signs are again lighted, and the pilot announces that we are preparing to land.
19 I am looking out the window and suddenly the plane enters clouds and I cannot see out the window.
20 The plane has stopped at the end of the runway and is sitting, waiting for instructions to take off.
21 The plane is descending to the runway for a landing. I feel the speed and see the ground getting closer.
22 The plane has taken off from the airport and banks as it changes direction. I am aware of the "tilt."
23 The plane starts down the runway, and the motors get louder as the plane increases speed and suddenly lifts off.

*This hierarchy was prepared by a client who initiated a self-desensitization project after reading a preliminary draft of this chapter. (Her case is described in more detail by Roscoe, Martin, and Pear, 1980.)

If a strong anxiety has occurred while you are constructing the hierarchy or developing your suds ratings, you might adopt one of two strategies: either discontinue your program and seek professional clinical help or continue your program but eliminate the five most anxiety-producing situations. After completing your desensitization program minus the five most anxiety-producing situations, you should then be able to develop a program for those items, since they will likely cause much less anxiety if you have successfully completed the earlier items.

LEARNING DEEP MUSCLE RELAXATION

Note 4

After you have constructed your hierarchy, you should next learn to relax all your muscles completely and to recognize when they are relaxed.[4] Do this by alternately tensing and relaxing your muscles while attending closely to the internal activities and sensations you are feeling at the time. Instructions for achieving deep muscle relaxation are presented in Table 24–2.

Note 5

It would be maximally effective if a friend with a low, even, soothing voice could record these relaxation instructions on tape. That way, you can listen to them rather than having to read them.[5] While your friend is reading the instructions, he or she should pause five seconds for each "(p)" that appears in them.

Let us assume that the instructions have been recorded on tape. You should now find a quiet, dimly lit, private setting with as few distracting stimuli as possible; a comfortable couch, bed, or reclining chair; and a time when you will not be interrupted for twenty to thirty minutes. Lie or sit on the couch, bed, or chair, which should support you with minimal use of your own muscles. Now turn on the tape recorder and follow the instructions.

After you have practiced the relaxation method on several different occasions, you will find that you are able to skip some of the steps and achieve the same deeply relaxed state in a shorter period of time. Eventually, you should be able to go directly to step 20 and achieve a completely relaxed state within a matter of minutes. We recommend that you gradually eliminate steps according to the following pattern:

1. Practice the entire 20 steps in Table 24–2 on at least three occasions spread over a minimum of two days.
2. Make a new tape recording consisting of steps 1, 8, 15, and 20. Use this new tape on at least three occasions spread over a minimum of two days.
3. Make a new tape consisting of steps 1 and 20. Use this new tape on at least two occasions spread over a minimum of one day.

After completing this program, which takes approximately one week, you should be able to relax totally in a matter of minutes. When you accomplish that goal, you are ready to begin the next phase of your self-desensitization

Table 24-2   Instructions to Be Recorded on Tape and Played to Achieve Deep Muscle Relaxation*

1   Listen closely to these instructions. They will help you to increase your ability to relax. Each time I pause, continue doing what you were doing before the pause. Now, close your eyes and take three deep breaths. (p) (p)

2   Make a tight fist with your left hand. Squeeze it tightly. Note how it feels. (p) Now relax. (p)

3   Once again, squeeze your left hand tightly and study the tension that you feel. (p) And once again, just relax and think of the tension disappearing from your fingers. (p) (p)

4   Make a tight fist with your right hand. Squeeze it as tightly as you can and note the tension in your fingers and your hand, and your forearm. (p) Now relax. (p)

5   Once again, squeeze your right fist tightly. (p) And again, just relax. (p) (p)

6   Make a tight fist with your left hand and bend your arm to make your left biceps hard. Hold it tense. (p) Now relax totally. Feel the warmth escape down your biceps, through your forearm, and out of your fingers. (p) (p)

7   Now make a tight fist with the other hand and raise your hand to make your right biceps hard. Hold it tightly, and feel the tension. (p) Now relax. Concentrate on the feelings flowing through your arm. (p) (p)

8   Now, squeeze both fists at once and bend both arms to make them totally tense throughout. Hold it, and think about the tension you feel. (p) Now relax, and feel the total warmth and relaxation flowing through your muscles. All the tension is flowing out of your fingertips. (p) (p)

9   Now, wrinkle your forehead and squint your eyes very tight and hard.** Squeeze them tight and hard. Feel the tension across your forehead and through your eyes. Now relax. Note the sensations running through your eyes. Just relax. (p) (p)

10   Okay, squeeze your jaws tight together and raise your chin to make your neck muscles hard. Hold it, bite down hard, tense your neck, and squeeze your lips really tight. (p) Now relax. (p) (p)

11   Now, all together, wrinkle up your forehead and squeeze your eyes tight, bite down hard with your jaws, raise your chin and tighten up your neck, and make your lips tight. Hold them all and feel the tension throughout your forehead, and eyes, and jaw, and neck, and lips. Hold it. Now relax. Just totally relax and enjoy the tingling sensations. (p) (p) (p)

12   Now, squeeze both your shoulders forward as hard as you can until you feel your muscles pulling tightly right across your back, especially in the area between your shoulder blades. Squeeze them. Hold them tight. Now relax. (p) (p)

13   Now squeeze your shoulders forward again and, at the same time, suck your stomach in as far as you can and tense your stomach muscles. Feel the tension throughout your stomach. Hold it. (p) Now relax. (p) (p)

14   Once more, squeeze your shoulder blades forward again, suck in your stomach as far as you can, tense your stomach muscles, and feel the tension throughout your upper body. Now relax. (p) (p)

15   Now, we are going to review all of the muscle systems that we have covered so far. First, take three deep breaths. (p) (p) Ready? Tighten up both fists and bend both of your arms to squeeze your biceps tight. Wrinkle your forehead and squeeze your eyes tight. Bite down hard with your jaws, raise your chin, and hold your lips tight. Squeeze your shoulders forward and suck in your stomach and push your stomach muscles against it. Hold them all. Feel the tremendous tension throughout. Now relax. Take a deep breath. Just feel the tension disappearing. Think about the total relaxation throughout all of your muscles—in your arms, in your head, in your shoulders, in your stomach. Just relax. (p) (p)

16   Now, let's go to your legs. Bring your left heel in tight toward your chair, push it down hard, and raise your toes so that your calf and your thigh are extremely tense. Squeeze your toes up and push your heel down hard. (p) Now relax. (p) (p)

17   One more time, bring your left heel in tight toward your chair, push it down hard, and raise

your toes so that your calf and your thigh are extremely tense. Push down on the heel and raise your toes. Now relax. (p) (p)

18 Now, bring your right heel in tight toward your chair and push it down and raise your toes so that your calf and your thigh are extremely tense. Push your heel down, squeeze your toes up, and squeeze your leg in tight. (p) Now relax. (p) (p)

19 Now, let's do both legs together. Squeeze your heels in tight toward your chair, push down on your heels, and raise your toes as high and as tight as you can. Hold it. (p) Now relax. (p) (p)

20 Now, take three deep breaths. (p) Now, tense all the muscles as they are named, exactly as you have practiced: left fist and biceps, right fist and biceps, forehead, eyes, jaw, neck, lips, shoulders, stomach, left leg, right leg. Hold it. (p) Now relax. (p) (p) Breathe in deeply three times and then repeat the total tensing and then the total relaxing, and while you are breathing in deeply and then tensing and then relaxing, notice how relaxed all of your muscles feel. Now tense (p) and relax (p). Now, breathe normally and enjoy the completely tension-free state of your body and muscles. (p) (p) (p) (p) (p) (p) Now turn the tape off.

---

*Each "(p)" represents a pause of five seconds. (The numerals should not be read out loud.)

**Individuals who wear contact lenses might want to remove them before doing this exercise.

program. You should *not* attempt to apply relaxation procedures in the actual fear-producing settings until you have completed the training. Even then, it would be best to wait until your self-desensitization program is progressing smoothly before making any unnecessary contacts with the actual fear-producing stimuli.

IMPLEMENTING THE SELF-DESENSITIZATION PROGRAM

Now that you have constructed your fear hierarchy and are able to relax completely within minutes, you are ready to start your program. This is done according to the following steps:

1. Find a quiet, private place that is free from distractions (preferably, the same place in which your relaxation practice sessions were conducted).
2. Place your stack of cards containing the fear items within easy reach. The cards should be in order, with the least fear-producing card on top and the most fear-producing card on the bottom.
3. Take several minutes and relax completely, as you have been practicing prior to this session.
4. When you are in a state of complete relaxation, take the card on top of the deck and look at the brief phrase that characterizes the situation that would normally cause some slight anxiety. Now turn the card over and look at the prompts that are to help you to visualize the first situation clearly and vividly. After looking at the prompts, close your eyes and try to imagine that you are actually in that situation, as prompted by your card. After about 10 seconds, place the card in a separate pile and relax totally. Relax for about 30 seconds, and during this time completely forget about the scene that you have just imagined. Think only of your muscles and how completely relaxed you feel while breathing deeply.

5. Now pick up the same card again, and then close your eyes and imagine that situation for at least 10 seconds. Put the card down in a separate place, and relax completely for another 30 seconds. During this time do not think of the scene that you were just imagining while in a relaxed state. After the 30 seconds are up, consider the amount of anxiety you felt while imagining this scene the second time. If you were able to imagine the scene with approximately five or fewer suds, then you are ready to proceed to card 2. If you felt more than five suds of anxiety, you should repeat the above routine once or twice more. If you felt less than five suds of anxiety, then relax for two minutes and repeat the procedure with the second card.

6. If you have great difficulty in imagining a scene, or in relaxing while imagining it, or if you feel more than 10 suds of anxiety, immediately stop imagining and induce deep muscle relaxation for a minute or two. Then repeat the item for only three to five seconds rather than a full 10 seconds.

7. If step 6 doesn't work, go back to the previous item and imagine that item for 20 seconds on two successive presentations of the item. Then, again try the item that caused the difficulty.

8. If you still have problems with a particular item, try to construct three new items with smaller steps between them to correct the difficulty encountered with that item. Proceed through the new items exactly as described.

9. In general, you should be able to proceed through one to four items per session. However, it is all right to go as slow as one item per session, if necessary. On the other hand, if you do not feel anxiety, you should not hesitate to go through as many as four items per session, or perhaps more.

10. Each session should begin with an item that was completed successfully in the previous session.

11. Sessions should not last more than about 20 minutes. Sessions might be conducted as frequently as twice per day and no less frequently than twice per week.

12. If you experience difficulties that do not yield to the corrective procedures in steps 6–8, cease self-desensitization attempts and seek professional clinical help.

It is important to keep track of your progress. Thus, at the end of each session, you should record on a separate sheet of paper the name and number of the particular items you imagined successfully, the number of exposures to each item successfully imagined, the suds ratings of the items completed in that session, and the date of the session. We also recommend that you graph your data in a way that is meaningful to you. To understand your progress better, you should also indicate the suds rating of the item when you first prepared your anxiety hierarchy and the final suds rating, which, ideally, will be less than five. In addition, if in real life you experience the actual situation represented by a successfully completed item, assess your suds rating in the real situation and compare it with your rating when imagining the situation. This will give you some indication of the success of your generalization to the natural environment. Table 24–3 shows the progress record and self-desensitization data taken by the client who prepared the fear-of-flying hierarchy shown in Table 24–1.

Table 24-3 Data Recorded by the Client Whose Fear-of-Flying Hierarchy Is Shown in Table 24-1.*

SESSION (AND DATE)	TASK	ORIGINAL SUDS RANKING[a]	IMMEDIATELY AFTER DESENSITIZATION	Contact 1 (Outbound flight: Aug. 26)	Contact 2 (Return flight: Sept. 6)
			SUDS RANKINGS OF ITEMS		
				WHEN ENCOUNTERED IN THE NATURAL ENVIRONMENT	
1 (Aug. 11)	Prepare hierarchy and do suds ranking on all items				
2 (Aug. 13)	Prepare cards				
3 (Aug. 14)					
4 (Aug. 15)	Learn deep muscle relaxation				
5 (Aug. 16)					
6 (Aug. 17)					
7 (Aug. 18)	Items: 1	0	0	0	0
	2	5	0	5[b]	—[c]
	3	6	0	6[b]	—[c]
	4	10	0	0	0
	5	13	0	0	—[c]
8 (Aug. 19)	6	17	0	0	0
	7	23	0	1	0
	8	27	0	0	0
	9	29	0	0	0
	10	30	0	0	0
	11	35	0	1	0
9 (Aug. 20)	12	38	0	0	0
	13	43	0	0	0
	14	46	0	0	0
10 (Aug. 21)	15	50	0	0	0
	16	60	0	0	0
	17	70	0	0	0

Continued

			SUDS RANKINGS OF ITEMS		
				WHEN ENCOUNTERED IN THE NATURAL ENVIRONMENT	
SESSION (AND DATE)	TASK	ORIGINAL SUDS RANKING[a]	IMMEDIATELY AFTER DESENSITIZATION	Contact 1 (Outbound flight: Aug. 26)	Contact 2 (Return flight: Sept. 6)
11 (Aug. 22)	18	75	0	0	0
	19	80	0	—[c]	—[c]
	20	90	0	1	0
12 (Aug. 23)	21	97	3	3	0
	22	99	9	9	10
	23	100	6	(25)5[d]	0

* For descriptions of the items, see the corresponding item numbers in Table 25-1.

[a]The original suds ranking was done during session 1.

[b]These items were encountered in the natural environment prior to desensitization training.

[c]These items were not encountered in the natural environment.

[d]When the plane suddenly moved from the end of the runway after having been stopped, the client was unprepared and a suds ranking of 25 resulted. However, she was able to recover her composure during the actual situation and reduce her anxiety to a suds ranking of 5.

WHEN TO SEEK PROFESSIONAL ASSISTANCE

Watson and Tharp (1972, p. 189) suggested that you should seek professional assistance if any of the following conditions are present:

1. Uncomfortable anxiety during the creation of the hierarchy.
2. Overlapping hierarchies, indicated by contradictory or paradoxical suds ratings of the items.
3. Inability to produce vivid imagery.
4. Inability to control the beginning or ending of an image.
5. Inability to desensitize high enough up on the hierarchy to meet your goals.

Wenrich, General, and Dawley (1976) also outlined several potential problems in systematic self-desensitization. Nevertheless, as indicated by Wenrich and others, there is evidence in support of the general recommendations of this chapter. It appears that individuals can often learn to overcome their own fears by following the specific procedures of self-desensitization.

STUDY QUESTIONS

1. Briefly explain the difference between systematic desensitization and systematic self-desensitization.

2. List the three main phases of a systematic self-desensitization project. Describe each in a paragraph or less.
3. What is a fear hierarchy (in two or three sentences)?
4. What is a suds rating? How are suds ratings used?
5. At the beginning of the section entitled "Learning Deep Muscle Relaxation," there are several suggestions that amount to using situational inducement. Briefly describe three such suggestions.
6. When carrying out a self-desensitization program, what should an individual do if the anxiety felt while imagining a particular scene is greater than 10 suds?
7. How fast should one go through the hierarchy in a self-desensitization program?
8. What are the conditions under which self-desensitization should be discontinued and professional advice sought?

SELF-MODIFICATION EXERCISE

Choose a particular undesirable fear or phobia that you have and attempt a self-desensitization program by following the procedures described in this chapter. Prepare a written report of your procedures and results.

EXTENDED DISCUSSION AND NOTES

1. Three other effective approaches to the treatment of phobias are reinforced practice, participant modeling, and flooding. As explained later (Chapter 26), all effective treatments involve either indirect or in vivo exposure to the feared stimulus. With *reinforced practice*, a phobic patient is praised by the therapist for showing progress in approaching the phobic stimulus through practice. This strategy almost always involves a shaping component as well. *Participant modeling* requires the client to be exposed to and actually practice gradually approaching phobic situations. However, social reinforcement is not emphasized. Instead, the critical variable is thought to be a therapist model who shows graded approaches to the phobic stimulus in the presence of the client. In *flooding*, the therapist tries to get the patient in the presence of the feared stimulus very early during therapy and to maintain exposure for long periods of time, such as an hour or more per session. The rational is that the conditioned fear response will extinguish (see Chapter 15). Although the feared stimulus may be presented in imagination, it is more usually presented in vivo. Leitenberg (1976) concluded that reinforced practice, participant modeling, and flooding have all been demonstrated to be more effective behavioral treatments of phobias than systematic desensitization. However, only systematic desensitization has been appropriately modified so as to be applicable in a self-management program.

2. This rating scale was first recommended by Wolpe and Lazarus (1966). They assumed that attaching numerical values to subjective evaluations of one's discomfort may help an individual to more consistently identify items in a hierarchy that are approximately the same distance apart in terms of the amount of anxiety they produce. However, one's skill at developing a suds rating will probably depend

upon the extent to which she has learned to label those private behaviors accurately. Although Skinner (1957) has provided a plausible theoretical account of how we learn to label private behaviors, research in this area is sadly lacking.

3. Although others have also recommended that the distance between items be approximately 5 to 10 suds (such as Wenrich and others, 1976, p. 28), this figure seems to be based on informal clinical observations rather than on rigorous empirical data.

4. Ever since Jacobson (1938) first described his relaxation method, a number of individuals have described different variations on the method. Cautela and Groden (1978), Davis, Eschelman, and McKay (1980), and Smith (1990) published comprehensive relaxation manuals. According to these authors, therapists, parents, and teachers, without prior training, can follow the illustrations and simple verbal descriptions of the procedures so that they can learn relaxation themselves and teach it to others.

5. On the basis of clinical observations, Goldfried and Davison (1976) suggested that having clients practice relaxation exercises at home without accompanying tapes as guides seldom does little good and may often be harmful.

STUDY QUESTIONS ON NOTES

1. Briefly describe three effective approaches for treating phobias, all of which involve therapist contact.
2. Why did Wolpe and Lazarus recommend using the suds scale?
3. How firm is the evidence that the starting distance between self-desensitization items should be 5 to 10 suds?
4. Who first described a procedure of deep muscle relaxation?

CHAPTER 25

Cognitive Behavior Modification

Although behavior modifiers have often tended to reject other psychological approaches (such as Freudian psychoanalysis), some blending has taken place between behavior modification and certain types of treatment collectively called *cognitive therapy*. The word **cognition** means "belief," "thought," "perception." Accordingly, cognitive therapists regard their approach to be primarily that of helping a client overcome his or her difficulties by getting rid of unproductive, debilitating thoughts or beliefs and adopting more constructive ones. Many behavior modifiers have noted certain similarities between the goals and procedures of cognitive therapists and their own. Cognitive therapists, in turn, have adopted some behavior modification methods. Out of this mutual appreciation has grown an area that has come to be known as *cognitive behavior modification* (see Meichenbaum, 1986). The purpose of this chapter is to describe briefly some of the procedures that are often considered to fall within this area. But first, let's take a look at "thinking" from a behavioral point of view.

"THINKING," "BELIEVING," AND PRIVATE BEHAVIOR

As we indicated in Chapter 15, there appear to be two important categories of behaviors. Operant behaviors, sometimes referred to as "voluntary" behaviors in everyday life, are controlled by the principles of operant conditioning. Reflexive or respondent behaviors, sometimes referred to as "involuntary" behaviors in everyday life, are influenced by the principles and procedures of respondent conditioning. Much of what we call "thinking" in everyday life can be described in terms of these two fundamental behavioral categories.

Try the following exercise. Close your eyes and imagine that you're sitting on a lawn chair in your backyard on a warm summer day. You look up and see the clear blue sky. Imagine a few white fluffy clouds drifting slowly along. Chances are that you will be able to form a clear image of the blue sky and the white fluffy clouds—so clear that you can almost see the colors. Thus, one type of thinking appears to consist of imagining in response to words— imagining so vividly that it can sometimes seem almost like the real thing. This probably comes about through Pavlovian conditioning. If you actually look at a clear blue sky, the color elicits activity in the visual system much as food elicited salivation in Pavlov's dogs. As you grew up, you experienced many trials in which the words "blue sky" were paired with actually looking at and seeing a blue sky. As a consequence, when you close your eyes and imagine that you are looking at a blue sky (with white fluffy clouds), the words likely elicit activity in your visual system so that you experience the behavior of "seeing" the actual scene. This has been referred to as "conditioned seeing" (Skinner, 1953). In a broader sense, we might think of "conditioned sensing." That is, just as we acquire, through experience, conditioned seeing, we also acquire conditioned hearing, conditioned smelling, and conditioned feeling. Consider the example described by Martin and Osborne (1989) in which an individual experienced numerous passionate sexual encounters with a partner who consistently used a very distinctive perfume. Then one day someone walked passed that individual in a department store wearing that same perfume. The individual immediately imagined seeing the partner (conditioned seeing), felt "tingly" all over (conditioned feeling), and even imagined that he heard the partner's voice (conditioned hearing). This sort of thing is also a part of what goes on during fantasy. To experience a fantasy or to read or listen to a story is, in some sense, to be there. It's as though you can see what the people in the story see, feel what they feel, and hear what they hear. We're able to do this because of many instances of conditioned sensing. Our long histories of associating words with actual sights, sounds, smells, and feelings enable us to experience the scenes which an author's words describe. The inside actions that occur when we're thinking are real—we're really seeing, or feeling, or hearing, when we respond to the words (Malott & Whaley, 1983).

Imaging (conditioned seeing) and other types of conditioned sensing constitute one type of thinking. Another type of thinking is simply self-directed verbal behavior, or self-talk. As we indicated in earlier chapters, our verbal behavior is taught to us by others through operant conditioning. We learn to speak because of effective consequences for doing so. As children, we learn to ask for such things as our favorite foods and the opportunity to watch our favorite cartoons, and we learn to say things that please Mom and Dad, aunts and uncles, and others. Much of our thinking is verbal behavior.

Thinking out loud is something that we learn to do as children because it helps us to perform tasks more efficiently (Roberts, 1979). When children first start attending school, they often say rules out loud to themselves to adjust to difficult tasks (Roberts & Tharp, 1980). When they are about five or six years old, however, they also begin to engage in subvocal speech in the sense that their self-talk begins to occur below the spoken level (Vygotski, 1978). We learn to talk silently to ourselves at a very early age largely because we encounter punishers when we think out loud (Skinner, 1957).

For example, teachers in school require children to think to themselves because thinking out loud disturbs the other students. As another example, naturally distressed reactions from others teach us to keep certain thoughts to ourselves. When you go to a party, upon being introduced to the hostess, you might say, "Boy, is that an ugly dress!" But you probably won't say it out loud; instead you will just "say it to yourself" or "think" it. Because much of our thinking goes on at a level that is not observable by others, we refer to it as *covert*, or *private*. It may include private respondent behavior (conditioned sensing), private operant behavior (self-talk), or both. Although private behavior is more difficult to "get at," we assume that in other respects it is the same as public behavior; that is, the principles and procedures applicable to private behavior are fundamentally the same as those that apply to public behavior. In short, we assume that they are the principles and procedures of operant and respondent conditioning.

Often, an instance of what we would refer to as thinking includes both respondent and operant components. To illustrate, consider the following example (described by Martin & Osborne, 1989). One of the authors grew up on a farm just outside of a small town. He attended school in the town and it was very important to him to be accepted by the town children. One of the town kids, Wilf, frequently teased him about being a "farmer." "Hey, gang," Wilf would say, "Here comes Garry the farmer. Hey, Garry, do you still have cow dung on your boots?" Now imagine that it's Saturday afternoon and Garry and his family are getting ready to go to town. Garry will be going to the Saturday afternoon matinee at the Roxy Theatre with the rest of the gang (a big deal since they didn't yet have TV on the farm). Garry says to himself, "I wonder if Wilf will be there?" (operant thinking). Garry can picture Wilf clearly (conditioned seeing) and can imagine Wilf teasing him about being a farmer (both operant thinking and conditioned hearing). Thoughts of the aversive experience elicit unpleasant feelings (a reflexively learned response). Garry reacts by paying special attention to his appearance in the hope that appearing citified will give Wilf nothing to say.

You can see that, contrary to the impression given in many introductory psychology courses, behavior modifiers do not ignore what goes on inside the person. While it is true that the great majority of studies in behavior modification have been concerned with observable behavior, more and more behavior modifiers have taken an interest in dealing with private behavior. In doing so, they have also tended to avoid certain everyday words, such as "thinking" and "believing," that are used quite freely by other social scientists. Although such words serve well in everyday conservation, there are usually more precise ways of talking about behavior and behavioral procedures. (For a discussion of situations in which everyday language is more suitable than behavioral language, and vice versa, see Pear, 1983.) As we have just illustrated, the word "thinking" might refer to public behavior, private behavior, operant behavior, respondent behavior, or some mixture of these. It is more precise to refer to the actual behavior of interest (whether it is private or public, respondent or operant). Moreover, to use special words such as "thinking" and "believing" to refer to private behavior implies that the principles and procedures applicable to private behavior are fundamentally different from those that apply to public behavior.

However, as indicated above, we believe that the principles and procedures of operant and respondent conditioning apply to private behavior as well as to public behavior. Although this assumption is currently unproved, it does appear to be scientifically and practically useful. In Chapter 23 we described how one of the authors, in a self-control jogging program, increased his antifatigue thoughts by following them with thoughts of a highly reinforcing activity. Although the effect was probably not as strong as it would have been had his jogging been immediately reinforced with the actual experiences that he merely imagined, no new principles had to be introduced to account for the effect. In Chapter 24, we described how a client self-desensitized her fear of flying by imagining the fear-producing situations while in a relaxed state. Presumably, the private "seeing behavior" (imagining) was so similar to actually seeing the fear-producing situations that the relaxation response generalized to those situations.

In each of these cases, as well as in a number of other examples presented in this book, private behavior was modified to bring about desired changes in public behavior. In no case, however, was it necessary to assume

Note 1   that private behavior is fundamentally different from public behavior.[1] In no case was it necessary to use vague terms such as "believing" and "thinking" to distinguish private behavior from public behavior. On the contrary, the treatments used were based on the assumption that the same general principles and procedures are applicable to both public and private behavior.

From this point of view of public and private behavior, we will describe some details of an actual case. We will then discuss some methods that others have called "cognitive" procedures.

CAROL'S CASE*

"I'm a failure. I feel ugly and useless. I keep thinking about not being able to keep a man, not being able to have a husband. I get really down and I

*This case is based on a report by Martin (1982), and is paraphrased from Martin and Osborne, 1989.

don't want to do anything. And then I start crying," Carol explained to Dr. Martin. "Sometimes at work, when I'm thinking of how Fred left me, I go to the bathroom and cry. Sometimes I can't stop crying for a whole hour."

Carol and Fred had been engaged for three years. Three months before she began her sessions with Dr. Martin, Fred had left Carol for another woman. Since then, Carol had suffered obsessive thoughts about Fred and about herself. These occurred on a daily basis and Carol was in danger of losing her job.

At the end of her first session with Dr. Martin, Carol agreed that each time she thought about Fred for more than a couple of minutes, she would record her thoughts on an index card. Carol also agreed to collect some specific photographs and to bring them to the next session. One week later, Carol and Dr. Martin carefully examined the observations that she had collected on the index cards. They agreed on a rating scale to evaluate each of her days with respect to her thoughts about her former boyfriend. A score of 5 was considered a very bad day and a score of 0 was considered a very good day. If Carol reported feeling very unhappy, she couldn't stop thinking of Fred for a long period of time, and she cried for a total of one hour or more, then she assigned that day a score of 5. If, on the other hand, she experienced only fleeting thoughts of Fred during the day, and such thoughts were not particularly disturbing, then the day was assigned a score of 0. Specific guidelines were also agreed upon for scores of 1,2,3, and 4. These latter scores were assigned as the unhappy thoughts and duration of crying during the day increased from the guidelines for scoring 0 to the guidelines for scoring 5. Her ratings for that first week of assessment averaged 4.2—a very unhappy week for Carol.

Carol agreed to implement the following procedure. Each time she experienced a thought characteristic of those that caused her to cry, she would stop what she was doing, clasp her hands, close her eyes, and silently yell "Stop!" to herself. Then she would open her eyes and take five photographs from her purse. The photographs were arranged in a particular order and encircled by a rubber band. With Dr. Martin's guidance, she had written specific statements on the back of each of them. With the photographs facing down, she looked at the back of the first one and read, "I'm my own boss. My life is ahead of me. I can do what I want to do." She turned the photo over and looked at her picture taken at the airport the previous year, before departure on a trip alone on which she had had a great time. For the next 5 to 10 seconds, she thought about how much she would like to travel again, and about the fun that she had had on her previous trip. Carol continued in this way with the four remaining photographs, which were prepared similarly to that described above. Following this entire procedure, which required approximately one to two minutes to complete, Carol recorded the problem thoughts on her index card and returned to her previous activities. She was also instructed to vary the positive thoughts when viewing the photographs at different times.

The results of the program are shown in Figure 25–1. At the begin-

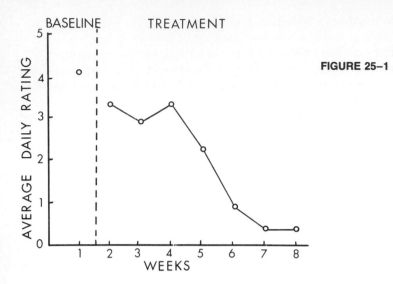

FIGURE 25–1 Average daily rating of the occurrence of obsessive thoughts by Carol. Each data point represents the average of the daily ratings assigned to obsessive thoughts by Carol, averaged across seven days of the week. A high rating indicates that obsessive thoughts were highly prevalent during the day. A low rating indicates the absence of obsessive thoughts. Reprinted with permission from Martin (1982).

ning of treatment, Carol still had some unhappy days, but her decreasing scores showed that she was improving. After eight weeks, Carol decided that she no longer needed help.

This case is similar in several respects to many of the reports in the cognitive behavior modification literature. The treatment procedures emphasized thought-stopping (described in more detail later in this chapter) and stimulus control. Thought-stopping was conceptualized as a stimulus change designed to terminate immediately the undesirable behaviors in whatever setting they occurred. In that same setting, the photographs and instructions controlled both respondent images and operant self-talk. The photographs elicited a variety of images that were considered incompatible with the unhappy thoughts. The instructions prompted coping self-statements to compete with the undesirable self-talk about Fred, her former boyfriend. Note that no attempt was made to program reinforcing consequences following the desirable private thoughts. The immediate consequences of "thinking" desirable alternative thoughts was a self-recording response on an index card. Independent of whether or not the self-recording functioned as a conditioned reinforcer, it was assumed that the content of the desirable thoughts would be reinforcing in and of themselves. Moreover, it was assumed that as Carol continued behaving in her natural environment, she would encounter a variety of natural reinforcers following the desirable alternative private behaviors. Thus, as with many cognitive behavior modification procedures, the thrust of the therapeutic manipulations emphasized stimulus control. Another way in which this case is characteristic of many cognitive behavior modification studies is that it relied on self-recording of private behaviors to demonstrate effectiveness.

SOME COGNITIVE PROCEDURES

A major theoretical assumption of cognitive therapy is that individuals interpret and react to events in terms of their perceived significance, that is, that human behavior is mediated by cognition. A second theoretical assumption is that cognitive deficiencies can cause emotional disorders. It follows from these assumptions that the primary focus of therapy is a fundamental change in a client's cognitions. Thus, cognitive therapists and cognitive behavior modifiers speak of achieving desirable changes in a client's behavior (including emotional behavior) by altering thought patterns, beliefs, attitudes, and opinions. Their methods, however, deal mainly with the client's private verbal behavior and images relating to himself and the world around him. Much of the evidence supporting the effectiveness of these techniques comes from case studies like Carol's rather than from well-controlled experiments.

ELLIS'S RATIONAL-EMOTIVE THERAPY

Cognitive behavior modification has received strong impetus from the well-known cognitive therapist Albert Ellis (see, for example, Ellis, 1984; Ellis & Bernard, 1985). A psychotherapist trained originally in Freudian psychoanalytic methods, Ellis became very disillusioned with those methods. He found that, although his clients perhaps gained some insight into their problems by remembering and talking about their childhood experiences, this insight was of little value in solving their problems. Ellis became convinced that the solutions were to be found in the situations in which the problems are encountered, not in the client's distant past. In shifting the focus of treatment to the client's present environment, Ellis developed what he called rational-emotive therapy.

As its name suggests, ***rational-emotive therapy*** is based on the premise that there is a very close connection between what we say to ourselves and how we feel. According to Ellis, most everyday emotional problems (and related behaviors) stem from irrational statements that people make to themselves when events in their lives are not the way they would like them to be. People tend to "catastrophize": they tell themselves that things are so horrible they can't possibly "stand it." Basically, Ellis's approach is to teach his clients to counteract such "irrational" self-statements with more positive and realistic statements. To do this, Ellis directly challenges irrational ideas of a client, and models rational reinterpretations of disturbing events. For example, a client might be taught to tell himself that, although his situation may be annoying or inconvenient, it is not catastrophic, and, moreover, there are usually things that he can do to improve it. (For example, see Figure 25–2.)

Ellis (1984) has emphasized that, despite being considered a cognitive therapist, he also uses a wide variety of behavioral methods when working with clients. For example, an important component of rational-emotive ther-

FIGURE 25–2 An exaggerated example of rational-emotive therapy.

apy involves in vivo "homework" assignments in which clients learn how to overcome their behavioral deficits as well as verbally counteract their negative self-statements. Bandura (1977, p. 190) has suggested that the corrective homework assignments may be more important than attempts to change the client's self-verbalizations, since there is little evidence that the latter approach produces large or consistent improvements in the behavior. Nevertheless, on the basis of his clinical experience, Ellis reports that rational-emotive therapy has been used successfully with a wide variety of problems, such as depression due to a broken love affair (the client may be telling himself that he simply cannot live without the love of a particular person); extreme fears, such as speech anxiety (the client may be telling herself that it would be absolutely horrible if some members of the audience thought poorly of her speaking skills); impotence (the client may be "sabotaging" his sexual arousal and enjoyment by telling himself that he must perform well to prove that he is a "true" man); homosexuality (the client may be telling himself that it is better to make love with another man than to risk the "terrible fate" of being rejected by a woman); and lack of self-confidence and subsequent failures (the client may be telling herself that she will inevitably fail at whatever she attempts, and that such failure will only prove once again what a rotten person she is). An interesting question that has yet to be tested scientifically is the extent to which people really do tell themselves such things. Although rational-emotive therapy was originally developed to help clients overcome their emotional disturbances, it has also developed into a personality theory that attempts to show people how to achieve healthy personal adjustment (Ellis, 1978). For a review of rational-emotive therapy, see Zettle and Hayes (1980). For a practical guide to rational-emotive therapy, see Dryden and DiGiuseppe (1990).

BECK'S COGNITIVE THERAPY

Aaron T. Beck (1976), independently of Ellis, has developed a cognitive therapy procedure that is similar to RET (rational-emotive therapy). Since Beck has specialized primarily in the treatment of depression, his cognitive therapy has been developed mainly for the treatment of that particular problem. However, as the title of his 1976 book (*Cognitive Therapy and the Emotional Disorders*) implies, he has applied his approach to a wide variety of problems, including manic states, anxiety neuroses, hysteria, obsessional disorders, psychosomatic disorders, and phobias (see Beck, Emery, & Greenberg, 1985). In addition, Beck has written a self-help book for couples that shows how they can use cognitive therapy to improve their relationships (Beck, 1988).

According to Beck (1976), neurotic individuals (i.e., people with "emotional disorders") engage excessively in aberrant, fallacious, or dysfunctional thinking, and this is what causes their problems. Among the various types of dysfunctional thinking are the following: (1) *dichotomous thinking*, which is thinking in absolute terms; for example, assuming that one is a failure if one gets any grade less than an "A"; (2) *arbitrary inference*, which is drawing a conclusion on the basis of inadequate evidence; for example, misinterpreting a frown on the face of a passerby to mean that the passerby disapproves of him or her; (3) *overgeneralization*, which is reaching a general conclusion on the basis of too few instances; for example, assuming that a single failure means that one cannot succeed at anything; and (4) *magnification*, which is exaggerating the meaning or significance of a particular event; for example, believing that it is terrible or catastrophic not to obtain something that one wants very badly.

The first step in Beck's procedure is to have the client identify clearly the dysfunctional thoughts and maladaptive assumptions that are causing his or her problem. Once the debilitating thought or assumption has been identified, there are several methods that are used in counteracting it and thus alleviating the problem. A major technique used by Beck is *reality checking* or *hypothesis testing*. After the client has identified the debilitating belief or thought and has learned to distinguish it as a hypothesis rather than as reality, he or she is then in a position to test it experimentally. If, for example, the client believes that everyone he meets turns away from him in disgust, the therapist might help him to devise a system for judging other people's facial expressions and body language so that the client can determine objectively whether the thoughts behind his problem are indeed accurate. In addition, the therapist would provide social reinforcement for carrying out the assessment. Presumably in most cases the client would discover that his thinking was erroneous and, upon correcting it, would solve his problem. In addition he would have learned how to solve or prevent other emotional problems by developing appropriate ways of thinking about the occurrences in his life.

Like Ellis, Beck uses various homework assignments that often contain liberal doses of behavior modification procedures such as those described previously in this text. It is therefore difficult to say how much of the success of his therapy, if any, is due to the cognitive procedures.

Some of the similarities between Beck's approach and RET can be seen from the description just given. Both approaches assume that the client's difficulty is caused by some type of inappropriate thought pattern. Both agree that the problem may stem from the client's tendency to "catastrophize" (to exaggerate unpleasant events); however, Beck does not emphasize this factor nearly as much as Ellis does. This is illustrated in an example that Beck, Rush, Shaw, and Emery (1979, p. 154) cited of a depressed student who expressed the belief that she would not be accepted by any of the colleges to which she had applied, despite the fact that she ranked close to the top in her high school class. Beck and colleagues note that the therapist might have used either of two different RET techniques to dissuade the student from her maladaptive thinking. The therapist might have challenged the student's belief that her worth as a person depended on her entrance into college or the therapist might have challenged the student's assumption that it would be a great catastrophe if she did not enter college. Beck and co-workers maintain, however, that both these approaches would provide, at best, only temporary relief to the student because they would not get at the root of the problem —namely the student's illogical pattern of thinking about herself that led her, in this case, to assume that she was a poor student despite the evidence to the contrary. (In fairness to Ellis, Beck and co-workers pointed out in a note that Ellis has stated that he would not necessarily be bound by the methods they attributed to RET. According to Ellis, "RET does *not* have one special way of questioning and disputing." This is true of Beck's cognitive therapy as well, which makes it extremely difficult for therapists to apply the recommended procedures consistently and for other authors to describe them accurately.)

MEICHENBAUM'S SELF-INSTRUCTIONAL METHODS

Donald Meichenbaum (1977, 1986), one of the leading cognitive behavior modifiers, has strongly emphasized the role of self-instruction (that is, telling oneself what to do in various situations) in bringing about desired behavior changes. Like Ellis, he teaches clients to recognize their negative self-state-ments and to counteract them with more realistic, positive statements (see Meichenbaum, 1986). In addition, he uses the relaxation method (described in Chapter 24) and other behavior modification techniques. In general, his approach centers on teaching the client to instruct himself or herself to engage in appropriate "coping" behavior in situations that cause anxiety or stress. The emphasis is more on coping with the negative emotions than on com-pletely eliminating them. For example, following treatment, one phobic client said, "It [self-instructing] makes me able to be in the situation, not to be comfortable, but to tolerate it. I don't talk myself out of being afraid, just out of appearing afraid. . . . You immediately react to the thing you're afraid of and then start to reason with yourself. I talk myself out of panic" (Meichen-baum, 1986, p. 372).

The client is taught to respond to certain stimuli produced by the stressful situation, and by his own behavior in that situation, as S^Ds for en-gaging in appropriate self-instruction. The coping behavior generally includes counteracting negative self-statements and inducing relaxation in the presence of the stressful situation. Sometimes it also involves reinterpreting one's emotions—that is, saying things to oneself that presumably make the negative emotions less aversive. For example, the client may be instructed to say to himself, "The reason my heart beats fast and my legs feel wobbly when I'm with a woman I like is because I'm sexually aroused, not because I'm terribly afraid"; or "The fact that I'm anxious before giving a speech doesn't mean I'm going to blow it—my anxiety is just a way of preparing me to be alert and do a good job." The client is also instructed to make reinforcing self-statements immediately after he has successfully coped with the stressful sit-uation (for example, "I did it!" and "Wait until I tell my therapist about this!").

To help the client develop coping skills before he deals with stressful situations in the natural environment, the therapist may give him "*stress in-oculations*" (Meichenbaum, 1985). These are stressful stimuli, such as unpre-dictable electric shocks or gruesome films, to which the client is exposed in the therapy setting. During these stressful situations, the client practices ap-propriate coping skills. Another tactic is for the client to recall stressful sit-uations (for example, visits to the dentist) with which he has previously coped and to generalize these coping techniques to the stressful situations with which he is presently unable to cope.

Besides working with adults, Meichenbaum has also used self-instruc-tional techniques in helping hyperactive and withdrawn children to manage their behavior (see Meichenbaum, 1986).

PROBLEM SOLVING

Teaching people how to proceed through logical reasoning to satisfactory solutions to personal problems is another approach that is sometimes consid-ered to fall within the area of cognitive behavior modification. D'Zurilla and

Goldfried (1971) outline the following five general steps in personal problem solving:

1. *General orientation.* The client is encouraged to recognize problems and to realize that it is possible to deal with them by acting systematically rather than impulsively. The client may be taught to recognize problems by being presented with common examples of them and/or by being asked to describe such situations that she has encountered in her own life.

2. *Problem definition.* When asked to specify the problem, most clients reply in very vague terms—for example, "I've been very upset lately." By specifying the history of the problem and the variables that seem to be controlling it, it is generally possible to define the problem more precisely. For example, a close analysis might indicate that what is upsetting the client is that she shares an apartment with a very untidy roommate, and she can't stand the "mess" she feels forced to live in.

3. *Generation of alternatives.* After defining the problem precisely, the client is instructed to "brainstorm" possible solutions—that is, to "let her mind run free" and to think of as many solutions as she can, no matter how farfetched. For example, possible solutions that she might come up with are (a) to move, (b) to self-desensitize to messiness, (c) to speak assertively to her roommate about keeping the place neat, (d) to try to shape neat behavior in her roommate, (e) to negotiate a behavioral contract with her roommate, (f) to throw her roommate's things out the window, and (g) to throw her roommate out the window.

4. *Decision making.* The next step is to examine the alternatives carefully, eliminating those that are obviously unacceptable, such as (f) and (g). She should then try to estimate the likely effectiveness and the likely short-range and long-range consequences of the remaining alternatives. On the basis of these considerations, she should select the alternative that seems most likely to provide the optimum solution, and (with the help of the therapist) devise a plan for carrying it out.

5. *Verification.* When the plan is put into effect, does it solve the problem? That is, is the client satisfied? If not, the problem-solving sequence must be started again and another solution attempted.

Foxx and Faw (1990) described a program for teaching problem-solving skills to psychiatric patients and discussed how generalization of these skills might be enhanced. In addition, D'Zurilla (1986) and Nezu and Nezu (1989) described how the problem-solving approach might be applied to a variety of clinical interventions.

THOUGHT STOPPING

Thought stopping (Wolpe, 1958) is used in cases in which a person engages in persistent, obsessive private verbal behavior that he or she cannot seem to control. (This, you will recall, is one of the procedures used in the case of Carol, described earlier in this chapter.) The procedure involves, first, instructing the client to think the obsessive thought. The therapist then suddenly yells "Stop!" Immediately, according to anecdotal clinical reports, the undesirable private verbal behavior ceases. After a few such trials demonstrate the effectiveness of the procedure, the client himself is instructed to yell "Stop!" while he is engaging in the undesirable private behavior. Again, the behavior ceases. Over trials, the self-instruction "Stop!" is faded to the private level so that eventually the client can "turn off" the undesirable private behavior simply by "yelling" "Stop!" silently to himself.

Masters and others (1987, p. 440) list the following discrete steps as being typically involved in thought stopping:

1. First, the therapist interrupts the client's overt thoughts.
2. Next, the therapist interrupts the client's covert thoughts.
3. Then the client interrupts his or her covert thoughts.
4. Finally, the client covertly interrupts his or her covert thoughts.

Although there have been a number of reports of successful applications of thought-stopping, most of these have involved only a few clients and the use of other procedures that may actually have been responsible for the improvement. Thus, the evidence for the effectiveness of thought-stopping is, at present, weak (Masters and others, 1987).

Although thought stopping has been generally used to manage obsessive private verbal behavior, Cautela and Wisocki (1977, p. 259) claim that it "may also be employed with feelings and images as well as several overtly observable behaviors." They also acknowledge that empirical support for the effectiveness of the procedure is weak.

OTHER "COGNITIVE" TECHNIQUES

It appears that all the principles and procedures discussed in this book can be applied privately (see Cautela & Kearney, 1986), although *it is by no means clear that it is effective to do so.*[2] As expressed by Craighead, Kazdin, and Mahoney (1980, p. 154):

Note 2

> A number of covert techniques have been derived from operant conditioning principles. For example, one technique referred to as *covert reinforcement* requires an individual to imagine engaging in some response he or she wishes to increase, such as speaking up in groups. After the response is imagined, the individual imagines some reinforcing event taking place, such as skiing down a mountain. The procedure is designed to increase the probability that the client will engage in the imagined target behaviors. There are additional covert techniques such as *covert extinction, covert punishment*, and *covert modeling*, which are conducted entirely in imagination. With each technique the imagery of the client is guided by instructions from the therapist.

Although some people consider the above procedures to be cognitive (as opposed to behavioral), Latimer and Sweet (1984, p. 13) pointed out that "the covert conditioning therapies arose within the field of behavior therapy and were based on existing learning (i.e., conditioning) theories." We believe they can be described in terms of private operant and respondent behaviors.

CONCLUDING COMMENTS

Although the behavioral applications we have described briefly in this chapter are usually called "cognitive," and although they are often said to be directed toward modifying thoughts, beliefs, and attitudes, their distinguishing characteristic seems to be that they deal with private verbal behavior and images **Note 3** as well as with public behavior.[3] They do not appear to involve any behavior principles besides those discussed in the previous chapters of this book. All behavior practitioners should be open to innovative procedures for helping people change their behavior. At the same time, there are advantages to **Note 4** examining such procedures from a consistent behavioral viewpoint.[4]

STUDY QUESTIONS

1. Cognitive behavior modification is a blend of what two types of treatment?
2. What does the word "cognition" mean?
3. Describe an example of "respondent thinking."
4. Describe an example of "operant thinking."
5. In what way did Carol's case involve stimulus-control procedures?
6. Why have behavior modifiers tended to avoid certain everyday language words, such as "thinking" and "believing"?
7. Do reputable behavior modifiers deny the existence and importance of private behaviors? Discuss.
8. Describe several examples cited in this chapter and Chapter 23 in which individuals' private behaviors influenced their public behaviors.
9. What basic assumption do the authors of this text make about public and private behavior?
10. What are two major assumptions of cognitive therapy?
11. With what do cognitive therapists and cognitive behavior modifiers mainly deal?
12. What is rational-emotive therapy? Who developed it?
13. According to Ellis, RET has been used successfully to improve what types of problems? Explain briefly.
14. According to Beck, what causes problems for neurotic individuals? Describe some examples.
15. Describe the basic steps in Beck's cognitive therapy.
16. Describe some similarities and a difference between Beck's approach and Ellis's RET.
17. How does Meichenbaum's self-instructional approach differ from Ellis's RET?
18. What are "stress inoculations"?
19. In two or three sentences each, outline the five steps of problem solving described by D'Zurilla and Goldfried.

20. Outline the procedure of thought-stopping
21. Why is covert reinforcement considered a cognitive technique?
22. In half a page or less, outline the authors' view of cognitive techniques, as described in this chapter.
23. Choose a hypothetical problem and describe how you think it might be modified through the use of covert reinforcement.
24. Choose a hypothetical problem and describe how you think it might be modified through the use of covert extinction.
25. Choose a hypothetical problem and describe how you think it might be modified through the use of covert punishment.
26. Choose a hypothetical problem and describe how you think it might be modified through the use of covert modeling.

EXTENDED DISCUSSION AND NOTES

1. Thinking (primarily self-talk and imaging) consitutes one type of private behavior. Another important category of private behavior is our feelings. As we indicated in Chapter 15, our feelings—made up of activity of the autonomic nervous system, such as breathing, heart rate, and glandular secretions—are the respondent component of emotional behavior. As illustrated by the work of Joseph Cautela and his colleagues, thinking and feeling as private behaviors are a proper subject matter for behavior modifiers and can readily be dealt with in terms of operant and respondent conditioning principles (Cautela & Kearney, 1986, 1990).

2. In a number of studies, the results favor procedures that require the performance of the target behavior rather than covert representations of it. For example, research on flooding and systematic desensitization indicates that a greater anxiety reduction is obtained when clients are actually exposed to the anxiety-provoking stimuli as opposed to merely imagining representations of those stimuli (Crowe, Marks, Agress, & Leitenberg, 1972; Emmelkamp & Wessels, 1975; Sherman, 1972; Stern & Marks, 1973). Also, participant modeling in which a subject observes a modeling sequence and then overtly performs the modeled behaviors is more effective in influencing the subsequent performance of those behaviors than if the subject merely observes or imagines a model (see Roper, Rachman, & Marks, 1975; Thase & Moss, 1976).

   On the other hand, Kazdin (1980a) found no difference between covert modeling and role rehearsal for improving on self-report and behavioral measures of assertiveness and self-efficacy. In the covert modeling condition, a subject imagined a person similar to himself or herself in age, and of the same sex, as a model in a treatment scene that called for an appropriate measure of assertiveness. Subjects narrated aloud what was imaged. In the role rehearsal group, the subjects actually acted out the treatment situations with the therapist. Thus, as indicated by this and other studies (Hersen, Kazdin, Bellack, & Turner, 1979; McFall & Twentyman, 1973), overt rehearsal does not always lead to greater behavior change than does covert or symbolic rehearsal.

3. In addition, cognitive behavior modifiers deal largely with what Skinner (1969) calls "rule-governed behavior (Zattle & Hayes, 1982)." As indicated previously, rules are verbal stimuli that describe specific contingencies of reinforcement. Because rules can function as S^Ds, a highly verbal person may not require many exposures to a particular contingency to respond appropriately to it. She may, for example, construct a rule describing the contingency and then respond to the rule rather than directly to the contingency itself. Or she may respond appropriately to someone else's description without herself having had any direct exposure at all to the contingency. Thus, for example, presenting a person with statistics showing that air travel is much safer than traveling by car may help to counteract that person's fear of flying—provided that the person has previously been successful in obtaining reinforcement or avoiding punishment by responding to similar descriptions of empirical data.

4. Some writers have voiced much stronger criticisms of cognitive behavior therapy approaches, implying that such approaches are either incorrect or unnecessary and are essentially a waste of time (see Greenspoon & Lamal, 1978; Ledwidge, 1978, 1979; Rachlin, 1977; Skinner, 1977; Wolpe, 1976, 1989). In an excellent review article covering the years from 1970 to 1983, Latimer and Sweet (1984) examined whether the cognitive components of treatment produce greater treatment gains than those obtained by behavioral procedures of established efficacy. They restricted their review to studies of clinical populations or of populations with clinically significant problems. Also, they did not consider the covert conditioning therapies, which they include as standard behavioral procedures. Of 11 studies reviewed, five compared a behavioral treatment of known effectiveness to the same treatment *plus* the cognitive procedures to be evaluated. None of these studies demonstrated a clinically significant contribution for the cognitive procedures. The remaining seven studies compared various cognitive therapy components to standard behavioral treatments. Four of these studies demonstrated the behavioral methods to be superior, one demonstrated the cognitive method to be superior, and two studies found no difference in the effects of the cognitive and behavioral methods that were compared. The review by Latimer and Sweet suggests that the success of cognitive behavior modification has been largely due to the standard behavioral methods, and that added components considered cognitive do not provide added effectiveness.

STUDY QUESTIONS ON NOTES

1. Why are thinking and feeling proper subject matters for behavior modification?

2. When behavior modifiers speak of private behavior, to what are they referring?

3. Which are more effective, procedures that require overt performance of the target behavior or those that rely on covert rehearsal of the target behavior? Defend your answer.

4. From this chapter, give three examples of how cognitive behavior modifiers rely on the presence of rule-governed behavior in the repertoires of their clients.

5. Does the literature on cognitive procedures indicate that adding cognitive components to behavior modification procedures can increase the effectiveness of those procedures? Justify your answer.

CHAPTER 26

Areas of **Clinical Behavior Therapy**

As indicated in Chapter 2, behavior modification is being used increasingly in the treatment of clinical disorders. In this chapter we give a brief overview of ways in which the principles and techniques described in the preceding chapters are being applied to treat some of the most frequently encountered adult psychological disorders. Our intention here is not to teach you how to actually treat these disorders yourself, nor to provide an exhaustive review of behavioral treatments of these disorders. Rather, our intention is to give you a brief introduction to the major areas in the field of clinical behavior modification and to indicate how some principles and techniques are being applied in these areas.

The disorders to be discussed here are given more detailed coverage in several excellent books (e.g., Barlow, 1985; Seligman, 1990), and the reader interested in more specific information concerning these disorders and their treatment is referred to those texts.

ANXIETY DISORDERS: FOCUS ON AGORAPHOBIA

Probably the most common anxiety disorder is *generalized anxiety disorder*—extreme anxiety or panic attacks for which no consistent antecedent stimulus can be readily identified. In addition, all phobias, such as discussed in Chapters 15 and 24, are considered anxiety disorders. One of the most debilitating anxiety disorders is *agoraphobia*, which is a fear of going out in public. Agoraphobia is a convenient type of anxiety disorder for us to focus on because it contains many features that are present in other types of anxiety disorders.

Agoraphobics are characterized by an intense fear of being in public places from which escape might be difficult or help unavailable if the person is suddenly incapacitated. The individual therefore avoids leaving the home for any purpose, at least if not accompanied by someone whom he or she trusts. This leads to increasing constriction of the individual's normal activities, thus preventing the individual from performing daily functions that most of us consider routine and necessary—going to a job, grocery shopping, and so forth.

TREATMENT

Note 1

Exposure Methods.   As with all phobias, the major component of treatment is exposure to the feared stimuli. Two types of exposure may be used: (1) indirect exposure, involving imaginal (as in systematic desensitization) or symbolic (e.g., films of fear-eliciting stimuli) procedures; and (2) direct or in vivo exposure.[1] Direct exposure may be either sudden, or graduated. The data indicate that direct exposure produces larger effects immediately after treatment (see Barlow, Leitenberg, Agras, & Wincze, 1969; Emmelkamp & Wessels, 1975; Mavissakalian & Barlow, 1981), but that by three to six weeks after the termination of therapy, therapeutic gains from indirect exposure tend to have "caught up" to those from direct exposure (Mathews, Johnston, Lancashire, Munby, Shaw, & Gelder, 1976; Mathews, Teasdale, Munby, Johnston, & Shaw, 1977; Munby & Johnston, 1980). This appears to be due to the fact that clients who have gone through indirect exposure eventually begin to engage in direct exposure on their own.

Interpersonal Factors.   Treating clients in small groups often appears to be beneficial, since the group members give each other support (Hand, Lamontagne, & Marks, 1974). Similarly, involving a friend or spouse in the treatment can be very beneficial (Munby & Johnston, 1980).

Homework.   Practice between sessions appears to be a critical therapeutic ingredient. Involvement of the client's spouse can be especially useful with regard to helping the client with these homework assignments.

Drugs.   There is evidence that the use of antidepressants such as tricyclics and monoamine oxidase, which inhibit panic reactions, can enhance the initial effect of exposure-based treatments.

OBSESSIVE-COMPULSIVE DISORDERS

An *obsessive-compulsive* disorder is one in which the client is bothered either by repetitive thoughts, images, or impulses, or by repetitive overt actions. Often the repetive overt actions appear to be reinforced by reduction in the anxiety that appears to be concomitant with (or perhaps engendered by) the repetitive thoughts, images, or impulses. The repetitive private behavior—that is, the thoughts, images, or impulses—is often referred to as "obsessive," while the repetitive public behavior is often referred to as "compulsive." However, the distinction between obsessive and compulsive is probably somewhat arbitrary.

TREATMENT

Aversion Procedures.   A number of aversion procedures have been tried on obsessive-compulsive disorders, including punishment (Kenny, Mowbray, & Lalani, 1978; Kenny, Solyom, & Solyom, 1973); McGuire & Vallance, 1964), thought stopping (Emmelkamp & Kwee, 1977; Stern, 1978; Stern, Lipsedge, & Marks, 1975), covert sensitization (Wisocki, 1970), and aversion relief (Solyom & Kingstone, 1973; Marks, Crowe, Drewe, Young, & Dewhurst, 1969). Although there has been some limited success with these techniques, they have not proved to be impressively effective.

Anxiety Reduction.   As mentioned above, obsessive-compulsive disorders often appear to be maintained by the anxiety reduction that occurs when the obsessive-compulsive behavior is engaged in. This suggests that the disorder can be corrected by eliminating the anxiety on which it is based. The main procedure for doing this has been systematic desensitization, and it seems to have produced benefits in 30 to 40 percent of the clients on whom it has been tried (Beech & Vaughn, 1978; Cooper, Gelder, & Marks, 1965). Flooding in imagination and implosion have also been used with obsessive-compulsive clients, but also with limited success (McCarthy, 1972; Emmelkamp & Kwee, 1977; Steketee, Foa, & Grayson, 1982).

Exposure and Response Prevention.   A procedure that appears to be especially effective is exposure to the feared situation while preventing the compulsive behavior from occurring. For example, clients with washing rituals are requested to touch their particular "contaminated" objects while refraining from ritualizing, regardless of the strength of their urge to do so. Typically, as with systematic desensitization, a hierarchy of least-feared to most-feared stimuli is used. Lasting improvement appears to be obtained in 65 to 75 percent of individuals given this treatment (Rachman & Hodgson, 1980). During treatment, there appears to be little difference between the effects of direct and indirect exposure; however, direct exposure appears to be more effective in maintaining gains (Foa, Steketee, Turner, & Fisher, 1980).

Cognitive Behavior Modification.   Little research has been done on the effects of adding a cognitive component to exposure. However, one study compared graduated exposure in vivo with exposure preceded by self-instructional training and found no difference between conditions (Emmelkamp, van der Helm, van Zanten, & Plochy, 1980).

Drugs. There is evidence that clomipramine and behavioral treatment combined is more effective than either of these alone (Marks, Stern, Mawson, Cobb, & McDonald, 1980).

FAILURE TO COPE WITH STRESS

All of us experience many stressful events throughout the course of a day, a week, or a month. For example, having to take an exam, interviewing for a job, or simply driving to work are at least somewhat stressful for most of us. Some circumstances are more stressful than others; for example, being involved in military combat or a natural catastrophe such as an earthquake are clearly very stressful experiences. Most people cope with ordinary, and even large amounts of stress, in an effective manner; however, some individuals are quite debilitated by stress, either because the stressful events in their lives are too intense or numerous, or because they are unable to cope with more ordinary types of stressful events. It appears that such individuals can benefit from behavioral treatments for managing stress; and, indeed, even individuals who cope adequately with stressful events can probably benefit from training in stress management.

TREATMENT

Rosenthal and Rosenthal (1985) have developed a comprehensive approach to treating stress that incorporates many principles and procedures of behavior modification. For example, they teach their clients to relax when encountering stressful situations. The relaxation methods they teach include yoga and transcendental meditation, as well as Jacobson's (1938) progressive muscle relaxation described in Chapter 24. They also encourage their clients to establish a daily physical exercise regimen, since they feel that a healthy, well-developed body enables one to resist more effectively the physical effects of stressful situations. They provide assertion training to their clients to help them manage maladaptive anger. In addition, they use cognitive behavior modification to alter verbalizations of the client that often produce or exacerbate stressful situations.

DEPRESSION

Everyone has probably experienced depression at some point in his or her life. Typically, it occurs as a result of the loss of an important source of reinforcement in one's life; for example, a job, a love affair, or a loved one. The depression usually lifts after a while, as other sources of reinforcement become available. However, some individuals remain depressed most of the time, often for no apparent external reason. Because this causes suffering and can be quite debilitating, such individuals require treatment.

TREATMENT

Aaron T. Beck is one of the leading specialists in the treatment of depression. We have already discussed the cognitive therapy that he and his colleagues developed (see Chapter 25). Beck uses a number of cognitive and behavioral techniques in treating depression.

Evoking and Testing Automatic Thoughts. The therapist and client jointly try to determine the thoughts that precede such emotions as anger, sadness, and anxiety by attempting to elicit these emotions, or having the client recall or imagine situations that elicited these emotions. The client is then encouraged to operationally define and test the validity of the automatic thoughts through a process called *reality checking or hypothesis testing.* For example, a client who has the automatic thought "I'm a failure in math" may define failure as "being unable to obtain a grade of 'C' after studying as long and hard as the average student." Thus, if the client does the indicated amount of study and receives a "C" or better, the automatic thought is proved wrong.

Identifying and Testing Maladaptive Assumptions. A maladaptive assumption is more general than automatic thoughts, and is usually not verbalized. Some examples are "In order to be happy, I must have a wife," and "I'm nobody if I don't have a job." Maladaptive assumptions are tested by having the client examine their logic, by having the client gather evidence against the assumption, or in various other ways.

Scheduling of Activities. The client is provided with homework assignments to increase his or her mastery of various activities. If necessary, the therapist subdivides the activity into graduated segments that the client can master readily.

Cognitive Rehearsal. The client pictures or imagines each step involved in the completion of a particular task.

Self-reliance Training. Depressed individuals frequently neglect even such routine tasks as showering or bathing, bedmaking, house cleaning, cooking, and shopping. In such cases, homework assignments are directed toward reestablishing these behaviors.

Role Playing and Role Reversal. By acting out the role of themselves (role playing) in various situations, clients learn appropriate overt behavior, automatic thoughts, and emotional behavior in those situations. By acting out the role of others responding to them (role reversal), clients can test out automatic thoughts they have concerning how others see them, which can cause clients to make less severe judgments about themselves. For example, a client who felt that store clerks thought she was inept changed this negative view of herself when she played the role of a salesclerk waiting on her.

Diversion Techniques. Clients are taught to engage in various behaviors, such as physical, social, play, and work activities, that compete with negative self-thoughts.

ALCOHOLISM

Alcoholism is a common problem in our society. Not only does the alcoholic injure his or her health, but under the influence of alcohol, a person may engage in behaviors that are upsetting or dangerous to others. Treatment is difficult because of the addictive nature of alcohol and because the client often does not remember the disturbing behaviors that he or she engaged in as a result of being intoxicated.

TREATMENT

Aversive Conditioning. As mentioned in Chapter 15, aversive conditioning is based on respondent conditioning. Aversive conditioning for alcoholism involves pairing the sight, smell, or taste of alcohol with electrical or chemical aversive stimuli. It has produced some limited success, but no longer constitutes the main component of most behavior modification treatment programs for alcoholism.

Stimulus Exposure and Extinction. This approach attempts to eliminate the client's urges or cravings to consume alcohol. The client is exposed repeatedly to stimuli associated with alcohol, while simultaneously alcohol consumption is prevented or limited. Case studies have indicated some promise for this approach (e.g., Blakey & Baker, 1980).

Contingency Management. This approach involves making positive reinforcement or the avoidance of aversive events contingent on abstinence. These contingencies are administered by agents in the client's environment. For example, the client's spouse (Miller, 1972) or the legal system (Haynes, 1973) may be used to administer contingencies. The more consequences that are applied, the more effective the program is likely to be. For example, impressive results have been obtained in a program in which access to all significant reinforcers (job, friends, family, apartment) is contingent on abstinence (Azrin, 1976; Hunt & Azrin, 1973).

Social Learning. This approach focuses on helping the client alter his or her lifestyle (Marlatt & Gordon, 1985) or learn the coping skills necessary to limit or abstain from alcohol consumption (Miller, 1978; Miller, Taylor, & West, 1980; Sobell & Sobell, 1973). (Social learning theory is described in Chapter 27).

Behavioral Systems Model.   A behavioral systems model bases treatment on a detailed assessment of all the variables that might affect the client's drinking behavior, including the manner in which these variables interact. The variables are classified according to categories or systems on the basis of their source (e.g., whether they are located in the client or in significant others) and whether they are antecedent, organismic, or consequent. Examples of antecedent variables that might be considered are "nagging" by one's spouse and problem-solving failure; examples of organismic variables are withdrawal symptoms produced by abstinence and retaliation fantasies of the spouse; examples of consequences for drinking are decreases in alcohol-withdrawal symptoms, labeling self as competent, and reinforcement from spouse. Those variables that are most susceptible to control and are likely to yield the best results are then dealt with by means of appropriate behavioral procedures, which might include skills training, stimulus control, consequence control, and cognitive procedures.

OBESITY

Obesity has been estimated to afflict 15 to 50 percent of us (Bray, 1976; Van Itallie, 1979). It is considered a problem not merely because it detracts from one's physical appearance according to the standards of our culture, but also because the obese individual is at increased risk for serious health problems. The causes of obesity are complex and not well understood. While many behaviorists once believed that obesity was the result of reinforcement for overeating, it now appears that physiological factors are involved in many, if not all, cases of obesity. Two major physiological theories of obesity are set-point theory and fat-cell theory. According to set-point theory, all humans and animals tend to regulate their weight around a biologically fixed level that cannot be altered by environmental manipulation (Keesey, 1980). According to fat-cell theory, one's tendency to gain weight is determined by the number of fat cells in one's body (Nisbett, 1972). Both theories, which are not necessarily incompatible, imply that weight loss will be very difficult for the obese individual and that there will be a strong tendency to gain back any weight that is lost.

Note 2   Regardless of the causes of obesity, it appears that in many cases it can be treated effectively with behavioral methods.[2]

TREATMENT

Contemporary treatment strategies for obesity incorporate a number of components (Brownell & Foreyt, 1985; LeBow, 1981, 1989).

Self-monitoring.   Clients keep daily records of the foods they eat and their caloric contents. In addition, they keep charts of their daily caloric intake and their body weights. The charts are posted in a conspicuous place in the home (see Chapter 18), and the client brings his or her records and data to therapy sessions for discussion with the therapist.

Stimulus Control. Clients restrict their at-home eating to a specific location, so that only the stimuli present in that location (e.g., the kitchen table) control eating behavior (see Chapter 8).

Changing Eating Behavior. Eating rate is reduced by having clients lay down utensils between bites, drink water during the meal, or take short breaks between courses (see Chapter 7).

Behavioral Contracts. Clients sign a contract in which they agree to lose a certain amount of weight in a specified period of time (e.g., 1 to 2 pounds each week), in return for which they receive money or some other desired item that they have given up for this purpose (see Chapter 23).

Exercise. Most behavioral obesity programs emphasize the importance of exercise in helping to achieve and maintain an optimum weight. Naturally, behavioral methods are important in helping people (obese or otherwise) initiate and follow a regular exercise program.

Very Low Calorie Diets. The use of very low calorie diets in combination with behavioral methods has produced impressive results, both in terms of initial weight loss and maintenance of weight loss (Lindner & Blackburn, 1976; Wadden, Stunkard, Brownell, & Dey, 1984). Patients undergoing these special diets must, however, be given a thorough physical examination prior to initiating the diet and must be seen regularly by a physician during the program.

MARITAL DISTRESS

Simply put, marital distress can be said to be present when marriage partners have a low ratio of positive to negative interactions. The goal of behavioral marital therapy, therefore, is to increase the rate of positive interactions and decrease the rate of negative interactions (Jacobson & Moore, 1981; Wood & Jacobson, 1985).

TREATMENT

Behavioral marital therapy typically proceeds according to the following stages (Wood & Jacobson, 1985).

Instigation of Positive Exchanges. Each spouse is asked to increase behaviors that are pleasing to the other partner.

Communication and Problem-Solving Training. Clients learn effective communication skills, and then learn to use them to systematically identify and solve problems in their relationship (see Chapter 16; also Bornstein & Bornstein, 1986). Beck (1988) has described how automatic thoughts and maladaptive assumptions can be involved in many types of communication problems in relationships and has recommended treating these problems with cognitive therapy similar to that which he uses in the treatment of depression (see pp. 361–362 and 373–374).

Generality. There are three main components to obtaining generality of the effects of treatment: (1) clients learn to monitor their relationship for specific critical signs of a relapse; (2) clients are encouraged to continue using the problem-solving techniques that they learned in therapy; (3) input from the therapist is decreased gradually rather than terminated abruptly.

SEXUAL DYSFUNCTION: FOCUS ON LOW SEXUAL DESIRE

Behavioral treatment of sexual dysfunctions began in the late 1950s (Semans, 1956; Wolpe, 1958). Types of sexual dysfunctions that have been treated successfully with behavioral methods include lack of excitement and failure to obtain orgasm. Most of these cases respond extremely well to graduated in vivo exposure (Masters & Johnson, 1970; Wolpe, 1958; LoPiccolo, 1978). However, therapists are now begining to encounter problems that are more difficult to treat, and that therefore require a combination of techniques. A notable example is that of low or inhibited sexual desire, which is increasingly being reported in men as well as women (Friedman & Hogan, 1985).

TREATMENT

Friedman (1983) has developed a model for treating inhibited sexual desire that integrates four therapeutic components.

Experiential/Sensory Awareness Exercises. These are exercises that are used to help clients verbalize unacknowledged feelings about sex (e.g., anxiety, anger, or disgust).

Insight. The client is helped to identify correctly, or at least to not misidentify, the variables responsible for his or her problem.

Cognitive Behavior Modification. The client is taught to alter irrational thoughts that inhibit his or her sexual desire.

Behavioral Assignments. As the effects of the above variables are decreased, the client is given behavioral assignments on which to work, the main ingredient of which is graduated in vivo exposure.

PERSONALITY DISORDERS

Personality may be defined as one's characteristic mode of interacting with others. If one typically interacts in ways that are extremely maladaptive or dysfunctional, one may speak of a *personality disorder*. The third edition revised of the *Diagnostic and Statistical Manual* (DSM III-R) of the American Psychological Association classifies a number of personality disorders. For example, the *avoidant personality disorder* exhibits a hypersensitivity to potential rejection or shame; the *antisocial personality disorder* manifests extreme disregard for others; the *dependent personality disorder* displays excessive dependence on others.

TREATMENT

Turkat and Meyer (1982; see Turkat & Maisto, 1985) have developed a behavioral approach to personality disorders that proceeds as follows. First, all presenting complaints are specified. Then the therapist devises a hypothesis concerning the mechanism underlying (or variables producing) the presenting complaints. Next the therapist makes predictions of other difficulties that the client might experience, which permits the therapist to test the validity of his or her hypothesis. Once the underlying mechanism has been correctly identified, the therapist devises a behavioral treatment strategy to correct the problem. For example, if all or part of the underlying mechanism in a case of avoidant personality disorder is fear of criticism by authority figures (perhaps stemming from severe punishment as a child), the therapist might select systematic desensitization as one component of treatment.

STUDY QUESTIONS

1. List nine frequently encountered adult psychological disorders.
2. Define *generalized anxiety disorder*. Define *agoraphobia*.
3. What is the major component of the treatment of phobias? List and briefly describe the two major types of this component. Which type seems to work better, and what is a likely reason for this?
4. What are *obsessive-compulsive disorders*? What is the distinction between "obsessive" and "compulsive," and how valid is this distinction?
5. What two types of treatment appear to work best with obsessive-compulsive disorders? What may account for the effectiveness of these treatments?
6. Briefly describe Rosenthal and Rosenthal's approach to treating stress.
7. Briefly describe the major components of Beck's treatment of depression.
8. Of the various approaches to treating alcoholism, which would you tend to favor least? Which would you tend to favor most? Justify your answers to these questions.
9. Describe two major physiological theories of obesity.
10. List and briefly describe the major components of contemporary strategies for treating obesity.

11. List and briefly describe the stages according to which behavioral marital therapy typically proceeds.
12. List and briefly describe the four therapeutic components of Friedman's model for treating inhibited sexual desire.
13. Define *personality*. Define *personality disorder*. List and briefly describe three personality disorders.
14. Briefly describe Turkat and Meyer's approach to treating personality disorders.

EXTENDED DISCUSSION AND NOTES

1. Williams and Chambless (1990) found that agoraphobic clients who saw their therapists as being more self-confident, caring, and involved showed more approach during in vivo exposure. The experimenters speculated:

> It appears that the therapists' ability to handle difficult situations confidently may provide clients with assurance that they, too, can cope with stressful situations. Clients also may be more willing to enter feared situations if they are guided by someone who seems to genuinely care about their feelings and their experiences as they undergo the intervention. [p. 114]

2. Agras, Taylor, Feldman, Losch, and Burnett (1990) studied the use of a hand-held computer in the treatment of obesity. The computer contained a number of functions. In addition to prompting the client to set daily caloric intake and exercise goals and providing feedback on his or her success in achieving the goal each day, the computer contained a function for planning meals, a trainer to promote slow eating, a message function for providing motivating and reinforcing statements at appropriate times, and a graphic function that plotted daily caloric intake, amount of exercise, and weight over a two-week "moving-window" period. The experimenters found that a group that used the computer without additional therapy or group support lost as much weight as did a group that used the computer with group support and a group that did not use the computer and received therapy. Although the weight loss in all three groups was modest, the results suggest that computer therapy holds promise for the future, given the development of more sophisticated computers and more effective computer therapy programs.

STUDY QUESTIONS ON NOTES

1. Explain why the personal characteristics of a therapist conducting in vivo exposure might be important.
2. Describe the functioning of a hand-held computer used for the treatment of obesity. How effective has this computer been shown to be?

CHAPTER 27

Giving It All Some Perspective: **A Brief History**

This chapter traces some of the highlights of the remarkable early growth of the field of behavior modification. The chapter should be read with the following qualifications in mind:

    a. Although we describe behavior modification as developing primarily through two major and separate lines of influence, there are obvious cross-influences, blends, and offshoots, and it might be possible to make a case for somewhat different histories.

    b. We identify what we consider to be major highlights of the recent development of behavior modification; we do not attempt a complete historical account.

Note 1
    c. Behavior modification as we know it today is primarily a product of the 1960s and 1970s. Very few historical highlights prior to the 1950s are discussed.[1]

Note 2
    d. In this chapter we describe mainly historical highlights in the U.S.[2]

THE TWO MAJOR LINES OF DEVELOPMENT

THE OPERANT-CONDITIONING ORIENTATION

Note 3
In 1938, B. F. Skinner[3] published his book *The Behavior of Organisms*, in which he described the results of experiments on the lever-pressing behavior of rats for food or water reinforcement and, on the basis of his findings, outlined the basic principles of operant behavior. This pioneering work gradually influenced other experimental psychologists to begin studying the effects of contingencies of reinforcement on the behavior of rats and other animals.

In 1950, Keller and Schoenfeld wrote an introductory psychology text, *Principles of Psychology*, that was unlike any other text of its kind. Keller and Skinner had been graduate students together at Harvard University, and the Keller and Schoenfeld text was inspired largely by the work and writings of Skinner. *Principles of Psychology* contributed significantly to the development of the field of behavior analysis. Although less well known outside Skinnerian and operant circles, this influential introductory text had a tremendous impact **Note 4**   within the operant tradition.[4]

In 1953, Skinner published *Science and Human Behavior*. In this book he offered his interpretation of how the basic behavioral principles (which had been researched on lower organisms and which are described in Part II of this text) influence the behavior of people in all kinds of everyday situations. Although there was very little supporting data for Skinner's generalizations to humans, his interpretations influenced others to begin examining the effects of reinforcement variables on human behavior in a number of experimental and applied settings. The results of these efforts led to much of what has been described in this text as behavior modification. The highlights of this development prior to the 1980s are presented in the top panel of Table 27–1. (See Chapter 2 for discussion of developments in behavior modification since 1980.)

Many of the reports in the 1950s were demonstrations that positive reinforcement and extinction affect human behavior in predictable ways and/or case demonstrations that an application of a behavioral program could effect a desired behavior change. For example, Fuller (1949) reported that an institutional, bedridden, profoundly retarded adult could be taught to raise his right arm to a vertical position when arm movements were appropriately shaped and a warm sugar-milk solution was used as the reinforcer. Greenspoon (1955) demonstrated that a simple social consequence (saying "mmm-hmm") could influence college students to say certain types of words (see Chapter 3, note 3). Azrin and Lindsley (1956), two of Skinner's graduate students, demonstrated that jellybean reinforcement could influence pairs of young children to cooperate in playing a simple game. Each of these experiments demonstrated that consequences influence human behavior in predictable ways. None of these experiments, however, was primarily practically oriented. One of the first published reports of the 1950s that concerned practical, applied problems was that of Ayllon and Michael (1959). With Michael as his Ph.D. dissertation advisor, Ayllon conducted a number of behavioral demonstrations at the Saskatchewan Hospital, a psychiatric institution in Weyburn, Saskatchewan. These demonstrations showed how staff could use procedures such as reinforcement, extinction, and escape and avoidance conditioning to modify behaviors such as delusional talk, refusals to eat, and various disruptive behaviors.

Following Ayllon and Michael's article and several subsequent papers published by Ayllon and his colleagues from their work at Weyburn, similar demonstrations of behavioral control began to appear with some frequency

Table 27-1 Some Historical Highlights of Behavior Modification and Behavior Therapy Prior to 1980

	PRE-1950s	1950s	EARLY AND MIDDLE 1960s
OPERANT-CONDITIONING (SKINNERIAN) ORIENTATION	Some basic research and theory (Skinner, 1938)	Two major texts (Keller & Schoenfeld, 1950; Skinner, 1953) Some human studies and applications: profoundly retarded (Fuller, 1949), schizophrenics (Lindsley, 1956), psychotics (Ayllon & Michael, 1959), verbal conditioning (Greenspoon, 1955), stuttering (Flanagan, Goldiamond, & Azrin, 1958) A basic operant research journal, with some applications (*Journal of the Experimental Analysis of Behavior*, 1958–)	Some major university training centers Several books of readings (e.g., Ulrich, Stachnik, & Mabry, 1966) More applications, many to "resistant" populations: e.g., retardation (Birnbrauer, Bijou, Wolf, & Kidder, 1965; Girardeau & Spradlin, 1964), autism (Ferster & DeMyer, 1962; Lovaas, 1966; Wolf, Risley, & Mees, 1964), hyperactivity (Patterson, 1965), delinquency (Schwitzgebel, 1964), psychotics (Isaacs, Thomas, & Goldiamond, 1960; Haughton & Ayllon, 1965) Child development (Bijou & Baer, 1961)
OFFSHOOTS AND MIXTURES			Premack principle (Premack, 1965) Coverant control (Homme, 1965) Precision teaching (Lindsley, 1966) Modeling (Bandura & Walters, 1963) A major book of readings (Ullmann & Krasner, 1965), An applied journal (*Behavior Research and Therapy*, 1963–) Covert sensitization (Cautela, 1966)
RESPONDENT-CONDITIONING (AND HULLIAN AND WOLPEAN) ORIENTATION	Some basic research and theory (Pavlov, 1927; Watson & Rayner, 1920) An early application of fear desensitization (Jones, 1924) An early application of assertion training (Salter, 1949)	Two major texts (Dollard & Miller, 1950; Wolpe, 1958) Applications of systematic desensitization, assertion training, and aversion therapy to a variety of phobias and behavioral excesses Comparisons of behavior therapy and psychotherapy (Eysenck, 1959)	Some major university training centers Several books of readings (e.g., Eysenck, 1960; Franks, 1964) More applications of systematic desensitization, assertion training, and aversion therapy to a variety of classic neurotic behaviors and sexual disorders

Table 27-1 (continued)

LATE 1960s	1970s
Additional major university training centers Isolated undergraduate and graduate courses in many universities Additional books describing applied research and procedures applicable to a variety of areas: e.g., education (Skinner, 1968), parenting (Patterson & Gullion, 1968), community work (Tharp & Wetzel, 1969), mental hospitals (Schaefer & Martin, 1969) Additional applications to a variety of areas, including self-control, delinquency, university teaching, marriage counseling, sexual behaviors, and academic skills An applied journal (*Journal of Applied Behavior Analysis*, 1968–)	Many "how-to-do-it" books in a variety of areas (see note 5) Behavior modification procedures described for many "traditional" areas of psychology (e.g., social, developmental, personality, abnormal, and clinical) Many other "helping professions" adopting behavior modification procedures (see Chapter 2) Wide variety of individual, institutional, and community applications and research
Token economies (Ayllon & Azrin, 1968b) Contingency contracting (Homme, Csanyi, Gonzales, & Rechs, 1969) Formulation of social learning theory (Bandura, 1969) Two major books (Bandura, 1969; Franks, 1969) Implosive therapy (Stampfl & Levis, 1967)	Emergence of cognitive behavior modification, social learning theory, and eclectic behavior therapy Numerous behavior modification-behavior therapy conferences and workshops Concern for behavior modification-behavior therapy as a profession, and for controls against misapplications Mixed paraprofessional and professional organizations (e.g., Association for Behavior Analysis, 1974–) Professional organizations (Association for the Advancement of Behavior Therapy, 1970–; Behavior Research and Therapy Society, 1970–; European Association of Behavior Therapy, 1971–) More journals specializing in behavior modification (see note 6)
Several major university training centers Additional books (e.g., Wolpe, 1969) More applications to phobias, anger, asthmatic attacks, frigidity, homosexuality, insomnia, speech disorders, exhibitionism, and other behaviors	Many additional books, publications and training workshops; much additional research

in the early 1960s (see Table 27–1). This early work was characterized by two features: (1) much of it was done with very resistant populations (such as the mentally retarded, autistic children, and severely regressed psychotics) that had not received a great deal of successful input from traditional psychology, and (2) many of the applications took place in institutional or highly controlled settings. A notable exception to this early trend is Bijou and Baer's (1961) interpretation of child development from a strictly behavioral perspective.

In 1965, Ullmann and Krasner published their very influential collection of readings, *Case Studies in Behavior Modification* (see the "offshoots and mixtures" panel in Table 27–1). This appears to be the first book with "behavior modification" in its title. In addition to collecting a number of case histories and research reports by other authors, Ullmann and Krasner compared behavior modification and the behavioral model with more traditional psychotherapeutic strategies and the medical model. Although their book is not just in the operant tradition, since they also included many studies and discussions in the Pavlovian–Hullian tradition (to be discussed in the next section of this chapter), it undoubtedly had a significant impact on furthering behavior modification and providing, in one source, information on much of the preliminary work in this area.

In the late 1960s, the operant-conditioning orientation began to spread throughout the Western Hemisphere. Several university training centers were developed, many universities initiated at least one or two courses in behavior modification at both the graduate and undergraduate levels, and applications spread to normal school settings, to university teaching, to homes, and to other populations and settings.

By the 1970s, the operant orientation had grown tremendously. Increasingly, this approach is referred to as *applied behavior analysis*. It is somewhat surprising to find contemporary textbooks that suggest that this approach has been used primarily on client populations with "limited cognitive capacity" and where considerable environmental control is a potential characteristic of the treatment procedures. Although this was true in the 1950s and 1960s, numerous applications now occur in almost all walks of life.

THE RESPONDENT-CONDITIONING (AND HULLIAN AND WOLPEAN) ORIENTATION

Late in the nineteenth century, the Russian physiologist I. P. Pavlov conducted experiments on digestion, which won him the Nobel Prize in medicine in 1904. While doing this research, Pavlov discovered that stimuli other than food could elicit salvation if the stimuli had been paired with food. This discovery led him to carry out an intensive investigation of what today is termed Pavlovian, classical, or respondent conditioning (see Chapter 15). Results of this work were published in a classic book titled *Conditioned Reflexes* (Pavlov, 1927). In 1913, John B. Watson published a very influential paper in which he argued that most human activities could be explained as learned habits. After becoming familiar with the work of Pavlov (and another Russian physiologist, I. Bechterev), Watson (1916) adopted the conditioned reflex as the unit of habit and argued that most complex activities were due to respondent conditioning (this, of course, was before Skinner distinguished between operant and respondent conditioning). At that time, some of his extreme and unsupported generalizations shook the foundations of much of traditional psychology. Watson followed his 1916 paper with a classic experiment in which he demonstrated that human emotional reactions could be condtioned in an experimental setting (Watson & Rayner, 1920; see Chapter 15 of the present text).

During the next 20 years, a number of somewhat isolated reports of the application of respondent-conditioning procedures to various behaviors appeared in the literature (for a list of many of these, see Yates, 1970). None of these applications, however, appears to have had any sustained impact on the development of behavior modification as we know it today.

Another influence closely related to the respondent-conditioning orientation was the work of the American learning theorist Clark Hull (1943, 1952). Hull, an early contemporary of Skinner, developed a "learning theory" that tended to capitalize on both operant conditioning as described by Skinner and respondent conditioning as described by Pavlov, meshed together in a theory that did not distinguish between the two types of conditioning. According to Hull, reinforcement was involved in Pavlovian as well as in operant conditioning. Hull did not attempt to interpret a wide variety of human behavior to the extent that Skinner did (compare Hull, 1952, with Skinner, 1953). However, two other psychologists, Dollard and Miller (1950), translated a variety of Freudian psychodynamic concepts (which, despite their lack of empirical support, were extremely popular in those days) into the language of Hull's learning theory.

Within this Pavlovian–Hullian tradition, two significant developments occurred in the 1950s, both no doubt influenced to some extent by Dollard and Miller's book and by the learning theory of Edwin Guthrie (1935). One development occurred in South Africa, where Joseph Wolpe began some research and theorizing that drew heavily on Pavlovian conditioning, Hullian theory, and the earlier work of Watson, Mary Cover Jones, and the British psysiologist Sir Charles Sherrington. Sherrington (1947) had noted that if one group of muscles is stimulated, an antagonistic muscle group will be inhibited—and vice versa. He called this *reciprocal inhibition* and postulated it to be a general process acting throughout the nervous system. Wolpe extended the principle of reciprocal inhibition to state that if a response that is incompatible with fear or anxiety can be made to occur to a stimulus that normally produces fear or anxiety, then that stimulus will cease to elicit the fear reaction. In 1958, Wolpe published his first book on reciprocal inhibition. It was to provide a major force in the launching of the modern era of the respondent tradition of behavior therapy. Wolpe used relaxation responses, sexual responses, and assertion responses to reciprocally inhibit fear or anxiety. (When relaxation is used, the treatment procedure is typically called systematic desensitization; see Chapter 15.)

Also during the 1950s, Hans Eysenck in England was instrumental in criticizing traditional Freudian psychoanalytic-treatment procedures and advocating learning-theory procedures as alternatives.

In 1960, Eysenck published a book of readings, *Behaviour Therapy and the Neuroses*, in which he presented a number of case histories where variations of reciprocal-inhibition and respondent-conditioning procedures were used in clinical therapy. The respondent-conditioning orientation of behavior therapy has occasionally been referred to as the "Wolpe–Eysenck" school.

In the early 1960s, Wolpe moved to the United States. He began a program at Temple University in which he trained therapists in his particular version of behavior therapy. In 1963, Eysenck founded the journal *Behaviour Research and Therapy*, which publishes operant-oriented studies as well as studies with a Pavlovian flavor. As indicated in the bottom panel of Table 27–1, behavior therapy within the respondent orientation grew quite rapidly in the 1960s and 1970s and developed applications to a variety of phobic and neurotic disorders. On June 30, 1984, the behavior therapy unit at Temple University Medical Center ceased to exist. Wolpe (1985) attributed termination of the unit to misunderstanding of behavior therapy by psychodynamic psychotherapists. Wolpe, however, continues to be a major force in the field.

MIXTURES AND OFFSHOOTS OF THE TWO MAJOR ORIENTATIONS

Much of behavior modification and behavior therapy clearly falls within either the operant orientation or the Pavlovian–Hullian–Wolpean orientation. Most other developments tend to be offshoots of one or the other of these traditions or fall in a gray area somewhere in-between (see the "offshoots and mixtures" panel of Table 27–1).

In addition to the two major orientations, two broad theoretical models of behavior modification emerged in the 1970s: social learning theory and cognitive behavior modification. Characteristics of *social learning theory* were outlined by Julian Rotter in 1954 in his book *Social Learning and Clinical Psychology*. The most influential of the social learning theorists, however, has been Albert Bandura (1969, 1977, 1986). This approach is "social" in the sense that it places great emphasis on the social contexts in which behavior is acquired and maintained. In addition to basic principles of respondent and operant conditioning, Bandura has strongly emphasized the importance of *observational learning*. By watching other people act and by observing what happens to them, we can then imitate their behavior. (Also, see previous discussion of modeling in Chapter 16.) Bandura believes that this type of learning can occur without external reinforcement, although he agrees that external reinforcement might be necessary to influence an individual to perform the behavior. Bandura also emphasizes "cognitive mediational processes" as an important influence on behavior. Based on prior experience with environmental influences as well as on current perceptions of environmental events, an individual is said to develop cognitive rules and strategies that can serve to determine future actions. An important cognitive mediational process, for example, is what Bandura calls self-efficacy (Bandura, 1982). This refers to a belief that one can perform adequately in a particular situation. In Bandura's words, "Given appropriate skills and adequate incentives . . . efficacy expectations are a major determinant of peoples' choices of activities, how much effort they will expend, and how long they will sustain effort in dealing with stressful situations" (Bandura, 1977, p. 194).

A cognitive framework for therapy was contained in Bandura's (1969) book. However, *cognitive behavior modification*, as represented by individuals such as Ellis, Beck, and Meichenbaum (see Chapter 25), is currently considered an approach separate from social learning theory. Moreover, most people would not see cognitive behavior modification as a mixture or an offshoot of the operant orientation or the Pavlovian–Hullian–Wolpean orientation. Nevertheless, it represents one of four current conceptual approaches within behavior therapy. While social learning theory emphasizes the regulation of behavior by external stimulus events, environmental consequences, and "cognitive mediational processes," cognitive behavioral clinicians deal primarily with assumed "cognitive mediation" of behavior—individuals' interpretations of what is happening around them.

In addition to these four theoretical models of behavior modification, a large group of practicing behavior therapists ascribe to an eclectic approach. Lazarus (1971) has been considered as representative of this position. Referring to what he calls "multimodal" behavior therapy, Lazarus (1971, 1976) argues that the practicing clinician should not restrict himself or herself to a particular theoretical framework, but rather, should use a variety of behavioral techniques along with psychoanalytic and other traditional clinical techniques, provided that they have some empirical support.

As indicated by this brief discussion of current conceptualizations of behavior modification, there is some disagreement among behavior modifiers on theoretical issues. Nevertheless, there is also considerable agreement.

All behavior practitioners should be open to innovative procedures for helping people to change their behavior. However, as we emphasized in Chapter 25 on cognitive behavior modification, there are advantages to examining such procedures from a consistent behavioral viewpoint. In our view, the procedures practiced by therapists who claim allegiance to the various conceptual approaches do not at present appear to involve any behavioral principles beyond those studied by basic researchers in the areas of operant and Pavlovian conditioning.

BEHAVIOR THERAPY AND BEHAVIOR MODIFICATION COMPARED _____

Although many writers use the terms "behavior modification" and "behavior therapy" interchangeably, there are some differences in their historical derivations. It appears that Lindsley, Skinner, and Solomon (1953) were the first to use the term "behavior therapy." They did so in a report describing some research in which psychotic patients in a mental hospital were reinforced with candy or cigarettes for pulling a plunger. However, those within the operant orientation subsequently made little use of the term (at least, until the 1970s). Although Lazarus (1958) next used the term "behavior therapy" when he applied it to Wolpe's reciprocal inhibition framework, the term became popular among those within the Pavlovian–Hullian–Wolpean orientation after Eysenck (1959) used it to describe procedures published by Wolpe. The first use of the term "behavior modification" appears to be in a chapter by R. I. Watson (1962). Since that time, many writers have distinguished between behavior modification, with its roots in operant conditioning, and behavior therapy, with its roots in Pavlovian conditioning and Hullian theory. Others, however, have not made that distinction consistently. Ullmann and Krasner (1965), for example, frequently used "behavior modification" and "behavior therapy" interchangeably. Also, critics tended to lump operant psychology with other learning theories (Chomsky, 1959) and behavior modification with Pavlovian conditioning, behavior therapy, conditioning therapy, and learning-based therapies (see, for example, Breger & McGaugh, 1965). It has been argued that critiques and historical accounts of behavior modification–behavior therapy that do not clarify the particular orientation being discussed (such as Mash, 1974) are often misleading (Martin, 1974). The distinctions that have tended to characterize the uses of the two terms are presented in Table 27–2. In spite of these historical distinctions, for which there is a fair amount of agreement, the terms often appear to be used interchangeably.

THE FUTURE OF BEHAVIOR MODIFICATION _____

Behavior modification has been applied to nearly all conceivable kinds of individual and social problems. Moreover, more and more of these applications have been concerned with prevention and social engineering in addition to amelioration of existing problems. There is no doubt that the "helping" professions are increasingly adopting behavior modification procedures, including such professions as social work, medicine, rehabilitation medicine, nursing, education, preventive dentistry, psychiatric nursing, psychiatry, public health, and clinical and community psychology. Applications are also occurring with increasing frequency in such areas as business, industry, sports, physical education, recreation, and the promotion of healthy lifestyles (see

Table 27-2 A Comparison of the Uses of the Terms "Behavior Therapy" and "Behavior Modification"

BEHAVIOR THERAPY	BEHAVIOR MODIFICATION
1 The term is used most often by followers of the Pavlovian–Hullian–Wolpean orientation and followers of the cognitive orientation (who tend to use it interchangeably with the term "cognitive behavior modification").	The term is used most often by followers of the operant orientation.
2 The term tends to be used by behavioral psychologists and psychiatrists who are concerned primarily with treatment in traditional clinical settings.	The term tends to be used by behavior specialists in schools, homes, and other settings that are not primarily the domain of the clinical psychologist and psychiatrist.
3 The term tends to be used to refer to behavioral treatments conducted in the therapist's office by means of verbal interaction ("talk therapy") between therapist and client.	The term tends to be used for behavioral treatments carried out in the natural environment as well as in special training settings.
4 The term is associated with an experimental foundation that is based primarily on human studies in clinical settings.	The term tends to be associated with an experimental foundation in basic operant research with animals and humans, in addition to experimental studies in applied settings.

Chapter 2). The immediate future of behavior modification appears to be very bright. Some day, a thorough knowledge of behavioral techniques may become an accepted necessity in our culture and will be taught to children in elementary school along with good hygiene and physical fitness. Perhaps these children will grow up to see a world in which good applications of behavioral principles will be second nature to everyone and will result in a happy, informed, skillful, productive culture without war, poverty, prejudice, or pollution.

STUDY QUESTIONS

1. Cite seven general statements that might answer the question "What is behavior modification?" (see Chapter 1).
2. How did Skinner's early work influence the initial development of behavior modification?
3. Discuss Keller's contribution to the development of behavior modification (see text and note 4).
4. Many of the early reports in the operant tradition in the 1950s were straightforward experiments that demonstrated that consequences influence human behavior. Briefly, describe two such experiments.

5. Briefly describe one of the first published reports (a very influential one) that concerned practical applications within the operant tradition.

6. What is the *Journal of the Experimental Analysis of Behavior*?

7. The publications of the early 1960s within the operant orientation seem to have been characterized by two features. What were they?

8. Was the very influential book *Case Studies in Behavior Modification* strictly within the operant orientation? Why or why not?

9. What concept did J. B. Watson adopt from Pavlov? How did Watson use this concept?

10. What behavior-therapy procedure do we credit to Joseph Wolpe?

11. What role did Hans Eysenck play in the development of behavior therapy in the 1950s?

12. What are the names of seven behavior modification-behavior therapy journals?

13. Briefly, describe four current conceptual (or theoretical) models of behavior modification.

14. Describe four differences in the usage of the terms "behavior therapy" and "behavior modification" (see Table 27–2).

15. If someone suggested, "Behavior modification is okay for some limited types of problems," what would you say?

16. Of the four conceptual models of behavior modification, which do you think has influenced Martin and Pear most strongly? (*Hint*: They're the authors of this book.) Cite evidence to justify your answer.

EXTENDED DISCUSSION AND NOTES

1. For a discussion of the history of behavior modification from the early 1900s to the 1960s, see MacMillan (1973). More detailed discussion of the Pavlovian influences on the development of behavior therapy can be found in Franks (1969) and Yates (1970). The most complete history of behavior modification was written by Kazdin (1978).

2. In the 1950s, important historical developments in behavior modification occurred concurrently in three countries: in South Africa, where Wolpe conducted his pioneering work on systematic desensitization; in England, where Eysenck spurred on the behavior modification movement by emphasizing dissatisfaction with traditional methods of psychotherapy; and in the United States, where Skinner and his colleagues were working within the operant-conditioning orientation. However, during the 1960s and early 1970s, most of the major books and research papers in behavior modification and behavior therapy were based on developments in the U.S. For example, three of the first four major behavior-therapy journals were published in the U.S. and contained primarily U.S. articles (*Journal of Applied Behavior Analysis*, 1968-; *Behavior Therapy*, 1970-; *Behavior Therapy and Experimental Psychiatry*, 1970–). Although the fourth journal (*Behaviour Research and Therapy*, 1963–) was edited by Eysenck in England, it too contained a large number of U.S. research reports. During the 1970s, however, behavior modification became a truly worldwide movement. For example, significant developments have occurred in Australia, the Dominican Republic, England, Holland, Israel, Norway, Spain, and Sweden (Brownell, 1981); in Germany (Stark, 1980); in Canada (Martin,

1981); in Brazil, Chile, Colombia, Mexico, and Venezuela (Ardila, 1978, 1982), in Sri Lanka (DeSilva & Simarasinghe, 1985); in France (Agathon, 1982); in Argentina (Blanck, 1983); in Ghana (Danguah, 1982); in Italy (Meazzini & Rovetto, 1983); in Thailand (Mikulis, 1983); in New Zealand (Singh & Blampied, 1983); and in Japan (Yamagami, Okuma, Morinaga, & Nakao, 1982).

3. Burrhus Frederick Skinner was born on March 20, 1904, in Susquehanna, Pennsylvania. At the time of his death on August 18, 1990, in Cambridge, Massachusetts, at the age of 86, Skinner was the world's best-known living psychologist and its leading behaviorist.

   After receiving his bachelor of arts degree with a major in English at Hamilton College in upstate New York, Skinner was a somewhat unsuccessful writer during the next two years in New York City's Greenwich Village, and in Europe. He then entered Harvard to study psychology and received his doctorate in 1931. It was at Harvard that he formed a friendship with Fred Keller, a friendship that was to last over 60 years. After being a postdoctoral fellow at Harvard, and then teaching at the University of Minnesota and at Indiana University, Skinner returned to Harvard as a professor in 1947. He remained associated with Harvard until his death.

   Skinner had a remarkable career and received numerous awards including the Distinguished Scientific Award from the American Psychological Association (1958), the President's National Medal of Science (1968), and the Humanist of the Year Award from the American Humanist Society (1972). In addition to his basic theoretical and experimental contributions, Skinner published a utopian novel, *Walden Two* (1948), worked on a project to teach pigeons to guide missiles during World War II (Skinner, 1960), and developed the concept of programmed instruction and teaching machines (Skinner, 1958). Skinner continued to be active throughout his academic career, publishing his most recent book in 1989 (*Recent Issues in the Analysis of Behavior*). He leaves a tremendous legacy: his influence on psychology is as significant as Galileo's on physics and Darwin's on biology.

4. In 1961, Keller journeyed to Brazil where he pioneered the first operant-conditioning course in that country and contributed immeasurably to the development of behavior modification there. Also while there, he and his Brazilian colleagues pioneered the Personalized System of Instruction, a behavior modification approach to university teaching that is revolutionizing college instruction (see Chapter 2). At the second annual meeting of the Association for Behavior Analysis (Chicago, 1976), tribute was paid to Skinner and Keller together. They were referred to as the mother and father of behavior modification, with Skinner the master experimenter and theoretician, and Keller the master teacher.

5. These how-to-do-it books cover such areas as toilet-training (Azrin & Foxx, 1974), eliminating nervous habits (Azrin & Nunn, 1977), teaching social behavior to young children (McGinnis & Goldstein, 1990; Shephard, 1973), quitting smoking (Pomerleau & Pomerleau, 1977; Shipley, 1985), dieting (LeBow, 1988; Stuart, 1978), helping women to become orgasmic (Heiman, LoPiccolo, & LoPiccolo, 1976), controlling alcoholic drinking (Miller & Muñoz, 1976), behavioral assessment with retarded children (Hardy, Martin, Yu, Leader, & Quinn, 1981), communication between couples (Gottman, Natarius, Gonso, & Markman, 1976), treating elderly persons (Hussian & Davis, 1986), encouraging pre-teens to think about the challenges of adolescence (Parkinson, 1986), helping adolescents to develop self-management skills (Brigham, 1989a, 1989b), managing stress (Neidhardt, Weinstein, & Co 1985), and developing self-improvement skills in a variety of areas (Martin & Osborne, 1989; Watson & Tharp, 1989).

6. Wyatt, Hawkins, and Davis (1986) examined the assertion heard from some psychologists of nonbehavioral persuasion, that behavior modification is dead. Wyatt and others argued that it is very much alive, vital, and growing. A part of the evidence in support of their argument is the increasing abundance of journals that are primarily behavioral in orientation. In addition to the three journals listed in Table 27–1, Wyatt and colleagues identified the following behavior-modification journals: *Education and Treatment of Children* (1969– ; originally *School Applications of Learning Theory*), *Behavior Therapy* (1970–), *Journal of Behavior Therapy and Experimental Psychiatry* (1970–), *Behaviorism* (1972–), *Behavioral Psychotherapy* (1973), *Mexican Journal of Behavior Analysis* (1975–), *Behavioral Engineering* (1976), *Japanese Journal of Behavior Therapy* (1976–), *Behavior Modification* (1977–), *La Technologie du Comportment* (1977–), *Journal of Organizational Behavior Management* (1978–), *The Behavior Analyst* (1978–), *The Behavior Therapist* (1978–), *Behavioral Assessment* (1979–), *Child and Family Behavior Therapy* (1979– ; originally *Child Behavior Therapy*), *Journal of Psychopathology and Behavioral Assessment* (1979– ; originally *Journal of Behavioral Assessment*), *Applied Research in Mental Retardation* (1980–), *Behavior Analysts and Social Action* (1980– ; originally *Behaviorists for Social Action*), *Journal of Precision Teaching* (1980–), *Analysis and Intervention in Developmental Disabilities* (1981–), *Behavioral Counselling Quarterly* (1981–), *Behavioral Processes* (1981– ; originally *Behavior Analysis Newsletters*), and *Behavioral Residential Treatment* (1986). In 1987, *Applied Research in Mental Retardation* and *Analysis and Intervention in Developmental Disabilities* were collapsed into one journal—*Research in Developmental Disabilities*.

STUDY QUESTIONS ON NOTES

1. Name three countries that were important in the development of behavior modification in the 1950s, and the person most associated with this development in each of these countries.
2. Cite three of Skinner's contributions other than his basic research and theoretical writings.
3. List five areas in which "how-to-do-it" behavior-modification books have been written.
4. What evidence is there that the literature of behavior modification, and hence behavior modification itself, is still growing and developing?

CHAPTER 28

Ethical Issues

Throughout this book we have emphasized the ethical or moral concerns that one should always bear in mind when applying behavior modification. It would be a great tragedy if this powerful new scientific technology were somehow to be used in ways that harmed rather than helped humanity. Because this is a real danger, it is fitting that we devote the final chapter of this book to a more detailed discussion of ethical concerns.

The history of civilization is a continuous story of the abuse of power. Throughout the ages, various groups have used the reinforcers and punishers at their disposal to control the behavior of less powerful groups (groups who had fewer reinforcers and punishers to deliver, or who lacked the means to deliver them contingent on selected target behaviors). The effect of this tradition has generally been to increase the reinforcements occurring to the more powerful at the expense of those occurring to the less powerful. From time to time, as the proportion of total reinforcement allotted to them steadily dwindled, groups subjected to this abuse of power have successfully revolted against their oppressors and have modified existing social structures, or established new ones, to check or eliminate the possibility of future abuses. Constitutions, bills of rights, and related political documents of modern states can be viewed as formal specifications of contingencies designed to control the behavior of those who control the behavior of others. In Western democracies, for example, we have moved from the era of the divine right of kings to one of "government by laws, not men." Moreover, with the introduction of periodic popular elections, the people who are controlled by those who make the laws can exert a certain measure of reciprocal control: they can vote them out of office. While in socialist and communist countries the revolutionary process concentrated on eliminating certain economic abuses rather than establishing democracy, many of these countries are apparently also now becoming more democratic. Nevertheless, the new social designs and practices that have emerged thus far have invariably fallen short of their objective; power continues to be abused throughout the world.

Because of this cultural history, and because of people's personal experiences with others who have abused their power (that is, used it for their own benefit and to the disadvantage of those over whom they exerted control), people have learned to react negatively to all overt attempts to control behavior. This negative reaction is so strong that those who would control our behavior usually find that their efforts are more successful when they disguise their aims (as when advertisers, for example, use the "soft sell" rather than "hard sell" or when people who want to change our opinion on an issue contrive to make it appear that we arrived at the new opinion essentially by ourselves). It should not be surprising, therefore, that the emergence of behavior modification has evoked many negative reactions, ranging from suspicion to outright hostility. Behavior modification is the technology based on the science that studies the factors that control behavior. This being the case, it is no secret that behavior modification is based on two propositions: (1) behavior can be controlled, and (2) it is desirable to do so to achieve certain objectives. Never before have such far-reaching techniques of behavior control been expressed so explicitly and advocated so strongly.

Some behavior modifiers, noting that terms such as "control" often evoke violently negative reactions to behavior modification, would prefer to use terms that have less of an emotional impact. They suggest, for example, substituting "influence" for "control," because they feel that the former term will help behavior modification become more acceptable to the vast majority of people. However, the weaker term may have the opposite effect: it may lead people to underestimate the real power of behavior modification and hence the dangers associated with its development, widespread use, and potential abuse.

Extreme wariness is a healthy reaction to any new, far-reaching advance in science or technology. Perhaps civilization would be in less danger if more precautions had been taken early in the development of, say, atomic energy. The solution to the present problems stemming from scientific and technological advances, however, does not lie in attempting to turn the clock back to a seemingly more secure, prescientific era. Science and technology are not the problem. They are merely highly sophisticated means that people have developed for solving problems. The real problem is that people frequently misuse these tools. This is, of course, a behavioral problem. It would seem, therefore, as Skinner (1953, 1971) has argued, that the science of behavior is the logical key to the solution of that problem. As with other powerful sciences and technologies, however, behavior modification can be misused. It therefore appears that it will be necessary to use behavior modification to control itself.

This line of reasoning leads us to a rather ironic conclusion: the fear of behavior modification may be a major impediment to the control of behavior modification. Either because of this fear, or simply as a result of misunderstanding, behavior modification has frequently been subjected to invalid ethical criticisms. To put behavior modification in its proper ethical perspective, first we discuss some of the most frequently heard criticisms and attempt to explain why we believe they are invalid. Then we turn to the question of how safeguards can be imposed on behavior modification to ensure that it will always be used in the best interests of humanity.

CRITICISMS OF BEHAVIOR MODIFICATION

ARGUMENT THAT BEHAVIOR CAN'T BE COMPLETELY CONTROLLED

Whatever its logical merits, the doctrine of free will provides a certain amount of comfort to many who fear behavioral control. Basically, the doctrine states that a person can act independently of the environmental and genetic factors that influence his or her behavior. The doctrine is generally presented more as a criticism of the science of behavior than as a criticism of the technology based on that science. However, it is also directed against behavior modification, in the sense that, if behavior is not completely determined, then it cannot be completely controlled; hence (the implication seems to be), it is pointless to attempt to discover laws of behavior, let alone to attempt to use those laws to control behavior.

Besides tending to be comforting, the doctrine of free will has the added advantage that it can never be proved false. Even if behavior is completely determined, it is improbable that all of the laws determining it will be discovered or that they will ever be used to obtain complete control over behavior. Perfect prediction and control seem not to be achievable in physics, so it is unlikely that they will be achievable in the behavioral sciences.

Whether or not behavior is *completely* determined by environmental and genetic factors (everyone agrees that it is at least partially determined by these factors) makes for interesting philosophical discussions. From a practical point of view, however, it may make little difference one way or the other. The important point seems to be that the amount of potential control over behavior is steadily increasing, as a result of new discoveries in behavioral science and refinements in behavioral technology. Therefore, denying that complete control is possible (if used as an argument against behavior modification) constitutes somewhat of a "head-in-the-sand" attitude toward the fact that behavior modification is already a powerful technology and is expanding rapidly.

ARGUMENTS AGAINST DELIBERATELY CONTROLLING BEHAVIOR

Note 1   It is sometimes argued that all attempts to control behavior are unethical.[1] A moment's reflection, however, shows that the goal of any social help profession (such as education, psychology, and psychiatry) can be achieved only to the extent that the practitioners of that profession exert control over behavior. The goal of education, for example, is to change behavior so that students will respond differently to their environment than they would had they not been educated. To teach a person to read, for example, is to change her behavior in such a way that she responds to signs, newspapers, books, and so forth in a manner that is different from the way in which she responded prior to being able to read. The goals of counseling, psychological treatment, and psychiatry likewise involve changing people's behavior so that they can function more effectively than they did prior to receiving professional help.

Many members of social help professions do not like to think that they are controlling behavior. They prefer to see themselves as merely helping their clients to achieve control over their own behavior. Establishing self-control, however, is also a form of behavior control. One simply teaches an individual to emit behavior that controls other behavior in some desired fashion. To do that, it is necessary to control the behavior involved in self-control. In other words, it is necessary to control the behavior that controls other behavior. The social help practitioner may object that this is nevertheless not control on his or her part because the external influence over the client's behavior is withdrawn as soon as the practitioner is sure that the client is able to manage his or her own behavior. Actually, as we have emphasized repeatedly throughout this book, the practitioner has simply shifted the control to the natural environment. One may speak of this as "withdrawing control," but the control still continues, even though its form has changed. If the practitioner has been successful in achieving the behavioral objectives, the desired behavior will be maintained, and in that sense the practioner's control over the behavior will persist.

Some people will grant that social help practitioners necessarily engage in the control of behavior, but will nevertheless argue that it is wrong to deliberately plan to control behavior. They regard planning to be "cold" and "mechanical" and feel that it interferes with warm, loving "spontaneous" relationships that should exist between persons. It is difficult to determine where this objection to planning comes from, since we know of no logical or empirical evidence that supports it. On the contary, many behavior modification programs that we know of are characterized by friendly, warm interactions between the individuals involved. Good behavior modifiers are genuinely interested in their clients as persons, and seem to find the time to interact with them on a personal level, just as other social-help practitioners do. There is no doubt that some people show behavior that appears to be "cold" and "mechanical." However, it is our impression that such people are no more common among behavior modifiers than they are among any subgroup of those in the "helping professions" with other orientations.[2]

Note 2

A lack of planning, on the other hand, can be disastrous. For illustrations of this, refer to Part II, where we gave numerous examples of how behavioral principles and processes can work to the disadvantage of those who are ignorant of them or who do not plan for them. If a behavior practitioner is not skillful in constructing programs for developing desirable behavior, he or she is very apt unwittingly to introduce contingencies that develop undersirable behavior.

ARGUMENTS AGAINST THE METHODS OF BEHAVIOR MODIFICATION

There are those who agree that behavior is determined, accept the idea that planning for behavior change is desirable, but nevertheless object to certain methods of behavior modification. Often, this view stems from the mistaken belief that behavior modifiers must confine themselves to a very small number of methods that are appropriate only to very simple behavior problems. On the contrary, behavior modification consists of a wide variety of methods that scientific research has indicated are effective in changing behavior. This is a very large set of methods (as the contents of this book demonstrate), and the behavior modifier is therefore in a good position to select the method that is likely to do the most good and the least harm in the treatment of any given problem.

Nevertheless, behavior modifiers often encounter objections to methods that they have judiciously selected. The objection is sometimes purely emotional, as when, for example, the use of reinforcement is said to constitute "bribery." the problem with this objection is that it is not based on a valid argument. It is merely name calling—attaching a negative label to something one wishes to discredit. To be valid, the argument must show that the use of the procedure is likely to have an undesirable result. For example, one might argue that a child who has become accustomed to receiving tokens for completing schoolwork will thereby be hindered in learning to do the schoolwork without receiving tangible reinforcement. Of course, much evidence that we now have fails to support this argument. Even if the opposite were the case, however, the argument would not refute behavior modification. It would merely cause a particular procedure to be questioned. One would then have to decide whether the advantages of using the procedure outweigh its disadvantages relative to the advantages and disadvantages of some other procedure. By comparing different procedures in this way, one eventually selects the procedure that seems best suited to the problem at hand.

ETHICAL SAFEGUARDS _____

As we indicated at the beginning of this chapter, behavior modification can be of great value to humanity but it also has the potential to be harmful. To promote the former and prevent the latter, we must build ethical safeguards into the practice of behavior modification. How this can be done is the topic of this section. But first we must be clear on what we mean by "ethics."

From a behavioral point of view, the term *ethics* refers to certain standards of behavior that are developed by a culture and that promote the survival of that culture (Skinner, 1953, 1971). For example, stealing is considered unethical or wrong in many cultures because of the disruptive effect it has on the culture. It is not necessarily the case, however, that people in those cultures decided to declare stealing wrong because of its disruptive effect. It might be that, among a number of cultures that existed at a particular time before recorded history, behaving honestly in relation to material goods happened to be socially reinforced and stealing happened to be punished in some of these cultures but not in others (just as different cultures happened to reinforce different types of religious beliefs). Cultures in which honest behavior toward material possessions was not reinforced and stealing not punished, however, tended not to survive. There are a number of possible reasons for this. Perhaps the members of these cultures put so much effort into fighting each other that their cultures were fatally vulnerable to invasions from other cultures. Perhaps the members of these cultures spent so much time fighting each other that they did not have enough time left over to produce an adequate amount of food for themselves. Perhaps, due to the constant fighting and bickering, these cultures were so unreinforcing to their members that the members defected in large numbers to other cultures, so that their former cultures became extinct due to lack of membership. Whatever the case, many cultures survived that reinforced nonstealing behavior and punished stealing—that is, cultures that considered nonstealing ethical or right and stealing unethical or wrong.

Thus, ethics has evolved as part of our culture in much the same way that the parts of our bodies have evolved; that is, ethics has contributed to the survival of our culture in much the same way that, for example, fingers and an opposable thumb have contributed to the survival of our species. This is not to say that people do not, at times, deliberately decide to formulate ethical rules for their culture. On the contrary, it is part of this cultural evolutionary process that at some point in the process some members of a culture begin to engage in such behavior due to the fact that they have been conditioned to work toward the survival of their culture. One way in which to work toward the survival of one's culture is to formulate and enforce (through reinforcement as well as punishment) a code of ethics that strengthens that culture.

Behavior modification is so new that ethical standards pertaining specifically to the changes in the culture it has brought about are still in the early stages of their evolution. Indeed, as indicated earlier in this chapter, some people have regarded the whole approach of behavior modification to be unethical. That stage, however, seems to be passing—which is fortunate, since, as Skinner (1953, p. 446) stated, "The current culture which . . . is most likely to survive is . . . that in which the methods of science are most effectively applied to the problems of human behavior." Various groups and organizations have addressed the ethical issues involved in such applications. Two highly reputable organizations that have done so are the Association for the Advancement of Behavior Therapy and the American Psychological Association.

In 1977, in its journal *Behavior Therapy*, the Association for the Advancement of Behavior Therapy published a set of basic ethical questions that one should always ask with regard to any behavior modification or behavior-therapy program. These questions are reprinted in Table 28–1 and should be examined carefully. As can be seen from the table, most of these points have been made frequently throughtout this book, especially in Chapter 21. If you are carrying out a behavior modification program and must answer no to any of these questions, it is extremely likely that the ethics of what you are doing would be considered questionable by any recognized group of behavior modifiers or behavior therapists. It should be noted, as well, that these ethical questions are relevant not only to behavior modifiers and behavior therapists, but to all providers of human services.

In 1978, a comprehensive report (Stolz and associates, 1978) on the ethical issues involved in behavior modification was published by a commission appointed by the American Psychological Association. A primary conclusion of the commission was that persons engaged in any type of psychological intervention should subscribe to and follow the ethics codes and standards of their professions. For members of the American Psychological Association and the Canadian Psychological Association, the current version of the ethics code is the American Psychological Association's Ethical Principles of Psychologists (1981). An additional policy statement of the American Psychological Association of relevance to psychological interventions is the Specialty Guidelines for the Delivery of Services (1981).

The report by the commission (Stolz and associates, 1978) considered the following issues across a number of different types of settings in which behavior modification is applied:

1. Identification of the client
2. Definition of the problem and selection of the goals
3. Selection of the intervention method
4. Accountability
5. Evaluation of the quality of the psychologist and the intervention
6. Record keeping and confidentiality
7. Protection of the client's rights
8. Assessment of the place of research in the therapeutic setting

Table 28-1 Ethical Issues for Human Services*

The focus of this statement is on critical issues of central importance to human services. The statement is not a list of prescriptions and
proscriptions.

On each of the issues described, ideal interventions would have
maximum involvement by the person whose behavior is to be changed,
and the fullest possible consideration of societal pressures on that person, the therapist, and the therapist's employer. It is recognized that the
practicalities of actual settings sometimes require exceptions and that
there certainly are occasions when exceptions can be consistent with
ethical practice.

In the list of issues, the term "client" is used to describe the
person whose behavior is to be changed; "therapist" is used to describe the professional in charge of the intervention; "treatment" and
"problem," although used in the singular, refer to any and all treatments and problems being formulated with this checklist. The issues are
formulated so as to be relevant across as many settings and populations
as possible. Thus, they need to be qualified when someone other than
the person whose behavior is to be changed is paying the therapist, or
when that person's competence or the voluntary nature of that person's
consent is questioned. For example, if the therapist has found that the
client does not understand the goals or methods being considered, the
therapist should substitute the client's guardian or other responsible person for "client," when reviewing the issues listed.

A Have the goals of treatment been adequately considered?
  1 To ensure that the goals are explicit, are they written?
  2 Has the client's understanding of the goals been assured by having the client restate them orally or in writing?
  3 Have the therapist and client agreed on the goals of therapy?
  4 Will serving the client's interests be contrary to the interests of
other persons?
  5 Will serving the client's immediate interests be contrary to the
client's long term interest?
B Has the choice of treatment methods been adequately considered?
  1 Does the published literature show the procedure to be the best
one available for that problem?
  2 If no literature exists regarding the treatment method, is the
method consistent with generally accepted practice?
  3 Has the client been told of alternative procedures that might be
preferred by the client on the basis of significant differences in
discomfort, treatment time, cost, or degree of demonstrated
effectiveness?
  4 If a treatment procedure is publicly, legally, or professionally controversial, has formal professional consultation been obtained, has
the reaction of the affected segment of the public been adequately considered, and have the alternative treatment methods been
more closely reexamined and reconsidered?
C Is the client's participation voluntary?
  1 Have possible sources of coercion on the client's participation
been considered?

Table 28-1 (Cont.)   Ethical Issues for Human Services*

    2 If treatment is legally mandated, has the available range of treatments and therapists been offered?

    3 Can the client withdraw from treatment without a penalty or financial loss that exceeds actual clinical costs?

D When another person or an agency is empowered to arrange for therapy, have the interests of the subordinated client been sufficiently considered?

    1 Has the subordinated client been informed of the treatment objectives and participated in the choice of treatment procedures?

    2 Where the subordinated client's competence to decide is limited, have the client as well as the guardian participated in the treatment discussions to the extent that the client's abilities permit?

    3 If the interests of the subordinated person and the superordinate persons or agency conflict, have attempts been made to reduce the conflict by dealing with both interests?

E Has the adequacy of treatment been evaluated?

    1 Have quantitative measures of the problem and its progress been obtained?

    2 Have the measures of the problem and its progress been made available to the client during treatment?

F Has the confidentiality of the treatment relationship been protected?

    1 Has the client been told who has access to the records?

    2 Are records available only to authorized persons?

G Does the therapist refer the clients to other therapists when necessary?

    1 If treatment is unsuccessful, is the client referred to other therapists?

    2 Has the client been told that if dissatisfied with the treatment, referral will be made?

H Is the therapist qualified to provide treatment?

    1 Has the therapist had training or experience in treating problems like the client's?

    2 If deficits exist in the therapist's qualifications, has the client been informed?

    3 If the therapist is not adequately qualified, is the client referred to other therapists, or has supervision by a qualified therapist been provided? Is the client informed of the supervisory relation?

    4 If the treatment is administered by mediators, have the mediators been adequately supervised by a qualified therapist?

*Adopted May 22, 1977 by the board of directors of the Association for Advancement of Behavior Therapy. This statement on Ethical Issues for Human Services was taken from the Membership Directory of the Association For Advancement of Behavior Therapy and is reprinted by permission of the association.

The settings that were considered were outpatient settings, institutions, schools, prisons, and society. We describe some of the commission's major points briefly with regard to these issues. In addition, although the commission did not do so, we indicate briefly how these issues pertain to the survival of our culture—since, as noted, this is the criterion against which our ethical standards will ultimately be judged.

1. IDENTIFICATION OF THE CLIENT

The identification of the client is usually quite obvious in outpatient settings, since the person who pays for the service is also the person whose behavior is to be modified. In other settings, such as prisons or mental hospitals, this is typically not the case. In those settings, behavior modifiers might be hired by the institutions to control the behavior of the inmates. Therefore the type of oppression described at the beginning of this chapter could occur. One possible destructive outcome of this is rebellion. For example, as we have seen in many news reports, oppressive control in prisons generates rebellions that are quite costly to society. In addition, it is most unlikely that the type of control that generates such rebellions will facilitate socially constructive behavior in prisoners after they are released from prison. Oppressive control in schools usually leads to somewhat more subtle forms of rebellion, such as vandalism, truancy, and dropping out, but they are still very costly to society.

While institutionalized individuals such as mental patients, geriatric patients, and severely retarded people usually lack the means to rebel, oppressive treatment of these people is also harmful to the culture. The major reason for this is that a culture that treats some of its members badly is likely, through the process of generalization, to treat other members badly. This point has been aptly expressed by a liberal politician who noted that the ultimate test of a society is how it treats those in the dawning of life, those in the twilight of life, and those in the shadows of life (children, the aged, and the severely handicapped, respectively). A culture that does not treat these groups very well may flourish in the short run, but its long-run chances for survival are likely to be quite weak.

Everything we know and have taught about behavior modification in this book seems to indicate that simply resolving to treat various individuals and groups in ethical ways is not a sufficient guarantee that they will be so treated. Contingencies of reinforcement must be arranged to make this happen. One way in which to arrange such contingencies is through *countercontrol*. Countercontrol is "the reciprocal of control: It is the influence the controllee has on the controller by virtue of access to suitable reinforcers" (Stolz and associates, 1978, p. 19).

It is generally agreed that an important form of countercontrol is that in which the client (defined as the person whose behavior is being controlled) is an active participant in both the design and the implementation of the behavior modification program. In situations in which this is not possible (cases of severe retardation), competent impartial third parties (ombudspersons, representatives of the community) who can act on behalf of the client should be involved in crucial decisions concerning the program design and implementation.

2. DEFINITION OF THE PROBLEM AND SELECTION OF THE GOALS

Defining the problem and selecting the goals are dependent on the values of the individuals involved. For example, some people consider homosexual tendencies to be a problem that should be eliminated; others do not. It is therefore important that these values be specified clearly. In the words of the commission, "In all settings, ethical protection will be enhanced if all those involved specify, to the extent possible, those reinforcers that may be functioning to control their own behavior. The professional and the professional's employer might, for example, specify their systems of values and attitudes relating to the client's problem" (Stolz and associates, p. 22). Ideally, the values on which the goals are based should be consistent with the long-term good of society. Strangely, however, the commission stated that "in practice there is no way to determine either what the long-term good of society is or what impact any immediate decision will have in the long run" (p. 22). This statement has been criticized by Krohn-Bonem and Bonem (1980), who note that it is inconsistent with practices in other areas of applied science, such as agriculture and medicine, where estimates of the long-term good of society play an important role in the decisions that are made. Although the future cannot be predicted with absolute certainty, this should not prevent us from

Note 3   using the best information available to attempt to influence it favorably.[3]

3. SELECTION OF THE INTERVENTION METHOD

Behavior modifiers should use the most effective, empirically validated methods with the least discomfort and least harmful side effects. To this end, it is generally agreed that behavior modifiers should use positive reinforcement rather than aversive techniques wherever possible. It is also generally agreed that behavior modifiers should use the least intrusive and restrictive interventions possible. However, there is a problem in defining the terms "intrusive" and "restrictive."

Note 4   To the extent that they mean "aversive," this recommendation simply repeats what has already been said.[4] Sometimes, however, these terms are said to refer to the amount of control in a situation, so that a more intrusive and restrictive situation involves more control than does a less intrusive or restrictive situation. As we have indicated already, however, behavior is always controlled. The issue may be that of minimizing artificial or contrived control in favor of control by natural contingencies of reinforcement. The desirability of this approach was stressed in Chapter 12 and elsewhere in this text.

4. ACCOUNTABILITY

Accountability refers to the fact that the professional must be held responsible for producing satisfactory results. The first step in being accountable is for the behavior modifier to describe clearly his or her credentials and qualifications to the client. Accountability, after a program has been initiated, has been emphasized throughout this text wherever we have discussed the importance of keeping accurate data (for example, see Chapter 18), for this is the only way in which one can tell that satisfactory results are indeed being obtained. Recording of data should not be limited to the target behavior; one should also take data on other relevant behaviors to ensure that no undesirable side effects are being produced by the treatment procedures. Feedback from individuals concerned directly with the welfare of the client should also be obtained regarding the effectiveness of the program. The establishment of impartial ethical review committees that formally ensure the accountability of behavior modifiers for their programs is also an important safeguard (see Krapfl, 1975). Such committees might function most effectively if they are appointed by, and report to, a public organization that is concerned with the welfare of the clients. Finally, as described in Chapter 21, behavior modifiers are encouraged to sign treatment contracts with their clients as a way of ensuring accountability.

5. THE QUALITY OF THE PSYCHOLOGIST AND THE INTERVENTION

Although behavior modifiers and behavior therapists have several professional organizations, only the Association for Behavior Analysis (ABA) has taken steps to develop formal, standardized procedures for evaluating a person's competence to practice behavior modification. We recommend that if you are carrying out a behavior modification project, you should obtain supervision from a recognized professional in the field if you are not a recognized professional. Probably the most widely recognized criterion of professional status is membership in the local state or provincial psychological (or other appropriate professional) association. In addition, one should always ensure that the procedures being used are consistent with the most up-to-date literature in the recognized behavior modification and behavior therapy journals.

6. RECORD KEEPING AND CONFIDENTIALITY

While behavior modifiers should always take good records, they should exercise utmost discretion in whom they permit to see those records to protect the client from undue control. Only those who are concerned directly with the progress of the client should have access to the client's records. Of course, the client should have access to his or her own records, if for no other reason than the value that such feedback has in furthering the goals of the program.

7. PROTECTION OF THE CLIENT'S RIGHTS

There is a good deal of overlap between this issue and issue 1. Rights are rules that increase the reinforcers available to an individual in a society and decrease potential aversive stimuli. Taking rights away from individuals, or giving rights to some (such as therapists) at the expense of others (such as clients), may decrease the long-range chances of a society's survival. One way in which to help ensure that client's rights are protected is through ethical review committees composed of professionals and members of the community who evaluate the ethics of proposed programs. Another is to stipulate that no program is to be carried out on a client who has not given informed consent (that is, consent based on knowledge of the procedures to be used and their probable effects) to participate in that program. There are, however, problems with the concept of "informed consent"; namely, it involves verbal behavior that, like other behavior, is under the control of the environment. Hence it may be manipulated in a particular fashion that may not be in the best interests of the client. The stipulation of informed consent probably provides only a partial check on the ethics of a program. In addition, there are many individuals for whom the stipulation is inapplicable (for example, severely retarded individuals).

8. THE PLACE OF RESEARCH IN THERAPEUTIC SETTINGS

As we have emphasized throughout this book, behavior modification and research go hand in hand. It is important and highly ethical to conduct research to ensure that every client is receiving the most effective treatment possible. One must be very careful in conducting this research, however, so as not to interfere with a client's progress. For example, if it is clear that a client is benefiting from a particular program, a long reversal phase would not be appropriate. Even if it is not completely clear that the client is benefiting from the program, some design other than an ABA design (a multiple-baseline or a multi-element design) might be more appropriate for testing the effectiveness of the program (see Chapter 20).

CONCLUSIONS

Behavior modification has great potential to be used for the good of society and perhaps may even be used to eliminate the oppression of some humans by others that has characterized all societies from the dawn of recorded history to the present.

One important responsibility of all behavior modifiers is to help educate the general public with respect to behavior modification so that they can deal with it more effectively. An informed public is probably the best safeguard against possible abuses of behavior modification. All behavior modification programs should be open to public scrutiny. In this regard, it is ironic that some of the aspects of behavior modification that have been most responsible for public alarm over behavior modification are those that provide the surest safeguards against its misuse. Behavior modification necessarily implies the specification of target behaviors and the methods to be used in establishing those behaviors. This makes it relatively easy to examine the goals and methods of any program and to question and criticize them.

Another important responsibility of behavior modifiers is to develop ethical safeguards for behavior modification to ensure that it is always used wisely and humanely and does not become a new tool in the oppression that has thus far characterized the human species. Of all the safeguards discussed, the most fundamental is countercontrol.

There are several ways in which to incorporate countercontrol into a behavior modification program. These include frequent opportunities for clients to discuss and negotiate aspects of the program with the behavior modifiers; having clients or their representatives participate fully in programming decisions; accepting feedback on the effectiveness of the program from individuals who are concerned directly with the welfare of the client; and the signing of a client-therapist contract that outlines clearly the objectives and methods of treatment, the framework for the service to be provided, and contingencies for remuneration that may be forthcoming to the therapist (as described in Chapter 21). Perhaps the best way for behavior modifiers to help develop effective countercontrol throughout society is to spread their skills as widely as possible. It should be rather difficult to use behavioral science to the disadvantage of any group whose members are well versed in the principles and tactics of behavior modification.

STUDY QUESTIONS

1. Describe in behavioral terms how the history of civilization is a story of the continuous abuse of power. From your knowledge of history or current events, give an example of this abuse.
2. From your knowledge of history or current events, give an example of what often happens when the reinforcements occurring to one group in a society

fall below a certain critical level relative to the reinforcements occurring to another group in that society.

3. From a behavioral point of view, how might we account for constitutions, bills of rights, and related political documents of modern states?

4. Explain why we tend to react negatively to all overt attempts to control our behavior.

5. Why and how do people who would control our behavior disguise their aims? Give an example of this that is not in the text.

6. State two propositions on which behavior modification is based.

7. Discuss whether behavior modifiers should tone down their language so as not to use terms (such as "control") that frighten many people.

8. Why is extreme wariness a healthy reaction to any new, far-reaching development in science or technology? Cite and discuss an example of this.

9. Why is the doctrine of free will not a valid criticism of attempts to develop a technology of behavior?

10. Explain why all social help professions are involved in the control of behavior, whether or not their practitioners realize it. Give an example.

11. Discuss the relative merits of planning versus not planning for behavior change.

12. Discuss three ethical arguments against the methods of behavior modification and the validity of these arguments.

13. What does the term "ethics" mean from a behavioral point of view?

14. Describe how ethics has evolved as a part of our culture.

15. What was a primary conclusion of the comprehensive report by Stolz and associates on the ethical issues involved in behavior modification?

16. Discuss countercontrol. Why is it important?

17. Is it practical to suggest that the goals of behavior modification programs should be consistent with the long-term good of society? Discuss.

18. What should be the characteristics of intervention methods used by behavior modifiers?

19. Discuss three possible meanings of "intrusive" and "restrictive" interventions.

20. Discuss how behavior modifiers can avoid using "intrusive" and "restrictive" interventions.

21. Discuss three ways in which behavior modifiers can ensure their accountability.

22. Discuss some steps that might be taken to help ensure the quality of behavioral interventions.

23. How can clients rights be protected in behavior therapy?

24. Discuss ways in which countercontrol might be incorporated into behavior modification programs.

25. Briefly explain why it should be rather difficult to use behavior modification to the detriment of any group whose members are well versed in the principles and tactics of behavior modification.

PRACTICE EXERCISE _____

Make a fairly detailed list of ethical guidelines that behavior modifiers should follow.

EXTENDED DISCUSSION AND NOTES

1. Skinner (1971) argued that we can trace this attitude, at least in part, to the influence of eighteenth-century revolutionaries and social reformers. To counteract the aversive control utilized by tyrants, these activists developed the concept of "freedom." It was, said Skinner, a very worthwhile concept in its time, for it helped to spur people to break away from aversive forms of control. Now, however, we have moved into an era in which positive reinforcement is a more predominant means of control (and will perhaps become increasingly so with the growth of behavior modification). The concept of "freedom" has therefore outlived its social usefulness. Indeed, it is harmful, in that it tends to prevent us from seeing how our behavior is controlled by positive reinforcement. It also tends to impede the development of a behavioral technology that can help us to solve many of civilization's current problems. Moreover, it encourages the view that some people deserve more "dignity" than others because of their achievements, whereas in actuality one's achievements (or failures to achieve) are due to one's conditioning history and genetic predispositions. Hence, the title of Skinner's book: *Beyond Freedom and Dignity* (1971).

2. In fact, in controlled clinical trials, behavior therapists have been rated by observers as significantly more empathic and supportive than nonbehavioral clinicians (Greenwald and others, 1981; Sloan and others, 1975). Moreover, in the absence of a warm and empathic relationship, clients simply will resist complying with the requests by behavior therapists for conducting various self-monitoring and homework assignments (Hersen, 1983; Martin & Worthington, 1982; Messer & Winokur, 1984).

3. Prilleltensky (1989, 1990) has argued that psychology as a whole, including behavior modification, has too readily accepted and promoted the status quo rather than questioning whether the status quo is really always best for human welfare. An example from the early days of behavior modification would be that of teaching children in school to sit quietly at their desks, as though there were some intrinsic merit in this behavior. Perhaps it is the rule that children in school should always be seated quietly at their desks that should be changed rather than the children. Prilleltensky argues that we should study how the status quo comes to be accepted and how we can redirect our efforts to changing it, rather than our clients, when this is more consistent with human welfare.

4. Brazier and MacDonald (1981) have described a continuum of procedures ranging from positive to negative, with placement of a procedure on the continuum based on subjective notions of degree of aversiveness. Their model, presented in Figure 28–1, lists the procedures and the level of authority required for implementing these procedures. Currently being employed at a community behavioral services program in Alberta involving residential and day programs for developmentally handicapped people, the model represents a potentially useful strategy for ensuring ethical and effective decision making in behavioral programming.

STUDY QUESTIONS ON NOTES

1. Discuss Skinner's view that we must go "beyond freedom and dignity" if civilization is to solve some of its most difficult problems.

LEAST (+)		MOST (−)
Procedures		
Reinforcement		
Modeling		
Verbal instructions		
Physical assistance		
Reinforced practice		
	Extinction	
	Social disapproval	
	Overcorrection	
	Time-out (contingent observation)	
	Response cost	
	Required relaxation	
	Required exercise	
	Physical restraint	
		Time-out (seclusion)
		Mechanical restraint
		Food deprivation
		Noxious chemicals
		Electric shock
Level of Authority		
Client	Client	Client
Front-line supervisor	Front-line supervisor	Front-line supervisor
	Unit supervisor	Unit supervisor
		Agency director
		Physician

*This model for selecting procedures appeared in an article on ethical decision making by Brazier and MacDonald (1981), and is reprinted with the permission of the authors, and the publisher of *Journal of Practical Approaches to Developmental Handicap.*

FIGURE 28–1   Procedures ranging from "least" to "most" restrictive and the level of authority required for their use.*

2. Do the data support the notion that behavior modifiers are "cold and mechanical" in their treatment of clients? Explain.

3. Describe two examples in which behavior modification might be used inappropriately, in your opinion, to support the status quo. Why do you think this use of behavior modification would be inappropriate?

4. Describe Brazier and MacDonald's procedure for ensuring ethical and effective decision making in behavioral programming.

References

AAMR. Revises Policy on Aversive Procedures. (1990). *AAMR News and Notes, 3(4)*, 5.

ACKER, L. E., GOLDWATER, B. C., & AGNEW, J. L. (1990). Sidney Slug: A computer simulation for teaching shaping without a laboratory animal. *Teaching of Psychology, 17*(2), 130–132.

ADER, R., & COHEN, N. (1982). Behaviorally conditioned immunosuppression and murine systemic lupis erythematosus. *Science, 215*, 1534–1536.

ADER, R., & COHEN, N. (1985). CNS-immune system interactions: Conditioning phenomena. *Behavioral and Brain Sciences, 8*, 379–426.

AGATHON, M. (1982). Behavior therapy in France, 1976–1981. *Journal of Behavior Therapy and Experimental Psychiatry, 13*, 271–277.

AGRAS, W. S. (1987). Presidential address: Where do we go from here? *Behavior Therapy, 18*, 203–217.

AGRAS, W. S., TAYLOR, C. B., FELDMAN, D. E., LOSCH, M., & BURNETT, K. F. (1990). Developing computer-assisted therapy for the treatment of obesity. *Behavior Therapy, 21*, 99–109.

AIRAPETYANTZ, E., & BYKOV, D. (1966). Physiological experiments and the psychology of the subconscious. In T. Verhave (Ed.), *The Experimental Analysis of Behavior* (pp. 140–157). New York: Appleton-Century-Crofts.

ALBERTO, P. A., & TROUTMAN, A. C. (1990). *Applied behavior analysis for teachers: Influencing student performance*, 3rd ed. Columbus, OH: Charles E. Merrill.

ARDILA, R. (1978). Behavior modification in Latin America. In M. Hersen, R. M. Eisler, & P. M. Miller (Eds.), *Progress in behavior modification*, Vol. 6 (pp. 124–142). New York: Academic Press.

ARDILA, R. (1982). International developments in behavior therapy in Latin America. *Journal of Behavior Therapy and Experimental Psychiatry, 13*, 15–20.

ARRICK, C. M., VOSS, J., & RIMM, D. C. (1981). The relative efficacy of thought-stopping and covert assertion. *Behaviour Research and Therapy, 19*, 17–24.

AUBUCHON, P., HABER, J. D., & ADAMS, H. E. (1985). Can migraine headaches be modified by operant pain techniques? *Journal of Behavior Therapy and Experimental Psychiatry, 16*, 261–263.

AXELROD, S., & APSCHE, J. (Eds.). (1983). *The effects of punishment on human behavior.* New York: Academic Press.

AXELROD, S., HALL, R. V., WEIS, L. & ROHRER, S. (1974). Use of self-imposed contingencies to reduce the frequency of smoking behavior. In M. J. Mahoney & C. E. Thoresen (Eds.), *Self-control: Power to the person* (pp. 77–85). Monterey, CA: Brooks/Cole.

AYLLON, T., & AZRIN, N. H. (1968a). Reinforcer sampling: A technique for increasing the behavior of mental patients. *Journal of Applied Behavior Analysis, 1*, 13–20.

AYLLON, T., & AZRIN, N. H. (1968b). *The token economy: A motivational system for therapy and rehabilitation.* New York: Appleton-Century-Crofts.

AYLLON, T., & MICHAEL, J. (1959). The psychiatric nurse as a behavioral engineer. *Journal of the Experimental Analysis of Behavior, 2*, 323–334.

AYLLON, T., MILAN, M. A.., ROBERTS, M. D., & McKEE, M. (1979). *Correctional rehabilitation and management: A psychological approach.* New York: John Wiley.

AZRIN, N. H. (1967). Pain and aggression. *Psychology Today, 1*(1), 27–33.

AZRIN, N. H. (1976). Improvements in the community-reinforcement approach to alcoholism. *Behaviour Research and Therapy, 14*, 339–348.

AZRIN, N. H., and BESALEL, V. A. (1980). *How to use over-correction.* Lawrence, KS: H and H Enterprises.

AZRIN, N. H. & FOXX, R. M. (1971). A rapid method of toilet training the institutionalized retarded. *Journal of Applied Behavior Analysis, 4*, 89–99.

AZRIN, N. H., & FOXX, R. M. (1974). *Toilet training in less than a day.* Champaign, IL: Research Press.

AZRIN, N. H., & HOLZ, W. C. (1966). Punishment. In W. K. Honig (Ed.), *Operant behavior: Areas of research and application* (pp. 380–447). New York: Appleton-Century-Crofts.

AZRIN, N. H., & LINDSLEY, O. R. (1956). The reinforcement of cooperation between children. *Journal of Abnormal and Social Psychology, 52*, 100–102.

AZRIN, N. H., NUNN, R. G., (1973). Habit reversal: A method of eliminating nervous habits and tics. *Behaviour Research and Therapy, 11*, 619–628.

AZRIN, N. H., & NUNN, R. G., (1977). *Habit control in a day.* New York: Simon & Schuster.

AZRIN, N. H., NUNN, R. G., & FRANTZ, S. E. (1980). Habit reversal vs. negative practice treatment of nervous tics. *Behavior Therapy, 11*, 169–178.

AZRIN, N. H., SISSON, R. W., MEYERS, R., & GODLEY, N. (1982). Alcoholism treatment by disulfiram and community reinforcement therapy. *Journal of Behavior Therapy and Experimental Psychiatry, 13(2)*, 105–112.

AZRIN, N. H., & WESOLOWSKI, M. D. (1975). The use of positive practice to eliminate persistent floor sprawling by profoundly retarded persons. *Behavior Therapy, 6*, 627–631.

BAER, D. M. (1984). Does research on self-control need more control? *Analysis and Intervention in Developmental Disabilities, 4*, 211–218.

BAER, D. M., PETERSON, R. F., & SHERMAN, J. A. (1967). The development of imitation by reinforcing behavioral similarity to a model. *Journal of the Experimental Analysis of Behavior, 10*, 405–416.

BAER, D. M., & WOLF, M. M. (1970). The entry into natural communities of reinforcement. In R. Ulrich, T. Stachnik, & J. Mabry (Eds.), *Control of human behavior,* Vol. 2 (pp. 319–324). Glenview, IL: Scott, Foresman.

BAER, D. M., WOLF, M. M., & RISLEY, T. R. (1968). Some current dimensions of applied behavior analysis. *Journal of Applied Behavior Analysis, 1*, 91–97.

BAER, D. M., WOLF, M. M., & RISLEY, T. R. (1987). Some still current dimensions of applied behavior analysis. *Journal of Applied Behavior Analysis, 20*, 313–329.

BAILEY, J. S., TIMBERS, G. D., PHILLIPS, E. L., & WOLF, M. M. (1971). Modification of articulation errors of pre-delinquents by their peers. *Journal of Applied Behaviour Analysis, 3*, 265–281.

BAILEY, J. S., WOLF, M. M., & PHILLIPS, E. L. (1970). Home-based reinforcement and the modification of pre-delinquents' classroom behavior. *Journal of Applied Behavior Analysis, 3*, 223–233.

BALDWIN, J. D., & BALDWIN, J. I. (1986). *Behavior principles in everyday life*, 2nd ed. Englewood Cliffs, NJ: Prentice-Hall.

BANDURA, A. (1965). Influence of models' reinforcement contingencies in the acquisition of imitative responses. *Journal of Personality and Social Psychology, 1*, 589–595.

BANDURA, A. (1969). *Principles of behavior modification*. New York: Holt, Rinehart & Winston.

BANDURA, A. (1977). *Social learning theory*. Englewood Cliffs, NJ: Prentice-Hall.

BANDURA, A. (1982). Self-efficacy mechanism in human agency. *American Psychologist, 37*, 122–147.

BANDURA, A. (1986). *Social foundations of thought and action: A social-cognitive theory.* Englewood Cliffs, NJ: Prentice-Hall.

BANDURA, A., & WALTERS, R. H. (1963). *Social learning and personality development.* New York: Holt, Rinehart & Winston.

BARLOW, D. H. (1980). Behavior therapy: The next decade. *Behavior Therapy, 11*, 315–328.

Barlow, D. H. (Ed.). (1985). *Clinical handbook of psychological disorders: A step-by-step treatment manual.* New York: Guilford.

BARLOW, D. H., & HAYES, S. C. (1979). Alternating treatment design: One strategy for comparing the effects of two treatments in a single subject. *Journal of Applied Behavior Analysis, 2*, 199–210.

BARLOW, D. H., HAYES, S. C., & NELSON, R. O. (1984). *The scientist practitioner: Research and accountability in clinical and educational settings.* New York: Pergamon.

BARLOW, D. H., & HERSEN, M. (1984). *Single-case experimental design: Strategies for studying behavior change*, 2nd ed. New York: Pergamon.

BARLOW, D. H., LEITENBERG, H., AGRAS, W. S., & WINCZE, J. P. (1969). The transfer gap in systematic desensitization: An analogue study. *Behaviour Research and Therapy, 7*, 191–197.

BARON, A., & GALIZIO, M. (1983). Instructional control of human operant behavior. *Psychological Record, 33*, 495–520.

BARONE, D. F. (1982). Instigating additional self-modification projects after a personal adjustment course. *Teaching of Psychology, 9*, 111.

BARRERA, M., & GLASGOW, R. (1976). Design and evaluation of a personalized instruction course in behavioral self-control. *Teaching of Psychology, 3*, 81–83.

BECK, A. T. (1976). *Cognitive therapy and the emotional disorders.* New York: International Universities Press.

BECK, A. T. (1988). *Love is never enough: How couples can overcome misunderstandings, resolve conflicts, and solve relationship problems through cognitive therapy.* New York: Harper & Row.

BECK, A. T., EMERY, G., & GREENBERG, R. L. (1985). *Anxiety disorders and phobias: A cognitive perspective.* New York: Basic Books.

BECK, A. T., RUSH, J., SHAW, B., & EMERY, G. (1979). *Cognitive therapy of depression.* New York: Guilford.

BECKER, W. C. (1986). *Applied psychology for teachers: A behavioral-cognitive approach.* Chicago: Science Research Associates, Inc.

BEECH, H. R., & VAUGHN, M. (1978). *Behavioral treatment of obsessional states.* New York: John Wiley.

BELCASTRO, F. P. (1985). Gifted students and behavior modification. *Behavior Modification, 9*, 155–164.

BELLACK, A. S. (1986). Schizophrenia: Behavior therapy's forgotten child. *Behavior Therapy, 17*, 199–214.

BELLACK, A. S., & HERSEN, M.   (1978). Chronic psychiatric patients: Social skills training. In M. Hersen & A. S. Bellack (Eds.), *Behavior therapy in the psychiatric setting* (pp. 167–195). Baltimore: William & Wilkins.

BELLACK, A. S., & HERSEN, M.   (1988). *Behavioral assessment: A practical handbook*, 3rd ed. New York: Pergamon.

BELLACK, A. S., TURNER, S. M., HERSEN, M., & LUBER, R. F.   (1984). An examination of the efficacy of social skills training for chronic schizophrenic patients. *Hospital and Community Psychiatry, 35*, 1023–1028.

BELLAMY, G. T., HORNER, R. H., & INMAN, D. P.   (1979). *Vocational habilitation of severely retarded adults: A direct service technology.* Baltimore: University Park Press.

BENTALL, R. P., LOWE, C. F., & BEASTY, A.   (1985). The role of verbal behavior in human learning. II: Developmental differences. *Journal of the Experimental Analysis of Behavior, 47*, 165–181.

BERNSTEIN, L., BERNSTEIN, R. S., & DANA, R. H.   (1974). *Interviewing: A guide for health professionals*, 2nd ed. New York: Appleton-Century-Crofts.

BIJOU, S. W., & BAER, D. M.   (1961). *Child development: A systematic and empirical theory*, Vol. 1. New York: Appleton-Century-Crofts.

BIRNBRAUER, J. S., BIJOU, S. W., WOLF, M. M., & KIDDER, J. D.   (1965). Programmed instruction in the classroom. In L. P. Ullmann & L. Krasner (Eds.), *Case studies in behavior modification* (pp. 358–363). New York: Holt, Rinehart & Winston.

BLAKEY, R., & BAKER, R.   (1980). An exposure approach to alcohol abuse. *Behaviour Research and Therapy, 18*, 319–326.

BLANCK, G.   (1983). *Behavior therapy in Argentina.* AAPC Ediciones, Buenos Aires.

BLECHMAN, E. A., & BROWNELL K.(Eds.).   (1989). *Handbook of behavioral medicine for women.* New York: Pergamon.

BLIMKE, J., GOWAN, G., PATTERSON, P., & WOOD, N.   (1984). Sport and psychology: What ethics suggest about practice. *Sports Science Periodical on Research and Technology in Sport*, Ottawa, Ontario: Coaching Association of Canada.

BORKOVEC, T. D., WILKINSON, L., FOLENSBEE, R., & LERMAN, C.   (1983). Stimulus control applications to the treatment of worry. *Behaviour Research and Therapy, 21*, 247–251.

BORNSTEIN, P. H., & BORNSTEIN, M. T.   (1986). *Marital therapy: A behavioral-communications approach.* New York: Pergamon.

BOSTOW, D. E., & BAILEY, J. B.   (1969). Modification of severe disruptive and aggressive behavior using brief timeout and reinforcement procedures. *Journal of Applied Behavior Analysis, 2*, 31–37.

BOUDEWYNS, P. A., FRY, T. J., & NIGHTINGALE, E. J.   (1986). Token economy programs in VA medical centers: Where are they today? *The Behavior Therapist, 6*, 126–127.

BRANTNER, J. P., & DOHERTY, M. A.   (1983). A review of time-out: A conceptual and methodological analysis. In S. Axelrod and J. Apsche (Eds.), *The effects of punishment on human behavior* (pp. 87–132). New York: Academic Press.

BRAY, G. A.   (1976). *The obese patient.* Philadelphia: Saunders.

BRAZIER, B., & MACDONALD, L.   (1981). Ethical decision-making in behavioral programming: A continuum of procedures. *Journal of Practical Approaches to Developmental Handicap, 4*(3), 11–13.

BREGER, L., and MCGAUGH, J. L.   (1965). Critique and reformulation of "learning theory" approaches to psychotherapy and neurosis. *Psychological Bulletin, 63*, 338–358.

BRIGHAM, T. A.   (1980). Self-control re-visited: Or why doesn't anyone actually read Skinner anymore? *The Behavior Analyst, 3*, 25–33.

BRIGHAM, T. A.   (1982). Self-management: A radical behavioral perspective. In P. Karoly & F. H. Kanfer (Eds.), *Self-management and behavior change: From theory to practice.* New York: Pergamon.

BRIGHAM, T. A. (1989a). *Managing everyday problems.* New York: Guilford.

BRIGHAM, T. A. (1989b). *Self-management for adolescents: A skills training program.* New York: Guilford.

BROWNELL, K. D. (1981). Report on international behavior therapy organizations. *The Behavior Therapist, 4,* 9–13.

BROWNELL, K. D., & FOREYT, J. P. (1985). Obesity. In D. H. Barlow (Ed.), *Clinical handbook of psychological disorders: A step-by-step treatment manual* (pp. 299–343). New York: Guilford.

CALHOUN, J. F. (1977). *Abnormal psychology: Current perspectives,* 2nd ed., (p. 381). New York: Random House.

CAMPBELL, D. T., & STANLEY, J. C. (1963). Experimental and quasi-experimental designs for research and teaching. In N. L. Gage (Ed.), *Handbook of research on teaching* (pp. 171–246). Chicago: Rand McNally.

CATALDO, M. F., & COATES, T. J.(Eds.). (1986). *Health and industry: A behavioral medicine perspective.* New York: John Wiley.

CATANIA, A. C. (1975). The myth of self-reinforcement. *Behaviorism, 3,* 192–199.

CATANIA, A. C. (1976). Self-reinforcement revisited. *Behaviorism, 4,* 157–162.

CATANIA, A. C., MATTHEWS, B. A., & SHIMOFF, E. (1982). Instructed versus shaped human verbal behavior: Interactions with nonverbal responding. *Journal of the Experimental Analysis of Behavior, 38,* 233–248.

CAUDILL, B. D., & LIPSCOME, T. R. (1980). Modelling influences on alcoholics' rates of alcohol consumption. *Journal of Applied Behavior Analysis, 13,* 355–365.

CAUTELA, J. R. (1966). Treatment of compulsive behavior by covert desensitization. *Psychological Record, 16,* 33–41.

CAUTELA, J. R. (1977). *Behavior analysis forms for clinical intervention.* Champaign, IL: Research Press.

CAUTELA, J. R. (1981). *Behavior analysis forms for clinical intervention,* Vol. 2. Champaign, IL: Research Press.

CAUTELA, J. R., & GRODEN, J. (1978). *Relaxation: A comprehensive manual for adults, children, and children with special needs.* Champaign, IL: Research Press.

CAUTELA, J. R., & KEARNEY, A. (1986). *The covert conditioning handbook.* New York: Springer.

CAUTELA, J. R., & KEARNEY, A. J. (1990). Behavior analysis, cognitive therapy, and covert conditioning. *Journal of Behavior Therapy and Experimental Psychiatry, 21,* 83–90.

CAUTELA, J. R., & UPPER, D. E. (1975). The process of individual behavior therapy. In M. Hersen, R. M. Eisler, & P. M. Miller (Eds.), *Progress in behavior modification,* Vol. 1. New York: Academic Press.

CAUTELA, J. R., & WISOCKI, P. A. (1977). The thought stopping procedure: Description, application, and learning theory interpretations. *The Psychological Record, 2,* 255–264.

CHOMSKY, N. A. (1959). A review of B. F. Skinner's Verbal Behavior, *Language, 35,* 26–58.

CHUNG, S. H. (1965). Effects of delayed reinforcement in a concurrent situation. *Journal of the Experimental Analysis of Behavior, 8,* 439–444.

CIAPANI, E. (1985). An analysis of a partial task training strategy for profoundly retarded institutionalized clients. *Journal of Behavior Therapy and Experimental Psychiatry, 16,* 49–55.

CIMINERO, A. R. (1977). Behavioral assessment: An overview. In A. R. Ciminero, K. S. Calhoun, & H. E. Adams (Eds.), *Handbook of behavioral assessment* (pp. 3–13). New York: John Wiley.

CIPANI, E. (Ed.). (1989). *The treatment of severe behavior disorders: Behavior analysis approaches.* Washington, DC: American Association on Mental Retardation.

COHEN, R., DeJAMES, P., NOCERA, B., & RAMBERGER, M. (1980). Application of a simple self-instruction procedure on adult exercise and studying: Two case reports. *Psychological Reports, 46,* 443–451.

COOPER, J., & AXSOM, D. (1982). Effort justification in psychotherapy. In G. Weary & H. L. Mirels (Eds.), *Integrations of clinical and social psychology* (pp. 214–230). New York: Oxford University Press.

COOPER, J. E., GELDER, M. G., & MARKS. I. M. (1965). Results of behavior therapy in 77 psychiatric patients. *British Medical Journal, 1,* 1222–1225.

CORMIER, W. H., & CORMIER, L. S. (1979). *Interviewing strategies for helpers: A guide to assessment, treatment and evaluation.* Monterey, CA: Brooks/Cole.

CORTE, H. E., WOLF, M. M., & LOCKE, B. J. (1971). A comparison of procedures for eliminating self-injurious behavior of retarded adolescents. *Journal of Applied Behavior Analysis, 4,* 201–213.

CRAIGHEAD, W. E., KAZDIN, A. E., & MAHONEY, M. J. (1980). *Behavior modification: Principles, issues, and applications.* Boston: Houghton Mifflin.

CROWE, M. J., MARKS, I. M., AGRESS, W. S., & LEITENBERG, H. (1972). Time limited desensitization, implosion and shaping for phobic patients: A cross-over study. *Behaviour Research and Therapy, 10,* 319–328.

DANAHER, B. G. (1977). Research on rapid smoking: Interim summary and recommendations. *Addictive Behavior, 2,* 151–166.

DANGUAH, J. (1982). The practice of behavior therapy in West Africa: The case of Ghana. *Journal of Behavior Therapy and Experimental Psychiatry, 13,* 5–13.

DANIEL, R. F., & POLSTER, R. A. (1984). *Parent training: Foundations of research and practice.* New York: Guilford.

DARDIG, J. C., & HEWARD, W. L. (1976). *Sign here: A contracting book for children and their parents.* Kalamazoo, MI: Behaviordelia.

DAVIS, M., ESCHELMAN, E. R. & McKAY, M. (1980). *The relaxation and stress-reduction workbook.* Richmond, CA: New Harbinger Publications.

DAY, W. (1983). On the difference between radical and methodological behaviorism. *Behaviorism, 11,* 89–102.

DECI, E. L., & RYAN, R. M. (1985). *Intrinsic motivation and self-determination in human behavior.* New York: Plenum.

DEITZ, S. M., & MALONE, L. W. (1985). Stimulus control terminology. *The Behavior Analyst, 8,* 259–264.

DEITZ, S. M., & REPP, A. C. (1973). Decreasing classroom misbehavior through the use of DRL schedules of reinforcement. *Journal of Applied Behavior Analysis, 6,* 457–463.

DEMCHAK, M. (1990). Response prompting and fading methods: A review. *American Journal on Mental Retardation, 94,* 603–615.

DERICCO, D. A., & NIEMANN, J. E. (1980). In vivo effects of peer modelling on drinking rate. *Journal of Applied Behavior Analysis, 13,* 149–152.

DERISI, W. J., & BUTZ, G. (1975). *Writing behavioral contracts: A case simulation practice manual.* Champaign, IL: Research Press.

DE SILVA, P., & SIMARASINGHE, D. (1985). Behavior therapy in Sri Lanka. *Journal of Behavior Therapy and Experimental Psychiatry, 16,* 95–100.

DEVANY, J. M., HAYES, S. C., & NELSON, R. O. (1986). Equivalence class formation in language-able and language-disabled children. *Journal of the Experimental Analysis of Behavior, 46,* 243–257.

Diagnostic and statistical manual of mental disorders: DSM I. (1952). Washington, DC: American Psychiatric Association.

Diagnostic and statistical manual of mental disorders: DSM II, 2nd ed. (1968). Washington, DC: American Psychiatric Association.

Diagnostic and statistical manual of mental disorders: DSM III, 3rd ed. (1980). Washington, DC: American Psychiatric Association.

Diagnostic and statistical manual of mental disorders: DSM III-R, 3rd ed. (1987). Washington, DC: American Psychiatric Association.

DICKINSON, A. M.   (1989). The detrimental effects of extrinsic reinforcement on "intrinsic motivation." *The Behavior Analyst, 12*, 1–16.

DOLEYS, D. M., MEREDITH, R. L., & CIMINERO, A. R. (Eds.).   (1982). *Behavioral psychology and medicine and rehabilitation: Assessment and treatment strategies.* New York: Plenum.

DOLLARD, J., & MILLER, N. E.   (1950). *Personality and psychotherapy.* New York: McGraw-Hill.

DONAHUE, J. A., GILLIS, J. H., & KING, H.   (1980). Behavior Modification in sport and physical education: A review. *Journal of Sport Psychology, 2*, 311–328.

DORSEY, M. F., IWATA, B. A., ONG, P., & McSWEEN, T. E.   (1980). Treatment of self-injurious behavior using a water mist: Initial response suppression and generalization. *Journal of Applied Behavior Analysis, 13*, 343–353.

DRYDEN, W., & DiGIUSEPPE, R.   (1990). *A primer on rational-emotive therapy.* Champaign, IL: Research Press.

DUNLAP, G.   (1990). The goals of intervention. *AAMR News and Notes, 3*, 5.

DUSH, D. M., HIRT, M. L., & SCHROEDER, H.   (1983). Self-statement modification with adults: A meta-analysis. *Psychological Bulletin, 94*, 408–422.

D'ZURILLA, T. J.   (1986). *Problem-solving therapy: A social competence approach to clinical intervention.* New York: Springer.

D'ZURILLA, T. J., & GOLDFRIED, M. R.   (1971). Problem solving and behavior modification. *Journal of Abnormal Psychology, 78*, 107–126.

ELLIS, A.   (1978). Rational emotive theory: Toward a theory of personality. In R. J. Corsini (Ed.), *Readings in current personality theories.* Itasca, IL: Peacock.

ELLIS, A.   (1984). *Rational-emotive therapy and cognitive behavior therapy.* New York: Springer.

ELLIS, A., & BERNARD, M. E. (Eds.).   (1985). *Clinical applications of rational-emotive therapy.* New York: Plenum.

EMMELKAMP, P. M. G., & KWEE, K. G.   (1977). Obsessional ruminations: A comparison between thought-stopping and prolonged exposure in imagination. *Behaviour Research and Therapy, 15*, 441–444.

EMMELKAMP, P. M. G., VAN DER HELM, M., VAN ZANTEN, B. L., & PLOCHY, I.   (1980). Contributions of self-instructional training to the effectiveness of exposure *in vivo*: A comparison with obsessive-compulsive patients. *Behaviour Research and Therapy, 18*, 61–66.

EMMELKAMP, P. M. G., & WESSELS, H.   (1975). Flooding in imagination versus flooding in vivo: A comparison with agoraphobics. *Behaviour Research and Therapy, 13*, 7–15.

Ethical principles of psychologists (1981). *American Psychologist, 36*, 633–638.

ETZEL, B., & LeBLANC, J.   (1979). The simplest treatment alternative: The law of parsimony applied to choosing appropriate instructional control and errorless learning procedures for the difficult-to-teach-child. *Journal of Autism and Developmental Disabilities, 9*, 361–382.

EYSENCK, H. J.   (1959). Learning theory and behavior therapy. *Journal of Mental Science, 105*, 61–75.

EYSENCK, H. J. (Ed.).   (1960). *Behaviour therapy and the neuroses.* London: Pergamon.

FAVELL, J. E., AZRIN, N. H., BAUMEISTER, A. A., CARR, E. G., DORSEY, M. F., FOREHAND, R., FOXX, R. M., LOVAAS, O. I., RINCOVER, A., RISLEY, T. R., ROMANCZYK, R. G., RUSSO, D. G., SCHROEDER, S. R., & SOLNICK, J. V.   (1982). The treatment of self-injurious behavior. *The Behavior Therapist, 13*, 529–554.

FAWCETT, S. B., & MILLER, L. K.   (1975). Training public-speaking behavior: An experimental analysis and social validation. *Journal of Applied Behavior Analysis, 8*, 125–135.

FEIST, J., & BRANNON, L.   (1988). *Health psychology: An introduction to behavior and health.* Belmont, CA: Wadsworth.

FERSTER, C. B., & DeMYER, M. K.   (1962). A method for the experimental analysis of the behavior of autistic children. *The American Journal of Orthopsychiatry, 32,* 89–98. Reprinted in L. P. Ullmann & L. Krasner (Eds.). (1965), *Case studies in behavior modification.* (pp. 121–129). New York: Holt, Rinehart & Winston.

FERSTER, C. B., & PERROTT, M. C.   (1968). *Behavior principles.* New York: Appleton-Century-Crofts.

FERSTER, C. B., & SKINNER, B. F.   (1957). *Schedules of reinforcement.* New York: Appleton-Century-Crofts.

FLANAGAN, B., GOLDIAMOND, I., & AZRIN, N.   (1958). Operant stuttering: The control of stuttering behavior through response-contingent consequences. *Journal of the Experimental Analysis of Behavior, 1,* 173–177.

FLORA, S. R.   (1990). Undermining intrinsic interest from the standpoint of a behaviorist. *The Psychological Record, 40,* 323–346.

FOA, E. B., STEKETEE, G., TURNER, R. M., & FISHER, S. C.   (1980). Effects of imaginal exposure to feared disasters in obsessive-compulsive checkers. *Behaviour Research and Therapy, 18,* 449–455.

FOWLER, S. A.   (1988). The effects of peer-mediated interventions on establishing, maintaining, and generalizing children's behavior changes. In R. H. Horner, G. Dunlap, & R. L. Koegel (Eds.), *Generalization and maintenance: Lifestyle changes in applied settings* (pp. 143–170). Baltimore: Paul H. Brookes.

FOX, L.   (1962). Effecting the use of efficient study habits. *Journal of Mathetics, 1,* 75–86. Reprinted in R. Ulrich, T. Stachnik, and J. Mabry (Eds.) (1966), *Control of Human Behavior,* Vol. 1 (pp. 85–90). Glenview, IL: Scott, Foresman.

FOXX, R. M., & BECHTEL, D. R.   (1982). Overcorrection. In M. Hersen, R. M., Eisler, & P. M. Miller (Eds.) *Progress in behavior modification,* Vol. 13 (pp. 227–288). New York: Academic Press.

FOXX, R. M., & FAW, G. D.   (1990). Problem-solving skills training for psychiatric inpatients: An analysis of generalization. *Behavioral Residential Treatment, 5,* 159–176.

FOXX, R. M., & SHAPIRO, S. T.   (1978). The timeout ribbon: A non-exclusionary timeout procedure. *Journal of Applied Behavior Analysis, 11,* 125–136.

FRANKS, C. M.   (1964). *Conditioning techniques in clinical practice and research.* New York: Springer.

FRANKS, C. M. (Ed.).   (1969). *Behavior therapy: Appraisal and status.* New York: McGraw-Hill.

FREDERICKSEN, L. W.   (1982). *Handbook of organizational behavior management.* New York: John Wiley.

FREDERIKSEN, L. W., & LOVETT, F. B.   (1980). Inside organizational behavior management: Perspectives on an emerging field. *Journal of Organizational Behavior Management, 2* 193–203.

FREEDMAN, J. L.   (1984). Effect of television violence on aggressiveness. *Psychological Bulletin, 96,* 227–246.

FRIEDMAN, J. M.   (1983). *A treatment program for low sexual desire.* Unpublished doctoral dissertation, State University of New York at Stony Brook, Stony Brook, NY.

FRIEDMAN, J. M., & HOGAN, D. R.   (1985). Sexual dysfunction: Low sexual desire. In D. H. Barlow (Ed.), *Clinical handbook of psychological disorders: A step-by-step treatment manual* (pp. 417–461). New York: Guilford.

FRIEDRICH-COFER, L.   (1986). Television violence and aggression: The debate continues. *Psychological Bulletin, 100,* 364–371.

FRIMAN, P. C., & ALTMAN, K.   (1990). Parent use of DRI on high rate disruptive behavior: Direct and collateral effects. *Research in Developmental Disabilities, 11,* 249–254.

FULLER, P. R.   (1949). Operant conditioning of a vegetative human organism. *American*

Journal of Psychology, 62, 587–590. Reprinted in L. P. Ullmann & L. Krasner (Eds.). (1965), *Case studies in behavior modification* (pp. 337–339). New York: Holt, Rinehart & Winston.

FUREDY, J. J., & RILEY, D. M. (1987). Human Pavlovian autonomic conditioning and the cognitive paradigm. In G. Davy (Ed.), *Cognitive processes and Pavlovian conditioning in humans.* (pp. 1–25). New York: John Wiley.

GARCIA, J., ERVIN, F. R., & KOELLING, R. A. (1966). Learning with prolonged delay of reinforcement. *Psychonomic Science, 5*, 121–122.

GARCIA, J., HANKINS, W. G., & RUSINIAK, K. W. (1974). Behavioral regulation of a milieu interne in man and rat. *Science, 185*, 824–831.

GARCIA, J., & KOELLING, R. A. (1966). Relation of cue-to-consequence in avoidance learning. *Psychonomic Science, 4*, 123–124.

GAYLORD-ROSS, R. J., & HOLVOET, J. (1985). *Strategies for educating students with severe handicaps.* Boston: Little, Brown.

GELFAND, D. M., HARTMANN, D. P. LAMB, A. K., SMITH, C. L., MAHAN, M. A., & PAUL, S. C. (1974). Effects of adult models and described alternatives on children's choice of behavior management techniques. *Child Development, 45*, 585–593.

GELLER, E. S., WINETT, R. A., & EVERETT, P. B. (1982). *Preserving the environment: New strategies for behavior change.* New York: Plenum.

GILES, T. R. (1990). Bias against behavior therapy in outcome reviews: Who speaks for the patient? *The Behavior Therapist, 13*, 86–90.

GIRARDEAU, F. L., & SPRADLIN, J. E. (1964). Token rewards on a cottage program. *Mental Retardation, 2*, 345–351.

GLASGOW, R. E., & ROSEN, G. M. (1978). Behavioral bibliotherapy: A review of self-help behavior therapy manuals. *Psychological Bulletin, 85*, 1–23.

GLASGOW, R. E., & ROSEN, G. M. (1979). Self-help behavior therapy manuals: Recent developments in clinical usage. *Clinical Behavior Therapy Review, 1*, 1–20.

GLASGOW, R. E., SWANEY, K., & SCHAFER, L. (1981). Self-help manuals for the control of nervous habits: A comparative investigation. *Behavior Therapy, 12*, 177–184.

GLYNN, E. L., & THOMAS, J. D. (1974). Effect of cueing on self-control of classroom behavior. *Journal of Applied Behavior Analysis, 7*, 299–306.

GLYNN, S. M. (1990). Token economy approaches for psychiatric patients: Progress and pitfalls over 25 years. *Behavior Modification, 14*, 383–407.

GOETZ, E. M., & BAER, D. M. (1973). Social control of form diversity and the emergence of new forms in children's block building. *Journal of Applied Behavior Analysis, 6*, 105–113.

GOLDFRIED, M. R., & DAVISON, G. C. (1976). *Clinical behavior therapy.* New York: Holt, Rinehart & Winston.

GOLDIAMOND, I. (1965). Self-control procedures in personal behavior problems. *Psychological Reports, 17*, 851–868. Reprinted in R. Ulrich, T. Stachnik, & J. Mabry (Eds.). (1966), *Control of human behavior*, Vol. 1 (pp. 115–127). Glenview, IL: Scott, Foresman.

GOLDIAMOND, I. (1975). The constructional approach to self-control. In A. Schwartz & I. Goldiamond (Eds.), *Social Casework: A behavioral approach.* (pp. 67–138). New York: Columbia University Press.

GOLDIAMOND, I. (1976). Self-reinforcement. *Journal of Applied Behavior Analysis, 9*, 509–514.

GORMALLY, J., BLACK, S., DASTON, S., & RARDIN, D. (1982). The assessment of binge eating severity among obese persons. *Addictive Behaviors, 7*, 47–55.

GOTTMAN, J., NOTARIUS, C., GONSO, J., & MARKMAN, H. A. (1976). *A couples' guide to communication.* Champaign, IL: Research Press.

GOWAN, G. R., BOTTERILL, C. D., & BLIMKE, J. (1979). Bridging the gap between sport science and sport practice. In P. Klavora & J. Daniel (Eds.), *Coach, athlete & sport psychologist.* Toronto: School of Physical and Health Education, University of Toronto.

GRAZIANO, A. M. (1975). Futurants, coverants and operants. *Behavior Therapy, 6,* 421–422.

GREEN, C. W., REID, D. H., WHITE, L. K., HALFORD, R. C., BRITTAIN, D. P., & GARDNER, S. M. (1988). Identifying reinforcers for persons with profound handicaps: Staff opinion vs. systematic assessment of preferences. *Journal of Applied Behavior Analysis, 21,* 31–43.

GREENSPOON, J. (1951). *The effect of verbal and nonverbal stimuli on the frequency of members of two verbal response classes.* Unpublished Ph.D. dissertation, Indiana University.

GREENSPOON, J. (1955). The reinforcing effect of two spoken words on the frequency of two responses. *American Journal of Psychology, 68,* 409–416.

GREENSPOON, J. (1976). *The sources of behavior: Abnormal and normal.* Monterey, CA: Brooks/Cole.

GREENSPOON, J., & LAMAL, P. A. (1978). Cognitive behavior modification—Who needs it? *Psychological Record, 28,* 343–351.

GREENWALD, D. P., KORNBLITH, S. J., HERSEN, M., BELLACK, A. S., & HIMMELHOCH, J. M. (1981). Differences between social skills, therapists and psychotherapists in treating depression. *Journal of Consulting and Clinical Psychology, 49,* 757–759.

GRIFFITH, R. G., & SPREAT, S. (1989). Aversive behavior modification procedures and the use of professional judgment. *The Behavior Therapist, 12,* 7, 143–146.

GROSS, A. M., & DRABMAN, D. S. (1990). *Handbook of clinical behavioral pediatrics.* New York: Plenum.

GUESS, D., HELMSTETTER, E., TURNBULL, H. R. III, & KNOWLTON, S. (1986). *Use of aversive procedures with persons who are disabled: An historical review and critical analysis.* Seattle: The Association for Persons With Severe Handicaps.

GUESS, D., TURNBULL, H. R. III, & HELMSTETTER, E. (1990). Science, paradigms, and values: A response to Mulick. *American Journal on Mental Retardation, 95,* 157–163.

GUESS, D., SAILOR, W., RUTHERFORD, G., & BAER, D. M. (1968). An experimental analysis of linguistic development: The productive use of the plural morpheme. *Journal of Applied Behavior Analysis, 1,* 297–306.

GUTHRIE, E. R. (1935). *The psychology of human learning.* New York: Harper & Row.

HAINS, A. H., & BAER, D. M. (1989). Interaction effects in multi-element designs: Inevitable, desirable, and ignorable. *Journal of Applied Behavior Analysis, 22,* 57–69.

HALAS, E., & EBERHARDT, M. (1987). Blocking and appetitive reinforcement. *Bulletin of the Psychonomic Society, 25,* 121–123.

HALL, B. L. (1980). Editorial. *Journal of Organizational Behavior Management, 2,* 145–150.

HALL, S. M. (1980). Self-management and therapeutic maintenance: Theory and research. In P. Karoly & J. Steffan (Eds.), *Improving the long-term effects of psychotherapy* (pp. 263–300). New York: Gardiner Press.

HALPERN, A. S., IRVIN, L. K., & LANDMAN, J. T. (1979). Alternative approaches to the measurement of adaptive behavior. *American Journal of Mental Deficiency, 84,* 304–310.

HAND, I., LAMONTAGNE, Y., & MARKS, I. M. (1974). Group exposure (flooding) in vivo for agoraphobics. *British Journal of Psychiatry, 124,* 588–602.

HANDLEMAN, J. S. (1986). A glimpse at current trends in the education of autistic children. *The Behavior Therapist, 7,* 137–139.

HARDY, L., MARTIN, G., YU, D., LEADER, C., & QUINN, G. (1981). *Objective behavioral assessment of the severely and moderately mentally handicapped: The OBA.* Springfield, IL: Charles C. Thomas.

HARING, T. G., & KENNEDY, C. H. (1990). Contextual control of problem behavior in students with severe disabilities. *Journal of Applied Behavior Analysis, 23,* 235–243.

HARRIS, C. S., & McREYNOLDS, W. T. (1977). Semantic cues and response contingencies in self-instructional control. *Journal of Behavior Therapy and Experimental Psychiatry, 8,* 15–17.

HARRIS, D. V., & HARRIS, B. L. (1984). *The athlete's guide to sports psychology.* New York: Leisure Press.

HARRIS, F. R., WOLF, M. M., & BAER, D. M. (1964). Effects of adult social reinforcement on child behavior. *Young Children, 20,* 8–17. Reprinted in R. Ulrich, T. Stachnik, & J. Mabry (Eds.). (1966), *Control of Human Behavior,* Vol. 1 (pp. 130–137). Glenview, IL: Scott, Foresman.

HAUGHTON, E., & AYLLON, T. (1965). Production and elimination of symptomatic behavior. In L. P. Ullmann & L. Krasner (Eds.), *Case studies in behavior modification* (pp. 94–98). New York: Holt, Rinehart & Winston.

HAWKINS, R. C., & CLEMENT, P. (1980). Development and construct validation of a self-report measure of binge eating tendencies. *Addictive Behaviors, 5,* 219–226.

HAWKINS, R. P. (1979). The functions of assessment: Implications for selection and development of devices for assessing repertoires in clinical, educational, and other settings. *Journal of Applied Behavior Analysis, 12,* 501–516.

HAWKINS, R. P. (1989). Developing potent behavior change technologies: An invitation to cognitive behavior therapists. *The Behavior Therapist, 12,* 126–131.

HAWKINS, R. P. & DOTSON, V. A. (1975). Reliability scores that delude: An Alice in Wonderland trip through the misleading characteristics of interobserver agreement scores in interval recording. In E. Ramp & G. Semp (Eds.), *Behavior analysis: Areas of research and application* (pp. 359–376). Englewood Cliffs, NJ: Prentice-Hall.

HAYES, S. C. (1989a). Nonhumans have not yet shown stimulus equivalence. *Journal of the Experimental Analysis of Behavior, 51,* 385–392.

HAYES, S. C. (1989b). *Rule-governed behavior: Cognition, contingencies, and instructional control.* New York: Plenum.

HAYES, S. C., BROWNSTEIN, A. J., ZETTLE, R. D., ROSENFARB, I., & KORN, Z. (1986). Rule-governed behavior and sensitivity to changing consequences of responding. *Journal of the Experimental Analysis of Behavior, 45,* 237–256.

HAYES, S. C., & NELSON, R. O. (1986). *Conceptual foundations of behavioral assessment.* New York: Guilford.

HAYNES, S. N. (1973). Contingency management in a municipally-administered antiabuse program for alcoholics. *Behavior Therapy and Experimental Psychiatry, 4,* 31–32.

HEFFERLINE, R. F., KEENAN, B., & HARFORD, R. A. (1959). Escape and avoidance conditioning in human subjects without their observation of the response. *Science, 130,* 1338–1339.

HEFFERNAN, T., & RICHARDS, C. S. (1981). Self-control of study behavior: Identification and evaluation of natural methods. *Journal of Counselling Psychology, 28,* 361–364.

HEIMAN, J., LoPICCOLO, L., & LoPICCOLO, J. (1976). *Becoming orgasmic: A sexual growth program for women.* Englewood Cliffs, NJ: Prentice-Hall.

HERMANN, J. A., MONTES, A. I., DOMINGUEZ, B., MONTES, F., & HOPKINS, B. L. (1973). Effects of bonuses for punctuality on the tardiness of industrial workers. *Journal of Applied Behavior Analysis, 6,* 563–570.

HERSEN, M. (1976). Historical perspectives in behavioral assessment. In M. Hersen & A. S. Bellack (Eds.), *Behavioral assessment: A practical handbook.* New York: Pergamon.

Hersen, M. (Ed.). (1983). *Outpatient behavior therapy: A clinical guide.* New York: Grune & Stratton.

Hersen, M. (1989). *Innovations in child behavior therapy.* New York: Springer.

Hersen, M., & Barlow, D. H. (1976). *Single case experimental designs: Strategies for studying behavior change.* Elmsford, NY: Pergamon.

Hersen, M., & Bellack, A. S. (1981). *Behavioral assessment: A practical handbook,* 2nd ed. Elmsford, NY: Pergamon.

Hersen, M., & Bellack, A. S. (Eds.). (1985). *Handbook of clinical behavior therapy with adults.* New York: Plenum.

Hersen, M., Kazdin, A. E., Bellack, A. S., & Turner, S. M. (1979). Effects of live modelling, covert modelling, and rehearsal on assertiveness in psychiatric patients. *Behaviour Research and Therapy, 17,* 369–377.

Hersen, M., & Last, C. G. (Eds.). (1985). *Behavior therapy casebook.* New York: Springer.

Hersen, M., & Turner, S. M. (1984). DSM III and behavior therapy. In S. M. Turner & M. Hersen (Eds.), *Adult psychopathology and diagnosis.* New York: John Wiley.

Hildebrand, R. G., Martin, G. L., Furer, P., & Hazen, A. (1990). A recruitment of praise package to increase productivity levels of developmentally handicapped workers. *Behavior Modification, 14,* 97–113.

Homme, L. E. (1965). Perspectives in psychology: XXIV. Control of coverants, the operants of the mind. *Psychological Record, 15,* 501–511.

Homme, L. E., Csanyi, A. P., Gonzales, M. A., & Rechs, J. R. (1969). *How to use contingency contracting in the classroom.* Champaign, IL: Research Press.

Horan, J. J., & Johnson, R. G. (1971). Coverant conditioning through a self-management application of the Premack principle: Its effect on weight reduction. *Journal of Behavior Therapy and Experimental Psychiatry, 2,* 243–249.

Hugdahl, K., & Ohman, A. (1977). Effects of instruction on acquisition and extinction on electrodermal responses to fear-relevant stimuli. *Journal of Experimental Psychology: Human Learning and Memory, 3,* 608–618.

Hull, C. L. (1943). *Principles of behavior.* New York: Appleton-Century-Crofts.

Hull, C. L. (1952). *A behavior system.* New Haven, CT: Yale University Press.

Hunt, G. M., & Azrin, N. H. (1973). A community-reinforcement approach to alcoholism. *Behavior Research and Therapy, 11,* 91–104.

Hussian, R. A., & Davis, R. L. (1986). *Responsive care: Behavioral interventions with elderly persons.* Champaign, IL: Research Press.

Irey, P. A. (1972). *Covert sensitization of cigarette smokers with high and low extraversion scores.* Unpublished master's thesis, Southern Illinois University.

Israel, A. C., Stolmaker, L., & Adrian, C. A. G. (1985). The effects of training parents in general child management skills on a behavioral weight loss program for children. *Behavior Therapy, 16,* 169–180.

Issacs, W., Thomas, J., & Goldiamond, I. (1960). Application of operant conditioning to reinstate verbal behavior in psychotics. *Journal of Speech and Hearing Disorders, 25,* 8–12. Reprinted in R. Ulrich, T. Stachnik, & J. Mabry (Eds.), *Control of human behavior,* Vol. 1 (pp. 199–202). Glenview, IL: Scott, Foresman.

Iwata, B. A., Pace, G. M., Kalsher, M. J., Cowdery, G. E., & Cataldo, M. F. (1990). Experimental analysis and extinction of self-injurious escape behavior. *Journal of Applied Behavior Analysis, 23,* 11–27.

Jacobs, H. E., Kardashian, S., Kreinbring, R. K., Ponder, R., & Simpson, A. P. (1984). A skills-oriented model for facilitating employment among psychiatrically-disabled persons. *Rehabilitation Counselling Bulletin, 28,* 87–96.

Jacobson, E. (1938). *Progressive relaxation.* Chicago: University of Chicago Press.

Jacobson, N. S., & Moore, D. (1981). Spouses as observers of the events in their relationship. *Journal of Consulting and Clinical Psychology, 49,* 269–277.

Johnson, K. R., & Ruskin, R. S. (1977). *Behavioral instruction: An evaluative review.* Washington, DC: American Psychological Association.

JOHNSON, S.P., WELCH, T.M., MILLER, L.K., & ALTUS, D.E. (1991). Participatory management: Maintaining staff performance in a university housing cooperative. *Journal of Applied Behavior Analysis, 24,* 119–127.

JOHNSON, W. G. (1971). Some applications of Homme's covert control therapy: Two case reports. *Behavior Therapy, 2,* 240–248.

JOHNSTON, J. M. (1979). On the relation between generalization and generality. *The Behavior Analyst, 2,* 1–6.

JOHNSTON, J. M. (1985). Controlling professional behavior: A review of *The effects of punishment on human behavior* by Axelrod and Apsche. *The Behavior Analyst, 8,* 111–119.

JOHNSTON, J. M., & PENNYPACKER, H. S. (1981). *Strategies and tactics of human behavioral research.* Hillsdale, NJ: Lawrence Erlbaum.

JONES, M. C. (1924). The elimination of children's fears. *Journal of Experimental Psychology, 7,* 383–390.

JORDAN, J., SINGH, N. N., & REPP, A. C. (1989). An evaluation of gentle teaching and visual screening in the reduction of stereotypy. *Journal of Applied Behavior Analysis, 22,* 9–22.

JOSEPHSON, W. L. (1987). Television violence and children's aggression: Testing the priming, social script, and disinhibition predictions. *Journal of Personality and Social Psychology, 53,* 882–890.

KANFER, F. H., & GAELICK, L. (1986). Self-management methods. In F. H. Kanfer & A. P. Goldstein (Eds.), *Helping people change: A textbook of methods,* 3rd ed. New York: Pergamon.

KANFER, F. H., & GRIMM, L. G. (1980). Managing clinical change: A process model of therapy. *Behavior Modification, 4,* 419–444.

KANNER, L. (1943). Autistic disturbances of affective contact. *Nervous Child, 2,* 217–250.

KAPLAN, S. J. (1986). *The private practice of behavior therapy: A guide for behavioral practitioners.* New York: Plenum.

KAPROWY, E. A. (1975). *Primary reinforcement, a token system, and attention criteria and feedback procedures with profound retardates in a verbal training classroom.* Unpublished Ph.D. dissertation, University of Manitoba.

KAROL, R. L., & RICHARDS, C. S. (1978, November). *Making treatment effects last: An investigation of maintenance strategies for smoking reduction.* Paper presented at the meeting of the Association for the Advancement of Behavior Therapy, Chicago.

KARRAKER, R. (1977). Self versus teacher selected reinforcers in a token economy. *Exceptional Children, 43,* 454–455.

KAU, M. L., & FISCHER, J. (1974). Self-modification of exercise behavior. *Journal of Behavior Therapy and Experimental Psychiatry, 5,* 213–214.

KAYSER, J. E., BILLINGSLEY, F. F., & NEEL, R. S. (1986). A comparison of in-context and traditional approaches: Total task, single-trial vs backward chaining, multiple-trials. *Journal of The Association for Persons with Severe Handicaps, 11,* 28–38.

KAZDIN, A. E. (1973a). Methodological and assessment considerations in evaluating reinforcement programs in applied settings. *Journal of Applied Behavior Analysis, 6,* 517–531.

KAZDIN, A. E. (1973b). The effect of vicarious reinforcement on attentive behavior in the classroom. *Journal of Applied Behavior Analysis, 6,* 72–78.

KAZDIN, A. E. (1977a). *The token economy: A review and evaluation.* New York: Plenum.

KAZDIN, A. E. (1977b). Assessing the clinical or applied importance of behavior change through social validation. *Behavior Modification, 1,* 427–451.

KAZDIN, A. E. (1978). *History of behavior modification.* Baltimore: University Park Press.

KAZDIN, A. E. (1980a). Covert and overt rehearsal and elaboration during treatment in the development of assertive behavior. *Behaviour Research and Therapy, 18,* 191–201.

KAZDIN, A. E. (1980b). *Research design in clinical psychology.* New York: Harper & Row.

KAZDIN, A. E. (1983). Psychiatric diagnosis, dimensions of dysfunction, and child behavior therapy. *Behavior Therapy, 14,* 73–99.

KAZDIN, A. E. (1989). *Behavior modification in applied settings,* 4th ed. Homewood II: Dorsey Press.

KAZDIN, A. E. (1985). The token economy. In R. M. Turner & L. M. Ascher (Eds.), *Evaluating behavior therapy outcome.* New York: Springer.

KAZDIN, A. E., & ERICKSON, L. M. (1975). Developing responsiveness to instructions in severely and profoundly retarded residents. *Journal of Behavior Therapy and Experimental Psychiatry, 6,* 17–21.

KAZDIN, A. E., & HARTMANN, D. P. (1978). The simultaneous treatment design. *Behavior Therapy, 9,* 912–922.

KAZDIN, A. E., & POLSTER, R. (1973). Intermittent token reinforcement and response maintenance in extinction. *Behavior Therapy, 4,* 386–391.

KAZDIN, A. E., & WILSON, G. T. (1978). *Evaluation of behavior therapy: Issues, evidence, and strategies.* Cambridge, MA: Ballinger.

KEESEY, R. E. (1980). A set point analysis of the regulation of body weight. In A. J. Stunkard (Ed.), *Obesity.* Phildelphia: Saunders.

KELLER, F. S. (1968). Good-bye, teacher. . . . *Journal of Applied Behavior Analysis, 1,* 79–89.

KELLER, F. S., & SCHOENFELD, W. N. (1950). *Principles of psychology.* New York: Appleton-Century-Crofts.

KELLER, F. S., & SHERMAN, J. G. (1982). The PSI handbook: Essays on personalized instruction. Lawrence, KS: TRI Publications.

KELLEY, H. H. (1983). Love and commitment. In H. H. Kelley, E. Berscheid, A. Christensen, J. H. Harvey, T. L. Houston, G. Levinger, E. McClintock, L. A. Peplau, & D. R. Peterson (Eds.), *Close relationships* (pp. 265–314). New York: W. H. Freeman.

KELLY, J. A. & LAMPARSKI, D. M. (1985). Outpatient treatment of schizophrenics: Social skills and problem-solving. In M. Hersen & A. S. Bellack (Eds.), *Handbook of clinical behavior therapy with adults* (pp. 485–508). New York: Plenum.

KENNY, F. T., MOWBRAY, R. M., & LALANI, S. (1978). Faradic disruption of obsessive ideation in the treatment of obsessive neurosis. *Behavior Therapy, 9,* 209–221.

KENNY, F. T., SOLYOM, L., & SOLYOM, C. (1973). Faradic disruption of obsessive ideation in the treatment of obsessive neurosis. *Behavior Therapy, 4,* 448–451.

KILLEEN, P. R. (1985). Reflection on a cumulative record. *The Behavior Analyst, 8,* 177–183.

KINKADE, K. A. (1973). *A Walden Two experiment: The first five years of Twin Oaks community.* New York: William Morrow.

KINSNER, W., & PEAR, J. J. (1988). Computer-aided personalized system of instruction for the virtual classroom. *Canadian Journal of Educational Communication, 17,* 21–36.

KIRCHER, A. S., PEAR, J. J., & MARTIN, G. (1971). Shock as punishment in a picture-naming task with retarded children. *Journal of Applied Behavior Analysis, 4,* 227–233.

KOHLER, F. W., & GREENWOOD, C. R. (1986). Toward a technology of generalization: The identification of natural contingencies of reinforcement. *The Behavior Analyst, 9,* 19–26.

KOOP, S., MARTIN, G., YU, D., & SUTHONS, E. (1980). Comparison of two reinforcement strategies in vocational-skill training of mentally retarded persons. *American Journal of Mental Deficiency, 84,* 616–626.

KRAPFL, J. E. (1975). Accountability for behavioral engineers. In W. S. Wood (Ed.), *Issues in evaluating behavior modification* (pp. 219–236). Champaign, IL: Research Press.

KROHN-BONEM, M., & BONEM, E. J. (1980). Why a rational approach to ethics? A review of Ethical Issues in Behavior Modification, by S. B. Stolz & associates, *The Behavior Analyst, 3*(2), 57–62.

KYMISSISS, E., & POULSON, C. L. (1990). The history of imitation in learning theory: The language acquisition process. *Journal of the Experimental Analysis of Behavior, 54,* 113–127.

LAMAL, P. A. (1989). The impact of behaviorism on our culture: Some evidence and conjectures. *The Psychological Record, 39,* 529–535.

LAST, C. G., & HERSEN, M. (Eds.) (1988). *Handbook of anxiety disorders.* New York: Pergamon

LATIES, V. G., & WEISS, B. (1963). Effects of a concurrent task on fixed interval responding in humans. *Journal of the Experimental Analysis of Behavior, 6,* 431–436.

LATIMER, P. R., & SWEET, A. A. (1984). Cognitive vs. behavioral procedures in cognitive behavior therapy: A critical review of the evidence. *Journal of Behavior Therapy & Experimental Psychiatry, 15,* 9–22.

LAZARUS, A. A. (1958). New methods in psychotherapy: A case study. *South African Medical Journal, 32,* 660–664.

LAZARUS, A. (1971). *Behavior therapy and beyond.* New York: McGraw-Hill.

LAZARUS, A. A. (1976). *Multi-model behavior therapy.* New York: Springer.

LEBOW, M. D. (1981). *Weight control: The behavioral strategies.* New York: John Wiley.

LEBOW, M. D. (1984). *Child obesity: A new frontier of behavior therapy.* New York: Springer.

LEBOW, M. D. (1988). *The thin plan: An honest alternative to rollercoaster weight loss.* Champaign, IL: Life Enhancement Publications.

LEBOW, M. D. (1989). *Adult obesity therapy.* New York: Pergamon.

LEDWIDGE, B. (1978). Cognitive behavior modification—A step in the wrong direction. *Psychological Bulletin, 85,* 353–375.

LEDWIDGE, B. (1979). Cognitive behavior modification or new ways to change minds: Reply to Mahoney & Kazdin. *Psychological Bulletin, 86,* 1050–1053.

LEITENBERG, H. (1973). The use of single-case methodology in psychotherapy research. *Journal of Abnormal Psychology, 82,* 87–101.

LEITENBERG, H. (1976). Behavioral approaches to treatment of neurosis. In H. Leitenberg, (Ed.), *Behavioral Modification and behavior therapy* (pp. 124–167). Englewood Cliffs, NJ: Prentice-Hall.

LEVINE, F. M., & FASNACHT, G. (1974). Token rewards may lead to token learning. *American Psychologist, 29,* 816–820.

LIEBERT, R. N. (1986). Effects of television on children and adolescents. *Journal of Developmental and Behavioral Pediatrics, 7,* 43–48.

LIEBERT, R. N., & PAULOS, R. W. (1975). Television and personality development: The socializing effects of an entertainment medium. In A. Davids (Ed.), *Child personality and psychopathology: Current topics, Vol. II,* New York: Wiley.

LINDNER, P. G., & BLACKBURN, G. L. (1976). An interdisciplinary approach to obesity using fasting modified by protein-sparing therapy. *Obesity/Bariatric Medicine, 5,* 198–216.

LINDSLEY, O. R. (1956). Operant conditioning methods applied to research in chronic schizophrenia. *Psychiatric Research Reports, 5,* 118–139.

LINDSLEY, O. R. (1966). An experiment with parents handling behavior at home. *Johnstone Bulletin, 9,* 27–36.

LINDSLEY, O. R., SKINNER, B. F., & SOLOMON, H. C. (1953). *Studies in behavior therapy: Status report I.* Waltham, MA: Metropolitan State Hospital.

LINSCHEID, T. R., IWATA, B. A., RICKETTS, R. W., WILLIAMS, D. E., & GRIFFIN, J. C. (1990). Clinical evaluation of the self-injurious behavior inhibiting system (SIBIS). *Journal of Applied Behavior Analysis, 23*, 53–78.

LOGAN, D. L. (1970). A "paper money" token system as a recording aid in institutional settings. *Journal of Applied Behavior Analysis, 3*, 183–184.

LOPICCOLO, J. (1978). Direct treatment of sexual dysfunction. In J. LoPiccolo & L. LoPiccolo (Eds.), *Handbook of sex therapy* (pp. 1–17). New York: Plenum.

LOVAAS, O. I. (1966). A program for the establishment of speech in psychotic children. In J. K. Wing (Ed.), *Early childhood autism* (pp. 115–144). Elmsford, NY: Pergamon.

LOVAAS, O. I. (1977). *The autistic child: Language development through behavior modification.* New York: Irvington.

LOVAAS, O. I. (1982, August). An overall evaluation of the young autism project. Paper presented to the American Psychological Association, Washington, DC.

LOVAAS, O. I., NEWSOM, C., & HICKMAN, C. (1987). Self-stimulatory behavior and perceptual development. *Journal of Applied Behavior Analysis, 20*, 45–68.

LOVAAS, O. I., SCHAEFFER, B., & SIMMONS, J. Q. (1965). Building social behavior in autistic children by use of electric shock. *Journal of Experimental Research in Personality, 1*, 99–109.

LOVAAS, O. I., & SMITH, T. (1988). Intensive behavioral treatment with young autistic children. In B. B. Lahey & A. E. Kazdin (Eds.), *Advances in clinical child psychology*, Vol. XI, New York: Plenum.

LOVAAS, O. I., & SMITH, T. (1989). A comprehensive behavioral theory of autistic children: Paradigm for research and treatment. *Journal of Behavior Therapy and Experimental Psychiatry, 20*, 17–20.

LOVE, S. R., MATSON, J. L., & WEST, D. (1990). Mothers as effective therapists for autistic children's phobias. *Journal of Applied Behavior Analysis, 23*, 379–385.

LOWE, C. F. (1979). Determinants of human operant behaviour. In M. D. Zeiller & P. Harzem (Eds.), *Advances in analysis of behaviour: Vol. 1. Reinforcement and the organization of behaviour* (pp. 159–192). Chichester, England: John Wiley.

LOWE, C. F., BEASTY, A., & BENTALL, R. P. (1983). The role of verbal behavior in human learning: Infant performance on fixed interval schedules. *Journal of the Experimental Analysis of Behavior, 39*, 157–164.

LOWTHER, R. M., & MARTIN, G. L. (1980). Multiple settings and trainers for programming generalization of a social response of severely retarded persons. *Behavior Research of Severe Developmental Disabilities, 1*, 131–145.

LUBETKIN, B. S., RIVERS, P. C., & ROSENBERG, C. N. (1971). Difficulties of disulfiram therapy with alcoholics. *Quarterly Journal of Studies on Alcohol, 32*, 118–171.

LUCE, S. C., DELQUADRI, J., & HALL, R. V. (1980). Contingent exercise: A mild but powerful procedure for suppressing inappropriate verbal and aggressive behavior. *Journal of Applied Behavior Analysis, 13*, 583–594.

LUDWIG, A. M., LEVINE, J. A., & STARK, L. H. (1970). *LDS and alcoholism.* Springfield, IL: Charles C. Thomas.

LUTHANS, F., & KREITNER, R. (1985). *Organizational behavior modification and beyond: An operant and social learning approach.* Glenview, IL: Scott, Foresman.

MACE, F. C., PAGE, T. J., IVANCIC, M. T., & O'BRIEN, S. (1986). Effectiveness of brief timeout with and without contingent delay: A comparative analysis. *Journal of Applied Behavior Analysis, 19*, 79–86.

MACKENZIE-KEATING, S. E., & MCDONALD, L. (1990). Overcorrection: Reviewed, revisited, and revised. *The Behavior Analyst, 13*, 39–48.

MACMILLAN, D. L. (1973). *Behavior modification in education.* New York: Macmillan.

MADSEN, C. H., BECKER, W. C., THOMAS, D. R., KOSER, L., & PLAGER, E. (1970). An analysis of the reinforcing function of "sit down" commands. In R. K. Parker (Ed.), *Readings in educational psychology.* Boston: Allyn & Bacon.

MADSEN, C. H., Jr., & MADSEN, C. R. (1974). *Teaching discipline: Behavior principles towards a positive approach.* Boston: Allyn & Bacon.

MAGER, R. F. (1972). *Goal analysis.* Belmont, CA: Fearon Publishers.

MAHONEY, M. J., & THORESON, C. E. (1974). *Self-control: Power to the person.* Belmont, CA: Brooks/Cole.

MALETSKY, B. M. (1974). Behavior recording as treatment: A brief note. *Behavior Therapy, 5,* 107–111.

MALOTT, R. (1984). Rule-governed behavior, self-management, and the developmentally disabled. *Analysis and Intervention in Developmental Disabilities, 4,* 199–209.

MALOTT, R. W., & WHALEY, D. L. (1983). *Psychology.* Holmes Beach, FL: Learning Publications.

MARHOLIN, D. II, LUISELLI, J. K., & TOWNSEND, N. M. (1980). Overcorrection: An examination of its rationale and treatment effectiveness. In M. Hersen, R. M. Eisler, & P. M. Miller (Eds.), *Progress in behavior modification,* Vol. 9, (pp. 49–80). New York: Academic Press.

MARKS, I. M., CROWE, E., DREWE, E., YOUNG, J., & DEWHURST, W. G. (1969). Obsessive-compulsive neurosis in identical twins. *British Journal of Psychiatry, 15,* 991–998.

MARKS, I. M., STERN, R. S., MAWSON, D., COBB, J., & McDONALD, R. (1980). Clomipramine and exposure for obsessive-compulsive rituals. *British Journal of Psychiatry, 136,* 1–25.

MARLATT, G. A., & GORDON, J. R. (Eds.). (1985). *Relapse prevention: Maintenance strategies in the treatment of addictive behaviors.* New York: Guilford.

MARLATT, G. A., & PARKS, G. A. (1982). Self-management of addictive disorders. In P. Karoly & F. H. Kanfer (Eds.), *Self-management and behavior change: From theory to practice* (pp. 443–488). New York: Pergamon.

MARTIN, G. A., & WORTHINGTON, E. L. (1982). Behavioral homework. In M. Hersen, R. M. Isler, & P. M. Miller (Eds.), *Progress in behavior modification,* Vol 13 (pp. 197–226). New York: Academic Press.

MARTIN, G. L. (1972). Teaching operant technology to psychiatric nurses, aides, and attendants. In F. W. Clark, D. R. Evans, & L. A. Hamerlynck (Eds.), *Implementing behavioral programs for schools and clinics* (pp. 63–87). Champaign, IL: Research Press.

MARTIN, G. L. (1974). Varieties of behaviour modification: A comment. *The Canadian Psychologist, 15,* 378–381.

MARTIN, G. L. (1975). Brief time-outs as consequences for errors during training programs with autistic and retarded children: A questionable procedure. *The Psychological Record, 25,* 71–89.

MARTIN, G. L. (1981). Behavior modification in Canada in the 1970's. *Canadian Psychology, 22,* 7–22.

MARTIN, G. L. (1982). Thought stopping and stimulus control to decrease persistent disturbing thoughts. *Journal of Behavior Therapy and Experimental Psychiatry, 13(3),* 215–220.

MARTIN, G. L., ENGLAND, G., KAPROWY, E., KILGOUR, K., & PILEK, V. (1968). Operant conditioning of kindergarten-class behavior in autistic children. *Behaviour Research and Therapy, 6,* 281–294.

MARTIN, G. L., & HRYCAIKO, D. (Eds.), (1983). *Behavior modification and coaching: Principles, procedures, and research.* Springfield, Il: Charles C. Thomas.

MARTIN, G. L., KOOP, S., TURNER, C., & HANEL, F. (1981). Backward chaining versus total task presentation to teach assembly tasks to severely retarded persons. *Behavior Research of Severe Developmental Disabilities, 2,* 117–136.

MARTIN, G. L., & LUMSDEN, J. (1987). *Coaching: An effective behavioral approach.* St. Louis, MO: Times Mirror/Mosby.

MARTIN, G. L., MCDONALD, S., & OMICHINSKI, M. (1971). An operant analysis of response interactions during meals with severely retarded girls. *American Journal of Mental Deficiency, 76*, 68–85.

MARTIN, G. L., & OSBORNE, J. G. (Eds.). (1980). *Helping in the community: Behavioral Applications.* New York: Plenum.

MARTIN, G. L., & OSBORNE, J. G. (1989). *Psychological adjustment to everyday living.* Englewood Cliffs, NJ: Prentice-Hall.

MARTIN, G. L., & TREFFRY, D. (1970). Treating self-destruction and developing self-care with a severely retarded girl: A case study. *Psychological Aspects of Disability, 17*, 125–131.

MASH, E. J. (1974). Has behavior modification lost its identity? *Canadian Psychologist, 15*, 271–280.

MASTERS, J. C., & DRISCOLL, S. A. (1971). Children's "imitation" as a function of the presence or absence of a model and the description of his instrumental behaviors. *Child Development, 42*, 161–170.

MASTERS, J. C. BURRISH, T. G., HOLLON, S. D., & RIMM, D. C. (1987). *Behavior Therapy: Techniques and Empirical Findings*, 3rd ed. Orlando, FL: Harcourt Brace Jovanovich.

MASTERS, W. H., & JOHNSON, V. E. (1970). *Human sexual inadequacy.* Boston: Little, Brown.

MATHEWS, A. M., JOHNSTON, D. W., LANCASHIRE, M., MUNBY, M., SHAW, P. M., & GELDER, M. G. (1976). Imaginal flooding and exposure to real phobic situations: Treatment outcome with agoraphobic patients. *British Journal of Psychiatry, 129*, 363–371.

MATHEWS, A. M., TEASDALE, J., MUNBY, M., JOHNSTON, D., & SHAW, P. (1977). A home-based treatment program for agoraphobia. *Behavior Therapy, 8*, 915–924.

MATSON, J. L. (1990). *Handbook of behavior modification with the mentally retarded*, 2nd ed. New York: Plenum.

MAVISSAKALIAN, M., & BARLOW, D. H. (Eds.). (1981). *Phobia: Psychological and pharmacological treatment.* New York: Guilford.

MAWHINNEY, T. C. (1990). Decreasing intrinsic "motivation" with extrinsic rewards: Easier said than done. *Journal of Organizational Behavior Management, 11(1)*, 175–191.

MCCARTHY, B. W. (1972). Short-term implosive therapy: Case study. *Psychological Reports, 30*, 589–590.

MCFALL, R. M. (1970). The effects of self-monitoring on normal smoking behavior. *Journal of Consulting and Clinical Psychology, 35*, 135–142.

MCFALL, R. M., & TWENTYMAN, C. T. (1973). Four experiments on the relative contribution of rehearsal, modelling, and coaching to assertion training. *Journal of Abnormal Psychology, 81*, 199–218.

MCGEE, J. J., MENOLASCINO, F. J., HOBBS, D. C., & MENOUSEK, P. E. (1987). *Gentle teaching: A nonaversive approach for helping persons with mental retardation.* New York: Human Sciences Press.

MCGINNIS, E., & GOLDSTEIN, A. P. (1990). *Skill streaming in early childhood: Teaching prosocial skills to the preschool and kindergarten child.* Champaign, IL: Research Press.

MCGUIRE, R. J., & VALLANCE, M. (1964). Aversion therapy by electric shock: A simple technique. *British Medical Journal, 1*, 151–153.

MCINNIS, T. (1976). Training and maintaining staff behaviors in residential treatment programs. In R. L. Patterson (Ed.), *Maintaining effective token economies* (pp. 32–68). Springfield, IL: Charles C. Thomas.

MCLAUGHLIN, T. F., BURGESS, N., & SACKVILLE-WEST, L. (1981). Effects of self-recording and matching on academic performance. *Child Behavior Therapy, 3*, 17–27.

MEAZZINI, P., & ROVETTO, F. (1983). Behavior therapy: The Italian way. *Journal of Behavior Therapy and Experimental Psychiatry, 14*, 5–9.

MEICHENBAUM, D. H. (1977). *Cognitive behavior modification: An integrative approach.* New York: Plenum.

MEICHENBAUM, D. (1986). *Stress inoculation training.* New York: Pergamon.

MEICHENBAUM, D. (1986). Cognitive behavior modification. In F. H. Kanfer & A. P. Goldstein (Eds.), *Helping people change: A Textbook of methods*, 3rd ed. (pp. 346–380). New York: Pergamon.

MELIN, L., & GOTESTAM, K. G. (1981). The effects of rearranging ward routines on communication and eating behaviors of psychogeriatric patients. *Journal of Applied Behavior Analysis, 14*, 47–51.

MERMELSTEIN, R., LICHTENSTEIN, E., & MCINTYRE, K. (1983). Partner support and relapse in smoking cessation programs. *Journal of Consulting and Clinical Psychology, 51*, 465–466.

MESSER, S. B., & WINOKUR, M. (1984). Ways of knowing and visions of reality in psychoanalytic therapy and behavior therapy. In H. Arkowitz & S. B. Messer (Eds.), *Psychoanalytic therapy and behavior therapy: Is integration possible?* (pp. 63–100). New York: Plenum.

MEYER, L. H., & EVANS, I. M. (1989). *Nonaversive intervention for behavior problems: A manual for home and community.* Baltimore: Paul H. Brookes.

MEYERSON, L., & MICHAEL, J. (1964). Hearing by operant conditioning procedures. *Proceedings of the International Congress on Education of the Deaf*, 238–242.

MICHAEL, J. (1974). Statistical inference: Mixed blessing or curse? *Journal of Applied Behavior Analysis, 7*, 647–653.

MICHAEL, J. (1975). Positive and negative reinforcement, a distinction that is no longer necessary; or, a better way to talk about bad things. *Behaviorism, 3*, 33–44.

MICHAEL, J. (1982). Distinguishing between discriminative and motivational functions of stimulus. *Journal of the Experimental Analysis of Behavior, 37*, 149–155.

MICHAEL, J. (1986). Repertoire-altering effects of remote contingencies. *The Analysis of Verbal Behavior, 4*, 10–18.

MICHAEL, J. (1987). Symposium on the experimental analysis of human behavior: Comments by the discussant. *The Psychological Record, 37*, 37–42.

MIDGLEY, M., LEA, S. E. G., & KIRBY, R. M. (1989). Algorithmic shaping and misbehavior in the acquisition of token deposit by rats. *Journal of the Experimental Analysis of Behavior, 52*, 27–40.

MIKULIS, W. L. (1983). Thailand and behavior modification. *Journal of Behavior Therapy and Experimental Psychiatry, 14*, 93–97.

MILLENSON, J. R. (1967). *Principles of behavioral analysis.* New York: Macmillan.

MILLER, P. M. (1972). The use of behavioral contracting in the treatment of alcoholism: A case report. *Behavior Therapy, 3*, 593–596.

MILLER, W. R. (1978). Behavioral treatment of problem drinkers: A comparative outcome study of three controlled drinking therapies. *Journal of Consulting and Clinical Psychology, 46*, 74–86.

MILLER, W. R., & MUNOZ, R. F. (1976). *How to control your drinking.* Englewood Cliffs, NJ: Prentice-Hall.

MILLER, W. R., TAYLOR, C. A., & WEST, J. C. (1980). Focus versus broad-spectrum behavior therapy for problem drinkers. *Journal of Consulting and Clinical Psychology, 48*, 590–601.

MILTENBERGER, R. G., FUQUA, R. W., & MCKINLEY, T. (1985). Habit reversal with muscle tics: Replication and component analysis. *Behavior Therapy, 16*, 39–50.

MOORE, J. (1990). On the "causes" of behavior. *Psychological Record, 40*, 469–480.

MORGANSTERN, K. P. (1973). Implosive therapy and flooding procedures: A critical review. *Psychological Bulletin, 79*, 318–334.

Morganstern, K. P. (1974). Issues in implosive therapy: Reply to Levis. *Psychological Bulletin, 81*, 380–382.

Morrison, R. L., & Bellack, A. S. (1984). Social skills training. In A.S. Belleck (Ed.), *Schizophrenia: Treatment, management, and rehabilitation* (pp. 247–280). Orlando, FL: Grune & Stratton.

Mowrer, O. H. (1938). Apparatus for the study and treatment of enuresis. *American Journal of Psychology, 51*, 163–166.

Mowrer, O. H. (1960). *Learning theory and behavior.* New York: John Wiley.

Muehlenhard, C. L., Koralewski, M. A., Andrews, S. L., & Burdick, C. A. (1986). Verbal and non-verbal cues that convey interest in dating: Two studies. *Behavior Therapy, 17*, 404–419.

Munby, J., & Johnston, D. W. (1980). Agoraphobia: The long-term follow-up of behavioral treatment. *British Journal of Psychiatry, 137*, 418–417.

Murphy, G. (1978). Overcorrection: A critique. *Journal of Mental Deficiency Research, 22*, 161–173.

Murrell, M., Hardy, M. A., & Martin, G. L. (1974). Danny learns to match digits with the number of objects. *Special Education in Canada, 49*, 20–23.

Nathan, P. E. (1987). DSM-III-R and the behavior therapist. *The Behavior Therapist, 10*, 203–205.

Neidhardt, E. J., Weinstein, M. S., & Conry, R. F. (1985). *Managing stress: A complete self-help guide.* Vancouver, BC: International Self-Counsel Press.

Nezu, A. M., & Nezu, C. M. (Eds.) (1989). *Clinical decision-making in behavior therapy: A problem-solving perspective.* Champaign, IL: Research Press.

Nihira, K., Foster, R., Shellhaas, M., & Leland, H. (1969). AAMD *Adaptive Behavior Scale, Revised.* Washington, DC: American Association on Mental Deficiency.

Nisbett, R. E. (1972). Hunger, obesity, and the ventromedial hypothesis. *Psychological Review, 79*, 433–453.

Nordquist, V. M. (1971). The modification of a child's enuresis: Some response-response relationships. *Journal of Applied Behavior Analysis, 4*, 241–247.

Norton, G. R. (1977). *Parenting.* Englewood Cliffs, NJ: Prentice-Hall.

O'Banion, A. R., & Whaley, D. L. (1981). *Behavioral contracting: Arranging contingencies of reinforcement.* New York: Springer.

O'Brien, R. M., Dickenson, A. M., & Rosow, M. P. (Eds). (1982). *Industrial behavior modification: A management handbook.* New York: Pergamon.

O'Brien, S., & Repp, A. C. (1990). Reinforcement-based reductive procedures: A review of 20 years of their use with persons with severe or profound retardation. *The Journal of the Association for Persons with Severe Handicaps, 15*, 148 –159.

O'Connor, R. (1969). Modification of social withdrawal through symbolic modeling. *Journal of Applied Behavior Analysis, 2*, 15–22.

Ohman, A., Dimberg, U., & Ost, L. G. (1984). Animal and social phobias: Biological constraints on learned fear responses. In S. Reiss & R. Bootzin (Eds.), *Theoretical issues in behavior therapy.* New York: Academic Press.

O'Leary, K. D. (1984). The image of behavior therapy: It is time to take a stand. *Behavior Therapy, 15*, 219–233.

O'Leary, K. D., Becker, W. C., Evans, M. B., & Saudargas, R. A. (1969). A token reinforcement program in a public school: A replication and systematic analysis. *Journal of Applied Behavior Analysis, 2*, 3–13.

Olenick, D. L., & Pear, J. J. (1980). Differential reinforcement of correct responses to probes and prompts in picture-naming training with severely retarded children. *Journal of Applied Behavior Analysis, 13*, 77–89.

Orlick, T. (1986a). *Coaches training manual to psyching for sport.* Champaign, IL: Human Kinetics.

Orlick, T. (1986b). *Psyching for Sport.* Champaign, IL. Human Kinetics.

OSKAMP, S. (1984). *Applied social psychology*. Englewood Cliffs, NJ: Prentice-Hall.

PAGGEOT, B., KVALE, S., MACE, F. C., & SHARKEY, R. W. (1988). Some merits and limitations of hand-held computers for data collection. *Journal of Applied Behavior Analysis, 21*, 429.

PALLOTTA-CORNICK, A. (1978). A comparison of backward and forward chaining to teach packaging and assembly tasks to severely and moderately retarded clients in a sheltered workshop. Unpublished master's thesis, University of Manitoba.

PAQUIN, N.J.R. (1982). Daily monitoring to eliminate a compulsion. In H. L. Newman, J. T. Huber, & D. R. Diggins (Eds.), *Therapies for adults: Depressive, anxiety, and personality disorders*. (pp. 266–268). San Francisco: Jossey-Bass.

PARKINSON, R.W. (1986). *Growing up on purpose*. Champaign, IL: Research Press.

PASSMAN, R. (1977). The reduction of procrastinative behaviors in a college student despite the "contingency fulfillment problems": The use of external control in self-management techniques. *Behavior Therapy, 8*, 95–96.

PATTERSON, C. J., & MISCHEL, W. (1975). Plans to resist distraction. *Developmental Psychology, 11*, 369–378.

PATTERSON, G. R. (1965). An application of conditioning techniques to the control of a hyperactive child. In L. P. Ullmann & L. Krasper (Eds.), *Case studies in behavior modification* (pp. 370–375). New York: Holt, Rinehart & Winston.

PATTERSON, G. R., & GULLION, M. E. (1968). *Living with children: New methods for parents and teachers*. Champaign, IL: Research Press.

PAUL, G. L., & LENTZ, R. J. (1977). *Psychosocial treatment of chronic mental patients: Milieu vs. social learning programs*. Cambridge: Harvard University Press.

PAVLOV, I. P. (1927). *Conditioned reflexes: An investigation of the physiological activity of the cerebral cortex*. Trans. G. V. Anrep. London: Oxford University Press.

PAWLICKI, R., & GALOTTI, N. (1978). A tic-like behavior case study emanating from a self-directed behavior modification course. *Behavior Therapy, 9*, 671–672.

PEAR, J. J. (1983). Relative reinforcements for cognitive and behavioral terminologies. *The Psychological Record, 33*, 20–25.

PEAR, J. J., & ELDRIDGE, G. D. (1984). The operant-respondent distinction: Future directions. *Journal of the Experimental Analysis of Behavior, 42*, 453–467.

PEAR, J.J., & KINSNER, W. (1988). Computer-aided personalized system of instruction: An effective and economical method for short and long distance education. *Machine-Mediated Learning, 2*, 213–237.

PEAR, J. J., & LEGRIS, J. A. (1987). Shaping of an arbitrary operant response by automated tracking. *Journal of the Experimental Analysis of Behavior, 47*, 241–247.

PD Supports Ban on Corporal Punishment. (1990). *Practitioner Focus, 4(2)*, 5, 8.

PERIN, C. T. (1943). The effect of delayed reinforcement upon the differentiation of bar responses in white rats. *Journal of Experimental Psychology, 32*, 95–109.

PERKINS, D. G. & PERKINS, F. M. (1976). *Nail-biting and cuticle-biting: Kicking the habit*. Richardson, TX: Self-Control Press.

PERRI, M. G., & RICHARDS, C. S. (1977). An investigation of naturally occurring episodes of self-controlled behaviors. *Journal of Consulting Psychology, 24*, 178–183.

PERRY, M. A., FURUKAWA, M. J. (1986). Modeling. In F. H. Kanfer & A. P. Goldstein (Eds.), *Helping people change* 3rd ed. New York: Pergamon.

PHILLIPS, E. L. (1968). Achievement Place: Token reinforcement procedures in a homestyle rehabilitation setting for "pre-delinquent" boys. *Journal of Applied Behavior Analysis, 1*, 213–223.

PHILLIPS, E. L., PHILLIPS, E. A., FIXSEN, D. L., & WOLF, M. M. (1973). Behavior shaping works for delinquents. *Psychology Today, 7* (1), 75–79.

PHILLIPS, E. L., PHILLIPS, E. A., WOLF, M. M., & FIXSEN, D. L. (1973). Achievement

Place: Development of the elected manager system. *Journal of Applied Behavior Analysis, 6,* 541–546.

PLIMPTON, G. (1965), ERNEST HEMINGWAY. In G. Plimpton (Ed.), *Writers at work: The Paris Review interviews* (pp. 215–239). Second series. New York: Viking.

POCHE, C., BROUWER, R., & SWEARINGEN, M. (1981). Teaching self-protection to young children. *Journal of Applied Behavior Analysis, 14,* 169–176.

POCHE, C., YODER, P., & MILTENBERGER, R. (1988). Teaching self-protection to children using television technique. *Journal of Applied Behavior Analysis, 21,* 253–261.

POLING, A., & FUQUA, R. W. (1986). *Research methods in applied behavior analysis.* New York: Plenum.

POMERLEAU, O.F., & POMERLEAU, C. S. (1977). *Break the smoking habit: A behavioral program for giving up cigarettes.* Champaign, IL: Research Press.

POPOVITCH, D. (1981). *Effective educational and behavioral programming for severely and profoundly handicapped students: A manual for teachers and aides.* Baltimore: Paul H. Brookes.

POTTER, B. A. (1980). *Turning around: The behavioral approach to managing people.* New York: Amacom.

POUTHAS, V., DROIT, S., JACQUET, A. Y., & WEARDEN, J. H. (1990). Temporal differentiation of response duration in children of different ages: Developmental changes in relations between verbal and nonverbal behavior. *Journal of the Experimental Analysis of Behavior, 53,* 21–31.

POWELL, J., MARTINDALE, A., & KULP, S. (1975). An evaluation of time-sample measures of behavior. *Journal of Applied Behavior Analysis, 8,* 463–469.

POWERS, R. B., & OSBORNE, J.G. (1976). *Fundamentals of behavior.* St. Paul, MN: West.

PREMACK, D. (1959). Toward empirical behavioral laws. I: Positive reinforcement. *Psychological Review, 66,* 219–233.

PREMACK, D. (1965). Reinforcement theory. In D. Levin (Ed.), *Nebraska symposium on motivation: 1965* (pp. 123–180). Lincoln: University of Nebraska Press.

PRILLELTENSKY, I. (1989). Psychology and the status quo. *American Psychologist, 44,* 795–802.

PRILLELTENSKY, I. (1990). Enhancing the social ethics of psychology: Toward a psychology at the service of social change. *Canadian Psychology, 31,* 310–319.

PRUE, D. M., KRAPFL, J. E., NOAH, J. C., CANNON, S., & MALEY, R. F. (1980). Managing the treatment activities of state hospital staff. *Journal of Organizational Behavior Management, 2,* 165–181.

QUARTI, C., & RENAUD, J. (1964). A new treatment of constipation by conditioning: A preliminary report. In C. M. Franks (Ed.), *Conditioning techniques in clinical practice and research* (pp. 219–227). New York: Springer.

RACHLIN, H. (1977). A review of M.J. Mahoney's *Cognition and behavior modification. Journal of Applied Behavior Analysis, 10,* 369–374.

RACHMAN, S., & HODGSON, R. (1980). *Obsessions and compulsions.* Englewood Cliffs, NJ: Prentice-Hall.

RAE, S., MARTIN, G. L., & SMYK, B. (1990). A self-management package versusa group exercise contingency for increasing on-task behavior of developmentally handicapped workers. *Canadian Journal of Behavioral Science, 22,* 45–58.

REDD, W. H., & BIRNBRAUER, J. S. (1969). Adults as discriminative stimuli for different reinforcement contingencies with retarded children. *Journal of Experimental Child Psychology, 7,* 440–447.

REED, S. D. (1990). Behavioral medicine and behavior change. In F. H. Kanfer, & A. P. Goldstein (Eds.), *Helping people change: A textbook of methods,* 4th ed. New York: Pergamon.

REID, D. H., PARSONS, M. B., & GREEN, C. W. (1989). Treating aberrant behavior through effective staff management: A developing technology. In E. Cipani (Ed.), *The treatment of severe behavior disorders*. Washington, DC: American Association on Mental Deficiency.

REPP, A. C., DEITZ, S. M., & DEITZ, D. E. (1976). Reducing inappropriate behaviors in classrooms and individual sessions through DRO schedules of reinforcement. *Mental Retardation, 14*, 11–15.

REPP, A. C., KARSH, K. G., FELCE, D., & LUDEWIG, D. (1989). Further comments on using hand-held computers for data collection. *Journal of Applied Behavior Analysis, 22*, 336–337.

REPP, A. C., & SINGH, N. (1990). *Perspectives on the use of nonaversive and aversive interventions for persons with developmental disabilities*. Sycamore, IL: Sycamore Publishing Co.

RESCORLA, R. (1987). A Pavlovian analysis of goal-directed behavior. *American Psychologist, 42*, 119–129.

RICHARDS, C. S. (1976). Improving study behaviors through self-control techniques. In J. D. Krumboltz & C. E. Thoresen (Eds.), *Counselling Methods* (pp. 462–467). New York: Holt, Rinehart & Winston.

RILLIG, M. (1977). Stimulus control and inhibitory processes. In W. K. Honig & J. E. R. Staddon (Eds.), *Handbook of operant behavior* (pp. 432–480). Englewood Cliffs, NJ: Prentice-Hall.

RISLEY, T., & WOLF, M. (1966). Experimental manipulation of autistic behaviors and generalization into the home. In R. Ulrich, T. Stachnik, & J. Mabry (Eds.), *Control of human behavior* (pp. 193–198). Glenview, IL: Scott, Foresman.

ROBERTS, R. N. (1979). Private speech in academic problem-solving: A naturalistic perspective. In G. Zevin (Ed.), *The development of self-regulation through private speech* (pp. 295–323). New York: John Wiley.

ROBERTS, R. N., & THARP, R. G. (1980). A naturalistic study of children's self-directed speech in academic problem-solving. *Cognitive Research and Therapy, 4*, 341–353.

ROPER, G., RACHMAN, S., & MARKS, I. (1975). Passive and participant modeling in exposure treatment of obsessive compulsive neurotics. *Behavior Research and Therapy, 13*, 271–279.

ROQUE, G. M., & ROBERTS, M. C. (1989). A replication of the use of public posting in traffic speed control. *Journal of Applied Behavior Analysis, 22*, 325–330.

ROSCOE, B., MARTIN, G. L, & PEAR, J. J. (1980). Systematic self-desensitization of fear of flying: A case study. In G. L. Martin & J. G. Osborne (Eds.), *Helping in the community: Behavioral applications* (pp. 345–352). New York: Plenum.

ROSEN, J. C. (1981). Self-monitoring in the treatment of diurnal bruxism. *Journal of Behavioral Therapy and Experimental Psychiatry, 12*, 347–350.

ROSENTHAL, T. L., & ROSENTHAL, R. H. (1985). Clinical stress management. In D. H. Barlow (Ed.), *Clinical handbook of psychological disorders: A step-by-step treatment manual* (pp. 145–205). New York: Guilford.

ROTH, D., BIELSKI, R., JONES, M., PARKER, N., & OSBORN, G. (1982). A comparison of self-control therapy and anti-depressant medication in the treatment of depression. *Behavior Therapy, 13*, 133–144.

ROTTER, J. B. (1954). *Social learning and clinical psychology*. Englewood Cliffs, NJ: Prentice-Hall.

ROVETTO, F. (1979). Treatment of chronic constipation by classical conditioning techniques. *Journal of Behavior Therapy and Experimental Psychiatry, 10*, 143–146.

RUSCH, F. R., & KAZDIN, A. E. (1981). Toward a methodology of withdrawal designs for the assessment of response maintenance. *Journal of Applied Behavior Analysis, 14*, 131–140.

RUTHERFORD, R. B. (1984). *Books in behavior modification and behavior therapy*. Scottsdale, AZ: Robert B. Rutherford.

SACKETT, D. L., & SNOW, J. C. (1979). The magnitude of compliance and noncompliance. In R. B. Haynes, D. W. Taylor, & D. L. Sackett (Eds.), *Compliance in health care.* Baltimore: Johns Hopkins University Press.

SAILOR, W., & GUESS, D. (1983). *Severely handicapped students: An instructional design.* Boston: Houghton Mifflin.

SAJWAJ, T., LIBET, J., & AGRAS, S. (1974). Lemon-juice therapy: The control of life-threatening rumination in a six-month-old infant. *Journal of Applied Behavior Analysis, 7,* 557–563.

SALMON, D. J., PEAR, J. J., & KUHN, B. A. (1986). Generalization of object naming after training with picture cards and with objects. *Journal of Applied Behavior Analysis, 19,* 53–58.

SALTER, A. (1949). *Conditioned reflex therapy.* New York: Creative Age Press.

SCHAEFER, H. H., & MARTIN, P. L. (1969). *Behavioral Therapy.* New York: McGraw-Hill.

SCHROEDER, S. R. (1972). Parametric effects of reinforcement frequency, amount of reinforcement, and required response force on sheltered workshop behavior. *Journal of Applied Behavior Analysis, 5,* 431–441.

SCHWITZGEBEL, R. L. (1964). *Streetcorner research: An experimental approach to juvenile delinquency.* Cambridge: Harvard University Press.

SCOTT, R. W., PETERS, R. D., GILLESPIE, W. J., BLANCHARD, E. B., EDMUNDSON, E. D., & YOUNG, L. D. (1973). The use of shaping and reinforcement in the operant acceleration and deceleration of heart rate. *Behaviour Research and Therapy, 11,* 179–185.

SELIGMAN, L. (1990). *Selecting effective treatments: Comprehensive systematic guide to treating adult mental disorders.* San Francisco: Jossey-Bass.

SEMANS, J. H. (1956). Premature ejaculation: A new approach. *Southern Medical Journal, 49,* 353–357.

SEMB, G., & SEMB, S. A. (1975). A comparison of fixed-page and fixed-time reading assignments in elementary school children. In E. Ramp & G. Semb (Eds.), *Behavior analysis: Areas of research and application* (pp. 233–243). Englewood Cliffs, NJ: Prentice-Hall.

SHELTON, J. L., & LEVY, R. L. (1981). *Behavioral assignments and treatment compliance: A handbook of clinical strategies.* Champaign, IL: Research Press.

SHEPHARD, W. C. (1973). *Teaching social behavior to young children.* Champaign, IL: Research Press.

SHERER, M., FRIEDMAN, R., ROLIDER, & VAN HOUTEN, R. (1984). The effects of a saturation enforcement campaign on speeding in Haifa, Israel. *Journal of Police Science and Administration, 12,* 425–430.

SHERMAN, A. R. (1972). Real life exposure as a primary therapeutic factor in the desensitization treatment of fear. *Journal of Abnormal Psychology, 19,* 19–28.

Sherman, J. G., Ruskin, R. S., & Semb, G. B. (Eds.). (1982). *The Personalized System of Instruction: 48 Seminal Papers.* Lawrence, KS: TRI Publications.

SHERRINGTON, C. S. (1947). *The integrative action of the central nervous system.* Cambridge: Cambridge University Press.

SHIFFMAN, S. (1984). Coping with temptations to smoke. *Journal of Consulting and Clinical Psychology, 52,* 261–267.

SHIMOFF, E., MATTHEWS, B. A., & CATANIA, A. C. (1986). Human operant performance: Sensitivity and pseudosensitivity to contingencies. *Journal of the Experimental Analysis of Behavior, 46,* 149–157.

SHIPLEY, R. H. (1985). *Quit smart: A guide to freedom from cigarettes.* Durham, NC: J. B. Press.

SIDMAN, M. (1953). Avoidance conditioning with brief shock and no exteroceptive warning signal. *Science, 118,* 157–158.

SIDMAN, M. (1960). *Tactics of scientific research.* New York: Basic Books.

SIDMAN, M. (1971). Reading and auditory-visual equivalence. *Journal of Speech and Hearing Research, 14,* 5–13.

SIDMAN, M., & TAILBY, W. (1982). Conditional discrimination vs. matching to sample: An expansion of the testing paradigm. *Journal of the Experimental Analysis of Behavior, 37,* 5–22.

SIEDENTOP, D. (1978). The management of practice behavior. In W. F. Straub (Ed.), *Sport psychology: An analysis of athletic behavior* (pp. 42–61). Ithaca, NY: Mouvement Publications.

SIEDENTOP, D., & TAGGART, A. (1984). Behavior analysis in physical education and sport. In W. L. Heward, T. E. Heron, D. S. Hill, & J. Trapp-Porter (Eds.), *Focus on behavior analysis in education* (pp. 104–113). Columbus, OH: Charles E. Merrill.

SIMEK, T. C., & O'BRIEN, R. M. (1981). *Total golf: A behavioral approach to lowering your score and getting more out of your game.* Huntington, NY: B-Mod Associates.

SIMONS, A. D., MURPHY, G. E., LEVINE, J. L., & WETZEL, R. D. (1986). Cognitive therapy and pharmacotherapy for depression. *Archives of General Psychiatry, 43,* 43–48.

SINGH, N., & BLAMPIED, N. M. (1983). Behavior modification in New Zealand. In M. Hersen, R. M. Eisler, & P. M. Miller (Eds.), *Progress in behavior modification,* Vol. 14 (pp. 173–218). New York: Academic Press.

SKINNER, B. F. (1938). *The behavior of organisms.* New York: Appleton-Century-Crofts.

SKINNER, B. F. (1948). *Walden two.* New York: Macmillan.

SKINNER, B. F. (1953). *Science and human behavior.* New York: Macmillan.

SKINNER, B. F. (1956). A case history in scientific method. *American Psychologist, 11,* 221–223.

SKINNER, B. F. (1957). *Verbal behavior.* New York: Appleton-Century-Crofts.

SKINNER, B. F. (1958). Teaching machines. *Science, 128,* 969–977.

SKINNER, B. F. (1960). Pigeons in a pelican. *American Psychologist, 15,* 28–37.

SKINNER, B. F. (1968). *The technology of teaching.* New York: Appleton-Century-Crofts.

SKINNER, B. F. (1969). *Contingencies of reinforcement: A theoretical analysis.* New York: Appleton-Century-Crofts.

SKINNER, B. F. (1971). *Beyond freedom and dignity.* New York: Knopf.

SKINNER, B. F. (1974). *About behaviorism.* New York: Knopf.

SKINNER, B. F. (1977). Why I am not a cognitive psychologist. *Behaviorism, 5,* 1–10.

SKINNER, B. F. (1989). *Recent issues in the analysis of behavior.* Columbus, OH: Charles E. Merrill.

SKINNER, B. F., & VAUGHAN, N. E. (1983). *Enjoy old age: A program of self-management.* New York: W. W. Norton.

SLOAN, R. B., STAPLES, F. R., CRISTOL, A. H., YORKSTON, N. J., & WHIPPLE, K. (1975). *Psychotherapy versus behavior therapy.* Cambridge: Harvard University Press.

SMITH, J. C. (1990). *Cognitive-behavioral relaxation training: A new system of strategies for treatment and assessment.* New York: Springer.

SOBELL, M. B., & SOBELL, L. C. (1973). Alcoholics treated by individualized behavior therapy: One year treatment outcome. *Behavior Research and Therapy, 11,* 599–618.

SOHN, D., & LAMAL, P. A. (1982). Self-reinforcement: Its reinforcing capability and its clinical utility. *Psychological Records, 32,* 179–203.

SOLYOM, L., & KINGSTONE, E. (1973). An obsessive neurosis following morning glory seed ingestion treated by aversion relief. *Journal of Behavior Therapy and Experimental Psychiatry, 4,* 293–295.

Specialty guidelines for the delivery of services. (1981). *American Psychologist, 36,* 639–685.

SPINELLI, P. R., & PACKARD, T. (1975, February). *Behavioral self-control delivery systems.*

Paper presented at the National Conference on Behavioral Self-Control, Salt Lake City.

SPOONER, F. (1984). Comparisons of backward chaining and total task presentation in training severely handicapped persons. *Education and Training of the Mentally Retarded, 19,* 15–22.

STADDON, J. E. R., & SIMMELHAG, V. L. (1971). The "superstition" experiment: A reexamination of its implications for the principles of adaptive behavior. *Psychological Review, 78,* 3–43.

STAINBACK, W. C., PAYNE, J. S., STAINBACK, S. B., & PAYNE, R. A. (1973). *Establishing a token economy in the classroom.* Columbus, OH: Charles E. Merrill.

STAMPFL, T. G., & LEVIS, D. J. (1967). Essentials of implosive therapy: A learning-theory-based psychodynamic behavioral therapy. *Journal of Abnormal Psychology, 72,* 496–503.

STARK, M. (1980). The German Association of Behavior Therapy. *The Behavior Therapist, 3,* 11–12.

STEKETEE, G., FOA, E. G., & GRAYSON, J. B. (1982). Recent advances in the treatment of obsessive-compulsives. *Archives of General Psychiatry, 39,* 1365–1371.

STEPHENS, C. E., PEAR, J. J., WRAY, L. D., & JACKSON, G. C. (1975). Some effects of reinforcement schedules in teaching picture names to retarded children. *Journal of Applied Behavior Analysis, 8,* 435–447.

STERN, R., & MARKS, I. M. (1973). Brief and prolonged flooding. *Archives of General Psychiatry, 28,* 270–276.

STERN, R. S. (1978). Obsessive thoughts: The problem of therapy. *British Journal of Psychiatry, 133,* 200–205.

STERN, R. S., LIPSEDGE, M. S., & MARKS, I. M. (1975). Obsessive ruminations: A controlled trial of thought-stopping technique. *Behavior Research and Therapy, 11,* 659–662.

STOKES, T. F., & BAER, D. M. (1977). An implicit technology of generalization. *Journal of Applied Behavior Analysis, 10,* 349–367.

STOLZ, S. B., & associates. (1978). *Ethical issues in behavior modification.* San Francisco: Jossey-Bass.

STOLZ, S. B., WIENCKOWSKI, L. A., & BROWN, B. S. (1975). Behavior modification: A perspective on critical issues. *American Psychologist, 30,* 1027–1048.

STUART, R. B. (1971). Assessment and change of the communication patterns of juvenile delinquents and their parents. In R. D. Rubin, H. Fernsterheim, A. A. Lazarus, & C. M. Franks (Eds.), *Advances in behavior therapy* (pp. 183–196). New York: Academic Press.

STUART, R. B. (1975). *Client-therapist treatment contract.* Champaign, IL: Research Press.

STUART, R. B. (1978). *Act thin, stay thin.* New York: W. W. Norton.

SULZER-AZAROFF, B., & REESE, E. P. (1982). *Applying behavior analysis: A program for developing professional competence.* New York: Holt, Rinehart & Winston.

TAYLOR, S. E. (1990). Health psychology: The science and the field. *American Psychologist, 45,* 40–50.

THARP, R. G., & WETZEL, R. J. (1969). *Behavior modification in the natural environment.* New York: Academic Press.

THASE, M. E., & MOSS, M. K. (1976). The relative efficacy of covert modelling procedures and guided participant modelling on the reduction of avoidance behavior. *Journal of Behavior Therapy and Experimental Psychiatry, 7,* 7–12.

THIERMAN, G. J., & MARTIN, G. L. (1989). Self-management with picture prompts to improve quality of household cleaning by severely mentally handicapped persons. *International Journal of Rehabilitation Research, 12,* 27–39.

THOMAS, D. L. & MILLER, L. K. (1980). Helping college students live together. Democratic decision-making versus experimental manipulation. In G. L. Martin & J. G. Osborne (Eds.). (1980), *Helping in the community: Behavioral applications* (pp. 291–305). New York: Plenum.

THORESON, C. E., & MAHONEY, M. J. (1974). *Behavioral self-control.* New York: Holt, Rinehart & Winston.

TIFFANY, S. T., MARTIN, C. & BAKER, R. (1986). Treatments for cigarette smoking: An evaluation of the contributions of aversion and counselling procedures. *Behavior Research and Therapy, 24,* 437–452.

TIMBERLAKE, W., & LUCAS, G. A. (1985). The basis of superstitious behavior: Chance contingency, stimulus substitution, or appetitive behavior? *Journal of the Experimental Analysis of Behavior, 44,* 279–299.

TODD, F. J. (1972). Coverant control of self-evaluative responses in the treatment of depression: A new use for an old principle. *Behavior Therapy, 3,* 91–94.

TODD, J. T., MORRIS, E. K., & FENZA, K. M. (1989). Temporal organization of extinction-induced responding in preschool children. *The Psychological Record, 39,* 117–130.

TORGRUD, L. J., & HOLBORN, S. W. (1990). The effects of verbal performance descriptions on nonverbal operant responding. *Journal of the Experimental Analysis of Behavior, 54,* 273–291.

TOUCHETTE, P. E., & HOWARD, J. S. (1984). Errorless learning: Reinforcement contingencies and stimulus control transfer in delayed prompting. *Journal of Applied Behavior Analysis, 17,* 175–188.

TROLLOPE, A. (1946). *An autobiography.* London: Williams & Norgate.

TURKAT, I. D., & MAISTO, S. A. (1985). Personality disorders: Application of the experimental method to the formulation and modification of personality disorders. In D. H. Barlow (Ed.), *Clinical handbook of psychological disorders: A step-by-step treatment manual* (pp. 502–570). New York: Guilford.

TURKAT, I. D., & MEYER, V. (1982). The behavior-analytic approach. In P. Wachtel (Ed.), *Resistance: Psychodynamic and behavioral approaches* (pp. 157–184). New York: Plenum.

TURKKAN, J. S. (1989). Classical conditioning: The new hegemony. *Behavioral and Brain Sciences, 12,* 121–179.

TURNER, R. M., & ASCHER, L. M. (Eds.). (1985). *Evaluating behavior therapy outcome.* New York: Springer.

TURNER, R. M., DITOMASSO, R. A., & DELUTY, M. (1985). Systematic desensitization. In R. M. Turner, & L. M. Ascher (Eds.), *Evaluating behavior therapy outcome.* New York: Springer.

ULLMANN L. P., & KRASNER, L. (Eds.). (1965). *Case studies in behavior modification.* New York: Holt, Rinehart & Winston.

ULRICH, R., STACHNIK, T., & MABRY. J. (Eds.). (1966). *Control of human behavior,* Vol. 1. Glenview, IL: Scott, Foresman.

UPPER, D., CAUTELA, J. R., & BROOK, J. M. (1975). Behavioral self-rating checklist. Described in J. R. Cautela & D. Upper, The process of individual behavior therapy. In M. Hersen, R. M. Eisler, & P. M. Miller (Eds.), *Progress in behavior modification,* Vol. 1 (pp. 275–305). New York: Academic Press.

VAN HOUTEN, R. (1983). Punishment: From the animal laboratory to the applied setting. In S. Axelrod & J. Apsche (Eds.), *The effects of punishment on human behavior.* New York: Academic Press.

VAN HOUTEN, R., & NAU, P. A. (1981). A comparison of posted feedback and increased police surveillance on highway speeding. *Journal of Applied Behavior Analysis, 14,* 261–271.

VAN ITALLIE, T. B. (1979). Obesity: Adverse effects on health and longevity. *American Journal of Clinical Nutrition, 32,* 2723–2733.

VYGOTSKY, L. S. (1978). *Mind and society.* Cambridge: Harvard University Press.

WACKER, D., MCMAHON, C., STEEGE, M., BERG, W., SASSO, G., & MELLOY, K. (1990). Applications of a sequential alternating treatments design. *Journal of Applied Behavior Analysis, 23,* 333–339.

WADDEN, T. A., STUNKARD, A. J., BROWNELL, K. D., & DEY, S. C. (1984). The treatment of moderate obesity by behavior modification and very-low-calorie diets. *Journal of Consulting and Clinical Psychology, 52*, 692–694.

WAHLER, R. G., WINKEL, G. H., PETERSON, R. F., & MORRISON, D. C. (1965). Mothers as behavior therapists for their own children. *Behaviour Research and Therapy, 3*, 113–124.

WALKER, C. E., HEDBERG, A., CLEMENT, P. W., & WRIGHT, L. (1981). *Clinical procedures for behavior therapy.* Englewood Cliffs, NJ: Prentice-Hall.

WALKER, G. R. (1989). Gentle teaching: A behavior analytic perspective. *The Behavior Therapist, 12*, 225–226.

WALKER, H. M., & BUCKLEY, N. K. (1972). Programming generalization and maintenance of treatment effects across time and across setting. *Journal of Applied Behavior Analysis, 5*, 209–224.

WALLACE, I. (1971). *The writing of one novel.* Richmond Hill, Ontario: Simon & Schuster (Pocket Books).

WALLACE, I., & PEAR, J. J. (1977). Self-control techniques of famous novelists. *Journal of Applied Behavior Analysis, 10*, 515–525.

WARD, W. D., & STARE, S. W. (1990). The role of subject verbalization in generalized correspondence. *Journal of Applied Behavior Analysis, 23*, 129–136.

WASSERMAN, E. A. (1989). Pavlovian conditioning: Is temporal contiguity irrelevant? *American Psychologist, 44*, 1550–1551.

WATSON, D. L., & THARP, R. G. (1972). *Self-directed behavior: Self-modification for personal adjustment.* Monterey, CA: Brooks/Cole.

WATSON, D. L., & THARP, R. G. (1989). *Self-directed behavior: Self-modification for personal adjustment,* 4th ed. Monterey, CA: Brooks/Cole.

WATSON, J. B. (1913). Psychology as the behaviorist views it. *Psychological Review, 20*, 158–177.

WATSON, J. B. (1916). The place of the conditioned reflex in psychology. *Psychological Review, 23*, 89–116.

WATSON, J. B. (1930). *Behaviorism,* Revised Edition. Chicago: University of Chicago Press.

WATSON, J. B., & RAYNER, R. (1920). Conditioned emotional reactions. *Journal of Experimental Psychology, 3*, 1–14. Reprinted in R. Ulrich, T. Stachnik, & J. Mabry (Eds.), *Control of Human Behavior*, Vol. 1 (pp. 66–69). Glenview, IL: Scott, Foresman.

WATSON, R. I. (1962). The experimental tradition and clinical psychology. In A. J. Bachrach (Ed.), *Experimental foundations of clinical psychology.* New York: Basic Books.

WEARDEN, J. H. (1988). Some neglect problems in the analysis of human operant behavior. In G. Davey & C. Cullen (Eds.), *Human operant conditioning and behavior modification* (pp. 197–224), Chichester, England: John Wiley.

WEBSTER, D. R., & AZRIN, N. H. (1973). Required relaxation: A method of inhibiting agitative-disruptive behavior of retardates. *Behaviour Research and Therapy, 11*, 67–78.

WEIHER, R. G., & HARMON, R. E. (1975). The use of omission training to reduce self-injurious behavior in a retarded child. *Behavior Therapy, 6*, 261–268.

WEINER, H. (1962). Some effects of response-cost upon human operant behavior. *Journal of the Experimental Analysis of Behavior, 5*, 201–208.

WEINER, H. (1963). Response-cost and the aversive control of human operant behavior. *Journal of the Experimental Analysis of Behavior, 6*, 415–421.

WEISZ, G., & BUCHER, B. (1980). Involving husbands in treatment of obesity—effects on weight loss, depression, and marital satisfaction. *Behavior Therapy, 11*, 643–650.

WELCH, M. W., & GIST, J. W. (1974). *The open token economy system: A handbook for a behavioral approach to rehabilitation.* Springfield, IL: Charles C. Thomas.

WELCH, S. J., & PEAR, J. J. (1980). Generalization of naming responses to objects in the natural environment as a function of training stimulus modality with retarded children. *Journal of Applied Behavior Analysis, 13,* 629–643.

WELD, E. M., & EVANS, I. M. (1990). Effects of part versus whole instructional strategies on skill acquisition and excess behavior. *American Journal on Mental Retardation, 94,* 377–386.

WENRICH, W., GENERAL, D., & DAWLEY, H. (1976). *Self-directed systematic desensitization.* Kalamazoo, MI: Behaviordelia.

WHALEY, D. L., & MALOTT, R. W. (1971). *Elementary principles of behavior.* New York: Appleton-Century-Crofts.

WHITE, G. D., NIELSEN, G., & JOHNSON, S. M. (1972). Timeout duration and the suppression of deviant behavior in children. *Journal of Applied Behavior Analysis, 5,* 111–120.

WITT, J. C., ELLIOT, S. N., & GRESHAM, F. M. (1988). *Handbook of behavior therapy in education.* New York: Plenum.

WHITMAN, T. L., SCIBIK, J. W., & REID, D. H. (1983). *Behavior modification with the severely and profoundly retarded: Research and application.* New York: Academic Press.

WICKES, I. G. (1958). Treatment of persistent enuresis with the electric buzzer. *Archives of Disease in Childhood, 33,* 160–164. Reprinted in R. Ulrich, R. Stachnik, & J. Mabry (Eds.) (1966), *Control of human behavior* (pp. 151–156). Glenview, IL: Scott, Forsman.

WIELKIEWICZ, R. M. (1986). *Behavior management in the schools: Principles and procedures.* New York: Pergamon.

WILCOXIN, H. C., DRAGOIN, W. B., & KRAL, P. A. (1971). Illness-induced aversions in rat and quail: Relative salience of visual and gustatory cues. *Science, 171,* 826–828.

WILLIAMS, C. D. (1959). The elimination of tantrum behavior by extinction procedures. *Journal of Abnormal and Social Psychology, 59,* 269.

WILLIAMS, K. E., & CHAMBLESS, D. L. (1990). The relationship between therapist characteristics and outcome of *in vivo* exposure treatment for agoraphobia. *Behavior Therapy, 21,* 111–116.

WILLIAMS, R. L., & LONG, J. D. (1982). *Toward a self-managed lifestyle,* 3rd ed. Boston: Houghton Mifflin.

WILSON, G. T. (1982). Adult disorders. In G. T. Wilson & C. M. Franks (Eds.), *Contemporary behavior therapy: Conceptual and empirical foundations.* New York: Guilford.

WINSTON, A. S., & BAKER, J. E. (1985). Behavior analytic studies of creativity: A critical review. *The Behavior Analyst, 8,* 191–205.

WISOCKI, P. A. (1970). Treatment of obsessive-compulsive behavior by covert sensitization and covert reinforcement: A case report. *Journal of Behavior Therapy and Experimental Psychiatry, 1,* 233–239.

WOLF, M. M. (1978). Social validity: The case for subjective measurement or how applied behavior analysis is finding its heart. *Journal of Applied Behavior Analysis, 11,* 203–214.

WOLF, M. M., HANLEY, E. L, KING, L. A., LACHOWICZ, J., & GILES, D. K. (1970). The timer-game: A variable interval contingency for the management of out-of-seat behavior. *Exceptional Children, 37,* 113–117.

WOLF, M. M., RISLEY, T., & MEES, H. (1964). Application of operant conditioning procedures to the behavior problems of an autistic child. *Behavior Research and Therapy, 1,* 305–312.

Wolfensberger, W. (Ed.) (1972). *Normalization: The principle of normalization in human services.* Toronto: National Institute of Mental Retardation.

WOLPE, J. (1958). *Psychotherapy by reciprocal inhibition.* Stanford, CA: Stanford University Press.

WOLPE, J. (1969) *The practice of behavior therapy*. Elmsford, NY: Pergamon.

WOLPE, J. (1976). Behavior therapy and its malcontents—II: Multimodal electricism, cognitive exclusivism, and 'exposure' empiricism. *Journal of Behavior Therapy and Experimental Psychiatry, 7*, 109–116.

WOLPE, J. (1982) *The practice of behavior therapy*, 3rd ed. New York: Pergamon.

WOLPE, J. (1985). Requiem for an institution. *The Behavior Therapist, 8*, 113.

WOLPE, J. (1989). The derailment of behavior therapy: A tale of conceptual misdirection. *Journal of Behavior Therapy and Experimental Psychiatry, 20*, 3–15.

WOLPE, J. (1990). *The practice of behavior therapy*, 4th ed. New York: Pergamon.

WOLPE, J., & LANG, P. J. (1964). A fear survey schedule for use in behaviour therapy. *Behaviour Research and Therapy, 2*, 27–30.

WOLPE, J., & LAZARUS, A. A. (1966). *Behavior therapy techniques: A guide to the treatment of neuroses*. Elmsford, NY: Pergamon.

WOOD, L. F., & JACOBSON, N. S. (1985). Marital distress. In D. H. Barlow (Ed.), *Clinical handbook of psychological disorders: A step-by-step treatment manual* (pp. 344–416). New York: Guilford.

WOOD, Y. R., HARDIN, M., & WONG, E. (1984, January). *Social network influences on smoking cessation*. Paper presented at the meeting of the Western Psychological Association, Los Angeles.

WRIGHTON, P. A. (1978). *Comparative effects of demerit tokens, response cost, and timeout to decrease self-stimulatory behavior during posture training with severely and profoundly retarded women*. Unpublished doctoral dissertation, University of Manitoba.

WYATT, W. J., HAWKINS, R. P., & DAVIS, P. (1986). Behaviorism: Are reports of its death exaggerated? *Behavior Analyst, 9*, 101–105.

YAMAGAMI, T., OKUMA, H., MORINAGA, Y., & NAKAO, H. (1982). Practice of behavior therapy in Japan. *Journal of Behavior Therapy & Experimental Psychology, 13*, 21–26.

YATES, A. J. (1970). *Behavior therapy*. New York: John Wiley.

YU, D., MARTIN, G. L., SUTHONS, E., KOOP, S., & PALLOTTA-CORNICK, A. (1980). Comparisons of forward chaining and total task presentation formats to teach vocational skills to the retarded. *International Journal of Rehabilitation Research, 3*, 77–79.

ZEILER, M. D. (1971). Eliminating behavior with reinforcement. *Journal of the Experimental Analysis of Behavior, 16*, 401–405.

ZETTLE, R. D. (1990). Rule-governed behavior: A radical behavioral answer to the cognitive challenge. *The Psychological Record, 40*, 41–49.

ZETTLE, R. D., & HAYES, S. C. (1980). Conceptual and empirical status of rational-emotive therapy. In M. Hersen, R. M. Eisler, & P. N. Miller (Eds.), *Progress in behavior modification*, Vol. 9 (pp. 125–166). New York: Academic Press.

ZETTLE, R. D., & HAYES, S. C. (1982). Rule-governed behavior: A potential theoretical framework for cognitive behavioral therapy. In P. C. Kendall (Ed.), *Advances in cognitive behavioral research and therapy, Vol 1.*, New York: Academic Press.

ZIEGLER, S. G. (1987). Effects of stimulus cueing on the acquisition of groundstrokes by beginning tennis players. *Journal of Applied Behavior Analysis, 20*, 405–411.

ZIMMERMAN, E. H., & ZIMMERMAN, J. (1962). The alteration of behavior in a special classroom situation. *Journal of Experimental Analysis of Behavior, 5*, 59–60.

ZLUTNICK, S., MAYVILLE, W. J., & MOFFAT, S. (1975). Modification of seizure disorders: The interruption of behavioral chains. *Journal of Applied Behavior Analysis, 8*, 1–12.

ZOHN, J.C., & BORNSTEIN P. H. (1980). Self-monitoring of work performance with mentally retarded adults: Effects upon work productivity, work quality, and on-task behavior. *Mental Retardation, 18*, 19–25.

Author Index

Subject Index